ALGORITHMIC RULE BY LAW

With the promise of greater efficiency and effectiveness, public authorities have increasingly turned to algorithmic systems to regulate and govern society. In *Algorithmic Rule By Law*, Nathalie Smuha examines this reliance on algorithmic regulation and shows how it can erode the rule of law. Drawing on extensive research and examples, Smuha argues that outsourcing important administrative decisions to algorithmic systems undermines core principles of democracy. Smuha further demonstrates that this risk is far from hypothetical or one that can be confined to authoritarian regimes, as many of her examples are drawn from public authorities in liberal democracies that are already making use of algorithmic regulation. Focusing on the European Union, Smuha argues that the EU's digital agenda is misaligned with its aim to protect the rule of law. Novel and timely, this book should be read by anyone interested in the intersection of law, technology and government.

Nathalie A. Smuha is a legal scholar and philosopher at the KU Leuven Faculty of Law, where she examines the impact of digital technology on human rights, democracy and the rule of law. She is a member of the Leuven AI Institute and the Digital Society Institute and a member of the board of trustees of the Academy of European Law. She has held visiting positions at the University of Chicago and the University of Birmingham, and she has taken up an Emile Noël Fellowship at NYU School of Law. Previously, she worked at the European Commission and practised law as a member of the Brussels Bar and the New York Bar. Professor Smuha is also editor of *The Cambridge Handbook on the Law, Ethics and Policy of AI*.

Algorithmic Rule By Law

HOW ALGORITHMIC REGULATION IN THE PUBLIC SECTOR ERODES THE RULE OF LAW

NATHALIE A. SMUHA
KU Leuven Faculty of Law

CAMBRIDGE
UNIVERSITY PRESS

CAMBRIDGE
UNIVERSITY PRESS

Shaftesbury Road, Cambridge CB2 8EA, United Kingdom

One Liberty Plaza, 20th Floor, New York, NY 10006, USA

477 Williamstown Road, Port Melbourne, VIC 3207, Australia

314–321, 3rd Floor, Plot 3, Splendor Forum, Jasola District Centre, New Delhi – 110025, India

103 Penang Road, #05-06/07, Visioncrest Commercial, Singapore 238467

Cambridge University Press is part of Cambridge University Press & Assessment, a department of the University of Cambridge.

We share the University's mission to contribute to society through the pursuit of education, learning and research at the highest international levels of excellence.

www.cambridge.org
Information on this title: www.cambridge.org/9781009427463

DOI: 10.1017/9781009427500

First published 2025

A catalogue record for this publication is available from the British Library.

Library of Congress Cataloging-in-Publication Data
NAMES: Smuha, Nathalie A., author.
TITLE: Algorithmic rule by law : how algorithmic regulation in the public sector erodes the rule of law / Nathalie A. Smuha, KU Leuven Faculty of Law.
DESCRIPTION: Cambridge, United Kingdom ; New York, NY : Cambridge University Press, 2024. | Includes bibliographical references and index.
IDENTIFIERS: LCCN 2024001824 (print) | LCCN 2024001825 (ebook) | ISBN 9781009427463 (hardback) | ISBN 9781009427470 (paperback) | ISBN 9781009427500 (epub)
SUBJECTS: LCSH: Rule of law. | Rule of law–European Union countries. | Algorithms–Social aspects. | Information technology–Law and legislation.
CLASSIFICATION: LCC K3171 .S66 2024 (print) | LCC K3171 (ebook) | DDC 340/.15181–dc23/eng/20240129
LC record available at https://lccn.loc.gov/2024001824
LC ebook record available at https://lccn.loc.gov/2024001825

ISBN 978-1-009-42746-3 Hardback

Contents

Detailed Contents

Figures

Illustrations of Algorithmic Regulation

(*continued*)

(*continued*)

Purpose (Name)	Authority	Country	Page
Admission Post Bac	French Ministry of Education	France	172, 278
Child welfare assessment	Allegheny's Child Welfare Agency	US	183, 185
Profiling offenders (HART)	Durham Constabulary	UK	185
Welfare fraud detection	Community level	Netherlands	187
Calculation of (A-level) grades	Office of Qualifications and Examinations Regulation	UK	188
Facial recognition	South Wales Police Force	UK	193
Suspicious bank activity detection (STIR)	National Revenue Administration	Poland	196
Assessment of migrant detention	Immigration and Customs Enforcement	US	200
Number plate recognition	National law enforcement	Belgium	203
Surveillance cameras	City of Antwerp	Belgium	204
Biometric identification databases	Ministry of Interior & Directorate of Security	Afghanistan	204
Concentrix System	HM Revenue and Customs	UK	219
Systeem Risico Indicatie (SyRi)	Tax authority and others	Netherlands	257, 280
Travel information and authorisation system (ETIAS)	Frontex	EU	308

Preface

To say that it is challenging to write a book on a topic that is continuously in flux is an understatement. Certainly, this work focuses on the larger picture painted by the impact of algorithmic regulation on the rule of law, thus ensuring the relevance of its insights regardless of technological evolutions – or so I hope. Nevertheless, both the technology and the laws I examined incessantly shifted shape. This meant that, if I cherished the hope of ever publishing this book, I had to find a way to deal with its ever-changing scope, and I had to let go of the idea that I could eternally integrate the latest legal and technological developments into its pages.

When I first started this research project, the General Data Protection Regulation had just entered into force, and there was nary a soul at the European Commission who thought a new regulation, let alone an AI-specific regulation, was needed. The High-Level Expert Group on AI, which I coordinated at the time, had only just commenced its mandate to write non-binding Ethics Guidelines for Trustworthy AI, and most citizens in Europe and elsewhere barely had an idea of the technology's existence (and of the fact that they were unknowingly already using it or subjected to it on a daily basis).

By the time I was halfway through my research, the European Commission published a proposal for a regulation on AI, thus radically changing the stakes. I eagerly started analysing its aptness to deal with the rule of law challenges I had already identified in the meantime, only to be sorely disappointed. Those challenges were not the object of the Commission's attention (nor that of anyone else for that matter, unfortunately). Two days before I defended my doctoral thesis on which this book is largely based, the Council of the European Union formally adopted its comments on the Commission's proposal, introducing a number of substantive changes to the original text. These changes also included some language on 'general-purpose AI', to correct the Commission's wholly understandable omission of tackling the concerns arising from applications like ChatGPT, still inexistent when the proposed AI Act was published in 2021.

A few months after my doctoral defence, the European Parliament finally got its (AI) act together too, and published its own amendments to the Commission's proposal, introducing yet another set of (arguably more sweeping) changes. Most importantly, it included a broad number of provisions that I, together with others, had fiercely advocated for in a stern critique on the original proposal. While this somewhat assuaged my initial disappointment, it soon remained evident that many of the problems I initially outlined remained unsolved. The finalisation of the AI Act and the noticeable sense of relief that followed its adoption – despite the many flaws it contains – thus only made me more determined to relay the results of my research in this book, and to caution against the mistaken optimism that EU legislation is now sufficiently comprehensive to tackle the threat of algorithmic rule by law. Evidently, both the law and the technology continue to evolve, and this book's cut-off point is July 2024. Only time will tell what the future of AI governance will bring; yet it is my hope that this book will contribute to its improvement.

Acknowledgements

Over the past years, I was fortunate to benefit from the help and inspiration of a large number of people, without which my doctorate, and hence this book, would not have seen the light of day.

I must start with Geert Van Calster, my *doktorvater* who welcomed me with open arms at KU Leuven in 2017. He provided me with freedom and support to shape my own – slightly atypical – path, and cheered for me every step of the way. I also wish to thank Bart Raymaekers, my co-supervisor, who already noted my passion for philosophy when I was a mere bachelor student, and who encouraged me to pursue it ever since. Karen Yeung has been an invaluable addition to this team of supervisors, and a guardian angel. She not only elevated the quality of this work with her brilliant insight and push for excellence, but she has also been a role model to me ever since I met her.

Next, I would like to thank the members of my doctoral examination committee. Elise Muir and Peggy Valcke, two leading illustrations of female power in academia, offered their guidance, advice, feedback and bighearted support all along the way, for which I sincerely thank them. I also wish to thank Iris van Domselaar for her time and kind encouragement, and for showing how beautiful and necessary the marriage of law and philosophy can be. Wouter Devroe and Ilse Samoy deserve gratitude not only for chairing the examination committee but also for welcoming more AI-related activities at the Faculty. I would like to thank Mark Coeckelbergh and Luc De Raedt, who were members of my supervisory committee, and whose insightful feedback on earlier drafts of my thesis challenged my thinking and undoubtedly enriched its results.

During the course of my doctoral degree in law, I also pursued a degree in philosophy, which inspired this work and can be seen as complementary thereto. I therefore wish to warmly thank Roger Vergauwen and Luc Anckaert, who supervised and stimulated my philosophical endeavours.

My colleagues at KU Leuven (both at the Faculty of Law and the Leuven Institute for AI) and at New York University School of Law not only supported me academically but also offered laughter and friendship, which made my work on this book so much more enjoyable. I owe special thanks to Federico Jorge Gaxiola Lappe, the very first reader of this manuscript, and the best possible teammate one can imagine.

Outside of academia, I wish to thank the people who contributed to the AI policy experience I gained on the ground. Many thanks go to my former colleagues at the European Commission, and the members of the High-Level Expert Group on AI. At the Council of Europe, I wish to thank the great team I got to work with, and the lovely members of the CAHAI. Many thanks also to the people at the OECD, UNICRI and UNESCO, and to the passionate people at AI4Belgium.

There is another set of people I wish to highlight, and these are the fantastic members of the AI Summer School family. It has been a privilege to get to know them and to share the programme's interdisciplinary experience together.

I also owe thanks to the Flanders Research Foundation (FWO) for granting me a fellowship to conduct this research, and for providing me with the flexibility to pursue policy activities on the side, which significantly contributed to this work. Many thanks also go to NYU's Jean Monnet Center for International and Regional Economic Law & Justice, where I wrapped up this book as an Emile Noël Fellow, and to the Belgian American Educational Foundation.

Yet the greatest thanks go to my family and friends, who stood by me all these years and who provided me with continuous encouragement and perspective. I hope they realise how grateful I am for their (non-academic) support, in countless different ways, which not only contributed to this book but immensely enriched my life. Large chunks of this book were written in a small town in France called Grabels, a place that merits special acknowledgement, as do the people who made my writing time there so enjoyable. Thank you.

Table of Cases

EUROPEAN COURT OF HUMAN RIGHTS

Advance Pharma sp. z o.o v Poland, Application no. 1469/20, 3 February 2022
Amuur v France, Application no. 19776/92, 25 June 1996
Breyer v Germany, Application no. 50001/12, 30 January 2020
Broniowski v Poland, Application no. 31443/96, 22 June 2004
Buhuceanu and others v Romania, Applications nos. 20081/19 and 20 others, 23 May 2023
Burden v the United Kingdom GC, Application no. 13378/05, 29 April 2008
Catt v The United Kingdom, Application no. 43514/15, 24 January 2019
Engel and Others v The Netherlands, Application nos. 5100/71; 5101/71; 5102/71; 5354/72; 5370/72, 8 June 1976
Evans v the United Kingdom, Application no. 6339/05, 10 April 2007
Georgia v Russia (I), Application no. 13255/07, 3 July 2014
Golder v the United Kingdom, Application no. 4451/70, 21 February 1975
Hämäläinen v Finland, Application no. 37359/09, 26 July 2014
Hassan v the United Kingdom, Application no. 29750/09, 16 September 2014
Hatton v the United Kingdom, Application no. 36022/97, 8 July 2003
Husayn (Abu Zubaydah) v Poland, Application no. 7511/13, 24 July 2014
Ivinović v Croatia, Application no. 13006/13, 18 September 2014
Klass and Others v Germany, Application no. 5029/71, 6 September 1978
M.M. v the United Kingdom, Application no. 24029/07, 13 November 2012
Malone v United Kingdom, Application no. 8691/79, 2 August 1984
Sunday Times v United Kingdom (no. 1), Application no. 6538/74, 26 April 1979

COURT OF JUSTICE OF THE EUROPEAN UNION

Case 26-62, Van Gend & Loos, 5 February 1963, EU:C:1963:1
Case 6-64, Flaminio Costa v ENEL, 15 July 1964, EU:C:1964:66
Case 294/83, Parti écologiste 'Les Verts' v European Parliament, 23 April 1986, EU:C:1986:166
Case 46/87 and 227/88, Hoechst v Commission, 21 September 1989, ECLI:EU:C:1989:337
Opinion 2/94 of the Court, Accession to the ECHR, 18 March 1996, ECLI:EU:C:1996:140
Case C-376/98, Germany v European Parliament and Council, 5 October 2000, ECLI:EU:C:2000:544
Case C-60/00, Carpenter, 11 July 2002, ECLI:EU:C:2002:434
Case C-50/00 P, Unión de Pequeños Agricultores v Council of the European Union, 25 July 2002, ECLI:EU:C:2002:462
Case C-101/01, Bodil Lindqvist, 6 November 2003, ECLI:EU:C:2003:596
Case C-496/99 P, Commission v CAS Succhi di Frutta, 29 April 2004, ECLI:EU:C:2004:236
Case C-36/02, Omega, 14 October 2004, ECLI:EU:C:2004:614
Case C-389/05, Commission v France, 17 July 2008, ECLI:EU:C:2008:411
Case C-169/07, Hartlauer v Wiener Landesregierung, 10 March 2009, ECLI:EU:C:2009:141
Joined Cases C-261/07 and C-299/07, VTB-VAB NV, 23 April 2009, ECLI:EU:C:2009:244
Case C-203/08, Sporting Exchange Ltd v Minister van Justitie, 3 June 2010, ECLI:EU:C:2010:307
Case C-208/09, Wittgenstein, 22 December 2010, ECLI:EU:C:2010:806
Case C-617/10, Ackerberg v Hans Åkerberg Franson, 26 February 2013, ECLI:EU:C:2013:105
Joined Cases C-584/10 P, C-593/10 P and C-595/10 P, Commission and Others v Kadi, 18 July 2013, EU:C:2013:518
Case C-583/11 P, Inuit Tapiriit Kanatami and Others v Parliament and Council, 3 October 2013, EU:C:2013:625
Case C-274/12 P, Telefónica v Commission, 19 December 2013, EU:C:2013:852
Joined Cases C-293/12 and C-594/12, Digital Rights Ireland and Seitlinger and Others, 8 April 2014, ECLI:EU:C:2014:238
Case T-402/13, Orange v European Commission, 25 November 2014, ECLI:EU:T:2014:99
Opinion 2/13 of the Court, Accession to the ECHR, 18 December 2014, EU:C:2014:2454
Case C-362/14, Schrems v Data Protection Commissioner, 6 October 2015, EU:C:2015:650

Case C-216/18 PPU, LM, 25 July 2018, EU:C:2018:586
Joined Cases C-293/17 and C-294/17, Coöperatie Mobilisation for the Environment, 7 November 2018, ECLI:EU:C:2018:882
Case C-619/18, Commission v Poland, 15 November 2018, ECLI:EU:C:2018:910
Case C-573/17, Popławski, 24 June 2019, ECLI:EU:C:2019:530
Case C-311/18, Data Protection Commissioner v Facebook Ireland and Maximillian Schrems, 16 July 2020, ECLI:EU:C:2020:559
Joined Cases C-354/20 PPU and C-412/20 PPU, 17 December 2020, EU: C:2020:1033
Case C-470/19, Friends of the Irish Environment Limited v Commissioner for Environmental Information, 15 April 2021, ECLI:EU:C:2021:271
Case C-901/19, CF, DN v Bundesrepublik Deutschland, 10 June 2021, ECLI:EU:C:2021:472
Case C-791/19 R, Commission v Poland, 15 July 2021, ECLI:EU:C:2021:596
Case C-204/21 R, Commission v Poland, 27 October 2021, ECLI:EU:C:2021:878
Case C-156/21, Opinion AG Campos Sánchez-Bordona, Hungary v European Parliament and Council of the European Union, 2 December 2021, ECLI: EU:C:2021:974
Case C-156/21, Hungary v Parliament and Council (Full Court), 16 February 2022, ECLI:EU:C:2022:97
Case C-157/21, Poland v Parliament and Council, 16 February 2022, ECLI: EU:C:2022:98
Joined Cases C-562/21 PPU and C-563/21 PPU, 22 February 2022, ECLI: EU:C:2022:100
Order of the President of the Court in Case C-657/21, European Parliament v European Commission, 8 June 2022
Case C-817/19, Ligue des droits humains v Conseil des ministres (PNR Case), 21 June 2022, ECLI:EU:C:2022:491
Case C-480/21, W O and J L v Minister for Justice and Equality, Order of the Court of 12 July 2022, ECLI:EU:C:2022:592
Case C-204/2, Commission v Poland, 5 June 2023, ECLI:EU:C:2023:442
Case C-107/23 PPU, Lin, 24 July 2023, ECLI:EU:C:2023:606
Case C-634/21, OQ v SCHUFA Holding AG, 7 December 2023, ECLI:EU: C:2023:957

NATIONAL COURTS

Netherlands

De Stichting Werkgroep Behoud de Peel v het college van gedeputeerde staten van Noord-Brabant, Raad Van State, 201600614/1/R2; 201600617/1/R2; 201600618/1/R2; 201600620/1/R2; 201600622/1/R2 en 201600630/1/R2, 17 May 2017, ECLI:NL:RVS:2017:1259

Stichting A4 met Vaart et al. v de minister van Infrastructuur en Waterstaat, Raad Van State, 201602958/1/R6, 18 July 2018, ECLI:NL:RVS:2018:2454
Hoge Raad, nr. 17/01448, 17 August 2018; ECLI:HR:2018
NJCM et al. en FNV v Staat der Nederlanden (SyRI Judgment), 2020, Rechtbank Den Haag C-09-550982-HA ZA 18-388, ECLI:NL:RBDHA:2020:865

US

K.W. v Armstrong, 298 FRD 479, D. Idaho 2014
Dobbs v Jackson Women's Health Organization, 597 U.S. 2022

UK

R (Bridges) v CCSWP and SSHD, 4 September 2019, High Court, Case no.: CO/4085/2018, [2019] EWHC 2341 (Admin)
R (Bridges) v CCSWP and SSHD, 11 August 2020, Court of Appeal (Civil Division), Case no.: C1/2019/2670, [2020] EWCA Civ 1058

Abbreviations

AFR	automated facial recognition
AI	artificial intelligence
API	application programming interface
CAI	Council of Europe Committee on AI
CAHAI	Council of Europe Ad Hoc Committee on AI
CFREU	Charter of Fundamental Rights of the European Union
CJEU	Court of Justice of the European Union
DMA	Digital Markets Act
DPIA	data protection impact assessment
DSA	Digital Services Act
ECHR	European Convention for the Protection of Human Rights and Fundamental Freedoms
ECJ	European Court of Justice
ECtHR	European Court of Human Rights
EPPO	European Public Prosecutor's Office
EU	European Union
FRIA	fundamental rights impact assessment
GC	General Court
GDPR	General Data Protection Regulation
LED	Law Enforcement Directive
OLAF	European Anti-Fraud Office
PSED	Public Sector Equality Duty
SWP	South Wales Police Force
TEU	Treaty on European Union
TFEU	Treaty on the Functioning of the European Union

1

Introduction

1.1 ALIGNING ALGORITHMIC REGULATION AND THE RULE OF LAW

1.1.1 *The Algorithmic Leviathan*

> … why may we not say, that all Automata (Engines that move themselves by springs and wheeles as doth a watch) have an artificiall life? For what is the Heart, but a Spring; and the Nerves, but so many Strings; and the Joynts, but so many Wheeles, giving motion to the whole Body, such as was intended by the Artificer? Art goes yet further, imitating that Rationall and most excellent worke of Nature, Man. For by Art is created that great LEVIATHAN called a COMMON-WEALTH, or STATE, (in latine CIVITAS) which is but an Artificiall Man; though of greater stature and strength than the Naturall, for whose protection and defence it was intended;
>
> *Thomas Hobbes, Leviathan, 1651*[1]

In the seventeenth century, Thomas Hobbes famously argued in favour of a strong, undivided and absolute sovereign – poetically captured by a reference to the biblical Leviathan[2] – who would safeguard society against a war of all against all.[3] Through the establishment of a social contract, citizens would agree to give up certain freedoms in exchange for the peace and security that the powerful sovereign would

[1] Thomas Hobbes, *Leviathan: Or the Matter, Forme and Power of a Commonwealth, Ecclesiasticall and Civil (1651)* (Project Gutenberg 2002) <www.gutenberg.org/files/3207/3207-h/3207-h.htm>, introduction.

[2] In Jewish theology, Leviathan is a powerful mastodontic creature, sometimes represented as a sea serpent or whale-like monster, mentioned inter alia in the Book of Job. Scholars have debated its meaning, yet it is often seen as "symbolizing God's power and sovereignty over against Job's impotence because he cannot restrain or catch them. Thus, Job has no right to challenge God concerning his justice in running the world". See Mark R Sneed, *Taming the Beast: A Reception History of Behemoth and Leviathan* (De Gruyter 2021) 2. Following Hobbes' work, the term has been used to refer to highly powerful entities or absolute states.

[3] Hobbes (n 1).

provide. Following Hobbes' influential work, the term Leviathan – still conjuring up the image of an all-mighty state[4] – has been used to refer to authoritarian regimes.[5] However, it is increasingly also applied to liberal democracies of which it is argued that their executive branch of power (and public administration in particular) has become overly powerful.[6] More recently, the term is also deployed in the context of public authorities' increased reliance on algorithmic systems, which have proven to be a highly potent and effective tool to exercise and amass power – giving rise to the so-called *Algorithmic Leviathan*.[7] Today, a mounting number of states – regardless of their political form of organisation – are arguably starting to qualify for this appellation.

In essence, algorithmic systems enable the automation of tasks through various techniques, from simple rule-based algorithms to more complex knowledge-driven and data-driven methods, including artificial intelligence (AI).[8] Such systems are increasingly used by public and private actors alike for a range of functions, from the recommendation of books that consumers might like to purchase online or the prediction of crime hotspots, to the approval of a loan. Given the impact they have on their environment and on people subjected to their outputs, algorithmic systems are hence tools through which one can wield power[9] and through which one can

4 Merriam-Webster's online definition of 'leviathan' is: (1) (a) a sea monster defeated by God in various scriptural accounts, (b) a large sea animal; (2) the political state, especially a totalitarian state having a vast bureaucracy; and (3) something large or formidable. See www.merriam-webster.com/dictionary/leviathan. The online Cambridge Dictionary instead keeps it at: something or someone that is extremely large and powerful. See https://dictionary.cambridge.org/dictionary/english/leviathan. The online Oxford Advanced Learner's Dictionary refers to: (1) a very large sea monster and (2) a very large and powerful thing, complemented with the example of 'the leviathan of government bureaucracy'. See www.oxfordlearnersdictionaries.com/definition/english/leviathan_1?q=leviathan.

5 See, for instance, Ji Li, 'The Leviathan's Rule by Law' (2015) 12 Journal of Empirical Legal Studies 815.

6 See, for instance, Cass R Sunstein and Adrian Vermeule, *Law and Leviathan: Redeeming the Administrative State* (Harvard University Press 2020).

7 The algorithmic Leviathan is characterised by Köning as a "'*giant machine' that operates in the background, that brings together and harnesses the combined power of a multitude of individuals, and that makes possible coordination outcomes which the individuals themselves could not attain without it*" in 'Dissecting the Algorithmic Leviathan: On the Socio-Political Anatomy of Algorithmic Governance' (2020) 33 Philosophy & Technology 467. See also Malcolm Langford, 'Taming the Digital Leviathan: Automated Decision-Making and International Human Rights' (2020) 114 AJIL Unbound 141. The term has, however, also been used to denote private actors, e.g. in Kathleen Creel and Deborah Hellman, 'The Algorithmic Leviathan: Arbitrariness, Fairness, and Opportunity in Algorithmic Decision-Making Systems' (2022) 52 Canadian Journal of Philosophy 26.

8 I will provide an extensive description of these techniques in Section 2.1.

9 See also, e.g., Karen Yeung, 'Why Worry about Decision-Making by Machine?' in Karen Yeung and Martin Lodge (eds), *Algorithmic Regulation* (Oxford University Press 2019); Pratyusha Kalluri, 'Do Not Ask If Artificial Intelligence Is Good or Fair, Ask How It Shifts Power' (2020) 583 Nature 169; Gry Hasselbalch, *Data Ethics of Power* (Edward Elgar Publishing 2021).

regulate – whereby regulation is understood, broadly, as a means to manage risk or influence behaviour to achieve a pre-specified goal.[10]

Regulation can, however, also be understood more narrowly: as a means *used by a public authority* to influence behaviour or to manage risk *through law*.[11] Public authorities[12] of the executive branch of power – tasked with the implementation, application and enforcement of law – increasingly deploy algorithmic systems to regulate in this narrower sense. Across the European Union (EU), Member States have, for instance, started deploying algorithmic systems to assist in decision-making regarding the initiation of tax fraud investigations, the allocation of social welfare

[10] This definition is drawn from Julia Black in 'Learning from Regulatory Disasters' (2014) 24 LSE Law, Society and Economy Working Papers 3 <http://eprints.lse.ac.uk/60569/1/WPS2014–24_Black.pdf>, following its adoption by Karen Yeung in 'Algorithmic Regulation: A Critical Interrogation' (2018) 12 Regulation & Governance 505, 507.

[11] Lawrence Lessig famously identified four different modalities of regulation of which law – traditionally seen as *the* regulatory modality – is only one, the others being: social norms, the market and the architecture or design of technological applications. See Lawrence Lessig, 'The Law of the Horse: What Cyberlaw Might Teach' (1999) 113 Harvard Law Review 501. See also Roger Brownsword, 'Technological Management and the Rule of Law' (2016) 8 Law, Innovation and Technology 100; Mireille Hildebrandt, 'Algorithmic Regulation and the Rule of Law' (2018) 376 Philosophical Transactions of the Royal Society A: Mathematical, Physical and Engineering Sciences 20170355, 4; Nathalie A Smuha, 'From a "Race to AI" to a "Race to AI Regulation": Regulatory Competition for Artificial Intelligence' (2021) 13 Law, Innovation and Technology 57, 60.

[12] Public authorities can be defined as bodies established by public law, whether at national, regional or local level, for the purpose of providing a public service or acting in the public interest, as well as any private law bodies vested with such powers. See, e.g., the Council of Europe, *The Administration and You – A Handbook* (Conseil de l'Europe 2018). This definition is also used in, e.g., 'Recommendation CM/Rec(2007)7 of the Committee of Ministers to Member States on Good Administration 2007' (CM/Rec(2007)7), Article 1. In EU legislation, the scope of 'public authority' typically depends on the particular context. For instance, in Directive 2003/4/EC of the European Parliament and of the Council of 28 January 2003 on public access to environmental information, a 'public authority' is defined in Article 2(2) as (a) government or other public administration, including public advisory bodies, at national, regional or local level; (b) any natural or legal person performing public administrative functions under national law, including specific duties, activities or services in relation to the environment; and (c) any natural or legal person having public responsibilities or functions, or providing public services, relating to the environment under the control of a body or person falling within (a) or (b). The Directive explicitly enables Member States to exclude 'bodies or institutions when acting in a judicial or legislative capacity' and hence to render the Directive only applicable to public administrations. See in this regard also Case C-470/19, *Friends of the Irish Environment Limited v Commissioner for Environmental Information*, 15 April 2021. Compare this with the approach taken in the Data Governance Act, where instead the concept of 'public sector body' was used, defined as the State, regional or local authorities, bodies governed by public law or associations formed by one or more such authorities, or one or more such bodies governed by public law. See Article 2(17) of Regulation (EU) 2022/868 of the European Parliament and of the Council of 30 May 2022 on European data governance and amending Regulation (EU) 2018/1724 (Data Governance Act) 2022 (OJ L).

benefits, the risk assessment of children's well-being, the profiling of criminals, and a range of other administrative acts.[13]

While reliance on algorithmic systems raises intricate ethical and legal questions in private and public contexts alike, in this book, I will be focusing on this narrower type of regulation, and particularly on how public authorities rely on such systems to inform or take administrative acts. Drawing on a definition from the Council of Europe, administrative acts comprise (1) legal acts, of both individual and general application, (2) physical acts of the administration taken in the exercise of public authority which may affect the rights or interests of natural or legal persons; and (3) situations of refusal to act or an omission to do so in cases where a public authority is under an obligation to act.[14] It is through these acts that the executive branch of power regulates individuals, and directly and significantly impacts their lives. As this book will demonstrate, by increasingly outsourcing the adoption of administrative acts to algorithmic systems, the executive can not only act more efficiently but also more powerfully, hence transforming into an *Algorithmic Leviathan*. Given this specific focus – and being well aware that other scholars have used the term more broadly[15] – in this book I will reserve the term *algorithmic regulation* to denote public authorities' use of algorithmic systems to inform or take administrative acts.

The benefits of algorithmic systems are well known. Their use to automate administrative acts can improve productivity, lead to cost savings, and generate

[13] Maciej Kuziemski and Gianluca Misuraca, 'AI Governance in the Public Sector: Three Tales from the Frontiers of Automated Decision-Making in Democratic Settings' (2020) 44 Telecommunications Policy 101976.

[14] See Committee of Ministers of the Council of Europe, 'Recommendation Rec(2004)20 of the Committee of Ministers to Member States on Judicial Review of Administrative Acts' 2. Since the EU lacks a harmonised definition of administrative acts at the level of Member States, I opted to draw on this well-established definition by the Council of Europe. Note, however, that, under EU law, administrative acts taken by EU authorities are typically denoted as 'regulatory acts of individual or general application' (as opposed to 'legislative acts' which in principle only refers to acts adopted through the ordinary or especial legislative procedure). See, e.g., Camilla Buchanan, 'Long Awaited Guidance on the Meaning of "Regulatory Act" for Locus Standi under the Lisbon Treaty' (2012) 3 European Journal of Risk Regulation 115.

[15] See, e.g., the definition by Mireille Hildebrandt as "*standard-setting, monitoring and behaviour modification by means of computational algorithms*", in Hildebrandt, 'Algorithmic Regulation and the Rule of Law' (n 11) 2. Consider also Karen Yeung's conceptualisation of algorithmic regulation as

> decisionmaking systems that regulate a domain of activity in order to manage risk or alter behavior through continual computational generation of knowledge from data emitted and directly collected (in real time on a continuous basis) from numerous dynamic components pertaining to the regulated environment in order to identify and, if necessary, automatically refine (or prompt refinement of) the system's operations to attain a prespecified goal

in Yeung, 'Algorithmic Regulation' (n 10) 507. Yeung's conceptualisation is not only broader (since it also encompasses regulation by private actors) but also narrower (as it does not include regulation through basic knowledge-driven algorithmic systems).

efficiency gains, particularly by operating at scale.[16] Against the background of an aging civil servants' population, an increasing workload and widespread budget cuts, it is thus no wonder that public authorities are strongly incentivised to adopt this technology on a large scale, as part of the EU's digital agenda[17] and the broader impetus to digitalise the public sector.[18] The European Union's recovery plan – the "*largest stimulus package ever*", aiming to "*rebuild a post-COVID-19 Europe*"[19] – even explicitly includes a pillar on 'digital transformation' that Member States need to integrate in their recovery plans to receive a financial contribution.[20] Reference is thereby made to investments in "*government ICT solutions, e-services, applications*", including the "*use of advanced technologies (such as high performance computing, cybersecurity or artificial intelligence) for public services and decision making*".[21]

While the potential of algorithmic regulation is clear, the technology can also cause significant harm.[22] This risk is inherent to the use of *any* technology, yet the features of algorithmic regulation – and the exercise of power that they enable, along with the delegation of human authority and control over impactful decisions – raises particular threats.[23] First of all, algorithmic systems are shaped by human programmers, and they can hence reflect the prejudices and biases of these programmers, or of the data selected by these programmers to train them on, which can lead to

[16] See, e.g., OECD, *The Path to Becoming a Data-Driven Public Sector* (OECD 2019) <www.oecd-ilibrary.org/governance/the-path-to-becoming-a-data-driven-public-sector_059814a7-en>.

[17] European Commission, 'A Digital Agenda for Europe' (2010) Communication from the Commission to the European Parliament, the Council, the European Economic and Social Committee and the Committee of the Regions COM/2010/0245 final; European Commission, '2030 Digital Compass: The European Way for the Digital Decade' (2021) Communication from the Commission to the European Parliament, the Council, the European Economic and Social Committee and the Committee of Regions COM/2021/118 final.

[18] The Commission's Coordinated Plan on AI of 2021, for instance, explicitly seeks to "*make the public sector a trailblazer for using AI*". European Commission, 'Coordinated Plan on Artificial Intelligence: 2021 Review. Fostering a European Approach to Artificial Intelligence' (2021) Annex to the Communication from the Commission to the European Parliament, the European Council, the Council, the European Economic and Social Committee and the Committee of the Regions COM(2021) 205 final 46.

[19] See the European Commission's website, detailing the recovery plan: https://ec.europa.eu/info/strategy/recovery-plan-europe_en.

[20] See Article 3(b) of Regulation (EU) 2021/241 of the European Parliament and of the Council of 12 February 2021 Establishing the Recovery and Resilience Facility 2021, OJ L 57.

[21] Ibid., Annex VII.

[22] Drawing on Feinberg, in this book I conceptualise harm as a wrongful setback to or thwarting of an interest, which can also include harm in the non-physical sense, such as the breach of a right. See Joel Feinberg, 'Harm to Others – Introduction', in his *The Moral Limits of the Criminal Law – Volume 1: Harm to Others* (Oxford University Press 1984).

[23] See, e.g., Cathy O'Neil, *Weapons of Math Destruction* (Penguin Books Ltd 2017); Virginia Eubanks, *Automating Inequality: How High-Tech Tools Profile, Police and Punish the Poor* (Picador 2019); Timnit Gebru, 'Race and Gender' in Markus D Dubber, Frank Pasquale and Sunit Das (eds), *The Oxford Handbook of Ethics of AI* (Oxford University Press 2020); Smuha, 'From a "Race to AI" to a "Race to AI Regulation"'n 11.

discriminatory outcomes.[24] Algorithmic systems also process vast amounts of (personal) data, based on which they can instantly categorise and profile individuals, infer new (sensitive) information about them, and intrude their personal sphere.[25] Furthermore, algorithmic systems can be used in an opaque manner, which might make it more difficult to identify and address potential unintended errors or prejudices. More importantly, such opacity can also conceal the possible risk that they are *deliberately* designed in a biased, intrusive or erroneous way.[26] Due to the scale and speed at which these systems can be used, the consequences when something goes wrong can be enormous.[27]

Unsurprisingly then, the increased adoption of algorithmic systems is met with increased concern. As a growing body of scholarship has analysed, the use of such systems can adversely impact the rights and interests of individuals subjected to their output, for instance by breaching their right to privacy and their right to non-discrimination.[28] When considering the context of the public sector in particular, the use of algorithmic systems also gives rise to domain-specific challenges. Public authorities that rely on such systems to inform or take administrative acts might hamper individuals' social, economic and cultural rights (e.g. by wrongly denying social welfare benefits), their right to asylum (e.g. by wrongly denying an asylum application), their right to liberty and due process (e.g. by wrongly arresting them) and other rights and freedoms that should be protected and respected by the state.

1.1.2 *Algorithmic Regulation and the Rule of Law*

Reliance on algorithmic regulation can also affect broader societal interests which do not necessarily correspond to, or which go well beyond, individual harm. This can be clarified by distinguishing three types of harm – whereby harm is defined

[24] See, e.g., Gabbrielle M Johnson, 'Algorithmic Bias: On the Implicit Biases of Social Technology' (2021) 198 Synthese 9941; Frederik J Zuiderveen Borgesius, 'Discrimination, Artificial Intelligence, and Algorithmic Decision-Making' (Council of Europe – Directorate General of Democracy 2018).

[25] See, e.g., Paul De Hert and others, 'Legal Safeguards for Privacy and Data Protection in Ambient Intelligence' (2009) 13 Personal and Ubiquitous Computing 435.

[26] See, e.g., Jenna Burrell, 'How the Machine "Thinks": Understanding Opacity in Machine Learning Algorithms' (2016) 3 Big Data & Society 205395171562251.

[27] See, e.g., Karen Yeung, 'Responsibility and AI: A Study of the Implications of Advanced Digital Technologies (Including AI Systems) for the Concept of Responsibility within a Human Rights Framework', Prepared by the Expert Committee on human rights dimensions of automated data processing and different forms of artificial intelligence (MSI-AUT), DGI(2019)05, 2019.

[28] See, e.g., Max Vetzo, JH Gerards and Remco Nehmelman, *Algoritmes en grondrechten* (Boom juridisch 2018); Council of Europe Ad Hoc Committee on Artificial Intelligence – CAHAI, 'Feasibility Study' (Council of Europe 2020) CAHAI(2020)23; European Union Agency for Fundamental Rights, 'Getting the Future Right – Artificial Intelligence and Fundamental Rights in the EU' (European Union Agency for Fundamental Rights 2020) <https://fra.europa.eu/en/publication/2020/artificial-intelligence-and-fundamental-rights>.

broadly as the thwarting of an interest[29] – namely individual, collective and societal harm.[30]

Individual harm occurs when one or more interests of an individual are thwarted. When public services, for instance, seek to detect tax fraud and rely on a biased algorithmic system, which disproportionally flags people with a migration background as risky and leads to biased output, this can hamper the interest of the individual who is subjected to the system, and her right not to be unjustly discriminated against.

Collective harm occurs when one or more interests of a collective or group of individuals are thwarted. Just as a collective consists of the sum of individuals, so too might this harm consist of the sum of harms suffered by members of the collective. The use of the biased fraud detection system can, for instance, give rise to collective harm where it thwarts the interest of a collective of people (in this case, those with a migration background who are subjected to the system) not to be unjustly discriminated against.

Societal harm occurs when one or more interests of society are thwarted. It is hence not concerned with the interests of a particular individual or an interest shared by a collective of individuals. Instead, it concerns harm to an interest held by society at large, going over and above the sum or accumulation of individual interests.[31] In the above example, a third type of harm is in fact at play. Whether individuals have a migration background or not, and whether they are subjected to this particular algorithmic system or not, they share an interest to live in a society in which the state treats people equally and exercises its power non-arbitrarily. Otherwise, they would live in fear that the state might treat *them* unequally next. That interest is different from the interest not to be unjustly discriminated against, and can hence be distinguished from the individual or collective harm done to those directly subjected to the system. Societal harm may well include instances of individual and collective harm, yet it has an impact beyond it and can hence be assessed as a sui generis type of harm.[32] The distinction between these types of harm matters, since legal mechanisms that are tailored to protect against individual and collective harm may not necessarily be apt to also protect us against forms of societal harm.[33]

[29] I made this distinction previously in Nathalie A Smuha, 'Beyond the Individual: Governing AI's Societal Harm' (2021) 10 Internet Policy Review 3.

[30] As mentioned *supra* in note 22, I draw on the conceptualisation of harm by Joel Feinberg, whereby 'interests' include rights but are not limited thereto. Some, but not all, wrongful setbacks to interests are protected by law. It should also be noted that the concept of harm is not static. It changes over time, along with the normative framework of a given society. See, e.g., Joanne Conaghan, 'Law, Harm and Redress: A Feminist Perspective' (2002) 22 Legal Studies 319.

[31] See in this regard also Yeung, 'Responsibility and AI' (n 27).

[32] This is inspired by Émile Durkheim's conceptualisation of society as a sui generis entity. See Émile Durkheim, *L'éducation morale* (Alcan 1925).

[33] The importance of considering the societal adverse impact of the use of AI and other digital technologies was already stressed by other scholars. See, e.g., Mireille Hildebrandt, *Smart*

In liberal democracies, the executive branch of power is responsible for implementing and enforcing laws that are, in principle, adopted by the legislative branch through a pluralistic democratic process. Depending on the policy area, public authorities will have a margin of discretion when implementing those laws, and they may have delegated powers to enact laws themselves, yet whenever they exercise public power, they remain bound by the rule of law.[34] However, as this book will demonstrate, when public authorities implement and enforce the law through algorithmic regulation, this may – inadvertently or deliberately – undermine the rule of law. The rule of law is a core societal interest in constitutional liberal democracies, and any adverse impact thereon can be conceptualised as a *societal harm*, as it goes beyond the harm to an individual right.

So what is the rule of law? The rule of law implies that government officials and citizens alike are bound by legal rules, and that nobody stands above the law. In the context of the public sector, it requires public authorities to adopt administrative acts based on established rules rather than arbitrary whims.[35] The rule of law thus tames public power, as it sets the legal boundaries within which public authorities can legitimately exercise their power.[36] Let me, however, stress that, beyond this general description, there is no universal agreement on what this concept precisely entails.[37] Drawing on legal sources and scholarship, in this book I will propose a more detailed account of the rule of law in the specific context of *liberal democracies*[38] –

Technologies and the End(s) of Law (Edward Elgar Publishing 2015); Yeung, 'Responsibility and AI' (n 27); Julie E Cohen, *Between Truth and Power: The Legal Constructions of Informational Capitalism* (Oxford University Press 2019); Carissa Véliz, *Privacy Is Power* (Bantam Press 2020); Salomé Viljoen, 'A Relational Theory of Data Governance' (2021) 131 The Yale Law Journal 573; Bart van der Sloot and Sascha van Schendel, 'Procedural Law for the Data-Driven Society' (2021) Information & Communications Technology Law 1. Reference can also be made to the work of Omri Ben-Shahar, who conceptualised the notion of 'data pollution' as one that goes beyond individual interests, and hence requires different legal mechanisms to tackle its risks. See Omri Ben-Shahar, 'Data Pollution' (2019), 11 Journal of Legal Analysis 104.

34 Denis James Galligan, 'Discretionary Powers in the Legal Order', in his *Discretionary Powers: A Legal Study of Official Discretion* (Oxford University Press 1990). See also more generally Bart Raymaekers, *Ethiek, recht en samenleving.* (LannooCampus 2013).

35 See e.g. Brian Z Tamanaha, *On the Rule of Law: History, Politics, Theory* (Cambridge University Press 2004); David Dyzenhaus, 'Preventive Justice and the Rule-of-Law Project' in Andrew Ashworth, Lucia Zedner and Patrick Tomlin (eds), *Prevention and the Limits of the Criminal Law* (Oxford University Press 2013).

36 Martin Krygier, 'The Rule of Law: Pasts, Presents, and Two Possible Futures' (2016) 12 Annual Review of Law and Social Science 199; Wojciech Sadurski, 'Rule of Law v. the Rule of Men and Women: What's in the Distinction?: A Short Essay for Martin Krygier' (2019) 11 Hague Journal on the Rule of Law 377.

37 Joseph Raz, 'The Law's Own Virtue' (2019) 39 Oxford Journal of Legal Studies 1, 1.

38 It is important to emphasise this context here since – as I will discuss *infra*, in Section 3.1 – the conceptualisation of the rule of law in liberal democracies does not fully align with its conceptualisation in authoritarian regimes.

given that my analysis is concerned with the EU in particular – and I will emphasise its close alignment with human rights and democracy.

Crucially, by virtue of the legal boundaries it establishes, the rule of law enables the protection of human rights and safeguards human liberty and dignity. Moreover, by enabling legislative and judicial oversight over executive action, the rule of law also counters authoritarian tendencies and ensures that governments respect the democratic process. Accordingly, in constitutional liberal democracies, the law plays a *protective* role, which public authorities must safeguard when carrying out their tasks.[39] In the EU legal order, the rule of law consists of a number of principles that public authorities must respect, including the principles of legality and legal certainty, the prohibition of the arbitrary use of executive power, the principle of equality before the law, effective judicial review of executive action, and the separation of powers.[40] As I will argue in this book, the fulfilment of these principles can be undermined when public authorities rely on algorithmic regulation.

Algorithmic regulation requires a translation from legal text-based rules to machine-readable code to enable the automation of the law's application. This translation process encompasses important normative and political decisions of legal interpretation, rather than mere technical actions. When this process contains errors or mistranslations, encompasses prejudices, occurs arbitrarily, encroaches on people's rights, or infringes hierarchically higher legal norms, this dilutes the protective function of the law. Given the scale at which algorithmic regulation is deployed, such dilution can be *systemic* rather than exceptional. That is because the infrastructure put in place for the implementation of algorithmic systems allows for instantaneous mass-decision-making, without the need for human intervention. This also means that, overnight, the parameters of algorithmic systems can be technically adapted by the executive authority that uses them, at the push of a button, thereby immediately affecting all people that are subjected thereto, without the need to inform or to convince (potentially critical) public officials of the changes made. Moreover, the opacity of algorithmic systems can make legislative, judicial and public oversight over how the law is applied through these systems highly difficult.

Over the longer term, this may therefore not only exacerbate the asymmetry of power between the government and its citizens, but also between the executive branch, on the one hand, and the judicial and legislative branch, on the other hand. The latter may no longer be able to ensure that constitutional checks and balances are in place. Both of these asymmetries open the door to the risk that algorithmic

39 See also Werner Schroeder, 'The European Union and the Rule of Law – State of Affairs and Ways of Strengthening', in Werner Schroeder (ed.), *Strengthening the Rule of Law in Europe: From a Common Concept to Mechanisms of Implementation* (Hart Publishing 2016).

40 I will discuss these principles extensively in Section 3.3, where I will examine the conceptualisation of the rule of law in the EU legal order to build the normative analytical framework of this book.

regulation incrementally increases executive power, diminishes public accountability, and erodes the rule of law. At worst, algorithmic regulation can in this way become a tool that enables authoritarian and illiberal practices,[41] thereby furthering the power of the Algorithmic Leviathan.

At least two scenarios are thinkable. Under a first scenario, a state may resort to the implementation of algorithmic regulation with ill intentions, at scale, to augment its power under the guise of enhancing the efficiency of the public sector, all the while avoiding public scrutiny. It can, for instance, creatively translate law to code and program algorithms in a manner favourable to government supporters, yet unfavourable to dissidents, minority groups or anyone the state considers falling outside the 'norm'. Under a second scenario, a state may resort to algorithmic regulation with good intentions, yet without proper attention to the risks that can arise therefrom – out of ignorance, negligence, recklessness, or even plain delusion. While the current well-intentioned government may not seek to abuse the vulnerabilities it creates, in the meantime, individuals subjected to the system can nevertheless be harmed, the rule of law's principles might be undermined, and – albeit inadvertently – an infrastructure is put in place that can easily be abused by a next, less well-intentioned government. Evidently, neither of those two scenarios are desirable, and a third one should be ensured: one in which appropriate safeguards exist to counter this threat.

1.1.3 *The EU's Rule of Law Crisis and the Rule* by *Law*

Such safeguards are not only important for the citizens of individual Member States but for the European Union as a whole. After the disastrous occurrence of World War II – initiated by an authoritarian state – the Union was brought to life as a project of state cooperation with the aim of preventing future wars. Originally, this cooperation was primarily economic in nature, focusing on the establishment of a common market.[42] Yet, over the years, the EU developed into an "*autonomous legal*

[41] For a definition of illiberal and authoritarian practices, I draw on the conceptualisation proposed by Marlies Glasius. She defines authoritarian practices as "*patterns of action that sabotage accountability to people over whom a political actor exerts control, or their representatives, by means of secrecy, disinformation and disabling voice*" and distinguishes these from "*illiberal practices, which refer to patterned and organized infringements of individual autonomy and dignity*". She notes that, "*although the two kinds of practice often go together in political life, the difference lies in the type of harm effected: authoritarian practices primarily constitute a threat to democratic processes, while illiberal practices are primarily a human rights problem*". See Marlies Glasius, 'What Authoritarianism Is . . . and Is Not: A Practice Perspective' (2018) 94 International Affairs 515, 517. See also Marlies Glasius and Marcus Michaelsen, 'Illiberal and Authoritarian Practices in the Digital Sphere' (2018) 12 International Journal of Communication 3795.

[42] See in this regard e.g. Catherine Barnard, *The Substantive Law of the EU: The Four Freedoms* (6th edn, Oxford University Press 2019).

order"[43] with a "*complete system of legal remedies and procedures*"[44] and cooperation going well beyond economic integration. Underpinning this legal order is the rule of law, enshrined in Article 2 Treaty on European Union (TEU) as a foundational Union value that is common to all Member States. Having been called "*one of the most elusive*"[45] and even an "*essentially contested*"[46] concept in legal scholarship, in the EU legal order, the rule of law is a constitutional tenet[47] consisting of various principles which are inherently linked to human rights and democracy, both of which are likewise listed in Article 2 TEU as core EU values.[48]

Given the interdependence of EU Member States, the erosion of the rule of law in one Member State is problematic for the Union as a whole. As noted by the European Commission, "*if the rule of law is not properly protected in all Member States, the Union's foundation stone of solidarity, cohesion, and the trust necessary for mutual recognition of national decisions and the functioning of the internal market as a whole, is damaged.*"[49] Various direct and indirect legal mechanisms therefore exist not only in national law but also in the EU legal order to help ensure that Member States respect the rule of law.[50] The fact that these protection mechanisms are not an unnecessary luxury is exemplified by the backsliding of the rule of law in several

43 See e.g. Opinion 2/13 of the Court (Full Court), EU Accession to the ECHR [2014], EU:C:2014:2454. See also Koenraad Lenaerts, 'The Autonomy of European Union Law' [2018] Il Diritto dell'Unione Europea 617.

44 See Case C-294/83, *Parti écologiste 'Les Verts' v European Parliament* [1986], EU:C:1986:166, §23; Case C-50/00 P, *Unión de Pequeños Agricultores v Council of the EU* [2002], ECLI:EU:C:2002:462, §40.

45 Armin von Bogdandy and Michael Ioannidis, 'Systemic Deficiency in the Rule of Law: What It Is, What Has Been Done, What Can Be Done' (2014) 51 Common Market Law Review 59, 62.

46 Jeremy Waldron, 'The Rule of Law as an Essentially Contested Concept' in Jens Meierhenrich and Martin Loughlin (eds), *The Cambridge Companion to the Rule of Law* (Cambridge University Press 2021).

47 See, e.g., Laurent Pech, 'The Rule of Law as a Well-Established and Well-Defined Principle of EU Law' [2022] Hague Journal on the Rule of Law.

48 In short: without the rule of law, human rights cannot be duly protected, and the integrity of the democratic process cannot be ensured. Commenting on the entwinement of human rights, democracy and the rule of law, the Council of Europe even went as far as noting that,

> The fact that the three concepts, taken together, form a single fundamental objective for the Council of Europe makes it less necessary for it to adopt a particular definition of the rule of law. Such an exercise of disentangling notions that are so closely intertwined and mutually supportive might even be risky in terms of overlooking essential human rights and democratic requirements and aspects

See Council of Europe, 'The Council of Europe and the Rule of Law' (Council of Europe 2008) CM(2008)170 5. Nevertheless, I shall propose a definition of the rule of law in Chapter 4.

49 European Commission, 'Communication from the Commission to the European Parliament, the European Council and the Council: Further Strengthening the Rule of Law within the Union – State of Play and Possible Next Steps' (Brussels, 3 April 2019) COM/2019/163 final.

50 These mechanisms are discussed more extensively *infra*, in Chapter 5.

Member States and the growing popularity of authoritarian governance approaches, which is increasingly referred to as a 'rule of law' crisis.[51]

Indeed, in a number of Member States, the rise of populist parties has led to government actions aimed at increasing the executive's power and deliberately eroding the rule of law, for instance by violating the principle of equality and non-discrimination, undermining judicial independence, and obstructing the separation of powers.[52] Crucially, some Member States have deliberately introduced legislation to advance authoritarian and illiberal ends, using the guise of the law's legitimacy precisely to undermine the rule of law.[53] Such perversion of the rule of law – which dismantles its essential role to protect human rights and democracy – has been referred to as rule *by* law. Under the rule by law, the law is merely a formal tool that legitimises executive action, regardless of whether it adversely impacts people's rights or obstructs public accountability. The law is hence reduced to playing a purely instrumental role rather than a protective one, and can even be used to foster illiberal and authoritarian practices.

This phenomenon is not limited to the European Union. Elsewhere in the world too, liberal democracies are increasingly under threat, with illiberal and authoritarian tendencies on the rise.[54] Rather than through coups d'état or sweeping regime changes, these developments are taking place in an incremental way. Huq and Ginsburg have denoted this phenomenon as 'constitutional retrogression', which they define as "*a process of incremental (but ultimately still substantial) decay in the three basic predicates of democracy – competitive elections, liberal rights to speech*

[51] Laurent Pech and Kim Lane Scheppele, 'Illiberalism Within: Rule of Law Backsliding in the EU' (2017) 19 Cambridge Yearbook of European Legal Studies 3; von Bogdandy and Ioannidis (n 45).

[52] See Renáta Uitz, 'Lessons from Sexual Orientation Discrimination in Central Europe' (2012) 60 American Journal of Comparative Law 235. For recent examples, see, e.g., Piotr Maciej Kaczynski, 'Poland, a LGBT-Free Zone?' *www.euractiv.com* (21 October 2021) < www.euractiv.com/section/politics/short_news/poland-a-lgbt-free-zone/>; Reuters, 'Hungary Restricts Sales of LGBT-Themed Children's Books' *Reuters* (6 August 2021) <www.reuters.com/world/europe/hungary-orders-shops-cover-up-lgbt-themed-childrens-books-2021-08-06/>.

[53] See, for instance, Zsolt Körtvélyesi, 'The Illiberal Challenge in the EU: Exploring the Parallel with Illiberal Minorities and the Example of Hungary' (2020) 16 European Constitutional Law Review 567; Łukasz Bojarski, 'Civil Society Organizations for and with the Courts and Judges – Struggle for the Rule of Law and Judicial Independence: The Case of Poland 1976–2020' (2021) 22 German Law Journal 1344.

[54] See, e.g., David Murakami Wood, 'The Global Turn to Authoritarianism and After' (2017) 15 Surveillance & Society 357; Zack Beauchamp, 'Call It Authoritarianism' (*Vox*, 15 June 2021) <www.vox.com/policy-and-politics/2021/6/15/22522504/republicans-authoritarianism-trump-competitive>; Protect Democracy, 'The Authoritarian Playbook – How Reporters Can Contextualize and Cover Authoritarian Threats as Distinct from Politics-as-Usual' (2022) <protectdemocracy.org/project/playbook-media-primer>. Outside the EU, one can, for instance, also point to the rule of law crisis in Israel, where planned judicial reforms – seemingly eroding the judiciary's independence – have sparked public outcry. See, in this regard, Arieh Saposnik and Natan Aridan, 'Introduction: Judicial Overhaul and Political Upheaval in Israel' (2023) 28 Israel Studies 1.

and association, and the rule of law".[55] They juxtapose this against 'authoritarian reversion', which concerns the "*wholesale, rapid collapse into authoritarianism*"[56] and which – contrary to constitutional retrogression – does not have the advantage of operating under the guise of legality. Indeed, the threat of constitutional retrogression stems precisely from the veneer of the legality through which governments can advance illiberal and authoritarian practices. Crucially, however, the rule *by* law can also be the result of negligent government action, whereby the adverse effects that certain laws can have on human rights and democracy are carelessly overlooked and left unaddressed. Evidently, such negligence can also be exploited by actors with illiberal or authoritarian intentions.

As a response to these developments, over the past decade, the European Union has strengthened its 'rule of law toolbox' by introducing several soft law mechanisms[57] aimed at monitoring the status of the rule of law in EU Member States,[58] as well as introducing new legislation. This includes the Conditionality Regulation adopted in 2020,[59] which enables the suspension of payments to Member States in which rule of law breaches seriously risk affecting the management of EU funds. The European Commission also launched several infringement procedures based on Article 258 TFEU against Member States' actions that undermined principles of the rule of law and misused the power of law to advance authoritarian and illiberal practices.[60] In addition, the European Parliament adopted several resolutions concerning the 'rule of law' situations in two Member States, and asked the Council to determine that a clear risk of a serious breach of EU values was present. In this manner, it hoped to trigger the mechanism of Article 7 TEU, which can lead to the suspension of a Member State's voting rights when it undermines one of the values listed in Article 2 TEU.[61]

Yet, despite their necessity, the effectiveness of the EU's rule of law protection mechanisms – especially in countering the risks raised by algorithmic

55 Aziz Huq and Tom Ginsburg, 'How to Lose a Constitutional Democracy' (2018) 65 UCLA Law Review 78, 96.

56 ibid 83.

57 See in this regard European Commission, 'A New EU Framework to Strengthen the Rule of Law' (2014) Communication from the Commission to the European Parliament and the Council COM/2014/0158 final.

58 Consider, for instance, the EU Justice Scoreboard and the annual Rule of Law Reports.

59 Regulation 2020/2092 of the European Parliament and of the Council of 16 December 2020 on a general regime of conditionality for the protection of the Union budget 2020 (OJ L).

60 Barbara Grabowska-Moroz, 'The Systemic Implications of the Vertical Layering of the Legal Orders in the EU for the Practice of the Rule of Law' (Reconnect – Reconciling Europe with its Citizens through Democracy and Rule of Law 2020); Sergio Carrera and Valsamis Mitsilegas, 'Upholding the Rule of Law by Scrutinising Judicial Independence' (CEPS 2018); Schroeder (n 39).

61 See, e.g., Joelle Grogan and others, 'The Crystallisation of a Core EU Meaning of the Rule of Law and Its (Limited) Normative Influence beyond the EU' (Reconnect – Reconciling Europe with its Citizens through Democracy and Rule of Law 2021).

regulation – can be questioned. Soft-law instruments lack teeth; the procedures foreseen in the Conditionality Regulation – much like infringement procedures – are lengthy, only provide solace ex post, and require a clear link to EU law which – in an area concerning Member States' public authorities – is not always straightforward; and the Article 7 TEU mechanism that can suspend Member States' voting rights is in a deadlock as it requires unanimity. The hope therefore rests primarily with (new) secondary legislation to mitigate potential concerns, especially if the aim is doing so ex ante. Thus far, no such legislation exists to specifically mitigate risks emanating from the use of algorithmic regulation by public authorities, though a number of rules already apply to the (automated) processing of personal data, most notably the General Data Protection Regulation (GDPR).[62] While offering some protection, the European Commission acknowledged that the GDPR – along with other existing rules at the EU level – currently does not provide sufficient protection against the adverse effects arising from the use of algorithmic regulation.[63] And while the ongoing rule of law crisis demonstrates that states do not need algorithmic regulation to erode the rule of law, the use of such systems can nevertheless exacerbate existing concerns and raise new ones, particularly over the longer term and systemically so.

In 2021, the European Commission proposed a new regulation laying down harmonised rules on AI (the "AI Act") to bridge certain gaps in existing legislation and better protect individuals' "*safety, health and fundamental rights*", particularly when "*high-risk*" AI systems are used.[64] The AI Act, which was adopted in spring 2024, also covers a number of algorithmic applications used in the public sector. In theory, the AI Act has been established to introduce new protection mechanisms that mitigate the adverse effects of algorithmic regulation on the rule of law. However, I will argue that, in practice, it falls short in providing effective protection.[65] The requirements it imposes are woefully deficient and rely to a large extent

[62] Regulation (EU) 2016/679 of the European Parliament and of the Council of 27 April 2016 on the Protection of Natural Persons with Regard to the Processing of Personal Data and on the Free Movement of Such Data, and Repealing Directive 95/46/EC (General Data Protection Regulation). See also the Law Enforcement Directive, which contains similar principles for the processing of personal data for law enforcement purposes: Directive (EU) 2016/680 of the European Parliament and of the Council of 27 April 2016 on the protection of natural persons with regard to the processing of personal data by competent authorities for the purposes of the prevention, investigation, detection or prosecution of criminal offences or the execution of criminal penalties, and on the free movement of such data, and repealing Council Framework Decision 2008/977/JHA 2016.

[63] European Commission, 'White Paper on Artificial Intelligence – A European Approach to Excellence and Trust', COM(2020) 65 final, Brussels, 19 February 2020.

[64] European Commission, Proposal for a Regulation Laying Down Harmonised Rules on Artificial Intelligence, COM(2021) 206 final, Brussels, 21 April 2021. See also page 264 (n 174).

[65] See *infra*, Section 5.4.

on a weak self-certification mechanism by AI providers.[66] Moreover, the AI Act focuses primarily on individual harms as opposed to societal harms and ignores the broader rule of law risks arising from algorithmic regulation.[67]

1.1.4 *Bridging Two Agendas and Countering* Algorithmic Rule by Law

Considering the above, the European Union appears to adopt a somewhat schizophrenic approach. On the one hand, through its *rule of law agenda*, it seeks to prevent and mitigate the erosion of the rule of law by national authorities. On the other hand, through its *digital agenda*, it supports and even requires those same authorities to adopt algorithmic regulation at scale, despite the fact that this can – deliberately or inadvertently – undermine the rule of law. The following question thus arises: can these two agendas be aligned? Put differently, does the EU have sufficient safeguards in place to avoid that algorithmic regulation – amidst a rule of law crisis – leads to a dilution of the law's protective function in liberal democracy?

This question has thus far largely been ignored in scholarship. Following the same schizophrenic line, ample legal research has analysed the erosion of the rule of law in liberal democracies,[68] including in EU member states[69] – yet this strand of research did not assess how this problem can be exacerbated by algorithmic regulation. Likewise, abundant legal research has mapped the risks raised by algorithmic systems, particularly focusing on how their use can affect individual (human) rights and interests, such as the right to non-discrimination or the right to privacy. While scholarship has mainly focused on harm to human rights,[70] increasingly, attention is also given to harm to democracy, typically focusing on algorithms in the context of elections and social media,[71] or on the way in which they are used in regimes that

66 Nathalie A Smuha and others, 'How the EU Can Achieve Legally Trustworthy AI: A Response to the European Commission's Proposal for an Artificial Intelligence Act' (Social Science Research Network 2021) <https://papers.ssrn.com/abstract=3899991>.

67 Smuha, 'Beyond the Individual' (n 29), section 6.

68 Huq and Ginsburg (n 55); Glasius (n 41); Kim Lane Scheppele, 'Autocratic Legalism' [2018] The University of Chicago Law Review 545.

69 Amichai Magen and Laurent Pech, 'The Rule of Law and the European Union' in Christopher May and Adam Winchester (eds), *Handbook on the Rule of Law* (Edward Elgar Publishing 2018).

70 See, e.g., Langford (n 7); Nathalie A Smuha, 'Beyond a Human Rights-Based Approach to AI Governance: Promise, Pitfalls, Plea' [2020] Philosophy & Technology; Tiberiu Dragu and Yonatan Lupu, 'Digital Authoritarianism and the Future of Human Rights' (2021) 75 International Organization 991.

71 See, e.g., Anita Gurumurthy and Deepti Bharthur, 'Democracy and the Algorithmic Turn' (2018) 15 Sur – International Journal on human Rights 39; M Brkan, 'Artificial Intelligence and Democracy' (2019) 2 Delphi – Interdisciplinary Review of Emerging Technologies 66; Steven Feldstein, 'How Artificial Intelligence Is Reshaping Repression' (2019) 30 Journal of Democracy 40.

are already authoritarian.[72] Moreover, the impact of algorithmic systems on the rule of law is likewise progressively examined,[73] yet mostly in the context of due process and 'administrative justice'[74] for individuals. Hitherto, a comprehensive and systematic assessment of the impact of algorithmic regulation on the rule of law as a core value underpinning liberal democracy is still missing. Accordingly, the relationship between both challenges – and more particularly the risk that algorithmic regulation can erode the rule of law and exacerbate authoritarian and illiberal tendencies – remains underexamined.[75]

This is problematic for several reasons. First, by considering these challenges as separate issues, the full impact of the adoption of algorithmic regulation in the current political climate – in which liberal democracy and the rule of law are under threat not only outside but also within the EU – remains underexplored. Second, without a mapping of this impact, potential legal solutions to ensure that algorithmic regulation is aligned with the rule of law rather than undermining it, remain underexamined. Third, as demonstrated by the lack of attention to the rule of law in the AI Act, this risk does not sufficiently appear on the radar of the EU legislator who now established a new legal framework for algorithmic systems which will set the tone for how such systems are used in the years and decades to come. Fourth, in the meantime, the adoption of algorithmic regulation by public authorities is becoming ever more widespread, leading to the implementation of a digital infrastructure with potentially irreversible effects for EU citizens and the EU legal order.

The picture that emerges when considering both lines of scholarship simultaneously, is a combination of two problems that might reinforce each other: one, the fact that the rule of law is increasingly being turned into a rule *by* law in liberal democracies, and two, the fact that algorithmic regulation can weaken public accountability and undermine the law's protective function. The introduction of

72 H Akın Ünver, 'Artificial Intelligence, Authoritarianism and the Future of Political Systems' (Centre for Economics and Foreign Policy Studies 2018).

73 See, e.g., Brownsword (n 11); Emre Bayamlıoğlu and Ronald Leenes, 'The "Rule of Law" Implications of Data-Driven Decision-Making: A Techno-Regulatory Perspective' (2018) 10 Law, Innovation and Technology 295; Hildebrandt, 'Algorithmic Regulation and the Rule of Law' (n 11); Gabriele Buchholtz, 'Artificial Intelligence and Legal Tech: Challenges to the Rule of Law' in Thomas Wischmeyer and Timo Rademacher (eds), *Regulating Artificial Intelligence* (Springer International Publishing 2020).

74 Steven M Appel and Cary Coglianese, 'Algorithmic Governance and Administrative Law' in Woodrow Barfield (ed), *The Cambridge Handbook of the Law of Algorithms* (Cambridge University Press 2020); Michèle Finck, 'Automated Decision-Making and Administrative Law' in Peter Cane and others (eds), *The Oxford Handbook of Comparative Administrative Law* (Oxford University Press 2020).

75 An important contribution has been made by Glasius and Michaelsen, who conceptualised illiberal and authoritarian practices in the digital sphere (n 41). While their argument to focus on such *practices* in all states rather than only on authoritarian *regimes* is refreshing, their categorisation of "*threats to citizens in the digital sphere*" into: "*(1) arbitrary surveillance, (2) secrecy and disinformation, and (3) violation of freedom of expression*" is too limited, as it does not capture the wider range of rule of law related risks that algorithmic systems can raise.

algorithmic regulation under the guise or the misguided belief of 'efficiency' might hence reinforce a rule by law and open the door to the exacerbation of illiberal and authoritarian tendencies – which I will conceptualise as the threat of *algorithmic rule by law*. Algorithmic rule by law raises issues beyond those captured by the concepts of *technological management*[76] or the *rule of algorithm*.[77] Regulation is implemented and enforced through algorithmic systems, yet the fact that the veneer of legality is preserved while the law's protective functions are being hollowed out, incrementally and opaquely, is what makes the situation even more problematic. Like the clueless frog in a pot of water that is slowly brought to boil, this veneer of legality might blind us to the fact that the values we hold dear are nevertheless undermined – carelessly or wilfully.

Accordingly, in this book, I seek to connect these two lines of scholarship and to bridge the gap they leave open. To do so, I will first conceptualise the rule of law in the EU legal order and distil from it the concrete requirements that public authorities must meet when exercising public power. I will draw on these requirements to develop a normative analytical framework that allows me to conduct a comprehensive analysis of how algorithmic regulation can adversely affect public authorities' adherence to the rule of law. To carry out this analysis, I will examine concrete illustrations of how algorithmic regulation is already used by public authorities in liberal democracies today. Based on my observations, I will conceptualise the threat of *algorithmic rule by law*, and set out the key features that render it a danger for the rule of law – and for the normative infrastructure of liberal democracy more generally. Finally, I will assess the safeguards provided by EU law against this threat, in light of the broader rule of law crisis. My purpose is hence to highlight potential legal gaps in protection that the EU legislator must address to ensure that algorithmic regulation is aligned with the rule of law and does not exacerbate authoritarian and illiberal practices. Moreover, since the adoption of algorithmic regulation and the erosion of the rule of law are global phenomena, the analysis that I carry out in this book – while EU-focused – could also be of relevance beyond the European Union.

Admittedly, the rule of law relies on much more than a protective legal system and necessitates an enabling societal culture in which it can flourish.[78] Indeed, "*a widely shared cultural belief that the law should rule is the essential element of the rule of law – and that is the hardest to achieve*".[79] While I hence do not claim that bridging the gaps in the EU legal framework will be *sufficient* to protect the rule of

[76] See, for instance, Brownsword (n 11).

[77] See, e.g., Michael Meyer-Resende and Marlene Straub, 'The Rule of Law versus the Rule of the Algorithm' [2022] Verfassungsblog <https://verfassungsblog.de/rule-of-the-algorithm/>.

[78] See also Leanne McKay, *Toward a Rule of Law Culture: Exploring Effective Responses to Justice and Security Challenges* (Adewale Ajadi and Vivienne O'Connor eds, United States Institute of Peace 2015).

[79] Tamanaha (n 35) 247.

law against the adverse effects of algorithmic regulation, I will nonetheless argue that it is a *necessary* condition to achieve this.

1.2 RESEARCH APPROACH

1.2.1 *Objectives, Questions and Hypotheses*

As introduced above, in this book, I seek to connect two developments that are currently taking place in the European Union. The first concerns the increased use of algorithmic regulation by public authorities. The second concerns the erosion of the rule of law and the rise of authoritarian and illiberal tendencies in liberal democracies, including in EU Member States. It is not my purpose to claim that these developments are causally linked. Rather, I seek to analyse and demonstrate how the former might reinforce the latter, and to assess whether the European Union's legal framework is armed against this threat. The objective of this book is therefore to examine how the use of algorithmic regulation by public authorities can adversely impact adherence to the rule of law, and to investigate what role EU law can play to counter this risk. Its corresponding research question is formulated as follows: *What safeguards does the EU have in place to avoid that reliance on algorithmic regulation by public authorities – amidst a rule of law crisis – undermines the rule of law and results in algorithmic rule by law?*

To answer this research question, I will formulate an answer to four sub-questions, each corresponding to a more specific objective, which will be dealt with in a dedicated chapter of this book:

(a) What is algorithmic regulation, and how is it deployed by public authorities?

To answer this question, I will examine the technical and societal aspects relating to algorithmic regulation and assess the various ways in which public authorities rely thereon in the functioning of their tasks, in particular to inform or take administrative acts (Chapter 2).

(b) How can the rule of law be conceptualised in the EU legal order, and which requirements does it impose on public authorities that are part of the executive branch of power?

To answer this question, I will look at legal theory and legal sources of EU law to conceptualise the rule of law in the context of the executive branch of power, and distil the requirements it imposes on public authorities. On that basis, I can subsequently develop a normative analytical framework to evaluate the alignment of public action with the rule of law's requirements (Chapter 3).

(c) How is the rule of law impacted by public authorities' reliance on algorithmic regulation and how can this impact, and the harm corresponding thereto, be conceptualised?

To answer this question, I will conduct a systematic impact analysis of algorithmic regulation on the rule of law's requirements, based on the normative framework developed under the second question. Drawing on that analysis, I will then be able to formulate a theory of harm that captures the way in which algorithmic regulation can transform the rule of law into a rule by law instead, leading to the threat that I will conceptualise as 'algorithmic rule by law' (Chapter 4).

(d) What safeguards does the EU legal framework provide against such harm, and to which extent can these safeguards counter the threat of algorithmic rule by law?

To answer this question, I will critically assess the legal protection mechanisms that existing and upcoming EU legislation provides against the conceptualised harm, and examine whether and how these mechanisms potentially fall short of their protective purpose (Chapter 5).

These questions are underpinned by four hypotheses, which I will be examining more closely throughout this book:

(a) Algorithmic regulation is increasingly used by public authorities across the EU, yet besides generating opportunities, it also poses risks, not only to individual but also to societal interests.
(b) The rule of law plays an essential role in liberal democracies, as it enables the protection of human rights and the democratic process. When the rule of law is undermined, this also opens the door to illiberal and authoritarian practices.
(c) Given the specific features of algorithmic systems, public authorities' reliance on algorithmic regulation can undermine the rule of law and foster a rule by law approach instead, which can also affect respect for human rights and democratic accountability.
(d) The EU legal framework – including the new AI Act – currently provides insufficient legal protection against the risks posed by public authorities' reliance on algorithmic regulation.

1.2.2 *Methodology*

While this book focuses on the extent to which legal mechanisms in the EU legal order can protect the rule of law against the risks posed by algorithmic regulation, it also deals with matters that fall outside the legal domain. In addition to legal scholarship, I will therefore be drawing on other disciplines too, including philosophy of law, ethics, public administration and critical data studies. After this introductory chapter, my inquiry proceeds as follows:

In Chapter 2, I offer a primarily *descriptive* account of algorithmic regulation, the technology that stands central in this book. I start by examining its building blocks –

namely, algorithmic systems – and discuss their technical and societal aspects alike. Subsequently, I describe how public authorities are organised – and more particularly, how administrative acts are adopted within bureaucratic administrations – to further an understanding of the role that algorithmic regulation can play within their organisation. In this chapter, I primarily draw on insights from computer science, critical data studies and public administration.

In Chapter 3, I set out the *normative* analytical framework of this book by conceptualising the rule of law in the EU legal order and concretising it into requirements that public authorities must meet when adopting administrative acts – including when they rely on algorithmic regulation to do so. To develop this normative framework, I draw on legal theory as well as legal sources, including primary and secondary EU law, case law from the Court of Justice of the European Union (CJEU) and from the European Court of Human Rights (ECtHR), EU soft law and sources from the Council of Europe that contribute to the EU understanding of the rule of law. The rule of law requirements that I distil from these sources will serve as the normative guide of this book.

In Chapter 4, drawing on the analytical framework developed in Chapter 3, I *evaluate* the impact of algorithmic regulation on the rule of law by systematically analysing how each of its requirements can be adversely affected. To concretise this analysis, I draw not only on theoretical scholarship but also on concrete illustrations[80] of algorithmic systems that are already used by public authorities today, or that have been used in the past, and examine how these illustrations interact with the identified rule of law requirements. Since this book aims at identifying possible adverse effects of algorithmic systems, I specifically focus on examples that engendered such effects, and purposely limit my investigation to the technology's use in liberal democracies, to demonstrate that these effects are not limited to authoritarian regimes. Moreover, rather than conducting an in-depth case study of one or two examples, I offer a broader overview of various cases in which algorithmic regulation is used across different public sector domains, with the aim of drawing more general conclusions. Based on my observations, I subsequently conceptualise a corresponding theory of harm, which I denote as algorithmic rule by law. Importantly, the examples of how algorithmic regulation has been used in the past do not allow me to conclude that reliance thereon by public authorities *necessarily* has an adverse impact on the rule of law. However, they do enable me to argue that algorithmic regulation *can* have an adverse impact, and that such impact must be dealt with if the aim is to protect the rule of law and safeguard the protective role it plays in liberal democracies.

In Chapter 5, I *evaluate* the safeguards provided by the existing EU legal framework, by looking at EU regulation aimed at protecting the rule of law, and EU

80 A schematic overview of these illustrations can be found *supra* at the start of this book, at page xiii.

regulation aimed at protecting individuals against the risks raised by reliance on automated data analysis and decision-making. Guided by the analysis carried out in Chapter 4, I critically assess the extent to which such regulation provides adequate protection against the identified harm, so as to ensure that the normative requirements identified in Chapter 3 are preserved.

Finally, in Chapter 6, I summarise my research results, identify avenues for further research, and draw concluding remarks.

1.2.3 *Scope of This Book*

This book will focus on public authorities' use of algorithmic systems to inform and adopt administrative acts, and examine how such use can affect the rule of law as conceptualised in the EU legal order. While the subject of this book is vast, I necessarily had to limit its scope in several ways.

First, although 'public authorities' are at times understood broadly as encompassing all state-related institutions, I will only focus on the use of algorithmic systems by the executive branch of power. This scope limitation by no means implies that the use of algorithmic regulation by entities belonging to the legislative or the judicial branch of power does not pose rule of law-related risks – quite the contrary. Yet, within the public sector, algorithmic systems are currently primarily used by the executive branch of power. Moreover, their impact on individual and societal interests – including the rule of law – is especially notable in the context of administrative acts, which hence motivated my focus.

Second, and related thereto, when conceptualising the rule of law and analysing how algorithmic regulation might affect this value, I will only examine the requirements it imposes on public authorities that are part of the executive branch of power. The rule of law is, however, more broadly applicable, and it also entails obligations for the legislative and judicial branch of power, and for natural and legal persons. While those obligations can also be impacted by reliance on algorithmic regulation, this falls outside the scope of this book.

Third, this book will only deal with algorithmic systems that operate based on techniques that are currently available or of which it is relatively certain that they will become available in the next years. I shall hence not be focusing on more futuristic or sci-fi scenarios of algorithmic regulation of which, based on the current state of the art, it is uncertain or unlikely that they will materialise. In fact, this book aims to demonstrate that concrete threats to the rule of law already emanate from the use of algorithmic systems that exist today. Furthermore, many illustrations of algorithmic regulation which I draw on in this book concern the automation of tasks based on methods that already exist since decades, without necessarily drawing on more recent approaches such as machine learning or generative AI systems. As my analysis will reveal, even basic algorithmic systems – which, in view of their relative simplicity, would not necessarily fall under the AI umbrella[81] – can pose a threat to the rule of law when deployed irresponsibly by public authorities.[82]

Fourth, it is acknowledged that algorithmic regulation can generate not only societal *harm* but also societal *benefits*. Moreover, I do not exclude that algorithmic regulation can be used in a manner that not merely respects but even promotes the rule of law.[83] However, I will not be examining such uses of algorithmic regulation in this book. Instead, this book primarily examines the harm raised by such technology and will not extensively analyse its benefits, except more sporadically to explain the rationale behind its uptake by public authorities. Furthermore, no cost–benefit analysis of algorithmic regulation will be made, given that such a utilitarian approach – which hinges on the quantifiability of costs and benefits – is difficult to reconcile with the nature of the impact that will be assessed. This book therefore focuses on a qualitative analysis of the impact of algorithmic regulation on the rule of law rather than a quantitative one.

Fifth, while I will be focusing on the potential adverse effects of algorithmic regulation, I will not be making a detailed comparison between the risks of algorithmic decision-making and the risks of human decision-making. Yet my choice for a

[81] As will be extensively discussed *infra*, in Section 2.1.5, Artificial Intelligence (AI) can be seen as an umbrella term for various technologies rather than only comprising one specific technology.

[82] Today's algorithmic systems (to the extent they are considered 'intelligent' enough to be called AI, see *infra* Section 2.1.5) all belong to the category of so-called narrow AI. Narrow AI is programmed to carry out a specific task in a specific domain, such as diagnosing a particular type of cancer or winning a game of Alpha Go. While a narrow AI system can be highly intelligent in carrying out its task and in some situations even able to surpass human performance, it is unable to perform functions outside its programmed scope. A system programmed to win Alpha Go, even if defeating the best human player in the world, will, for instance, not be able to recommend a movie or take out the dog for a walk. While this does not mean that narrow AI cannot produce results that are unexpected by its developers (for instance through the misalignment of values in the optimisation function of the system), its capacities and limitations entirely rest upon the humans that programmed it. Narrow AI can be contrasted with so-called general AI, which is characterised by its ability to autonomously carry out a multitude of complex tasks across various domains, including a level of moral sentience that renders it an independent agent. Today, no general AI system exists (even if certain researchers are actively working towards its creation and attracting significant funding for this endeavour, though this remains a minority). The rise of generative AI systems in late 2022 and early 2023 has led some authors to suggest that the advent of generative AI is growing nearer, yet others have criticised this stance as merely feeding a hype, as also generative AI applications like ChatGPT or DALL·E (discussed *infra* under Section 2.1.3) lack all sentience. This book is exclusively concerned with narrow AI.

[83] Consider, for instance, the use of algorithmic systems to track and investigate human rights violations (including violations by governments) which can facilitate their challenge in court. See also, e.g., Jay D Aronson, 'The Utility of User-Generated Content in Human Rights Investigations' in Molly K Land and Jay D Aronson (eds), *New Technologies for Human Rights Law and Practice* (Cambridge University Press 2018); John Emerson, Margaret L Satterthwaite and Anshul Vikram Pandey, 'The Challenging Power of Data Visualization for Human Rights Advocacy' in Molly K Land and Jay D Aronson (eds), *New Technologies for Human Rights Law and Practice* (Cambridge University Press 2018).

focus on the former does not imply a denial or disregard of the latter. Human beings can also make mistakes, be biased, act non-transparently, and inadvertently or deliberately undermine liberal democratic values. Some people therefore argue that, since both methods of decision-making imply risks, one must draw a comparison and make a trade-off, often followed by the contention that 'at least algorithmic systems can be de-biased' or 'be fixed' or 'rendered transparent'. In this book, I touch upon these contentions only sporadically, not only because thorough comparisons fall outside its scope, but also because I believe it makes no sense to juxtapose human and algorithmic decision-making. As I will demonstrate in this book, algorithmic decision-making *is* human decision-making, since algorithmic systems – along with their outcomes – are entirely shaped by the people that develop and use them. I therefore consider algorithmic decision-making to be an extension of human decision-making – embedding all its benefits and flaws – yet at a much faster speed and on a much wider scale, which means it can exacerbate these flaws and render them *systemic*.

Sixth, it should be noted that the Council of Europe, too, has adopted a binding legal instrument to regulate the impact of algorithmic system on human rights, democracy and the rule of law.[84] Though the contours of this convention are still new at the time of writing this book,[85] its scope largely overlaps with the AI Act, albeit at a much more general level. Since the Council of Europe's convention also aims to address issues pertaining to the rule of law, its content is likewise of relevance for the concerns discussed in this book. I will, however, not be examining this instrument, as my analysis is confined to the EU legal order. While the acquis of the

[84] The Committee of Ministers of the Council of Europe established a Committee on AI (CAI) and mandated it with the drafting of a legal instrument for this purpose, which will take the form of a (framework) convention. See 'Terms of Reference of the Committee on Artificial Intelligence (CAI) Set up by the Committee of Ministers under Article 17 of the Statute of the Council of Europe and in Accordance with Resolution CM/Res(2021)3 on Intergovernmental Committees and Subordinate Bodies, Their Terms of Reference and Working Methods' (Council of Europe Committee of Ministers 2021) CM(2021)131-addfinal <https://rm.coe.int/cai-terms-of-reference/1680a7b90b>.

[85] The basis for the new convention is the work of the Council of Europe's Ad Hoc Committee on AI (CAHAI), which received a mandate from the Committee of Ministers to carry out its tasks from 2019 to 2021. The CAHAI first drafted a Feasibility Study on a legal framework for the design, development and application of AI in December 2020 (n 28). Subsequently, in December 2021, it also adopted a document that sets out the possible elements for the Council of Europe's future legal framework, see 'Possible Elements of a Legal Framework on Artificial Intelligence, Based on the Council of Europe's Standards on Human Rights, Democracy and the Rule of Law' (Council of Europe 2021) CM(2021)173-add <https://rm.coe.int/possible-elements-of-a-legal-framework-on-artificial-intelligence/1680a5ae6b>.
In July 2023, its successor, the Committee on AI (CAI), published a working draft of the (framework) convention, which was criticised for strongly watering down the substantive provisions proposed by the CAHAI. The convention's final version (which did not remedy this criticism) was adopted on 17 May 2024. See Council of Europe Framework Convention on Artificial Intelligence and Human Rights, Democracy and the Rule of Law [Vilnius, 5.IX.2024], <https://rm.coe.int/1680afae3c>.

Council of Europe plays an important role in the EU's conceptualisation of the rule of law – and will hence be discussed in Chapter 3 – its regulatory initiatives on AI fall outside the scope of this work.

Seventh, as briefly introduced above, algorithmic regulation can affect a myriad of interests, of which the rule of law and its requirements are but one example. An alternative research project could have focused on the impact of algorithmic regulation on human rights, and on how EU human rights law deals therewith. While such an examination falls outside the scope of this book, I will on several occasions highlight the relationship between the rule of law and human rights, which – within the normative infrastructure of liberal democracies – are inherently entwined.

Finally, the risks raised by public authorities' reliance on algorithmic regulation can also be tackled through (existing or new) legislation at Member State level, for instance through administrative law provisions or more tailored legislation. This book will, however, consider legal gaps at the EU level only. One can question the choice for a focus on EU law regarding matters that appear to be primarily a Member State affair. Yet, as I explained above, Member States' adherence to the rule of law matters for the Union at large, as it is essential for the success of the European integration project, the enforcement of EU law, and the establishment of mutual trust amongst Member States. Moreover, while some Member States might have national rules in place that provide some protection against the adverse impact of algorithmic regulation,[86] others do not, or only inadequately so, whereas EU citizens should be protected in *all* EU Member States. For these reasons – and given also the looming EU harmonisation of national rules on algorithmic systems – my focus will be the EU legal framework. This means that I will not be evaluating (the legal safeguards afforded by) national administrative law and national variations of the principles of good administration, despite the fact that they can help counter the developments that this book will problematise.

1.2.4 *Relevance*

The relevance of this book is threefold. First, it aims to formulate a systematic conceptualisation of the adverse effects of algorithmic regulation, moving beyond a discussion of mere harm to individual interests – which are most prevalent in the current scholarship – towards a theory of harm that encompasses the erosion of the rule of law. Millions of euros are currently being invested into the uptake of algorithmic regulation by public authorities all over Europe, including through

[86] See, for instance, the *loi pour une République numérique* in France (LOI no. 2016–1321 du 7 octobre 2016 pour une République numérique), which introduces a range of provisions relating to the use of algorithmic systems and data, and which introduces additional protection mechanisms for citizens (including transparency measures) when public authorities deploy algorithmic systems.

funding coming from the EU recovery plan. Given public authorities' role in steering and governing society, it is essential to ensure that the implementation of this technology – with wide-ranging impact on individuals, collectives and society – occurs in a manner that respects the core values of the EU rather than undermining them.

Second, this book aims to bridge scholarship on the risks of algorithmic regulation with scholarship on the rule of law crisis in the EU – and on the broader rise of authoritarian and illiberal tendencies in constitutional liberal democracies. By mapping how the former can exacerbate the latter – and seeking to align the EU's digital agenda with the EU's rule of law agenda – this book makes a novel contribution to legal scholarship and seeks to stimulate further research in this area.

Third, this book aims to critically assess the current and proposed EU legal framework that applies to the use of algorithmic regulation by public authorities. It thereby seeks to contribute to EU policymaking in the field, by providing insights to the EU legislator and other relevant actors regarding legal gaps that must be addressed.

2

Algorithmic Regulation

As its name indicates, algorithmic regulation relies on the automation of regulatory processes through algorithms. Examining the impact of algorithmic regulation on the rule of law hence first requires an understanding of how algorithms work. In this chapter, I start by focusing on the technical aspects of algorithmic systems (Section 2.1), and complement this discussion with an overview of their societal impact, emphasising their societal embeddedness and the consequences thereof (Section 2.2). Finally, I examine how and why public authorities rely on algorithmic systems to inform and take administrative acts (Section 2.3), before drawing some conclusions for subsequent chapters (Section 2.4).

2.1 TECHNICAL ASPECTS

To get a better grasp of the technical processes that underlie algorithmic regulation, I will start by explaining what algorithms are (Section 2.1.1). Subsequently, I examine two commonly distinguished categories of algorithmic approaches, namely those based on reasoning, also referred to as knowledge-driven systems (Section 2.1.2) and those based on learning, also referred to as data-driven systems (Section 2.1.3). After comparing their respective strengths and weaknesses, I emphasise that the distinction between both should not be seen as strict, since many systems are composed of a combination of techniques, and the trend in the field is evolving towards hybrid systems (Section 2.1.4). I conclude with a discussion on the relationship between algorithmic systems and artificial intelligence, and a technical conceptualisation of algorithmic regulation for the purpose of this book (Section 2.1.5).

2.1.1 *Algorithms*

Algorithms are most commonly described as finite sequences of defined instructions, aimed at solving a problem.[1] These instructions can be expressed in computer code, which enables the algorithm's execution by a computer program. In this way, algorithms enable human beings to automate processes that they would otherwise need to undertake themselves, from a simple repetitive task to a complex calculation, or the analysis of heaps of information. An algorithm is hence shaped by whichever is the human-defined objective behind it, or the problem one aims to solve.[2] Over time, researchers have sought to address problems of varying complexity through algorithmic systems – understood as systems that are comprised of multiple algorithms – from automatically translating text from one language to another, or distinguishing between different human voices, to calculating the individual tax rates of the entire population. Algorithmic systems are increasingly used to take over tasks which would be considered as requiring 'intelligence' if carried out by a human being.[3] Accordingly, the term artificial intelligence – which I will discuss further in Section 2.1.5 – can be seen as an umbrella term for different algorithmic techniques aimed at carrying out 'intelligent' functions.[4]

In its simplest form, an algorithm relies on certain *input* that is provided, after which the algorithm – or the sequence of step-by-step *instructions* expressed in code – is executed, which ultimately results in an *output*.[5] Figure 2.1 on the next page provides a visual abstraction of this process.

1 The concept of 'algorithm' dates back to antiquity and was primarily associated with the computation of mathematical functions. The first algorithm is considered to have originated with Euclid around 300 BC and served to compute the greatest common divisor of two integers. Etymologically, the word 'algorithm' stems from the ninth-century Persian Muḥammad ibn Mūsā al-Khwārizmī (Latinised as 'Algorithmi'), a polymath who – amongst many other achievements – popularised algebra and presented the first systematic solution of linear and quadratic equations. It is, however, only in the nineteenth century that algorithms also started to be considered as a function that could be executed by a computer. The first such algorithm was written by writer and mathematician Lady Ada Lovelace sometime between 1842 and 1843, long before the first modern computer was built. See WW Rouse Ball, *A Short Account of the History of Mathematics* (4th edn, Dover Publications 1908) 129; Stuart Jonathan Russell and Peter Norvig, *Artificial Intelligence: A Modern Approach* (3rd edn, Pearson 2016) 8. With the advent of modern computers in the twentieth century, algorithmic functions started being used as an automation technique. For a further discussion of the definition of algorithms, see, e.g., Thomas H Cormen and others, *Introduction to Algorithms* (3rd edn, MIT Press 2009).

2 See in this regard also Michael Veale, 'Governing Machine Learning That Matters' (PhD thesis, University College London, 2019), 29.

3 See also Nils J Nilsson, *The Quest for Artificial Intelligence: A History of Ideas and Achievements* (Cambridge University Press 2009).

4 See also Russell and Norvig (n 1).

5 See, e.g., Cormen and others (n 1). See also Woodrow Barfield and Jessica Barfield, 'An Introduction to Law and Algorithms' in Woodrow Barfield (ed), *The Cambridge Handbook of the Law of Algorithms* (Cambridge University Press 2020) 4.

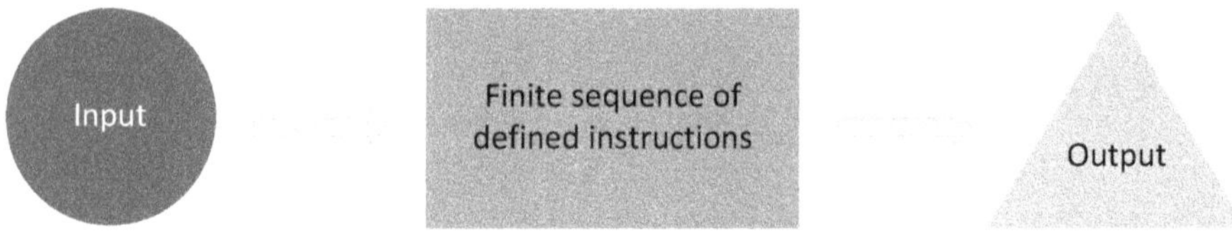

FIGURE 2.1 Abstraction of an algorithm.

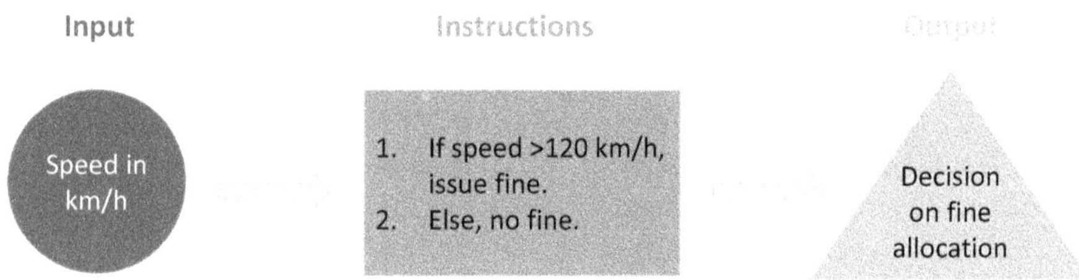

FIGURE 2.2 Abstraction of an algorithmic system to automate the decision to issue a fine.

An algorithm can be compared to a cooking process: it requires ingredients (input), step-by-step directions of how to prepare and cook these ingredients (instructions), resulting in a – hopefully delicious – dish (output). The shape and content of the input, instructions and output will depend on the algorithm's context and purpose, just as the ingredients, cooking instructions and resulting dish will depend on what one intends to cook.

To provide an example, I may wish to automate the issuing of a fine to highway drivers who drive too fast. They should, however, only be fined when they exceed the maximum speed limit, which on Belgian highways is 120 km/h. To this end, I could develop an algorithmic system that uses as input the measured km/h that the car drives. If I do not want to manually insert those km/h into the system, I could equip the system with a sensor that enables it to automatically measure the speed and thereby facilitate the provision of its input. In terms of instructions, I will need to write out in code that, once the speed limit is exceeded, a fine should be issued. Finally, the resulting output would be a concrete decision to issue a fine (or not) to the driver in question. Of course, I could also decide to include additional input and instructions to the system so that I not only automate the decision of issuing a fine but also the subsequent step of looking up the driver's address, and notifying her that a fine should be paid within a certain timeframe – yet in its simplest form, this algorithmic process comes down to Figure 2.2.

The outcome of an algorithmic system can thus be used to make a decision without the need for further human intervention, such as in the above example. This can be referred to as *algorithmic decision-making*, since it concerns a decision-making process that is automated through an algorithm.[6] Although I may be physically present when a driver crosses the speed limit, I will not necessarily be prompted to first verify the system's input, nor will I need to confirm that a fine should indeed be issued. Instead, I have outsourced that decision to the algorithmic system. The outcome of such system, however, need not necessarily be a final decision. Algorithms can also be used for a range of other functions or sub-tasks, from executing a simple calculation, to computing a prediction, recommendation or categorisation,[7] which can then inform a subsequent human or algorithmic decision.

The above algorithmic system could, for instance, also be tweaked to produce as output a recommendation of whether or not to issue a fine, which a human being then needs to approve, rather than an actual fining decision. This is sometimes denoted as an *algorithmic recommendation system*. Moreover, it is also possible that an algorithmic system is used to merely support a sub-part of a decision, based on which a human being can then decide to take a particular action. For instance, an algorithmic system can be used to automatically determine the speed at which a car was driven, without also being programmed to issue a recommendation to fine the driver when that speed reaches the limit. Nevertheless, I may use that piece of information to determine whether the speed limit was exceeded and whether a fine should be issued. This can be referred to as a more general *algorithmic decision-support system*, since the system is used to support a decision, without making an explicit recommendation or taking a final decision.[8]

Collectively, the algorithmic decision-making system, recommendation system and support system described above enable *algorithmic regulation*, since they are deployed by a public authority to inform or take an administrative act (namely, issuing a fine). In this book, I will hence deploy the term *algorithmic regulation* to cover all three types of systems. However, when discussing concrete examples, and whenever the distinction is relevant, I will indicate whether it concerns an algorithmic system that *adopts* (takes) or that *informs* (recommends or supports) an administrative act.

An obvious advantage of using an algorithmic system instead of manually measuring the driving speed and issuing corresponding fines is the fact that the process can be applied at much larger scale and speed, so that many more drivers can be controlled and fined where needed and unwanted behaviour can be reduced. Moreover, I no longer always need to be physically present at the place of the event,

6 See, for instance, Theo Araujo and others, 'In AI We Trust? Perceptions about Automated Decision-Making by Artificial Intelligence' (2020) 35 AI & Society 611, 611–12.

7 This variety of functions is, for instance, reflected in the definition of 'AI' of the European Commission, the European Commission's High-Level Expert Group on AI, the AI Act and the OECD, to which I will return in subsequent sections.

8 See, for instance, Anne Kaun, 'Suing the Algorithm: The Mundanization of Automated Decision-Making in Public Services through Litigation' [2021] Information, Communication & Society 1, 5.

but can instead be at my office and work on another matter in the meantime. However, since the delegation of tasks to algorithmic systems also entails, to a certain degree, the delegation of responsibility for tasks originally undertaken by human beings, reliance thereon can give rise to several ethical and legal questions, depending on the task at stake. As long as I am using an algorithmic system to automatically activate my heater when the temperature falls below 20°C, this algorithmisation does not lead to much consternation. Yet the algorithmisation of tasks that have more significant consequences for individuals, collectives and society evidently needs to be handled with greater care. In the example above, for instance, all three of the systems – although differentiable in the part of the task that they automate – can entail consequences for drivers who may be subjected to a fine.

Various algorithmic approaches can be used to automate tasks, and these can be classified in several ways. A commonly made distinction concerns algorithmic systems focused on *reasoning* – sometimes referred to as *knowledge-driven* systems – and those focused on *learning* – sometimes referred to as *data-driven* systems.[9] Yet it must be stressed that the boundaries of these categories are not uniformly set, and that algorithmic systems can also draw on different approaches simultaneously or on approaches that do not neatly fall under one or the other category. With this caveat in mind, in what follows I will set out the main features of knowledge-driven and data-driven systems, respectively. Rather than giving a comprehensive account of the wide set of techniques falling under each of these approaches, the discussion below will be succinct, aimed only at providing the reader with a basic understanding of how these systems might operate the context of algorithmic regulation.

2.1.2 *Knowledge-Driven Systems*

As their name implies, knowledge-driven systems start from a certain knowledge model of reality that is represented through code, based on which the algorithm can subsequently reason. Two elements are core in this regard. The first concerns a knowledge base, which can contain facts, observations and other types of data that represent a coded model of reality. Such knowledge must be 'translated' so that it can be processed by an algorithmic system – also known as *knowledge*

[9] Luc De Raedt, 'De artificiële-intelligentierevolutie en de impact ervan' in Pieter d'Hoine and Bart Pattyn (eds), *Wetenschap in een veranderende wereld: Lessen voor de eenentwintigste eeuw* (1st edn, Universitaire Pers Leuven 2020) 286. Note that others have proposed a classification of algorithmic systems based on large paradigms within the research domain of AI, including the symbolic school, the Bayesian school, the analogisers, the neural or connectionist school and the evolutionary school. See Pedro Domingos, *The Master Algorithm: How the Quest for the Ultimate Learning Machine Will Remake Our World* (1st edn, Penguin 2017).

representation.[10] The second element concerns coded instructions about how the system can analyse, combine and draw inferences based on that knowledge to solve a problem – known as *knowledge manipulation* or simply *reasoning*.[11] These instructions are typically codified in the system through symbolic rules that set out the relationships between the symbols and establish how the system can deduce information, engage in planning and scheduling activities, search through knowledge bases, and optimise solutions.[12] How the developer of the system translates knowledge and rules into code is hence key, as is the extent to which the codified knowledge is correct or based on appropriate assumptions and beliefs. Given the important role that pre-established rules play in these systems, they are sometimes also referred to as 'rule-based systems'.

Rule-based systems were the dominant paradigm up until the 1980s and are therefore also known as 'traditional' or 'good, old-fashioned' AI.[13] They have, for instance, successfully been programmed to win a game of chess from the world chess champion,[14] as the rules of chess-playing are well delineated and can hence be represented in code with relative ease. Such systems can also be used by public services to assist in decision-making on the allocation of social welfare benefits. To this end, information about the income, family situation and legal status of individuals first needs to be represented in code – along with other information that determines whether or not an individual is eligible to receive benefits. In addition, the relevant legislation that stipulates the criteria and conditions under which individuals can receive benefits also needs to be translated to symbols and rules. On that basis, the system can subsequently infer a citizen's benefits eligibility, calculate the corresponding amount and provide as output a recommendation or

[10] See also Ronald J Brachman and Hector J Levesque, *Knowledge Representation and Reasoning* (Elsevier 2004). Knowledge representation can occur through symbolic or non-symbolic methods, though the former is more prevalent.

[11] See also M Michalewicz, ST Wierzchoń and MA Kłopotek, 'Knowledge Acquisition, Representation & Manipulation in Decision Support Systems' (arXiv, 23 May 2017) <http://arxiv.org/abs/1705.08440>. Note that the use of the term 'manipulation' in this technical context is thus not the same as the use of the term in a social or legal context, which, according to the *Cambridge Online Dictionary*, rather connotes "*controlling someone or something to your own advantage, often unfairly or dishonestly*".

[12] See High-Level Expert Group on AI, 'A Definition of AI: Main Capabilities and Scientific Disciplines', Brussels, April 2019, <www.digital-strategy.ec.europa.eu/en/library/definition-artificial-intelligence-main-capabilities-and-scientific-disciplines>, 3.

[13] Nan Duan, Duyu Tang and Ming Zhou, 'Machine Reasoning: Technology, Dilemma and Future' in *Proceedings of the 2020 Conference on Empirical Methods in Natural Language Processing: Tutorial Abstracts* (Association for Computational Linguistics 2020) 1 <www.aclweb.org/anthology/2020.emnlp-tutorials.1>.

[14] See also Brian P Bloomfield and Theo Vurdubakis, 'IBM's Chess Players: On AI and Its Supplements' (2008) 24 The Information Society 69; Feng-Hsiung Hsu, *Behind Deep Blue: Building the Computer that Defeated the World Chess Champion* (Princeton University Press 2022).

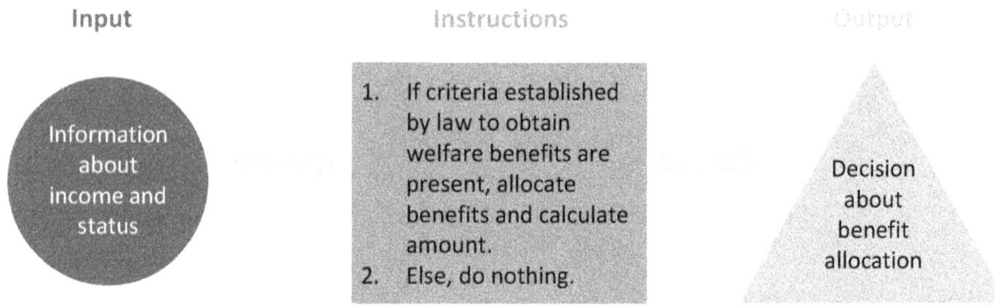

FIGURE 2.3 Abstraction of a knowledge-driven system to automate welfare benefits allocation.

decision on whether benefits should be allocated and how high the amount should be – as represented in Figure 2.3.[15]

Given their reliance on finite and discrete symbols and logical rules, reasoning processes are typically interpretable. The reasoning steps of the algorithm – which can have varying forms of complexity – can be retraced, which makes the algorithmic process relatively transparent and explainable (at least for technical experts, who should then be able to communicate about how this process works to those subjected thereto). This traceability also makes it possible to verify whether some important information has potentially been overlooked, or whether the legal rules about benefits eligibility, which were translated into symbolic rules, have been interpreted correctly. At the same time, reasoning techniques in principle presuppose that the steps or rules that need to be taken to solve a problem are – at least to a certain extent – already known.[16] Similarly, they presuppose the existence of human expertise in the domain to which the problem relates.[17] In situations where the rules that apply are pre-established by law, relatively precise and relatively easily codifiable in symbols, this need not pose major issues – even though, as we shall see in Chapter 4, the translation from legal rules to code poses fundamental challenges.[18] However, in situations where the rules that govern the situation are not (yet) known, vague or uncertain, a knowledge-driven approach that is based on simplistic rules may not be effective.

[15] As will be discussed in Section 4.1, algorithmic systems are already used by several governments for this purpose. See also Paul Henman, 'Digital Technologies and Artificial Intelligence in Social Welfare Research: A Computer Science Perspective' in Michael Adler (ed), *Research Agenda for Social Welfare Law, Policy, Practice and Impact* (Edward Elgar Publishing 2022).

[16] See, e.g., Birte Glimm and Yevgeny Kazakov, 'Classical Algorithms for Reasoning and Explanation in Description Logics' in Markus Krötzsch and Daria Stepanova (eds), *Reasoning Web. Explainable Artificial Intelligence*, vol 11810 (Springer International Publishing 2019).

[17] See also James P Ignizio, *Introduction to Expert Systems: The Development and Implementation of Rule-Based Expert Systems* (McGraw-Hill 1991).

[18] See in this regard also Mireille Hildebrandt, 'Law as Information in the Era of Data-Driven Agency' (2016) 79 The Modern Law Review 1.

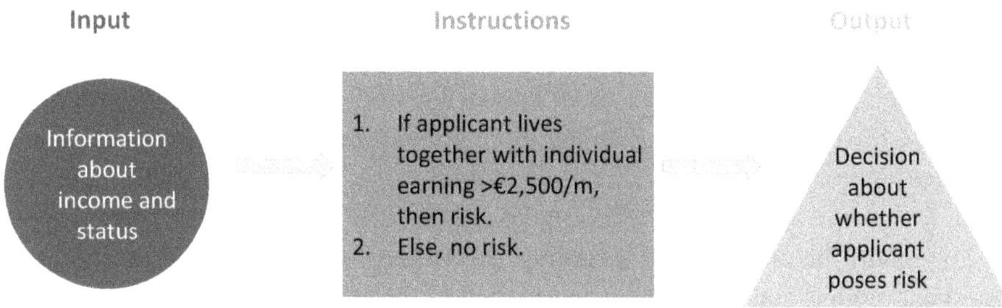

FIGURE 2.4 Abstraction of a knowledge-driven system to identify the risk of social welfare fraud.

Consider, in this regard, an example in the same sphere: an algorithmic process to assess the risk that individuals commit social welfare or tax fraud. While the majority of taxpayers and welfare applicants act in good faith, in every country, there will be individuals who commit fraudulent acts to pay less than they owe, or to receive more than they should.[19] Since public resources are limited, and not every individual can or should be investigated for fraud, one may consider developing an algorithmic system that can help identify or predict the risk of fraud, in order to prioritise those cases for investigation. Yet, while I can probably reuse a lot of the information on citizens that I had gathered for the previous example, this task may be more difficult to delegate to a rule-based knowledge-driven system. What are the rules that I would need to codify to identify a potential risk of fraud? Fraudulent types of behaviour do not always occur in easily describable steps.[20] I could make an attempt by codifying the rule that anyone who applies for welfare benefits yet lives together with someone earning more than 2,500 EUR/month poses a risk of fraud, as shown in Figure 2.4. However, with this type of rule, the output – namely, the decision on whether I need to further investigate that applicant – risks being both overly inclusive and exclusive.

[19] The detection of welfare fraud is a major application of algorithmic regulation. Its deployment aims to offset the costs incurred for the development of an algorithmic fraud detection system by the money that can be saved through the optimisation of fraud detection. See also Marvin van Bekkum and Frederik Zuiderveen Borgesius, 'Digital Welfare Fraud Detection and the Dutch SyRI Judgment' [2021] European Journal of Social Security 13882627211031256; Rikke Frank Jørgensen, 'Data and Rights in the Digital Welfare State: The Case of Denmark' [2021] Information, Communication & Society 1.

[20] This has not stopped public authorities from doing so anyway, as showcased by the example of the 'fraudescore-algorithm' used in the Netherlands up until 2020 (and in some municipalities even thereafter still). The system relied on predetermined criteria to calculate the risk of fraud, which included, for instance, the level of education of citizens, the fact that they worked as a hairdresser or taxi driver, and the neighbourhood they lived in. See also 'Junk Science Underpins Fraud Scores' (*Lighthouse Reports*, 25 June 2022) <www.lighthousereports.nl/investigation/junk-science-underpins-fraud-scores/>; 'Verboden fraudescores bleven in gebruik bij gemeenten' *NRC* (25 June 2022) <www.nrc.nl/nieuws/2022/06/25/profileren-verboden-fraudescores-bleven-in-gebruik-bij-gemeenten-a4134660>. I will come back to this example in Section 4.1.

Taking a rule-based approach may pinpoint me somewhat in the right direction, but will still require me to take into account that this rule may be too general to yield effective results. Of course, the more knowledge and experience I gain, the more I can use this knowledge to formulate more tailored rules, and perhaps also to add some exceptions to the rule. However, fraudulent techniques might change over time, so I would constantly need to update those rules.

To remedy the problem of uncertainty, recourse can be made to probabilistic and statistical models that can help make predictions based on the knowledge that I do have, and thereby cover certain knowledge gaps and reduce uncertainty.[21] These models are increasingly being researched and tailored for use in the context of knowledge-driven approaches. By relying on these models, the rigidity of more simplistic 'rule-based' systems that merely apply a static rule to a knowledge base can be diminished. Probabilistic and statistical models can hence be seen as lying somewhere in between knowledge-driven and data-driven systems.

Importantly, the knowledge on which the system reasons needs to be transformed into machine-readable code.[22] Depending on the size of the knowledge base, the potentially informal nature of the knowledge, and the relationships that need to be represented between the various symbols that represent the knowledge, this can be quite laborious. In the context of algorithmic regulation, whenever the legal rules that need to be translated are vague or open to multiple understandings – which is not infrequent, given the inherent openness and interpretability of language – certain interpretative decisions will need to be taken in advance, to the exclusion of others. Furthermore, if knowledge about certain aspects of the problem is lacking, it cannot be represented. Unless this is remedied through approaches that provide more flexibility, this will mean that – when a specific situation arises that deviates from the codified norm and for which no explicit alternative rule has been foreseen – the system is unlikely to provide a solution. Notwithstanding this restraint, knowledge-driven systems are used profusely in virtually all societal domains, and are able to assist in tasks of high complexity.

2.1.3 *Data-Driven Systems*

Researchers also explored other routes to perform 'intelligent' tasks, focusing on *data-driven* approaches instead. Rather than codifying a certain model of knowledge

[21] See, e.g., Judea Pearl, 'Graphical Models for Probabilistic and Causal Reasoning' in A Tucker and others (eds), *Computing Handbook* (2014).

[22] This task has also been referred to as 'handcrafted knowledge', which reflects the manual labour that is typically associated therewith. See John Launchbury, 'A DARPA Perspective on Artificial Intelligence' (DARPA, February 2017) <www.darpa.mil/about-us/darpa-perspective-on-ai>.

in advance, data-driven systems "*let the data speak*"[23] and infer the model from the data instead. Accordingly, these models typically allow for more flexibility and adaptability since, by *learning* from the data, the system will be able to adjust to new situations. Though already explored earlier, data-driven systems primarily gained traction after the 1980s, when the capabilities of knowledge-driven systems seemed to be hitting their limits.[24] Especially from the twenty-first century onwards, data-driven approaches started booking new successes and led to several major breakthroughs in the field – particularly those relying on machine-learning techniques.[25] It is for this reason that some AI definitions *only* refer to learning-based systems.[26]

The recent successes of those systems are largely linked to the enhanced availability of data and in particular 'big data', which can be defined as "*large volumes of extensively varied data that are generated, captured, and processed at high velocity*".[27] A growing number of tools enable the collection and analysis of data in digital – and hence easily perusable – format, by means of sensor-embedded objects, phones and computers, and the Internet of Things (IoT) more generally.[28] The fact that the processing power of computers significantly improved – thus enabling more and faster computations, and the fact that the storage of large volumes of data became more affordable, likewise contributed to the success of data-driven systems.

There are various types of data-driven techniques. Generally speaking, such techniques aim to infer the rules that should be followed from (a large number of) examples contained in a dataset, which can be labelled or not. The algorithm is thus tasked with inferring the rules (or function) behind the data and to create a

[23] Already in 1973, the French mathematician Jean-Paul Benzécri introduced the idea of "*letting the data speak for themselves*", stressing that "*Le modèle doit suivre les données, non l'inverse*" in J-P Benzécri, *L'analyse des données 2: L'analyse des correspondances* (Dunod 1973). See also François Husson, Julie Josse, and Gilbert Saporta, 'Jan de Leeuw and the French School of Data Analysis' (2016) 73(6) Journal of Statistical Software 16.

[24] Even earlier, in the late 1950s, seminal papers by – amongst others – Ray Solomonoff laid down the groundwork for inductive inference systems, which helped pave the way for modern machine learning approaches. See also David Restrepo Amariles, 'Algorithmic Decision Systems: Automation and Machine Learning in the Public Administration' in Woodrow Barfield (ed), *The Cambridge Handbook of the Law of Algorithms* (Cambridge University Press 2020).

[25] De Raedt (n 9) 286.

[26] Some authors, for instance, explicitly exclude reasoning-based systems from the term 'algorithmic systems', which they reserve for data-driven systems only (as opposed to 'information systems' which can be reasoning-based), such as in Lukas Lorenz, Albert Meijer and Tino Schuppan, 'The Algocracy as a New Ideal Type for Government Organizations: Predictive Policing in Berlin as an Empirical Case' (2021) 26 Information Polity: The International Journal of Government & Democracy in the Information Age 71.

[27] Wendy Arianne Günther and others, 'Debating Big Data: A Literature Review on Realizing Value from Big Data' (2017) 26 The Journal of Strategic Information Systems 191. See also Roger Clarke, 'Big Data, Big Risks' (2016) 26 Information Systems Journal 77.

[28] Alem Čolaković and Mesud Hadžialić, 'Internet of Things (IoT): A Review of Enabling Technologies, Challenges, and Open Research Issues' (2018) 144 Computer Networks 17.

model that should identify the relationship between the various datapoints provided to the system (for instance, inputs and outputs). By analysing a large set of examples (*training phase*), and by continuously tweaking the model based on those examples to better fit the dataset's curve, the function can be determined with ever more accuracy. Once the model has been developed based on training data, whenever the system is confronted with new input, the model can be used to predict that new input's corresponding output (*use phase*). In addition, there will typically also be a *testing phase* in between, to see how well the model performs before deploying it at scale.

The fact that data-driven systems are able to 'learn' a model from the data they are provided, does not take away the fact that these systems likewise rely on human coding. After all, the algorithms still hinge on instructions pertaining to the development of the model, and the use of the model to categorise or cluster new data. Yet the representation of reality itself will in principle not be codified in advance, nor will the instructions set out how such representation can be manipulated to achieve a certain result. This absence of the codification of knowledge and rules that set out the relationship between different knowledge elements also means that data-driven systems are typically not able to pick up *causal* relations between input and output (though this is a growing topic of research).[29] Instead, the inferred relationship between input and output is one of *correlation*. As to inferring the model, different techniques exist. A distinction is often made between supervised, unsupervised and reinforcement learning techniques – each of which is briefly discussed below.[30]

Under *supervised learning*, an algorithm is instructed to analyse training data examples that consist of input–output pairs which are explicitly labelled or scored, and to infer a model therefrom. The labelling typically occurs by a human being prior to the dataset's use. Based on the model that is inferred from the original examples, the system will have learned how to classify new examples. The performance of the system will typically increase over time, as the analysis of more data can allow it to infer more granular rules and improve the model.

For an example of such a method, I suggest revisiting the algorithmic system used to assess the risk of social welfare fraud. Instead of using a rule-based algorithm and programming rules that are likely to be under- and over-inclusive, I can instead try to teach the system to distinguish between fraudulent and non-fraudulent applications, as represented in Figure 2.5 on the next page. To develop the system, I could train it on a dataset containing information about past welfare benefits applicants, as well as an indication (or label) of whether they committed fraud in the past or not. Crucially, I would need a sufficiently large dataset, with enough examples of both

[29] See also Judea Pearl, 'The Seven Tools of Causal Inference, with Reflections on Machine Learning' (2019) 62 Communications of the ACM 54; Sema K Sgaier, Vincent Huang and Grace Charles, 'The Case for Causal AI' (2020) 18 Stanford Social Innovation Review 50.

[30] See also Igor Kononenko and Matjaž Kukar, *Machine Learning and Data Mining* (Woodhead Publishing 2007).

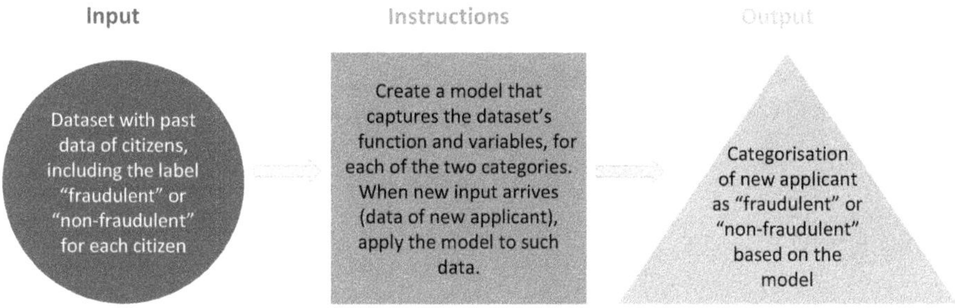

FIGURE 2.5 Abstraction of a supervised data-driven system to predict the propensity of fraud.

types of categories.[31] On that basis, I would instruct the algorithm to create a model that seeks to deduce the relevant variables for each of the two categories. When a new applicant subsequently submits an application to receive benefits, I can then use that model to predict which of the two categories – fraudulent or not – best captures the pattern of the applicant's profile. The final output would consist of the categorisation of that applicant in the corresponding category. If the applicant would be categorised in the 'fraudulent' category, I may treat this application with extra suspicion, and investigate it further before accepting it.

Alternatively, it may well be that I would like the system to discover fraudulent features that I did not think of myself. In that case, I can turn to *unsupervised learning* techniques. Under unsupervised learning, the data based on which the algorithm is trained does not contain pre-assigned labels. Instead, the algorithm analyses the unlabelled dataset by looking for potential patterns therein, and by developing a model based on those patterns. This model can, for instance, result in the clustering of data into categories with similar features, or the detection of certain anomalies within a given dataset. These techniques are hence useful to explore certain rules or clusters that were not previously identified within a dataset.[32]

When looking for welfare fraud, rather than explicitly labelling examples, I could let the algorithm create a model based on past data from citizens, and let it identify clusters of datapoints or anomalies in the dataset that may reveal potential correlations with fraud – as represented in Figure 2.6 on the next page. For instance, the data analysis might reveal that a large majority of past fraudulent applicants refused to provide public authorities with information about their financial situation when

[31] Note that, in practice, sufficient (representative) examples are not always available, which undermines the ability to generalise and can hence stand in the way of the system's proper functioning.

[32] *Deep learning* algorithms are an example thereof. They rely on *artificial neural networks*, modelled loosely after the way in which the neurons in a human brain work. The term 'deep' is a reference to the fact that these networks consist of multiple layers. Such algorithms are prevalently used for the detection of certain features in an unlabelled dataset (though they can also be used with labelled datasets).

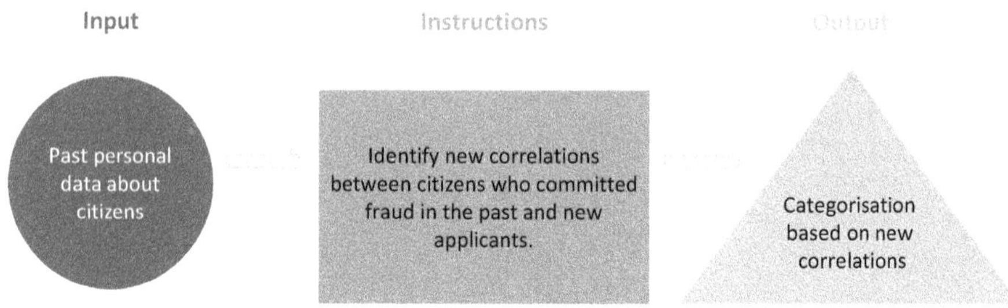

FIGURE 2.6 Abstraction of an unsupervised data-driven system to predict the propensity of fraud.

asked. A model can then be created based on the identified correlations, which I could subsequently use to assess the fraud propensity of a new applicant by verifying whether one of the identified patterns is also present there. Also in this example, the final output – based on the model's prediction of fraud propensity or not – can be a recommendation to treat a certain application with suspicion. A civil servant may choose to follow this recommendation or not. Alternatively, the recommendation can also be formalised into a decision to automatically take further investigative steps, without leaving any margin of appreciation in this respect.

A beneficial feature of unsupervised learning methods is not only the reduced workload – since the training set need not be labelled in advance – but also the fact that patterns can be identified which human beings did not previously consider or perceive. At the same time, this technique requires a larger dataset to produce successful results, and it can also lead to the identification of patterns that are irrelevant, erroneous or useless, precisely because there are no prior labels that indicate what is of value to solve the problem.[33] In the example above, it may well be that the data analysis reveals that a majority of past fraudulent applicants owned a cat, and a majority of past non-fraudulent applicants owned a dog. It would, however, be a far stretch to automatically treat all new applications from cat-owners as suspicious due to the mere fact that such a correlation was picked up. As I discuss in the next section, beyond the risk of spurious correlations,[34] the lack of labels also means that the data clustering can occur in a manner that deviates from non-discrimination law, by, for instance, taking into account prohibited grounds of discrimination, such as gender or nationality.[35]

[33] Algorithmic systems can also be run on *semi-supervised* learning methods aiming to combine the assets of both techniques. As the name implies, under semi-supervised learning, part of the training data is labelled, while the other part is left unlabelled.

[34] Tyler Vigen, *Spurious Correlations* (Hachette Books 2015).

[35] See in this regard also European Union Agency for Fundamental Rights (ed), *Handbook on European Non-Discrimination Law* (Publications Office of the European Union 2018).

Finally, I should also mention a third learning technique, called *reinforcement learning*.[36] This approach aims at enabling an algorithmic system (denoted as 'the agent') to learn which decision it should take through a reward mechanism, given uncertainty about the system's environment and given an objective – represented by a value function – that needs to be maximised. The system is instructed to observe the *state* of an environment and to identify the optimal *action* to alter the environment's state in such a way that the receipt of a *reward* signal is maximised. Since the system's aim is to maximise accumulative reward signals rather than an immediate reward, it learns to identify the course of action yielding the best results over the longer term.[37]

Unlike supervised learning, there are no labelled pairs of input–output examples to train the system. Instead, the model considers state–action pairs, and the extent to which they yield a certain reward. This reward feedback – typically in the form of a numerical score – allows the model to be tweaked so as to increase its success in achieving the value. Each time, the system needs to balance the exploitation of knowledge it gained from previous modelling attempts, with the exploration of new action methods that were not yet tried but could yield a (higher) reward.[38] By repeating the process of analysing the result of an action on the environment's state and the corresponding reward, the model can thus come closer to maximise the value that represents the objective over the long term.[39]

An example of a reinforcement learning system is a chatbot deployed by a public authority to provide citizens with answers to some frequently asked questions, as represented in Figure 2.7 on the next page. It can draw on an initial dataset of past questions and answers, but also on a wider collection of information concerning the public authority's functioning that may be of use for citizens. The chatbot can be programmed to seek feedback from the citizen at the end of the conversation to evaluate whether the provided answers satisfied the citizen's inquiries. This feedback can be used to improve the chatbot's answer whenever a similar question is asked by a citizen in the future.

The upside of this technique is the fact that one does not need to undertake the laborious task of labelling input–output pairs, one does not need to have complete information about the environment and one does not need to give continuous feedback about the model's performance, since this is only done for the totality of the outcome (in the example above, the quality of the chatbot's final answer). An important downside, however, is the risk that the algorithm may compute a

36 See for instance Richard S Sutton and Andrew G Barto, *Reinforcement Learning: An Introduction* (2nd edn, The MIT Press 2018).

37 See also LP Kaelbling, ML Littman and AW Moore, 'Reinforcement Learning: A Survey' (1996) 4 Journal of Artificial Intelligence Research 237.

38 Sutton and Barto (n 36) 3.

39 Csaba Szepesvári, *Algorithms for Reinforcement Learning* (Morgan & Claypool Publishers 2010).

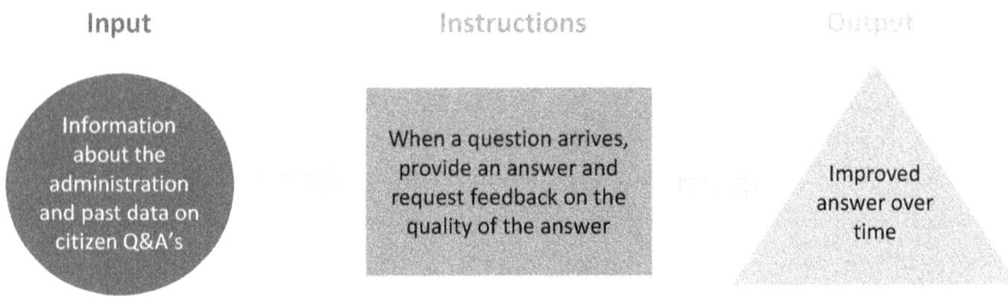

FIGURE 2.7 Abstraction of a data-driven system to automate and improve the answering of citizen questions.

model that merely pursues 'reward hacking', namely, the maximisation of the reward signal, while oblivious to the fact that intermediate actions to achieve that reward may be undesirable or cause undesirable consequences.[40] The way in which the objective – or the value function – is defined, is hence essential.

Finally, let me also make a brief note about *large language models* or LLMs, which are learning-based models that are designed to both 'comprehend' and generate text. These models are trained on a very large dataset of text examples, which in some cases span virtually all text that can be found on the internet.

The model is trained to infer and predict which sequence of words constitutes the most sensible response to a prompt provided by the user, based on the prompt's context. Just as with other learning-based models, LLMs consist of large strings of numbers (weights) which are 'interpreted' and executed by code. When the model is trained, it slightly adjusts these weights based on what it has 'learned', allowing it to improve its predictions of the next suitable word(s) in light of the overall context. It is precisely the capability of large language models to take such context into account that explains the success of their predictions, and hence of their performativity. These models have also been referred to as foundational models, as they are typically trained on a broad range of data rendering them capable of performing various general tasks, which makes them a suitable 'foundation' to build new applications in a more cost-effective manner, without the need to develop a model from scratch. Indeed, the models can be finetuned to serve more particular purposes, for instance by feeding them with domain-specific datasets to adapt them to certain contexts (e.g. in the area of law or medicine) or to adapt them to specific language types (e.g. therapeutical conversations).

Since LLMs are typically further trained on the inputs they receive from their users, they heavily rely on reinforcement learning by human feedback. By virtue of their ability to predict relevant word sequences, LLMs can be used to power chatbots, such as ChatGPT (by OpenAI), Bing Chat (by Microsoft), Bard (by

40 See also Yinlong Yuan and others, 'A Novel Multi-Step Reinforcement Learning Method for Solving Reward Hacking' (2019) 49 Applied Intelligence 2874.

Google) and Llama (by Meta). Beyond text, similar approaches also drive applications that enable the generation of images, videos, and audio. Since the interfaces of these generative models are specifically designed to enable their use by non-experts, the wide availability of the systems – often free or at low cost – arguably lead to a major breakthrough in the public's awareness of the technology's transformative impact on society. Jumping on this hype, it should come as no surprise that public authorities too have been exploring how they can use LLM-powered chatbots to facilitate their interactions with citizens to more efficiently deliver their services. In October 2023, the UK government, for instance, announced that it would launch an AI chatbot to help Britons pay their taxes and access their pensions, based on a model that would be powered by OpenAI.[41]

2.1.4 *Comparing Approaches*

Bearing in mind the above description of knowledge- and data-driven algorithms, we can now make a few comparisons. Firstly, when knowledge-driven systems merely rely on the codification of symbols and rules, they can be relatively inflexible, since they do not deal very well with new and uncertain situations that deviate from the coded model. This is, however, different for knowledge-driven systems that also draw on probabilistic and statistical methods, as they can extrapolate from the known information to make predictions that can contribute to a solution, despite the potential uncertainty or knowledge gaps. Data-driven systems are typically more flexible, as they enable the inference of models that can evolve over time in light of new data that is fed into the system. Yet the models established through data-driven systems or through statistical methods can subsequently be used for reasoning, thus underscoring the fact that systems need not only focus on one approach or another.[42]

The fact that data-driven systems do not require a coded description of what the data represent by translating knowledge into symbols and symbolic rules has been an important contributor to the successes they booked, especially in domains where the representation of codified knowledge is more difficult. Indeed, over the last decade, learning-based approaches have, for instance, been responsible for significant advances in computer vision (or methods to acquire and analyse images and videos), computer hearing (or methods to acquire and analyse sound data like music or

[41] See James Titcomb and Matthew Field, 'Sunak to Launch AI Chatbot for Britons to Pay Taxes and Access Pensions' The Telegraph (28 October 2023) <www.telegraph.co.uk/business/2023/10/28/rishi-sunak-launch-ai-chatbot-pay-taxes-access-pensions/>. This announcement was seen by some as an answer to the huge pressure on the call centers of the UK's Revenue and Customs departments, as citizens were faced with very long waiting times.

[42] It has also been argued that there exists "*a conceptual continuity between algebraically rich inference systems, such as logical or probabilistic inference, and simple manipulations, such as the mere concatenation of trainable learning systems*"; see Léon Bottou, 'From Machine Learning to Machine Reasoning' (2014) 94 Machine Learning 133.

speech), and computer touch (or methods to acquire and analyse tactile information). Furthermore, especially when using unsupervised learning techniques, learning algorithms can help identify patterns and categorisations that humans did not previously perceive or consider, which can lead to useful new insights.[43]

However, the use of data-driven systems also has drawbacks. First, the inherently probabilistic nature of their outcomes means that there will always be a margin of error. In some situations, such algorithms can achieve a very high level of accuracy in their predictions, yet it may be that the dataset on which the system was trained did not present an accurate representation of real-life situations, thus reducing the system's accuracy and utility outside the lab.[44] The output may also be false or entirely estranged from reality, which is especially problematic in the context of generative models that produce text or images which come across as highly realistic. It has been noted that data-driven algorithms can be "*statistically impressive*", yet they remain "*individually unreliable*".[45] That said, knowledge-driven algorithms are not free from error either: if the knowledge that the system should reason upon is not correctly represented by the human programmer, the outcome will be equally flawed.

Second, certain data-driven algorithms – especially those relying on deep learning methods[46] – suffer from a lack of transparency and interpretability, which has been referred to as the so-called 'black box' problem. Such systems "*internalise data in ways that are not easily audited or understood by humans*", for instance due to the "*complexity of the algorithm's structure*", or because they rely "*on geometric relationships that humans cannot visualise*".[47] This means that human developers and deployers of such algorithms cannot always explain how a certain outcome was achieved, and why it was achieved.[48] This can be contrasted with the interpretability of knowledge-driven systems which, in light of their typically predetermined symbolic rules, provide better insight into how and why a certain output is provided.

Third, while data-driven algorithms can identify patterns and correlations between data points that humans might not have recognised, they are in principle unable to establish *causal* relationships between those points, which may lead

[43] Yavar Bathaee, 'The Artificial Intelligence Black Box and the Failure of Intent and Causation' (2018) 31 Harvard Journal of Law & Technology 890, 891.

[44] See, e.g., David Thogmartin, 'Ensuring Reliable AI in Real World Situations' (Deloitte 2022), <www2.deloitte.com/content/dam/Deloitte/de/Documents/Innovation/DELO-8505%20Trustworthy%20AI%20Robust%20and%20Reliable_KS6.pdf>.

[45] Launchbury (n 22).

[46] See also Yoshua Bengio, Aaron Courville and Ian Goodfellow, *Deep Learning* (The MIT Press 2016).

[47] Bathaee (n 43) 901.

[48] Cynthia Rudin and Joanna Radin, 'Why Are We Using Black Box Models in AI When We Do Not Need To? A Lesson from an Explainable AI Competition' (2019) 1 Harvard Data Science Review 2 <https://hdsr.mitpress.mit.edu/pub/f9kuryi8/release/6>.

to spurious correlations, a risk inherent to virtually all statistical models.[49] Furthermore, the lack of symbolically represented knowledge also renders data-driven systems unable to contextualise the information they process. This means that certain logical facts that are evident for human beings ('common sense'), may not be picked up by the system. In addition, the system can also 'learn' in ways that the developers did not predict or intend, which may lead to unforeseen adverse consequences.[50]

Finally, data-driven algorithms have a higher vulnerability to adversarial attacks. By inserting deceptive input into the system – which can go unnoticed by the human eye – one can deliberately confuse the model created by the system and thereby compromise its output.[51] While certain defence techniques exist against those attacks, such as data manipulation constraints, the risk nevertheless remains that the system's vulnerabilities are exploited, and that the results computed by the system become unreliable.[52] The high complexity of the models and the decreased transparency mentioned above, can also render the detection of those attacks more difficult.

In sum, knowledge-driven and data-driven techniques each have a set of capabilities that enable the automation of (intelligent) tasks. When seeking to solve a problem through an algorithmic system, the choice of technique will hence be determined by the type of problem, the existing knowledge and expertise about the problem, the availability of (representative) data, the characteristics one wishes to prioritise when seeking a solution to execute the task and – most importantly – the budget. One does not necessarily need to choose between one technique or another, as various methods exist to remedy the constraints of each, by combining reasoning techniques with learning-based approaches. Data-driven models can be used to help predict how the sought-after data could look like, after which the outcome of that prediction can serve as a basis for further reasoning and analysis through symbolic rules.[53] This demonstrates that the distinction between knowledge- and data-driven techniques is not always clear-cut. In fact, the most recent research trend focuses on hybrid systems, whereby knowledge- and data-driven techniques are combined.[54]

[49] See also Vigen (n 34). With complex data-driven systems, the so-called 'curse of dimensionality' – first coined by Richard Bellman – can make this risk more prominent. See Richard Bellman, *Dynamic Programming* (Princeton University Press 1957).

[50] See, e.g., Gina Neff and Peter Nagy, 'Talking to Bots: Symbiotic Agency and the Case of Tay' [2016] International Journal of Communication 4915.

[51] See, e.g., Marco Barreno and others, 'Can Machine Learning Be Secure?', in *Proceedings of the 2006 ACM Symposium on Information, Computer and Communications Security* (Association for Computing Machinery 2006), <www.dl.acm.org/doi/10.1145/1128817.1128824>.

[52] See, e.g., Luis Muñoz-González and Emil C. Lupu, 'The Security of Machine Learning Systems', in Leslie F. Sikos (ed), *AI in Cybersecurity*, Intelligent Systems Reference Library (Springer International Publishing, 2019), 47 and following.

[53] Duan, Tang and Zhou (n 13) 2.

[54] De Raedt (n 9) 300. See also Gary Marcus and Ernest Davis, *Rebooting AI: Building Artificial Intelligence We Can Trust* (Penguin Random House 2020).

2.1.5 *AI Systems*

Before concluding this technical chapter, there is one more term I wish to expand on in the context of algorithmic regulation, namely artificial intelligence (AI) – the importance of which has been described as "*more profound than electricity or fire*".[55] World leaders have stated that "*whoever becomes the leader in this sphere will become the ruler of the world*",[56] and the European Parliament's Special Committee on Artificial Intelligence in a Digital Age even claimed that it can be "*thought of as the fifth element after air, earth, water and fire*".[57] Aside from the hype that these hyperbolic statements represent, what does this technology consist of, and how does it relate to the algorithmic systems I described in the previous sections?

As noted above, AI can be understood as an umbrella term for a range of 'intelligent' technological applications. The pursuit of intelligent machines is almost as ancient as human history,[58] yet the first time the term AI was used dates back to the now-famous 1956 Dartmouth Workshop, considered to mark the birth of 'AI' as a field of research.[59] While all AI systems are composed of algorithms, not all algorithmic systems necessarily fall under the AI umbrella. As the term indicates, to be considered 'artificially intelligent', a system would need to perform a task that is typically associated with *intelligence*, rather than merely constituting the simple *automation* of a task. What is considered an 'intelligent' task may vary significantly based on the person to whom the question is asked, and the discipline they are trained in. A philosopher might define the term quite differently from a schoolteacher or a lawyer. More importantly, AI experts, too, tend to define this technology in different ways. In their seminal AI handbook, Russell and Norvig, for instance, identify definitions that focus on the ability of a machine to think or the ability act

[55] Uttered by Sundar Pichai, CEO of Google, in 2018. See Catherine Clifford, 'Google CEO: A.I. Is More Important than Fire or Electricity' *CNBC* (1 February 2018) <www.cnbc.com/2018/02/01/google-ceo-sundar-pichai-ai-is-more-important-than-fire-electricity.html>.

[56] Uttered by Vladimir Putin, President of the Russian Federation, in 2017. See James Vincent, 'Putin Says the Nation that Leads in AI "Will Be the Ruler of the World" – The Verge' *The Verge* (4 September 2017) <www.theverge.com/2017/9/4/16251226/russia-ai-putin-rule-the-world>.

[57] Stated by the European Parliament's Special Committee on Artificial Intelligence in a Digital Age (AIDA), 'Draft Report on Artificial Intelligence in a Digital Age' (European Parliament 2021) (2020/2266(INI)) 9.

[58] See also Pamela McCorduck, *Machines Who Think* (2nd edn, A K Peters, Ltd 2004).

[59] The workshop proposal described the project as aiming:

> to proceed on the basis of the conjecture that every aspect of learning or any other feature of intelligence can in principle be so precisely described that a machine can be made to simulate it. An attempt will be made to find how to make machines use language, form abstractions and concepts, solve kinds of problems now reserved for humans, and improve themselves.

See John McCarthy and others, 'A Proposal for the Dartmouth Summer Research Project on Artificial Intelligence', 31 August 1955, *AI Magazine*, 27(4), 2006, 12.

humanly, versus definitions focusing on their ability to think or act *rationally*.[60] The latter definition is more prominently used among AI researchers nowadays, as it can more easily be formalised by virtue of an AI system's optimisation function, through which the system can be tasked to select those actions that are expected to maximise its utility.[61]

In essence, one could consider algorithmic systems on a spectrum. One extreme contains algorithms with only a very minimal set of instructions, too basic or simplistic to be considered 'intelligent'. The other extreme contains algorithms that are highly complex and sophisticated, and would be considered 'intelligent' by virtually all researchers. Yet, when it comes to algorithmic systems situated in the middle part of the spectrum, researchers do not always agree on whether the system would be considered 'intelligent' or not, and the perception thereof also tends to change over time.[62] There is no fixed rule as regards *how many* or *which type of* instructions an algorithmic system must contain in order to be called an 'AI' system.

Since the term AI is currently widely used, and since the European Union's regulatory initiative is titled 'the AI Act', let me discuss some AI definitions put forward in the context of EU policy, and examine how these compare with the description above. In this regard, it must be borne in mind that the conceptualisation of 'AI' has not only an academic or scientific relevance, but also a political one. The scope of the regulatory requirements that legislators may impose on 'AI' systems will after all depend on how they define 'AI'. Furthermore, the definition of AI also has a societal relevance, as it contributes to framing the broader narrative around the impact of AI in society.[63] Consider, for instance, the way in which the European Parliament's Delvaux report frames AI, evoking the context of "*Mary Shelley's* Frankenstein's Monster" and "*the story of Prague's Golem*",[64] and cautioning that "*humankind stands on the threshold of an era when ever more sophisticated robots, bots, androids and other manifestations of artificial intelligence ('AI') seem to be poised to unleash a new industrial revolution*".[65] The Report further states that "*ultimately there is a possibility that in the long-term, AI could surpass human intellectual capacity*",[66] and makes the much-commented suggestion to create "*a specific legal status for robots in the long run, so that at least the most sophisticated*

[60] Russell and Norvig (n 1) 2.
[61] De Raedt (n 9) 286.
[62] This phenomenon relates to the so-called *AI effect*, whereby a type of application that was originally considered as 'intelligent' becomes so commonplace that it is no longer considered sufficiently intelligent to still warrant the designation 'AI'. See also McCorduck (n 58).
[63] See in this regard Bilel Benbouzid, Yannick Meneceur and Nathalie Alisa Smuha, 'Quatre nuances de régulation de l'intelligence artificielle: Une cartographie des conflits de définition' (2022) 232–33 Réseaux 29.
[64] Mady Delvaux, 'Report with Recommendations to the Commission on Civil Law Rules on Robotics (2015/2103(INL))' (European Parliament 2017) A8–0005/2017 §A.
[65] ibid §B.
[66] ibid §Q.

autonomous robots could be established as having the status of electronic persons responsible for making good any damage they may cause"[67] – a suggestion that was rejected by the European Commission. However, the Commission did follow up on the report's proposal to establish a definition of AI and to draft ethics guidelines to guide use of the technology.

To this end, it set up a High-Level Expert Group on AI in June 2018 composed of fifty-two experts from various domains, tasked with the drafting of Ethics Guidelines for AI as well as Policy and Investment Recommendations.[68] As part of its tasks, the Expert Group set up a working group to establish a definition of AI – an exercise that took just as long as agreeing on AI ethics principles – which resulted in the following formulation:

> Artificial intelligence (AI) systems are software (and possibly also hardware) systems designed by humans[69] that, given a complex goal, act in the physical or digital dimension by perceiving their environment through data acquisition, interpreting the collected structured or unstructured data, reasoning on the knowledge, or processing the information, derived from this data and deciding the best action(s) to take to achieve the given goal. AI systems can either use symbolic rules or learn a numeric model, and they can also adapt their behaviour by analysing how the environment is affected by their previous actions.[70]

The following elements can already be distilled from this definition. First, as will be stressed in the next section, the Expert Group emphasised that systems are designed by human beings. This means that they do not 'overcome' us passively but that they are an active creation of persons who are therefore also responsible for their consequences.[71] Second, the definition takes into account that there is no 'single' AI system.[72] It indicates that AI systems can 'use symbolic rules', as in the case of knowledge-driven systems, thus not limiting the term AI only to data-driven systems. Accordingly, AI is considered an overarching concept covering a range of

[67] ibid §59(f).

[68] European Commission, 'High-Level Expert Group on Artificial Intelligence' (*Shaping Europe's Digital Future – European Commission*) <https://ec.europa.eu/digital-single-market/en/high-level-expert-group-artificial-intelligence>. See also Nathalie A Smuha, 'The EU Approach to Ethics Guidelines for Trustworthy Artificial Intelligence' (2019) 20 Computer Law Review International 97.

[69] The footnote in the definition states that: "*Humans design AI systems directly, but they may also use AI techniques to optimize their design.*" It was added by the Expert Group to reflect the fact that AI systems can sometimes also be programmed to develop new algorithms.

[70] High-Level Expert Group on AI, 'A Definition of AI: Main Capabilities and Scientific Disciplines' (n 12).

[71] See also Nathalie A Smuha, 'Laten we intelligenter zijn wanneer we het over Artificiële Intelligentie hebben' (*Knack Data News*, 11 March 2020) <https://datanews.knack.be/ict/nieuws/laten-we-intelligenter-zijn-wanneer-we-het-over-artificiele-intelligentie-hebben/article-opinion-1574905.html>.

[72] Nathalie A Smuha, 'From a "Race to AI" to a "Race to AI Regulation": Regulatory Competition for Artificial Intelligence' (2021) 13 Law, Innovation and Technology 57.

technologies that have certain properties in common, namely their ability to reason on or learn from the data provided to them, and to "*act in the physical or digital dimension*" based on such data. As regards data-driven systems, the definition indicates that AI systems can 'adapt their behaviour' over time[73] based on what they 'learn',[74] which is in turn dependent on how they have been programmed to do so by a human being. Lastly, the definition also mentions hardware, thereby indicating that knowledge- and data-driven algorithms can also be incorporated into hardware to design machines that can carry out physical tasks, which is the aim of the field of robotics.

While the European Commission endorsed the Expert Group's *Ethics Guidelines*, it did not retain the above definition in its subsequent proposal for a new AI regulation, published two years later in April 2021. Instead, it suggested a somewhat different definition of AI, encompassing "*software that is developed with one or more of the techniques and approaches listed in Annex I and can, for a given set of human-defined objectives, generate outputs such as content, predictions, recommendations, or decisions influencing the environments they interact with*".[75] Like the High-Level Expert Group, the Commission's definition stressed that the objectives of AI are 'human-defined', also indicating a difference in style with the Delvaux report.[76] At the same time, the Commission's original proposal suggested to exhaustively list in annex I the specific techniques and approaches that should fall under the AI Act's scope, so as to enhance legal certainty. These concerned:

(a) Machine learning approaches, including supervised, unsupervised and reinforcement learning, using a wide variety of methods including deep learning;
(b) Logic- and knowledge-based approaches, including knowledge representation, inductive (logic) programming, knowledge bases, inference and deductive engines, (symbolic) reasoning and expert systems;
(c) Statistical approaches, Bayesian estimation, search and optimisation methods.

73 They can do this in an autonomous manner, yet only once they are programmed to do so by a human being.

74 Besides formal definitions provided by governmental organisations, consider also the definition(s) provided by Russell and Norvig in their influential Handbook on AI (n 1).

75 European Commission, Proposal for a Regulation of the European Parliament and the Council laying down harmonised rules on Artificial Intelligence (Artificial Intelligence Act) and amending certain Union legislative acts 2021 [COM(2021) 206 final].

76 This point can be criticised, since AI systems can also be programmed to set objectives autonomously (in light of certain restraints and/or elements of information provided to them). Some hence argued that these systems might fall outside the scope of the Commission's AI definition. However, one can counter-argue that, even for those systems, there is still a programming phase during which a human being sets out the system's objectives at a more abstract level, to be further concretised by the system later on, and hence that they do fall under the definition's scope.

Accordingly, the Commission originally opted for a broad general definition of AI, while simultaneously meticulously specifying the underlying techniques that would actually be caught. This implies a focus on the technical approach behind the systems and their specific research discipline classification rather than their properties or effects. The idea behind listing these techniques under an annex was to ensure flexibility in the future, in case new approaches come along that do not neatly fit under the existing ones – even if list-based definitional approaches inevitably risk being both over- and under-inclusive. Stakeholders have therefore proactively been seeking to influence the regulation's definition of AI prior to its adoption.[77]

A number of actors have argued that the Commission's original definition was too broad.[78] Some argued that only data-driven approaches – and more specifically machine-learning applications – should be covered by the proposed AI Act,[79] while others proposed that at least the approaches listed under point (c) should be excluded.[80] In addition, it has been argued that not only AI systems but also other technologies that can be used for similar tasks should be included, to ensure a 'level playing field' between different technologies.[81] Evidently, a narrower definition also

[77] During the trilogue negotiations about the AI Act, both the Council of the European Union and the European Parliament have been discussing whether the approach of listing AI techniques in annex I of the AI Act should be maintained or whether this list should be removed in favour of a (broader) definition in the main body of the regulation. See, e.g., Luca Bertuzzi, 'Artificial Intelligence Definition, Governance on MEPs' Menu' (*Euractiv*, 8 November 2022) <www.euractiv.com/section/digital/news/artificial-intelligence-definition-governance-on-meps-menu/>. Ultimately, they decided to opt for the latter option. I will also return to this point *infra* when discussing the AI Act in more detail, in Section 5.4.

[78] Consider, for instance, the feedback by Digital Europe (a leading trade association representing digitally transforming industries in Europe) stating that: "*The definition of 'artificial intelligence' set in the AI Act is too wide. The proposed definition encompasses many software technology applications, even when they pose no major concerns around data, opaqueness, safety and reliability. It notably includes within AI techniques 'logic-based and statistical approaches, Bayesian estimation, search and optimisation methods'*". 'DIGITALEUROPE's Initial Findings on the Proposed AI Act' (DIGITALEUROPE 2021) <www.digitaleurope.org/resources/digitaleuropes-initial-findings-on-the-proposed-ai-act/>.

[79] See, e.g., the position of the Slovenian presidency as reported by AlgorithmWatch, 'European Council and Commission in Agreement to Narrow the Scope of the AI Act' (*AlgorithmWatch*, 23 November 2021) <https://algorithmwatch.org/en/eu-narrow-scope-of-ai-act/>.

[80] Huawei, 'Huawei Response on the European Commission's Proposal for a Regulation of the European Parliament and of the Council Laying Down the Harmonised Rules on Artificial Intelligence (Artificial Intelligence Act) and Amending Certain Union Legislative Acts' (*European Commission – Have your say*, August 2021) <https://ec.europa.eu/info/law/better-regulation/have-your-say/initiatives/12527-Artificial-intelligence-ethical-and-legal-requirements/F2665442_en>.

[81] 'Feedback to the European Commission's Regulation Proposal on the Artificial Intelligence Act' (DigitalPoland 2021) <https://digitalpoland.org/en/blog/2021/08/feedback-to-the-european-commission-s-regulation-proposal-on-the-artificial-intelligence-act>. As I also noted elsewhere, "*the adoption of a strict rule that imposes burdensome obligations on AI deployers to minimise certain risks, would not cover a manifestation of the same risk by other types of technology, and*

narrows down the scope of systems that are subjected to regulatory requirements and scrutiny. It is therefore no surprise that a regulatory battleground emerged around this definition, which continuously shifted in shape during the course of the negotiations on the AI Act between the European Parliament and Council.[82]

The two latter institutions decided to eliminate the Commission's annex with AI approaches and techniques, and to solely include a (slightly altered) definition in the regulation's main text. In the final version of the AI Act, which entered into force on 1 August 2024, Article 3(1) reads: "'*AI system' means a machine-based system designed to operate with varying levels of autonomy, that may exhibit adaptiveness after deployment and that, for explicit or implicit objectives, infers, from the input it receives, how to generate outputs such as predictions, content, recommendations, or decisions that can influence physical or virtual environments*". This definition has the advantage of being closer to the one proposed by the OECD[83] and is therefore seemingly more reflective of the slowly emerging global definitional consensus. It also lists the 'actions' that AI systems can be programmed to undertake based on the input they are provided, such as making recommendations and predictions, or taking decisions, and it explicitly includes the concept of 'autonomy'.

I will come back to the AI Act's definition of AI in Section 5.4 where I analyse the regulation in more detail. At this stage, suffice it to say that this definition may come across as rather broad, but that the actual regulatory scope of the AI Act is significantly narrowed down by the regulation's Recital 12, which distinguishes it from 'simpler traditional software systems or programming approaches' and from 'systems that are based on the rules defined solely by natural persons to automatically execute operations', neither of which should fall under the AI Act's scope. Furthermore, its scope is also narrowed down by the specific AI-applications listed under its substantive provisions, since not all systems that fall under the AI definition are also subjected to new regulatory requirements.

Importantly, this book is not interested in the definitional conundrums of AI, but rather in the adverse effects that the use of algorithmic regulation – by virtue of the scaled and automated decision-making it enables – may have on the rule of law and its principles, regardless of the underlying technique used for this purpose. Data-driven approaches are often considered to be more problematic than knowledge-driven approaches, given their reliance on potentially biased or erroneous datasets,

might merely push AI deployers towards the use of other tools to achieve the same problematic end", in Smuha, 'From a "Race to AI" to a "Race to AI Regulation"' (n 72) 64.

82 For a discussion of this battleground, and its various definitional camps, see, e.g., Benbouzid, Meneceur and Smuha (n 63).

83 In its policy documents, the OECD defines AI systems as follows: "*An AI system is a machine-based system that can, for a given set of human-defined objectives, make predictions, recommendations, or decisions influencing real or virtual environments. AI systems are designed to operate with varying levels of autonomy.*" See OECD, 'Recommendation of the Council on Artificial Intelligence' (2019) OECD/LEGAL/0449 <https://legalinstruments.oecd.org/en/instruments/OECD-LEGAL-0449>.

their dynamic and evolving nature, their greater opacity, and their relative novelty – which also means less time has passed to develop appropriate mitigation measures for their risks. I could hence have opted to limit my investigation to the way in which public authorities rely on data-driven systems only, and leave aside the use of knowledge-driven systems. However, as noted above – the distinction between both is not firm, since systems can rely on both approaches, and on intermediary probabilistic approaches. Furthermore, as already hinted at, and as I will discuss further below, knowledge-driven approaches, too, can pose significant risks, even those that are only based on very crude rules. While they typically benefit from a higher degree of intelligibility and a greater level of control and predictability, their use can still cause substantial societal harm. Moreover, public authorities tend to rely both on knowledge- and data-driven approaches to automate administrative acts.

Consequently, in this book I will focus on algorithmic systems in general. Where the distinction between different approaches is relevant (for instance in light of a specific risk or drawback arising therefrom) I will mention whether the system is primarily knowledge- or data-driven. Rather than trying to set boundaries around which techniques are sufficiently 'intelligent' to fall under the AI umbrella, I will limit my use of the term AI altogether by reserving it only for my discussion of the AI Act in Section 5.4, given the Act's heavy reliance on this term. In the remainder of the book, I will instead examine the deployment of algorithmic regulation by public authorities to inform or take administrative acts, regardless of the underlying approach or technique they rely on. Collectively, I will refer to the use of such systems as *algorithmic regulation*. With these technical aspects in mind, let me now consider the societal aspects of those systems.

2.2 SOCIETAL ASPECTS

In the section above, I described the building blocks of algorithmic systems, and focused on their technical aspects in isolation. In reality, algorithmic systems do not operate in a vacuum and cannot be reduced to their technical characteristics. As noted in the Introduction, they can regulate their environments, govern social relationships and steer human behaviour – and are often explicitly designed to do so.[84] This is because they are always already embedded in a broader infrastructure, which is composed not just of the system's software, but also of the wider network of individuals, organisations, cultures, languages, laws and customs in which they are designed, developed and used. In other words, algorithmic systems are 'socio-

[84] In this regard, it can also be pointed out that algorithmic systems can serve as a tool to 'nudge' individuals. Karen Yeung speaks of 'hypernudge', since data-driven systems particularly enable the channelling of "*user choices in directions preferred by the choice architect through processes that are subtle, unobtrusive, yet extraordinarily powerful*", "*due to their networked, continuously updated, dynamic and pervasive nature*". See Karen Yeung, '"Hypernudge": Big Data as a Mode of Regulation by Design' (2017) 20 Information, Communication & Society 118.

technical' systems, as they have an influence on, and are influenced by, their societal environment.[85] When public authorities implement algorithmic regulation, they do so with a certain purpose, which involves the concrete effects it can have beyond the algorithmic system. For instance, they count on the system to enhance the efficiency of their organisational processes, to improve the accuracy of their decisions, or to help predict or analyse societal phenomena based on which they can optimise their actions.

In what follows, I therefore examine this mutual influencing process further by providing a characterisation of algorithmic systems that emphasises their socio-technical nature (Section 2.2.1). Following this characterisation, I discuss various consequences associated with reliance on algorithmic systems, including the risk of error (Section 2.2.2), the risk of bias (Section 2.2.3), the impact on human agency (Section 2.2.4), the dependency of algorithmic systems on data and proxies (Section 2.2.5) and the potential opacity surrounding their use (Section 2.2.6). Keeping these elements in mind will enable a better understanding, in subsequent chapters, of the impact of algorithmic regulation on societal interests, including on the rule of law.

2.2.1 *Algorithmic Systems as Socio-technical Infrastructure*

The intuition that the design, development and use of a technology is not a mere technical matter, but also a normative and political matter, is far from new. Already in 1964, Lewis Mumford juxtaposed *democratic technics* with *authoritarian technics*. He argued that certain technologies, and particularly systems used for automation, lend themselves more easily to authoritarian tendencies in society given their scale, their centralised and controlling nature, and their focus on efficiency and speed instead of human individuality.[86] Over the past decades, scholarship on the relationship between technology and society has been burgeoning, producing theoretical frameworks that draw on a variety of disciplines.[87]

[85] High-Level Expert Group on AI, 'Ethics Guidelines for Trustworthy AI' (European Commission 2019) <https://digital-strategy.ec.europa.eu/en/library/ethics-guidelines-trustworthy-ai>; Gordon Baxter and Ian Sommerville, 'Socio-Technical Systems: From Design Methods to Systems Engineering' (2011) 23 Interacting with Computers 4; Andreas Theodorou and Virginia Dignum, 'Towards Ethical and Socio-Legal Governance in AI' (2020) 2 Nature Machine Intelligence 10; Shakir Mohamed, Marie-Therese Png and William Isaac, 'Decolonial AI: Decolonial Theory as Sociotechnical Foresight in Artificial Intelligence' [2020] 33 Philosophy & Technology, 659; Pekka Ala-Pietilä and Nathalie A Smuha, 'A Framework for Global Cooperation on Artificial Intelligence and Its Governance' in Bertrand Braunschweig and Malik Ghallab (eds), *Reflections on Artificial Intelligence for Humanity* (Springer International Publishing 2021); Gry Hasselbalch, *Data Ethics of Power* (Edward Elgar Publishing 2021).

[86] Lewis Mumford, 'Authoritarian and Democratic Technics' (1964) 5 Technology and Culture 1.

[87] See also Hanseth and Monteiro, who rely on actor-network theory to examine the societal implications of standardisation processes for information infrastructures, and mention other relevant theoretical frameworks, from structuration theory and phenomenology to hermeneutics and Habermas' theory of communicative action: Ole Hanseth and Eric Monteiro,

A chief insight of this scholarship, albeit still controversial for some,[88] concerns the fact that technology is not neutral[89] but that it embodies normative and political choices on the part of its designers, developers and users, which shape the technology's affordances.[90] These choices can not only be judged by the extent to which the technology is effective in reaching its goals, but also by how it can alter or entrench power structures and impact human relationships. By virtue of being part of a society, technical systems are inherently interwoven therein and influenced thereby. Yet, once created, they exert an influence on society in turn. This influence can have various modalities. It can be deliberate or accidental, known or obscure, significant or minor, positive or negative (and is often mixed), and it can manifest itself in the short or in the longer term. To expose this influence, both the social forces behind the technology and the technology's particular characteristics should be assessed,[91] as each of these elements can contribute thereto.

A well-known example of a deliberate way in which artifacts have been designed to exert a particular influence on society, concerns Robert Moses' low-hanging bridges on Long Island.[92] Their height prevented public buses – and the people of colour or lower-income passengers they typically carried – from accessing public beaches that were primarily intended for the recreation of white middle- and upper-class citizens, who could pass the low-hanging bridges with their cars.[93] Another example, which is not deliberate yet nevertheless highly worrisome, concerns the way in which cars are designed by using crash-test dummies that reflect the average height and size of men, not taking into account the anatomy of women. This renders it 47 per cent more likely for a woman that is involved in a car crash to be

'Inscribing Behaviour in Information Infrastructure Standards' (1997) 7 Accounting, Management and Information Technologies 183, 185.

88 Some authors still adhere to the notion that technology – by virtue of its inanimate nature – is inherently neutral, and that one can only make normative or political judgments about the society in which the technology is used or about the person that uses it, rather than about the technology itself. See, e.g., Joseph C Pitt, '"Guns Don't Kill, People Kill"; Values in and/or Around Technologies' in Peter Kroes and Peter-Paul Verbeek (eds), *The Moral Status of Technical Artefacts*, vol 17 (Springer Netherlands 2014). See also Boaz Miller, 'Is Technology Value-Neutral?' (2021) 46 Science, Technology, & Human Values 53.

89 Melvin Kranzberg, 'Technology and History: "Kranzberg's Laws"' (1995) 15 Bulletin of Science, Technology & Society 5.

90 In this context, the affordance of a technology can be described as the quality that defines its possible uses or that makes clear how it can or should be used. See in this regard also Mireille Hildebrandt, *Smart Technologies and the End(s) of Law* (Edward Elgar Publishing 2015); Julie E Cohen, 'Affording Fundamental Rights: A Provocation Inspired by Mireille Hildebrandt' (2017) 4 Critical Analysis of Law 76.

91 Langdon Winner, 'Do Artifacts Have Politics?' (1980) 109 Daedalus 121, 123.

92 However, see also the critical account of Bernward Joerges, 'Do Politics Have Artefacts?' (1999) 29 Social Studies of Science 411.

93 Winner (n 91) 124. See also Lawrence Lessig, 'The Law of the Horse: What Cyberlaw Might Teach' (1999) 113 Harvard Law Review 501, 543.

seriously injured, and 71 per cent more likely for her to be moderately injured, than for a man.[94]

As I will elaborate in the next sections, this holds true not only for physical artefacts, but also for digital technologies – including algorithmic systems. An example of how the combined use of physical and digital technology can deliberately co-contribute to a societal impact, is found in Flanders. Since February 2021, Flemish municipalities have the competence to penalise excessive speed themselves by means of a fine, so as to increase the enforcement of speed limits. However, for smaller towns, the costs to set up automatised speed traps to measure cars' driving speed are prohibitively high. Enter private companies. Through a contractual arrangement with several towns, a number of companies agreed to bear the installation costs of the automatised speed traps in exchange for a lumpsum of €24 for every fine the town issued. Of course, such business model implies that the more fines are issued, the more profit is made.[95] The companies therefore contractually stipulated with the towns that physical infrastructures meant to discourage drivers from driving fast, such as speed bumps and chicanes, as well as priority arrangements for cyclists, are to be removed and not to be reintroduced for at least six years.[96] After media reports and public outrage, the Home Office Minister annulled the contracts, citing the adverse impact on 'the public interest' and the importance of the town's autonomy as a justification for the annulment.[97]

This example illustrates in a disconcertingly clear way how physical and digital infrastructure can be used to optimise one goal (e.g. private profits) over another (e.g. road safety in the public interest). In other words: the design, development, use, interplay, as well as the governance and ownership of infrastructure is not merely of technical but also of societal relevance. Moreover, it shows that the societal embeddedness of technology also translates into physical power by those who design, develop and deploy the system, over those who are subjected to the system. In sum, technological normativity shapes possibilities for action,[98] both for those who actively make use of the system, and for those who are subjected to the system.

I described above how algorithms essentially consist of a given input, instructions and output. Moreover, they depend on the physical infrastructure that enables their

94 Caroline Criado Perez, 'The Deadly Truth about a World Built for Men – From Stab Vests to Car Crashes' *The Guardian* (23 February 2019) <www.theguardian.com/lifeandstyle/2019/feb/23/truth-world-built-for-men-car-crashes>. See also Caroline Criado Perez, *Invisible Women: Exposing Data Bias in a World Designed for Men* (Vintage Publishing 2020).

95 Yannick Verberckmoes, 'Mogen verkeersboetes een verdienmodel zijn? Volgens experts is een grens overschreden' *De Morgen* (12 December 2021) <www.demorgen.be/gs-b72e332e>.

96 Matthias Verbergt, 'Privébedrijf achter trajectcontroles doet verkeersdrempels verdwijnen' (*De Standaard*) (11 December 2021) <www.standaard.be/cnt/dmf20211210_97898448>.

97 'Bart Somers vernietigt systeem trajectcontrole Bonheiden' *De Standaard* (14 January 2022) <www.standaard.be/cnt/dmf20220114_94712942>.

98 Laurence Diver, 'Interpreting the Rule(s) of Code: Performance, Performativity, and Production' [2021] MIT Computational Law Report 2 <https://law.mit.edu/pub/interpretingtherulesofcode/release/1>.

functioning and, in particular as regards data-driven systems, the data they are fed. All of these individual elements, including the designers and owners behind it, therefore influence the system's impact on those subjected to its use. Constitutive of these elements are human choices, such as the choice of what to optimise the system for, what data to use and how to categorise and label it, what elements to dismiss, how to translate knowledge to code, how to use and present the system's output, and how to communicate the system's capabilities. These choices also pertain to which programming language to use – bearing in mind that the affordance of language we code in also shapes how we think, for instance in terms of coding solutions – and at the meta-level, how to design and develop programming languages and the Application Programming Interfaces (APIs) through which they can be used.[99]

The implicit and explicit choices regarding all of these elements contribute to the system's influence on society, rendering the human beings that make these choices – and that are positively or adversely affected thereby – part of the system's broader socio-technical infrastructure.[100] These choices are often invisible as they are not always rendered explicit, and tend to correspond to what Susan Star calls 'the study of boring things'.[101] She gives the example of the physical infrastructure of our sewer system which may undoubtedly sound like a 'boring thing' to study and analyse, yet nevertheless constitutes an important element of modern cities' utilities and reveals a lot of information about how we live and how society is organised. We barely notice this infrastructure's existence, unless or until it breaks down and no longer functions as it should.[102] Star suggests that perhaps, "*if we stopped thinking of computers as information highways and began to think of them more modestly as symbolic sewers*", the realm of the functional and value-laden choices behind them might become more visible.[103]

What Star notes about IT systems in general also applies to algorithmic systems. In fact, the term *system* already implies this infrastructural nature, typically referring

[99] ibid 19.

[100] Furthermore, the three elements mentioned above – input, instructions and output – each of which are essentially abstractable to patterns of zeroes and ones, also hinge on a physical infrastructure that enables these patterns to be processed in the first place, including the human labour that goes into creating them: from tangible components such as processors and batteries that make up a computer's hardware, to data storage centres that consume a significant amount of energy, and connections to private and public networks to exchange information (for instance through optic fibre cables running across oceans), all of which are likewise subjected to human design, development and use choices. For a detailed overview, see Kate Crawford and Vladan Joler, 'Anatomy of an AI System: The Amazon Echo as an Anatomical Map of Human Labor, Data and Planetary Resources' (*Anatomy of an AI System*, 2018) <www.anatomyof.ai>.

[101] Susan Leigh Star, 'The Ethnography of Infrastructure' (1999) 43 American Behavioral Scientist 377, 377.

[102] Hasselbalch (n 85) 18.

[103] Star (n 101) 379.

to a set of things that work interdependently as parts of a broader mechanism or an interconnected network that forms a united whole.[104] This notion hence emphasises that algorithmic systems are not isolated entities, but embedded in an overarching *system*, and part of a broader socio-technical infrastructure.[105]

To conclude, in order to understand the societal impact of algorithmic systems beyond the technical elements described above, it is useful to render visible at least part of the human choices (and hence the power structures) that underlie their design, development and use. Considered holistically, algorithmic systems are more than just the sum of their individual components, as the interplay of these components engenders societal effects.[106] When analysing how algorithmic regulation is used in the public sector, I will therefore keep this broader dimension in mind. In the remainder of this section, I discuss some of the consequences of the societal embeddedness of algorithmic systems.

2.2.2 *Risk of Human Error*

When people apologise for a blunder by stating that they are 'only human', this seems to imply that non-human machines could be programmed without this 'human' tendency of making mistakes. Indeed, one of the ideas that drive the uptake of algorithmic systems in society is the fact that human errors and mistakes could be avoided or minimised, as a machine could carry out tasks without, for instance, becoming tired, drunk, ill or simply overlooking something. However, since the developers of algorithmic systems are 'only human' too, this is wishful thinking. Mistakes can occur throughout various instances of an algorithmic system's lifecycle, for instance when gathering or selecting input, labelling or categorising data, translating knowledge and rules to code, designing the system's optimisation function, interpreting the system's output, or applying it in practice. Some mistakes will be easily noticeable and potentially also easily correctible. Others might be more difficult to spot and, especially if the system is used on a large scale, may cause significant damage before the mistake is rectified.

Consider the example of an algorithmic system to help allocate medical benefits, deployed by the Idaho Department of Health and Welfare. The system was set up to

[104] See the definition of 'system' in the Merriam-Webster online dictionary, <www.merriam-webster.com/dictionary/system>.

[105] There is a related notion that is worth pointing out at this stage as well, namely the *systemic* effects – positive or negative – that algorithmic systems can give rise to. Precisely because algorithmic systems are part of a broader infrastructure that allows them to be used and relied upon in a systemic way, their impact is typically not limited to an isolated node of society, but can affect all of the elements that the system is interconnected with – and vice-versa – be it tangible physical items, individuals, organisations or intangible practices and norms.

[106] Rónán Kennedy, 'The Rule of Law and Algorithmic Governance' in Woodrow Barfield (ed), *The Cambridge Handbook of the Law of Algorithms* (1st edn, Cambridge University Press 2020) 215.

administer the state's Development Disabilities Waiver programme, which establishes a personalised annual budget for individuals in need to contribute to their living costs. The personalised budget was calculated based on a number of data-points, including a review of medical records, information gathered during a visit at the individual's place, and an evaluation of the individual's 'Scale of Independent Behavior'.[107] All of this information first had to be manually inputted into the system, which entails a first layer of risk for human error. The information can accidentally be inputted incorrectly, or it can be gathered in an erroneous manner (for instance in case the evaluator misinterprets someone's ability to independently perform a task and hence attaches a wrong score to this criterion). Next, based on the inputted information, the system was programmed to make a budget decision that was supported by a data-driven model which aimed to predict the individual's budget needs. The model in question was, however, deficient. In some instances, it *decreased* the budget of people whose medical needs had *increased*, indicating a structural flaw with serious consequences.[108] Ultimately, the combination of various mistakes in the system led to budget reductions for a large number of individuals in need, without explanation, which forced those who were affected to start a class action to seek redress.[109]

Mistakes can also occur when data pulled from different databases loses its original contextual integrity and thereby no longer accurately reflects reality,[110] or when an organisation relies on data that reveals a spurious correlation[111] yet erroneously interprets this as having a causal relationship. In the previous section, I gave the fictitious example of the fraud propensity of dog- versus cat-owners. Consider, however, the non-fictitious correlation that has been identified between US per capita cheese consumption and the number of people who die by becoming entangled in their bedsheets (correlation of 94.71 per cent between 2000 and 2009).[112] One should hope that no public authority would believe that introducing cheese consumption restrictions will also lead to fewer deaths. More generally, mistakes can also arise when a reasoning process relies on the mistranslation of knowledge to code, or when the model or optimisation function of an algorithmic

[107] See Restrepo Amariles (n 24) 288. See also Ryan Calo and Danielle Keats Citron, 'The Automated Administrative State: A Crisis of Legitimacy' (2021) 70 Emory Law Journal 797, 801.

[108] See *K.W. v Armstrong*, 298 FRD 479 (D. Idaho 2014). For a thorough discussion of this case, see Restrepo Amariles (n 24) 287 and following.

[109] ibid 289–90.

[110] ibid 292.

[111] Spurious correlations can be defined as "*false indicators of causality, typically arising when an extraneous variable that affects two other variables is omitted*". See Imad A Moosa, 'Blaming Suicide on NASA and Divorce on Margarine: The Hazard of Using Cointegration to Derive Inference on Spurious Correlation' (2017) 49 Applied Economics 1483.

[112] See Vigen (n 34). See also 'Beware Spurious Correlations' [2015] *Harvard Business Review* <https://hbr.org/2015/06/beware-spurious-correlations>.

system is based on erroneous underlying assumptions about society that may not be easily verifiable – a point discussed further below.

Even basic algorithmic systems that do not rely on data-driven models or multiple datasets can contain errors which may lead to disastrous consequences. The example of the UK's Post Office scandal, which involved reliance on a faulty software called Horizon to carry out transaction, accounting and stocktaking tasks, is a testimony to this.[113] Due to bugs in the software, the amounts reported sometimes indicated shortfalls of thousands of pounds, which the Post Office took at face value and – rather than considering that the system was flawed – used as a basis to prosecute postmasters, some of whom ended up in prison following convictions for false accounting and theft.[114] Accordingly, insufficient attention to errors in the software's programming led to great human tragedy, which was only redressed two decades after the facts, when some of the falsely convicted postmasters already served many years in prison, lost their marriages or died.[115]

In sum, just as mistakes can occur when human beings make decisions, so can mistakes occur when human beings design, develop and use algorithmic tools to inform or make decisions. Yet due to their *systemic* nature, the mistakes that occur in the context of algorithmic systems can lead to *systemic* types of harm, a point I will come back to in Chapter 4.

2.2.3 *Risk of Bias*

Another concern typically associated with human action and decision-making is 'bias'. As human subjects, we are not isolated entities, but inherently influenced by our societal surroundings. Our education, upbringing, culture, social circles, language and societal roles shape our thoughts, opinions and values. While we can try to detach ourselves from these influences and seek an 'objective' point of view to consider facts and events, our inherent positionality in the world – including our motivations, ambitions and relationships – means that we inevitably look at the world from a certain angle. Our biases are not necessarily problematic, as they enable us to draw on our knowledge and experience to make sense of the world around us.[116] However, bias can also be fallacious and cloud our rational judgment,

[113] 'Post Office Scandal: What the Horizon Saga Is All About' *BBC News* (22 July 2021) <www.bbc.com/news/business-56718036>.

[114] Mitchell Clark, 'Bad Software Sent Postal Workers to Jail, Because No One Wanted to Admit It Could Be Wrong' (*The Verge*, 23 April 2021) <www.theverge.com/2021/4/23/22399721/uk-post-office-software-bug-criminal-convictions-overturned>.

[115] Zoe Darling, 'More than 30 Victims of Post Office IT Scandal Died without Justice' (*The Justice Gap*, 15 February 2022) <www.thejusticegap.com/more-than-30-victims-of-post-office-it-scandal-died-without-justice/>.

[116] See also Endre Begby, 'The Epistemology of Prejudice' (2013) 2 Thought: A Journal of Philosophy 90; Thomas L Griffiths, 'Understanding Human Intelligence through Human Limitations' (2020) 24 Trends in Cognitive Sciences 873.

as well as having a discriminatory effect on the people we interact with or make decisions about.

One of the proclaimed benefits of algorithmic regulation is the fact that – unlike human beings – algorithmic systems do not suffer from human biases and achieve more objective decision-making, hence diminishing the risk of unjust discrimination.[117] After all, algorithmic systems lack moral agency and are hence not inherently motivated by their own self-interests or by prejudices in the way human beings are. Yet the myth that algorithmic systems generate purely objective outcomes has by now been busted, as it is widely acknowledged that they can reflect the prejudices and cognitive biases of their makers and users. Bias can also manifest itself through the data fed into the system.[118] If a facial recognition system is only trained on datasets showing pictures of white men, the system will not be able to recognise women and people of colour as accurately.[119] Accordingly, the outcomes of algorithmic systems, and the biases they reflect, hinge on the human decisions that lie at their origin. The fact that a broad range of societal domains, and hence also the knowledge about or data collected from these domains, are still plagued by inequalities and historic discriminations, renders the unchecked use of algorithmic systems liable to perpetuate and even exacerbate unjust bias – at scale.

Consider the by now well-known example of Amazon's data-driven algorithmic system built to evaluate the CVs of incoming applicants. The choice of the system's designers to rely on data from previous (successful) applicants, which were primarily white males, to train the algorithm's model resulted in the algorithm assigning lower scores to incoming female CVs, and hence to discriminate applicants based on their gender.[120] The outcome of this design choice was unlikely deliberate, yet had an adverse impact on numerous individuals, as the non-representative dataset led to unlawful discrimination.[121] One can also raise questions about the fact that most

[117] See, e.g., David Moschella, 'Machines Are Less Biased than People' (*Verdict*, 12 November 2019) <www.verdict.co.uk/ai-and-bias/>.

[118] Harini Suresh, 'The Problem with "Biased Data"' (*Medium*, 26 April 2019) <https://medium.com/@harinisuresh/the-problem-with-biased-data-5700005e514c>; Frederik J Zuiderveen Borgesius, 'Strengthening Legal Protection against Discrimination by Algorithms and Artificial Intelligence' [2020] The International Journal of Human Rights 1; Eirini Ntoutsi and others, 'Bias in Data-Driven Artificial Intelligence Systems – An Introductory Survey' (2020) 10 WIREs Data Mining and Knowledge Discovery e1356.

[119] Joy Buolamwini and Timnit Gebru, 'Gender Shades: Intersectional Accuracy Disparities in Commercial Gender Classification', in *Proceedings of Machine Learning Research* (2018) <http://proceedings.mlr.press/v81/buolamwini18a/buolamwini18a.pdf>; Timnit Gebru, 'Race and Gender' in Markus D Dubber, Frank Pasquale and Sunit Das (eds), *The Oxford Handbook of Ethics of AI* (Oxford University Press 2020); Ntoutsi and others (n 118).

[120] Jeffrey Dastin, 'Amazon Scraps Secret AI Recruiting Tool That Showed Bias against Women' *Reuters* (San Francisco, 10 October 2018) <www.reuters.com/article/us-amazon-com-jobs-automation-insight-idUSKCN1MK08G>.

[121] Consider also the research undertaken by journalists from Bavarian Broadcasting who examined an algorithmic application developed by a Munich-based start-up that analyses videos from job applicants based on their tone of voice, language, gestures and facial expressions, in

algorithmic voice assistants, such as Amazon's Alexa, Apple's Siri or Microsoft's Cortana, typically have a female name and voice by default, thereby – consciously or not – risking to reinforce the societal paradigm of female subservience.[122]

Evidently, the risk of biased decision-making is also present without reliance on algorithmic regulation. It has therefore been argued by some that, since the decision-making process of algorithmic systems can at least be rendered transparent by 'printing out and examining the program' so as to 'de-bias' it (unlike the thought processes of biased public officials) algorithmic regulation remains the better option.[123] Without taking a stance on which option is 'best', it must be pointed out that the prejudices embedded in algorithmic systems are not always visible or easily perceivable, for instance when they arise from reliance on proxies that are only indirectly discriminating, or from biased assumptions underpinning the system's design choices or the selection of the data. Moreover, as I noted in Section 2.1, the decision-making process of algorithmic systems using deep-learning techniques are not intelligible, hence making it challenging to assess their potentially biased character. Finally, the significant difference in terms of the decision-making's *scale* should be pointed out. Unlike a public official handling individual cases, in just a few seconds a biased algorithmic system can inform or adopt impactful administrative acts for thousands or even millions of citizens. Accordingly, those behind the proverbial wheel of the algorithmic system – its designers, developers and users – carry an important responsibility in this respect.

2.2.4 *Opacity*

One of the reasons it can be difficult to detect and mitigate the risk of errors or bias in the context of algorithmic systems is the fact that they can suffer from a

order to make the application process *"faster, but also more objective and fair"*. The application's evaluation of candidates was found to be easily swayed by appearances in the video, such as the fact that an applicant wears glasses or a headscarf, or the presence of a painting or bookshelf against the wall, or the lighting quality of the video – all of which should in principle be irrelevant for a job applicant's evaluation. See Bavarian Broadcasting, 'Objective or Biased' (*BR*), 2021 <https://interaktiv.br.de/ki-bewerbung/en/>.

122 Caitlin Chin and Mishaela Robison, 'How AI Bots and Voice Assistants Reinforce Gender Bias' (*Brookings*, 23 November 2020) <www.brookings.edu/research/how-ai-bots-and-voice-assistants-reinforce-gender-bias/>. As a response to such criticism, many AI-enabled voice assistants are now also equipped with male voices.

123 See, for instance, the contention by Boden that

> many people – for instance, those who are female, working class, Jewish, disabled, or black – encounter unspoken (and often unconscious) prejudice in their dealings with official or professional bodies. An AI welfare advisor, for example, would not be prejudiced against such clients unless its data and inferential rules were biased in the relevant ways. A program could, of course, be written so as to embody its programmer's prejudices, but the program can be printed out and examined, whereas social attitudes cannot.

See Margaret A Boden, 'The Social Impact of Artificial Intelligence' in Ray Kurzweil (ed), *The Age of Intelligent Machines* (Cambridge University Press 1990) 451.

transparency deficit. As pointed out in Section 2.1.3, certain data-driven systems are also denoted as 'black-box' systems, given the unexplainable nature of their inner decision-making processes.[124] This problem is less manifest with knowledge-driven systems, which are typically more interpretable. The notion that algorithmic systems are opaque should thus be nuanced, especially when making general statements. Broadly speaking, a lack of transparency in the context of algorithmic systems can manifest itself in at least three non-exclusive ways, concerning, respectively: (1) the fact that an algorithmic system is used, (2) the way in which it is used and (3) the way in which it works.

First, public authorities that rely on algorithmic systems to inform or adopt administrative acts can omit to communicate, or choose to obscure, the fact that they deploy such systems. Given the system's digital and hence potentially frictionless nature, individuals may not always be aware of the fact that they are being subjected to a (partially) automated decision-making process.[125] This need not be problematic, especially if the decisions made by the system do not affect people in any meaningful way. If a Flemish-speaking public official uses an algorithmic translation tool to draft an email in French rather than asking a colleague for help, this is unlikely to affect anyone's rights or interests, and unlikely needs to be rendered explicit. If, however, that public official outsources the decision of whether a citizen should receive social welfare benefits to an algorithmic system, the omission to communicate about this is a different matter, since this information is valuable to a citizen wanting to challenge the decision, particularly if she suspects error or bias. I will come back to this issue in subsequent chapters when analysing the impact of algorithmic regulation on the rule of law. Suffice it to state here that this type of opacity is human-chosen, and does not depend on the technical specificities of the system.[126]

Second, there can be opacity around the way in which an algorithmic system is used. This concerns, for instance, opacity around the type of data fed into the system, what the system was optimised for, which assumptions underly the system's design, and how the outcomes of the system are used by the public authority that

[124] See, e.g., Frank Pasquale, *The Black Box Society: The Secret Algorithms that Control Money and Information* (Harvard University Press 2015).

[125] Think of remote facial recognition systems that might scan our faces without us being aware of this, but also of online psychographic targeting that can be used to manipulate us into buying certain products or believing disinformation. See also Kate Crawford, *Atlas of AI* (Yale University Press, 2021), 109.

[126] Furthermore, it can also be noted that algorithmic systems can be deliberately used to pretend they are a human being rather than a machine, in light of their ability to be programmed so as to mimic human behaviour – for instance in the form of a chatbot. When not transparently communicated about, such opaque use of algorithms can adversely affect interests such as privacy, autonomy and dignity. See, e.g., Catelijne Muller, 'The Impact of Artificial Intelligence on Human Rights, Democracy and the Rule of Law' (Council of Europe 2020) CAHAI(2020)06-fin <www.coe.int/en/web/artificial-intelligence/cahai>.

deploys it. These value-laden choices are rarely made transparent, which strengthens the idea that those choices do not exist. That idea is mistaken, yet it risks overshadowing the fact that the systems' developers and deployers, who are usually already in a position of power, can retain power precisely through the non-contestable configuration of these systems.[127]

Third, there can be opacity around the algorithmic system's inner workings. This is where the black-box problem truly comes in.[128] For certain data-driven systems, it cannot be explained how their internal decision-making processes work, given the high level of complexity of the model's functions. This renders it difficult to evaluate whether the processes followed by the system are based on robust and fair assumptions and comply with existing legislation.[129] However, even when such inscrutable systems are used, transparency regarding the two other points above remains possible, and can already enhance the possibility to exercise oversight over the system. Information can in any case be provided about the way in which the system was designed and developed, what it was optimised for, which input was selected, which techniques were used, and how the system was tested for potential bias or inaccuracies. It should hence be ensured that this third type of opacity is not used as a pretence to also maintain *human-chosen* opacity to avoid public scrutiny.[130] Moreover, to address the challenges of this third type of opacity, a research domain has developed itself around the notion of 'explainable AI', aimed at rendering such models more intelligible and at enabling developers and deployers of these systems to gain more insights into their internal processes.[131]

Finally, it has been claimed that the choice between using a black box model and an interpretable model often comes down to making a trade-off between accuracy and interpretability since, despite their opaque nature, in some situations deep learning models can generate more accurate results.[132] However, this juxtaposition is not always accurate. Researchers have shown that, in some situations, a similar level of accuracy can also be reached with more interpretable models, and that this binary choice can hence be a false (and potentially misleading) dichotomy.[133]

[127] See in this regard also Steven Feldstein, *The Rise of Digital Repression: How Technology Is Reshaping Power, Politics, and Resistance* (Oxford University Press 2021).

[128] Bathaee (n 43).

[129] Jenna Burrell, 'How the Machine "Thinks": Understanding Opacity in Machine Learning Algorithms' (2016) 3 Big Data & Society 1.

[130] Crawford (n 125) 12.

[131] See in this regard, e.g., Andrea Vedaldi and others, *Explainable AI: Interpreting, Explaining and Visualizing Deep Learning* (Springer 2019); Pantelis Linardatos, Vasilis Papastefanopoulos and Sotiris Kotsiantis, 'Explainable AI: A Review of Machine Learning Interpretability Methods' (2021) 23 Entropy 18.

[132] See for instance High-Level Expert Group on AI, 'Ethics Guidelines for Trustworthy AI' (n 85) 18.

[133] Rudin and Radin (n 48) 7.

2.2.5 *Dependency on Data and Proxies*

Algorithmic systems are highly dependent on data. For knowledge-driven systems, this dependency may be less pronounced, as the system's functioning often relies on a pre-articulated model of reality that is codified into the system, yet this model ultimately also consists of machine-readable data based on which the system can reason. For data-driven systems this dependency is far more explicit, as they rely on (very large) datasets to derive a model in the first place. This also implies that the quality of the system's output strongly hinges on the quality and accuracy of the data it is fed during the training, testing and use phase. Public authorities' reliance on such systems in policy-making can be accompanied by the belief that, if only we have enough data about a certain phenomenon, we can use data-driven techniques to make normative decisions. This has also been referred to as *dataism* or "*a belief in data as the enabler of a better, more effective, and objective society*".[134] While the term dataism sounds almost spiritual, its definition actually corresponds rather well to so-called *evidence-based* approaches of public decision-making, grounded in 'data' and 'science',[135] which often comes down to statistical analysis.

While this is of course a lofty goal, it is important to keep in mind that "*data are not the facts themselves, but rather traces or marks of these facts*".[136] Moreover, the facts that data represents "*are about a phenomenon of interest, which is chosen by an observer from a number of different possibilities*",[137] and hence cannot be said to reflect an Archimedean perspective. Likewise, the design and development of algorithmic models rely on "*socially derived perceptions and understandings, not fixed universal, physical laws*".[138] This implies the potential existence of a gap between the data and model on the one hand, and the reality that they represent on the other hand.[139] Accordingly, when developing a model or drawing inferences from a dataset, this gap needs to be kept in mind. Moreover, even when this gap is

[134] Heather Broomfield and Lisa Reutter, 'In Search of the Citizen in the Datafication of Public Administration' (2022) 9 Big Data & Society 1, 3. See also Jose van Dijck, 'Datafication, Dataism and Dataveillance: Big Data between Scientific Paradigm and Ideology' (2014) 12 Surveillance & Society 197.

[135] See, e.g., Gary Banks, 'Evidence-Based Policy Making: What Is It? How Do We Get It?' (2009) SSRN ANU Public Lecture Series, Productivity Commission <https://papers.ssrn.com/abstract=1616460>.

[136] Wolfgang Pietsch, *Big Data* (1st edn, Cambridge University Press 2021) 11.

[137] ibid.

[138] Kyle Eischen, 'Opening the "Black Box" of Software: The Micro-Foundations of Informational Technologies, Practices and Environments' (2003) 6 Information, Communication & Society 57, 61. See also Katherine Fink, 'Opening the Government's Black Boxes: Freedom of Information and Algorithmic Accountability' (2018) 21 Information, Communication & Society 1453, 1454.

[139] A common aphorism in statistics that acknowledges this limitation states that 'all models are wrong', even if 'some are useful'. See also George EP Box, 'Science and Statistics' (1976) 71 Journal of the American Statistical Association 791.

minimal, and the dataset can be said to provide an adequate representation of reality, one must consider that a precise reproduction of reality may not always be desirable from a normative point of view. As explained above, in many societal domains, historic inequalities persist, which will also be reflected in the data collected about that domain, necessitating a cautious approach when using data about how things *are* to make predictions, recommendations or decisions about how things *should be*.

Unfortunately, the push for technocratic governance, which "*assumes that complex societal problems can be deconstructed into neatly defined, structured and well-scoped problems that can be solved algorithmically and in which political realities play no role*",[140] sometimes leads to a conflation of the positive and the normative. This can also be referred to as the *is–ought fallacy*.[141] Let me clarify with an example. Consider the use of an algorithmic system by a public authority to assist in hiring new officials at a Ministry.[142] It is one thing for this system to help assess whether a formal eligibility criterion for the job (for instance, having a specific degree) has been met. In this case, the system is not asked to help determine which grounds should render a job candidate eligible or right for the job, but merely to assess whether the already explicitly defined prerequisite is attained. It is, however, another thing for the system to help determine, for instance based on data of past hired public officials and how well they perform, which candidate should be interviewed.

The first algorithmic task can be said to belong to the positive realm. Someone already took a normative decision by deciding that one must have a specific degree to be eligible for the job, and the algorithm is merely deployed to peruse data to determine whether this is the case. The second task, however, belongs to the normative realm. The ministry here outsources the normative decision of what makes a public official 'right for the job' to the algorithmic system, which will in turn rely on the optimisation function and the data it was fed. The underlying normative grounds of the algorithmic recommendation may not be transparent here (perhaps the fact that they have much prior work experience or, to revisit the above example of Amazon,[143] the fact that they are male), because it is not necessarily known which factors were flagged by the algorithmic system as relevant, yet it comes down to a normative decision nonetheless. As I discussed

[140] Marijn Janssen and George Kuk, 'The Challenges and Limits of Big Data Algorithms in Technocratic Governance' (2016) 33 Government Information Quarterly 371, 372.

[141] The articulation of this fallacy is notably ascribed to David Hume. See David Hume, *A Treatise of Human Nature: Being an Attempt to Introduce the Experimental Method of Reasoning into Moral Subjects and Dialogues Concerning Natural Religion [1739]* (LA Selby-Bigge ed, Clarendon Press 1896). See also Max Black, 'The Gap Between "Is" and "Should"', (1964) 73(2) *The Philosophical Review* 165–81.

[142] I have taken this example from annex III of the AI Act mentioned above, which classifies such systems as high risk.

[143] See *supra*, Section 2.2.3.

elsewhere,[144] when humans seek to understand the best approach to deal with a problem, they already – often implicitly – have an idea of what the ideal outcome would be, based on their values and preferences. While algorithmic systems can help determine what the best course of action might be given a value X, they will never be able to determine the value that humans should strive for *as such*. Thinking otherwise is a naive approach at best, and leads to a dangerous discharge of responsibility at worst.

In addition, it should be borne in mind that not everything can easily or fully be captured by data. Complex social phenomena are not readily translatable to quantifiable metrics, and hence typically require the mediation of indicators, metrics and proxies.[145] Since hardly any social phenomenon can be entirely reduced to metrics and indicators, something risks getting lost when translating information about such phenomena into a format that can be algorithmically computed and analysed.[146] This intangible information deficit is also problematic in the context of algorithmic regulation, which is dependent on the quality of these indicators and proxies, and on the soundness of the assumptions underlying their use.[147] Moreover, it places the official or authority responsible for the identification and collection of these indicators in a position of power (albeit typically a hidden one) since they can not only frame the problem that needs analysis, but also the norm or ideal that the system should seek to optimise, as well as indications that may constitute a deviation of the norm.

Consider the example of an algorithmic system used by a public authority to predict which individuals might commit fraud, and hence where it should focus its limited resources. While a person's 'propensity to commit fraud' is difficult to quantify, there are some elements that will typically be used to provide an indication thereof, such as possible previous convictions of fraud, missing documents, unusual transactions or past complaints. These elements are more easily quantifiable and data-fiable and could thus be used as a proxy for 'the propensity to commit fraud', which is what the public authority is ultimately after. Crucially, however, the chosen proxies are not always reflective of the sought-after phenomenon: this will depend

[144] Nathalie A Smuha, 'The Human Condition in an Algorithmized World: A Critique through the Lens of 20th-Century Jewish Thinkers and the Concepts of Rationality, Alterity and History' (Institute of Philosophy, KU Leuven 2021) 12.

[145] Sally Engle Merry, 'Measuring the World: Indicators, Human Rights, and Global Governance' (2011) 52 Current Anthropology S83; Viktor Mayer-Schönberger and Kenneth Cukier, *Big Data: A Revolution That Will Transform How We Live, Work, and Think* (Houghton Mifflin Harcourt 2013).

[146] See also Geoffrey C Bowker and Susan Leigh Star, 'Building Information Infrastructures for Social Worlds – The Role of Classifications and Standards' in Toru Ishida (ed), *Community Computing and Support Systems: Social Interaction in Networked Communities* (Springer 1998); Luke Stark, 'Algorithmic Psychometrics and the Scalable Subject' (2018) 48 Social Studies of Science 204.

[147] Rachel Thomas and David Uminsky, 'The Problem with Metrics Is a Fundamental Problem for AI' [2020] Ethics of Data Science Conference 2020 <http://arxiv.org/abs/2002.08512>.

on the soundness of the assumptions made by the system's developers.[148] Furthermore, even if the indicators are well-chosen (by being relevant to analyse the phenomenon in question) they remain mere indicators: in practice, a citizen might very well have missing documents and make unusual transactions, yet nevertheless not in the slightest be prone to commit fraud. In short, the human condition cannot simply be reduced to numerical utility functions.[149] It must therefore be ensured that such a reductionist approach to human beings – and to social phenomena more generally – does not ignore relevant and essential aspects of their humanity for the sake of speed and efficiency. This is especially important when the proxies and indicators are not based on actual behaviour or facts about the citizen in question, but on correlations that were identified with other individuals and groups.[150]

Finally, it must be noted that the data analysed by data-driven systems typically concerns information about individualisable human beings, in which case it is considered to be 'personal data'.[151] The personalisation of administrative acts essentially relies on public authorities' ability to collect data about citizens, and to use such data to profile them and draw inferences about their character, preferences or behaviour.[152] As the combination of different data-sets might yield new possibilities for analysis and insights, authorities are incentivised to both collect more data and

[148] Furthermore, certain proxies may be relevant in theory, but are illegal to take into account in practice given that they can lead to unjust discrimination. A hypothetical study might indicate, for instance, that over the past fifty years women were overall less creditworthy than men (without necessarily explaining the historical reasons for this). While, on that basis, banks could choose to make the assumption that sex is a valid indicator of someone's creditworthiness, they are in principle not allowed to take this factor into account in their evaluation, since sex is a prohibited discrimination ground.

[149] Foreword by Danielle Allen, x, in Hannah Arendt, *The Human Condition* (University of Chicago Press (2019) 1958).

[150] See in this regard also Sandra Wachter and Brent Mittelstadt, 'A Right to Reasonable Inferences: Re-Thinking Data Protection Law in the Age of Big Data and AI' (2019) 2 Columbia Business Law Review 494; Eduard Fosch-Villaronga and others, 'A Little Bird Told Me Your Gender: Gender Inferences in Social Media' (2021) 58 Information Processing & Management 102541.

[151] Under EU General Data Protection Regulation ("GDPR"), such information is broadly defined as "*any information that relates to an identified or identifiable living individual*". See European Parliament and Council Regulation (EU) 2016/679 of the European Parliament and of the Council of 27 April 2016 on the protection of natural persons with regard to the processing of personal data and on the free movement of such data, and repealing Directive 95/46/EC (General Data Protection Regulation) 2016.

[152] Such predictions not only rely on the data of the individual that is being assessed, but also on the data of many other individuals, and how their traits correlate. On algorithmic profiling, see, e.g., Mireille Hildebrandt and Bert-Jaap Koops, 'The Challenges of Ambient Law and Legal Protection in the Profiling Era' (2010) 73 Modern Law Review 428; Stefanie Hänold, 'Profiling and Automated Decision-Making: Legal Implications and Shortcomings' in Marcelo Corrales, Mark Fenwick and Nikolaus Forgó (eds), *Robotics, AI and the Future of Law* (Springer 2018). See also Omri Ben-Shahar, 'Data Pollution' (2019), 11 Journal of Legal Analysis 104 and Salomé Viljoen, 'A Relational Theory of Data Governance' (2021) 131 The Yale Law Journal 573.

keep it stored for a longer time, in case an opportunity arises to use it in another context.[153] Clearly, this creates tensions with the fundamental rights to privacy and data protection,[154] as the incentive to gather and analyse data from as many individuals as possible de facto leads to mass surveillance.[155] As I discuss further below,[156] the EU has legislation in place to protect individuals when their personal data is processed. However, this does not take away the fact that mass personal data-collection is taking place on a daily basis, which increases the asymmetry of information and hence also the asymmetry of power between government and citizen. It goes beyond this book to provide a thorough description of the impact of algorithmic regulation on the rights to privacy and data protection, yet it must be highlighted as an important factor when considering its societal aspects, since this impact considerably influences society's shape and direction.[157]

2.2.6 *Impact on Human Agency*

Human agency denotes the capacity of human beings to act in a particular situation or environment, and is typically associated with the notion that they can do so intentionally and autonomously.[158] Agency is traditionally also linked to responsibility since, generally speaking, one can only be deemed responsible for situations in which one has a certain level of agency.[159] Since the very raison d'être of algorithmic systems is to take over tasks from human beings to make their lives 'easier' or 'better',

153 For a commercial actor, these insights could focus on the way in which a certain service or product can best be commercially marketed based on individuals' preferences. For a law enforcer, these insights could focus on the physical places in which most crimes occur, and where police resources should hence be prioritised. See also Crawford (n 125) 95.

154 These rights are respectively protected by Articles 7 and 8 of the Charter of Fundamental Rights of the European Union, as well as by secondary legislation – including, for instance, the abovementioned GDPR.

155 See Karen Yeung, 'Five Fears about Mass Predictive Personalization in an Age of Surveillance Capitalism' (2018) 8 International Data Privacy Law 258; Shoshana Zuboff, *The Age of Surveillance Capitalism: The Fight for a Human Future at the New Frontier of Power* (1st edn, PublicAffairs 2019).

156 See *infra*, Section 5.3, focusing particularly on the GDPR and the LED.

157 See also Paul De Hert and others, 'Legal Safeguards for Privacy and Data Protection in Ambient Intelligence' (2009) 13 Personal and Ubiquitous Computing 435; Bart Custers, 'Data Dilemmas in the Information Society: Introduction and Overview' in Bart Custers and others (eds), *Discrimination and Privacy in the Information Society*, vol 3 (Springer Berlin Heidelberg 2013) <http://link.springer.com/10.1007/978-3-642-30487-3_1>; Julie E Cohen, 'Turning Privacy Inside Out' (2019) 20 Theoretical Inquiries in Law 1.

158 See, e.g., Markus Schlosser, 'Agency' in Edward N Zalta (ed), *The Stanford Encyclopedia of Philosophy* (Winter 2019, Stanford University 2019) <https://plato.stanford.edu/archives/win2019/entries/agency/>.

159 See, for instance, Aristoteles, *Nicomachean Ethics* (Terence Irwin tr, Hackett 1999), section III.1 1109b30. See also Maureen Sie, 'Self-Knowledge and the Minimal Conditions of Responsibility: A Traffic-Participation View on Human (Moral) Agency' (2014) 48 The Journal of Value Inquiry 271; Mark Balaguer, *Free Will* (MIT Press 2014).

their impact on human agency is a given, as humans essentially outsource their capacity of action to the system.[160] As long as they have agency regarding the act of outsourcing, and regarding the consequences attached thereto, this need not be an issue. Conversely, the loss of such agency might also hamper their sense of responsibility.[161] The link between reliance on algorithmic systems and human responsibility – and in particular, the risk of a negative correlation between both – has extensively been discussed in scholarship.[162] I will not attempt to reproduce this discussion here, but will merely make some observations on how the deployment of algorithmic systems can impact the agency of the deployers of algorithmic systems in the public sector – an environment that is typically marked by hierarchical relationships.[163]

For this purpose, let me recall an experiment carried out by Stanley Milgram in the 1960s, to assess how obediently people act under 'authority', as this experiment likewise involved the mediation of a machine.[164] Individuals were asked to administer increasingly high electric shocks to a volunteer, whenever that volunteer answered a question erroneously. While the shocks were fake, the grim results of his experiment indicated that there was a high rate of individuals who, sitting behind a machine and faced with the choice to obey to authority or refrain from hurting another person (even upon that person's specific request to stop), all too often opted for the former.[165] Milgram analysed the results of the – multiple variations of his – experiment and drew a number of conclusions that are also of relevance when considering the societal aspects of algorithmic systems.

First of all, Milgram observed that "*distance, time and physical barriers neutralise the moral sense*".[166] The further away the individual was from the volunteer

[160] See in this regard also European Group on Ethics in Science and New Technologies (EGE), 'Statement on Artificial Intelligence, Robotics and "Autonomous" Systems', March 2018, <https://op.europa.eu/en/publication-detail/-/publication/dfebe62e-4ce9-11e8-be1d-01aa75ed71a1>, 9.

[161] See, e.g., Gerben Meynen, 'Why Mental Disorders Can Diminish Responsibility: Proposing a Theoretical Framework' in Bert Musschenga and Anton van Harskamp (eds), *What Makes Us Moral? On the Capacities and Conditions for Being Moral* (Springer Netherlands 2013).

[162] See, for instance, Jaana Hallamaa and Taina Kalliokoski, 'How AI Systems Challenge the Conditions of Moral Agency?' in Matthias Rauterberg (ed), *Culture and Computing* (Springer International Publishing 2020). See also Elena Popa, 'Human Goals Are Constitutive of Agency in Artificial Intelligence (AI)' (2021) 34 Philosophy & Technology 1731.

[163] I discuss the organisational environment of public decision-making in more detail in Section 2.3.

[164] Stanley Milgram, *Obedience to Authority: An Experimental View* (Harper Perennial 2009).

[165] Milgram also refers to the obedience to authority organised through bureaucratic organisation in Nazi Germany, and the actions of Adolf Eichmann who – pursuant to Hannah Arendt's account – banalised the evil he committed by stating that he was simply obeying orders. This 'thoughtlessness' and banalisation of evil is discussed by Arendt in Hannah Arendt, *Eichmann in Jerusalem: A Report on the Banality of Evil* (Viking Press 1963); Hannah Arendt, *Lectures on Kant's Political Philosophy* (University of Chicago Press 1982).

[166] Milgram (n 164) 157.

subjected to the shock, the higher the obedience rate, despite the moral concern.[167] In the context of algorithmic regulation, there is typically a physical distance between the person responsible for the system and the individual subjected thereto. Indeed, the system is meant to take over tasks from human beings, providing them with the possibility to monitor these tasks from a distance. However, as Milgram noted, this physical distance also facilitates an emotional distance from the individual subjected to the system, and hence from responsibility in case the individual is adversely impacted by the system's outcomes.

Second, Milgram also explains that the individuals who participated in his experiment automatically adopted a number of internal mechanisms or 'buffers' to cope with the tension they faced in an ethically unclear situation, and to divest themselves of moral responsibility. One of those mechanisms concerns deference to a hierarchically higher authority that imposed the decision. In the context of algorithmic regulation, one can point to the fact that algorithmic systems often tend to have a sense of authority, due to their typically superior computational capabilities as well as their aura of objectivity, since they are based on technical rules and mathematical functions rather than on 'biased' human decisions.[168] Reference can also be made to the known risk of automation bias, or the propensity for human beings to favour suggestions made by automated systems and to ignore contradictory information made without automation, even if correct.[169] In a more banal sense, the fact that the public authority's hierarchy decided that decisions should henceforth be informed or taken through algorithmic systems can also constitute an act of authority through which public officials can divest responsibility. It inevitably constraints their individual agency, thus potentially making them feel less responsible for the system's problematic outcomes.

Third, Milgram describes "*the tendency of the individual to become so absorbed in the narrow technical aspects of the task that he loses sight of its broader consequences*".[170] The fact that the problematic act becomes fragmented (the official is no longer the sole person behind the act and is no longer directly faced with its consequences, but there is a chain of actions in between, mediated by technology) likewise facilitates the act's execution.[171] Similarly, when it comes to algorithmic

[167] See ibid. Milgram explicitly refers to the set-up of the experiment and the role that technology played therein: "*While technology has augmented man's will by allowing him the means for the remote destruction of others, evolution has not had a chance to build exhibitors against these remote forms of aggression to parallel those powerful inhibitors that are so plentiful and abundant in face-to-face confrontations.*"

[168] See also Linda J Skitka, Kathleen L Mosier and Mark Burdick, 'Does Automation Bias Decision-Making?' (1999) 51 International Journal of Human-Computer Studies 991.

[169] Mary Cummings, 'Automation Bias in Intelligent Time Critical Decision Support Systems' [2014] AIAA 1st Intelligent Systems Technical Conference.

[170] Milgram (n 164) 7.

[171] Milgram calls this a dangerously typical situation in complex societies: "*it is psychologically easy to ignore responsibility when one is only an intermediate link in a chain of evil action but is far from the final consequences of the action. Even Eichmann was sickened when he toured the*

regulation, it can be noted that algorithmic systems are often composed of different components that interact with each other within a broader network or chain, which further alienates the system's designer or deployer from its consequences and facilitates the evasion of responsibility. This has also been discussed in scholarship as the difficulty of the *many hands* problem[172] which, in the context of algorithmic systems, is only intensified by the opacity surrounding the different types of (inter-acting) conducts and systems.[173]

Finally, one can also point out Milgram's warning that individuals tend to de-humanise the persons affected by their action by attributing impersonal qualities to those persons, and thereby making it easier to cope with the role of 'hurter'. In the context of algorithmic regulation, the affected person is typically an unknown plurality of citizens, reduced to numeric abstractions and data-points in the system and hence also de-humanised in a more literal sense. All of these elements individually as well as collectively should be carefully taken into consideration when outsourcing impactful decisions about human beings to algorithmic systems. With this in mind, let us now explore how algorithmic regulation is relied upon by public authorities.

2.3 ALGORITHMIC REGULATION IN THE PUBLIC SECTOR

Previously, I described the building blocks of algorithmic regulation, namely algorithmic systems, and I discussed their technical and societal aspects. Since this book is concerned with the use of algorithmic regulation by *public authorities of the executive branch of power*, in this section I conduct a closer examination of how these authorities operate. A better understanding of the bureaucratic environment in which administrative acts are adopted, and of the inherent challenges associated with such an environment, is an important prerequisite to examine the role that algorithmic regulation can play therein. Therefore, in this section, I start by setting out how public authorities are organised and describe the key features of their bureaucratic environment (Section 2.3.1), as well as the pitfalls associated therewith (Section 2.3.2). Subsequently, I discuss the role of administrative discretion, and its ability to mitigate some of bureaucracy's pitfalls (Section 2.3.3). I then examine the history of public authorities' reliance on algorithmic systems (which is not a new

concentration camps, but to participate in mass murder he had only to sit at a desk and shuffle papers." See ibid 11.

[172] Dennis F Thompson, 'Designing Responsibility: The Problem of Many Hands in Complex Organizations' in Jeroen van den Hoven, Seumas Miller and Thomas Pogge (eds), *Designing in Ethics* (1st edn, Cambridge University Press 2017). See also Jennifer Cobbe, Michael Veale, and Jatinder Singh, 'Understanding Accountability in Algorithmic Supply Chains' (2023), Proceedings of the 2023 ACM Conference on Fairness, Accountability, and Transparency, 1186–97.

[173] See in this regard Nathalie A Smuha, 'Beyond the Individual: Governing AI's Societal Harm' (2021) 10 Internet Policy Review 10–11.

phenomenon) and discuss how the logic of such systems resonates with the logic of bureaucracy (Section 2.3.4). Finally, I conclude with an assessment of the reasons underlying public authorities' embrace of algorithmic regulation (Section 2.3.5).

A caveat must, however, be made. While this section provides a broad overview of the operations and use of algorithmic regulation by public authorities, such overview should not be generalised for all EU Member States. Each Member State has its own legal and administrative traditions, and its own pace of technological uptake. This also means that the internal practices and cultures of their public authorities, including their deployment of algorithmic regulation, vary significantly.[174] Even within the same Member State, notable differences in technological uptake exist when comparing one public authority with another. Let me therefore stress that my observations on the use of algorithmic regulation by public authorities are general in nature rather than representing a meticulous description of the situation in every public authority in the EU, given the large diversity of such uptake.

2.3.1 *The Organisation of Public Authorities*

The executive branch of power is responsible for the execution of laws, and its competences are often characterised as having a residual character, encompassing "*anything that is neither legislative nor judicial*".[175] Historically, the executive has been in charge of law enforcement, warfare and national security, as well as tax collection. Yet from the late nineteenth century onwards, with the rise of the welfare state, its competences significantly expanded, covering also the governance of welfare programmes, economic state interventions, and the regulation of societal risks – such as the risks raised by new technologies to public health or safety.

Increasingly, the general laws and policies adopted by the legislative branch of power required more sophisticated implementation techniques, whereby the executive branch became competent to adopt a growing range of administrative acts, both of individual and general application, often necessitating more specific knowledge or technical expertise.[176] To exercise these more specialised functions, a large

[174] See in this regard also European Commission. Joint Research Centre, *AI Watch, Artificial Intelligence for the Public Sector: Report of the "3rd Peer Learning Workshop on the Use and Impact of AI in Public Services", 24 June 2021* (Publications Office 2021) <https://data.europa.eu/doi/10.2760/162795>.

[175] Robert Schütze, *European Constitutional Law* (Cambridge University Press 2012) 221.

[176] See Sean Gailmard and John W Patty, 'Formal Models of Bureaucracy' (2012) 15 Annual Review of Political Science 353. Note that the role and place of experts in bureaucracy and in policy-making more generally (including reliance on external experts when it concerns highly specialised scientific domains) is much debated – especially in light of the greater call for public participation in policy-making by non-experts – but will not be discussed further in this book.

organisation of expert administrators was built, denoted as bureaucracy.[177] As stated by Francesca Bignami, the nineteenth century can be described as one "*of great optimism in the ability of public servants and the bureaucratic form of organisation to pursue the common good and advance the interests of society as a whole*".[178] Public officials working at public authorities are (largely) unelected, but they in principle operate under the supervision and control of the government's (largely) elected members.[179]

Bureaucracy has most famously been conceptualised by Max Weber in his work *Economy and Society*, as part of his broader reflections on modernity and the birth of the rational state.[180] Weber's conceptualisation of bureaucracy should be seen as an 'ideal type' or 'analytical concept' rather than as a factual description of how public authorities function.[181] He examined how the bureaucratic organisation of public administration was able to legitimise social control through legal-rational means, as opposed to more traditional or feudal forms of domination.[182] While not devoid of criticism,[183] Weber's work is still a cornerstone of public

177 This does not mean that bureaucratic forms of state organisation did not exist before. See in this regard Peter Crooks and Timothy H Parsons (eds), *Empires and Bureaucracy in World History: From Late Antiquity to the Twentieth Century* (Cambridge University Press 2016).

178 Francesca Bignami, 'From Expert Administration to Accountability Network: A New Paradigm for Comparative Administrative Law' (2011) 59 American Journal of Comparative Law 859, 862.

179 Accordingly, the expansion of the executive's tasks and the concomitant establishment of public administration also marked the start of a distinction between the 'political' component of the executive ('political executive') and the 'administrative' component of the executive ('administrative executive' or 'bureaucracy'). This has raised concerns around the 'unaccountable' nature of civil servants (especially those working in executive agencies, who typically work more independent from politically elected officials), despite the public power they wield and the impact their decisions can have on citizens. However, elections are but one manner of organising accountability, and a rich body of administrative law – together with broader constitutional principles – has ensured various accountability mechanisms for public administrators. See, e.g., Andrew B Whitford, 'Decentralization and Political Control of the Bureaucracy' (2002) 14 Journal of Theoretical Politics 167; Anya Bernstein and Cristina Rodriguez, 'The Accountable Bureaucrat' (2023) 132 Yale Law Journal 1600. See also, e.g., Gillian E Metzger, 'Legislatures, Executives, and Political Control of Government' in Peter Cane and others (eds), *The Oxford Handbook of Comparative Administrative Law* (Oxford University Press 2020) 697. See also Denis J Galligan, 'Public Administration and the Tendency to Authoritarianism' in András Sajó (ed), *Out of and into Authoritarian Law* (Brill – Nijhoff 2002) 193.

180 Note that this work was published after Weber's death, by his wife Marianne. See also Glynn Cochrane, *Max Weber's Vision for Bureaucracy: A Casualty of World War I* (Springer International Publishing 2018) 68.

181 See, e.g., Lorenz, Meijer and Schuppan (n 26) 73. See also Johan P Olsen, 'Maybe It Is Time to Rediscover Bureaucracy' (2006) 16 Journal of Public Administration Research and Theory 1, 2.

182 Chris Muellerleile and Susan L Robertson, 'Digital Weberianism: Bureaucracy, Information, and the Techno-Rationality of Neoliberal Capitalism' (2018) 25 Indiana Journal of Global Legal Studies 187, 192.

183 See, for instance, the discussion by Harro Höpfl of the many inconsistencies in Weber's conceptualisation of bureaucracy, drawing on similar critiques from other scholars in 'Post-

administration research[184] and proves helpful in discerning how public authorities operate today,[185] since "*bureaucracies continue to be pillars of public service provision*".[186]

Several features have been distinguished as characteristic of modern bureaucracy.[187] While these features are grouped differently by various commentators,[188] the most notable are:

- Efficiency: the optimisation of working methods and resources in order to achieve the desired goals in the most efficient manner;
- Legality: the legitimation of administrative action through formalised rules, standards and procedures;
- Rationality: the execution of tasks based on expert knowledge and reason, and the gathering of further knowledge to advance the organisation's goals and create an institutionalised memory;[189]
- Objectivity and impartiality: the application of laws and procedures to all subjects equally, without privileging certain individuals or groups;
- Impersonality: the execution of tasks driven by impersonal official obligations rather than by personal interests or emotions – or *sine ira et studio*, as Weber put it;[190]

bureaucracy and Weber's "Modern" Bureaucrat' (2006) 19 Journal of Organizational Change Management 8. See also the critique that Weber's conceptualisation was hardly original, and largely drawn from earlier work by Hegel, in Cochrane (n 180) 72 and following.

[184] See Erin L Borry and Tina Kempin Reuter, 'Humanizing Bureaucracy: Applying the Human Rights-Based Approach to Weber's Bureaucracy' (2022) 5 Perspectives on Public Management and Governance 164, 164.

[185] While some scholars claimed that public administration is no longer organised bureaucratically, but rather in terms of market structure or network structure, these claims have been rebutted and incorporated into an understanding of modern public organisation as carrying mixed features which include but are not limited to those structures. See also Olsen (n 181); Höpfl (n 183).

[186] Rik Peeters and Arjan Widlak, 'The Digital Cage: Administrative Exclusion through Information Architecture – The Case of the Dutch Civil Registry's Master Data Management System' (2018) 35 Government Information Quarterly 175, 176. See also Olsen (n 181).

[187] It should be stressed that there does not exist a uniform conceptualisation of bureaucracy. Note in this regard also Claude Lefort's statement that "*Bureaucracy appears as a phenomenon that everyone talks about, feels and experiences, but which resists conceptualization*", in Claude Lefort, 'What Is Bureaucracy?' (1974) 22 Telos: Critical Theory of the Contemporary 31.

[188] See, e.g., Höpfl (n 183); Olsen (n 181); Lorenz, Meijer and Schuppan (n 26); Borry and Reuter (n 184) 165.

[189] Rationality has been defined and used by scholars in many different ways. As regards the use of the term by Weber, Kalberg, for instance, identified four related but distinct types of rationality. See Stephen Kalberg, 'Max Weber's Types of Rationality: Cornerstones for the Analysis of Rationalization Processes in History' (1980) 85 The American Journal of Sociology 1145.

[190] Meaning 'without hatred or passion'. See Max Weber, *Economy and Society (1968)* (Keith Tribe tr, Harvard University Press 2019) 353.

- Hierarchy: the establishment of relationships of super- and subordination, including the importance of loyalty and obedience to hierarchical authority;
- Specialisation: the organisation of tasks based on specific jurisdictional and competence areas, driven by a functional division of labour.

Note that, beyond this set of formal or procedural features, bureaucracy has also been described more substantively as "*an expression of cultural values and a form of governing with intrinsic value*", whereby "*administration is based on the rule of law, due process, codes of appropriate behavior, and a system of rationally debatable reasons*".[191] Public officials' obedience to authority is therefore seen as the other side of the same rule of law-coin, as it legitimises their actions and ensures their accountability to society at large. Moreover, their duty to act in the public interest[192] renders them "*guardians of constitutional principles, the law, and professional standards*.[193] Evidently, this duty also raises questions on the relationship between, on the one hand, the 'public' interests or values that public authorities should advance and, on the other hand, the 'individual' interests or values that private persons might hold dear – especially in a pluralistic society.[194]

Over the last century, the organisation of public authorities has known several waves of reform, inspired by neoclassical and private management ideas.[195] This has led to the privatisation of services and an embrace of market competition, whereby citizens have become "*a collection of customers with a commercial rather than a political relationship to government, and legitimacy is based on substantive performance and cost efficiency*".[196] Despite these reforms, the core features of bureaucracy were retained, and most particularly the focus on procedural rationality and the efficient execution of tasks.[197] Indeed, as noted by Galligan, "*the premise of efficient administration in implementing the policies of government remains the dominant paradigm*".[198] In what follows, I will therefore be using the notion of bureaucracy and public administration interchangeably.

2.3.2 The Pitfalls of Bureaucracy

A lot has been written about the downsides of bureaucracy, and it goes well beyond the scope of this book to reconstruct those rich debates here. I therefore limit myself

191 Olsen (n 181) 3.
192 See in this regard also Barry Bozeman, *Public Values and Public Interest: Counterbalancing Economic Individualism* (Georgetown University Press 2007).
193 Olsen (n 181) 3.
194 See in this regard also Sebastiaan P Tijsterman and Patrick Overeem, 'Escaping the Iron Cage: Weber and Hegel on Bureaucracy and Freedom' (2008) 30 Administrative Theory & Praxis 71.
195 See Kennedy (n 106) 210.
196 Olsen (n 181) 6.
197 Muellerleile and Robertson (n 182).
198 Galligan, 'Public Administration and the Tendency to Authoritarianism' (n 179) 192.

here to a brief analysis of how some of the core features of public administration can run counter to the normative ideals of liberal democracy, as this will be relevant for my subsequent examination of the impact of algorithmic regulation on the rule of law. Such analysis also enables a better understanding of the challenges that are *inherent* to bureaucracy, as opposed to the challenges that are raised or exacerbated by algorithmic regulation in particular.

Despite the benefits that Weber identified with the bureaucratic form of organisation, he also acknowledged it might pose certain threats to substantive values such as individual freedom, and the risk of a concentration of power.[199] For instance, in related work,[200] he noted that an overly instrumental conception of rationality can result in a *stahlhartes Gehäuse* or *iron cage* in which people are subjected to rules and procedures without ensuring that the substantive values these rules are supposed to serve are actually achieved.[201]

This echoes an oft-made distinction between two types of rationality, namely procedural and substantive rationality.[202] As explained by Muellerleile and Robertson, *substantive rationality* is the value-laden framework that people draw on to determine their actions in a particular situation, typically based on their individual ethical perspective.[203] Conversely, *procedural rationality* draws on scientific and economic calculation, and is based on a depersonalised set of codified rules, laws and regulations, which is typical in bureaucratic organisations. When the execution of actions becomes a mere instrumental undertaking, without regard for their practical impact and the extent to which they advance the goals and values they should secure, procedural rationality can undermine substantive rationality, to the detriment of the values intrinsic thereto.

This risk has been raised by various scholars. In particular, it has been pointed out that the impersonal nature of bureaucracy (or the 'rule of nobody', as bureaucracy was called by Hannah Arendt[204]) can lead to a 'disinterestedness' that erodes public officials' sense of responsibility and morality, which can turn into amorality[205]

[199] Borry and Reuter (n 184) 165. See also Kari Palonen, 'Max Weber's Reconceptualization of Freedom and Foundations' (1999) 27 Political Theory 523; Terry Maley, 'Max Weber and the Iron Cage of Technology' (2004) 24 Bulletin of Science, Technology & Society 69.

[200] Max Weber, *The Protestant Ethic and the Spirit of Capitalism (1905)* (Stephen Kalberg tr, Blackwell 2002).

[201] See also Peter Baehr, 'The "Iron Cage" and the "Shell as Hard as Steel": Parsons, Weber, and the Stahlhartes Gehäuse Metaphor in the Protestant Ethic and the Spirit of Capitalism' (2001) 40 History and Theory 153; Tijsterman and Overeem (n 194); Peeters and Widlak (n 186).

[202] See, e.g., Arre Zuurmond, *De Infocratie: Een Theoretische en Empirische Heroriëntatie Op Weber's Idealtype in Het Informatietijdperk* (Phaedrus 1994) 4.

[203] Muellerleile and Robertson (n 182) 195.

[204] Hannah Arendt, *On Violence* (Harcourt Brace and Company 1970).

[205] See in this regard, for instance, the critique formulated by MacIntyre in his seminal work 'After Virtue' (*After Virtue: A Study in Moral Theory (1981)* (Bloomsbury Academic 2015). See also Ron Beadle and Geoff Moore, 'MacIntyre on Virtue and Organization' (2006) 27 Organization Studies 323; Matthew Sinnicks, 'Leadership after Virtue: MacIntyre's Critique of Management

(or worse, immorality). One of the most fervent critiques of rational-legal bureaucracy has been formulated by Zygmunt Bauman in his *Modernity and the Holocaust.*[206] According to Bauman, the features of modern bureaucracy, particularly the emphasis on efficiency and procedural rationality, and the specialisation of tasks which risks obliterating the overall result of one's actions, can undermine the possibility for moral action by individuals working for the state.[207] Bauman called attention to the 'important role' that bureaucratic culture played in the Holocaust (also commented on by Hannah Arendt in her characterisation of Eichmann as an amoral bureaucrat[208]), and characterised modern bureaucracy as 'a moral sleeping pill'.[209] As summarised by du Gay, "*for Bauman, the essence of bureaucratic structure and process' is the dissociation of 'instrumental rational criteria' from 'moral evaluations' of the ends they serve*",[210] leading to the threat of moral discharge and the dehumanisation[211] of those subjected to the impersonally applied procedures.[212]

It has also been argued that, precisely because of its emphasis on procedural rationality and rule-following, the organisation of public administration carries an inherent risk of authoritarianism, and a neglect of the rights of individuals.[213] As, for instance, noted by Galligan, "*administrative bureaucracies are naturally governed by procedural rigidity and a disregard for individualized differences; efficiency and self-interest prevail over fairness, and secrecy militates against explanation and justification*".[214] Accordingly, public administration can be considered as more than a mere 'neutral' instrument to carry out public policies. Instead, by virtue of its inherent features, it can rather be seen as a mode of organisation that can *aggravate* potential authoritarian and illiberal elements already contained in the laws it implements.[215]

Reconsidered' (2018) 147 Journal of Business Ethics 735. See also See also Camilla Stivers, 'Rule by Nobody: Bureaucratic Neutrality as Secular Theodicy' (2015) 37 Administrative Theory & Praxis 242; Hannah Spector, 'Bureaucratization, Education and the Meanings of Responsibility' (2018) 48 Curriculum Inquiry 503.

206 Zygmunt Bauman, *Modernity and the Holocaust* (Polity Press 1989). See also Smuha, 'The Human Condition in an Algorithmized World' (n 144) 35.

207 Paul du Gay, *In Praise of Bureaucracy: Weber, Organization, Ethics* (SAGE Publications 2000), chapter 2 in particular.

208 Arendt, *Eichmann in Jerusalem: A Report on the Banality of Evil* (n 165).

209 Bauman (n 206) 26.

210 Du Gay (n 207).

211 See also Borry and Reuter (n 184). Reference can also be made to Section 2.2.6, where I discussed similar concerns voiced by Stanley Milgram.

212 While these statements might seem condemning, it should be noted that both Arendt and Bauman have nuanced their critique of bureaucracy by conducting more in-depth investigations into its merits and pitfalls, which goes beyond the space I can allocate to this subject in this book.

213 Denis James Galligan, 'Discretionary Powers in the Legal Order', in his *Discretionary Powers: A Legal Study of Official Discretion* (Oxford University Press 1990).

214 Galligan, 'Public Administration and the Tendency to Authoritarianism' (n 179) 187.

215 ibid. It should be noted that more nuanced stances have been taken in this regard. For instance, Claude Lefort, another philosopher who opposed totalitarianism and engaged in a critical examination of the role of bureaucracy in the political sphere, drew on Weber to reject

Others have taken up bureaucracy's defence, arguing that bureaucratic objectivity "*entails a trained capacity to treat people as 'individual' cases, i.e. apart from status and ascription, so that the partialities of patronage and the dangers of corruption might be avoided*".[216] Moreover, one could also consider bureaucracy's "*instituted blindness to inherited differences in status and prestige*" as "*a source of democratic equalization*".[217] Du Gay also nuances the above, by pointing out that the distinction between formal and substantive rationality has not been deployed by Weber and that it may be artificial since, in practice, a distinction between 'means versus ends' is not always straightforward.[218] Rules can, after all, be designed with the specific aim of protecting and enhancing substantive rights and values, and can contribute to the institutionalisation of public accountability.

Furthermore, it has also been argued that an over-emphasis on *substantive* rationality might overlook the fact that there exists a plurality of (often conflicting) values.[219] Bureaucracy can allow the state to remain 'neutral' and maintain its legitimacy in a pluralistic society, precisely because it focuses on procedural rationality and efficiency, and thereby enables "*the expression and protection of a broader range of conflicting values held to be important by human beings*".[220] While the theme of state neutrality has been widely debated,[221] it should be noted that Weber considered value conflict to be an inherent feature of modernity,[222] and he was hopeful that democratic institutions, through an agonistic political process, could

the claim that "*the development of bureaucracies must affect the nature of a political and economic regime, no matter how necessary they might seem once certain conditions are fulfilled*". He noted that,

> On the contrary, Weber claims that the numerical importance of this form of organization does not in any way determine its relation to power. The proof is that the state bureaucracy accommodates itself to diverse regimes – as demonstrated by France, where the state bureaucracy has remained remarkably stable. The proof lies also in the fact that during war, the bureaucratic staff of a conquered country is used by the foreign power, and continues to carry out its administrative tasks. In principle, bureaucracy is indifferent to the interests and values of a political system, i.e., it is an organ at the service of rulers located somewhere between the rulers and those who are ruled.

See Lefort (n 187). At the same time, the indifference of bureaucracy to the values of a political system does not exclude the fact that its mode of organisation can enhance the excesses of authoritarian governance approaches, as argued by Galligan.

216 Du Gay (n 207).

217 ibid.

218 ibid.

219 This plurality of values – and the fact that these values can be irreconcilable – was already acknowledged by Weber too. According to him, this irrevocability was furthered by the broader disenchantment of modernity, and the erosion of the role of religion and more traditional sources of moral authority as unifying factor. See in this regard also Michael W Spicer, 'Public Administration in a Disenchanted World: Reflections on Max Weber's Value Pluralism and His Views on Politics and Bureaucracy' (2015) 47 Administration & Society 24, 27.

220 ibid 25.

221 See in this regard also Stivers (n 205).

222 Spicer (n 219) 32.

address these conflicts. Consequently, he believed in the power of democratic control to mitigate the pitfalls of the 'iron cage', and insisted on the need to make space for politics and democratic oversight amidst and alongside bureaucracy.[223]

Interestingly, the two views I just outlined on bureaucracy's merits and pitfalls foreshadow an important tension that is inherently part of society's reliance on legal rules and procedures to exert social control, which will be closely examined in this book. On the one hand, we require abstract rules of general application, to ensure the law's impartiality ('procedural rationality'). On the other hand, we also require that the application of those general rules results in individual justice,[224] in light of the concrete particularities of each person and situation, and the way in which different values and interests matter to them ('substantive rationality'). Based on the discussion above, it can be concluded that a combination of both is warranted, albeit not always evident, and that political oversight based on a democratic process is an important mechanism to foster this.

In addition to external oversight, there are other mechanisms that can curb the risks evoked above. One such mechanism is ensuring the 'internal morality' of public authorities. Notably, "*Weber did not see bureaucrats, particularly civil servants, simply as mindless automatons but believed them perfectly capable of ethically principled conduct within their own proper sphere of action*".[225] He also emphasised their ethical duties and their need for 'moral discipline'.[226] Indeed, normativity can also play a role *inside* public authorities, by incorporating substantive principles within the organisation of bureaucracy and requiring public officials to adhere thereto.[227] As I shall discuss extensively in Chapter 3, these substantive principles can be distilled from the more general commitment to the rule of law, and from other core tenets of liberal democracy.[228] Another mechanism concerns administrative discretion, which is prevalent in public authorities' day-to-day organisation and can be used to soften the rigidity of procedural rules.[229] Since discretion will be an important theme in this book, especially when discussing its relationship with algorithmic regulation, let me dissect this concept more closely in the next section.

[223] See Max Weber, *Weber: Political Writings* (Peter Lassman and Ronald Speirs eds, Cambridge University Press 1994) 222. See also Palonen (n 199) 532; Spicer (n 219) 35.

[224] See in this regard also Reuben Binns, 'Human Judgment in Algorithmic Loops: Individual Justice and Automated Decision-Making' (2022) 16 Regulation & Governance 197, which will also be discussed *infra*, in Section 4.2.

[225] Spicer (n 219) 34.

[226] ibid.

[227] Denis James Galligan, 'Senses of Discretion', in his *Discretionary Powers: A Legal Study of Official Discretion* (Oxford University Press 1990) 5.

[228] Typically, these principles are concretised through the branch of administrative law.

[229] Galligan, 'Discretionary Powers in the Legal Order' (n 213); Tony Evans, 'Professionals and Discretion in Street-Level Bureaucracy' in Peter Hupe, Michael Hill and Aurélien Buffat (eds), *Understanding Street-Level Bureaucracy* (Bristol University Press 2015).

2.3.3 *Administrative Acts in between Rules and Discretion*

In essence, discretion provides public authorities with a certain level of autonomy when making a decision amongst a variety of options, based on their assessment and judgment.[230] It can be defined as "*a power which leaves an administrative authority some degree of latitude as regards the decision to be taken, enabling it to choose from among several legally admissible decisions the one which it finds to be the most appropriate*".[231] When exercising discretion, public authorities still do so within the confines of the law, which led Dworkin to state that "*discretion, like the hole in a doughnut, does not exist except as an area left open by a surrounding belt of restriction. It is therefore a relative concept. It always makes sense to ask, 'Discretion under which standards?'*"[232] Unsurprisingly, the expansion of the modern state and the increase in government functions, including the increase of legislation that needs to be implemented and applied by the executive, also led to an expansion of discretionary power.

Discretion can arise in different circumstances. The most common one relates to the tension I indicated above, between the general nature of legal rules on the one hand, and the need for their individual application on the other hand. When determining a desirable policy outcome or goal, it is impossible for the legislator to determine in advance all the particular situations that may arise, and to provide precise instructions to the executive as to how it should act in each of these situations. Public authorities therefore typically have some discretion as to how precisely they will implement and enforce generally applicable rules and policies. In this sense, discretion is a side-effect of organising social control based on a system of legal rules.

However, discretion is more than a side-effect, since it can also be seen as "*a positive way of conferring powers where it is important that officials have more freedom as to the way they are to be exercised than a detailed set of rules might allow*".[233] In some situations, applying a general rule to advance a just cause, without the possibility of tempering its concrete impact in potentially unforeseen or unanticipated circumstances, can actually lead to injustice. On the one hand, securing

[230] Galligan notes that the emphasis in discretion should not lay on the fact that public authorities have *autonomy*, but rather that they have scope for judgment and personal assessment – which also implies the need to rely on reason. See 'Senses of Discretion' (n 227) 8.

[231] This definition is drawn from the Council of Europe. See Committee of Ministers of the Council of Europe, 'Recommendation No. R (80) 2 of the Committee of Ministers Concerning the Exercise of Discretionary Powers by Administrative Authorities', 1980.

[232] See Ronald Dworkin, *Taking Rights Seriously* (Harvard University Press 1978) 31. See also Tony Evans and John Harris, 'Street-Level Bureaucracy, Social Work and the (Exaggerated) Death of Discretion' (2004) 34 British Journal of Social Work 871, 881; Mireille Hildebrandt, 'Algorithmic Regulation and the Rule of Law' (2018) 376 Philosophical Transactions of the Royal Society A: Mathematical, Physical and Engineering Sciences 20170355, 5.

[233] Galligan, 'Senses of Discretion' (n 227) 2.

public services for millions of citizens naturally requires a certain level of organisation and systematisation. On the other hand, any system will also inevitably overlook the uniqueness of the individual cases that it systematises.

This dilemma was also discussed by Emmanuel Levinas, famous for his emphasis on the primacy of ethics in human relationships and the responsibility we have for the 'other'.[234] He considered it inevitable that any system seeking to ensure justice for the many can become dehumanising precisely by approaching individuals in a general rather than an individualised manner.[235] Indeed, within such a system, "*the other is no longer the unique person offering himself to the compassion of my responsibility, but an individual within a logical order or a citizen of a state in which institutions, general laws, and judges are both possible and necessary*".[236] This leads to the danger that the other is "*extinguished in the system of universal laws*".[237] While this danger does not imply that all systematisation of public services should be rejected, it does mean that the system needs to be continually corrected and perfected against its own harshness.[238] This permanent correction of the system, however, cannot be expected to come from another *system*. Instead, Levinas believes it can be found in acts of 'little goodness', which he juxtaposes against a systematised 'Goodness'.[239] The little goodness is "*a goodness outside of every system, every*

[234] See also Emmanuel Levinas, *Autrement qu'être ou au-delà de l'essence* (11th edn, Le Livre de Poche (2019) 1974); Emmanuel Levinas, *Le temps et l'autre* (11th edn, Presses Universitaires de France (2014) 1979).

[235] Emmanuel Levinas, *Is It Righteous to Be?: Interviews with Emmanuel Levinas* (Jill Robbins ed, Stanford University Press 2001). See also Luc Anckaert, 'Ethics of Responsibility and Ambiguity of Politics in Levinas's Philosophy' (2020) 97 Problemos 61.

[236] Lévinas, *Is It Righteous to Be?* (n 235) 116.

[237] ibid.

[238] ibid 206–07. See also Luc Anckaert, 'Goodness without Witnesses: Vasily Grossman and Emmanuel Levinas' in Michael Fagenblat and Arthur Cools (eds), *Levinas and Literature* (De Gruyter 2020) 230.

[239] In this regard, Levinas draws on the novel *Life and Fate* by Vasily Grosman (written in 1959 but only published in 1980). *Life and Fate* details events during the Second World War and provides (comparative) perspectives about the totalising regimes of Nazism and Stalinism. A few characters in the novel – especially Ikonnikov, described as a 'holy fool' – showcase "isolated acts of senseless kindness", which stand in stark opposition to the great totalitarian visions of "the Good". Levinas recounts the significance thereof as follows:

> Grossman's eight hundred pages offer a complete spectacle of desolation and dehumanization … Yet within that decomposition of human relations, within that sociology of misery, goodness persists. There is a long monologue where Ikonnikov – the character who expresses the ideas of the author – casts doubt upon all social sermonizing, that is, upon all reasonable organization with an ideology, with plans … Every attempt to organize humanity fails. The only thing that remains undying is the goodness of everyday, ongoing life. Ikonnikov calls that 'little act of goodness' … This 'little goodness' is the sole positive thing … [I]t is a goodness outside of every system, every religion, every social organization.

See Levinas, *Is It Righteous to Be?* (n 235) 89. See also Michael L Morgan, *The Cambridge Introduction to Emmanuel Levinas* (Cambridge University Press 2011) 23.

religion, every social organization".[240] It is "*a correction of the impersonality of a system that both tries to realize justice but also disregards the invisible tears of people who, despite all their efforts, fall outside of this whole*".[241]

In the context of public authorities' application of the law, it is this little goodness, this case-by-case correction to ensure justice in individual situations where the application of general laws might lead to injustice, that can be likened to the role of discretion. Indeed, discretion enables public officials to exercise a 'little goodness' that softens the hard edges of a generalised legal system. This is precisely why hardship clauses are sometimes incorporated in government policies, allowing public authorities to provide relief from the law's application or to deviate from its implementation based on the specific individual circumstances.[242] In this sense, discretion can counter the excesses of procedural rationality, by ensuring that rules are not applied overly rigidly, but with due regard to the ends they aim to serve, based on substantive rationality. It hence provides space to make trade-offs between different interests and values in a particular situation, without the need for the legislator to always anticipate those situations.

Discretion can arise due to other factors too. Certain risks that the legislator seeks to prevent or mitigate arise in situations of inherent complexity or uncertainty, requiring more comprehensive assessments by experts to identify the best course and timing of action. For instance, in the area of technology regulation, the legislator typically sets out a legal framework with general safety norms that should be met, but relies on public authorities and their risk analyses to develop more specific standards, procedures and guidelines. Furthermore, the fact that public authorities inevitably have limited resources at their disposal means they must optimise these resources in a way that allows them to reach their goals in the most efficient manner by setting certain priorities. Discretion has therefore been "*long identified as necessary for administrative authorities to operate effectively within all modern legal systems*".[243]

Note that the role of discretion applies not only to the implementation of legislation at the national level, but also to the implementation of European law. Indeed, when the EU adopts new legislation, certain legal provisions may explicitly or implicitly enable Member Sates' public authorities to exercise some discretion as

[240] Levinas, *Is It Righteous to Be?* (n 235) 89.

[241] Anckaert (n 238) 230.

[242] For instance, the Dutch tax authorities allow citizens to apply for hardship relief in tax cases "*when the law has a consequence that was unintended*" and "*which the legislator would have been able to prevent if it had anticipated such consequence*" (as detailed on the Dutch government's website <www.government.nl/topics/paying-taxes/applying-for-hardship-relief-in-tax-cases>.

[243] Karen Yeung and Lee A Bygrave, 'Demystifying the Modernized European Data Protection Regime: Cross-Disciplinary Insights from Legal and Regulatory Governance Scholarship' (2022) 16 Regulation & Governance 137, 148; Galligan, 'Discretionary Powers in the Legal Order' (n 213).

regards the ways in which this legislation will be implemented at the national level. In this context, discretion hence also serves as a tool that allows individual Member States to make trade-offs between different values and interests in line with their national traditions, as long as they remain within the confines set out by the EU legislator and by primary EU law.[244]

Depending on the context in which public power is exercised, the executive's discretion can be more or less extensive. Let me concretise this with an example. Consider the legal rule in the area of Belgian migration law, which grants a migrant in Belgium the possibility to apply for a residence permit "*if exceptional circumstances justify the submission of this application in Belgium rather than abroad*".[245] In this case, discretion is rather vast: the law itself does not define a list of 'exceptional' circumstances, so it is up to the officials implementing the law to interpret this term, and to decide whether such circumstances are present. The relevant public authority (the Immigration Office, acting under the supervision of the 'political' executive) typically issues policy guidelines that set out which procedures will be followed in the implementation of this rule. On the government's website, one can, for instance, read that "*a long stay in Belgium, or integration into Belgian society, is not, in itself, an exceptional circumstance justifying an application for a residence permit in Belgium*".[246] This statement or policy reflects the executive's discretionary choice of implementing the law in this way rather than in another, as it is not an explicit part of the text adopted by the legislator. Had a more migration-friendly government been elected, this policy might, for instance, have been different.

Contrast this with the Belgian legal rule that for every child, regardless of income level, parents receive a standard sum of childcare benefits.[247] In this situation, the general rule to be applied is rather clear, and discretion is near inexistent: if an individual has a child, it is clear that the public official in charge needs to allocate that person the standard sum. However, even in this context, discretion is not *entirely* absent. One can still conceive that the responsible public authority may adopt guidelines or procedures that set out which type of evidence is accepted to prove the existence of a child, and which process must be followed to apply for such benefits if they are not allocated automatically. Accordingly, even within the scope of a single administrative act – the allocation of childcare benefits – public

[244] See Koen Lenaerts, Ignace Maselis and Kathleen Gutman, *EU Procedural Law* (Janek Tomasz Nowak ed, Oxford University Press 2015) 141.

[245] Article 9 bis of the Law of 15 December 1980 on access to the territory, residence, settlement and removal of foreign nationals.

[246] See the website of the Belgian Immigration Office: https://dofi.ibz.be/en/themes/third-country-nationals/residence-permit-articles-9-9bis-9ter/exceptional-circumstances.

[247] While these procedures are slightly different in Belgium's different regions, in Flanders this is governed by the Flemish Decree of 27 April 2018 (*Decreet tot regeling van de toelagen in het kader van het gezinsbeleid*), accessible at www.ejustice.just.fgov.be/mopdf/2018/07/31_1.pdf#Page140.

authorities can have discretionary competences over some of the act's aspects, and bound competences over other aspects.[248]

As regards the adoption of administrative decisions, Galligan identifies three elements to the decision-making process, each of which allows for the exercise of discretion: (1) finding facts, (2) setting standards and (3) applying the standards to the facts.[249] Discretion is often associated with the second element (requiring the interpretation of vague or ambiguous legislation, or the creation of more specific standards based on broad legislation), and third element (requiring an element of judgment and assessment, even if the way in which the standard must be interpreted is clear). However, even the first element already implies some discretion (e.g. how will evidence regarding the facts be gathered and assessed?). Accordingly, drawing on the example above, discretion not only arises as regards the final decision (e.g. the allocation of childcare benefits) but also in various intermediary steps (e.g. how can the existence of a child be proven, how is the application process for benefits organised, how is the allocation calculated, and so on).

To summarise, public authorities and officials exercise their functions and take administrative acts based on a set of rules, yet they always have a varying level of discretion at their disposal which enables them to carry out their tasks in a way that is, ideally, both efficient *and* just. Of course, this does not mean that discretion is always exercised in a sound manner. The autonomy afforded by discretion also opens the door for deviations of the law and potential abuses. This is why, in line with the principles of the rule of law that I will discuss in Chapter 3, public authorities typically also adopt guidelines or procedures that set out how public officials should exercise discretion, thereby enhancing the predictability and consistency of the law's application across various departments within the organisation. Moreover, democratic oversight and judicial review play an important role in ensuring that discretion – whether to apply, interpret or deviate from the general law – is used commensurably with the rule of law and other constitutional values and principles.

With this conception in mind of how public authorities carry out their functions and adopt administrative acts, in between rules and discretion, let me now examine the role that algorithmic systems can play in this context.

2.3.4 *From Bureaucracy to Algocracy*

The processing of information and the adoption of administrative acts based on such information is a core task of public authorities. As discussed above, the aspiration to do so efficiently, objectively and rationally already underpinned the nineteenth-century model of administrative bureaucracy and remained an important aim of

[248] Steven Van Garsse (ed), *Handboek Bestuursrecht* (Politeia 2016) 41.

[249] Galligan, 'Senses of Discretion' (n 227) 9.

public administrations ever since.[250] It is therefore no surprise that, as soon as affordable, algorithmic regulation became part and parcel of public authorities' working methods, aimed at rendering their information processing activities more efficient.

In this regard, Zuurmond highlights that *"bureaucracy and informatisation seem to go hand in hand"*.[251] Indeed, bureaucracy relies on the execution of administrative tasks based on expert knowledge and information, which in turn requires the collection of data – including data about legal subjects. According to Peeters and Widlak: *"as state tasks expanded, especially in welfare states, so did the number of registrations and their importance. Knowing your citizens has never been more important as when you try to decide who is eligible to student grants, social security, health care, social housing, or pensions"*.[252] Besides the collection of information, the need for the speedy processing of such information also set in motion a broader process of digitalisation. When public authorities started to deploy computer systems in the twentieth century, they realised that the information they sought to process first had to be converted from an analogue format to computer-readable code ('digitisation'). Only then, analytical and decision-making processes could be transformed to the digital realm too ('digitalisation').

Gradually, the image of bureaucrats sitting behind a stuffy pile of papers thus transformed into an image of bureaucrats sitting behind large computer screens. In early 2002, Bovens and Zouridis pointed out that *"window clerks are being replaced by Web sites, and advanced information and expert systems are taking over the role of case managers and adjudicating officers. Instead of noisy, disorganized decision-making factories populated by fickle officials, many of these executive agencies are fast becoming quiet information refineries, in which nearly all decisions are pre-programmed by algorithms and digital decision trees"*.[253] The uptake of algorithmic regulation in public administration is hence nothing new. Yet over time, public authorities *"experienced several leaps of technological innovation"*,[254] and the systems they relied upon became ever more sophisticated. Today, algorithmic regulation is not only based on basic decision trees, but also on more complex knowledge-driven systems and increasingly on data-driven systems too. Accordingly, a distinctive growth can be perceived both as regards the scale on which algorithmic regulation

[250] See Höpfl (n 183); Gailmard and Patty (n 176).

[251] Zuurmond (n 202) 2.

[252] Peeters and Widlak (n 186) 176.

[253] Mark Bovens and Stavros Zouridis, 'From Street-Level to System-Level Bureaucracies: How Information and Communication Technology Is Transforming Administrative Discretion and Constitutional Control' (2002) 62 Public Administration Review 174, 175.

[254] Dag Wiese Schartum, 'From Legal Sources to Programming Code: Automatic Individual Decisions in Public Administration and Computers under the Rule of Law' in Woodrow Barfield (ed), *The Cambridge Handbook of the Law of Algorithms* (1st edn, Cambridge University Press 2020) 302.

is used in the public sector, as well as the importance and impact of the acts that are being automated.[255]

Evidently, the introduction of algorithmic regulation also impacted the way in which public officials take decisions. Instead of making judgment calls regarding the application of the law to concrete situations, their role became increasingly focused on filling in electronic forms and templates, based on which an algorithm can compute certain outcomes. Bovens and Zouridis conceptualised this as a turn from 'street-level' bureaucracy (a term coined by Michael Lipsky to denote public officials interacting with and taking decisions about citizens)[256] to 'screen-level' bureaucracy. As the uptake of algorithmic regulation increased, and the computers assigned to public officials became a networked digital infrastructure that connects databases and processes across public authorities, 'screen-level' bureaucracy developed further into 'system-level' bureaucracy.[257] The advent of the internet and the Internet of Things also played an important role in this regard, as it progressively enabled citizens to directly provide information to public authorities (knowingly or not), thereby facilitating the collection of their data.

Today, reliance on algorithmic regulation can hence be called *systemic*, as it underpins the functioning of public authorities at large. Algorithmic systems can be used for a myriad of functions within public authorities, from the automated translation of text and the filtering of incoming mail, to the formulation of replies to citizen questions and the adoption of administrative acts. This does not mean that the adoption of administrative acts is necessarily *entirely* automatised. As noted in Section 2.1.1, algorithmic systems can be used for the *adoption* of administrative acts (decision-making sensu stricto), yet in most public authorities these systems are still primarily used to *inform* or *recommend* administrative acts. This also implies that, today, the collection, processing, analysis and assessment of data by public authorities, which lies at the heart of their decision-making processes, is primarily carried out by algorithms.

Initially, it was thought that the embrace of algorithmic systems would alter the nature of bureaucracy, or even lead to its collapse by giving rise to a radically new 'post-bureaucratic order'.[258] However, as already hinted at above and as noted by various scholars, "*rather than less bureaucracy, we seem to experience its propagation and expansion at every turn*".[259] Instead of being dissipated, the 'original' bureaucracy merely turned into an 'algorithmic' or 'digital' bureaucracy. Muellerleile and Robertson note that "*the digital bureaucracy is a world of data in motion, given*

[255] See also Caroline Lequesne-Roth, 'Livre blanc: La digitalisation du service public – Pour une éthique numérique inclusive' (Observatoire de l'éthique publique 2021).

[256] Michael Lipsky, *Street-Level Bureaucracy: Dilemmas of the Individual in Public Services* (Russell Sage Foundation 1980).

[257] Bovens and Zouridis (n 253) 178.

[258] Höpfl (n 183).

[259] Muellerleile and Robertson (n 182) 187.

direction and shape by new kinds of digital infrastructures – from codes to algorithms to platforms, whose digital footprint replaces the material archive, and whose experts are the new data scientists".[260] Lorenz and others even speak of an 'algocracy', arguing that, "*whereas the bureaucracy denotes the exercise of power through the office, the algocracy shows that power is exercised through algorithms*".[261]

The adoption of algorithmic systems by public authorities hence did not simply come down to the introduction of a new tool amongst others to rationalise public decision-making. It also fundamentally altered the organisation of public administrations[262] and brought along several side-effects. In Chapter 4, I will carry out an extensive analysis of the impact of those effects on one particular societal interest, namely the rule of law. In this section, already foreshadowing this analysis, I will only mention four general consequences of the uptake of algorithmic systems in the public sector.

First, one can observe that public authorities have increasingly formalised aspects of their decision-making processes, as such formalisation is necessary to express information and rules through computer-readable binary code.[263] As Bovens and Zouridis point out, "*a conditionally programmed legal framework will lend itself much easier to ICT applications than a goal-oriented legal framework*".[264]

Second, this algorithmisation also led to a reduction of discretion at the level of individual public officials. As previously described, algorithms rely on input and instructions to deliver certain outcomes, and are able to do so at scale. To benefit from these efficiencies of scale, public authorities hence seek to routinise and centralise processes.[265] Accordingly, "*many decisions are no longer made at the street level by the worker handling the case; rather, they have been programmed into the computer in the design of the software*".[266] Indeed, decisions are increasingly guided by algorithmic systems and databases,[267] whereby public officials are often "*no longer involved in handling individual cases, but direct their focus toward system development and maintenance, toward optimizing information processes, and toward creating links between systems in various organizations*".[268] This does not mean that administrative discretion has dissolved. Instead, the introduction of algorithmic regulation and the routinisation of decisions has pushed this discretion higher up the value chain, to the level of the designers and developers of the algorithmic

260 ibid 190.
261 Lorenz, Meijer and Schuppan (n 26) 72.
262 See also Kennedy (n 106).
263 Bovens and Zouridis (n 253) 178.
264 ibid 181.
265 See also Kennedy (n 106) 231.
266 Bovens and Zouridis (n 253) 177.
267 Lorenz, Meijer and Schuppan (n 26) 72.
268 Bovens and Zouridis (n 253) 178.

systems. I will come back to this point in the following chapters, given the implications this has on the rule of law.[269]

A third effect of the public sector's algorithmisation is the extensive process of quantification and datafication this brought along, particularly given the more recent uptake of data-driven systems.[270] Today, public authorities have more data than ever at their disposal to inform their policy and decision-making processes. Furthermore, the computational abilities of algorithmic systems allow them to process and analyse such data at unprecedented speed.[271] This also reinforces the bureaucratic tendency towards rationalisation, under the heading of 'evidence-based' decision-making. As Lorenz and others describe, the introduction of algorithmic systems "*enables government organizations to quantify the uncertainty inherent in decision-making processes on the basis of data analysis by expressing it as probability and to thereby further rationalize this process: even though there is no full certainty about a situation, a more rational choice can be made based on probabilities*".[272]

Finally, along with this rationalisation and datafication one can also discern a thoroughgoing formalisation of citizen registration and classification.[273] Algorithmic regulation typically requires that natural and legal persons are classified according to traits that are relevant for the regulation's application, based on the various data-points that have been collected about them. This classification can be inserted into the system manually, but it can also be generated through a data-driven system programmed to identify patterns and, on that basis, classify citizens into various categories, and evaluate or score them.[274] Since these classifications are used to inform administrative acts, their contours are not without substantive consequences.

As noted by Peeters and Widlak, "*classifications are by their very nature contested, because they are abstractions and simplifications of a complex social reality that highlight certain elements of that reality while ignoring others*".[275] However, while humans know that concepts and classifications are mere social constructs, and that they only represent a selective and partial aspect of that which is being classified, this cannot be said of algorithmic systems. For instance, my mother is not just a 'mother', but also a 'wife', a 'daughter', a 'colleague', a 'friend', a 'consumer', a 'reader', a

[269] See *infra*, particularly Section 4.1.3.

[270] Maciej Kuziemski and Gianluca Misuraca, 'AI Governance in the Public Sector: Three Tales from the Frontiers of Automated Decision-Making in Democratic Settings' (2020) 44 Telecommunications Policy 101976, 3.

[271] The gathering of data is also strongly promoted by international organisations such as the OECD, as it is believed that "*intelligent data usage offers a myriad of possibilities to fundamentally transform public sector activities, how services are designed, delivered and monitored*". See OECD, *The Path to Becoming a Data-Driven Public Sector* (OECD 2019) <www.oecd-ilibrary.org/governance/the-path-to-becoming-a-data-driven-public-sector_059814a7-en> 9.

[272] Lorenz, Meijer and Schuppan (n 26) 72.

[273] See also Hänold (n 152); Broomfield and Reutter (n 134).

[274] See also Lina Dencik and others, 'Data Scores as Governance: Investigating Uses of Citizen Scoring in Public Services' (Data Justice Lab, Cardiff University 2018).

[275] Peeters and Widlak (n 186) 176.

'Belgian', a 'woman' and more. Depending on the particular context, one or more aspects of an individual will be particularly focused on, for example to determine the applicability of certain legal rules, even if that aspect is but one part of a more comprehensive picture.[276] It is therefore possible, yet always partial, to place people and things into a category, even if we do so on a daily basis.[277]

These conventional concepts, limited as they may be to reflect the richness of reality, are how we structure our world, and – by extension – our legal system. Yet as long as we find ourselves in an intersubjective environment, we can draw attention to the limitations of these concepts, contest them, explain why a certain categorisation is erroneous, provide nuance, or ask for additional options or categories given that we share the concept's *meaning*.[278] Such explanation and contestation is not possible when classifications are made by an algorithmic system. Furthermore, the registration of information into databases also tends to reverse the burden of proof when seeking to correct such information. Indeed, "*once something is registered, it is considered 'true' according to the principles of formal bureaucracy*".[279] And, as discussed above, the larger the database, the more chance that datapoints are erroneously registered or classified, which can evidently affect administrative acts that are based on such erroneous information.

This hints to the fact that algorithmic regulation not only generates benefits, but that it can also reinforce some of the pitfalls we already encountered with bureaucracy. I will revisit this issue expansively in further chapters. At this stage, suffice it to conclude that the logic of bureaucracy and the logic of algorithmic systems (and particularly the efficiency-oriented informatisation, standardisation, and rationalisation they bring along) seem rather aligned. While the uptake of algorithmic regulation does impact the way in which public officials perform their tasks, the core features of bureaucratic organisation that underpin those tasks appear to have remained in place.

Before concluding this chapter on algorithmic regulation, let me briefly make explicit what I have thus far mostly implied, namely the benefits that public authorities aspire to materialise when adopting algorithmic regulation.

2.3.5 *Rationale of Algorithmic Regulation*

"*What if more poor families were to receive the state benefits they need? What if more patients' lives can be saved? What if more children could be protected from situations*

276 Consider, for instance, also the categorisation of behaviours that are 'legal' and 'illegal', or distinctions between people that are 'single', 'married' or 'divorced'. See in this regard also Larry Alexander, 'Scalar Properties, Binary Judgments' (2008) 25 Journal of Applied Philosophy 85.

277 Bowker and Star (n 146).

278 Smuha, 'The Human Condition in an Algorithmized World' (n 144) 31.

279 Peeters and Widlak (n 186) 176.

of abuse? What if more people can be rescued from imminent flooding? What if more terrorist attacks could be prevented?"[280] The OECD does not beat around the bush regarding the opportunities it sees in the adoption of algorithmic systems. As of yet, evidence of the concrete benefits of algorithmic regulation is scarce, particularly as regards data-driven systems, given the relative novelty of their scaled use.[281] As noted by van Noordt and Misuraca, "*many of the benefits ascribed to AI for the public sector are not always based on empirical data, but often rely only on assumptions*", rendering it difficult to validate and assess the actual benefits of the adoption of algorithmic regulation in public authorities.[282] In what follows, I discuss the aspired or expected benefits they generate, without taking the materialisation of such benefits for granted.

First, as already pointed out, the automated nature of algorithmic regulation means that its computations can be carried out on a vast scale (even population-wide), thereby enabling mass decision-making.[283] As Schartum notes,

> Of course, it is possible to imagine many more office buildings where thousands of men and women would do all the detailed processing of individual cases that are processed today by computers, but this alternative is not very realistic: Modern taxation systems, national social insurance schemes and management of many other welfare programs would not be feasible without the use of computers and the algorithmic law that is integrated in the software.[284]

Accordingly, by processing vast amounts of data in a short amount of time, algorithmic systems may increase the efficiency of processes, as the speed of their computations supersedes that of human decision-making. These efficiencies are also believed significantly to reduce costs given that "*cognitive technologies could free up hundreds of millions of public sector worker hours*".[285]

Second, the ability to peruse a large amount of data in a short amount of time also means algorithmic systems can help optimise decision-making processes.[286] Public authorities possess more data than ever before, yet this easily leads to an excess of

[280] OECD, 'A Data-Driven Public Sector: Enabling the Strategic Use of Data for Productive, Inclusive and Trustworthy Governance', vol 33 (2019) OECD Working Papers on Public Governance 6.

[281] Colin van Noordt and Gianluca Misuraca, 'Artificial Intelligence for the Public Sector: Results of Landscaping the Use of AI in Government across the European Union' [2022] 39 Government Information Quarterly 101714.

[282] ibid.

[283] See also Fleur Johns, 'Governance by Data' (2021) 17 Annual Review of Law and Social Science 53.

[284] Schartum (n 254) 301.

[285] Peter Viechnicki and William D Eggers, 'How Much Time and Money Can AI Save Government?' (Deloitte Center for Government Insights 2017).

[286] See Svenja Falk, *Digital Government: Leveraging Innovation to Improve Public Sector Performance and Outcomes for Citizens* (Springer Berlin Heidelberg 2016).

information when resources to analyse such data are limited. As Michèle Finck puts it, *"in an age of informational overload through the continuous generation of ever more data, computational learning may become the only means of making sense of data the quantity of which exceeds the capacities of human cognition"*.[287] As discussed above,[288] data-driven systems are indeed able to identify patterns in data that public officials may not be able to see, and can on that basis provide recommendations that could in principle enable public authorities to reach their goals more effectively. Consider the example of an algorithmic system used by the French tax authorities to identify non-declared swimming pools based on Google maps images, thereby recuperating about 10 million euros of non-paid taxes in a short amount of time.[289]

Third, algorithmic regulation is sometimes introduced with the explicit aim of reducing the risk of partial, erroneous, arbitrary, or biased decision-making, and to decrease the risk of corruption.[290] By codifying the application of rules designed to address these risks into algorithmic systems, an informational architecture is created that can prevent public officials to deviate from the law *by design*.[291] Furthermore, the automated application of legal rules could also lead to their more consistent application, as the same rule will no longer be applied by different public officials who might have their own interpretation or judgment.[292] It has been argued that, in this way, algorithmic regulation might not only enhance the law's effectiveness, but also public authority's legitimacy.[293]

Fourth, algorithmic systems could take over tasks that are highly repetitive and intellectually unstimulating for public officials, or tasks that are dangerous and would

[287] Michèle Finck, 'Automated Decision-Making and Administrative Law' in Peter Cane and others (eds), *The Oxford Handbook of Comparative Administrative Law* (Oxford University Press 2020) 659.

[288] See *supra* Section 2.1.3.

[289] 'La détection par intelligence artificielle de piscines non déclarées va être généralisée en France' *Le Monde.fr* (29 August 2022) <www.lemonde.fr/pixels/article/2022/08/29/experimentee-dans-neuf-departements-la-detection-de-piscines-non-declarees-par-intelligence-artificielle-va-etre-generalisee_6139439_4408996.html>.

[290] See for instance Nils Köbis, Christopher Starke and Iyad Rahwan, 'The Promise and Perils of Using Artificial Intelligence to Fight Corruption' [2022] Nature Machine Intelligence <www.nature.com/articles/s42256-022-00489-1>.

[291] See the discussion in this regard in Roger Brownsword, 'Technological Management and the Rule of Law' (2016) 8 Law, Innovation and Technology 100; Karen Yeung, 'Can We Employ Design-Based Regulation While Avoiding Brave New World?' (2011) 3 Law, Innovation and Technology 1.

[292] See also Thomas J Barth and Eddy Arnold, 'Artificial Intelligence and Administrative Discretion: Implications for Public Administration' (1999) 29 The American Review of Public Administration 332; Justin B Bullock, 'Artificial Intelligence, Discretion, and Bureaucracy' (2019) 49 The American Review of Public Administration 751.

[293] Irina Pencheva, Marc Esteve and Slava Jankin Mikhaylov, 'Big Data and AI – A Transformational Shift for Government: So, What Next for Research?' (2020) 35 Public Policy and Administration 24, 28.

unduly expose human beings to risks,[294] such as cleaning a nuclear site.[295] Reports that highlight the advantages of such systems typically emphasise that this frees up valuable time which public officials can spend on safer or more interesting tasks, or for better interactions with citizens in need, rather than replacing their jobs.[296]

Fifth, algorithmic regulation, especially when based on data-driven systems, can also enable the personalisation of administrative acts at lower cost, thereby reconciling the massive scale of decisions that public authorities must take, with the need for individual tailoring.[297] More generally, the algorithmisation of the public sector and establishment of well-kept interoperable databases should avoid the need for citizens to provide the same data multiple times to different authorities,[298] and might enable public authorities to provide their services proactively based on the information they have, without the need for a citizen to request a service, let alone the need to physically visit the authority's office.[299]

Importantly, all of these benefits must be considered against a background of increasing pressure that public officials face to 'do more with less'. Their responsibilities keep on increasing, while public spending is significantly being cut. As early as 2018, a survey conducted by McKinsey revealed that "*43 percent of all public sector transformation efforts over the past five years have had cost reduction as a core goal*".[300] The global recession and the war in Ukraine arguably only magnified this financial pressure. At the same time, I must underline that the aim to cut back public spending by adopting technology is by no means a new development. Already

[294] See, e.g., Kai-Fu Lee, 'AI's Real Impact? Freeing Us from the Tyranny of Repetitive Tasks' [2019] *Wired* <www.wired.co.uk/article/artificial-intelligence-repetitive-tasks>.

[295] H2020, 'The Robots Are Coming to Clean up Our Nuclear Sites' (*CORDIS – European Commission*), 2019. <https://cordis.europa.eu/article/id/358596-the-robots-are-coming-to-clean-up-our-nuclear-sites>. See also Rob Spencer, 'Got a Dirty, Dangerous, Dull Job? Let a Robot Do It and Keep Your Workers Safe' (2002) 20 Robotics World 14.

[296] As discussed further below, the introduction of algorithmic systems, however, often stems from a desire to cut costs – including personnel costs. In the abovementioned example of the French swimming-pool detection system, trade unions in fact expressed their concerns around the system's use, fearing that it will be used to avoid recruiting new officials in a context of a continuous decline in staff since several years. See 'La détection par intelligence artificielle de piscines non déclarées va être généralisée en France' (n 289).

[297] See Pascal D König, 'Dissecting the Algorithmic Leviathan: On the Socio-Political Anatomy of Algorithmic Governance' (2020) 33 Philosophy & Technology 467, 470. See also Horst Eidenmueller, 'Why Personalized Law?' (Social Science Research Network 2021) SSRN Scholarly Paper ID 3969934 <https://papers.ssrn.com/abstract=3969934>.

[298] See, e.g., OECD, *The Path to Becoming a Data-Driven Public Sector* (n 271). See also Schartum (n 254) 322.

[299] See, e.g., Regina Sirendi and Kuldar Taveter, 'Bringing Service Design Thinking into the Public Sector to Create Proactive and User-Friendly Public Services' in Fiona Fui-Hoon Nah and Chuan-Hoo Tan (eds), *HCI in Business, Government, and Organizations: Information Systems* (Springer International Publishing 2016).

[300] Tera Allas, Roland Dillon and Vasudha Gupta, 'A Smarter Approach to Cost Reduction in the Public Sector', McKinsey (8 June 2018) <www.mckinsey.com/industries/public-and-social-sector/our-insights/a-smarter-approach-to-cost-reduction-in-the-public-sector>.

in the 1980s, under the influence of the New Public Management movement (NPM) which espoused the integration of private sector management ideas into public administration,[301] algorithmic systems were increasingly embedded in public processes. NPM reinforced the ideal of efficiency and imbued it with private sector tools such as market-based mechanisms, performance indicators, outsourcing and procurement, customer-service orientation, but also budget cuts and performance management of staff. The adoption of digital technology was seen as an important part thereof.[302] While NPM has been subjected to criticism,[303] the push towards performance indicators and cost-savings remained, and similar ideas also permeated the subsequent 'digital-era governance' and 'e-governance' movements, which more explicitly focused on efficiency improvements through automated data analysis and electronic platforms.[304]

Furthermore, a strong push for the uptake of algorithmic systems in the public sector also came from the European Commission. In 2009, EU Member States signed the *Malmo Declaration on eGovernment*,[305] which the Commission implemented through the *European eGovernment Action Plan 2011–2015*[306] and the *eGovernment Action Plan 2016–2020*,[307] each underlining the need to accelerate the digital transformation of governments. The *Tallinn eGovernment Declaration* in 2017 added an important impetus for Member States and the Commission to continue investing in the modernisation of the public sector, seen as indispensable to increase "*the transparency, responsiveness, reliability, and integrity of public governance*".[308]

Most recently, with its Coordinated Plan on AI in 2019[309] and 2021,[310] the European Commission urged all EU Member States to adopt their own national

[301] Broomfield and Reutter (n 134) 3.
[302] Kennedy (n 106) 211.
[303] See also P Dunleavy, 'New Public Management Is Dead – Long Live Digital-Era Governance' (2005) 16 Journal of Public Administration Research and Theory 467.
[304] OECD, 'A Data-Driven Public Sector' (n 280) 9.
[305] 'Ministerial Declaration on EGovernment, Approved Unanimously in Malmö, Sweden, on 18 November 2009', Malmö, 2009, <www.mt.ro/web14/documente/date-deschise/reglementari/Ministerial-declaration-on-egovernment_Malmo_2009.pdf>.
[306] Communication from the Commission to the European Parliament, the Council, the European Economic and Social Committee and the Committee of the Regions: The European eGovernment Action Plan 2011–2015 – Harnessing ICT to promote smart, sustainable & innovative government 2010 (COM(2010) 743 final).
[307] Communication from the Commission to the European Parliament, the Council, the European Economic and Social Committee and the Committee of the Regions: EU eGovernment Action Plan 2016–2020 – Accelerating the digital transformation of government 2016 (COM(2016) 179 final).
[308] 'Tallinn Declaration on EGovernment at the Ministerial Meeting during Estonian Presidency of the Council of the EU on 6 October 2017', Talinn, 2017, <https://digital-strategy.ec.europa.eu/en/news/ministerial-declaration-egovernment-tallinn-declaration>.
[309] European Commission, 'Coordinated Plan on Artificial Intelligence', Brussels, 7.12.2018, COM(2018) 795 final.
[310] European Commission, 'Coordinated Plan on Artificial Intelligence: 2021 Review. Fostering a European Approach to Artificial Intelligence' Annex to the Communication from the

AI strategy, including a plan for the technology's adoption in the public sector.[311] The EU also explicitly finances the uptake of algorithmic regulation by Member States through the recovery and resilience facility that was established to meet the financial challenges raised by the Covid-19 pandemic,[312] and more indirectly through other EU budgets.[313] In sum, Member States have reasons enough to adopt algorithmic regulation, and it can only be expected that this trend will be accelerated in the years to come.

A caveat should be made, as the benefits aspired by algorithmic systems are not automatically achieved.[314] After all, the *actual* benefits of these systems entirely depend on how they are designed, developed and used, and whether they take into account the risks set out in previous sections. It is not because a system is developed or deployed with good intentions, that it is also developed and deployed in a good manner, with due attention to unintended consequences or problematic uses later on. Moreover, even when benefits are achieved, this does not mean they actually benefit *all*. Often, those who already find themselves in a beneficial position will be best placed to reap those benefits, whereas those who are in a vulnerable position may not necessarily be better off,[315] a point that I will revisit later on.

In addition, the capacities of algorithmic systems, and particularly systems defined as 'AI', are sometimes oversold,[316] and hyperbolic statements about their benefits, followed by disappointing results, are not uncommon.[317] Yet once significant investments have been made to establish an algorithmic regulation project, sunken costs and path dependencies render it difficult to abandon it, even if the output is not up

Commission to the European Parliament, the European Council, the Council, the European Economic and Social Committee and the Committee of the Regions COM(2021) 205 final 46.

311 It can be noted that these strategies often present the digital transformation as enabling 'progress' towards an ever-better human condition, a view that bears strong affinities with progressivism. See in this regard also Smuha, 'The Human Condition in an Algorithmized World' (n 144) 26.

312 Regulation (EU) 2021/241 of the European Parliament and of the Council of 12 February 2021 Establishing the Recovery and Resilience Facility.

313 Consider, for instance, the many AI projects funded through the H2020 and HorizonEurope research programmes of the European Union.

314 Smuha, 'The Human Condition in an Algorithmized World' (n 144) 10.

315 See also Sahajveer Baweja and Swapnil Singh, 'Beginning of Artificial Intelligence, End of Human Rights' (*LSE Human Rights*, 16 July 2020) <https://blogs.lse.ac.uk/humanrights/2020/07/16/beginning-of-artificial-intelligence-end-of-human-rights/>.

316 Kate Crawford also describes the phenomenon of so-called 'Potemkin AI', whereby a product is sold as an autonomous system for marketing purposes, but in fact primarily relies on human labour behind the scenes, often in very dire labour circumstances. See Crawford (n 125) 65.

317 A recent example is the use of algorithmic systems to help counter the Covid-19 pandemic. Soon after Covid-19 broke out, numerous tech developers enthusiastically started designing and deploying AI systems with great expectations of how these could be used against the virus. However, the results were disappointing, and AI was not able to deliver its promise. See in this regard Will Douglas Heaven, 'Hundreds of AI Tools Have Been Built to Catch Covid. None of Them Helped' (*MIT Technology Review*, 30 July 2021) <www.technologyreview.com/2021/07/30/1030329/machine-learning-ai-failed-covid-hospital-diagnosis-pandemic/>.

to standard. Finally, it is precisely the desire to reap the benefits of this technology, often with the explicit aim to increase individual and societal welfare, that can blind public authorities to its risks and that eventually gives cause to concerns.

2.4 CONCLUDING REMARKS

In the sections above, I delineated the concept of algorithmic regulation for the purpose of this book by discussing its technical and societal aspects, and by examining how public authorities rely thereon within their broader organisational environment. I started by describing algorithmic systems as the building blocks of algorithmic regulation, and explained that these are essentially comprised of *input*, algorithmic *instructions* and *output*. I distinguished knowledge-driven systems from data-driven systems and discussed some of the differences in both approaches, whilst simultaneously cautioning against their strict distinction, since algorithmic systems can rely on a mixed approach. Moreover, regardless of the underlying approach and of whether they are considered 'intelligent' enough to fall under the AI umbrella, the impact of these systems on individual, collective and societal interests can be significant, especially when used by public authorities. Therefore, I decided to focus my analysis on all algorithmic systems that are used by public authorities to inform or take administrative acts, regardless of their underlying approach.

Since algorithmic systems are not isolated entities but part of a broader environment, I complemented their technical description with a discussion of some of their societal characteristics, which cannot be seen as separate therefrom. It is only by clarifying the underlying socio-technical infrastructure in which these systems are embedded that the mutual influence of algorithmic systems and society upon each other can be made more visible. I therefore emphasised the need to examine the implicit and explicit human choices that underlie the systems' design and use – and hence their affordances – as well as the power relationships that shape these choices. The extent to which algorithmic systems are opaque, for instance, relies not merely on the technique underlying their functioning, but also on how developers and deployers communicate about the normative choices they made throughout the systems' design and use.

I also highlighted several risks associated with the use of algorithmic regulation, including human errors or mistakes, (unintended) bias and discriminatory outcomes, the impact on human agency, and emphasised the wide-ranging effects these risks can have given not only the systems' opacity but also the scale of their deployment. In addition, I discussed the systems' dependency on data, and the importance of keeping in mind that not all social phenomena can easily be captured by quantifiable metrics. This broader picture of the societal aspects of algorithmic systems, which also highlights their function as *regulatory* tools broadly speaking, is essential to understand the concrete effects they can have on their environment.

Finally, I examined how algorithmic regulation is used by, and influences the organisation of, public authorities. I first discussed how public authorities function, and highlighted their bureaucratic environment, observing that the logic of bureaucracy is in certain aspects very similar to the logic of algorithmic systems. Both 'systems' are underpinned by a drive towards procedural rationality and efficiency – to the potential detriment of substantial rationality. I also emphasised the important role of discretion in public decision-making – particularly the way in which it can counter some of the excesses of procedural rationality – and the need for public authorities to have both political oversight over their actions and an 'internal morality' to ensure they execute their tasks both efficiently *and* justly.

Across this chapter, I provided various illustrations of how algorithmic systems can be used in the public sector for a diversity of tasks, including managing public welfare programmes, conducting criminal investigations, evaluating asylum applications or assessing tax fraud. While most applications today are still primarily focused on *informing* rather than *adopting* administrative acts, the trend of ever-increased reliance on this technology provides strong indications that in the next decade, the automated adoption of administrative acts will become part and parcel of public administration. In this book, I will therefore analyse how the rule of law can be impacted by algorithmic regulation, conceptualised as the reliance on algorithmic systems either to *inform* or to *adopt* administrative acts. Having clarified what this practice entails, I can now move on to a conceptualisation of the rule of law.

3

The Rule of Law

Delineating the rule of law is a task worthy of several books in and of itself. Though it forms one of the core governance principles of modern states, the rule of law remains an elusive concept that has been defined in numerous ways throughout its rich history.[1] My aim here is not to recreate this history in all its glory. Instead, I merely seek to elucidate this concept for the purpose and context of this book. This means that my conceptualisation of the rule of law will be limited to its implications for the actions of public authorities and, more concretely, authorities that are part of the executive branch of power. As I already noted in the Introduction, while the rule of law also plays an important role in the organisation of relationships between private parties,[2] this falls outside the scope of my analysis.

In this chapter, I will first examine how the rule of law has been defined in legal theory, and how it has been distinguished from the rule *by* law, which is a distortion thereof (Section 3.1). Second, I will assess how the rule of law has been conceptualised in the context of the EU, as this book focuses primarily on the EU legal order (Section 3.2). In this regard, I will also draw on the acquis of the Council of Europe. The Council of Europe is a distinct jurisdictional order, yet it heavily influenced the 'EU' conceptualisation of the rule of law, and the EU regularly relies on Council of Europe sources in its own legal practices. Finally, I will draw on those findings to identify the rule of law's core principles and to distil the concrete requirements that

[1] See Aziz Z Huq, *The Rule of Law: A Very Short Introduction* (Oxford University Press 2024). Regarding the context of algorithmic regulation, see also Monika Zalnieriute and others, 'From Rule of Law to Statute Drafting: Legal Issues for Algorithms in Government Decision-Making' in Woodrow Barfield (ed), *The Cambridge Handbook of the Law of Algorithms* (Cambridge University Press 2020) 259.

[2] Indeed, citizens must obey the law too. As noted by James Madison in Federalist No. 51 (1788): "*in framing a government which is to be administered by men over men, the great difficulty lies in this: you must first enable the government to control the governed; and in the next place oblige it to control itself*". See Alexander Hamilton, James Madison, John Jay and Lawrence Goldman, *The Federalist Papers, October 1787–May 1788* (Oxford University Press 2008).

public authorities must fulfil to comply therewith (Section 3.3). Identifying these requirements – and the inherent challenges to achieve them – will subsequently allow me to build a normative analytical framework that I can use as a benchmark in Chapter 4 to assess how algorithmic regulation impacts the rule of law, and how it can lead to algorithmic rule by law.

3.1 A THEORETICAL INTRODUCTION TO THE RULE OF LAW

Before diving into primary sources of law, I will first consider how the rule of law has been conceptualised in legal theory and how it has been distinguished from other values, as this will provide a useful foundation to examine the role of this concept in the EU legal order later on. In this section, I start by setting out the various ways in which the rule of law has been defined thus far (Section 3.1.1) and conclude that – despite the fact that it is often conceptualised as a list of principles – there is something that can be called the 'spirit' of the rule of law which captures the protective role it plays in liberal democracies, beyond any formal list (Section 3.1.2). Building on this observation, I then distinguish between formal and substantive conceptions of the rule of law and underline that, in this book, the emphasis will lay on the latter (Section 3.1.3). Finally, I discuss the relationship between the rule of law and illiberal and authoritarian practices, by distinguishing the rule *of* law from the rule *by* law – a distinction that is central to this book's argument (Section 3.1.4).

3.1.1 *A Plethora of Definitions*

The idea behind the rule of law dates back at least to ancient times.[3] Aristotle alluded to it in several of his works and most famously in his *Politics*, where he insisted on a 'rule of law' rather than a 'rule of man',[4] given that "*he who bids the law rule may be deemed to bid God and Reason alone rule, but he who bids man rule adds an element of the beast; for desire is a wild beast, and passion perverts the minds of*

[3] The idea behind this notion arguably dates back even further, depending on which principles one considers to be part of the rule of law. The Code of Hammurabi, for instance, composed around 1755–1750 BC, already reflected a certain commitment to governance by law, based on general, clear and publicly known rules. See Larry May, *Ancient Legal Thought: Equity, Justice, and Humaneness from Hammurabi and the Pharaohs to Justinian and the Talmud* (Cambridge University Press 2019). Note also the statement by Amichai Magen and Laurent Pech that "*the idea and ideal of the rule of law has ancient roots in Babylonian, Hebraic, Hellenic, Roman, and in some respects Chinese political thought*", in 'The Rule of Law and the European Union' in Christopher May and Adam Winchester (eds), *Handbook on the Rule of Law* (Edward Elgar Publishing 2018) 235.

[4] Aristotle's reference to 'man' can be taken quite literally here. Under Greek 'democracy', women (as well as slaves and strangers) were not considered to be citizens with voting rights or any other privileges tied to the legal and political system. This remained true in virtually every subsequent century, up until the twentieth, when women were finally admitted to participation in political life.

rulers, even when they are the best of men".[5] For Aristotle, not only citizens, but also 'the guardians of the law' ought to obey the law.[6] A similar idea was espoused by other Greek thinkers. Mirko Canevaro offers the example of an oration by Hypereides, who led the Athenian resistance against King Philip II of Macedonia and Alexander the Great, stating that: "*For men to be happy they must be ruled by the voice of law, not the threats of a man; free men must not be frightened by accusation, only by proof of guilt; and the safety of our citizens must not depend on men who flatter their masters and slander our citizens but on our confidence in the law.*"[7]

Evidently, the notion of the rule of law in the fourth century BC does not fully coincide with its modern version(s), yet one can reasonably argue that its essence was already present back then. Both quotes express a clear opposition against governance through arbitrary rules that depend on the whims and interests of the people who happen to be in power. Both accounts argue in favour of governance through legal rules as a remedy against the arbitrariness of man. And both consider that, by placing confidence in 'the voice the law', which subjects rulers and the ruled alike to norms that are stable and bidding to reason, the corrupting nature of power can be curbed, and the liberty of citizens can be protected. This is also the spirit behind the concept of the rule of law that was espoused by more modern theorists, both in the European continent and in the Anglo-American world.[8]

One of the most influential conceptualisations of the rule of law stems from A. V. Dicey, a nineteenth-century British constitutional theorist.[9] Of particular interest is Dicey's caution against arbitrary rule-setting by the executive power, which he pronounced against the background of the enlargement of the state and its functions, and the birth of modern bureaucracy.[10] He put forward three essential

5 Aristotle, *Politics* (Benjamin Jowett tr, Batoche Books 1999) 77. See also Jeremy Waldron, 'Is the Rule of Law an Essentially Contested Concept (in Florida)?' (2002) 21 Law and Philosophy 137, 142.

6 See Brian Z Tamanaha, *On the Rule of Law: History, Politics, Theory* (Cambridge University Press 2004) 8; Tom Bingham, *The Rule of Law* (Penguin Books 2011) 3.

7 Mirko Canevaro, 'The Rule of Law as the Measure of Political Legitimacy in the Greek City States' (2017) 9 Hague Journal on the Rule of Law 211, 213.

8 Rule of law-conceptualisations in the continent and Britain took different shapes, given the diverse political contexts in which they developed. A thorough discussion of these differences is not necessary for the purpose of this book, the more given that theorists from both sides of the pond undoubtedly influenced each other. Suffice it to say that the continental notions of the *Rechtsstaat* or *État de droit* typically embodied a more constitutional perspective – in emphasising the fact that the state's legality derives its exercise of power by means of law, and that the constitution can set certain limits on the kind of laws that can be adopted – whereas Anglo-American rule of law conceptions emphasised Parliament's sovereignty and the common law system of legal precedents. See, e.g., Martin Loughlin, *Foundations of Public Law* (Oxford University Press 2010) 315 and following.

9 Martin Loughlin goes as far as to say that it is no exaggeration to say Dicey invented the concept of the rule of law. See 'The Apotheosis of the Rule of Law' (2018) 89 The Political Quarterly 659, 659.

10 See also Mark Bovens and Stavros Zouridis, 'From Street-Level to System-Level Bureaucracies: How Information and Communication Technology Is Transforming Administrative Discretion and Constitutional Control' (2002) 62 Public Administration Review 177.

principles that underlie the 'rule or supremacy of the law' in the British legal system, namely: (1) the need to curb the exercise of arbitrary power by persons in authority (*non-arbitrariness of power*); (2) the subjection of every man, whatever his rank or condition, to the ordinary law of the realm by ordinary tribunals (*equality*);[11] and (3) the protection of individual rights through general rules of constitutional law based on common law remedies, rather than a written constitution or Bill of Rights (*general principles through common law*).[12] While, as I will discuss below, the first two principles resonate with other rule of law-conceptions in Europe, the third principle clearly denotes a dissociation from the continental legal system,[13] seemingly implying that the rule of law is inherently a common law concept. This view has been criticised,[14] yet for the purpose of this book, we can bracket this discussion and continue exploring other rule of law conceptions. After all, Dicey arguably did not intend to put forward a general constitutional theory, but rather aimed to set out the principles of 'British constitutional law'.[15]

Dicey was not the only one whose fears of an unbounded administrative state or Leviathan proved particularly conducive of rule of law-theorising.[16] For Friedrich Hayek, who explicitly drew on Dicey's work,

> nothing distinguishes more clearly conditions in a free country from those in a country under arbitrary government than the observance in the former of the great principles known as the Rule of Law. Stripped of all technicalities, this means that government in all its actions is bound by rules fixed and announced beforehand – rules which make it possible to foresee with fair certainty how the authority will use its coercive powers in given circumstances and to plan one's individual affairs on the basis of this knowledge.[17]

[11] Note, however, that this concept of equality is unlikely to be substantive in nature, but rather concerned with equal access to courts in a formal way, as argued by Paul Craig in 'Formal and Substantive Conceptions of the Rule of Law: An Analytical Framework' [1997] Public Law 467, 472.

[12] AV Dicey, *Introduction to the Study of the Law of the Constitution [1885]* (10th edn, Macmillan 1968). See also Craig (n 11) 470–474.

[13] Dicey believed that written legal documents such as bills of rights could all too easily be rescinded, and hence placed more faith in common law remedies, which he found more robust. See, e.g., James E Pfander, 'Dicey's Nightmare: An Essay on The Rule of Law' (2019) 107 California Law Review 737, 745.

[14] See, for instance, also Judith Shklar's critique that this formulation of the rule of law merely entails "*an outburst of Anglo-Saxon parochialism*" in Judith Shklar, 'Political Theory and the Rule of Law' in Allan C Hutchinson and Patrick Monahan (eds), *The Rule of Law: Ideal or Ideology?* (Carswell 1987) 5.

[15] Loughlin (n 9) 659.

[16] Bovens and Zouridis (n 10) 176.

[17] Friedrich A von Hayek, *The Road to Serfdom (1944)*, (Bruce Caldwell ed, Routledge 2008) 112. This definition is also cited by Joseph Raz as "*one of the clearest and most powerful formulations of the ideal of the rule of law*". See Joseph Raz, in 'The Rule of Law and Its Virtue' in his book *The Authority of Law: Essays on Law and Morality* (Oxford University Press 1979) 195.

Another influential account of the rule of law can be found in Lon Fuller's *The Morality of Law*, in which eight elements are put forward as "*the morality that makes law possible*".[18] These concern the fact that (1) there should be general rules that can be applied to concrete cases (*generality*), (2) the rules should be made public so that those subjected thereto can know them (*publicity*), (3) the rules should be adopted before they are being applied to concrete cases (*prospectivity*), (4) the rules should be clear and understandable (*intelligibility*), (5) the rules should not contradict each other (*consistency*), (6) it should be possible practically to conform to the rules (*conformability*), (7) the rules should be relatively stable over time (*stability*) and (8) the application and implementation of the rules by the state should correspond with the promulgated rules (*congruence*). Fuller's rule of law conceptualisation can be described as an anatomical or list-based approach, as it offers a list of features that the law should have to speak of its morality and hence of its legal character.

A similar approach was also embraced by Lord Bingham, whose list is slightly different.[19] His eight rule of law ingredients comprise the fact that: (1) the law must be accessible and so far as possible intelligible, clear and predictable (*accessibility*); (2) questions of legal right and liability should be resolved by application of the law rather than by arbitrary discretion (*non-arbitrariness*); (3) the laws of the land should apply equally to all, save to the extent that objective differences justify differentiation (*equality*); (4) public officers must exercise the powers conferred to them in good faith, fairly, for the purpose for which the powers were conferred, without exceeding those powers' limits, and not unreasonably (*fair and reasonable exercise of power*); (5) the law must afford adequate protection of human rights (*human rights*); (6) means must be provided for resolving, without prohibitive cost or inordinate delay, bona fide civil disputes (*means for dispute resolution*); (7) adjudicative procedures provided by law should be fair (*fair trial*); and (8) the rule of law requires compliance by the state with its obligations in international law as in national law (*respect for the international legal order*).

3.1.2 *The Spirit of the Rule of Law*

List-based approaches have been criticised as overly focusing on the formal features of the law, rather than considering the purpose that underlies these principles.[20] Without a consideration of the rule of law's underlying purpose, the danger exists that its principles are applied in a way that does not actually achieve their aims. Martin Krygier therefore argued in favour of a 'teleological' approach to the rule of law, inviting reflection on the overarching purpose or 'spirit' of this

[18] Lon L Fuller, *The Morality of Law* (Yale University Press 1969) 33–94. See also Margaret Jane Radin, 'Reconsidering the Rule of Law' (1989) 69 Boston University Law Review 781, 784.

[19] See Bingham (n 6).

[20] Rosalind Dixon, 'Rule of Law Teleology: Against the Misuse and Abuse of Rule of Law Rhetoric' (2019) 11 Hague Journal on the Rule of Law 461.

concept.[21] In short, a teleological approach focuses on the *why* rather than the *what*. Once we identified this 'why', we can use it as normative guidance for institutional design and action, rather than being fixated on the list of its constitutive elements. The question is hence: what is the purpose or spirit of the rule of law?

Of course, that goal may be manifold when considered from the point of view of various actors, and it is also likely to be defined differently by different people. Yet if we consider a contextual approach in light of this book and focus on the role it plays in the public sector, it can be reasonably argued that the rule of law entails a commitment to set limits to the exercise of public power in order to ensure legal accountability and to safeguard human liberty, dignity and agency.[22] By subjecting public authorities to the law and ensuring their actions can be reviewed against that law, natural and legal persons are protected against overly broad encroaches on their rights and freedoms. Moreover, the fact that public authorities are bound by rules that are proclaimed in advance also enables citizens to plan their lives in accordance with those rules.[23]

The chief merit of the teleological approach to the rule of law is that it puts this overarching purpose into perspective. The rule of law is not a goal in and of itself that should be fetishised, but a means that can help achieve other related values, such as the protection of human rights and public accountability, and thus democracy.[24] Based on that purpose, one can then logically derive that the features that the legal system must have in order to ensure the realisation of the rule of law's spirit, such as the need for public authorities to comply with the law and the ability to hold them to account when they do not, as well as the need for the law and its application to be foreseeable, accessible and intelligible. This order of things is important, as the rhetoric of the rule of law can also be abused. As noted by Dixon, given the complexity of the ideal of the rule of law, it is "*especially susceptible to superficial forms of abusive borrowing*", a practice she describes as "*involving the use of one or more related techniques, namely radical: (1) superficiality, (2) selectivity, (3) decontextualisation, and (4) anti-purposive usage in the application of liberal democratic*

[21] Martin Krygier, 'The Rule of Law: Pasts, Presents, and Two Possible Futures' (2016) 12 Annual Review of Law and Social Science 199. See also Martin Krygier, 'What's the Point of the Rule of Law?' (2019) 67 Buffalo Law Review 743.

[22] Jeremy Waldron, 'The Rule of Law' in Edward N Zalta (ed), *The Stanford Encyclopedia of Philosophy* (Summer 2020, Metaphysics Research Lab, Stanford University 2020) <https://plato.stanford.edu/archives/sum2020/entries/rule-of-law/>, chapter 6. See also Dixon (n 20) 461; Paul Dermine, 'The New Economic Governance of the Eurozone: A Rule of Law Analysis' (PhD thesis, Maastricht University 2020) 31. As will be discussed further in Chapter 5, according to Endicott and Yeung, this includes not only private agency but also public agency. See Timothy Endicott and Karen Yeung, 'The Death of Law? Computationally Personalized Norms and The Rule of Law' [2022] University of Toronto Law Journal 72(4), 373–402.

[23] See also Hayek (n 17).

[24] At least under the conception of the rule of law in constitutional liberal democracies, as further discussed *infra*.

norms".[25] When focusing solely on an anatomical or list-based approach, there is thus a risk that public authorities select only those principles on the list that suit them and that may be used precisely to undermine the underlying spirit of the rule of law. I will come back to this risk when distinguishing the rule *of* law from the rule *by* law.

3.1.3 *Formal and Substantive Notions of the Rule of Law*

Related to this discussion is the question whether the rule of law embodies only procedural aspects of the law, or whether it also covers substantive elements. Does the rule of law have anything to say about the law's substance, such as the fact that it should be compatible with human rights and with democratic principles? Or are 'human rights' and 'democracy' distinct notions that are not part of the rule of law's spirit? Glancing again over the descriptions above, one can note that respect for human rights is, for instance, featured in the 'ingredients list' proposed by Lord Bingham, but does not appear in the account of Lon Fuller. These conceptual differences lay at the heart of the distinction between *formal* and *substantive* notions of the rule of law, also referred to as *thin* and *thick* notions.[26]

Formal or thin conceptions of the rule of law attach importance to the procedural aspects of the law's promulgation (Was the law enacted through a valid procedure? Was the norm made public and is it sufficiently clear to safeguard legal certainty? Is the law administered by an impartial and independent tribunal?). However, as explained by Paul Craig, such conceptions "*do not seek to pass judgment upon the actual content of the law itself*".[27] This does not necessarily mean that those who support such thin conceptions do not care about matters like human rights and democracy. However, they consider these aspects to be embodied by values other than the rule of law. In contrast, substantive rule of law notions are 'thicker' since they suggest that any rule of law definition, in addition to formal requirements, should also comprise a minimum of substantive requirements regarding the *content* of the rules and the *type of procedure* to enact them. In fact, they believe such substantive requirements to be an *inevitable* part of the rule of law, since the line between substance and procedure is too blurred to draw, and both aspects are inherently entwined.[28]

The distinction between formal and substantive notions of the rule of law can arguably be seen as part of the broader distinction between two major strands in legal philosophy: positivism and naturalism. The former (on which the formalistic rule of law notion is based) holds that the authority of law stems from the validity of the

[25] Dixon (n 20) 462. See also Rosalind Dixon and David Landau, *Abusive Constitutional Borrowing: Legal Globalization and the Subversion of Liberal Democracy* (Oxford University Press 2021).

[26] See in this regard, e.g., Radin (n 18) 783; Craig (n 11); Brian Z Tamanaha, 'The History and Elements of the Rule of Law' [2012] Singapore Journal of Legal Studies 232.

[27] Craig (n 11) 467.

[28] Waldron (n 22).

procedures by which it is adopted, while the latter (corresponding to a substantive notion of the rule of law) holds instead that the authority of law *also* depends on a substantive standard based on which its content can and should be judged.[29] Hence, under a substantive view, immoral laws (such as those enacted in Nazi Germany, for instance) should not be considered as law at all, even if clear, publicly proclaimed and adopted by the established procedure. It is, in fact, precisely in reaction to these atrocious laws that naturalism started to gain more ground again after the Second World War.[30] Lord Bingham's explicit inclusion of respect for human rights as part of his rule of law-ingredients list reflects this view. As he explains: "*a state which savagely represses or persecutes sections of its people cannot in my view be regarded as observing the rule of law, even if the transport of the persecuted minority to the concentration camp or the compulsory exposure of female children on the mountain-side is the subject of detailed laws duly enacted and scrupulously observed*".[31]

While a substantive notion of the rule of law is intuitively attractive, opponents claim that it is unworkable as it presupposes an inherent element of justice or morality based on which a law should be judged to be considered as having the authority of law. Yet arguably, once we open the door to the law's contestation based on whether it is deemed moral or just, we *either* enable all legal subjects to oppose any law they consider to be 'unjust', *or* we at the same time need to proclaim that an objective standard of 'justice' exists. After all, by bringing in 'justice' as a substantive standard against which the law's authority should be judged, we also need to define that standard – and risk stumbling upon different conceptualisations thereof. Hence Carl Schmitt's critique on substantive notions of the law, which he describes as the idea that: "*law should above all be what I and my friends value*".[32]

Joseph Raz was likewise critical of overly thick rule of law conceptions: "*If the rule of law is the rule of the good law then to explain its nature is to propound a complete social philosophy. But if so the term lacks any useful function.*"[33] Proponents of a

[29] This sentiment is captured quite well by Martin Luther King Jr., who stated that "*an individual who breaks a law that conscience tells him is unjust, and who willingly accepts the penalty of imprisonment in order to arouse the conscience of the community over its injustice, is in reality expressing the highest respect for law*", in his 'Letter from Birmingham Jail', 1963.

[30] Ronald Dworkin has been one of the strongest opponents of positivism, pointing out the immoral excesses that an overly positivistic approach to law can engender. His discussion with HLA Hart, who instead defended legal positivism and the so-called 'rule of recognition' as the basis for legal validity, has been highly influential in legal philosophy and also left its mark on modern conceptualisations of the rule of law. See respectively, Ronald Dworkin, *Law's Empire* (Hart Publishing 1998); HLA Hart, *The Concept of Law* (3rd edn, Oxford University Press 2012). See also See also Scott J Shapiro, 'The "Hart-Dworkin" Debate: A Short Guide for the Perplexed' [2007] Public Law and Legal Theory Working Paper Series <https://law.yale.edu/sites/default/files/documents/pdf/Faculty/Shapiro_Hart_Dworkin_Debate.pdf>.

[31] Bingham (n 6) 67.

[32] Carl Schmitt, *Legality and Legitimacy [1932]* (Duke University Press 2004) 14.

[33] Raz (n 17) 211.

formal rule of law-notion therefore prefer to conceptualise it as a self-standing value, which remains distinct from values like democracy, human rights, justice or the more abstract 'good'. Tamanaha[34] and Waldron, too, express reservations, the latter claiming that

> once we open up the possibility of the Rule of Law's having a substantive dimension, we inaugurate a sort of competition in which everyone clamors to have their favorite political ideal incorporated as a substantive dimension of the Rule of Law. [...] The result is likely to be a general decline in political articulacy, as people struggle to use the same term to express disparate ideals.[35]

Consequently, Waldron argues that the rule of law is a so-called essentially contested concept,[36] defined by WB Gallie as concepts "*the proper use of which inevitably involves endless disputes about their proper uses on the part of their users*".[37] Others have gone further in their critique and suggested to do away with the concept altogether,[38] as they find it to be too vague, encompassing too many different things for different people, and thus ultimately 'meaningless'.[39]

[34] Tamanaha states that "*to insist that the rule of law requires human rights and democracy has the effect of defining the rule of law in terms of institutions that match liberal democracies*", which "*is unjustifiable. It smacks of stuffing the meaning of the rule of law with contestable normative presuppositions to produce a desired or presupposed outcome which is then imposed on everyone by definitional fiat*". Tamanaha (n 26) 234.

[35] Waldron (n 22).

[36] See Richard H Fallon, '"The Rule of Law" as a Concept in Constitutional Discourse' (1997) 97 Columbia Law Review 1, 6; Waldron, 'Is the Rule of Law an Essentially Contested Concept (in Florida)?' (n 5); Jeremy Waldron, 'The Rule of Law as an Essentially Contested Concept' in Jens Meierhenrich and Martin Loughlin (eds), *The Cambridge Companion to the Rule of Law* (Cambridge University Press 2021).

[37] WB Gallie, 'Essentially Contested Concepts' (1955) 56 Proceedings of the Aristotelian Society 167, 169.

[38] Shklar (n 14) 1. The reasoning goes as follows: if it is a concept that anyone can lay claim on regardless of the underlying practice or value, what purpose can the rule of law still serve? Also Martin Loughlin, drawing on Carl Schmitt's critique, cautions against rule of law-advocates who make a claim on this concept to brand their opponents as rule of law-enemies. According to him, the concept "*has value only for its aspirational qualities*" and "*although a coherent formulation of the general concept can be devised, this formulation is entirely unworkable in practice*". See Loughlin (n 8) 314.

[39] Loughlin (n 8) 314. Driving this point to the extreme, one could compare 'the rule of law' with concepts like 'the common good' or 'the public interest', which have likewise been criticised as inherently contested and vague, and prone to ideological abuse precisely because of their vagueness. See, e.g., Clarke E Cochran, 'Political Science and "The Public Interest"' (1974) 36 The Journal of Politics 327; Donna Dickenson, 'The Common Good' in Roger Brownsword, Eloise Scotford and Karen Yeung (eds), *The Oxford Handbook of Law, Regulation and Technology* (Oxford University Press 2017). Consider also Stephen Humphreys account, which criticises rule of law-rhetoric as a 'theatre' – empty, fungible and therefore (ab)used by certain countries to impose economic, political and social reforms on other countries behind the facade of 'rule of law promotion'. See Stephen Humphreys, *Theatre of the Rule of Law: Transnational Legal Intervention in Theory and Practice* (Cambridge University Press 2010).

While one can sympathise with these views to some extent, it would be a mistake to throw away the baby with the bathwater. In my view, the aspirational quality of the rule of law does not deduct from its value, nor does it deprive one from judging concrete government practices based on whether they respect, advance or impede this ideal. Rather than merely showing disaccord, the vast scholarly literature about the rule of law and its various conceptualisations can be seen as an attestation of its continuous importance in modern legal systems. Furthermore, the binary choice presented above is too simplistic. In modern liberal democracies, the values of human rights and democracy can unapologetically be identified as minimum substantive standards, without needing to navigate between the Scylla of bare proceduralism and the Charybdis of unbounded moral relativism. One does not need to open the door to infinite subjective sentiments of 'justice' to support a conceptualisation of the rule of law that requires public authorities to ensure the legal rules they adopt respect human rights and the democratic process. Certainly, the rule of law is an ideal type, as it is never fully achieved in practice.[40] Yet it represents something to be striven towards and can serve as a useful normative framework to guide public action – and to orientate my analysis in this book.

More importantly, as I will explain in Section 3.2, in the EU legal order, the rule of law is *more* than a normative principle. It is a value enshrined in both primary and secondary union law that all Member States and the EU itself must *legally* comply with.[41] This also counts for Member States of the Council of Europe, for whom compliance with the rule of law is a legally enshrined obligation, entwined with the obligation to comply with human rights and democracy.[42] Accordingly, while acknowledging the existence of both thick and thin notions of the rule of law in legal scholarship, this divergence does not stand in the way of rendering it both an aspirational value that should be striven towards, and a normative source from which concrete requirements can be derived that public authorities must legally abide by – including when they rely on algorithmic regulation. In what follows, I will thus dive into EU legal sources with the aim of distilling a more concrete conceptualisation of the rule of law in the context of the public sector to build my analytical framework.

Before doing so, I must however clarify one more theoretical point, namely the relationship between the rule of law on the one hand and authoritarian and illiberal practices on the other. As stated in the Introduction, the increase of such practices in modern liberal democracies – including in the EU – is a development that this book seeks to problematise. In the next section, I will therefore explain how they relate to the rule of law, and how this relationship informs the broader hypothesis of this

[40] Tamanaha (n 26) 234.

[41] Pekka Pohjankoski, 'Rule of Law with Leverage: Policing Structural Obligations in EU Law with the Infringement Procedure, Fines and Set-Off' (2021) 58 Common Market Law Review 1341.

[42] See Council of Europe, 'The Council of Europe and the Rule of Law' (Council of Europe 2008) CM(2008)170 5.

book, namely that public authorities' reliance on algorithmic regulation, in addition to potentially undermining the rule of law, can also dilute the law's protective function against illiberal and authoritarian tendencies in society.

3.1.4 *The Rule of Law and the Rule by Law*

In political theory, authoritarianism is typically juxtaposed to democracy, not to the rule of law. While many different definitions of these concepts exist, put very simply, in a democracy, those subjected to the law must be able to have a say in it.[43] How such 'say' is organised depends on the type of democratic system, of which numerous variations exist,[44] yet they all differ from authoritarian or autocratic regimes, where the law can be decided by a sole person or entity with absolute power, without accountability to the governed people.[45] Note that, in both of these descriptions, the law plays a role. Of course, in the latter, the ruler can also unilaterally decide to govern arbitrarily, based on whims rather than legal rules, and it is *that* precise feature, the absence of laws, that proponents of a thin conceptualisation of the rule of law consider to be its opposite.[46] For this reason, some scholars have argued that the rule of law is compatible with authoritarianism, and that some authoritarian states can be meaningfully said to adhere to the rule of law.[47]

Both in the past and in the future, states have indeed been relying upon laws (i.e., legal rules that were adopted in accordance with a given procedure[48]) to implement illiberal and authoritarian practices. However, proponents of a substantive notion of the rule of law would qualify such states as adhering to a rule *by* law instead. The rule by law embodies a purely formalistic notion of the law, whereby the power of the law serves to advance authoritarian and illiberal purposes which are incompatible with the spirit of the rule *of* law,[49] namely the aim of taming excessive public power and protect human liberty. Recall in this regard also the quote by Lord Bingham cited above. It is not because a state persecutes minorities through legal rules that it abides by the rule of law. Accordingly, while the rule *of* law entails the

43 See also Philippe C Schmitter and Terry Lynn Karl, 'What Democracy Is . . . and Is Not' (1991) 2 Journal of Democracy 75; Robert Alan Dahl, *On Democracy* (Yale University 1998).

44 See, for instance, Susan Rose-Ackerman, *Democracy and Executive Power: Policymaking Accountability in the US, the UK, Germany, and France* (Yale University Press 2021).

45 Victor V Ramraj, 'Democracy and Authoritarianism' in Peter Cane and others (eds), *The Oxford Handbook of Comparative Administrative Law* (Oxford University Press 2020).

46 See in this regard also Craig (n 11).

47 See, for instance, Tamanaha (n 26).

48 Which Hart would denote as 'secondary rules'. See Hart (n 30).

49 Of course, the distinction between the rule of law and the rule by law is only meaningful for those who consider the rule of law to encompass something that goes beyond mere procedural requirements. As Dyzenhaus explains, "*only if one holds to a fairly substantive or thick conception of the rule of law will one think that there is a point on a continuum where rule by law ceases to be in accordance with the rule of law*". See David Dyzenhaus, *The Constitution of Law: Legality in a Time of Emergency* (Cambridge University Press 2006) 42.

idea that *"the law should stand above every powerful person and agency in the land"*, the rule *by* law, *"in contrast, connotes the instrumental use of law as a tool of political power"*.[50]

The rule by law can hence be seen as a distortion of the rule of law, as it undermines the law's protective role. Governments can indeed deploy the law to legitimise their actions – even if oppressive or unjust – and to consolidate rather than to limit their power. As noted by Joseph Weiler: *"The rule of law, outside a democracy is simply the most effective instrument of authoritarianism and worse."*[51] Besides legal scholars, also the Council of Europe's Venice Commission (which, as we shall see below, is responsible for advising Member States on rule of law-related matters) underscored this distinction, stating that *"over time, the essence of the rule of law in some countries was distorted so as to be equivalent to 'rule by law', or 'rule by the law', or even 'law by rules'. These interpretations permitted authoritarian actions by governments and do not reflect the meaning of the rule of law today"*.[52] In its 2008 rule of law report, the Council of Europe's Committee of Ministers explained it as follows: *"There can be no democracy without the rule of law and respect for human rights; there can be no rule of law without democracy and respect for human rights, and no respect for human rights without democracy and the rule of law."*[53]

Already centuries ago, authors like de Tocqueville stressed that democracy is *more* than the mere rule of the majority, as this could lead to a so-called tyranny of the majority.[54] That is why the maintenance of a liberal democracy requires a deliberative process that enables participation and the protection of certain rights and liberties, including for minorities, that cannot simply be overturned by a majority – even if it does so by law.[55] Moreover, as already touched upon in Section 2.3, the relationship between the government and its citizens is also subjected to a set of principles that enable administrative justice and ensure the government can be held to account when infringing the law. In other words, whereas the rule *of* law underpins human rights and democracy, under the rule *by* law, the law merely provides a veneer of legality for actions that are not compatible therewith, as it

[50] Waldron, 'The Rule of Law' (n 22), chapter 4. As Waldron notes in the same chapter, some authors consider this distinction to be superfluous and defend the merits of a rule *by* law approach.

[51] Joseph HH Weiler, 'Not on Bread Alone Doth Man Liveth (Deut. 8:3; Mat 4:4): Some Iconoclastic Views on Populism, Democracy, the Rule of Law and the Polish Circumstance' in Armin von Bogdandy and others (eds), *Defending Checks and Balances in EU Member States*, vol 298 (Springer Berlin Heidelberg 2021) 5.

[52] Venice Commission, 'Report on the Rule of Law – Adopted by the Venice Commission at Its 86th Plenary Session' (2011) CDL-AD(2011)003rev-e 5.

[53] Council of Europe (n 42), §26.

[54] See Alexis de Tocqueville, *Democracy in America (1835)* (Barnes & Noble 2003).

[55] These rights can hence be shielded from the 'the democratic will'. See also Denis J Galligan, 'Public Administration and the Tendency to Authoritarianism' in András Sajó (ed), *Out of and into Authoritarian Law* (Brill–Nijhoff 2002) 190.

undermines the protective role that the law plays in safeguarding human rights and democracy.

Today, authoritarian tendencies are prevalent across the globe. Importantly, these tendencies are also surfacing in liberal democracies, and are eroding its normative pillars incrementally.[56] According to the authors of the Authoritarian Playbook,

> before the 1990s, authoritarian leaders bent on upending democracy typically came to power forcefully and swiftly, often by means of a military coup d'état. The moment democracy ceased to exist could be timestamped and reported on with a block headline. Yet for at least the last thirty years, the threats to democracy have evolved. Today, democracy more often dies gradually, as the institutional, legal, and political constraints on authoritarian leaders are chipped away, one by one.[57]

In other words, the threat hence comes from within, through the incremental erosion of legal protection mechanisms that are meant to safeguard the rule of law, democracy and human rights. Instead, the law is being used to bolster regimes that are moving away from liberal democracy, without (yet) meriting the connotation of an authoritarian regime.[58]

Authoritarian-minded leaders that know the rules of the game and are eager to uphold the veneer of legality, which facilitates international legitimacy and hence entails financial benefits,[59] are increasingly facilitating illiberal and authoritarian practices by adopting new laws or legal reforms, seemingly in 'full accordance with the law', yet at the same time undermining the law's protective function.[60] Furthermore, these practices typically occur cumulatively and incrementally rather

[56] See also David Murakami Wood, 'The Global Turn to Authoritarianism and After' (2017) 15 Surveillance & Society 357.

[57] Protect Democracy, 'The Authoritarian Playbook – How Reporters Can Contextualize and Cover Authoritarian Threats as Distinct from Politics-as-Usual' (2022) <protectdemocracy.org/project/playbook-media-primer> 5.

[58] These regimes have also been denoted as 'hybrid regimes', whereby "*the executive branch concentrates powers to the detriment of nonstate and opposition actors. Hybrid regimes are sometimes called 'competitive authoritarian' because, while the ruling party competes in elections (usually winning), the president is granted an array of autocratic powers that erode checks and balances.*" See Javier Corrales, 'The Authoritarian Resurgence: Autocratic Legalism in Venezuela' (2015) 26 Journal of Democracy 37, 37.

[59] See in this regard also Ken Godfrey, 'How the EU Can Better Avoid Bankrolling Authoritarianism' (*Carnegie Europe* 4 March 2021), <https://carnegieeurope.eu/2021/03/04/how-eu-can-better-avoid-bankrolling-authoritarianism-pub-83992>.

[60] The implementation of illiberal and authoritarian practices is thus legitimised by reference to the law, which has also been referred to as 'autocratic legalism' or – when accompanied by deliberate constitutional reforms with the same purpose – as 'constitution authoritarianism'. See in this regard Kim Lane Scheppele, 'Autocratic Legalism' [2018] The University of Chicago Law Review 545; Orlando Scarcello, 'Authoritarian Constitutionalism: An Oxymoron? The Case of Costantino Mortati's Early Writings (1931–1940)' (2021) 3/21 Jean Monnet Working Paper, <https://jeanmonnetprogram.org/wp-content/uploads/JMWP-03-Orlando-Scarcello.pdf>.

than through one sweeping reform, which keeps the harm they cause under the radar for a longer time, and can hence fail to mobilise sufficient opposition.

It is, however, important to note that the distortion of the rule of law into the rule *by* law need not necessarily stem from a deliberate intention to undermine the law's protective role. An overly rigid and disproportionately severe interpretation of the law can also lead to practices that run counter to the ideal of the rule of law. Reference can in this regard be made to the Venice Commission's Opinion of 2021[61] regarding the 'childcare allowance case' in the Netherlands, which I will discuss further in Chapter 4. In this case, the Dutch tax authorities applied an overly strict approach to the implementation of a law against alleged fraudsters, and targeted parents even without the proven intention of fraud, with disproportionate reimbursement claims for the so-called undue benefits they had received. The authority's (and later the courts')[62] reluctance to apply a hardship clause and ensure a proportionate balance of the interests at stake, tragically impacted a large number of families, causing 'unprecedented injustice' and irreparable damage.[63] In its opinion, the Venice Commission noted that it has "*consistently cautioned against considering 'the rule of law' as a purely formal concept in the meaning of 'rule by law' and not as a substantive concept, meaning that the law must be accompanied with guarantees against abuse of legal powers.*"[64] It also noted that an "*exercise of power that leads to substantively unfair, unreasonable, irrational or oppressive decisions violates the Rule of Law*" which, it concluded, "*has been done by several Dutch authorities*".[65] This demonstrates how the rule *by* law is not only the product of deliberate action, but can also be the consequence of negligence on behalf of public authorities to ensure that their exercise of power does not violate the rule of law.

Throughout this book, I will rely on the distinction between the rule of law and the rule by law, and argue that negligent or deliberately problematic reliance on algorithmic regulation might eventually foster *algorithmic rule by law*. I hence do not reserve this term solely for practices that consciously and purposely undermine the protective power of the law while upholding the veneer of legality, but also for practices that do so inadvertently by paying insufficient attention to this very risk. With this in mind, I will now examine how the rule of law is conceptualised in the European Union. While its entwinement with democracy and human rights is henceforth taken as a baseline, I still need to further concretise this 'elusive' concept[66] before I can distil therefrom the requirements that public authorities

[61] Mr Richard Barrett and others, 'The Netherlands: Opinion on the Legal Protection of Citizens' (Venice Commission 2021) Opinion no. 1031/2021 CDL-AD(2021)031.

[62] Also the Council of State's Administrative Jurisdiction Division, which carried out judicial reviews of the tax authority's actions, followed suit in this approach. See ibid, §16.

[63] Parliamentary Inquiry Committee, 'Unprecedented Injustice' (House of Representatives of the States General 2020) 35 510, no. 1.

[64] Barrett and others (n 61), §118.

[65] ibid, §118.

[66] Tamanaha (n 6) 3.

must fulfil when taking administrative acts and examining how reliance on algorithmic regulation can affect them.

3.2 THE RULE OF LAW IN THE EUROPEAN UNION

The rule of law is typically part of a national legal order, where it functions as a normative value or guiding principle for the institutional design of a nation state. Yet, ever since the rise of international and supranational organisations in the twentieth century, the rule of law has also been considered beyond the context of the nation state.[67] Many international organisations have this value incorporated into their mandate or into their policy agenda, for instance in the form of 'rule of law promotion initiatives'.[68] In addition, a number of non-governmental organisations have started mapping rule of law indicators and used this as a basis to create indexes that measure and compare states' compliance with the rule of law.[69] Arguably, the most important international organisation mandated to set rule of law standards is the Council of Europe. While the Council of Europe's legal order is distinct from that of the European Union, it has had a tremendous influence on the EU's understanding of the rule of law, and effectively shaped its EU conceptualisation. In this section, I therefore start with an introduction to the Council of Europe's work on the rule of law, and examine the authority it has in the European Union (Section 3.2.1). Next, I discuss the origins of the rule of law in the EU legal order (Section 3.2.2) and distinguish between its vertical and horizontal dimensions (Section 3.2.3). I then examine how the rule of law is conceptualised in primary sources of EU law and identify the six core principles associated therewith (Section 3.2.4). Finally,

67 Martin Loughlin even credits the increased international reliance on 'the rule of law' with the concept's revival after having been criticised for its 'contested nature'. See Loughlin (n 9) 664.

68 Such initiatives consist of development aid schemes, whereby adherence to the rule of law is typically set as a precondition to benefit from the aid. Rule of law promotion schemes have been the subject of heavy criticism, as their rule of law-definitions – upon which receipt of the aid depends – has been argued to encompass Western and capitalistic elements, hence 'sneaking in' a liberal economic agenda under the guise of a so-called neutral conception of the rule of law. For a detailed analysis and critique, see also Humphreys (n 39).

69 These rule of law-indexes are not devoid of criticism either since, to enable comparisons, they need to set a common standard for a not-commonly agreed upon concept. At the same time, these initiatives can build on existing literature and output by international organisations that sought to define the rule of law at global level, and allow for interesting insights not only as regards how countries fare comparatively to each other, but also how their scores decline or increase over time. One of the most well-known rule of law indexes is prepared by the World Justice Project and focuses on eight factors: Constraints on Government Powers, Absence of Corruption, Open Government, Fundamental Rights, Order and Security, Regulatory Enforcement, Civil Justice, and Criminal Justice. See, e.g., World Justice Project, 'Rule of Law Index 2020' (World Justice Project 2020) <https://worldjusticeproject.org/sites/default/files/documents/WJP-ROLI-2020-Online_0.pdf>. The European Commission's rule of law framework, discussed further below, takes a similar approach by considering how each EU member state performs based on a number of criteria (see *infra* Section 5.2).

I conclude with a discussion of the so-called EU 'rule of law crisis' and draw attention to the rule of law's fragility (Section 3.2.5).

3.2.1 *The Rule of Law and the Council of Europe*

When the Council of Europe was founded in 1949, the notion of the rule of law was already part of its establishing statute, stating in Article 3 that every member "*must accept the principles of the rule of law and of the enjoyment by all persons within its jurisdiction of human rights and fundamental freedoms*".[70] Pursuant to Article 8 of the Statute, any member of the Council of Europe which has seriously violated Article 3 may be suspended from its rights of representation, and can eventually even be expelled from the organisation.[71] The European Convention on Human Rights (ECHR), signed under the Council of Europe's auspices a year later, likewise evokes the rule of law in its preamble as part of a 'common heritage' of the governments of European countries. Since then, the Council of Europe produced a broad set of guidelines and recommendations regarding the rule of law, constituting one of its three pillars, together with democracy and human rights.[72] Accordingly, the idea of the rule of law as a concept that is common to signatory member states, and that can be given a common conception at the international level, started taking shape. This occurred not merely in theory, but through the explicit desire of states to work towards and commit to a common understanding of the rule of law, anchored in an international legally binding instrument.

In 1999, the Council of Europe established the European Commission for Democracy through Law (better known as the Venice Commission) which is an advisory body on constitutional matters.[73] Its 2011 report on the rule of law aimed at identifying a 'consensual definition' of this concept, in order to facilitate its interpretation and application. As already hinted at, the Venice Commission explicitly

[70] See Article 3 of the Statute of the Council of Europe 1949 (CETS 001).

[71] Note how the Treaty's preamble also reaffirms its member states' "*devotion to the spiritual and moral values which are the common heritage of their peoples and the true source of individual freedom, political liberty and the rule of law, principles which form the basis of all genuine democracy*". Following Russia's invasion of Ukraine on 24 February 2022, the Council of Europe's Committee of Ministers adopted a resolution to cease Russia's membership under Article 8 of the Statute. See Resolution CM/Res(2022)2 on the cessation of the membership of the Russian Federation to the Council of Europe, adopted by the Committee of Ministers on 16 March 2022 at the 1428ter meeting of the Ministers' Deputies.

[72] See also Jörg Polakiewicz and Julia Katharina Kirchmayr, 'Sounding the Alarm: The Council of Europe as the Guardian of the Rule of Law in Contemporary Europe' in Armin von Bogdandy and others (eds), *Defending Checks and Balances in EU Member States: Taking Stock of Europe's Actions* (Springer 2021) 361.

[73] Besides the forty-six Council of Europe Member States, the Venice Commission also counts representatives from fifteen other countries, namely Algeria, Brazil, Canada, Chile, Costa Rica, Israel, Kazakhstan, the Republic of Korea, Kosovo, Kyrgyzstan, Morocco, Mexico, Peru, Tunisia and the USA. Argentina, the Holy See, Uruguay and Japan have Observer Status.

rejects a thin conception of the rule of law, in favour of one that also embraces substantive elements, including respect for democracy and human rights. The report states that "*a consensus can now be found for the necessary elements of the rule of law*", namely: (1) legality, including a transparent, accountable and democratic process for enacting law; (2) legal certainty; (3) prohibition of arbitrariness; (4) access to justice before independent and impartial courts, including judicial review of administrative acts; (5) respect for human rights; and (6) non-discrimination and equality before the law. Based on those six elements, the Venice Commission subsequently prepared a rule of law-checklist to facilitate the evaluation of the condition of the rule of law in individual states.[74] The rule of law-checklist was subsequently endorsed by the Committee of Ministers and by the Council of Europe's Parliamentary Assembly.[75]

This work proved highly influential for the European Union, which came into existence a few years after the establishment of the Council of Europe. The EU acknowledged the Council of Europe's 'normative pre-eminence'[76] in the 2007 Memorandum of Understanding between the Council of Europe and the EU, stating that "*the Council of Europe will remain the benchmark for human rights, the rule of law and democracy in Europe*".[77] All EU Member States are also a member of the Council of Europe. At the same time, both institutions agreed to cooperate and complement each other's work as regards the protection of the rule of law based on common standards.[78] When building this book's normative framework and distilling concrete rule of law requirements for public authorities, I therefore

[74] Venice Commission, 'Rule of Law Checklist' (Council of Europe 2016) Study no. 711 / 2013 CDL-AD(2016)007rev.

[75] Parliamentary Assembly, 'Venice Commission's Rule of Law Checklist' (2017) Resolution 2187 (2017).

[76] Joelle Grogan and others, 'The Crystallisation of a Core EU Meaning of the Rule of Law and Its (Limited) Normative Influence beyond the EU' (Reconnect – Reconciling Europe with its Citizens through Democracy and Rule of Law 2021) 27.

[77] 'Memorandum of Understanding between the Council of Europe and the European Union' (Council of Europe 2007) 3 <https://rm.coe.int/16804e437b>.

[78] Note also that the EU is committed to accede to the European Convention for the Protection of Human Rights and Fundamental Freedoms (ECHR) and declared that fundamental rights – as guaranteed by the ECHR and as they result from the constitutional traditions common to the Member States – shall constitute general principles of EU law. See in this regard Article 6 (2) TEU, introduced in the Treaty after the CJEU's Opinion 2/94 in 1996 that the Treaty did not provide for the EU with the competence to enact rules on human rights or to conclude international conventions in this field, which meant that it also did not have the competence to accede to the ECHR – see *Opinion 2/94* (European Court of Justice, 28 March 1996). Nevertheless, when on the basis of this Treaty provision a draft accession agreement was subjected to the Court's review in 2014, the latter again issued a negative opinion, highlighting potential adverse effects on the autonomy of the EU legal order – see *Opinion 2/13* (European Court of Justice (Full Court), 18 December 2014). Negotiations between the EU and the Council of Europe were taken up again in 2019 and are still ongoing at the time of writing this book.

consider not only EU legal sources but also the output of Council of Europe bodies.[79]

Cooperation between the European Union and the Council of Europe became ever closer over the years,[80] particularly considering the EU's increasing competence in matters related to the Council of Europe's working sphere, including the rule of law, which thus started to play a role not only at the *national* and *international* level, but also at the *supranational* level. In fact, the establishment of the EU as a supranational legal order can be seen as a turning point for the rule of law. Under the auspices of the Council of Europe, Member States already accepted to adhere to common standards, as further developed in the case law of the European Court of Human Rights (ECtHR). However, one could argue that this adherence is 'softened' by the intergovernmental nature of the Council of Europe, as well as the margin of appreciation doctrine that offers national authorities some room for manoeuvre in fulfilling their obligations under the ECHR, precisely in light of the acknowledged difficulty of identifying uniform European standards for the rule of law and human rights across states.[81] In the European Union, however, an independent legal order arose with the competence to autonomously define legal concepts, harmonise legislation, and create laws that have direct effect in the national legal order. How then, did the rule of law take shape in the EU?

3.2.2 *The Rule of Law's Origins in the EU Legal Order*

Though the European Union came into being about seventy years ago, the concept of the rule of law only started to explicitly appear in its legal order halfway its existence.[82] The Union's origins lay in a willingness of Member States to cooperate on economic matters (from common policies for the coal and steel sector, to the establishment of a customs union and a common market), leaving matters like democracy, human rights and the rule of law at the national level, and at the

[79] The Charter of Fundamental Rights of the European Union (CFREU) also states that insofar as it contains rights that correspond to rights guaranteed by the ECHR, the meaning and scope of those rights shall be the same – without preventing Union law to provide more extensive protection (see Article 52(3) of the CFREU).

[80] It can also be noted that The Court of Justice of the European Union frequently cites the case law of the European Court of Human Rights (ECtHR) in its own judgments.

[81] See, e.g., Polakiewicz and Kirchmayr (n 72) 366.

[82] Admittedly, then-head of the European Economic Community Walter Hallstein coined the notion of 'a community based on law' in the 1960s, yet this concerned the governance of the Union itself, and was meant to indicate that the Union could only rely on law, not on any means of coercion, to enforce its rules. See Werner Schroeder, 'The European Union and the Rule of Law – State of Affairs and Ways of Strengthening', in his *Strengthening the Rule of Law in Europe: From a Common Concept to Mechanisms of Implementation* (Hart Publishing 2016) 5.

intergovernmental level of the Council of Europe.[83] Gradually, Member States embraced further integration, transforming the Union from a market-oriented project to a self-standing legal order in which human rights, democracy and the rule of law have come to play a central role,[84] greatly aided in this endeavour by the CJEU's case law.[85]

The seminal case in which the rule of law was first mentioned in the EU legal order is *Les Verts*, concerned with party political funding.[86] In this 1986 judgment, the CJEU formally stated that "*the European Economic Community is a Community based on the rule of law, inasmuch as neither its Member States nor its institutions can avoid a review of the question whether the measures adopted by them are in conformity with the basic constitutional charter, the Treaty*."[87] According to the Court, the Treaties established a "*complete system of legal remedies and procedures*" designed to review the legality of measures adopted in the Union, and to protect natural and legal persons against the application to them of general measures implemented either by EU institutions or by national authorities.[88] While *Les Verts* was concerned with the rule of law *horizontally*, dealing with the relationship between EU institutions rather than within EU Member States, it did hint at the fact that also the actions of Member States can be reviewed based on their conformity with EU law. In subsequent case law, the CJEU reiterated and firmly entrenched the Union's rule of law-basis.[89]

A few years later, in 1993, the rule of law was included as part of the so-called Copenhagen criteria which set out the conditions that aspiring EU Member States

[83] Magen and Pech note that the concept of the rule of law "*first entered treaty language in the context of Member State's efforts to speak in greater unison to the rest of the world, not as part of any intra-community constitutional discourse*" and that it was for a long time primarily seen as part of the Union's external action rather than a focal point of its internal policy. See Magen and Pech (n 3) 236.

[84] See also Case 6/64, *Costa v E.N.E.L.*, 15 July 1964, ECLI:EU:C:1964:66.

[85] Koen Lenaerts, Piet Van Nuffel and Tim Corthaut, *EU Constitutional Law* (Oxford University Press 2021) 16.

[86] *Parti écologiste 'Les Verts' v European Parliament* [1986] European Court of Justice C-294/83, EU:C:1986:166.

[87] ibid §23.

[88] ibid §23. See in this regard also the Court's seminal judgments in *Van Gend & Loos* and *Costa ENEL*, respectively establishing the principle of direct effect (meaning that natural and legal persons can directly invoke before a national court legal rights granted to them by EU law), and the principle of the primacy of EU law over the law of its Member States. See *Van Gend & Loos* [1963] European Court of Justice Case 26-62, EU:C:1963:1; *Flaminio Costa v ENEL* [1964] European Court of Justice Case 6-64, EU:C:1964:66.

[89] See, e.g., the Courts judgments in *Commission and Others v Kadi*, C-584/10 P, C-593/10 P and C-595/10 P, EU:C:2013:518, §66; *Inuit Tapiriit Kanatami and Others v Parliament and Council*, C-583/11 P, EU:C:2013:625, §91; and *Telefónica v Commission*, C-274/12 P, EU:C:2013:852, §56 *Maximillian Schrems v Data Protection Commissioner* [2015] European Court of Justice (Grand Chamber) C-362/14 §60.

should fulfil to be eligible for membership.[90] Yet it was not until the Treaty of Amsterdam, signed in 1997, that the rule of law was incorporated into primary EU law as one of the Union's founding 'principles' that are 'common to the Member States', alongside liberty, democracy, respect for human rights and fundamental freedoms – without, however, providing any definition of the concept.[91] When the Treaty of Lisbon was signed ten years later, the rule of law and the other founding principles became 'values' instead[92] yet obtained a more prominent place in the Treaty on European Union (TEU), right at the start in Article 2. The Lisbon Treaty likewise omitted the concept's definition, yet reiterated that it is considered a value common to all Member States. Pursuant to Article 21 TEU, the rule of law is also a 'principle' that the Union seeks to 'advance in the wider world', hence constituting a part of the EU's identity and objectives both internally and externally.[93] Whether called a value or principle, it is clear from both terms that the rule of law is considered an overarching guiding norm that requires concretisation through court interpretation or legislation in order to distil concrete obligations therefrom.[94]

3.2.3 *Vertical and Horizontal Dimensions*

When discussing the rule of law in the European Union, a distinction needs to be made between the various dimensions in which the rule of law plays a role. First, the rule of law can be examined at the level of EU Member States, dealing with the relationship between national institutions (legislative, executive and judicial) and national citizens (*vertically*).[95] Member States are required to comply with the rule of – both national and European – law.[96] However, since the EU constitutes an autonomous legal order,[97] one can also examine the rule of law at the level of the EU, dealing with the relationship between EU institutions (legislative, executive

[90] "*Membership requires that the candidate country has achieved stability of institutions guaranteeing democracy, the rule of law, human rights and respect for and protection of minorities, the existence of a functioning market economy as well as the capacity to cope with competitive pressure and market forces within the Union*". See 'Presidency Conclusions – Copenhagen European Council' (European Council 1993) <www.europarl.europa.eu/enlargement/ec/pdf/cop_en.pdf>.

[91] See also Roila Mavrouli, 'The Dark Relationship between the Rule of Law and Liberalism. The New ECJ Decision on the Conditionality Regulation' (2022) 7 European Papers 275, 276.

[92] For a discussion on the significance of this change in vocabulary, see Werner Schroeder, 'The Rule of Law as a Value in the Sense of Article 2 TEU: What Does It Mean and Imply?' in Armin von Bogdandy and others (eds), *Defending Checks and Balances in EU Member States*, vol 298 (Springer Berlin Heidelberg 2021) 110.

[93] Schroeder (n 82) 13.

[94] ibid 12.

[95] Note that this is also the level that the Council of Europe is focusing on.

[96] See Armin von Bogdandy and Michael Ioannidis, 'Systemic Deficiency in the Rule of Law: What It Is, What Has Been Done, What Can Be Done' (2014) 51 Common Market Law Review 59, 64.

[97] See Case 6-64, *Flaminio Costa v ENEL*, 15 July 1964, EU:C:1964:66.

and judicial) and EU citizens (*horizontally*).[98] Both of these layers are *internal* to the EU. These dimensions can further be distinguished from the rule of law's *external* dimension, which concerns the relationship between the EU and third countries, and between the institutions of those countries and their citizens. This dimension is primarily relevant for the EU's external action, such as rule of law-promotion activities in third countries pursuant to Article 21 TEU.

In this book, I will *not* be looking at the external dimension of the rule of law, nor will I consider the *horizontal* dimension of the rule of law in the EU.[99] At this point, it may therefore be useful to explain why, if my focus only lays on what happens at Member State level, I am nevertheless analysing the role of EU law. Surely there are national conceptions of the rule of law in all EU Member States, and national mechanisms to protect and enforce it in accordance with those conceptions. So why am I grounding my analysis in the EU legal order? Put differently: what does it matter from the perspective of EU law whether Member States, within their national jurisdictions, uphold the rule of law? I briefly answered this question in the Introduction, but this point merits some further clarification here.

It is true that the EU was not granted any 'general' competence regarding the 'rule of law'. This is not surprising, as the rule of law is expressed as a relatively abstract value. As is well known, pursuant to the principle of conferral enshrined in Article 5 TEU, the Union "*shall act only within the limits of the competences conferred upon it by the Member States in the Treaties to attain the objectives set out therein. Competences not conferred upon the Union in the Treaties remain with the Member States.*" Moreover, Article 4 TEU also states the Union's obligation to respect Member States' national identities, "*inherent in their fundamental structures, political and constitutional, inclusive of regional and local self-government. It shall respect their essential State functions, including ensuring the territorial integrity of the State, maintaining law and order and safeguarding national security.*" Accordingly, it can be assumed that Member States, though declaring the rule of law to be a value that is common to their traditions, did not wish to create a harmonised conceptualisation of the rule of law or to bestow the EU with competences to control the compatibility of their actions therewith *in general*. Arguably, the Council of Europe – through the jurisdiction of the ECtHR, based on the ECHR – already has a mandate to govern and clarify rule of law-related matters.

98 See Theodore Konstadinides, *The Rule of Law in the European Union: The Internal Dimension* (Bloomsbury 2017) 5.

99 In the EU, several entities can be said to constitute the Union's executive power – most prominently the European Commission – and the legality of their actions are reviewable by the CJEU. Insofar as they implement algorithmic systems in their decision-making processes, tensions can likewise arise with their obligation to adhere to the rule of law. This subject, however, merits a separate research project – one that can potentially build on the insights of the current one.

At the same time, the EU does have some more specific or indirect competences related to the rule of law (which I will come back to in Chapter 5), and it cannot be denied that respect for the rule of law, also at Member State level, is crucial for the success of the Union's project. There are several reasons for this. First, a large part of Union law has direct effect in Member States. EU law is hence integrated in national legal orders, enabling citizens to derive rights therefrom that are enforceable before national courts. The national level is hence not easily distinguishable from the European level, given the prevalence of EU law. Accordingly, "*deficient rule of domestic law automatically translates in deficient rule of EU law*".[100] Second, the European Union hinges on *mutual trust* between Member States – including trust in the fact that their public authorities act in accordance with human rights, democracy, the rule of law and other EU values.[101] This trust has highly practical consequences, as it, for instance, enables a Member State's court to extradite a citizen to another Member State pursuant to a European arrest warrant, or to engage in legal cooperation in asylum cases.[102] In other words, there are significant negative externalities involved for other Member States and the EU legal order as a whole if the rule of law is not observed.[103] Third, all citizens of Member States also have EU citizenship, which *inter alia* accords them with rights that they invoke when they move to another Member State, making it important for the sake of the enforcement of those rights that the host Member State respects the rule of law too. A weakening of the rule of law in one Member State hence not only affects the nationals of that state but also other EU citizens that moved there. In addition, more indirectly, it affects all those who reside in the EU by virtue of that state's "*participation in the EU's decision-making processes and in the adoption of norms that bind all in the EU*".[104] This is why, fourth, adherence to the rule of law is also a prerequisite to become an EU Member State.[105] It is thus reasonable to require Member States to keep respecting the rule of law also after they joined the EU.

In sum, regardless of whether there exists a common conception of the rule of law in all Member States, and regardless of whether there exists an autonomous 'EU' notion of the rule of law, adherence to this value by all Member States is part of their *common interest* – and it thus makes sense for EU law to play a role in ensuring this adherence. This is also why several mechanisms exist in the EU legal order to protect the rule of law at Member State level. The (in)existence of a commonly accepted notion of the rule of law in the EU hence does not affect my arguments, as

[100] von Bogdandy and Ioannidis (n 96) 64.
[101] Konstadinides (n 98) 17.
[102] Schroeder (n 82) 17.
[103] von Bogdandy and Ioannidis (n 96) 74.
[104] Laurent Pech and Kim Lane Scheppele, 'Illiberalism Within: Rule of Law Backsliding in the EU' (2017) 19 Cambridge Yearbook of European Legal Studies 3, 8.
[105] See 'Presidency Conclusions – Copenhagen European Council' (n 90). See also Petra Bárd and others, 'An EU Mechanism on Democracy, the Rule of Law and Fundamental Rights' (2016) CEPS Paper in Liberty and Security in Europe, 247.

they do not rely on the specific 'EU' nature of the rule of law, but on the underlying value it represents, which is expressed not only at supranational, but also at national and international level. My focus on the EU legal framework primarily stems from a desire to analyse not only how algorithmic regulation can affect the rule of law, but also to examine, within a concrete legal system, which safeguards exist to protect it. Yet as noted in the Introduction, the theory of harm that I will conceptualise has relevance far beyond the EU and can provide insights for all jurisdictions where the rule of law – along with democracy and human rights – is deemed important. To make my research inquiry tractable, I will hence presume there is an 'EU' conceptualisation of the rule of law, drawing on EU legal sources, while stressing that, even if no such distinct notion were to exist, this leaves my analysis intact, as my normative framework is generalisable beyond the European Union.

3.2.4 *The EU Conceptualisation of the Rule of Law*

As noted above, Article 2 TEU lists the rule of law as a foundational Union value, without a definition. Since this article distinguishes the rule of law from other values, such as respect for human rights and democracy, some have noted that this may indicate a 'thin' understanding of the rule of law in the European Union.[106] It would, however, seem short-sighted to claim that the EU adheres to a formal conceptualisation of the rule of law based on the mere fact that 'human rights' is listed alongside the rule of law rather than as part of it. In fact, a closer look at EU legal sources reveals a rather thick conception of the rule of law instead.

Starting with the CJEU's case law, one can note that judgments relating to the rule of law have been focusing primarily on two angles. The first concerns compliance with the rule of law at EU level – horizontally – where the availability of a complete system of remedies to ensure judicial protection of EU citizens against EU legal acts stands central. For instance, in the UPA case, the Court stated that "*the European Community is* [. . .] *a community based on the rule of law in which its institutions are subject to judicial review of the compatibility of their acts with the Treaty and with the general principles of law which include fundamental rights*".[107] This statement clearly indicates a thick conceptualisation of the rule of law, incorporating human rights-compliance.

The second angle of the Court's case law concerns compliance with the rule of law at Member State level or vertically. Member State authorities are not only obliged to respect the rule of *national* law, but also the rule of *EU* law, covering both primary and secondary EU legislation. Thus far, Member States' adherence to the principle of judicial impartiality and independence has received most

[106] See von Bogdandy and Ioannidis (n 96) 63.

[107] See Case C-50/00 P, *Unión de Pequeños Agricultores v Council of the European Union*, [2002] ECR I-6677, §38.

attention.[108] As this principle is concretised through the second paragraph of Article 19(1) TEU and Article 47 of the Charter of Fundamental Rights of the EU (the Charter or the CFREU),[109] the Court was able to flesh out its requirements in more details. This focus is not surprising. Not only are some Member States deliberately and rather overtly attempting to undermine this principle[110] (which lead to several Court challenges) but the independence of the national judiciary is also of particular importance in the EU legal order, given the role of national courts as 'first Union courts'.[111] One can also consider the principle of judicial independence as an overarching safeguard that can act as a last barrier against breaches of other rule of law principles. If a public authority arbitrarily uses its power, or if it breaches the principle of legal certainty and legality, the national court is the natural avenue to address this. As long as the functioning of the court hence occurs in an independent and impartial manner, other rule of law breaches can in theory be challenged (though, as I will discuss below, ex post protection mechanisms are insufficient safeguards in the context of algorithmic regulation, which requires ex ante safeguards instead).

The CJEU also clarified other principles of the rule of law, such as the principle of legality and legal certainty, and the obligation for the Commission – as part of the EU executive power – to state reasons for a decision.[112] While these cases dealt with the actions of EU institutions rather than Member States, they nevertheless show how the Court conceptualises the rule of law, and have been drawn upon by EU institutions when conceptualising the rule of law.[113]

[108] Rafał Mańko, 'ECJ Case Law on Judicial Independence' (European Parliamentary Research Service 2021) 2, <www.europarl.europa.eu/RegData/etudes/BRIE/2023/753955/EPRS_BRI(2023)753955_EN.pdf>.

[109] These two articles, respectively, establish that Member States shall provide remedies sufficient to ensure effective legal protection in the fields covered by Union law, and that everyone whose rights and freedoms guaranteed by the law of the Union are violated has the right to an effective remedy before a tribunal in compliance with the conditions laid down in that article.

[110] Barbara Grabowska-Moroz, 'The Systemic Implications of the Vertical Layering of the Legal Orders in the EU for the Practice of the Rule of Law' (Reconnect – Reconciling Europe with its Citizens through Democracy and Rule of Law 2020) 6. Also in Strasbourg, the principle of the independence of the judiciary has been fleshed out by the Court in several cases. See, for instance, the judgment concluding that the Civil Chamber of the Polish Supreme Court consisting of newly appointed judges is not an "independent and impartial tribunal established by law", in *Advance Pharma sp. z o.o v Poland* [2022] Application no. 1469/20.

[111] National courts have the competence (and obligation) to enforce EU law at national level and can for instance also initiate preliminary reference procedures. See also Lenaerts, Van Nuffel and Corthaut (n 85) 513.

[112] For an overview, see also Konstadinides (n 98) 105 and following.

[113] Reference can also be made to relevant case law of the ECtHR dealing with various rule of law principles and their implementation at national level. This case law has been an important source not only for the Venice Commission but also for the CJEU in its own case law. See, for instance, *Golder v The United Kingdom* [1975] European Court of Human Rights Application no. 4451/70; *Engel and Others v The Netherlands* [1976] European Court of Human Rights

Yet courts are not the only actors who helped conceptualise the rule of law in the EU. The European Commission offered the most comprehensive definition of the rule of law at EU level thus far when it launched the rule of law framework.[114] The framework acts as a complementary component to existing protection mechanisms (further discussed in Chapter 5) and forms the Commission's response to a set of authoritarian and illiberal practices undertaken by several EU Member States, thus clearly focusing on the rule of law's vertical dimension. According to the Commission, even though "*the precise content of the principles and standards stemming from the rule of law may vary at national level, depending on each Member State's constitutional system*", nevertheless, case law of the CJEU and of the ECtHR, "*as well as documents drawn up by the Council of Europe, building notably on the expertise of the Venice Commission, provide a non-exhaustive list of these principles and hence define the core meaning of the rule of law as a common value of the EU in accordance with Article 2 TEU*".[115]

These principles are virtually identical to the ones identified by the Council of Europe and include *legality*, which implies a transparent, accountable, democratic and pluralistic process for enacting laws; *legal certainty*; *prohibition of arbitrariness of the executive powers*; *independent and impartial courts*; *effective judicial review including respect for fundamental rights*; and *equality before the law*. In its 2019 Communication on 'Further strengthening the Rule of Law within the Union', the Commission added the principle of '*separation of powers*' to this list,[116] which also formed part of the rule of law's definition in its 2020 and 2021 rule of law reports setting out the status of adherence to this value in each Member State.[117] With that addition, it brought its own definition entirely in line with the definition proposed by the Venice Commission. A number of those principles – such as the

Application nos. 5100/71; 5101/71; 5102/71; 5354/72; 5370/72; *Amuur v France* [1996] European Court of Human Rights Application no. 19776/92.

114 European Commission, 'A New EU Framework to Strengthen the Rule of Law' (2014) Communication from the Commission to the European Parliament and the Council COM/2014/0158 final 6.

115 ibid 4.

116 European Commission, 'Communication from the Commission to the European Parliament, the European Council and the Council: Further Strengthening the Rule of Law within the Union – State of Play and Possible Next Steps' (European Commission 2019) Brussels, 3 April 2019, COM/2019/163 final,).

117 European Commission, '2020 Rule of Law Report: The Rule of Law Situation in the European Union' (European Commission 2020), Brussels, Brussels, 30 September 2020 COM(2020) 580 final; European Commission, 'The Rule of Law Situation in the European Union. 2021 Rule of Law Report' (European Commission 2021) Brussels, 20 July 2021, COM(2021) 700 final. Note that from 2022 onwards, the Rule of Law Reports no longer included a definition of the rule of law, likely pursuant to the adoption of the Conditionality Regulation, which is discussed further below.

principles of legal certainty, equality before the law, and respect for human rights – have also been recognised as general principles of EU law.[118]

In December 2020, the European Parliament and Council adopted the Conditionality Regulation.[119] This Regulation, which aims to protect the Union budget against adverse effects caused by breaches of the rule of law,[120] constitutes the first piece of EU legislation in which the rule of law is explicitly defined. I will discuss it more extensively in Chapter 5, but let me already emphasise here that the Regulation embraces a thick notion of the rule of law. Recital 3 states that,

> while there is no hierarchy among Union values, respect for the rule of law is essential for the protection of the other fundamental values on which the Union is founded, such as freedom, democracy, equality and respect for human rights. Respect for the rule of law is intrinsically linked to respect for democracy and for fundamental rights. There can be no democracy and respect for fundamental rights without respect for the rule of law and vice versa.[121]

In Article 2 of the Conditionality Regulation, the European Parliament and Council[122] have defined the rule of law precisely as the European Commission did in its rule of law reports, conceptualising it as "*including the principles of legality implying a transparent, accountable, democratic and pluralistic law-making process; legal certainty; prohibition of arbitrariness of the executive powers; effective judicial protection, including access to justice, by independent and impartial courts, also as regards fundamental rights; separation of powers; and non-discrimination and equality before the law.*"[123]

[118] Takis Tridimas, 'The General Principles of EU Law and the Europeanisation of National Laws' (2020) 13 Review of European Administrative Law 5.

[119] Regulation 2020/2092 of the European Parliament and of the Council of 16 December 2020 on a General Regime of Conditionality for the Protection of the Union Budget.

[120] Note that it is not aimed at directly penalising those rule of law breaches as such, for which other mechanisms exist. This was also stressed by the CJEU in a judgment that followed an action for annulment of the Conditionality Regulation by Hungary and Poland. See *Hungary v Parliament and Council* [2022] European Court of Justice (Full Court) C-156/21, EU:C:2022:97; *Poland v Parliament and Council* [2022] European Court of Justice (Full Court) C-157/21, EU:C:2022:98.

[121] Interestingly, Article 3 of the Conditionality Regulation also sets out actions that can be 'indicative' of breaches of the principles of the rule of law. These actions concern: (1) endangering the independence of the judiciary; (2) failing to prevent, correct or sanction arbitrary or unlawful decisions by public authorities, including by law enforcement authorities, withholding financial and human resources affecting their proper functioning or failing to ensure the absence of conflicts of interest; and (3) limiting the availability and effectiveness of legal remedies, including through restrictive procedural rules and lack of implementation of judgments, or limiting the effective investigation, prosecution or sanctioning of breaches of law. I will come back to this in Chapter 5, when I analyse the extent to which this Regulation provides protection against the adverse impact of algorithmic regulation on the rule of law.

[122] At least those Member States who did not seek to annul the Conditionality Regulation.

[123] Article 2(a) of the Conditionality Regulation.

In light of the above, I can conclude that these six principles collectively constitute the EU conceptualisation of the rule of law, which clearly encompasses not only formal but also substantive elements and is fully aligned with its conception at the Council of Europe. The rule of law is seen as a sine qua non for human rights and democracy, and as a value that merits being protected by EU law, also – or especially – when it risks being infringed at the level of Member States. Though conceptualisable as a list of principles, these should not be approached as a mere checklist, but as part of the rule of law's broader spirit, acknowledging its protective power and its ability to uphold the normative infrastructure of liberal democracy.

3.2.5 *The Rule of Law's Fragility: A Tale of Caution*

The existence of an EU definition of the rule of law does not mean that this definition is also universally respected by EU Member States. The fact that two Member States challenged the validity of the Conditionality Regulation provides an indication that the picture is not all rosy.[124] I have already alluded several times to the rise in authoritarian tendencies globally, and to the fact that the EU has been undergoing what commentators have called a 'rule of law crisis'.[125] In this section, I will elaborate on this crisis and discuss the main points of friction that lead to this grave denomination.

At the outset, let me reiterate that the rule of law is an ideal, or a value that should continuously be striven towards rather than one that can be perfectly achieved. No EU Member State can be said to meet its principles entirely – if only because, as I shall discuss in the next section, when examining these principles more closely, they are imbued with internal and external tensions that renders their achievement challenging.[126] Bearing this in mind, what now does this EU 'rule of law crisis' consist of? It frequently happens that Member States do not fulfil their obligations under EU law in a negligent or sporadic manner, for instance because they did not implement a directive within the set deadline, or because the national measures they adopted to implement an EU legal act were (inadvertently or deliberately) misinterpreted and hence concern an incorrect implementation. Such occasional infringements or minor non-alignments with European Union law are, however, not what legal scholars are currently apprehensive about. Instead, concerns are centred around more structural challenges to the rule of law, which are twofold in nature.

First, in several Member States, the primacy of EU law, and hence the alignment of national acts with the rule of *EU* law, is being challenged. Such challenges can be explicit or more implicit, and were, for instance, instigated by the

[124] See Case C-156/21, *Hungary v Parliament and Council (Full Court)*, 16 February 2022, EU:C:2022:98 and Case C-157/21, *Poland v Parliament and Council (Full Court)*, 16 February 2022, EU:C:2022:97.

[125] Schroeder (n 82); Pech and Scheppele (n 104); Grogan and others (n 76).

[126] See, in particular, Sections 3.3 and 3.4 of this book.

German and Polish Constitutional Courts,[127] the French Council of State,[128] as well as political parties.[129] To the extent that only one Member State institution is behind such challenge, this has in and of itself not (yet) caused major disturbances in the EU legal order.[130] The situation is, however, different in countries where the challenge of EU law's primacy is more structural in nature and shared by various institutions, or where it complements a wider challenge to the values of liberal democracy more generally, which is the second and, arguably, more worrisome type of concern.

Several Member States have indeed taken legislative initiatives that deliberately pursue illiberal or authoritarian practices and undermine the protective power of the law.[131] In such states, "*no longer are rule of law issues temporary and isolated deviations from a norm of compliance, which had been presumed. Instead, noncompliance with European values has become a principled ideological choice*."[132] Huq

[127] See, e.g., 'Brussels Closes Case against Germany in EU Law Supremacy Dispute' (*POLITICO*, 2 December 2021) <www.politico.eu/article/brussels-closes-case-against-germany-in-eu-law-supremacy-dispute/> 2; 'Explained: What Bombshell Polish Court Ruling Means for EU' (*POLITICO*, 8 October 2021) <www.politico.eu/article/explained-poland-court-ruling-european-union-eu/>. See also Pieter Cleppe, 'An Overview of National Top Courts Challenging the Supremacy of EU Law, Brussels Report' (*Brussels Report*, 12 October 2021) <www.brusselsreport.eu/2021/10/12/an-overview-of-national-top-courts-challenging-the-supremacy-of-eu-law/>.

[128] See, e.g., Theodore Christakis, 'French Council of State Discovers the "Philosopher's Stone" of Data Retention' (*about:intel*, 23 April 2021) <https://aboutintel.eu/france-council-of-state-ruling/>; Sharifullah Dorani, 'The Primacy of EU Law over French Law: EU Law Takes Precedence over National Law?' (CESRAN 23 November 2021) <https://cesran.org/the-primacy-of-eu-law-over-french-law-eu-law-takes-precedence-over-national-law.html>.

[129] See, e.g., Reuters, 'Poland's Kaczynski Says Primacy of EU Law Undermines Sovereignty' *Reuters* (18 September 2021) <www.reuters.com/world/europe/polands-kaczynski-says-primacy-eu-law-undermines-sovereignty-2021-09-18/>.

[130] Though they have been eagerly commented on by legal scholars. See, for instance, Mehrdad Payandeh, 'Constitutional Review of EU Law after Honeywell: Contextualizing the Relationship between the German Constitutional Court and the EU Court of Justice' (2011) 48 Common Market Law Review 9; Dana Burchardt, 'Backlash against the Court of Justice of the EU? The Recent Jurisprudence of the German Constitutional Court on EU Fundamental Rights as a Standard of Review' (2020) 21 German Law Journal 1; Panos Koutrakos, 'Longing for Less Interesting Times? The German Federal Constitutional Court and the Supremacy of EU Law' (2020) 45 European Law Review 293.

[131] See also Pech and Scheppele (n 104); Zsolt Körtvélyesi, 'The Illiberal Challenge in the EU: Exploring the Parallel with Illiberal Minorities and the Example of Hungary' (2020) 16 European Constitutional Law Review 567; Marcin Wiącek, 'Constitutional Crisis in Poland 2015–2016 in the Light of the Rule of Law Principle' in Armin von Bogdandy and others (eds), *Defending Checks and Balances in EU Member States*, vol 298 (Springer Berlin Heidelberg 2021); Maurits Meijers and Harmen van der Veer, 'MEP Responses to Democratic Backsliding in Hungary and Poland. An Analysis of Agenda-Setting and Voting Behaviour' (2019) 57 Journal of Common Market Studies 838.

[132] Kim Lane Scheppele, Dimitry Vladimirovich Kochenov and Barbara Grabowska-Moroz, 'EU Values Are Law, After All: Enforcing EU Values Through Systemic Infringement Actions by the European Commission and the Member States of the European Union' (2020) 39 Yearbook of European Law 3, 8.

and Ginsburg note that "*in both Hungary and Poland, for example, elected governments have recently hastened to enact a suite of legal and institutional changes that simultaneously squeeze out electoral competition, undermine liberal rights of democratic participation, and emasculate legal stability and predictability*".[133] The Polish reform of the judiciary which the Law and Justice Party initiated in 2015 after it gained majority control is a case in point. The government inter alia set up a disciplinary chamber to control Polish judges, undermined their ability to refer preliminary questions to the CJEU and lowered the retirement age of judges in an arbitrary way – thereby undermining their independence.[134] Hungary's reforms of both the Constitution and of the Constitutional Court are likewise frequently mentioned examples, and also in Romania challenges to the independence of the judiciary have raised concerns.[135] Yet also beyond the sphere of the judiciary, Member States have relied on the law to advance illiberal and authoritarian aims. Consider, for instance, the introduction of legislative proposals that curtail the rights of LGBTQ+ individuals in Hungary,[136] Poland[137] and Romania[138] that curb the

[133] Aziz Huq and Tom Ginsburg, 'How to Lose a Constitutional Democracy' (2018) 65 UCLA Law Review 78, 94. It should, however, be noted that in the Polish elections of October 2023, the opposition parties (consisting of the Civic Coalition, Third Way and The Left) managed to achieve a combined total vote of 54 per cent. Their ambition is to steer the country back towards a more liberal democratic course.

[134] See in this regard Case C-619/18, *Commission v Poland*, 15 November 2018, ECLI:EU:C:2018:910; C-791/19 R, *Commission v Poland*, 15 July 2021, ECLI:EU:C:2021:596; Case C-204/21 R, *Commission v Poland*, 27 October 2021, ECLI:EU:C:2021:878; Case C-204/2, *Commission v Poland*, 5 June 2023, ECLI:EU:C:2023:442. See also Gabriel N Toggenburg and Jonas Grimheden, 'Managing the Rule of Law in a Heterogeneous Context: A Fundamental Rights Perspective on Ways Forward' in Werner Schroeder (ed), *Strengthening the Rule of Law in Europe – From a Common Concept to Mechanisms of Implementation* (Hart Publishing 2016) 225.

[135] See, e.g., Zoltán Fleck, Nóra Chronowski and Petra Bárd, 'The Crisis of the Rule of Law, Democracy and Fundamental Rights in Hungary (Paper I)' (2022) 4 MTA Law Working Papers 1; 'Systemic Backsliding of the Rule of Law in Hungary: State Control' (*Netherlands Helsinki Committee*, 19 April 2022) <www.nhc.nl/systemic-backsliding-of-the-rule-of-law-in-hungary-state-control/>. See in this regard also Case C-107/23 PPU, Lin, 24 July 2023, ECLI:EU:C:2023:606.

[136] Reuters, 'Hungary Restricts Sales of LGBT-Themed Children's Books' *Reuters* (6 August 2021) <www.reuters.com/world/europe/hungary-orders-shops-cover-up-lgbt-themed-childrens-books-2021-08-06/>.

[137] Piotr Maciej Kaczynski, 'Poland, a LGBT-Free Zone?' *www.euractiv.com* (21 October 2021) <www.euractiv.com/section/politics/short_news/poland-a-lgbt-free-zone/>.

[138] As of early 2024, the law – inspired by the Hungarian law cited above – has been accepted by the Senate and lower House, but still needs to be formally approved, and hence has not yet entered into force. See also Reuters, 'Romania Must Reject Hungary-Style Anti-LGBT Bill, Rights Groups Say' *Reuters* (29 April 2022) <www.reuters.com/world/europe/romania-must-reject-hungary-style-anti-lgbt-bill-rights-groups-say-2022-04-29/>. In May 2023, Romania has also been condemned by the ECtHR for violating the rights of same-sex couples. See *Buhuceanu and others v Romania*, Applications nos. 20081/19 and 20 others, 23 May 2023.

activities of non-governmental organisations who scrutinise the government's actions,[139] or that undermine the plurality and freedom of media.[140]

In sum, the rule of law, and in particular its role to secure constitutional checks and balances and to protect other core values such as human rights and democracy, is being undermined not in an isolated but in a systemic manner. Furthermore, the Member States in question are using the law as a tool to do so, thus legitimising actions that infringe the values in Article 2 TEU while upholding a semblance of legality at national level. This can only be conceptualised as rule *by* law.

These developments should be considered against the background of a broader global crisis of liberal democracy, including the rise of nationalism, populism and the increased support for authoritarian modes of governance which are believed to be more 'efficient'.[141] For instance, in Belgium, a survey taken in September 2021 revealed that 37.4 per cent of the participants consider that 'our society would be better governed if the power were concentrated in the hands of a single leader'.[142] Amongst people aged twenty-five to thirty-four, this number even rose to 46.9 per cent.[143]

Overall, these developments demonstrate that the rule of law and the values of liberal democracy more generally are fragile. They can be eroded incrementally, almost invisibly, unless the isolated actions of Member States are looked at cumulatively.[144] Arguably, such gradual degradation is of even greater concern, as a sudden collapse may at least have the advantage of triggering a response from a sufficiently large group of people who refuse to have their rights and liberties stripped away. In contrast, an incremental attack on EU values – encased by a shell of legality through the perversion of the rule of law into rule by law – renders a large-scale mobilisation against such practices more difficult. Furthermore, as noted by Huq

[139] 'Hungarian Civil Society Raises Alarm over NGO Law Change' (*Euractiv*, 22 April 2021) <www.euractiv.com/section/justice-home-affairs/news/hungarian-civil-society-raises-alarm-over-ngo-law-change/>.

[140] See, e.g., Eva Połońska and Charlie Beckett (eds), *Public Service Broadcasting and Media Systems in Troubled European Democracies* (Springer International Publishing 2019).

[141] Bojan Bugarič, 'The Rise of Nationalist-Authoritarian Populism and the Crisis of Liberal Democracy in Central and Eastern Europe' in Uladzislau Belavusau and Aleksandra Gliszczynska-Grabias (eds), *Constitutionalism under Stress* (Oxford University Press 2020). This longing for a more centralised mode of governance is not new as such, and also marked the political sentiment at the beginning of the twentieth Century in several EU countries. See in this regard Scarcello (n 60).

[142] The survey, commissioned by the RTBF (the public service broadcaster of Belgium's French-speaking Community) was taken between 20 and 27 September 2021 by KANTAR, with an indicated maximum margin of error of 3.01 per cent. The results of the survey can be accessed through this link: https://ds.static.rtbf.be/article/attachment/10852475/9/3/3/2a279d7bcb6b412677b112d29b4cf053.pdf. For a discussion of these results, see also Aubry Touriel and Thomas Gadisseux, 'Sondage RTBF : un quart des Belges veulent la fin de notre démocratie parlementaire' *RTBF* (4 October 2021) <www.rtbf.be/article/sondage-rtbf-un-quart-des-belges-veulent-la-fin-de-notre-democratie-parlementaire-10852475>.

[143] ibid.

[144] Indeed, "*a constitutional liberal democracy can degrade without collapsing*". See Huq and Ginsburg (n 133) 94.

and Ginsburg, "*there will be cases where disputes arise as to whether a sufficient aggregate amount of backsliding has occurred*",[145] and this dispute can aptly be exploited by those who use the guise of the law to legitimise their problematic practices.

To counter these developments, the European Union has been exploring routes to not only mitigate but also prevent some of these concerns, and over the last decade it has enlarged its toolbox with several rule of law-monitoring mechanisms that can play a more proactive role.[146] In Chapter 5, I will discuss the rule of law-protection afforded by EU law in more detail when I examine the robustness of these mechanisms against the risks of algorithmic regulation. For now, suffice it to conclude that a cautionary approach is warranted, since observance of the rule of law, even in the EU, where a layered normative infrastructure exists to uphold this value, cannot be taken for granted.

3.3 THE RULE OF LAW AS NORMATIVE FRAMEWORK

Now that I analysed how the rule of law has been conceptualised in legal theory (Section 3.1) and in the EU legal order (Section 3.2), two conclusions can be drawn. First, the rule of law is an overarching concept, alternatingly denoted as a principle, idea, value or interest. It encompasses a range of principles that can be grouped in different ways and at different levels of generality. In the context of the public sector, these principles serve a common purpose, namely constraining public power and thereby also enabling such power by delineating its legal contours. Second, despite some conceptual differences, several principles seem to resurge in virtually all EU accounts of the rule of law and can hence be proposed as constituting its 'core content' in the context of the European Union's legal order. These are the principles of *legality*; *legal certainty*; *the prohibition of arbitrariness of the executive powers*; *equality before the law*; *effective judicial protection, with access to justice and review of government action by independent and impartial courts, also as regards human rights*; and *the separation of powers*.[147] The question is now: how can these still rather broad and general principles serve as the normative framework of my research? To recap, my aim in this chapter is to assess how public authorities should exercise power in a way that complies with the rule of law when they rely on algorithmic regulation. Only then can I assess how their use of algorithmic regulation risks undermining such compliance.

In this section, I will take these six rule of law principles as my starting point and examine the concrete requirements that public authorities must respect to align

[145] ibid 98.

[146] See European Commission, 'A New EU Framework to Strengthen the Rule of Law' (n 114). See also Toggenburg and Grimheden (n 134) 225.

[147] See *supra*, Section 3.2.5.

therewith. To do so, I draw on relevant legal sources from the European Union and the Council of Europe that concretise these principles and clarify what they imply for the executive branch of power.[148] Through their concretisation, these six principles will serve as this book's normative analytical framework. In Chapter 4, I will use this framework to analyse how public authorities' reliance on algorithmic regulation can affect each of these principles and put forward an overarching theory of harm to conceptualise this threat.

As part of this concretisation exercise, it is important to consider the challenges that public authorities *already* face when seeking to fulfil these six principles, regardless of any reliance on algorithmic regulation. Just as the rule of law is an ideal that is never entirely achievable, so are its principles, which contain some intrinsic tensions that impede their full realisation.[149] Therefore, in this section, for each principle – namely legality (Section 3.3.1); legal certainty (Section 3.3.2); the prohibition of arbitrariness (Section 3.3.3); equality before the law (Section 3.3.4); judicial review of government action and access to justice (Section 3.3.5); and the separation of powers (Section 3.3.6) – I will not only assess their relevant requirements for public authorities, but also the challenges that are an inherent part thereof.

3.3.1 *Legality*

3.3.1.a The Principle's Requirements

The principle of legality – sometimes also referred to as the principle of lawfulness – requires that public authorities recognise the 'supremacy of the law' and act in conformity therewith. While its focus often lays on conformity with the constitution[150] (which typically delineates the competences of different authorities), the principle of legality requires conformity with legislation more generally, be it at national, international or supranational level.[151] This also implies that Member States must act in conformity with European law, in light of their legal obligations under the EU Treaties. While the rule of law also requires that public authorities

[148] Some of these sources are non-binding – such as the previously mentioned Venice Commission's rule of law checklist, the European Commission's rule of law reports, or the Recommendations from the Council of Europe's Committee of Ministers – yet my reliance thereon is justified by the fact that they draw on or develop binding legal instruments and pertinent case law. It should be noted that my analysis aims at the development of a *normative* framework, without claiming that all the identified requirements are also *legally enforceable* before national or Union courts. I will discuss the legal framework – and the legal obligations of Member States at the level of the EU – in more detail *infra*, in Section 5.2.

[149] See also Tamanaha (n 26).

[150] Venice Commission (n 74), §44.

[151] See also Case C-496/99 P, *Commission v CAS Succhi di Frutta*, 29 April 2004, § 63: "*in a community governed by the rule of law, adherence to legality must be properly ensured*".

fulfil their duties in ensuring that private parties respect the law,[152] my analysis focuses on the duties of public authorities themselves.

The legality principle is first and foremost a formal principle, and hence does not dictate the substance of the law that must be complied with *as such*. However, both the European Union and the Council of Europe have stressed that, since their Member States have committed themselves to human rights legislation (including the EU Charter of Fundamental Rights and the European Convention on Human Rights), the legality principle de facto also encompasses the requirement to comply with human rights,[153] and that judicial review of the legality of government action also entails a review of its alignment with human rights. Accordingly, while 'respect for human rights' is listed as a separate value under Article 2 TEU, the legality principle does bring the need to comply with human rights under the wings of the rule of law.[154]

Importantly, public authorities must not merely 'comply' with the law; their actions must also be 'authorised' by law, thus implying the need to identify a legal basis to justify their acts.[155] Indeed, the powers of public authorities should be "*defined by law*", and this "*delineation of powers between different authorities*" should be "*clear*".[156] As implied by the Venice Commission's rule of law checklist, cases in which public authorities are allowed to operate without an explicit legal basis should be a rarity and duly justified, making it the exception.[157] Moreover, whenever legislative power is delegated to the executive, "*the objectives, contents, and scope of the delegation of power*" should be "*explicitly defined in a legislative act*".[158] Importantly, the principle of legality also applies when public authorities delegate

[152] For instance, the executive's duty to implement the law also means it should foresee sanctions against the law's non-compliance by private parties and prevent impunity. See also Venice Commission (n 74), §53–55.

[153] ibid. See, e.g., the checklist question: "*Do public authorities comply with their positive obligations by ensuring implementation and effective protection of human rights?*" at 18.

[154] As also argued by Paul Dermine, *The New Economic Governance of the Eurozone: A Rule of Law Analysis* (Cambridge University Press 2022).

[155] "State action must be in accordance with *and authorised by* the law." (emphasis added) in Venice Commission (n 74), §44. This is particularly important when the actions of public authorities limit individuals' human rights. Consider in this regard also the ECtHR's statement that

> the expression 'in accordance with the law' not only requires the impugned measure to have some basis in domestic law, but also refers to the quality of the law in question, requiring that it should be accessible to the person concerned and foreseeable as to its effects. For domestic law to meet these requirements, it must afford adequate legal protection against arbitrariness and accordingly indicate with sufficient clarity the scope and discretion conferred on the competent authorities and the manner of its exercise,

in the Judgment in *Catt v The United Kingdom*, Application no. 43514/15, 24 January 2019, §94. See also *M.M. v the United Kingdom*, Application no. 24029/07, 13 November 2012, §193.

[156] Venice Commission (n 74) 18.

[157] ibid.

[158] ibid 20.

their tasks to private actors. In that case, equivalent guarantees of legality should be established by law.[159]

Beyond compliance *with* and *action authorised by* the law, the principle of legality also requires public authorities to safeguard the legal and practical conditions for the law's correct implementation.[160] When public authorities implement laws and adopt administrative acts, they need to do so commensurably with the law's text and with respect to the principle of proportionality, as highlighted by the Recommendation of the Council of Europe's Committee of Ministers to Member States on good administration.[161] Concretely, this means that public authorities "*shall impose measures affecting the rights or interests of private persons only where necessary and to the extent required to achieve the aim pursued*".[162] Moreover, "*when exercising their discretion, they shall maintain a proper balance between any adverse effects which their decision has on the rights or interests of private persons and the purpose they pursue. Any measures taken by them shall not be excessive*".[163]

Finally, both the EU and the Council of Europe emphasise that the principle of legality also requires public participation and transparency[164] to ensure public authorities' accountability. Indeed, the Conditionality Regulation, for instance, states that the principle of legality implies "*a transparent, accountable, democratic and pluralistic law-making process*".[165] While it can be recalled that those adhering to a thin rule of law conception would consider these requirements as separate from the rule of law, it is clear that under its EU conceptualisation, the strong affinity with democracy is underscored, and a narrow conception of legality without democratic legitimacy is excluded. The Venice Commission's checklist also provides that the public ought to "*have access to draft legislation, at least when it is submitted to Parliament*", as well as "*a meaningful opportunity to provide input*".[166] It also

[159] ibid.

[160] Council of Europe (n 42), §45. See also the ECtHR Judgment in *Broniowski v Poland*, Application no. 31443/96, 22 June 2004, §184: "*The rule of law underlying the Convention and the principle of lawfulness in Article 1 of Protocol No. 1 require States not only to respect and apply, in a foreseeable and consistent manner, the laws they have enacted, but also, as a corollary of this duty, to ensure the legal and practical conditions for their implementation.*"

[161] See Committee of Ministers of the Council of Europe, 'Recommendation CM/Rec(2007)7 of the Committee of Ministers to Member States on Good Administration'.

[162] ibid 8.

[163] ibid.

[164] Compare the precise wording of the legality principle in Article 2 of the EU's Conditionality Regulation ("*legality implying a transparent, accountable, democratic and pluralistic law-making process*") with the formulation in §18 of the Venice Commission's Rule of Law Checklist ("*legality, including a transparent, accountable and democratic process for enacting law*").

[165] Article 2(a) of the Conditionality Regulation.

[166] Venice Commission (n 74) 13.

requires that, where appropriate, "*impact assessments [are] made before adopting legislation (e.g. on the human rights and budgetary impact of laws)*".[167]

Transparency and public participation[168] must, moreover, not only be ensured in the legislative phase, but also in the executive or implementation phase when public authorities adopt administrative acts.[169] Over the last decades, the idea of democratic participation in administrative processes has increasingly come to the forefront. As noted by Galligan, "*this regeneration of democratic practices within administration can have strong elements of discussion, negotiation, and compromise*", drawing on the model of deliberative democracy to bring together a plurality of interests and views in modern societies.[170] Since normative administrative acts through which public authorities concretise legislation can indeed affect a multitude of interests, methods of deliberative democracy can contribute to an understanding of how those interests could be balanced. Moreover, by ensuring that they act transparently and in a participatory manner, public authorities can enhance their accountability as well as elevate the quality of their acts, for instance through the solicitation of feedback on whether the act reaches its aims and does not cause unintended negative externalities.

3.3.1.b Challenges to the Principle of Legality

Bearing in mind these requirements, what are the tension points that can arise when public authorities seek to abide by the principle of legality? The first challenge can be found in the need to ensure a sufficiently clear and delineated legal basis for public authorities to act on. Rules of general application tend to be over- and under-inclusive, since they typically set out broad instructions in advance that will subsequently be applied to an indeterminate number of individual cases.[171] As also admitted by Scalia, "*all generalizations (including, I know, the present one) are to*

[167] ibid. In this regard, the checklist also refers to ECtHR *Hatton v the United Kingdom*, Application no. 36022/97, 8 July 2003, §128, stating that "*A governmental decisionmaking process concerning complex issues of environmental and economic policy such as in the present case must necessarily involve appropriate investigations and studies in order to allow them to strike a fair balance between the various conflicting interests at stake.*" See also *Evans v the United Kingdom*, Application no. 6339/05, 10 April 2007, § 64.

[168] Especially when it comes to ensuring public participation in decision-making that pertains to technological and scientific matters, the influential work of Sheila Jasanoff should be pointed out. See, e.g., Sheila Jasanoff, 'Technologies of Humility: Citizen Participation in Governing Science' (2003) 41 Minerva 223.

[169] See Committee of Ministers of the Council of Europe, 'Recommendation No. R (81) 19 of the Committee of Ministers to Member States on the Access to Information Held by Public Authorities'; 'Recommendation CM/Rec(2007)7 of the Committee of Ministers to Member States on Good Administration' (n 161).

[170] Galligan, 'Public Administration and the Tendency to Authoritarianism' (n 55) 197.

[171] See also Denis James Galligan, 'Fair Procedures in Discretionary Decisions', in his book *Discretionary Powers: A Legal Study of Official Discretion* (Oxford University Press 1990).

some degree invalid, and hence every rule of law has a few corners that do not quite fit".[172] Situations will hence inevitably arise that were not foreseen and that do not entirely conform to the normative assumptions behind the rule. Tamanaha therefore concludes that *"legality, which requires making decisions in accordance with rules, will in this manner occasionally produce non-optimal or undesirable results."*[173] While this may not be ideal, it is a price societies are willing to pay to avoid a situation of lawless or arbitrary decision-making. Moreover, as we saw in Section 2.3, when implementing legislation, public authorities can often rely on discretionary powers to ensure that the application of a general rule to a specific case remains proportionate and justified.

Second, as simple as the phrase 'acting in conformity with the law' may sound, its execution is not always straightforward. The broadness of legal rules often also leads them to be 'vague' and 'ambiguous'.[174] Moreover, the law is language based, which means it is inherently open for various interpretations.[175] Accordingly, one can argue that the determination of *how* public authorities must act in conformity with the law can be up for discussion, and depends on the way in which the law is interpreted – and by whom. This is where, yet again, the executive's discretion comes in. Rarely is a law so detailed and precise that no interpretative scope exists, hence necessarily implying a level of choice for public authorities to determine the law's meaning when implementing it. Despite such discretion, public authorities cannot interpret the law arbitrarily. They need to do so in a way that conforms to the normative aims of the law. Moreover, the textual openness and ambiguity of the law can also be considered its very strength, as this feature allows it to be applied to different individual cases, thus precluding the need to foresee detailed rules for every individual situation in advance (which may raise tensions with the principle of equality) and preventing the need to continuously update the law to match changed realities (which may raise tensions with the principle of legal certainty).[176]

[172] Antonin Scalia, 'The Rule of Law as a Law of Rules' (1989) 56 The University of Chicago Law Review 1175, 1177.

[173] Tamanaha (n 26) 241.

[174] See in this regard also Jeremy Waldron, 'Vagueness in Law and Language: Some Philosophical Issues' (1994) 82 California Law Review 509; Paul Craig, 'Legality: Six Views of the Cathedral' in Peter Cane and others (eds), *The Oxford Handbook of Comparative Administrative Law* (Oxford University Press 2020).

[175] Mireille Hildebrandt, 'The Adaptive Nature of Text-Driven Law' (2021) 1 Journal of Cross-disciplinary Research in Computational Law 1, 8 <https://journalcrcl.org/crcl/article/view/2>. See also Bronwen Morgan and Karen Yeung, *An Introduction to Law and Regulation: Text and Materials* (1st ed., Cambridge University Press 2007) 152.

[176] Hildebrandt (n 175). This is also the reason why critiques that "the law is always running behind the technology" are often incorrect, since the fact that a law does not mention a specific technology by name does not prevent it from regulating it. The generality of laws, and particularly their open textuality, is often precisely what enables their applicability to novel technologies. Consider for instance that the liability regime which is in place in many European countries today, is still strikingly similar to the one established by the Romans in

As regards the third challenge, I would like to recall the above discussion about the rule *of* law versus the rule *by* law. When legality is considered a goal in itself, namely a self-standing principle outside of the rule of law's overarching spirit, it embodies a formalistic conceptualisation of the law that considers its substance irrelevant, even if it may undermine important values like human rights and democracy. Legality then risks being reduced to legalism, which, as explained by Diver, in its strongest form can be seen as "*an ideology, according to which not only should rules be followed, but they should not be questioned or even interpreted beyond their apparent meaning*".[177] In the past, a rigid interpretation of the legality principle has been relied on to legitimise atrocious rules that were unmistakeably incompatible with the spirit of the rule of law.[178] As discussed above, this risk also exists today. Indeed, legal rules can be used as a means not to delineate public power but to expand it and to enhance public control over natural and legal persons.[179] It is therefore crucial that the implementation of the legality principle is not seen separately from the purpose of the rule of law, and from the values that are essential in liberal democracies, lest it be abused for authoritarian and illiberal ends.

3.3.2 *Legal Certainty*

3.3.2.a The Principle's Requirements

The principle of legal certainty is closely affined with and complementary to the principle of legality. Beyond the fact that the law should be respected and should authorise public actions, this principle focuses on the *qualities* that the law should have. Those qualities concern the law's accessibility, intelligibility, transparency and publicity, as well as its foreseeability.[180] As pointed out by Tamanaha, this "*enhances liberty of action or individual autonomy because people are advised of their permissible range of free action*", also pointing to a positive correlation between economic development on the one hand, and the predictability of the law and its application on the other.[181] This doctrine hence applies not only to legislation but also to

antiquity, despite the undeniable change and technological evolutions that the world has undergone since then.

177 Laurence Diver, 'Interpreting the Rule(s) of Code: Performance, Performativity, and Production' [2021] MIT Computational Law Report 2 <https://law.mit.edu/pub/interpretingtherulesofcode/release/1> 3.

178 See also Bingham (n 6) 67.

179 See *supra* Section 3.2.5.

180 See, e.g., the references to the Case *Sunday Times v United Kingdom* (no. 1), Application no. 6538/74, 26 April 1979, § 49 and *Malone v United Kingdom*, Application no. 8691/79, 2 August 1984, § 68, in Council of Europe (n 42), §46. These characteristics also appear, for instance, in Lon Fuller's influential account of the rule of law, as discussed *supra* in Section 3.1.1.

181 Tamanaha (n 26) 240.

administrative acts taken by public authorities, both as regards general and individual acts.[182]

Legal certainty requires public authorities to ensure stability when implementing the law, and to carry out their tasks in line with people's legitimate expectations, in a manner that is compatible with other legislation.[183] To achieve this, applicable laws and their implementation guidelines must be foreseeable as to their effects, through a sufficiently clear and precise formulation that enables natural and legal persons to organise their lives accordingly. A link can also be made to the principle of the non-arbitrary exercise of public power and the discussion of the executive's discretion, since "*a law which confers discretion to a state authority must indicate the scope of that discretion*" as well as "*the manner of its exercise with sufficient clarity, to give the individual adequate protection against arbitrariness*".[184] Finally, the law must also be applied in a consistent way, and when rules are changed, for instance because they are adapted to a changing reality, this needs to happen with a fair warning.[185]

3.3.2.b Challenges to the Principle of Legal Certainty

The implementation of the legal certainty principle is not devoid of challenges. First, as noted above, a fine line exists between a legal text that is so precise that it loses its general and broad applicability, and a text that is so imprecise that it ceases being conducive to legal certainty and lends itself to arbitrariness. Where and how this line must be drawn depends on the context and substance of the legal provisions. As regards the regulation of technology-related risks, for instance, the need for technical expertise typically drives legislators to opt for broad legal provisions, which can then be further specified by (specialised) public authorities through administrative acts. It is, however, important that those administrative acts still comply with the principle of legal certainty, by remaining relatively foreseeable and in any case consistent with the normative aims of the law they are based on. This issue is specifically addressed in the Venice Commission's checklist, which states that

> precaution in advance of dealing with concrete dangers has now become increasingly important; this evolution is legitimate due to the multiplication of the risks resulting in particular from the changing technology. However, in the areas where the precautionary approach of laws apply, such as risk law, the prerequisites for State action are outlined in terms that are considerably broader and more imprecise, but the Rule of Law implies that the principle of foreseeability is not set aside.[186]

[182] Venice Commission (n 74) 27.
[183] To return to Hayek's quote, the rule of law enables us "*to foresee with fair certainty how the authority will use its coercive powers in given circumstances and to plan one's individual affairs on the basis of this knowledge*". See Hayek (n 17) 112.
[184] Council of Europe (n 42), §46.
[185] Venice Commission (n 74) 26.
[186] ibid.

Second, the consistent application of the law by public authorities can also be a challenge, especially when authorities are decentralised and when the law's broadness leaves much scope for discretion. At a very practical level, the same law will often be applied to different individual cases by many different public officials, who might each have a different way of interpreting and implementing its provisions. In many situations, however, the risk of inconsistency is reduced by the adoption of implementation guidelines which public officials ought to follow, and by the hierarchical control that is typical of bureaucracy. Yet, there again, too much specification may shift the balance towards over-precision. Indeed, in certain situations, stability and consistency may lead to undesirable outcomes in the face of new or unforeseen circumstances that require flexibility. The Venice Commission therefore recalls that "*stability is not an end in itself: law must also be capable of adaptation to changing circumstances. Law can be changed, but with public debate and notice, and without adversely affecting legitimate expectations*".[187]

Consequently, just like the principle of legality, the principle of legal certainty comprises some inherent tensions, requiring a balance between consistency and adaptability. There is no uniform way of achieving this balance, as it depends on the particular context. Nevertheless, guidance must not be sought in the essentialisation or idealisation of either consistency or adaptability. Instead, it should be found in the overarching aim of this principle as part of the rule of law: ensuring that those subjected to the law can reasonably foresee the law's effects and plan their lives accordingly. This is the goal that public authorities should strive towards when implementing laws and adopting administrative acts.

3.3.3 *Non-arbitrariness of the Executive Powers*

3.3.3.a The Principle's Requirements

The prohibition of arbitrariness is arguably the clearest expression of the rule of law's aim to constrain public power and ensure it is exercised in line with the law. Concretely, it provides that public authorities cannot act arbitrarily or based on whims. Instead, they must act rationally and unbiasedly, in the public interest, and make sure that "*public officials carry out their duties in an impartial manner, irrespective of their personal beliefs and interests*".[188]

The EU Charter of Fundamental Rights expresses this principle, as part of the right to good administration, as follows: "*Every person has the right to have his or her affairs handled impartially, fairly and within a reasonable time by the institutions, bodies, offices and agencies of the Union.*"[189] As part of this provision, persons also

[187] ibid.

[188] See also the principle of 'impartiality' as part of 'Recommendation CM/Rec(2007)7 of the Committee of Ministers to Member States on Good Administration' (n 161), Article 4.

[189] Article 41(1) Charter of Fundamental Rights of the European Union.

have the right to be heard before a measure is taken that adversely affects them, and the right to have access to their file (while respecting the legitimate interests of confidentiality and of professional and business secrecy).[190] While the Charter's provision only applies to public authorities at EU level, it expresses requirements that can be found in the administrative rules of all EU Member States as regards the relationship between public authorities and natural and legal persons.

An important requirement derived from the principle of non-arbitrariness is that public officials should provide reasons or justifications for their decisions in a clear and understandable manner.[191] This allows those affected by their decisions to appraise the non-arbitrary nature thereof. The obligation to give reasons for public decisions – also enshrined as a right in Article 41(2)(c) of the EU Charter – is particularly important when they affect the rights or interests of individuals.[192] Conversely, an explicit obligation to express the reasons behind the adoption of an administrative act does not always exist for normative acts, or those that have a general rather than an individual application. In Belgium, for instance, no formal motivation requirement exists in such case.[193] Nevertheless, the absence of a formal motivation duty for general acts does not extinguish the need for such acts to be based on factually and legally acceptable motives, which need to be clear either from the act itself or at least from the administrative file.[194]

The prohibition of arbitrariness is especially important when public authorities have a (wide) margin of discretion. On the one hand, "*the complexity of modern society means that discretionary power must be granted to public officials.*"[195] On the other hand, this power ought to be exercised in a non-arbitrary manner, implying that measures taken by public authorities should be reasonable and proportionate.[196] Indeed, "*an exercise of power that leads to substantively unfair, unreasonable, irrational or oppressive decisions violates the rule of law*".[197] Accordingly,

[190] ibid Article 41(2).

[191] Venice Commission (n 74), §68.

[192] Also in this regard, the Council of Europe's Committee of Ministers issued further recommendations for member states' public authorities. See, e.g., Committee of Ministers of the Council of Europe, 'Resolution 77(31) on the Protection of the Individual in Relation to the Acts of Administrative Authorities'; 'Recommendation CM/Rec(2007)7 of the Committee of Ministers to Member States on Good Administration' (n 161).

[193] Steven Van Garsse (ed), *Handboek Bestuursrecht* (Politeia 2016) 36.

[194] This file consists of the entirety of the documents that pertain to the decision, including drafts of the decision, preliminary advices, minutes that were taken at meetings, email exchanges, reports or other relevant materials. See also ibid 36 and 84.

[195] Venice Commission (n 74) 29.

[196] See, for instance, Case C-389/05, *Commission v France*, 17 July 2008, ECLI:EU:C:2008:411, §94; Case C-169/07, *Hartlauer v Wiener Landesregierung*, 10 March 2009, ECLI:EU:C:2009:141,§64; and Case C-203/08, *Sporting Exchange Ltd v Minister van Justitie*, 3 June 2010, ECLI:EU:C:2010:307, §50.

[197] Venice Commission (n 74), §64. Note also the ample case law in this regard cited in the Checklist, e.g. *Husayn (Abu Zubaydah) v Poland*, Application no. 7511/13, 24 July 2014, §521; *Hassan v the United Kingdom*, Application no. 29750/09, 16 September 2014, §106; *Georgia v*

discretionary power requires clear legal restrictions, "*in particular when exercised by the executive in administrative action*".[198]

Already in 1980, the Council of Europe's Committee of Ministers adopted a Recommendation dealing with the exercise of discretionary power.[199] The Recommendation sets out six principles public authorities must respect whenever they exercise such power: they should not pursue a purpose other than that for which the power has been conferred; they must observe objectivity and impartiality, taking into account only the factors relevant to the particular case; they must observe the principle of equality before the law by avoiding unfair discrimination (which will be further discussed below); they should maintain a proper balance between any adverse effects which its decision may have on the rights, liberties or interests of persons and the purpose which it pursues; they must take their decision within a time which is reasonable having regard to the matter at stake; and they must apply any general administrative guidelines in a consistent manner while at the same time taking account of the particular circumstances of each case.

Finally, public authorities must also put in place mechanisms that can prevent, correct and sanction the arbitrary or abusive use of discretion.[200] This also includes, according to the EU rule of law report methodology, an anti-corruption framework, covering measures to ensure whistle-blower protection and to encourage the reporting of corruption, as well as the criminalisation of corruption as such.[201] Moreover, as regards public authorities' use of electronic databanks, "*precautions should be taken against any abuse or misuse of information*", making everyone concerned with the operation of electronic data processing in the public sector "*bound by rules of conduct aimed at preventing the misuse of data and in particular by a duty to observe secrecy*".[202]

3.3.3.b Challenges to the Principle of Non-arbitrariness

As regards the tensions that arise in the implementation of this principle, two aspects are particularly worth highlighting: first, tensions around the (overzealous faith) in

Russia (I), Application no. 13255/07, 3 July 2014, §182; *Ivinović v Croatia*, Application no. 13006/13, 18 September 2014, §40. For the CJEU, see, e.g., Case 46/87 and 227/88, *Hoechst v Commission*, 21 September 1989, ECLI:EU:C:1989:337, §19; and T-402/13, *Orange v European Commission*, 25 November 2014, ECLI:EU:T:2014:99, §89.

[198] Venice Commission (n 74) 29.

[199] Committee of Ministers of the Council of Europe, 'Recommendation No. R (80) 2 of the Committee of Ministers Concerning the Exercise of Discretionary Powers by Administrative Authorities', Adopted by the Committee of Ministers on 11 March 1980 at the 316th meeting of the Ministers' Deputies, 1980.

[200] Venice Commission (n 74) 29.

[201] European Commission, 'European Rule of Law Mechanism: Methodology for the Preparation of the Annual Rule of Law Report' (2020) 2.

[202] Committee of Ministers of the Council of Europe, 'Resolution (74) 29 on the Protection of the Privacy of Individuals Vis-a-Vis Electronic Data Banks in the Public Sector'.

rationality and efficiency and, second, tensions around the exercise of (excessive or insufficient) discretion. Let me discuss each in turn.

First, it can be recalled that the rise of the welfare state in the nineteenth century significantly expanded the competences of public administrations, which started organising themselves as hierarchical bureaucracies with the purpose of taking rational and objective decisions. There is, however, no such thing as 'objectivity' in public decision-making. As pointed out by Barth and Arnold, "*the issue in the public sphere is not to remove values from decisions. We know that in public policy, there is no such thing as an apolitical or valueless decision; all but the most narrowly technical decisions reflect value choices or biases by what is done and by what is not done.*"[203] Public authorities and officials are hence always coloured by the political processes that govern them in a direct way, and by the values and interests of the societal groups they are part of in a more indirect way. More generally, political values and policies lay at the basis of public decision-making, and thus also determine how decision-making processes take place and which goals they aspire to achieve. As noted above,[204] an overemphasis on procedural rationality, objectivity and efficiency hence risks obfuscating the fact that *all* public policy is grounded in normative values – whether those values are rendered explicit or not.

History has also shown that an overemphasis on rational procedures and efficiency, without critical attention to the substantive aims those procedures should attain, can lead to outcomes that are diametrically opposed to the spirit of the rule of law as cornerstone of liberal democratic societies.[205] Public authorities must hence make sure that their zeal for rational and efficient decision-making does not trump the social policies and values they are meant to achieve. While the requirement for rational and impartial decision-making should not be dismissed as unattainable, it is important to understand the normative assumptions that underlie the decision-making process and – in Weberian terms – to balance procedural rationality against substantive rationality. In this regard, the role of empathy[206] has been pointed out as a potential counterbalance against uncritical formal rationality in public decision-making. Yet the ability to let decisions be guided by empathy in addition to rationality also requires a certain level of discretion, which is imbued with similar tensions.

Indeed, the second challenge to the implementation of the prohibition of arbitrariness concerns the level of discretion that public officials ought to have when

[203] Thomas J Barth and Eddy Arnold, 'Artificial Intelligence and Administrative Discretion: Implications for Public Administration' (1999) 29 The American Review of Public Administration 332, 337.

[204] See *supra* Section 3.2.

[205] Recall in this regard the connection made by Bauman between excessive bureaucracy without normative underpinnings on the one hand, and the Holocaust on the other hand, in Zygmunt Bauman, *Modernity and the Holocaust* (Polity Press 1989).

[206] Sofia Ranchordas, 'Empathy in the Digital Administrative State' (2022) 71 Duke Law Journal 1341.

making decisions – a recurring dilemma in public governance theory, and one that I already touched upon in Section 2.3.3. As noted by HLA Hart, since "*we are men, not gods*", we should "*not cherish the conception of a rule so detailed that the question whether it applied or not to a particular case was always settled in advance, and never involved, at the point of actual application, a fresh choice between open alternatives.*"[207] It can also be recalled that the flexibility afforded by discretion can be used to keep the excesses of procedural rationality in check, and to ensure more meaningful policy outcomes.[208] At the same time, it is equally clear that discretion needs to be delimited to avoid that public authorities can subvert legislative authority by interpreting and applying general rules in an arbitrary or abusive manner.[209] Being at the mercy of public officials who can singlehandedly decide whether a right is accorded or denied, was precisely the bureaucratic nightmare scenario depicted by Hayek in his *Road to Serfdom*.[210]

Over time, public authorities have sought to decrease discretion at the level of public officials by routinising public decision-making processes through the adoption of detailed guidelines that public officials should follow. While this routinisation can contribute to the consistency of decision-making, decrease corruption and counter arbitrary actions, it also reduces the possibility for justified deviations, for instance when this would be beneficial to ensure substantive rationality, or to correct (unintended) adverse effects caused by the law's general nature.[211] In other words, there is a fine line between an *excess* and a *shortage* of discretion at the level of individual public officials, which requires careful balancing rather than overly strict formalisation in one way or the other, while keeping in mind that discretion ought to be used in the public interest.[212]

Finally, a third challenge arises when seeking to identify what exactly the 'public interest' is that public authorities should aim to achieve when performing their tasks and exercising discretion. While it is quite ingrained that the "*proper ends of government*" are "*promoting the common good and human well-being*",[213] it is far

[207] Hart (n 30) 128.

[208] See in this regard Lars Tummers and Victor Bekkers, 'Policy Implementation, Street-Level Bureaucracy, and the Importance of Discretion' (2014) 16 Public Management Review 527.

[209] Barth and Arnold (n 203) 332.

[210] Indeed, "*one of the major dilemmas with public administrators exercising discretion is that the public must rely on the 'public interestedness' of the administrator when we know that people and agencies can be motivated by self-interest.*" See Hayek (n 17). See also Michael C Munger, 'Self-Interest and Public Interest: The Motivations of Political Actors' (2011) 23 Critical Review 339.

[211] It has therefore been argued that, despite the arbitrariness risks attached thereto, "*front-line discretion is necessary to respond to the unexpected and to ensure that services are responsive to individual need*". See Tony Evans, 'Professionals and Discretion in Street-Level Bureaucracy' in Peter Hupe, Michael Hill and Aurélien Buffat (eds), *Understanding Street-Level Bureaucracy* (Bristol University Press 2015) 281.

[212] Van Garsse (n 193) 41.

[213] Cass R Sunstein and Adrian Vermeule, *Law and Leviathan: Redeeming the Administrative State* (Harvard University Press 2020) 5.

from self-evident how concepts like the public interest or the common good should be defined or interpreted.[214] It would take me too far to discuss here the vast scholarship that either criticises these concepts as empty vessels which can be abused by any ideology[215] or claims that they should be placed more prominently on policy agendas.[216] Suffice it to say that – in a modern heterogenous society where various people, groups and organisations have competing interests – identifying whether a measure is 'in the public interest or not' is not a straightforward exercise.

3.3.4 *Equality before the Law*

3.3.4.a The Principle's Requirements

The principle of equality before the law, often mentioned together with the principle of non-discrimination, is strongly affined with the prohibition of arbitrariness. While in Article 2 TEU the value of *equality* is listed in addition to, rather than as part of, the value of the rule of law, in the Conditionality Regulation it is nevertheless mentioned as one of the sub-principles of the rule of law's definition.[217] Equality is also a general principle of EU law recognised by the CJEU, enshrined in Title III of the EU Charter, and further concretised in secondary EU legislation.[218] Accordingly, compliance therewith can also be argued to fall under the rule of law's principle of legality, which requires Member States' actions to align with primary and secondary EU law. One could hence argue that thin and thick rule of law theorists alike must concede that in the EU, the principle of equality ought to be respected by public authorities.

Pursuant to this principle, public authorities must treat all individuals in an equal manner, and effectively protect them against discrimination. A number of discrimination grounds are explicitly prohibited by the EU Charter of Fundamental Rights[219]

214 See, e.g., Anthony Downs, 'The Public Interest: It's Meaning in a Democracy' (1962) 29 Social Research 1.

215 Note how Sorauf conceptualises it as a 'political *je ne sais quoi*', in Frank J Sorauf, 'The Public Interest Reconsidered' (1957) 19 The Journal of Politics 616.

216 See, e.g., Barry Bozeman, *Public Values and Public Interest: Counterbalancing Economic Individualism* (Georgetown University Press 2007).

217 Although Article 2 of the Conditionality Regulation considers this principle to be part of the rule of law, those adhering to a thin conception of the rule of law would not necessarily agree with this, particularly if it concerns a substantive understanding of equality.

218 See in this regard also Elise Muir, *EU Equality Law: The First Fundamental Rights Policy of the EU* (Oxford University Press 2018).

219 See Article 21 of the EU Charter: (1) Any discrimination based on any ground such as sex, race, colour, ethnic or social origin, genetic features, language, religion or belief, political or any other opinion, membership of a national minority, property, birth, disability, age or sexual orientation shall be prohibited. (2) Within the scope of application of the Treaties and without prejudice to any of their specific provisions, any discrimination on grounds of nationality shall be prohibited.

and by the European Convention on Human Rights.[220] In essence, the principle requires that persons in similar situations are treated equally and that different situations are treated differently. When public authorities violate this requirement, an effective remedy needs to be ensured so that this can be challenged in court.[221]

In the European Union, besides being a formal requirement, the principle of equality is also considered to be a substantive one, requiring the *substantively* equal treatment of persons.[222] This implies that in certain situations, the principle's application dictates that public authorities *must* make differentiations, namely when legal subjects are substantively finding themselves in unequal situations. However, whenever a differential treatment is applied, this should be objectively justified on the basis of a reasonable aim, and in conformity with the principle of proportionality.[223]

3.3.4.b Challenges to the Principle of Equality

One can immediately notice the challenge that is contained in that last sentence. When is a distinction objectively justified and when do people find themselves in a differing situation that warrants differential treatment, and when not? A link can be made here also to the more general problem of over- and under-inclusivity that is inherent to any general rule of law. Solving these questions typically requires a case-by-case analysis and balancing exercise. Evidently, such a balance needs to take place not only at the level of the legislature, when adopting legislation, but also at the level of the executive, when implementing legislation and adopting administrative acts. Public authorities hence need to express an objective and reasonable justification for any differential treatment, which ought to pursue a legitimate aim and showcase a reasonable relationship of proportionality between the means employed and the aim one seeks to realise.[224] The situation of the differently treated people must hence be *relevantly* differentiated.[225] When such differentiations are challenged in court, the assessment of the justifiability of differentiation often reflects "*local political, social and legal dimensions of the case as well as arguments made by claimants and alleged offenders*", revealing that there are "*very few clear-cut*

[220] See Article 14 ECHR: The enjoyment of the rights and freedoms set forth in this Convention shall be secured without discrimination on any ground such as sex, race, colour, language, religion, political or other opinion, national or social origin, association with a national minority, property, birth or other status.

[221] See European Union Agency for Fundamental Rights (ed), *Handbook on European Non-Discrimination Law* (Publications Office of the European Union 2018).

[222] Venice Commission (n 74) 19.

[223] ibid 32.

[224] ibid.

[225] Moreover, Strasbourg case law provides that "*contracting States enjoy a margin of appreciation in assessing whether and to what extent differences in otherwise similar situations justify a difference*". See in this regard *Burden v the United Kingdom GC*, Application no. 13378/05, 29 April 2008, §60; *Hämäläinen v Finland*, Application no. 37359/09, 26 July 2014, §108.

examples of static rules, requirements, or thresholds for defining the key concepts and groups underlying discrimination as a legal standard".[226]

In addition, it may also be challenging for persons who are affected by a public authority's unreasonable differentiation to remedy this situation, as it is not always evident that such differentiation is taking place. While laws and regulations of general application are in principle rendered public (given the transparency required by the principle of legal certainty and legality), individual acts taken by public authorities when they apply these laws to specific cases are typically not public.[227] Instead, they are often only communicated to the natural or legal person to which the act pertains, which means that it is not always easy for persons to ascertain that they are treated differently than others who are in a similar situation. Accordingly, the fulfilment of the requirement that an effective remedy must exist against discriminatory or unequal applications of the law depends on more than the mere existence of a ground of legal standing. It also necessitates a certain level of transparency by public authorities on how they interpret a general rule, and how they intend to apply it.

3.3.5 *Judicial Review*

3.3.5.a The Principle's Requirements

Like other principles, the principle of effective judicial review can be broken down into various sub-principles, which are sometimes presented separately, sometimes together. The Conditionality Regulation speaks of "*effective judicial protection, including access to justice, by independent and impartial courts, also as regards fundamental rights*",[228] while the Venice Commission frames it as "*access to justice before independent and impartial courts, including judicial review of administrative*

[226] Sandra Wachter, Brent Mittelstadt and Chris Russell, 'Why Fairness Cannot Be Automated: Bridging the Gap between EU Non-Discrimination Law and AI' (2021) 41 Computer Law & Security Review 105567, 8. See also their subsequent paper, Sandra Wachter, Brent Mittelstadt and Chris Russell, 'Bias Preservation in Machine Learning: The Legality of Fairness Metrics under EU Non-Discrimination Law' (2021) 123 West Virginia Law Review 735, in which they argue that "*the fundamental aim of the law is not only to prevent ongoing discrimination, but also to change society, policies, and practices to 'level the playing field' and achieve substantive rather than merely formal equality*". They also stress that tackling bias in algorithmic systems should go beyond fairness metrics that 'preserve' the status quo, but must aim at transforming existing societal biases so as to foster substantive equality.

[227] Under Belgian administrative law, for instance, administrative acts with a general application (regulations or normative acts) need to be rendered public by law, whereas individual acts only need to be communicated to the legal subjects to which the act pertains. See, e.g., Van Garsse (n 193) 38.

[228] Regulation 2020/2092 of the European Parliament and of the Council of 16 December 2020 on a general regime of conditionality for the protection of the Union budget (n 119), Article 2.

acts" and lists *respect for human rights* as a separate principle.[229] As my focus lays on distilling from these principles more specific requirements for the executive branch of power, I will set aside the sub-principles on "*access to justice*" and "*independent and impartial courts*",[230] and limit my attention here to the requirement of ensuring judicial review of administrative acts.

In essence, judicial review comprises a legality check that encompasses, but is not limited to, compliance of those acts with human rights law.[231] In the context of the European Union, this also implies the review of national authorities' compliance with primary and secondary EU law. More generally, judicial review also enables the verification of public authorities' compliance with the other rule of law principles listed above, including respect for legal certainty, the prohibition of arbitrary decision-making, and respect for the principle of equality. Given this overarching role in protecting the rule of law's principles, the importance of an effective judicial review mechanism can thus not be overstated. The ability to "*prevent, correct or sanction arbitrary or unlawful decisions by public authorities, including by law-enforcement authorities*" can indeed be seen as a sine qua non to protect the rule of law.[232] Without this ability, the rule of law would ultimately remain a dead letter. Importantly, judicial review must also be enabled for acts that are carried out by private actors on behalf of public actors.[233] Public authorities can thus not escape a review of the legality of their actions – or of their responsibility – by outsourcing their tasks to companies or other private organisations.

A legality review can be instigated by natural and legal persons in a direct way (by directly challenging the administrative act in question before a court) or in an indirect way (by invoking the illegality of the act indirectly in the context of a court proceeding to which the act is relevant).[234] Yet while they should always be entitled to seek judicial review of an act if it directly affects their rights and interest, natural

[229] Venice Commission (n 74) 11.

[230] It should, however, be noted that especially the latter was the object of much recent case law both before the Luxembourg and the Strasbourg Courts, given that judicial capture has been taking place in certain EU Member States. For an overview, see, e.g., Mańko (n 108); Dimitry V Kochenov and John Morijn, 'Strengthening the Charter's Role in the Fight for the Rule of Law in the EU: The Cases of Judicial Independence and Party Financing' (2021) 27 European Public Law 759.

[231] The Venice Commission's Checklist (at page 18) also explicitly requires, under the principle of legality, that "*public authorities comply with their positive obligations by ensuring implementation and effective protection of human rights*". It hence not only concerns a requirement not to infringe human rights, but also to abide by positive obligations to ensure their implementation and protection.

[232] As testified by the fact that the EU Conditionality Regulation also explicitly states in its Article 3 (b) that the failure of ensuring this "*may be indicative of breaches of the principles of the rule of law*" for the purpose of the Regulation.

[233] Venice Commission (n 74) 24.

[234] Moreover, when court proceedings are instigated and individuals have standing, the right to a fair trial must be respected, including the equality of arms. Ibid 45. See in this regard also Article 6 of the ECHR.

and legal persons do not always have standing to challenge an act that does not demonstrably directly and personally affects them (for instance when it concerns an administrative act of general applicability)[235] even if the act infringes one of the rule of law's principles and hence causes societal harm.[236] The absence of a so-called *actio popularis* (an action that existed in Roman law, which could be brought by a member of the public to protect 'the public interest') is therefore not incompatible with the principle of effective judicial review.[237] This despite the fact that "*leaving the possibility to ask for a review of constitutionality only to the legislative or executive branch of government may severely limit the number of cases and therefore the scope of the review*".[238]

In many jurisdictions (as is the case in Belgium, for instance[239]) judges have the obligation *not* to apply administrative acts in case they are illegitimate, yet that of course first requires a judge to assess the act's legality. Moreover, the court controlling public authorities' exercise of discretionary power should also have the "*powers of obtaining information as are necessary for the exercise of its function*".[240] Finally, if an administrative act (or act of negligence) by a public authority is found unlawful and private persons suffer damages, a remedy must be provided.[241]

3.3.5.b Challenges to the Principle of Effective Judicial Review

Vital as the principle of effective judicial review may be, the challenges accompanying its realisation are manifold. For instance, where public authorities have discretion, judicial review often takes on a more limited shape to avoid judges replacing policymakers – which would obstruct the principle of the separation of powers. Certainly, the act taken by the public authority needs to be *legal*, but as regards its

[235] Compare this with the problem of standing in EU Courts as regards the legality review of EU legal acts. See Koen Lenaerts, Ignace Maselis and Kathleen Gutman, *EU Procedural Law* (Janek Tomasz Nowak ed, Oxford University Press 2015) 312 and following.

[236] For instance, Article 22 of the Code of Good Administration recommended by the Council of Europe's Committee of Ministers foresees that "*private persons shall be entitled to seek, directly or by way of exception, a judicial review of an administrative decision which directly affects their rights and interests*".

[237] See in this regard also Venice Commission, 'Study on Individual Access to Constitutional Justice – Adopted by the Venice Commission at Its 85th Plenary Session' (Council of Europe 2011) CDL-AD(2010)039rev. For Belgium, see, e.g., Sabien Lust, *Rechtsbescherming Tegen de (Administratieve) Overheid. Een Inleiding* (die Keure 2014) 119.

[238] Venice Commission (n 74), §109.

[239] See Article 159 of the Belgian Constitution: "*Courts only apply general, provincial or local decisions and regulations provided that they are in accordance with the law.*" (official translation).

[240] Committee of Ministers of the Council of Europe, 'Recommendation No. R (80) 2 of the Committee of Ministers Concerning the Exercise of Discretionary Powers by Administrative Authorities' (n 199).

[241] 'Recommendation CM/Rec(2007)7 of the Committee of Ministers to Member States on Good Administration' (n 161), Article 23.

choice to pursue a particular discretionary policy or decision rather than another, judges can often only intervene if that policy or decision is (manifestly) *unreasonable*.[242] Any review is then limited to a review of legality, despite the fact that, in practice, public authorities can take actions that are *legal*, yet nevertheless cause a disproportionately adverse impact that could have been avoided with alternative policies.[243] Accordingly, whenever they have discretion (which, as discussed above, is often the case) public authorities may have a relatively broad margin of appreciation to evaluate the criteria based on which they pursue certain policies. The tension point here seems to lay between ensuring a sufficient level of judicial review that enables verification of the government's compliance with the rule of law, while at the same time also ensuring that the separation of powers is upheld and that judges do not take over the task of governments.

In addition, one can raise the difficulties regarding the right to have standing in court to ensure that an administrative act is reviewed, and the accessibility of such a review. Firstly, there may be situations where an administrative act adversely affects a societal interest, which does not necessarily bear a one-on-one relationship with a demonstrable adverse effect on an individual right or interest.[244] In that case, natural and legal persons would be prevented from challenging the act, unless national law explicitly grants standing for collective or public interest groups (the standing problem). Secondly, if individual harm remains unnoticed – recall, for instance, the situation mentioned under the principle of equality, where an individual is simply not aware of the fact that the public authority erroneously or wrongly distinguishes her case from a similar case meriting equal treatment – the problematic act will not be challenged (the knowledge problem).[245] Thirdly, the harm at the level of the individual may be perceived as insignificant, or in any case as too small in proportion to the costs that may be involved in challenging it, even if the act more significantly impacts a societal interest, thus rendering it unlikely that the individual

[242] See also Hasan Dindjer, 'What Makes an Administrative Decision Unreasonable?' (2021) 84 The Modern Law Review 265.

[243] Note that under Belgian law, for instance, the fact that a public authority used its discretionary power in a manner that does not pursue the public interest, but instead aligns with a private interest, is not enough ground to annul the decision if there are other justifications for the decision. See Van Garsse (n 193) 82.

[244] For the context of algorithmic regulation, which will be elaborated in the next chapter, see, e.g., Nathalie A Smuha, 'Beyond the Individual: Governing AI's Societal Harm' (2021) 10 Internet Policy Review 3; Bart van der Sloot and Sascha van Schendel, 'Procedural Law for the Data-Driven Society' (2021) Information & Communications Technology Law 1; Karen Yeung, 'Responsibility and AI – A Study of the Implications of Advanced Digital Technologies (Including AI Systems) for the Concept of Responsibility within a Human Rights Framework' (Council of Europe 2019) <https://rm.coe.int/a-study-of-the-implications-of-advanced-digital-technologies-including/168096bdab>.

[245] In this regard, it can be highlighted that an inherent asymmetry of information exists between public authorities on the one hand, and private persons on the other hand. I will discuss this issue further in Chapter 4.

will challenge the problematic act (the threshold problem). Fourthly, an individual can also acquiesce with a problematic act and waive the opportunity to invoke her protective right to review (perhaps because the act, while infringing the rule of law, is beneficial to her), thereby undermining the opportunity to remedy any *indirect* adverse effects of the act suffered by third parties (the egocentrism problem).

Finally, in the context of the European Union's 'rule of law crisis', one must also recall the importance of ensuring an independent and impartial judiciary.[246] Since this book focuses on the executive branch of power, I will not elaborate on this requirement here. I will point out, however, that Member States have been condemned by the CJEU and by the ECtHR precisely because they did not respect this principle.[247] Evidently, judges that are partial to the government and its administration will not be able to effectively carry out a judicial review of administrative acts and grant the protection that is due in this regard. For all those reasons, securing the principle of effective judicial review of government actions – including their respect for human rights – is not devoid of challenges.[248]

3.3.6 *Separation of Powers*

3.3.6.a The Principle's Requirements

The separation of powers aims at preventing the concentration of public power with one state entity. It does so by providing for checks and balances and thereby minimising the risk of unchecked power that can curb the rights and freedoms of citizens, erode democratic representation, and undermine public accountability. Not all legal theorists would consider it as a principle that is classifiable under the concept of the rule of law, and it is, for instance, absent from the 'ingredients list' of both Lon Fuller and Lord Bingham. At the same time, there is little doubt that the rule of law and the separation of powers are entwined. The separation of powers is therefore mentioned by both the EU and the Council of Europe in their rule of law conceptualisations, on par with the other rule of law principles. While the Venice Commission did not include separate questions for this principle in its rule of law checklist (presumably in light of the fact that the five other principles collectively contribute to the separation of powers), the European Commission's rule of law framework does contain a residual pillar named "*other institutional issues linked to checks and balances*", underlining that its abstract nature

[246] See Sergio Carrera and Valsamis Mitsilegas, 'Upholding the Rule of Law by Scrutinising Judicial Independence' (CEPS 2018).

[247] See also *supra*, Section 3.2.5.

[248] For the limitations of ad hoc judicial review of administrative action as a systematic safeguard against abuse of power, see also Harry Woolf, Jeffrey Jowell and Andrew P Le Sueur, *De Smith, Woolf and Jowell's Principles of Judicial Review* (Sweet & Maxwell 1999).

does not preclude its importance in the evaluation of countries' compliance with the rule of law.[249]

Distributing different public functions across different branches of power not only decentralises public power, but also enables one branch to 'check' and to 'balance out' the other.[250] Accordingly, the separation of powers is not a strict separation,[251] because its very aim is to enable mutual control, which requires a certain level of cooperation and transparency. Such control and cooperation occurs, in first instance, through the classical constitutional checks and balances of the *trias politica* doctrine. The legislative branch of power can keep the executive in check by organising parliamentary hearings and investigations, playing a role in the government's budget approvals, as well as more generally delimiting the contours in which the executive can operate when enacting laws.[252] The judicial branch of power can carry out a judicial review of the government's actions and hold it accountable if and when it transgresses the limits of its competences.[253]

Yet, besides the two other branches of power, citizens also play a critical role in keeping the government accountable. They do so by casting their vote during popular elections (though this is primarily relevant for the 'political' as opposed to the 'administrative' executive) and by challenging problematic government actions in court.[254] By extension, enabling a healthy civil society can also be considered as an essential requirement of this principle, given the contribution of civil society organisations to the checks and balances of and between the three branches of power.[255] Together with (independent) media,[256] civil society investigates, reports on, raises awareness of, and challenges government action in the

[249] This also comprises the theme of the "*quality of the public administration, and how authorities apply the law and implement court decisions*". See European Commission, 'The Rule of Law Situation in the European Union. 2021 Rule of Law Report' (n 117) 20, section 3.4.

[250] See also Richard Bellamy (ed), *The Rule of Law and the Separation of Powers* (Ashgate/Dartmouth 2005).

[251] It also implies loyal cooperation between the different state institutions. See also Justin Fox and Mattias Polborn, 'On the Separation of Executive and Legislative Powers: Executive Independence, Liberty, and Social Welfare' (2021) 33 Journal of Theoretical Politics 430.

[252] See in this regard also Alison L Young, *Democratic Dialogue and the Constitution* (Oxford University Press 2017).

[253] Rafael La Porta and others, 'Judicial Checks and Balances' (2004) 112 Journal of Political Economy 445. See also Guobin Zhu, *Deference to the Administration in Judicial Review: Comparative Perspectives* (Springer International Publishing 2019).

[254] See also Andreas Schedler, 'Conceptualizing Accountability' in Andreas Schedler, Larry Diamond and Marc F Plattner (eds), *The Self-Restraining State: Power and Accountability in New Democracies* (Lynne Rienner Publishers 1999).

[255] European Commission, '2020 Rule of Law Report: The Rule of Law Situation in the European Union' (n 117) 20.

[256] For reasons of time and space I will not consider the role of media in keeping public power in check, yet it should be noted that the European Commission's Rule of Law Report mentions the important role of media regulatory authorities and bodies, as well as the need for a framework to protect journalistic and other media activity from state inference, to investigate attacks on journalists, and to ensure access to public documents and information. See also

public interest – including, where possible, through public interest litigation in judicial review procedures. As the Commission's 2021 rule of law report states: "*An enabling framework for civil society allows for debate and scrutiny of those in power; and when their space to operate shrinks, it is a sign that the rule of law is at risk.*"[257]

In this regard, the requirement for public authorities to ensure transparency is vital. This requirement was already mentioned under the principle of legality (pertaining to the rule-making process) and under the principle of legal certainty (pertaining to the implementation process of legal rules), yet it can also be considered as essential for maintaining the separation of powers, as it enables the 'checks' it entails. The Council of Europe's Code of Good Administration explicitly includes the 'principle of transparency' in this context. It requires public authorities to "*ensure that private persons are informed, by appropriate means, of their actions and decisions which may include the publication of official documents. They shall respect the rights of access to official documents according to the rules relating to personal data protection.*"[258] Furthermore, in a specific Recommendation on access to information, the Council of Europe's Committee of Ministers also stresses that "*everyone within the jurisdiction of a member state shall have the right to obtain, on request, information held by the public authorities other than legislative bodies and judicial authorities*", and that "*access to information shall not be refused on the ground that the requesting person has not a specific interest in the matter*".[259]

Finally, the principle of the separation of powers can arguably also be understood as requiring a certain level of separation between public and private power. This aspect is not rendered explicit in the Venice Commission's rule of law checklist or in the European Commission's rule of law reporting, yet it is implicit, for instance, in requirements regarding a framework against corruption and conflicts of interests.[260] Private actors are often relied upon by public authorities to exercise public

European Commission, 'European Rule of Law Mechanism: Methodology for the Preparation of the Annual Rule of Law Report' (n 201) 2–3.

[257] European Commission, 'The Rule of Law Situation in the European Union. 2021 Rule of Law Report' (n 117) 20.

[258] See Article 10 of the 'Recommendation CM/Rec(2007)7 of the Committee of Ministers to Member States on Good Administration' (n 161) 9.

[259] Committee of Ministers of the Council of Europe, 'Recommendation No. R (81) 19 of the Committee of Ministers to Member States on the Access to Information Held by Public Authorities' (n 169) 2. For public authorities at the level of the EU, Article 42 of the EU Charter of Fundamental Rights also enshrines a right of access to documents. Note also that Article 11(2) TEU provides that "*The institutions shall maintain an open, transparent and regular dialogue with representative associations and civil society*". Moreover, Article 11(3) TEU states that "*The European Commission shall carry out broad consultations with parties concerned in order to ensure that the Union's actions are coherent and transparent.*" This underlines the importance of the principle of transparency at the level of the European Union, as well as its connection with the role of civil society.

[260] See in this regard also Paul R Verkuil, *Outsourcing Sovereignty: Why Privatization of Government Functions Threatens Democracy and What We Can Do about It* (Cambridge University Press 2007).

tasks. As noted above, such outsourcing does not divest the government of its responsibilities: the same rule of law guarantees must apply, regardless of whether the public task is executed by a public or private entity.

3.3.6.b Challenges to the Principle of the Separation of Powers

The first challenge to uphold the separation of powers can be found precisely in the requirement to separate public and private powers. For an increasing number of functions, public authorities have no choice but to rely on private actors, because they may lack the know-how, skills, expertise or data to execute a task.[261] As I will discuss below, this is particularly the case in the digital realm, for instance as regards development of algorithmic systems. Such dependency not only poses the risk that public and private interests are mingled, but it can also create a power imbalance in the advantage of large technology companies who are increasingly influential in the public sphere. This influence manifests itself both directly by developing tools for the government and more indirectly by establishing the infrastructure and standards that those tools rely on, which are often not transparent – including for the officials that use those tools.[262]

A second challenge lies in the fact that the balance amongst the various branches of power already seems to be skewed in favour of the executive branch of power. This is due to various reasons. One must, for instance, acknowledge the extensiveness of the tasks delegated by the legislative to the executive, especially in an ever more complex society, where regulatory trade-offs and risk assessments require detailed analyses that legislators are unable to conduct. As noted by Ackerman, "*consider, for example, the regulatory problems posed by environmental protection. Although democratic legislation can provide guiding principles, parliaments have neither the time nor the expertise to sift the changing scientific data in search of responsible regulatory solutions*".[263] More generally, the legislative branch is dependent on the executive to implement and apply its general laws, and the judicial branch is dependent on the executive to implement and apply its judgments. Furthermore, in many countries, the last decade has witnessed a further consolidation of executive power, be it in the context of the financial crisis, the Covid-19 pandemic or for other reasons.[264] There is also an inherent asymmetry of

[261] See Antonio Cordella and Leslie Willcocks, 'Outsourcing, Bureaucracy and Public Value: Reappraising the Notion of the "Contract State"' (2010) 27 Government Information Quarterly 82; Sonia Gantman, 'IT Outsourcing in the Public Sector: A Literature Analysis' (2011) 14 Journal of Global Information Technology Management 48.

[262] See also Linnet Taylor, 'Public Actors without Public Values: Legitimacy, Domination and the Regulation of the Technology Sector' (2021) 34 Philosophy & Technology 897.

[263] Bruce Ackerman, 'The New Separation of Powers' (2000) 113 Harvard Law Review 633, 696.

[264] See also Protect Democracy, 'The Authoritarian Playbook – How Reporters Can Contextualize and Cover Authoritarian Threats as Distinct from Politics-as-Usual' (2022) <protectdemocracy .org/project/playbook-media-primer>.

information between the different branches: the executive holds much more information than the other two branches, which can render the latter's control of the former difficult. The executive also holds and spends the state budget. Under a worst case scenario, it can deploy this budget to finance actions that fortify its position, slander political opposition and marginalise critics, restrict the scope of action of civil society organisations and gather ever more information about natural and legal persons to increase its control over them.

Evidently, the rule of law, together with secondary legislation that sets out, for instance, rules about budget spending or electoral advertisement, is specifically targeted at preventing this from happening, and limiting the executive's ability to consolidate its power at the expense of the legislative, the judiciary and civil society. However, that does not take away the fact that, once problematic actions have been undertaken, it can be difficult for the other branches of power to reverse them. Far from being hypothetical, the previous section clarified that this situation is unfolding itself in various states across the world where authoritarian practices are on the rise.

Finally, when considering the context of the European Union, it should be noted that the division of tasks between different branches of power is organised somewhat differently in each Member State, in light of diverse national constitutional traditions.[265] As there is hence not one model for the configuration of state institutions, it is not always straightforward to assess the extent to which a particular configuration may cross the line of the 'separation of powers'. This point is, unsurprisingly, also eagerly invoked by populist leaders who seek to diminish the separation of powers and to consolidate executive power under the guise of respecting the 'diversity of national traditions'.[266] Accordingly, lest such arguments be used to undermine the rule of law, it is important to maintain a balanced understanding of the separation of powers, which safeguards both the foundational values listed in Article 2 TEU, and Member States' national identities as protected by Article 4(2) TEU.[267]

[265] Janneke Gerards, 'Pluralism, Deference and the Margin of Appreciation Doctrine' (2011) 17 European Law Journal 80; Luigi Corrias, 'National Identity and European Integration: The Unbearable Lightness of Legal Tradition' (2016) 2016 1 European Papers – A Journal on Law and Integration 383. This is also perceivable when comparing legal and political institutions in liberal democracies outside the EU. Consider how certain judges in the United States are politically elected, which could elsewhere be perceived as a potential attempt to politicise and undermine the independence of courts. See also Kate Malleson and Peter H Russell, *Appointing Judges in an Age of Judicial Power: Critical Perspectives from around the World* (University of Toronto Press 2018).

[266] See also Oliver Mader, 'Enforcement of EU Values as a Political Endeavour: Constitutional Pluralism and Value Homogeneity in Times of Persistent Challenges to the Rule of Law' (2019) 11 Hague Journal on the Rule of Law 133.

[267] Article 4(2) TEU reads as follows: "*The Union shall respect the equality of Member States before the Treaties as well as their national identities, inherent in their fundamental structures, political and constitutional, inclusive of regional and local self-government. It shall respect their essential State functions, including ensuring the territorial integrity of the State, maintaining law and order and safeguarding national security*".

3.4 CONCLUDING REMARKS

In this chapter, I conceptualised the rule of law and drew on binding and non-binding legal sources from the European Union and the Council of Europe, as well as legal theory, to concretise its core principles into requirements that public authorities must abide by. By respecting these requirements, public authorities not only fulfil their rule of law obligations, but they also enable the protective role that the rule of law plays in constitutional liberal democracies, safeguarding both human rights and democracy. My analysis of the rule of law's six principles revealed that, just like the concept of the rule of law itself, these principles represent ideals that should be striven towards. Moreover, their fulfilment involves intrinsic challenges, given the normative tensions that are inherent to a pluralistic society governed by general rules requiring concrete application.

Some of these challenges are *external* to the concept of the rule of law. For instance, the increase in the executive's competences that accompanied the welfare state lead to what some have described as an (ever stronger) asymmetry of power between the executive, and the legislative and the judiciary.[268] I also noted how judicial review can be hampered by narrow standing rules, or by the fact that affected persons suffer from a knowledge gap or an incentive gap to initiate legal proceedings.[269] The fulfilment of the rule of law's principles by public authorities also depends on whether they can incorporate them into their internal normative systems, rather than seeing them as externally imposed.[270] Legal obligations can only take one so far; what matters at least as much is the social environment in which public authorities operate.[271] This also implies that public authorities must be allocated sufficient resources – both time-wise and in terms of adequate resourcing – to achieve their tasks in a diligent manner, and in a way that fosters not only procedural but also substantive rationality.

The achievement of the rule of law is however also dependent on overcoming certain *internal* challenges, which are part of the rule of law's very concept. Rather

[268] Reijer Passchier, *Artificiële intelligentie en de rechtsstaat* (Boom 2021).

[269] Galligan also notes that, more generally, "*there is reason to doubt that [judicial review] has more than marginal impact on the way administrative bodies operate*". See Galligan, 'Public Administration and the Tendency to Authoritarianism' (n 55) 198.

[270] Galligan puts it as follows:

> The problem can be put in terms of competing norms; the norms of administrative justice [such as the rule of law] are external and compete with norms that are generated internally. The assimilation of the external norms and their replacement of incompatible internal norms is difficult to achieve, and is a process about which we have limited knowledge. And yet that process is the key to countering the authoritarian tendencies within administrative bureaucracies.
>
> (ibid)

[271] Tamanaha conceptualises this as the need for a "*shared cultural belief*" in the rule of law, in (n 26) 246.

than being clear-cut, the requirements associated with its six principles are imbued with notions that are not always reconcilable and that necessitate delicate trade-offs. For instance, the principle of legality requires a balance between the law's broadness and prescriptiveness. It is only by setting out broader rules with general applicability that the law can be tailored to specific cases that are not all foreseeable in advance. The goal that this principle serves is, after all, not to essentialise and idealise the law, but to help achieve the rule of law's overarching aims. Similarly, the fact that public authorities must apply the law in a way that ensures legal certainty – including stability, foreseeability, consistency, publicity and intelligibility – serves the purpose of ensuring that individuals can autonomously and freely plan their lives in accordance with the law, with legitimate expectations about its effects. Yet this very purpose also implies that, sometimes, changed or unforeseen circumstances require a certain level of flexibility and adaptability to continue achieving the law's normative aims despite the new situation. Moreover, while clear procedures and routinised decision-making processes can help public officials to act in a non-arbitrary and non-discriminatory manner, some level of discretion remains necessary, as it enables officials to balance competing interests in specific situations and soften the law's hard edges.

In sum, there is a fine line between too little and too much precision, too little and too much stability, and too little and too much discretion. Overcoming these tensions may be a challenge, yet this should not be seen as a weakness of the rule of law, but rather as a strength – or, as Hildebrandt puts it, "*a feature, not a bug*".[272] By navigating these tensions and balancing them in concrete situations, the law can fulfil its protective role in an ever-changing environment. Public authorities should hence not seek to undo these tensions – or worse, to disguise them – but they should aim to strike, in each context, the right balance between extremes in order to safeguard the rule of law's spirit. Put differently, a marriage must be found between rules and discretion – whereby it should be stressed that marriage is a perpetual dance, not a one-shot game,[273] and that it requires continuous work rather than quick fixes. Certainly, it may not always be the happiest of marriages, but some mutual understanding is needed, for their divorce would either result in a rule *by* law (if the focus shifts entirely to the 'rules') or in no rules at all (if the focus shifts entirely to 'discretion'). The rule *of* law is thus the middle way that public authorities should strive for, by embracing rather than erasing the tensions inherent thereto.

[272] See Mireille Hildebrandt, 'Understanding Law and the Rule of Law: A Plea to Augment CS Curricula' (2021) 64 Communications of the ACM 28.

[273] This draws on a metaphor proposed by Karen Yeung.

4

From Rule of Law to Algorithmic Rule by Law

In Chapter 3, I concretised the six principles that constitute the rule of law in the EU legal order in order to develop a normative analytical framework for the purpose of this book's discussion. Drawing on this framework, in this chapter I can now revisit each of these principles and carry out a systematic assessment of how public authorities' reliance on algorithmic regulation can adversely affect them (Section 4.1). I then propose a theory of harm that conceptualises this threat, by juxtaposing the *rule of law* to the *algorithmic rule by law* (Section 4.2). Finally, I summarise these findings and outline the main elements that should be considered when evaluating the aptness of the current legal framework to address this threat (Section 4.3).

4.1 ALGORITHMIC REGULATION AND THE RULE OF LAW

How do the six rule of law principles fare under the increased use of algorithmic systems to inform and adopt administrative acts? In this section, I analyse respectively how such use affects the principle of legality (Section 4.1.1); legal certainty (Section 4.1.2); the prohibition of arbitrariness (Section 4.1.3); equality before the law (Section 4.1.4); judicial review of government action (Section 4.1.5); and the separation of powers (Section 4.1.6). While I assess each of these principles separately, it should be noted that their entwined nature and common purpose renders many observations relevant across the board.

In my evaluation, I draw not only on relevant scholarship, but also on concrete illustrations of how algorithmic regulation is already used by public authorities today. It should be noted that the variety of algorithmic systems deployed in the public sector is enormous, both in terms of technique and purpose, and in terms of application domain. In the sections below, in line with the research aims of this book, I have deliberately selected examples of algorithmic regulation that pose a risk to the rule of law (without claiming the inexistence of illustrations which do not demonstrate such risk). Moreover, I have specifically selected examples of algorithmic regulation in liberal democracies, to highlight that the risks posed thereby are not limited to autocratic regimes. Many of the examples concern the US and the UK, not only because they are frontrunners in the adoption of algorithmic regulation but also for the simple reason that, over the years, information about their adoption of algorithmic regulation has become publicly available. In fact, until today, in many EU countries information about public authorities' use of algorithmic systems is lacking, and research about their effects has not or barely been conducted. For this analysis, I hence selected my examples based on three criteria: (1) the algorithmic system is deployed by a public authority from a liberal democracy, (2) the examples represent uses of algorithmic regulation in different public sector domains and (3) there is some level of information available about the system's use and effects.

Based on my analysis of relevant scholarship and concrete illustrations, I conclude that, in certain situations, public authorities' reliance on algorithmic regulation can indeed hamper the six rule of law principles. This does not mean that all uses of algorithmic regulation *necessarily* lead to an adverse impact on the rule of law – or, more precisely, such generalisation cannot be concluded from my casuistical evaluation. However, it does imply that algorithmic regulation *can* lead to an adverse impact on the rule of law, and that this needs to be taken into account if the aim is to protect this value and the protective role of the law in liberal democracy.

4.1.1 *Legality*

As noted above, the primary requirement of the legality principle entails that public authorities and officials comply with the law, and that the measures they adopt for its implementation are congruent therewith, as well as proportionate. At first sight, reliance on algorithmic systems to inform or take administrative acts could contribute to the better fulfilment of this requirement. To the extent legal rules are structured around *if-then* premises, they could in theory lend themselves rather well to a transformation from text to code.[1] Moreover, reliance on algorithmic systems for the adoption of administrative acts could prevent that public officials deviate from the codified requirements and hence that they deviate from the law, since the relevant legal requirements can be codified straight into the architectural design of the system (*law-by-design*).[2]

[1] See Lawrence Lessig, *Code: And Other Laws of Cyberspace* (Basic Books 1999); Dag Wiese Schartum, 'From Legal Sources to Programming Code: Automatic Individual Decisions in Public Administration and Computers under the Rule of Law' in Woodrow Barfield (ed), *The Cambridge Handbook of the Law of Algorithms* (1st edn, Cambridge University Press 2020). See also Pascal D König 'Dissecting the Algorithmic Leviathan: On the Socio-Political Anatomy of Algorithmic Governance' (2020) 33 Philosophy & Technology 467, 470.

[2] See, e.g., Daria Gritsenko and Matthew Wood, 'Algorithmic Governance: A Modes of Governance Approach' (2022) 16 Regulation & Governance 45.

Indeed, the very ontology of code leads to the fact that, once legal rules are codified, their prescriptive nature actually becomes descriptive.[3] Legal rules are then no longer normatively guiding the actions or decisions of public officials, but they are applied almost in real time by an algorithmic system. This can be a desirable feature if the aim is to counter rule-deviating behaviour. Moreover, even where an algorithmic system is only used to inform an administrative act rather than to adopt one, public officials that intend to deviate from the algorithmic suggestion may face an additional hurdle to do so, as the deviation from a pre-codified norm typically requires an additional step, for instance in the form of a justification that enables one to override the system. Consequently, reliance on algorithmic systems could deter the deviation from codified norms in both direct and indirect ways, and thus theoretically also contribute to the deterrence of illegal or corrupt behaviour by public officials.[4] Unfortunately, these very 'advantages' can also be considered as problematic, and as potentially hindering the fulfilment of the legality principle.

4.1.1.a Lost in Translation

The aspiration to codify legal rules and concepts in order to automate administrative acts is not as forthright as it seems. Transforming legal text to code requires a translation process, as the law rests on linguistic concepts that embody social constructs, which are open ended in terms of their interpretability.[5] These concepts are naturally understood by human interpreters as belonging to a broader societal context, and as being multi-interpretable. Moreover, within legal texts, a wide variation exists in the use of language, from very open-ended and abstract principles to more specific and prescriptive formulations (evoking the well-known distinction between rules and principles, and their respective merits and pitfalls).[6]

Indeed, legal rules are inherently indeterminate, a feature that Julia Black notes as arising *"in part from the nature of language, in part from their anticipatory nature,*

[3] Laurence Diver, 'Interpreting the Rule(s) of Code: Performance, Performativity, and Production' [2021] MIT Computational Law Report 2 <https://law.mit.edu/pub/interpretingtherulesofcode/release/1> 6. As regards the law and its effects, it can be noted that Mireille Hildebrandt draws a distinction between the *descriptive* nature of [law as] speech acts (whereby legal terms can be used to *describe* a particular situation) and the *performative* nature of speech acts (whereby legal terms, when certain conditions are met, can give rise to '*legal effect*'). Both can, however, be distinguished from the mere *prescriptive* nature of legal terms, serving to provide *normative guidance* on how one ought to act, without immediately attaching legal effects to behaviour that deviates from such guidance. See in this regard Mireille Hildebrandt, *Law for Computer Scientists and Other Folk* (Oxford University Press 2020) 20–21.

[4] See, e.g., Per Aarvik, 'Artificial Intelligence – A Promising Anti-Corruption Tool in Development Settings?' (Chr Michelsen Institute 2019).

[5] See also HLA Hart, *The Concept of Law* (3rd ed., Oxford University Press 2012) 129.

[6] See in this regard Julia Black, *Rules and Regulators* (Clarendon 1997). See also Bronwen Morgan and Karen Yeung, *An Introduction to Law and Regulation: Text and Materials* (1st edn, Cambridge University Press 2007) 153 and following.

and in part because they rely on others for their application."[7] She therefore underlines the need for a 'sympathetic interpreter' of legal rules to ensure they are applied in the way that was intended. According to her, "*problems of inclusiveness and determinacy or certainty can be addressed by interpreting the rule in accordance with its underlying aim. By contrast, the purpose of the rule could be defeated if the rule is interpreted literally, if things suppressed by the generalization remain suppressed.*"[8] To make this more concrete, consider the example I provided in Section 2.3 regarding the legal rule in the area of Belgian migration law, which grants migrants in Belgium the possibility to apply for a residence permit under the condition that '*exceptional circumstances*' justify the submission of such application.[9] The legislator purposelessly used a broad legal term rather than making a list of all situations that are considered exceptional, thereby enabling the accommodation of circumstances that might not have been foreseen when the rule was adopted, yet which subsequently present themselves as exceptional and justify the granting of a residence permit. The interpreter of the rule, namely the relevant public authority, can hence interpret the term 'exceptional circumstance' in various ways,[10] as long as such interpretation is congruent with the law's purpose and with other legal norms.

Code, in contrast, is far more rigid. Ultimately it is expressed in zeroes and ones, and it hence requires substantially more precision.[11] This means that certain interpretative decisions need to be made *upfront*, since the rich openness of text cannot fully be captured in code. Accordingly, in the course of the codification process, some nuances and potential modes of interpretation will inevitably get lost in translation.[12] The legal concepts that are codified often concern complex social phenomena that cannot be readily expressed in a 'data-fiable' and computable

7 Black, *Rules and Regulators* (n 6) 10.

8 See ibid 12. See also the discussion *supra*, in Section 3.3.1. Julia Black puts it as follows,

> in forming the generalization, which is the operative basis of the rule, only some features of the particular event or object are focused on and are then projected onto future events, beyond the particulars which served as the paradigm or archetype for the formation of the generalization. The generalizations in rules are thus simplifications of complex events, objects or courses of behaviour. Aspects of those events will thus be left out, or 'suppressed' by the generalization. Further, the generalization, being necessarily selective, will also include some properties which will in some circumstances be irrelevant.
> (See ibid 7.)

9 Article 9 bis of the Law of 15 December 1980 on access to the territory, residence, settlement and removal of foreign nationals.

10 While the term 'exceptional circumstance' is fairly broad, as stressed *supra* in Section 2.3.3, also more precise legal concepts are open to multiple interpretations and might see their meaning change over time.

11 See also Bert-Jaap Koops, 'The (In)Flexibility of Techno-Regulation and the Case of Purpose-Binding' (2011) 5 Legisprudence 171.

12 Nathalie A Smuha, 'The Human Condition in an Algorithmized World: A Critique through the Lens of 20th-Century Jewish Thinkers and the Concepts of Rationality, Alterity and History' (Institute of Philosophy, KU Leuven 2021) 32.

format which, as alreadydiscussed, means that reliance on (inevitably imperfect) proxies is typically warranted, and that certain interpretative choices in this regard need to be made.[13] In the example of the migration law rule, if its application were to be automatised in the context of a hypothetical algorithmic recommendation system, a translation will need to be made from law to code as to what is considered an 'exceptional circumstance' so as to qualify for a residence application, and which proxies can help determine this. Inevitably, this translation will *include* circumstances that the interpreter is able and willing to anticipate when the system is developed, and *exclude* circumstances which the interpreter did not consider (or did not wish to consider). These normatively relevant choices will then be embedded into the system, and automatise the rule's interpretation as decided at that point in time.

The question is then: how exactly does this translation and interpretation process occur in the context of algorithmic regulation? Through which procedure is it decided how textual concepts are essentialised into binary code, and how is it decided which quantifiable proxies are adequate to capture non-readily codifiable phenomena? Who is responsible for these choices? How can it be ensured that they are made, in Black's words, by a 'sympathetic interpreter'? And who oversees these choices and makes sure that they comply with the law, and that the algorithmic rules through which they are implemented are congruent and proportionate?

In non-algorithmic context, the CJEU already cautioned against reliance on quantitative criteria to assess complex qualitative phenomena, stating that this threatens to reduce the protection that individuals may need. The case at hand concerned an application for subsidiary protection lodged by an individual, based on the asserted existence of a "*serious and individual threat by reason of indiscriminate violence in situations of armed conflict*".[14] The relevant public authority rejected the application based on a single quantitative criterion (the ratio between the number of casualties in the relevant area and the total number of individuals composing the population of that area) rather than conducting a comprehensive assessment of the particular circumstances of the individual case.[15] While this case

[13] See *supra*, Section 2.2.5.

[14] See in this regard Case C-901/19, CF, *DN v Bundesrepublik Deutschland*, 10 June 2021, ECLI: EU:C:2021:472, §15. See also the analysis of M van Harn and KM Zwaan, 'Kwantificeren is geen kwalificeren: de uitspraak van het Hof van Justitie inzake de vaststelling van willekeurig geweld (art. 15c-situaties)' (2021) 27 Nederlands tijdschrift voor Europees Recht 211.

[15] The Court stated in §35 of the judgment that

> The systematic application by the competent authorities of a Member State of a single quantitative criterion, which may be of questionable reliability in view of the specific difficulty of identifying objective and independent sources of information close to areas of armed conflict, such as a minimum number of civilian casualties injured or deceased, in order to refuse the grant of subsidiary protection, is likely to lead national authorities to refuse to grant international protection in breach of the Member States' obligation to identify persons genuinely in need of that subsidiary protection.

did not involve algorithmic regulation, it demonstrates how the same quantitative and restrictive logic that underpins algorithmic regulation can undermine the law's protection. Moreover, with the use of algorithmic systems, this problem only risks being exacerbated. First, such systems enable decision-making on a much wider scale. And second, the fact that such systems can rely on *multiple* quantitative criteria might give a false impression of higher accuracy and objectivity, even if these criteria might still concern factors that do not necessarily relate to the individual subjected to the system. What happens if this quantification becomes not only ubiquitous and normalised, but also automated? How do we ensure that the difference between 'calculating' and making a judgment or assessment is not forgotten precisely because of this normalisation?

If the system is primarily knowledge-driven, the choices made by the system's developers are in principle rendered explicit into the model, as they need to reflect on the criteria they will use before codifying. For instance, in the Belgian migration law example, choices would need to be made in advance as regards the type of circumstances or events that qualify as sufficiently 'exceptional' to justify a residence permit, and which datapoints can demonstrate the presence of such circumstances. Yet the question remains: who makes this choice? On which basis? How is it justified? How can it be ensured that this choice is made appropriately and in compliance with the law? And who verifies the interpretation of the law?

If the system is primarily data-driven, the codification of relevant criteria and categories is not always delineated in advance, but can be suggested by the system itself based on patterns it identifies in the data it is fed. The contours of the system's apprehended reality hence depend upon the patterns it may or may not pick up, which in turn depends on how the system was designed and how the data was gathered and selected in the first place.[16] Moreover, data-driven categorisations can subsequently be incorporated into knowledge-driven systems, using them as a basis for reasoning and inference-drawing. Accordingly, regardless of the type of system, the choices made by its developers regarding the dataset to be used, the design of the algorithm and the optimisation function will be highly relevant to influence the outcomes of the administrative act.

Importantly, information that may be evident for human beings (given the broader knowledge and 'common sense' that human beings have about society) may not necessarily be 'understood' by the algorithmic system, which can only rely on the concepts that it was trained on or programmed with, and has no understanding of the meaning behind those concepts.[17] This limitation can be problematic when it leads to an algorithmic outcome that is not congruent with the legal rule it is meant to apply, and hence does not align with the principle of legality.

[16] Smuha, 'The Human Condition in an Algorithmized World' (n 12) 32.

[17] See also Gary Marcus and Ernest Davis, *Rebooting AI: Building Artificial Intelligence We Can Trust* (Penguin Random House 2020).

An illustration of this problem can be found with Idaho's algorithmic system that was used to determine benefits budgets for disabled adults, as briefly mentioned in Chapter 2.[18] In the course of the class action litigation that was initiated by those who suddenly saw their budgets being cut, despite their medical needs, several deficiencies of the system came to the surface, including one that defied any logical human reasoning. As explained by Restrepo Amariles:

> Likely a product of the multi-collinearity issues, there were several regression coefficients wherein the algebraic sign was the opposite of that expected (that is, an input decreased the budget when one would expect it to increase instead). For example, an indication that a participant has "other neurological impairment(s)" reduced a self-directed budget by $8,095, and high-level needs for Total Support with Laundry and Assistance in Feeding similarly had negative impacts of $4,201 and $5,715, respectively. Decreasing a budget in response to more severe needs seems deeply counter-intuitive and indicates a structural flaw with the prediction tool.[19]

While for a human case assessor it would have been evident that people with additional impairments would require *more* rather than *less* monetary aid, the algorithmic system's flaw resulted in the exact opposite result, demonstrating that, inevitably, certain elements can get lost in translation.[20] Indeed, "*when a computer learns and consequently builds its own representation of a classification decision, it does so without regard for human comprehension*".[21]

4.1.1.b From Legality to Legalism

I observed in Chapter 3 how the rule of law is, in essence, a middle-ground between the rule *by* law (where rules are applied without any form of discretion and nuance, even if they may be unjust or lead to unjust results) and the total absence of rules. In this context, I also explained that there is a good reason why, to achieve the rule of law and the principle of legality, rules and discretion ought to coexist. However, an

[18] See *supra*, Section 2.2.2. See also Jay Stanley, 'Pitfalls of Artificial Intelligence Decisionmaking Highlighted in Idaho ACLU Case' (*American Civil Liberties Union*, 2 June 2017) <www.aclu.org/blog/privacy-technology/pitfalls-artificial-intelligence-decisionmaking-highlighted-idaho-aclu-case>.

[19] David Restrepo Amariles, 'Algorithmic Decision Systems: Automation and Machine Learning in the Public Administration' in Woodrow Barfield (ed), *The Cambridge Handbook of the Law of Algorithms* (Cambridge University Press 2020) 289.

[20] As previously noted, an algorithmic system will not be able to interpret legal concepts as social constructs that only reflect a partial view of the world, and will not understand the *meaning* behind the syntax. See in this regard also David Cole, 'The Chinese Room Argument' in Edward N Zalta (ed), *The Stanford Encyclopedia of Philosophy* (Winter 2020, Metaphysics Research Lab, Stanford University 2020) <https://plato.stanford.edu/archives/win2020/entries/chinese-room/>.

[21] Jenna Burrell, 'How the Machine "Thinks": Understanding Opacity in Machine Learning Algorithms' (2016) 3 Big Data & Society 1, 10.

overly rigid codified translation of the law risks reducing legality to a form of legalism,[22] precisely because of the lack of room for discretion and critical reflection about the underlying purpose that the rule should serve. As noted by Laurence Diver, code tends to be legalistic in light of its inherent 'ruleishness'.[23] And whereas in non-algorithmic settings the legalistic application of rules can be offset by accommodating nuanced interpretations and modes of application where need be, the rigidity of code does not easily enable such interpretative flexibility.[24]

Consider the example of Indiana, where a plan was launched in 2006 to outsource and automate the eligibility checks for several welfare programs, including Medicaid and food stamps. As explained by Virginia Eubanks, the tender request specified that the automation process aimed to "*reduce fraud, curtail spending, and move clients off the welfare rolls*".[25] This move followed the finding that two employees of the Family and Social Service Administration (FSSA) of Indianapolis had committed fraud, which lead politicians to claim that the welfare system was fraudulent and "*irretrievably broken*".[26] The hope was not only that automation would reduce the risk of fraud, cut costs and increase process efficiency (especially given the high workload on public officials and increasing backlogs), but it was also claimed that this would free up time for the remaining public officials to work more closely with clients.[27]

The algorithmic system was however riddled with system failures and technical errors, which led to erroneous denials of benefits, and made the application process far more difficult. Besides technical glitches and integration problems, Eubanks explains how one of the main causes of error was "*the result of inflexible rules that interpreted any deviation from the newly rigid application process, no matter how inconsequential or inadvertent (including missing a phone call from a caseworker) as an active refusal to cooperate*".[28] And once a refusal to cooperate was determined, this led to the straight denial of eligibility. Accordingly, through an overly legalistic interpretation and codification of rules, persons in need were automatically denied benefits, and caseworkers did not have the flexibility to easily remedy this problem where needed. Such use of algorithmic regulation hence led to a disproportionate application of the law, which runs counter to the principle of legality, which – as

[22] Definitions of legalism vary, yet Judith Shklar has influentially defined it as "*the ethical attitude that holds moral conduct to be a matter of rule following, and moral relationships to consist of duties and rights determined by rules.*" See Judith N Shklar, *Legalism: Law, Morals, and Political Trials* (Harvard University Press 1986) 1.

[23] Diver (n 3) 3.

[24] See also Zenon Bankowski and Burkhard Schafer, 'Double-Click Justice: Legalism in the Computer Age' (2007) 1 Legisprudence 31.

[25] Virginia Eubanks, *Automating Inequality – How High-Tech Tools Profile, Police and Punish the Poor* (Picador 2019) 46.

[26] ibid.

[27] ibid 47.

[28] ibid 51.

discussed above – requires public authorities to make "*a proper balance between any adverse effects which their decision has on the rights or interests of private persons and the purpose they pursue*".[29]

One might contend that this can be avoided by simply codifying better or plural interpretations of the law, based on the variability of potentially applicable situations. However, this would require the coders of the algorithmic system to foresee each and every possible situation that might emerge in the future in advance – which is impossible.[30] Choices therefore inevitably need to be made, and since algorithmic systems are not only based on pre-programmed algorithms but also lack any human understanding, it is not possible to question or challenge them by explaining that the situation at hand is not accommodated by the codified rules, or that it requires a different legal application. Moreover, even when the algorithmic system only *informs* an administrative act rather than adopting one, public officials may still be discouraged from deviating from the proposed outcome, thereby reinforcing a legalistic approach. This discouragement may stem from the pressure of KPI's that public officials need to meet in light of efficiency goals, such as the speedy handling of case files, from the lack of sufficient information or understanding about the system's operations to challenge its merits, or from more general deference to the system's 'cognitive superiority' and 'air of authority' arising from the 'objective' mathematical rules underlying its functioning.[31]

Notwithstanding the need to find a middle ground between rules and discretion, the 'ruleishness' of code risks skewing the balance entirely towards the *rules* side of the spectrum. This also leads to a problematic tension with the principle of proportionality, which is part of the legality principle and acts as a necessary softener of legal rules' rigidity. Indeed, public authorities have the responsibility to ensure that the measures they take when they apply general laws to individual cases are proportionate, and that they take into account the factors relevant to the case.[32] If no such proportionality assessment takes place and the law is mechanically applied, the hard edges of the over- and under-inclusive nature of law are left untouched, opening the door to adverse effects on those subjected to it.

This is precisely what happened in the Dutch child allowance case, which I briefly mentioned in Chapter 3.[33] After it was revealed in 2013 that a criminal

[29] Committee of Ministers of the Council of Europe, 'Recommendation CM/Rec(2007)7 of the Committee of Ministers to Member States on Good Administration' (2007) 8. See also *supra*, Section 3.3.1.

[30] Recall in this regard also the quote by HLA Hart that, after all, "*we are men, not gods*". See Hart (n 5) 128.

[31] See *supra*, Section 2.2.6.

[32] See also Committee of Ministers of the Council of Europe, 'Recommendation No. R (80) 2 of the Committee of Ministers Concerning the Exercise of Discretionary Powers by Administrative Authorities', Adopted by the Committee of Ministers on 11 March 1980 at the 316th meeting of the Ministers' Deputies, 1980.

[33] See *supra*, Section 3.1.5. See also Parliamentary Inquiry Committee, 'Unprecedented Injustice' (House of Representatives of the States General 2020) 35 510, no. 1.

scheme had defrauded the Dutch state of social aid payments for years, the Dutch tax authority doubled down on tackling fraud and started taking a more severe stance,[34] including in the area of childcare allowance, which is a means-based type of allowance. Applications for such allowance were only minimally verified, so that nearly any applicant would receive an 'advance' on the allowance, after which it would be verified if any revision of the paid allowance was needed and if any recovery was to be paid back to the state. At the time, the relevant law stated that: "*If a revision of an allowance or a revision of an advance results in an amount to be recovered or if a settlement of an advance with an allowance leads to this, the person concerned shall owe the entire amount of the recovery.*"[35] As the Venice Commission noted, "*this provision was interpreted by the Tax and Customs Administration as the so-called 'all or nothing approach', so that even if a parent had acted in good faith but neither the parent or the childminder could provide proof of hours used or parental contribution etc., the parent had to repay the full amount for the whole year*".[36] Evidently, the public authority's narrow interpretation of the legal rule led to high demands for repayment.[37] Yet this problem was exacerbated by the fact that it relied on an algorithmic system, enabling it to significantly scale up its investigations and targeting practices.[38]

When the dramatic consequences of this legalistic application of the law came to light, a Parliamentary investigation was conducted. Many families underwent significant financial hardship and, in some cases, children were even taken away from their parents who could no longer afford to take care of them, which resulted in child neglect. Commenting on how things could go so wrong for so long, the committee in charge of the investigation noted that "*the administrative justice system neglected its important function of safeguarding the legal rights of individual citizens*" inter alia by "*perpetuating the ruthless application of the legislation on childcare allowance, over and above what was prescribed by law*".[39] In its opinion on this case, the Venice Commission was particularly critical of the public authority's refusal to conduct a proportionality test[40] regarding the measures they were imposing and

[34] Richard Barrett and others, 'The Netherlands: Opinion on the Legal Protection of Citizens' (Venice Commission 2021) Opinion no. 1031/2021 CDL-AD(2021)031 4.

[35] See Article 26 of the General Act on Means-Tested Benefits, which entered into force in 2005. See ibid.

[36] ibid 4.

[37] According to the Venice Commission's Opinion, based on the Parliamentary Investigation, 15 per cent of the parents were subjected to repayment requests. See ibid 4.

[38] Which, as will be discussed *infra* in Section 4.1.4, also appear to have been potentially discriminatory.

[39] Parliamentary Inquiry Committee (n 33) 7.

[40] In addition, it should also be noted that the Venice Commission deplored the fact that the courts who reviewed the administrative decision did not apply a proportionality test – even though it is required by virtue of international law and the rule of law principles – for the mere reason that the legislator had excluded the application of such a test in the relevant legislation. See Barrett and others (n 34) 21.

their effect on the affected families. Instead, they blindly applied the law in a rigid and legalistic manner, leading to a rule *by* law approach rather than respecting the rule of law.[41]

While this case shows that public authorities do not need to rely on algorithmic systems to adopt an overly legalistic interpretation of the law, it also demonstrates that the use of such systems can drastically increase the scale of the law's legalistic application, and that it eliminates the possibility for a sound proportionality assessment of individual cases. Furthermore, besides making the scaled application of legalistic rules cheaper, the opaque nature and use of algorithmic systems also makes the identification and problematisation thereof more difficult, thus perpetuating the law's disproportionate application. In sum, by codifying a particular interpretation of text-natured law into code, the law's meaning becomes fixed and unitary, and is thereby essentialised. Without the possibility to correct the adverse effects of such over- and under-inclusivity, it becomes much more difficult to ensure a proportionate application of the law, and to ensure the alignment of algorithmic regulation with the rule of law.

4.1.1.c Loss of Process Transparency

Besides matters of interpretation and correctness, the question also arises of how the translation from law to code can take place in a manner that respects the principle of transparency. As noted in Chapter 3, transparency is a recurring requirement that can be found under the principle of legality (pertaining to the transparency of the law-making process), the principle of legal certainty (pertaining to the transparent character of the law itself) and the principle of non-arbitrariness (pertaining to the transparent nature of the law's application and the justification of its manner of implementation). My focus here is on the first of these. The translation from law to code can be seen as part of the law-making process, given that it constitutes the first step before public authorities can start applying it to legal subjects. The codification process of algorithmic regulation is typically not a public endeavour, but a rather 'technical' matter. Simply put: it belongs to the realm of coders,[42] by which I intend to denote technical experts (rather than trained public officials) who make choices about the system's design and development, including the datasets that will be used and the labels assigned to them, the algorithmic model that is deployed and its

[41] In its opinion about the childcare allowance case, it pointed to the Venice Commission's Rule of Law Checklist, which states that an 'exercise of power that leads to substantively unfair, unreasonable, irrational or oppressive decisions violates the Rule of Law'. It seems safe to conclude, as several Dutch authorities have done – including the Council of State's Administrative Jurisdiction Division in two judgments in 2019, that applying the 'all or nothing' approach falls under this definition. (See ibid 24.)

[42] See in this regard also the conceptualisation of the 'coding elite' by Jenna Burrell and Marion Fourcade, 'The Society of Algorithms' (2021) 47 Annual Review of Sociology 213.

optimisation function, and the translation process from legal text or other linguistic concepts to code.

These choices are often opaque, as the coders do not necessarily make their decisions (and the justification for those decisions) explicit. However, if there is no transparency about this process, it is far more difficult to exercise oversight over the executive's interpretative choices and ensure they respect the rule of law. More generally, transparency is also needed to ensure that the system does not contain errors, bugs, or erroneous translations that may be unintended yet can have an adverse impact.[43] Mistakes can happen, and errors also occur without any mediation from algorithmic systems. Yet errors can be reproduced in the systems that humans build, and in that case, the speed and scale of the system's decision-making process can render the error's effects much more problematic. In addition, the larger the amount and variety of data that public authorities gather and process about citizens, the more room there is for mistakes. As stated by Peeters and Widlak: "*There are few barriers for an error to diffuse via data exchange and exclude a citizen from services and overwhelm a citizen with administrative burdens. There are, however, many barriers for a correction to have the same, but opposite, automatic effect.*"[44]

While transparency is no panacea, providing insight about the interpretative choices of the translation, the data and proxies that are being used and the manner in which the system functions, at least makes it easier to identify and correct errors, and to discuss and possibly contest the validity of the assumptions underlying the algorithmic model. Yet public authorities do not always provide transparency about the systems they use, let alone about the translation process preceding their use. Consider, in this regard, the algorithmic system used in Belgium to assist with the identification of social security fraud, known as the OASIS tool.[45] The system is primarily data-driven and relies on large databases to profile citizens, including the categorisation of potential fraudsters.[46] As noted by Elise Degrave, the system targets "*mainly the poorest people*", focusing, for instance, on the detection of fraudulent labour providers and bankruptcies, and domicile fraud aimed at securing more social assistance than one is entitled to.[47] Degrave explains how her many attempts

[43] See also Karl de Fine Licht and Jenny de Fine Licht, 'Artificial Intelligence, Transparency, and Public Decision-Making' (2020) 35 AI & Society 917.

[44] Rik Peeters and Arjan Widlak, 'The Digital Cage: Administrative Exclusion through Information Architecture – The Case of the Dutch Civil Registry's Master Data Management System' (2018) 35 Government Information Quarterly 175, 176.

[45] Elise Degrave, 'The Use of Secret Algorithms to Combat Social Fraud in Belgium' (2020) 1 European Review of Digital Administration & Law 167.

[46] For an overview of algorithmic fraud detection in Belgian federal administrations, see Anthony Simonofski, Thomas Tombal and Pauline Willem, 'Policy Report on Big Data Policy of the Belgian Federal Administrations' (BELSPO 2020), <https://soc.kuleuven.be/io/digi4fed/doc/d1-2-policy-report-on-big-data-policy-of-the.pdf>.

[47] Degrave (n 45) 170–71. See also Elise Degrave and Amelie Lachapelle, 'Le droit d'accès du contribuable à ses données à caractère personnel et la lutte contre la fraude fiscale' (2014) 5 Revue générale du contentieux fiscal.

to gain more information about the system (through the exercise of her right to access to administrative documents) were unsuccessful, either because the authority considered "*the document could be a 'source of misunderstanding' within the meaning of the law on the publicity of the administration*" or because, upon appeal, the Commission for Access to Administrative Documents found that "*the authority addressed was not an administrative one and that the requirements of transparency did not therefore apply*".[48] She concludes that "*in short, information about OASIS seems to be hidden*", as "*we have not been able to access an official document clearly explaining this tool*".[49] If a highly educated law professor who is specialised in public information law does not manage to obtain information about an algorithmic system, one can imagine how much more difficult it must be for people who are in a more vulnerable position and even more likely to be adversely impacted by such a system.

In addition to the unwillingness to provide information, the non-transparency of algorithmic regulation can also be related to the private nature of the system's development process.[50] The example of the 'Children's Safeguarding Profiling System' used by the Hackney County Council (UK) is telling in this regard.[51] The system was developed in cooperation with Ernst & Young and tech company Xantura to identify children at risk of maltreatment and families who need additional support.[52] When researchers[53] submitted a Freedom of Information Request to the London Borough of Hackney, they received the following response:

> Xantura and London Borough of Hackney are working together to develop the system as development partners, but Xantura anticipates operating on a commercial basis. We believe that to reveal detailed workings of the system would be damaging to their commercial interests and, while the project is in pilot phase, of limited public use. We therefore believe that the public interest in seeing any operating

48 Degrave (n 45) 171.

49 ibid 172.

50 See also Jenna Burrell, 'How the Machine "Thinks": Understanding Opacity in Machine Learning Algorithms' (2016) 3 Big Data & Society 205395171562251, 639; Abe Chauhan, 'Towards the Systemic Review of Automated Decision-Making Systems' [2021] Judicial Review 1, 4.

51 Niamh McIntyre and David Pegg, 'Councils Use 377,000 People's Data in Efforts to Predict Child Abuse' *The Guardian* (16 September 2018) <www.theguardian.com/society/2018/sep/16/councils-use-377000-peoples-data-in-efforts-to-predict-child-abuse>.

52 Luke Stevenson, 'Artificial Intelligence: How a Council Seeks to Predict Support Needs for Children and Families' (*Community Care*, 1 March 2018) <www.communitycare.co.uk/2018/03/01/artificial-intelligence-council-seeks-predict-support-needs-children-families/>.

53 See Lina Dencik, Arne Hintz, Joanna Redden and Harry Warne, 'Data Scores as Governance: Investigating Uses of Citizen Scoring in Public Services' (Data Justice Lab, Cardiff University 2018) 59, <https://datajustice.files.wordpress.com/2018/12/data-scores-as-governance-project-report2.pdf>. See also Joanna Redden, Lina Dencik and Harry Warne, 'Datafied Child Welfare Services: Unpacking Politics, Economics and Power' (2020) 41 Policy Studies 507.

> manuals is outweighed by Xantura's commercial interests and exempt this part of the request under Section 43 of the Freedom of Information Act.[54]

Accordingly, the commercial interests of a private company, in charge of highly impactful decisions taken by a public authority in the public interest, were prioritised over transparency towards citizens.

Besides the risk of errors or unconscious bias, transparency can also help counter the risk of *intended* mistranslations. Indeed, as Plato's story of the ring of Gyges shows: a lack of transparency can not only cover up mistakes, but it can unfortunately also be exploited to increase power.[55] The deliberate codification of a rule into an unduly narrow, arbitrary or otherwise illegal interpretation can take place *either* by the private developers of the system, for instance with the aim of translating the rules in their private interests, *or* by the public authority, for instance with the aim of codifying an interpretation that helps it consolidate power or disadvantage political opponents, minorities or others that may challenge its actions. Countering this risk requires oversight during the design and translation phase, rather than only during the period that the system is already being deployed at scale.

At the same time, it must be acknowledged that the risk of abuse is an inevitable reality, and that any oversight and transparency measures will always be subject to limitations. Therefore, given the vastness of the adverse consequences in case things go wrong, there may be administrative acts for which the deployment of algorithmic regulation is undesirable altogether. Pursuant to the principle of legality's requirement to ensure a *participatory* law-making process,[56] the desirability of algorithmic regulation in light of its potential impact should be the subject of public deliberation.[57] This also implies that citizens should have a say about the administrative acts that can or should be algorithmised *prior* to the implementation of algorithmic regulation.

4.1.2 *Legal Certainty*

Legal rules need to be clear and sufficiently precise to make the way in which they will be applied predictable. Furthermore, they must be applied consistently, enabling legal subjects to have legitimate expectations about the rules they will be

[54] Aleksi Knuutila, 'Documents Relating to the Children's Safeguarding Profiling System – A Freedom of Information Request to Hackney Borough Council' (*WhatDoTheyKnow*, 15 January 2018) <www.whatdotheyknow.com/request/documents_relating_to_the_childr>.

[55] See Plato, *The Republic* (Benjamin Jowett tr, Dover Publications, Inc 2000) Book 2.

[56] See *supra*, Section 3.3.1.

[57] See also Venice Commission, 'Rule of Law Checklist' (Council of Europe 2016) Study no. 711/2013 CDL-AD(2016)007rev 13. Moreover, the need for public deliberation about algorithmisation has also been stressed in Nathalie A Smuha and others, 'How the EU Can Achieve Legally Trustworthy AI: A Response to the European Commission's Proposal for an Artificial Intelligence Act' (Social Science Research Network 2021) <https://papers.ssrn.com/abstract=3899991> 8.

subjected to and to plan their lives accordingly. At first glance, the application of legal rules by an algorithmic system rather than public officials can contribute to this requirement. As noted in Section 2.3, ensuring the consistent application of a rule is not straightforward when this occurs by mediation of countless public officials who may each have their own way of interpreting a rule, especially if they operate in a decentralised organisational structure.[58] While the routinisation of decision-making by promulgating detailed guidelines can diminish the risk of diverging interpretations, it cannot prevent this from happening altogether. Yet delegating the application of legal rules to an algorithmic system can in principle ensure greater consistency, since the codification process occurs in a centralised manner, with only one 'interpreter' – namely the machine, or rather, the coder – acting as mediator between the rule and *all* legal subjects. In practice, there are, however, several drawbacks that need to be pointed out.

4.1.2.a Fanciful Foreseeability

First, the consistent application of rules is but one of the requirements of the principle of legal certainty and should not be prioritised over the rule of law's overarching aims. It is possible that a change in circumstances or new societal developments require the adapted application of a rule to maintain its original purpose. This is why the rule of law requires that a balance be struck between stability and flexibility. However, once a particular interpretation of the law is codified and its execution is automatised, this balance risks being skewed, as the codification process stabilises and thereby essentialises the legal rule's interpretation.[59] This, in turn, makes it harder for public officials to apply the law to individual cases and adapt the law's interpretation to changing circumstances when needed.

One could counterargue that the system can be programmed to identify and apply different rules based on different situations, yet this still requires a codification of all possible situations in advance, as well as an ex ante decision of the way in which the rule will be applied in those cases. Moreover, there will inevitably be cases that fall outside these codified situations, and that will not be adequately dealt with based on those prior decisions.[60] Accordingly, those who will not fall into the pre-established categories of persons and rule applications risk encountering a significant disadvantage.[61] Contrary to a public official, the algorithmic system that informs or adopts the

[58] See also Nadine van Engen, Bram Steijn and Lars Tummers, 'Do Consistent Government Policies Lead to Greater Meaningfulness and Legitimacy on the Front Line?' (2019) 97 Public Administration 97; See also Andrew B Whitford, 'Decentralization and Political Control of the Bureaucracy' (2002) 14 Journal of Theoretical Politics 167.

[59] See also Diver (n 3) 9.

[60] See *supra*, Section 3.3.1.

[61] See in this regard also Peeters and Widlak (n 44); Smuha, 'The Human Condition in an Algorithmized World' (n 12) 32.

administrative act will not be able to take a more flexible and case-by-case approach to address this concern. It is therefore important that consistency is not fetishised in the name of legal certainty. Instead, it must be interpreted as one of various elements that can contribute to the rule of law's overarching aim, tailored to the specific context.

Consider, for instance, an algorithmic system deployed by public authorities in Poland to profile the unemployed and, based on their categorisation, decide on their eligibility for specific programmes aimed at helping them back to the job market through 'labour market programs'.[62] Essentially, the system calculated the 'employment potential' of unemployed individuals. The Polish Ministry of Labor and Social Policy hoped that the system would lead to a more efficient use of limited resources, by allocating more funds for "*those who are particularly distant from the labor market, and less for those who are able to handle finding a job easier*".[63] Besides 'efficiency', one of the reasons cited for the system's introduction was the fact that, previously, local labour offices were already undertaking a form of 'profiling', but they were doing so in an unstructured and inconsistent way. Therefore, "*it could have been the case that the standard or principles of assigning specific active labor market programs to the unemployed varied in different offices.*"[64] To remedy this, the algorithmic system henceforth centrally determined the questions that public officials should ask during their interviews with the unemployed, and subsequently automatically profiled them based on the inputted answers.

However, the Polish NGO Panoptykon who interviewed public officials working with the system and who conducted an extensive investigation, concluded that the proportion of people assigned to particular profiles still varied strongly from one labour office to another, even after the system's introduction.[65] This was, for instance, because public officials did not always interpret or explain the questions uniformly to the citizens "*especially considering high caseloads and time limits for one interview*",[66] nor did the citizens always interpret these questions uniformly, hence leading to differing types of answers and outcomes in similar situations and vice versa. Accordingly, the system failed to lead to 'consistency', demonstrating that the mere use of automated data processing in itself does not necessarily lead to such

62 See AlgorithmWatch, 'Automating Society Report 2020' (2020) 186, <https://automatingsociety.algorithmwatch.org/wp-content/uploads/2020/12/Automating-Society-Report-2020.pdf>.

63 Jędrzej Niklas, Karolina Sztandar and Katarzyna Szymielewicz, 'Profiling the Unemployed in Poland: Social and Political Implications of Algorithmic Decision Making' (Panoptykon 2015) 7, <www.ohchr.org/sites/default/files/Documents/Issues/Poverty/DigitalTechnology/LSE_appendix2.pdf>.

64 ibid 8.

65 As noted by the NGO: "*It turned out that the percentage share of the unemployed assigned to Profile II in the entire group of the unemployed varies among particular labor offices and ranges from 33% to as much as 96% in some offices. In the case of Profile III, this ratio ranges from 4% to 33%.*" See ibid 14.

66 ibid 28.

a result.[67] At the same time, the researchers of Panoptykon also observed that "*the use of algorithmic decision-making can help mask the shortcomings of a given public policy (such as an objective shortage of resources) by limiting options that are available to some categories of citizens and making the management of public resources less transparent*".[68]

It should, moreover, be considered that the concrete effects of a codified rule are not always foreseen or foreseeable in advance. Unintended and unknown bugs in the code might hamper legal certainty, and might lead to unwanted adverse consequences that the coders of the algorithmic system did not predict, let alone the people subjected to the system.[69] In that sense, foreseeability of the rule's application through codification may turn out to be a mere illusion. Furthermore, due to the scaled nature of the system's application, unpredicted adverse effects can affect a vast number of people at the same time. The example of an algorithmic system deployed by the Swedish Public Employment Service is telling in this regard. The system was used to verify whether people who received certain unemployment benefits remained eligible, thereby aiming to 'increase efficiency'.[70] However, due to a flaw in the system, about 70,000 unemployed individuals erroneously stopped receiving their benefits,[71] a flaw that had certainly not been anticipated by the coders when they programmed the system, or it would have been addressed *prior* to its use. Therefore, it is not because a line of code is executed consistently, that it also effectively leads to foreseeability and legal certainty. Also in Austria, public authorities' reliance on a similar algorithmic profiling system to categorise the unemployed based on their job prospects faced significant criticism.[72]

[67] Note that, in the meantime, the system has been scrapped. See Jedrzej Niklas, 'Poland: Government to Scrap Controversial Unemployment Scoring System' (*AlgorithmWatch*, 16 April 2019) <https://algorithmwatch.org/en/poland-government-to-scrap-controversial-unemployment-scoring-system/>.

[68] Niklas, Sztandar and Szymielewicz (n 63) 35. Also here, a request for public information submitted by an NGO, Panoptykon Foundation, was answered negatively, stating that information about the logic of the profiling is not considered 'public information'. It ultimately decided to challenge this decision in court until it managed to obtain information about the system's predetermined questions. See Niklas (n 67).

[69] See also Diver (n 3) 9.

[70] See 'DN Debatt. "Är Sverige Redo Att Låta Maskiner Fatta Besluten?"' *Dagens Nyheter* (17 February 2019) <www.dn.se/debatt/ar-sverige-redo-att-lata-maskiner-fatta-besluten/>.

[71] Tom Wills, 'Sweden: Rogue Algorithm Stops Welfare Payments for up to 70,000 Unemployed' (*AlgorithmWatch*, 25 February 2019) <https://algorithmwatch.org/en/rogue-algorithm-in-sweden-stops-welfare-payments/>.

[72] See, e.g., Doris Allhutter and others, 'Algorithmic Profiling of Job Seekers in Austria: How Austerity Politics Are Made Effective' (2020) 3 Frontiers in Big Data 1 <www.frontiersin.org/article/10.3389/fdata.2020.00005/full>. The system also faced heavy critique for being allegedly discriminatory, for instance against women and people with a disability, see Nicolas Kayser-Bril, 'Austria's Employment Agency Rolls out Discriminatory Algorithm, Sees No Problem' (*AlgorithmWatch*, 2019) <www.algorithmwatch.org/en/austrias-employment-agency-ams-rolls-out-discriminatory-algorithm/>.

Furthermore, when it comes to enhancing legal certainty, a distinction can be made between knowledge-driven and data-driven systems, as the aspired enhancement of consistency will primarily apply to the former (barring, of course, the abovementioned problems, as well as the fact that even in knowledge-driven systems rules can be incorporated that randomise certain outcomes, thereby diluting predictability). As discussed in Section 2.1, data-driven systems do not rely on an ex ante codified model, but instead hinge on a dataset in which patterns are identified and to which weights are assigned, based on which a model is subsequently derived. Accordingly, the rule's application relies on – and is adapted to – the data. The main strength of data-driven systems thus lies in their adaptability to new situations based on new data.[73] While this feature can counter the concern of over-stability and inflexibility, reliance on a data-driven system risks pushing the pendulum entirely the other way, towards too much adaptability and too little predictability. Persons subjected to a data-driven system may find it difficult to know in advance to which category the system will correlate them, and hence to which 'personalised' application of the rule they will be subjected to.

In addition, the rule's application will not hinge on a causal relationship between the rule and the person's behaviour or situation but based on the extent to which that person falls into one of the patterns that the system identified. This in turn depends on the behaviour and situations of persons with a similar profile (where such similarity could depend on factors that are entirely irrelevant to the rule itself). Yet this undermines the entire logic behind the law and its application. In principle, one should derive rights and obligations based on one's own action or situation, not based on how much one shows similarities with other people.[74] To give an example: the entitlement of an ill person to healthcare benefits should hinge on her specific needs rather than on the needs of those people that an algorithm happened to identify as showing certain similarities with her. As cautioned by Restrepo Amariles, the application of the law thereby "*ends up being transformed into a normative correlation of facts*", as citizens are subjected to rules based whether they fall into identified patterns and correlations.[75]

Furthermore, data-driven systems, too, carry certain limitations in terms of flexibility, as they are after all dependent on their programming language and the choices made by coders in terms of the system's design, datasets and model.[76] They are hence still predetermined to some extent, which opens the door to the same concerns, including the risk of bugs in the code that may render the system

[73] See *supra*, Section 2.1.3.

[74] See also Emre Bayamlıoğlu and Ronald Leenes, 'The "Rule of Law" Implications of Data-Driven Decision-Making: A Techno-Regulatory Perspective' (2018) 10 Law, Innovation and Technology 295, 296.

[75] Restrepo Amariles (n 19) 298.

[76] See also Elena Popa, 'Human Goals Are Constitutive of Agency in Artificial Intelligence (AI)' (2021) 34 Philosophy & Technology 1731.

unpredictable and potentially harmful. The fact that system developers typically lack the practice of meticulously tracing and documenting who made which design choices, and for which reasons, only adds to the problem. It complicates the identification of errors, but it also renders the system more vulnerable to (subsequent) non-documented tweaking. Even the system's designers may no longer remember which choices they made. On the one hand,[77] the agility of algorithmic systems and the inherent malleability of software and databases can be seen as a strength, since it allows for their continuous adaptation and improvement. Yet, on the other hand, such agility comes with a price, as the openness of the algorithmic system to continuous adaptation – without adequate traceability – undermines the ability of public authorities and those affected alike to have information about the system's (mal)functioning.[78]

This is an undervalued problem which undermines legal certainty, as also demonstrated by the 'means-testing' algorithmic system introduced in the UK to calculate and allocate welfare benefits, under the heading 'Universal Credit'.[79] Based on 'real-time' information on citizens, drawn from a range of sources and continuously updated, the system calculates each month how many benefits a person is entitled to receive. However, the "*calculation fails to factor in how frequently people are paid, leading it to overestimate their earnings in some months and underestimate them in others. This design flaw has caused irrational fluctuations and reductions in how much benefit people [] receive from month to month*",[80] hence leading to anything but 'certainty' for people about their rights. These fluctuations not only forced certain people to rely on food banks and take on debt to make ends meet, but the uncertainty of how many benefits they will receive each month – hinging on a non-transparent processing of datapoints – has also led to mental health problems and heightened anxiety.[81] In sum, lest public authorities pay due attention to these issues when they implement algorithmic systems for administrative acts, the aspired benefit of increased legal certainty and predictability may be merely fanciful.

4.1.2.b Problematic Preservation of the Past

As noted in Chapter 3, while legal certainty requires a certain level of stability, this requirement must not become so rigid that it undoes the potential for adaptability

77 See *supra*, Section 2.1.

78 Consider in this regard also the discussion *supra* on algorithmic systems as socio-technical infrastructure in Section 2.2, and on the inherent malleability of software in Section 4.1.2.a.

79 See in this regard Richard Pope, 'Universal Credit – Digital Welfare' (PT2 2020) <https://digitalwelfare.report/>.

80 'Automated Hardship: How the Tech-Driven Overhaul of the UK's Social Security System Worsens Poverty' (Human Rights Watch 2020) <www.hrw.org/report/2020/09/29/automated-hardship/how-tech-driven-overhaul-uks-social-security-system-worsens>.

81 ibid.

when a public official notices that the rule's application in a specific situation would undermine the intended purpose of the law. This can occur, for instance, because once the law is actually applied, it becomes clear that it raises unforeseen unintended consequences, or because the context and circumstances in which the law is applied changed in the meantime.[82] After all, the world is not static.

In the previous section, I discussed how the use of algorithmic regulation by public authorities might foster legalism. An additional characteristic of legalism as defined by Judith Shklar, is that it can be associated with a conservative ideology.[83] The rules we ought to conform to were inevitably established in the past, which in turn risks leading to a commitment to the preservation of this past. This can be problematic if those past rules are no longer apt to help us deal with changing developments in the here and now, including new insights about the adverse impact of previously ill-conceived rules, or the impact of new technological developments on society. Note how, in the context of algorithmic regulation, this problem is prevalent not only with knowledge-driven systems where rules are explicitly codified, but also in data-driven systems where rules are 'found' based on patterns identified in a dataset. As this dataset necessarily contains data from the past, a novel interpretation that does justice to evolving situations is near impossible to achieve without the intervention of human assessment and judgment.[84] It is this very ability of interpretative adaptability that risks getting lost, as the automation of administrative action prevents public officials to understand and apply the rules in a manner that meets the changing insights or needs of society.

As a counterargument, one can contend that the adaptation of legal interpretation to changing circumstances should not occur by officials who work for public administrations, but rather by legislators who can revise existing laws through the applicable legislative procedure. It must indeed be acknowledged that the separation of powers can come under pressure if government officials unilaterally decide to change the interpretation of the law as put down by the legislator *contra legem*, merely because they consider that certain circumstances changed. Such an action would be contrary to the rule of law. Yet that is not what this argument is about, for an adapted interpretation need not be *contra legem*, and the changed circumstance need not manifest itself at the level of the general rule but can arise at the level of a concrete situation to which public officials must apply the general rule.[85] It is at the level of the *latter* that discretion should be used – within the confines of the law and

82 See for instance Joanne Conaghan, 'Law, Harm and Redress: A Feminist Perspective' (2002) 22 Legal Studies 319.

83 See Shklar (n 22) 10. See also Robin West, 'Reconsidering Legalism' (2003) 88 Minnesota Law Review 119, 120.

84 See also supra, Section 2.2.3.

85 See supra, Section 3.3.2.

in a manner appropriate for the particular case – to ensure the law's purpose remains attainable.[86]

Finally, one might also contend that an adapted interpretation of a legal rule can be secured through litigation before a court rather than by public officials. While courts can indeed play an important role in this regard, the principle of the separation of powers persists – meaning that this interpretation cannot go *contra legem*, unless it violates a hierarchically higher norm (such as EU primary or secondary law). Moreover, courts can only intervene ex post when the damage of a problematically applied law has already occurred. This is why public authorities need to act diligently when they adopt measures to implement general laws, and need to ensure their measures are proportionate in the case at hand *before* the law's application.[87] While there is certainly a collective responsibility of all branches to adopt, apply and interpret laws in a manner that does not lead to unjust hardship,[88] this does not dilute the responsibility of public authorities whose actions most directly affect legal subjects.

4.1.2.c Loss of Implementation Transparency

When discussing the impact of algorithmic regulation on the legality principle, I explained how transparency regarding the rule-making process can be compromised. Yet in addition to such procedural transparency, also substantive transparency of the rules' content and the way they are implemented and applied may be at risk, which is precisely what the principle of legal certainty aims to protect. The law must be sufficiently clear, intelligible and precise, so that legal subjects can predict how it will affect them and how they need to change or adapt their behaviour to ensure it is in line therewith.[89] This also implies the need for clarity about how the law is *applied* by public authorities. However, if one recalls the earlier discussion about the opacity that often surrounds the use and parameters of algorithmic systems,[90] it is clear that this requirement can come under pressure.

If the law's application is mediated through algorithmic regulation, and if the way in which this system operates is not communicated (or, in case of certain data-driven systems, if its operations are unintelligible) how can the principle of legal certainty

[86] As the Venice Commission stated in its rule of law checklist: "*stability is not an end in itself: law must also be capable of adaptation to changing circumstances. Law can be changed, but with public debate and notice, and without adversely affecting legitimate expectations.*" Venice Commission, 'Rule of Law Checklist' (n 57), §60.

[87] See also *supra*, Section 3.3.3.

[88] This collective responsibility of all state institutions was also stressed by the Venice Commission in its Opinion on the Dutch child care allowance case. See, e.g., Barrett and others (n 34) 27.

[89] See *supra*, Section 3.2.2. See also Joseph Raz, 'The Rule of Law and Its Virtue', in his *The Authority of Law: Essays on Law and Morality* (Oxford University Press 1979).

[90] See *supra*, Sections 2.4.4 and 4.1.1.c.

be met? How can one have certainty not only about the law that will be applied, but also about the way in which public officials make use of their discretion when they apply the law? Without such transparency, there can be no oversight, whether by citizens or by other branches, of public authorities' actions that rely on algorithmic regulation, and hence no assurance that these actions are in line with human rights, democracy and the rule of law.

Though the need for transparency about the implementation of laws and policies by public authorities seems evident, the reluctance of providing information about algorithmic systems that are used *for this very purpose* shows this is not a given. This is evidenced by the various cases brought before courts due to the refusal of public authorities to offer information about the algorithmic systems they are using – including those that inform and take administrative acts. I have already discussed the opacity surrounding the Belgian OASIS tool,[91] yet one can also point out the obstacles faced by individuals who sought information about the abovementioned Polish unemployment profiling algorithm.[92] Accessing information was also an obstacle in the context of the Swedish Trelleborg algorithm dealing with the allocation of welfare benefits,[93] and the controversial French Admission Post Bac algorithm, which automatically assigned students to higher education institutions.[94] Also in the latter case, dismayed students were forced to sue the relevant public authority to enforce their public information right, after obtaining negative replies to their requests for information. Note that there is currently no uniform answer across the EU as to whether the source code of algorithmic systems deployed by public authorities is considered as public information that can be requested pursuant to an access to information request.

Of course, transparency on how public authorities implement legislation is *always* a challenge, given the inherent asymmetry of information between the government and its citizens. However, the use of algorithmic systems as intermediaries between public authorities and citizens can further diminish transparency by adding an additional layer of opacity, one that is not easily pierced.[95] Furthermore, as demonstrated by the example of Hackney's Child Risk Assessment System, the problem can be aggravated when the commercial or intellectual property rights of the private

91 Degrave (n 45).

92 Niklas, Sztandar and Szymielewicz (n 63).

93 This example is not discussed in this book, but see in this regard Anne Kaun, 'Suing the Algorithm: The Mundanization of Automated Decision-Making in Public Services through Litigation' [2021] Information, Communication & Society 1.

94 Restrepo Amariles (n 19) 284. See also Madeleine Thompson, 'The French Educational Algorithm of Inefficiency' (Brown Political Review 8 November 2016) <https://brownpoliticalreview.org/2016/11/french-educational-algorithm/>.

95 See also Ada Lovelace Institute, AI Now Institute, and Open Government Partnership, 'Algorithmic Accountability for the Public Sector' (2021) 7 <www.opengovpartnership.org/documents/algorithmic-accountability-public-sector/>.

company who developed the system are invoked.[96] This essentially comes down to the supremacy of a private interest (which can already be called dubious given the influence it implies of a private party over public policy), over a public interest. Beyond the concerns this might raise for individuals who are directly affected by the system, this problem is a societal one, as it reduces the possibility for government control more generally.[97]

These elements collectively reveal that the implementation of algorithmic systems to inform or take administrative acts does not unassumingly enhance legal certainty. Rather, it raises several challenges for the attainment of this principle, and risks making it more difficult to achieve the delicate balance between stability and adaptability, thereby potentially exacerbating the tensions that are already part of the rule of law.

4.1.3 *Non-arbitrariness*

As discussed in Section 3.3, the principle of non-arbitrariness requires public authorities to act in a non-arbitrary fashion, meaning impartially, reasonably, efficiently, fairly and timely. They should be able to justify their actions, and use their discretion in a way that balances the various interests involved, guided by the effects of the measures they adopt and taking into account the factors relevant to the case.[98] Moreover, public authorities should only use their power to attain the specific purpose for which it was granted to them,[99] and must put in place mechanisms against the risk of corruption and the potential abuse or misuse of discretion – including the abuse or misuse of (personal) information retained by the authorities.[100] With this recap in mind, how are these requirements affected by reliance on algorithmic systems to inform or take administrative acts?

96 See *supra*, Section 4.1.1.c.

97 For this reason, France introduced new legislation providing inter alia that – as a default – the use of algorithms in public decision-making should be made transparent to the public, and setting out minimum information that should be provided by public authorities. See LOI no. 2016-1321 du 7 octobre 2016. See also OECD, 'A Data-Driven Public Sector: Enabling the Strategic Use of Data for Productive, Inclusive and Trustworthy Governance', vol 33 (2019) OECD Working Papers on Public Governance 6, 40.

98 See Denis James Galligan, 'Discretionary Powers in the Legal Order', in his *Discretionary Powers: A Legal Study of Official Discretion* (Oxford University Press 1990).

99 See *supra*, Section 3.3.3.

100 Recall in this regard also Committee of Ministers of the Council of Europe, 'Recommendation No. R (87) 15 of the Committee of Ministers to Member States Regulating the Use of Personal Data in the Police Sector', Adopted by the Committee of Ministers on 17 September 1987 at the 410th meeting of the Ministers' Deputies (1987); Committee of Ministers of the Council of Europe, 'Recommendation No. R (91) 10 of the Committee of Ministers to Member States on the Communication to Third Parties of Personal Data Held by Public Bodies', Adopted by the Committee of Ministers on 9 September 1991 at the 461st meeting of the Ministers' Deputies (1991).

Prima facie, one might purport yet again that the introduction of algorithmic regulation can contribute to the attainment of this rule of law principle, for reasons already explored in previous sections. Reliance on algorithmic systems diminishes discretion at the level of individual public officials – which could potentially be used arbitrarily or in a way that overly deviates from the law – thereby also diminishing the risk of its arbitrary use. Instead, public officials' discretionary power could be replaced by 'evidence-based', streamlined and centralised automated suggestions and decisions. While these aspirations sound promising in theory, their promise entails more than one catch.

4.1.3.a Optimising Efficiency over Justice

A first catch relates to the aspiration of increased efficiency, which is an important goal of bureaucratic organisation more generally. Yet as hinted at above, the very alignment of bureaucratic and algorithmic logic can also obscure that an increase in 'efficiency' might come at the cost of substantive values that public authorities should strive for. An efficient administration is but one of the requirements under the non-arbitrariness principle and should be seen as a means rather than an end in itself – the actual end being: serving citizens in the public interest. By unduly focusing on efficiency, the underlying normative aims of public policies risk being pushed to the sideline, and this can have problematic consequences for the persons involved.

Recall the example of Indiana discussed earlier, where eligibility processes for several welfare programs were automated in an overly narrow manner. In addition to the automated denial of benefits, each time the system perceived a 'lack of cooperation' through something as banal as a missed phone call, Eubanks noted that "*performance metrics designed to speed eligibility determinations created perverse incentives for call centre workers to close cases prematurely*".[101] Indeed, "*timelines could be improved by denying applications and then advising applicants to reapply, which required that they wait an additional 30 or 60 days for a new determination*".[102]

This measuring of success by the number of cases that have been handled (which is quantifiable) rather than by whether people were adequately helped (which is a more difficult metric), also adds to the pressure placed on public officials. It prevents them from deviating from the system and reducing 'efficiency', even if this would contribute to other normative values. This problem was also highlighted by the officials who worked with the Polish unemployment system, which can be seen as another example of efficiency gone rogue. As mentioned above, the Polish unemployment agency deployed an algorithmic system to assist in decisions about whether and which unemployment aid and programmes would be offered to

[101] Eubanks (n 25) 51.
[102] ibid.

citizens, based on their 'employability'.[103] Also here, the aim of the system's implementation was the optimisation of public resources by rendering the process of resource allocation more efficient, and diminishing the risk of arbitrary decisions.

In practice, this 'efficiency' aim translated itself to profiling and categorising citizens in an automated way, including a category of people who were seen as 'lost cases' (in casu, Profile III). People categorised as such would not be eligible for the labour market programs designed to help them find employment, based on opaque and potentially discriminatory criteria.[104] Furthermore, despite the fact that the algorithmic system was introduced to reduce disparities among local offices by 'standardising' the process, empirical evidence suggests that this did not diminish the arbitrary nature of the categorisation. One reason for this was the fact that, during conversations with unemployed citizens, public officials had to deal with answers to questions that were not anticipated by the coders and hence not programmed in the algorithmic system. Based on interviews that Panoptykon conducted with public officials, it appeared that one of those questions concerned "*reasons making it difficult to take up work*", where answers like "*homelessness*" or "*criminal record*" were lacking and could hence not be processed by the system.[105] To remedy this problem:

> The first interviewed counselor suggested that if the unemployed admitted to being homeless, she would either chose 'too much competition' or 'health restrictions' and 'lack of job-seeking skills and self-presentation', depending if the obstacle is only the lack of formal place of residence ('employer does not want to hire persons without a residence address' [PUP 3]) or hygiene (a person 'is dirty and stinks' [PUP 3]). The second counselor explained that – since homelessness is usually accompanied by other difficulties – she would try to identify other relevant answers to this question, ignoring homelessness as a specific cause: for instance, 'health restrictions' or 'a lack of conviction about the necessity to take up a job' [PUP 6]. Another suggested solution was to make sure that a person is eventually included in Profile III as a person 'distant from the labor market', no matter what the result of the automated scoring will be
>
> [PUP 3].[106]

To defend this profiling practice, and the exclusion of Profile III persons from receiving any help, the authorities emphasised it would advance evidence-based decision-making, based on 'scientific methods' through the "*combination of an individual 'examination' of a person and econometric elements*".[107] The narrative that algorithmic regulation can supplant potentially arbitrary decisions by public

[103] See *supra*, Section 4.1.2.a.
[104] Niklas (n 67).
[105] Niklas, Sztandar and Szymielewicz (n 63) 28.
[106] ibid.
[107] ibid 7.

officials with 'objective data analysis' based on 'science' is a recurring theme, notwithstanding the fact that both the data and the indicators relied upon by an algorithmic system remain the result of human choices, and can hence likewise be biased.

Accordingly, both in the case of Indiana's welfare eligibility system and Poland's unemployment system, the aim of efficiency overshadowed the aim of ensuring that people who need help get help. In both cases, quantifiable economic targets were prioritised over social policies and values. And while the outcome of an automation process does not necessarily need to lead to such problematic prioritisation, these examples do demonstrate that the implementation of automation tools requires extra attention to this risk, especially in a bureaucratic environment which already lends itself to over-emphasising procedural rationality.[108]

4.1.3.b Reducing Explainability

To counter the risk of arbitrariness and to ensure compliance with the principle of legality, public authorities must justify the administrative acts they take. In the context of algorithmic regulation, this means that transparency about the underlying choices as regards the system's parameters, data and model design should be provided, so that individuals can understand the reasons behind the decision.[109] If this is lacking, those subjected to the system's outcomes are unable to assess the lawful nature of the action and to challenge it where need be. This also counts for the legislative and executive branch, who should be able to 'check and balance' the executive's power.

As explained in Chapter 2, when public authorities deploy algorithmic regulation that is based on knowledge-driven approaches, the system's operations are typically more intelligible and explainable.[110] In principle, this renders it more straightforward for authorities to provide an explanation.[111] However, even when knowledge-driven approaches are used, a meaningful explanation can still be missing if authorities neglect to provide information about the system's functioning. Indeed, as noted in Chapter 2, opacity need not be technical in nature, but can also stem from human choices. More importantly, in some situations, the public officials who deploy the system may not necessarily know or understand how the system functions, as they are typically not part of the development process. The example of the

[108] See *supra*, Section 2.3.

[109] See in this regard Melanie Fink and Michèle Finck, 'Reasoned A(I)Administration: Explanation Requirements in EU Law and the Automation of Public Administration' (2022) 47 European Law Review 376.

[110] See *supra*, Section 2.1.4.

[111] However, see also Mike Ananny and Kate Crawford, 'Seeing without Knowing: Limitations of the Transparency Ideal and Its Application to Algorithmic Accountability' (2018) 20 New Media & Society 973.

Polish unemployment algorithm was telling in this regard. Pursuant to a deliberate choice from the Polish Ministry, the public officials received no insight into the system's operations and the precise parameters that led to the recommended outcomes.[112] The interviews with the officials also revealed that citizens who requested an explanation about the system's functioning were treated with suspicion based on the mere fact that they asked for more information.[113]

When the decision-making process hinges on a data-driven model that provides recommendations based on deep learning or other 'non-explainable' methods, public authorities' duty to state the reasons for their administrative acts is even more difficult to fulfil. In those situations, even if they want to comply with their obligation, public officials may be unable to provide a meaningful explanation of the system's outcomes. The use of such systems therefore seems even more difficult to reconcile with the core tenet that public authorities should be able to motivate their decisions, and with the more general requirement of transparency that accompanies the practice of automated data processing pursuant to the GDPR. In past case law, the CJEU therefore distinguished algorithmic systems that deploy 'predetermined criteria' to profile citizens from systems that rely on machine learning approaches, given the opacity of the latter and the fact that "*it might be impossible to understand the reason why a given program arrived at a positive match.*"[114]

4.1.3.c Diminishing Discretion

Besides obscurity about what the system is optimised for, one can also raise questions over who decides about such optimisation, and how this happens. While the introduction of algorithmic regulation diminishes discretion at the level of individual public officials, it does not eliminate discretion entirely. Instead, discretion shifts to those who code the algorithmic system.[115] This means that normatively relevant decisions about the aims that public policies should be optimised for, or the quantitative criteria that should be considered in the context of taking an administrative act, are henceforth not taken by specialised public officials who are responsible for the administrative act, but by coders.[116] In many cases, these coders are private company employees to which the development of the algorithmic system was

[112] See Niklas, Sztandar and Szymielewicz (n 63) 32.

[113] ibid 31.

[114] See Case C-817/19, *Ligue des droits humains v Conseil des ministres* (PNR Case), ECLI:EU:C:2022:491, §195.

[115] See Mark Bovens and Stavros Zouridis, 'From Street-Level to System-Level Bureaucracies: How Information and Communication Technology Is Transforming Administrative Discretion and Constitutional Control' (2002) 62 Public Administration Review 174, 181.

[116] See Burrell and Fourcade (n 42) 223.

outsourced, since public authorities today often still lack the relevant know-how to do so in-house. In that case, discretion is essentially also outsourced.[117]

This means that algorithmic regulation radically alters the nature of discretion, as it can no longer function as a potential correction to the downsides of the law's general nature, and as a tool to ensure that, on a case-by-case basis, the administrative acts through which legislation is implemented are appropriate for the specific situation.[118] Instead, discretion is centralised, hierarchised and – literally and figuratively – systematised, thereby arguably losing its essence. If discretion is only present in decisions about how an algorithmic system that implements the law is codified, and if it is absent when it comes to the law's actual application to individual cases, then it is no longer capable to play its corrective role. Not when the system accidentally creates adverse effects for individuals and society. But also not when the system has been deliberately codified in a way that is incompatible with the rule of law's principles, including the legality principle which requires compliance with hierarchically higher norms such as human rights and EU law more generally.

Furthermore, embedding rules into a coded infrastructure can remove the possibility of deviating from the codified rule, even in cases where this may be necessary from a legal or moral perspective. This undermines public officials' agency and forces obedience to the rule through the infrastructure's architecture.[119] I have already discussed the risk of automation bias, and the relative ease with which individuals tend to rely on the authority of algorithmic systems, particularly given their superior computational skills.[120] This occurs even more in contexts of time pressure, when people do not have the time to double-check the system's suggestion, or in contexts of scarcity of information, when people lack the data or knowledge to assess the system's reliability. As pointed out by Hildebrandt, "*even in the case of decision-support instead of decision-making, human intervention becomes somewhat illusionary, because those who decide often do not understand the 'reasons' for the proposed decision. This induces compliance with the algorithms, as they are often presented as 'outperforming' human expertise.*"[121] Even when a system is 'merely' meant to inform an administrative act, it will in practice still render it difficult for

[117] See in this regard also Paul R Verkuil, *Outsourcing Sovereignty: Why Privatization of Government Functions Threatens Democracy and What We Can Do about It* (Cambridge University Press 2007).

[118] See also *supra*, Section 2.3.3.

[119] See in this regard also Arre Zuurmond, *De infocratie: Een Theoretische en empirische heroriëntatie op Weber's idealtype in het informatietijdperk* (Phaedrus 1994) 1. See also Karen Yeung, 'Can We Employ Design-Based Regulation While Avoiding Brave New World' (2011) 3 Law, Innovation and Technology 1.

[120] See *supra*, Section 2.2.6.

[121] Mireille Hildebrandt, 'Algorithmic Regulation and the Rule of Law' (2018) 376 Philosophical Transactions of the Royal Society A: Mathematical, Physical and Engineering Sciences 20170355, 2.

officials to deviate therefrom, as this typically requires an additional step of explanation to someone higher up the hierarchy to justify why a suggestion is not followed.

The constraints to deviate from the system can also come from other factors. Money will have been invested in the system's implementation to gain time and efficiency.[122] If public officials are still required to spend time on making their own assessment of a case, regardless of the system's recommendation, that investment will be less cost-efficient and might undermine possible KPIs that officials are required to fulfil. Indeed, through the impetus of the New Public Management approach, which introduced indicators and KPIs into public decision-making, officials may be even more incentivised to focus on the number of cases they can close, or the number of decisions they were able to take – regardless of whether these decisions also do justice to the situation at hand from a normative perspective.[123] Deviating from the algorithmic suggestion rather than simply ratifying might hence endanger the achievement of those KPIs.

The tendency to follow the algorithm's advice has also been corroborated, for instance, in the context of the KrimPro system used by the German Police in Berlin. KrimPro is a predictive policing system which displays predicted areas on a map showcasing the geographical distribution of the probable 'high-risk' areas in and around Berlin for domestic burglaries and other crimes, based on which decisions are taken regarding the optimisation of resources.[124] When researchers conducted in-depth interviews about the system's use and utility within the police forces, this revealed a relatively strong pressure to conform to the recommendations of the system. As one interviewee put it: "*I do not risk anything because even if I find it stupid and nothing happens there or even if something happens, it will not be my responsibility. I have not done anything wrong.*"[125] In this regard, Lorenz et al. note that

> if the police professionals who are responsible for fighting domestic burglaries reject the prediction and therewith additional units and a crime is committed that might

[122] See also Maciej Kuziemski and Gianluca Misuraca, 'AI Governance in the Public Sector: Three Tales from the Frontiers of Automated Decision-Making in Democratic Settings' (2020) 44 Telecommunications Policy 101976.

[123] In this regard, reference can be made to the vast academic literature which addresses the perverted impact of performance management in the public sector. For a general overview, see, e.g., F. Buschor, 'Performance Management in the Public Sector: Past, Current and Future Trends' (2013) 11 Tékhne 4. See also Ulrik Hvidman and Simon Calmar Andersen, 'Impact of Performance Management in Public and Private Organizations' (2014) 24 Journal of Public Administration Research and Theory 35.

[124] Lukas Lorenz, Albert Meijer and Tino Schuppan, 'The Algocracy as a New Ideal Type for Government Organizations: Predictive Policing in Berlin as an Empirical Case' (2021) 26 Information Polity: The International Journal of Government & Democracy in the Information Age 71, 77.

[125] Albert Meijer, Lukas Lorenz and Martijn Wessels, 'Algorithmization of Bureaucratic Organizations: Using a Practice Lens to Study How Context Shapes Predictive Policing Systems' (2021) 81 Public Administration Review 837, 842.

> have been prevented by these units, they put themselves in a bad light. On the other hand, the heads of the inspections do not risk anything when they just comply with the assessment provided by the KrimPro report and deploy additional units even if these extra efforts appear to be ineffective.[126]

A comparative study was conducted of an algorithmic system used by the Dutch police, where the relationship between the police officers and the algorithmic system appeared to be more collaborative rather than hierarchical. Meijer et al. note on this basis that "*two patterns of algorithmisation of government bureaucracy can be identified and that these patterns depend on dominant social norms and interpretations rather than the technological features of algorithmic systems.*"[127] In other words, reliance on algorithmic regulation need not necessarily lead to a heavy curbing of agency. However, in environments that are bureaucratic in nature and that already leave more limited scope for critical reflection, the use of such systems can reinforce these tendencies, including the push towards obedience to authority.

In this regard, Endicott and Yeung stressed that public agency is an important corollary of the government's legal accountability.[128] They conceptualise it as follows: "*the community must make itself capable of deciding and acting responsibly, by empowering and requiring officials and institutions to undertake demonstrably reasoned action on its behalf in certain crucial respects*".[129] As they convincingly argue, public agency is a prerequisite for a responsible government and hence for the rule of law, since "*no community can be ruled by law unless public agencies are empowered by the law to take reasoned decisions to make and to apply the law*".[130] However, when public authorities delegate administrative acts to algorithmic systems, either indirectly by uncritically relying on their recommendations, or directly by adopting an automated decision-process, such agency gets eroded. It not only gets eroded at the level of public officials, but it can also get eroded at the level of the public authority itself when it outsources the system's development to coders who work for a private company or who are in any case untrained to make judgments about administrative acts that can significantly affect individuals.

Importantly, a set-up which leaves little scope for judgment or critical reflection by public officials (and in fact discourages it) also risks detaching the human decision-maker from both the decision and its consequences. Recall in this regard the parallels with Milgram's experiment, which were discussed in Section 2.2.6, and particularly his warning that individuals tend to adopt certain 'buffers' to shield themselves from a sense of responsibility when their actions lead to adverse

[126] Lorenz, Meijer and Schuppan (n 124) 81.
[127] Meijer, Lorenz and Wessels (n 125) 837.
[128] Timothy Endicott and Karen Yeung, 'The Death of Law? Computationally Personalized Norms and the Rule of Law' [2022] University of Toronto Law Journal 72(4), 378.
[129] ibid.
[130] ibid 379.

consequences for those subjected thereto, especially if mediated by a machine.[131] This emotional detachment can be enhanced with physical distance between the decision-maker and the subject, as well as the many hands problem[132] discussed above. In sum, the diminished discretion and agency of public officials can – in the name of efficiency and an alleged reduction of arbitrary decision-making – undermine public officials' sense of responsibility for the administrative acts they take with algorithmic systems, and hence undermine the rule of law's overarching telos.

4.1.4 *Equality before the Law*

The principle of equality before the law requires public authorities to treat persons equally and in a non-discriminatory way. Natural and legal persons can only be treated unequally in case there is a justifiable ground or motivation for their differentiation.[133] As discussed in Chapter 3, one of the main challenges arising from the principle of equality centres on the question of *when* a differentiation is justifiable, and *when* the very lack of a differentiation may be considered unjustifiable.[134] In the context of algorithmic regulation, one can recall that the very purpose of algorithmic systems consists of making automated differentiations and categorisations between various types of data (including data about individuals) in order to apply legal rules to particular (categories of) cases in a more efficient, objective and speedy way. The question is therefore: how does reliance on algorithmic regulation contribute to this principle's attainment or to its challenge?

4.1.4.a Risk of Scaled Bias

Legal rules are abundant with categorisations and, as I discussed above, many of these categories are over- and under-inclusive given the law's general nature. One could hence contend that algorithmic regulation might help refine the law's overly rudimentary categorisations by conducting a more 'personalised' analysis of citizens' data and thereby contributing to *substantive* equality – especially when based on data-driven techniques that can identify distinctions that public officials could not easily perceive by themselves. Several scholars have put forward arguments along

[131] See *supra*, Section 2.2.5.

[132] ibid. See also, e.g., Dennis F Thompson, 'Designing Responsibility: The Problem of Many Hands in Complex Organizations' in Jeroen van den Hoven, Seumas Miller and Thomas Pogge (eds), *Designing in Ethics* (1st edn, Cambridge University Press 2017). See also Helen Nissenbaum, 'Accountability in a Computerized Society' (1996) 2 Science and Engineering Ethics 25.

[133] See *supra*, Section 3.3.4.

[134] See also Sandra Wachter, Brent Mittelstadt and Chris Russell, 'Why Fairness Cannot Be Automated: Bridging the Gap between EU Non-Discrimination Law and AI' (2021) 41 Computer Law & Security Review 105567.

these lines.[135] Ben-Shahar and Porat have, for instance, argued in favour of a technology-driven personalisation of the law.[136] The promise of algorithmic regulation in this context, as Endicott and Yeung observed, "*is that it could take social ordering beyond the crude, impersonal techniques of law, with its clumsy dependence on general rules*".[137] However, they also point out that this would pose significant challenges for the rule of law.[138]

In the context of the principle of equality, one can question to which extent the (more refined) categorisations or distinctions proposed by an algorithmic system are *justifiable* from a legal perspective, since the validity of categorisations (whether in the law or in the law's application) hinges upon their justifiability. It is here that the limits of algorithmic regulation come to the fore, for whether a distinction based on a certain criterion is justifiable or not cannot be determined by an algorithm. Algorithmic systems can propose categorisations based on data they receive, and hence based on data about how things *are*, but they will not be able to say anything about how things *should* be. Otherwise, this would constitute a conflation between the normative and the positive, thereby committing the error of the is–ought fallacy.[139]

When speaking of equality, it is also important to recall the discussion in Chapter 2 about algorithmic systems' risk of biased decision-making. While their machine-like nature and reliance on data may make it seem like they are neutral and objective decision tools, algorithmic systems merely reflect the values and value-laden choices that are embedded in their components and environment. This means that the systems' coders have a significant influence on the potential (unjust) bias that may be reflected in the system's outcomes, and on the validity of the distinctions and categorisations that the system will make (whether they pre-programmed these distinctions or whether these distinctions are derived from the

[135] Casey and Niblett noted, for instance that "*as technologies associated with big data, prediction algorithms, and instantaneous communication reduce the costs of discovering and communicating the relevant personal context for a law to achieve its purpose, the goal of a well-tailored, accurate, and highly contextualized law is becoming more achievable*." See Anthony Joseph Casey and Anthony Niblett, 'A Framework for the New Personalization of Law' (2019) 86 The University of Chicago Law Review 333, 335. See also Horst Eidenmüller and Gerhard Wagner, *Law by Algorithm* (Mohr Siebeck 2021).

[136] Omri Ben-Shahar and Ariel Porat, *Personalized Law: Different Rules for Different People* (Oxford University Press 2021). For an important critique on their arguments, see, e.g., Endicott and Yeung (n 128).

[137] Endicott and Yeung (n 128).

[138] As discussed *supra*, Section 2.2.5.

[139] The articulation of the is–ought problem is most notably ascribed to David Hume. See David Hume, *A Treatise of Human Nature: Being an Attempt to Introduce the Experimental Method of Reasoning into Moral Subjects and Dialogues Concerning Natural Religion [1739]* (LA Selby-Bigge ed, Clarendon Press 1896). See also Max Black, 'The Gap Between "Is" and "Should"' (1964) 73(2) *The Philosophical Review* 165–81; Nicoletta Bersier Ladavac, Christoph Bezemek and Frederick Schauer (eds), *The Normative Force of the Factual: Legal Philosophy between Is and Ought*, vol 130 (Springer International Publishing 2019).

data they gathered and labelled). A vast scholarship exists on how algorithmic regulation impacts the principle of equality and the right to non-discrimination, which I will not be repeating here.[140] Yet suffice it to note that reliance on biased algorithmic systems can lead to unjustifiable discrimination, regardless of how such bias manifests itself.

Consider the example of the algorithmic system used by Allegheny's child welfare agency in Pennsylvania, which was meant to enable the more efficient identification of families where children ran a risk of being neglected or abused, and hence to optimise resources by prioritising further investigations for those flagged families in particular.[141] Due to a biased design, the system flagged *"a disproportionate number of black children for a 'mandatory' neglect investigation, when compared with white children"*.[142] By deploying this system, Allegheny's child welfare agency not only inflicted harm at the level of the individual families that were affected thereby, but it also undermined the general principle of equality which is an essential societal interest. There can be no rule of law if the law is applied unequally to people based on the mere colour of their skin – and a breakdown of the rule of law is problematic for all members of society rather than just for those who are targeted by a specific system.

An additional problem in the context of (primarily data-driven) algorithmic systems concerns the risk of discrimination through proxies. Even if prohibited discrimination grounds such as ethnicity or gender are purposely *not* taken into consideration when training or deploying an algorithmic system, these grounds can still *implicitly* contribute to a biased outcome by virtue of their strong relationship with seemingly neutral datapoints.[143] Since the elimination of discrimination through proxies is notoriously difficult (eliminating data that is related to prohibited discrimination grounds can in fact result in a lack of sufficient data to carry out an analysis in the first place), this risk should always be considered when algorithmic regulation is used. In the case of Allegheny's system, researchers who received access to the relevant data and conducted an investigation of the system's deployment found that the algorithmic system *"on its own was more racially disparate than*

[140] See also Toon Calders and Indrė Žliobaitė, 'Why Unbiased Computational Processes Can Lead to Discriminative Decision Procedures' in Bart Custers and others (eds), *Discrimination and Privacy in the Information Society*, vol 3 (Springer Berlin Heidelberg 2013); Parliamentary Assembly of the Council of Europe (PACE), 'Recommendation 2183 (2020) on Preventing Discrimination Caused by the Use of Artificial Intelligence' (PACE 2020) Recommendation.

[141] See Dan Hurley, 'Can an Algorithm Tell When Kids Are in Danger?' *The New York Times* (2 January 2018) <www.nytimes.com/2018/01/02/magazine/can-an-algorithm-tell-when-kids-are-in-danger.html>.

[142] Sally Ho and Garance Burke, 'An Algorithm That Screens for Child Neglect Raises Concerns' *Associated Press* (29 April 2022) <https://apnews.com/article/child-welfare-algorithm-investigation-9497ee937e0053ad4144a86c68241ef1>.

[143] Frederik J Zuiderveen Borgesius, 'Discrimination, Artificial Intelligence, and Algorithmic Decision-Making' (Council of Europe – Directorate General of Democracy 2018) 13.

workers, both in terms of screen-in rate and accuracy".[144] While it is not disputed that human administrators can be biased too, this case illustrates that an algorithmic system can in some situations be even more biased, with as an additional feature the fact that its biased administrative decisions can be implemented instantaneously and at population scale.

This point can also be illustrated by revisiting the algorithmic system used in the Dutch childcare allowance case.[145] I have already noted how the public authority's narrow interpretation of the existing legal rule marked an excessive number of families as potential fraudsters even without any fraudulent intent, and led to high demands for repayment. In addition, the tax authority also relied on a data-driven algorithmic system that helped flag potential cases of fraud which it had learned from a dataset with examples of past correct and incorrect applications.[146] Problematically, "*one of the many indicators used to identify fraud cases was citizenship, and applicants with foreign origin were selected by the system for detailed scrutiny of their applications*".[147] Accordingly, the combination of a system that (1) codified a legal rule in an overly legalistic manner due to the excessively narrow interpretation thereof by the public authority, and that (2) relied on discriminatory criteria, led to a disproportionate targeting of people with a foreign background – many of which went through financial and social dramas.[148]

Also here, it can be pointed out that the Dutch tax authority need not have recourse to an algorithmic system to rely on a problematic proxy to identify fraudulent behaviour. Human beings are perfectly capable of using discriminating factors in their decision-making without any assistance from a machine. However, the automation of the process renders potentially *beneficial* deviations from the discriminatorily codified system more difficult, in addition to the vast scale on which a problematic proxy can be applied.

4.1.4.b Exacerbating Societal Inequality

It is precisely this scale that enables algorithmic systems to not only reproduce but also to exacerbate discriminatory tendencies in society. When data-driven systems are deployed to categorise natural and legal persons (whether as (in)eligible for benefits, or as (un)likely fraudsters, as criminals or as having other undesirable

144 Hao-Fei Cheng and others, 'How Child Welfare Workers Reduce Racial Disparities in Algorithmic Decisions', *CHI Conference on Human Factors in Computing Systems* (ACM 2022) 3 <https://dl.acm.org/doi/10.1145/3491102.3501831>.

145 See also Parliamentary Inquiry Committee (n 33).

146 See Autoriteit Persoonsgegevens, 'Onderzoeksrapport Belastingdienst/Toeslagen: De verwerking van de nationaliteit van aanvragers van kinderopvangtoeslag' (2020) z2018–22445, 14 <https://autoriteitpersoonsgegevens.nl/uploads/imported/onderzoek_belastingdienst_kinderopvangtoeslag.pdf>.

147 Barrett and others (n 34) 4.

148 See Parliamentary Inquiry Committee (n 33).

features) these systems necessarily rely on datasets that reflect a state of play from the past. This means that societal inequalities that are reflected in the datasets risk being perpetuated in the algorithmic system. Importantly, this risk is not limited to data-driven systems, since also in knowledge-driven systems the algorithmic categories can be based on biased assumptions. In addition, precisely due to historical inequalities, there is less data available about certain population groups (so-called data gaps), which tends to reduce the accuracy of algorithmic models and outcomes as concerns these populations.[149]

Algorithmic systems in administrative decision-making are often also deployed in contexts that are inclined to focus disproportionately on individuals or groups that are more vulnerable.[150] This is not surprising. After all, many of the public welfare programmes organised by public authorities are precisely targeted at helping the most vulnerable in society and ensure they can enjoy a range of social and economic rights.[151] At the same time, this very vulnerability can also turn them into targets when it comes to the assessment of risks – which can also be seen in examples of algorithmic regulation, such as the system used by Allegheny's child welfare agency. As explained by Eubanks, one of the risk assessment factors on which that system relied concerned the use of social services, like a parent's access to mental healthcare services in a clinic funded by Medicaid.[152] These clinics are obligated to report medical records to the state, which means their patient data can be analysed by state-deployed algorithmic systems – such as the Allegheny system. Importantly, Eubanks points out that private clinics – which are typically more expensive – are *not* obligated to share their records with the state. The algorithmic system would hence *not* pick up a parent's access to mental healthcare services – and the stigma and potential risks associated therewith – if the parent is wealthy enough to afford a private clinic.[153] Evidently, this also means that the system can disproportionately target people based on their financial situation.

For another example, consider the Harm Assessment Risk Tool (HART) used by law enforcers in Durham. The system was developed by researchers of the University of Cambridge together with Durham Constabulary, to help custody offers take decisions about offenders' eligibility for the so-called Constabulary's Checkpoint

[149] See in this regard also Rónán Kennedy, 'The Rule of Law and Algorithmic Governance' in Woodrow Barfield (ed), *The Cambridge Handbook of the Law of Algorithms* (1st edn, Cambridge University Press 2020) 216.

[150] See also Sofia Ranchordas and Luisa Scarcella, 'Automated Government for Vulnerable Citizens: Intermediating Rights' (2021) 30 William & Mary Bill of Rights Journal 373.

[151] This very vulnerability, however, often also leads to higher administrative burdens. See in this regard Julian Christensen and others, 'Human Capital and Administrative Burden: The Role of Cognitive Resources in Citizen-State Interactions' (2020) 80 Public Administration Review 127.

[152] See Eubanks (n 25) 147.

[153] See also J Khadijah Abdurahman, 'Birthing Predictions of Premature Death' [2022] Logic Magazine <https://logicmag.io/home/birthing-predictions-of-premature-death/>.

programme.[154] This programme essentially seeks to deal with an offence outside court prosecution, with the aim of reducing future offences by dealing with the underlying reasons of why a person may be committing a crime (such as drug or alcohol abuse, homelessness or mental health).[155] The system categorises offenders as low, medium or higher risk of re-offending, whereby those presenting a 'medium' level of risk can be eligible for the programme. However, concerns arose that the algorithm was "*discriminating people from poorer areas*",[156] for one of the factors taken into consideration by the model concerned a person's postal code.

A review of HART notes that

> the primary postcode predictor is limited to the first four characters of the postcode, and usually encompasses a rather large geographic area. Yet even with this limitation, one could argue that this variable risks a kind of feedback loop that may perpetuate or amplify existing patterns of offending. If the police respond to forecasts by targeting their efforts on the highest-risk postcode areas, then more people from these areas will come to police attention and be arrested than those living in lower-risk, untargeted neighbourhoods. These arrests then become outcomes that are used to generate later iterations of the same model, leading to an ever-deepening cycle of increased police attention.[157]

The mere fact that one resides in a given postcode only affected the system's outcome indirectly, in combination with other predictive criteria. Nevertheless, the system was altered to address the criticism that it risked categorising a disproportionate number of people from poorer neighbourhoods as high-risk and hence as ineligible for the rehabilitation programme.

To tackle these issues, a lot of research currently focuses on making algorithmic systems 'fairer' and 'eliminating bias'.[158] There are, however, no straightforward solutions to this problem, especially given the fact that 'fairness' can be conceptualised and defined in numerous ways.[159] Moreover, the fact that algorithmic bias is virtually always an emanation of underlying structural problems and societal inequalities indicates that mere technical fixes will be unable to sustainably address

[154] Marion Oswald and others, 'Algorithmic Risk Assessment Policing Models: Lessons from the Durham HART Model and "Experimental" Proportionality' (2018) 27 Information & Communications Technology Law 223, 225.

[155] Matt Burgess, 'UK Police Are Using AI to Inform Custodial Decisions – But It Could Be Discriminating against the Poor' (*Wired UK*, 1 March 2018) <www.wired.co.uk/article/police-ai-uk-durham-hart-checkpoint-algorithm-edit>.

[156] ibid.

[157] Oswald and others (n 154) 228.

[158] However, see also Ivo Emanuilov and Katerina Yordanova, 'Do You Believe in FAIR-y-Tales? An Overview of Microsoft's New Toolkit for Assessing and Improving Fairness of Algorithms' (*CITIP blog*, 14 July 2020) <www.law.kuleuven.be/citip/blog/do-you-believe-in-fair-y-tales-an-overview-of-microsofts-new-toolkit-for-assessing-and-improving-fairness-of-algorithms/>; Virginia Dignum, 'The Myth of Complete AI-Fairness' in Allan Tucker and others (eds), *Artificial Intelligence in Medicine* (Springer International Publishing 2021).

[159] See Wachter, Mittelstadt and Russell (n 134).

this problem. In that sense, the HART example is almost ironic: while the aim of the programme is to tackle the structural problems underlying crime, being part of a neighbourhood with structural problems risked reducing one's eligibility for this very programme. This showcases once again the limits of quantification as a substitute for qualification.

However, even when deploying a more basic algorithmic system that does not rely on elaborate data-analytics, public authorities can carry out *scaled* discriminatory decision-making. The example of a Dutch algorithmic system to detect welfare fraud – which was basically implemented through a sophisticated excel sheet – is a sad case in point. For years on end about 158 communities who looked for an efficient way to identify and investigate welfare fraud profiled individuals based on parameters that were plainly discriminatory. Although in 2020 the Ministry of Social Affairs spurred communities to stop using this system, noting that it breached the GDPR, researchers[160] revealed that – up until 2022 – a number of communities were still relying on it.[161] Indicators of potential fraud included factors like employment as a taxi driver or a hairdresser, residing in a low-income area, or having a low level of education.[162] As the researchers note, these variables have no statistical evidence but are merely a collection of past prejudices.[163] Furthermore, by analysing the source code, they also stumbled upon hidden fields with the option to profile individuals based on the indicators 'native' or 'foreigner', hence suggesting that, in the past, these systems might also have been used to discriminate people based on nationality. This makes it painfully clear that no complex machine learning systems are needed to adversely affect a large group of citizens with algorithmic regulation.

4.1.4.c Loss of Comparability

A final point to raise under the principle of equality, is the fact that the use of algorithmic systems to inform or take administrative acts also renders it more difficult to know that the equality principle is being infringed in the first place. One can recall the opacity that often surrounds the use of algorithmic regulation – including the fact that such technology is deployed, the parameters it considers, the

160 'Junk Science Underpins Fraud Scores' (*Lighthouse Reports*, 25 June 2022) <www.lighthousereports.nl/investigation/junk-science-underpins-fraud-scores/>.

161 See also 'Verboden fraudescores bleven in gebruik bij gemeenten' *NRC* (25 June 2022) <www.nrc.nl/nieuws/2022/06/25/profileren-verboden-fraudescores-bleven-in-gebruik-bij-gemeenten-a4134660>.

162 An interactive overview of the 'fraudescorekaart' was made available by the researchers who uncovered the algorithm's continued use, and can be found here: https://fraudescorekaart.lighthousereports.nl/#/.

163 Lighthouse Reports, 'People All over the Netherlands Have Been Flagged for Welfare Fraud Based on a Crude Spreadsheet & Some Unscientific Prejudices. How Do We Know? We Took the Algorithm Apart & Rebuilt It. Score Yourself & See' (2022), <https://twitter.com/LHreports/status/1540598392300179456>.

data it relies on, and the way in which textual legal concepts and rules have been translated to code. The lack of information about these elements also renders it challenging to assess – both by the people subjected to the system and by those who deploy it – whether the principle of equality is being respected.[164] Which type of data was fed into the algorithmic system, and upon which parameters does it rely to inform or take administrative decisions? If those parameters involve distinction grounds that directly or indirectly relate to a prohibited discrimination ground, or that are otherwise problematic, how can their use be challenged, and (how) can public authorities justify these distinctions? The asymmetry of information between those subjected to the system and those who design and develop it requires that the answer to these questions is made explicit, ideally proactively, in order to at least somewhat restore this imbalance.[165]

Potential clashes with the principle of equality are moreover not limited to the way in which an algorithmic system is developed, but can also arise from the way in which the system is used. The example of the system deployed by the UK's Office of Qualifications and Examinations Regulation (Ofqual) during the Covid-19 pandemic can illustrate this problem. After exams were cancelled in 2020 in light of the pandemic, high-school teachers were asked to predict what the A-level results of their high-school students would likely have been. Anticipating that those results would be overly optimistic, given that "*evidence suggests that estimated grades will tend towards over-estimation*",[166] Ofqual also deployed an algorithmic system which relied on basic statistical modelling to consider student grades from previous years as well as grades at national level for the same subjects, in order to 'objectivise' the process.[167] As a result, almost 40 per cent of the A-level grades predicted by teachers in England were downgraded.[168] Needless to say, the system's impact on students was significant, especially considering that their grade also determined whether they met the admission requirements set by higher education institutions.

Besides various types of criticism about the system's accuracy and design (on which Ofqual only provided transparency after the grades were assigned), one concern that raised tensions with the equality principle was the fact that the system was only used for schools with more than fifteen children taking an A-level subject.

[164] Emre Bayamlıoğlu, 'Contesting Automated Decisions: A View of Transparency Implications' (2018) 4 European Data Protection Law Review 433.

[165] See also Katherine Fink, 'Opening the Government's Black Boxes: Freedom of Information and Algorithmic Accountability' (2018) 21 Information, Communication & Society 1453.

[166] Ofqual, 'Awarding GCSE, AS, A Level, Advanced Extension Awards and Extended Project Qualifications in Summer 2020: Interim Report', Ofqual/20/6656/1, (13 August 2020), 16, <https://assets.publishing.service.gov.uk/media/5f3571778fa8f5173f593d61/6656-1_Awarding_GCSE__AS__A_level__advanced_extension_awards_and_extended_project_qualifications_in_summer_2020_-_interim_report.pdf>.

[167] For an extensive report setting out Ofqual's methodology, see ibid.

[168] Will Bedingfield, 'Everything That Went Wrong with the Botched A-Levels Algorithm' [2020] *Wired UK* <www.wired.co.uk/article/alevel-exam-algorithm>.

Where a school had five or fewer children taking an A-level subject, the grades were primarily based on the teacher's predictions, and where a school had between five and fifteen children taking an A-level subject, the grades were based on a combination of the teacher's prediction and the system's prediction.[169] Given the alleged over-estimation of teachers' scores, scores were thus higher for smaller classes – thereby disadvantaging state schools which typically have larger groups of students.[170] At the same time, reliance on the national average grades also led to the penalisation of students at excellent schools, who saw their results downgraded by virtue of an overall lower average.[171]

Given the public backlash against the system's use, the government ultimately decided to ignore the algorithmic predictions and rely only on the teacher's estimates. This was not a perfect solution either, as Ofqual pointed to the fact that:

> studies of potential bias in teacher assessment suggest that differences between teacher assessment and exam assessment results can sometimes be linked to student characteristics, including gender, age within year group, ethnicity, special educational needs, and having English as an additional language. However, such effects are not always seen, and when they are, they tend to be small and inconsistent across subjects.[172]

While human bias hence remained a risk, this was ultimately still preferred over the vastness of the risks presented by the use of the algorithmic system. Latent to this algorithmic antagonism was not only the wider scale of its (problematic) impact, but also its overreliance on statistical modelling, and the fact that it assessed students not only based on their own capabilities, but also on various parameters that did not directly relate to them – such as the size of their classroom and the level of their peers in other schools. In addition, the fact that Ofqual did not previously share detailed information about the system's methodology and parameters, and failed to conduct a prior public consultation to seek feedback, was strongly criticised, as this could have prevented or at least mitigated some of the concerns.

I already discussed the lack of transparency several times.[173] Yet with respect to the principle of equality, an additional risk can be pointed out, namely the potential loss of comparability between various individuals or groups of individuals. Challenging an administrative act in light of a presumed breach of the principle of equality requires that the subject of the act has information about the fact that other persons were treated differently, despite similar circumstances – or the same, despite

[169] See also the detailed analysis provided by Jeni Tennison, 'How Does Ofqual's Grading Algorithm Work?' (2020) <https://rpubs.com/JeniT/ofqual-algorithm>.

[170] Bedingfield (n 168).

[171] ibid.

[172] Ofqual (n 166) 16.

[173] The lack of transparency on the rule-making process was discussed in Section 4.1.1.c, and the lack of transparency about the law's application was discussed in Section 4.1.2.c.

different circumstances.[174] However, legal subjects are not always aware of the fact that a particular differentiation is taking place. While laws and regulations of general application are in principle rendered public – in view of the transparency required by the principle of legal certainty and legality – the individual acts taken by public authorities when they apply these laws to specific cases are not always public, which means that it is not always easy for persons to ascertain that they may be treated differently than others who are in a similar situation.

I therefore noted that the principle's requirement of an effective remedy against the discriminatory application of legislation also requires transparency by public authorities on how they interpret a general rule and how they intend to apply it. In a non-algorithmic context, such transparency can take the shape of the publication of administrative guidelines on the methodology used by public officials to apply legal rules to different categories of persons.[175] However, if these guidelines are replaced by more 'refined' or 'personalised' distinctions or categorisations undertaken by virtue of an algorithmic assessment, this means that subjects will not be able to easily compare the methodology applied in their case with the methodology that was applied to other persons – and thus the extent to which a potential difference in treatment was justified. As a consequence of this loss of comparability, the unequal treatment of persons through the differentiated application of general legislation might remain hidden under the algorithmic surface. Evidently, this also affects the possibility of challenging a breach of the principle of equality through the judicial review of administrative action, which I discuss in what follows.

4.1.5 *Judicial Review*

The judicial review of administrative acts aims at ensuring effective judicial protection against executive action that does not comply with the rule of law, including, as part of the legality principle, actions that infringe human rights.[176] In the previous sections, I started my discussion of how algorithmic regulation can impact the principles of the rule of law with an optimistic note, noting that, theoretically at least, it might in fact advance the fulfilment of the principle. How algorithmic systems could enhance the judicial review of administrative acts is not immediately evident, other than the abovementioned aim of preventing officials to deviate from the codified rule or from the algorithmically proposed outcome (which is not the same as preventing them from taking arbitrary or unlawful decisions).

Recall that the principle of judicial review is part of the broader principle of effective judicial protection and access to justice, and that it serves as an overarching point of oversight to ensure that any infringements that occur, despite all the rule of

[174] See *supra*, Section 3.3.4.
[175] See in this regard also Bovens and Zouridis (n 115).
[176] See *supra*, Section 3.3.5.

law requirements imposed on public authorities, can be remedied by means of a review by an independent judge.[177] The judge is hence the last soldier guarding respect for the various other principles that were already discussed, namely legality, legal certainty, non-arbitrariness of executive power and equality before the law.[178] The implementation of the principle of judicial review can, however, face a number of challenges.[179] Are these challenges aggravated by the deployment of algorithmic systems to inform or adopt administrative acts? For the reasons set out below, I believe the answer to that question is positive.

4.1.5.a Informational Limits for Review

To carry out the judicial review of an administrative act, the reviewing judge must have access to the necessary information to assess that act, including the legal basis on which it was grounded, the way in which it was adopted, and the reasons or justification for its adoption.[180] I have already explained that the deployment of algorithmic regulation can hinder the transparency of government action. Such transparency is not only important for those affected by the public authority's system (to decide whether or not they should challenge its use), but also for judges (to assess the action's conformity with the principles of the rule of law). Admittedly, depending on the type of administrative act and the level of discretion that the public authority has, judicial review may be limited in scope to avoid that a judge substitutes a public decision-maker.[181] However, even when judicial review is limited to a legality check, the judge still needs to be able to ensure that the way in which the public authority implemented and applied a general legal rule

[177] See in this regard also the Judgment of the ECtHR in Case of *Klass and Others v Germany*, Application no. 5029/71, 6 September 1978, where it stated in §55 that

> One of the fundamental principles of a democratic society is the rule of law, which is expressly referred to in the Preamble to the Convention (see the Golder judgment of 21 February 1975, Series A no. 18, pp. 16–17, para. 34). The rule of law implies, inter alia, that an interference by the executive authorities with an individual's rights should be subject to an effective control which should normally be assured by the judiciary, at least in the last resort, judicial control offering the best guarantees of independence, impartiality and a proper procedure.

It also underlined the importance thereof in the more recent case of *Breyer v Germany*, Application no. 50001/12, 30 January 2020, which likewise dealt with state surveillance, in §102.

[178] See in this regard Guobin Zhu, *Deference to the Administration in Judicial Review: Comparative Perspectives* (Springer International Publishing 2019).

[179] See *supra*, Section 3.3.5.b.

[180] The provision of such information can be seen as part of the cooperation that the different branches of the state must engage in to ensure checks and balances. See also Harry Woolf, Jeffrey Jowell and Andrew P Le Sueur, *De Smith, Woolf and Jowell's Principles of Judicial Review* (Sweet & Maxwell 1999).

[181] Hasan Dindjer, 'What Makes an Administrative Decision Unreasonable?' (2021) 84 The Modern Law Review 265.

occurred in accordance with the law, with respect for human rights, and in a non-arbitrary and proportionate manner.

If administrative action is taken or informed by an algorithmic system, the above-mentioned loss of transparency (both as regards the process of the rule-making and the rule's application to the concrete situation) is thus problematic for the proper exercise of judicial review. A judge that does not know the parameters that led to a decision, and the reasons grounding the decision, will not be able to assess whether these parameters contain an unlawful ground of discrimination, or whether those reasons are arbitrary. In this regard, merely providing the judge with the source code of the algorithmic system may not be of much help.[182] The overall majority of judges will not be able to interpret this code, and even if they could, this would still not offer them insight into how a concrete decision about the individual who challenges the act was adopted. The judge must hence be able to review the underlying logic of the system, including the parameters on which it is based.

Note that, in some cases, ensuring transparency about the system's operations might also imply the need to share information about how the general rules lying at the basis of the specific administrative act were translated from text to code, and whether this translation complies with the various rule of law principles. After all, this translation process plays an important role in the allocation (or potential narrowing down) of rights for natural and legal persons. These can also include specific rights that individuals derive from EU law, and for which they have a fundamental right to effective protection.[183] Public authorities must hence duly document this translation process and the various choices that were made in that context, since without such documentation, the principle of effective judicial review may be impeded.[184] Unfortunately, many public authorities currently do not pro-actively keep track of the normative choices that underlie the system's design and development (especially if the system's design was outsourced). The absence of such documentation practice is problematic not only from a (judicial) transparency perspective, but also from a security perspective. If there is no trace of *which* developer took *which* translation decision, the system is more vulnerable to (subsequent) traceless tweaking.

The problem lies, however, not only in the *ability* of judges to review the system, but also in their *willingness* to do so, which requires sufficient knowledge of the risks associated therewith and the openness to carry out a critical examination rather than

182 See in this regard also Ananny and Crawford (n 111).

183 Recall in this regard the importance of ensuring sufficient transparency to enable individuals to invoke their right to an effective judicial remedy, as also stressed by the CJEU in Case C-817/19, *Ligue des droits humains v Conseil des ministres* (PNR Case) (n 114) §195.

184 This is important in the context of all algorithmic systems, but may be even more problematic for systems that are meant to be 'dynamic' and 'agile'. Consider in this regard also the problematic example I mentioned *supra*, under Section 4.1.2, regarding the 'continuously updated' algorithmic system used for the UK's Universal Credit programme.

a mere deference to public authorities.[185] Consider in this regard the case brought by Edward Bridges, a civil liberties campaigner, against the South Wales Police Force (SWP) in the UK in order to challenge the police's use of automated facial recognition technology in public (through a pilot called 'AFR Locate').[186] Besides claiming that the use of this technology breached the right to privacy and data protection law, Mr Bridges also argued that it affected the right to equality and constituted an infringement of the 'Public Sector's Equality Duty',[187] since the authority "*failed to have regard to the possibility that use of the AFR software would produce a disproportionately higher rate of false positive matches for those who are women or from minority ethnic groups, such that use of AFR Locate would indirectly discriminate against those groups*".[188]

The High Court's assessment of this claim is telling of the difficulties one can encounter when seeking judicial review of public authorities' use of algorithmic regulation, and of the burden of proof one may need to meet. It stated that: "*In our view, and on the facts of this case there is an air of unreality about the Claimant's contention. There is no suggestion that as at April 2017 when the AFR Locate trial commenced, SWP either recognised or ought to have recognised that the software it had licenced might operate in a way that was indirectly discriminatory*".[189] It continued by stating that

> even now there is no firm evidence that the software does produce results that suggest indirect discrimination. Rather, the Claimant's case rests on what is said by Dr Anil Jain, an expert witness. In his first statement dated 30th September 2018, Dr Jain commented to the effect that the accuracy of AFR systems generally could depend on the dataset used to 'train' the system. He did not, however, make any specific comment about the dataset used by SWP or about the accuracy of the NeoFace Watch software that SWP has licensed. Dr Jain went no further than to say that if SWP did not know the contents of the dataset used to train its system 'it

[185] More generally, reference can also be made to the specific skills and virtues that judges should have in the context of adjudication, as well as their (ethical and legal) duties. See also, e.g., Iris van Domselaar, 'The Perceptive Judge' (2018) 9 Jurisprudence 71.

[186] See *R (Bridges) v CCSWP and SSHD*, 4 September 2019, High Court, Case no.: CO/4085/2018, [2019] EWHC 2341 (Admin). As the judgment states at §28, SWP deployed AFR Locate on about fifty occasions between May 2017 and April 2019 at a variety of large public events.

[187] This argument was based on section 149(1) of the UK's Equality Act 2010, which sets out the so-called 'Public Sector Equality Duty' and requires that

> a public authority must, in the exercise of its functions, have due regard to the need to (a) eliminate discrimination, harassment, victimisation and any other conduct that is prohibited by or under this Act; (b) advance equality of opportunity between persons who share a relevant protected characteristic and persons who do not share it; (c) foster good relations between persons who share a relevant protected characteristic and persons who do not share it.

[188] *R (Bridges) v CCSWP and SSHD* (n 186) §21.

[189] ibid §153.

would be difficult for SWP to confirm whether the technology is in fact biased'. The opposite is, of course, also true.[190]

Further in the judgment, the High Court also included the statement by Dr Jain: "I cannot comment on whether AFR Locate has a discriminatory impact as I do not have access to the data sets on which the system is trained and therefore cannot analyse the biases in those data sets. For the same reason, the defendant is not in a position to evaluate the discriminatory impact of AFR Locate."[191]

It is hard to find a more blatant example of how informational limitations can have an impact on the judicial review of public authorities' use of algorithmic systems. Furthermore, the High Court's stance aggravated the problem. It considered Mr Bridges' claim that the SWP insufficiently considered the risk that the system might suffer from bias and lead to indirect discrimination to have "*an air of unreality*" since he could not provide evidence of such discrimination, all the while acknowledging that he did not get access to the relevant datasets and that any evidence in this regard was hence unfeasible. Given this reasoning, it is hence no surprise that the High Court rejected Mr Bridges' arguments. The Court of Appeal, however, took the opposite stance. On the particular issue of the duty of equality, it stated: "*With respect to the Divisional Court, we do not consider that there is 'an air of unreality' about the Appellant's contention that there has been a breach of the PSED* [Public Sector Equality Duty]. *On the contrary, it seems to us to raise a serious issue of public concern, which ought to be considered properly by SWP.*"[192] Moreover, it underlined the informational limitations associated with the use of the algorithmic system by noting that "*Dr Jain cannot comment on this particular software but that is because, for reasons of commercial confidentiality, the manufacturer is not prepared to divulge the details so that it could be tested*".[193] Furthermore, the Court of Appeal found that the current legal framework was *not* sufficient to constitute a legal basis for the use of such technology and suffered from fundamental deficiencies.[194] Especially when compared to the findings of the High Court, the Court of Appeal's stance is a substantial improvement. It has, nevertheless, been argued that the Court of Appeal's judgment still failed to grasp the full significance of the technology's capabilities, and that its evaluation of the legal arguments was hence inadequate.[195] In sum, the courts' engagement with the capabilities and limitations of algorithmic regulation in the context of judicial review (and its impact on individual and societal interests) cannot

[190] ibid.
[191] ibid, §155.
[192] *R (Bridges) v CCSWP and SSHD*, 11 August 2020, Court of Appeal (Civil Division), Case no.: C1/2019/2670, [2020] EWCA Civ 1058, §173.
[193] ibid, §199.
[194] ibid, §91.
[195] See the discussion of this case in Karen Yeung, 'Constitutional Principles in a Networked Digital Society' [2022] SSRN Electronic Journal, 10 <www.ssrn.com/abstract=4049141>.

be taken for granted, and hinges on the judges' understanding of, and willingness to pay attention to, the specific risks arising therefrom.

Finally, recall that judicial review must also be available when public authorities delegate their tasks to a private entity.[196] Accordingly, whenever the development (or deployment) of an algorithmic system has been outsourced to a private company, public authorities should not be able to escape the need to provide information about the algorithmic system by reference to the private company's intellectual property rights. Instead, they must ensure that, where such rights exist, these do not hinder the judge's review of how the challenged administrative act came into being.

4.1.5.b Difficult Access to a Remedy

Before a legal dispute concerning an administrative act is heard in court, the individual subjected to the act must first have taken the step to challenge it and thus to request its judicial review. This means that she must already have knowledge of the fact that the act was potentially arbitrary or unlawful, or have sound arguments to make this case. If she lacks information on how the algorithmic system works, it will be difficult for her to make such arguments. It is here that the asymmetry of information between the individual subjected to the system and the system's developer or deployer can also lead to a stronger asymmetry of power, which in the context of judicial proceedings might also hamper access to justice and the equality of arms principle.[197] An individual may not always know that an algorithmic system lies at the basis of an administrative act affecting her. And even if she knows this fact,

[196] See Venice Commission, 'Rule of Law Checklist' (n 57), §45.

[197] See also Council of Europe Ad Hoc Committee on Artificial Intelligence – CAHAI, 'Feasibility Study' (Council of Europe 2020) CAHAI(2020)23, §23. In this regard, reference can also be made to the AERIUS rulings of the Dutch Council of State, concerning a software used by the relevant authority to calculate the deposition of nitrogen in the context of environmental impact assessments for agricultural projects (case references: Raad Van State, 17 May 2017, ECLI:NL:RVS:2017:1259; Raad Van State, 18 July 2018, ECLI:NL:RVS:2018:2454; and Hoge Raad, 17 August 2018; ECLI:HR:2018). That calculation formed the basis for a partially automated decision process to determine whether a project "*is likely to cause a significant deterioration or disturbance of a nitrogen-sensitive habitat located in a Natura 2000 site*", and hence whether a permit ought to be provided (see also Joined Cases C-293/17 and C-294/17, *Coöperatie Mobilisation for the Environment*, 7 November 2018, ECLI:EU:C:2018:882), in light of a preliminary reference procedure that arose in the case before the Council of State. When the outcomes of the software – which operated in an opaque manner – were challenged, the Dutch Council of State had the opportunity to stress the importance of the equality of arms principle whenever public authorities rely on algorithmic systems. Particularly, both at the lower and higher instance it was stated that whenever the decision of an administrative authority is the result of an automated process – even if only in part – and the affected party wishes to verify the correctness of the choices made during that automated process (including the verification of the data and assumptions used for this analysis) to potentially challenge it, the administrative authority must ensure that its choices, assumptions and data are *transparent* and *verifiable*.

she may still be in the dark as regards the system's functioning – and particularly how its suggestions or decisions come about. Yet as long as such information is not accessible, it will be more difficult for individuals to seek the judicial review of an administrative act that adversely impacts them and to obtain a remedy. For instance, in case a data-driven system is deployed, individuals would ideally need to have information about the potential patterns and categorisations that the system picked up, and how the system correlated their data with that of other persons. How else can they assess and – if need be – argue before a court that such correlations may be spurious or discriminatory?

I have already discussed several instances where public authorities refused to provide insight into the algorithmic systems they are using when informing or taking administrative acts. That such refusal can take extreme proportions is also illustrated by the STIR system (short for 'System Teleinformatyczny Izby Rozliczeniowej') used in Poland automatically to detect suspicious bank activities. The system, described by the Polish government as a 'warehouse of data', was adopted in 2017 and used by the Polish National Revenue Administration which was established that same year, when the government declared tax fraud to be a priority.[198] As explained by AlgorithmWatch, "*STIR can be accessed by analysts working in a special unit of KAS. Every day, reports from STIR land on their desks, which include information on transactions that were automatically labelled as suspicious as well as 'entities classified as high-risk groups using the financial sector for tax evasion'*".[199] Based on this information, it can then be decided to freeze the bank accounts of companies suspected of tax fraud – an administrative act that various companies already sought to challenge in court. These companies were, however, unable to challenge the outcomes of the algorithmic system as such, given a lack of information about its operations.

In 2017, the Polish government adopted a law that serves as the legal basis for this system, mandating the National Revenue Administration to establish relevant risk indicators. It, however, only did so in general terms.[200] While the opacity about the algorithm and its risk indicators was raised early on by civil society organisations, the law goes as far as qualifying the provision of information about the algorithm as an offence. In fact, "*the law introducing STIR states that disclosing or using algorithms or risk indicators, without being entitled to do so, is an offense. A person who discloses algorithms can be imprisoned for up to five years (if the act was unintentional, then a fine can be given).*"[201] On the one hand, one can understand, in the context of fighting tax fraud, the reluctance of the government to provide overly detailed information about how the algorithmic system operates, lest fraudsters can use this

[198] AlgorithmWatch (n 62) 179.
[199] ibid 180.
[200] ibid 181.
[201] ibid 185.

information to avoid being caught. On the other hand, however, the freezing of a company's bank account can have far-reaching consequences, and natural and legal persons should have sufficient information to be able to challenge the system in case doubts arise as to the legality of its outcomes. When sharing information about an algorithm's risk indicators is penalised with a prison sentence, one can question whether the balance between the government's legitimate aim to combat tax fraud and ensuring the possibility for judicial review is appropriately struck.

Evidently, the government should not be able to justify its decision to freeze a bank account merely based on the fact that an algorithmic system flagged one or more transactions as suspicious, without also explaining where the suspicion stems from. And the reviewing judge will still be able to ask the government to substantiate its decision – whether it was based on an algorithmic system or not. Yet such substantiation becomes more difficult if the system's flagging, for instance, hinges on the detection of 'unusual patterns' on a bank account, without an explanation as regards the causality between the pattern and the potential fraud. To which extent can a judge defer to the public authority's discretion to use algorithmic tools to identify a risk of fraud, even if the tool is opaque? What is the scope of the review that the judge must carry out? Does it suffice that the public authority – in this case, the Polish National Revenue Administration – provides a general list of potential risk indicators that may have been triggered? Or should the judge also be able to review the choices underlying the algorithmic decision-making tool? These are open questions that each judge might answer differently, yet they matter for the provision of an effective remedy for those subjected to the system and wishing to challenge not just its outcome as put forward by a public administration, but also its underlying assumptions, choices and inner workings.

An additional point to raise as regards the complication for natural and legal persons to obtain a remedy against an administrative act is that, in some jurisdictions, access to judicial review can be conditional upon the submission of a prior formal complaint with the public authority that took the challenged act. For instance, under Belgian law, an individual seeking the judicial review of an administrative act first needs to submit a formal complaint with that administration whenever a complaint mechanism is foreseen.[202] Note that the existence of a complaint procedure depends on the particular public authority, and that its modalities may differ from authority to authority.[203] Yet the mediation of algorithmic regulation might render the filing of a formal complaint more difficult. As noted elsewhere,[204] when an individual is adversely impacted by algorithmic regulation (for instance because of a miscategorisation, or because of the absence of a category that fits her case) the possibilities for re-interpretation, contestation and adaptation are close to

[202] See in this regard Steven Van Garsse (ed), *Handboek Bestuursrecht* (Politeia 2016).
[203] ibid.
[204] See also Smuha, 'The Human Condition in an Algorithmized World' (n 12) 36–37.

zero, as the system itself cannot be 'reasoned' with, and the relevant design choices have typically been made not by the public officials using the system, but by its coders.[205] Merely adding a public official as a 'human in the loop' will therefore not be of much help if that official subsequently uncritically refers back to the system.

4.1.5.c Lack of Systemic Review

When an individual does manage to successfully challenge a problematic administrative act in court and submit it to judicial review, the damage will already be done, in some cases irreversibly so. Recall in this regard the example of the UK Post Office scandal I mentioned in Chapter 2, where people wrongly accused of theft due to reliance on a flawed algorithmic system spent years in prison or even died before a court was able to set the record straight.[206] Or recall the example of the Dutch child care allowance scandal, where families were driven into poverty and went through emotional dramas before the problem was addressed.[207] This is why, in the context of algorithmic regulation, ex post judicial review is a necessary but insufficient safeguard.[208] Nevertheless, and setting the irreversibility of certain types of damage aside, judicial review does enable a judge to remedy the situation ex post by indemnifying those adversely affected and condemning the state if the rule of law's principles were breached.

When the administrative act that is being challenged was informed or taken through an algorithmic system, there is, however, an additional element to consider: judicial review in principle only applies to the administrative act pertaining to the individual that brought the case to court, and not to other administrative acts taken by the same, potentially flawed, system. This is, however, problematic, as the system's flaws may be systemic in nature, and risk causing systemic harm rather than mere individual harm.[209] As long as the root of the problem (namely the faulty design, development or deployment of the algorithmic system) is not addressed, adverse effects will remain, whether to other individual interests or to societal interests more generally. As observed by Abe Chauhan, "*deciding on individual cases distances courts from the root of the systemic error in decisions made by the*

[205] See also Burrell and Fourcade (n 42).

[206] See *supra*, Section 2.2.2.

[207] See *supra*, Sections 4.1.1 and 4.1.4.

[208] See also Joe Tomlinson, Kate Sheridan and Adam Harkens, 'Judicial Review Evidence in the Era of the Digital State' (2020) 4 Public Law 740.

[209] Karen Yeung, 'Responsibility and AI: A Study of the Implications of Advanced Digital Technologies (Including AI Systems) for the Concept of Responsibility within a Human Rights Framework' (Council of Europe, 2019) 63, <https://rm.coe.int/a-study-of-the-implications-of-advanced-digital-technologies-including/168096bdab>; Nathalie A Smuha, 'Beyond the Individual: Governing AI's Societal Harm' (2021) 10 Internet Policy Review 3; Bart van der Sloot and Sascha van Schendel, 'Procedural Law for the Data-Driven Society' (2021) Information & Communications Technology Law 1.

relevant department or authority as to the design and implementation of such systems. Each of these issues is exacerbated by the evidential difficulties created by opacity and the effect of automation bias."[210] Due to the jurisdictional limitations of the judicial review process, judges may hence not always be in the position to remedy the broader adverse impact of the system's problematic use. While some courts have started to accept the review of upstream decisions made in relation to algorithmic regulation,[211] such a remedy is not uniformly available, and the lack thereof renders the halting of public authorities' (intentional or unintentional) systemic infringement of the rule of law's principles more difficult. Once again, this emphasises the need for ex ante safeguards in the context of algorithmic regulation, but also for a reconsideration of mechanisms that would allow for more structural judicial remedies, so as to ensure that ex post review does not hinge on the shoulders of individual citizens. Systemic problems, after all, require systemic solutions.[212]

Finally, it must also be stressed that the judiciary depends on the executive branch to uphold its judgments. This led Montesquieu to state that "*of the three powers above mentioned, the judiciary is next to nothing*".[213] It is hence better to prevent rather than cure when it comes to keeping the executive power in check, especially if one recalls that in some EU Member States, authoritarian tendencies have already resulted in an erosion of the judiciary's independence.[214]

4.1.6 *Separation of Powers*

The last of the six rule of law principles concerns the separation of powers. In essence, this principle is aimed at avoiding a concentration of power by ensuring adequate checks and balances amongst the different branches.[215] In constitutional liberal democracies, each power should only exercise the functions that it is legally ascribed, with due regard for the protection of the rights and liberties of citizens, who should also be able to hold their government accountable.[216] In addition, the separation of powers can also be said to imply a separation of public power from private power, ensuring that public power is used in the public interest, rather than

[210] Chauhan (n 50) 5.

[211] ibid.

[212] See also Jennifer Cobbe, Michelle Seng Ah Lee and Jatinder Singh, 'Reviewable Automated Decision-Making: A Framework for Accountable Algorithmic Systems', *Proceedings of the 2021 ACM Conference on Fairness, Accountability, and Transparency* (Association for Computing Machinery 2021).

[213] See Baron de Montesquieu, *The Spirit of the Laws* (1748) (Thomas Nugent tr, Hafner Publishing Company 1949). This extract was later also quoted by Alexander Hamilton in Federalist Paper 78 (1788).

[214] See *supra*, Section 3.2.5.

[215] See *supra*, Section 3.3.6.

[216] Andreas Schedler, 'Conceptualizing Accountability' in Andreas Schedler, Larry Diamond and Marc F Plattner (eds), *The Self-Restraining State: Power and Accountability in New Democracies* (Lynne Rienner Publishers 1999).

in the interest of private parties. If we now examine how this principle fares in light of the public authorities' increased reliance on algorithmic regulation, one can intuitively imagine that this may affect the power dynamics between the different branches of power and between the state and its citizens. Considering all that has already been discussed under the previous principles, let me focus on three points in particular.

4.1.6.a Strengthening the Executive

To begin with, one can note that the use of algorithmic regulation strengthens the power of the executive branch in several ways. First, it provides the executive with the possibility to adopt administrative acts at a faster speed and scale, thereby enabling it to exercise its decision-making power on many more natural and legal persons at the same time.[217] Second, it enables the executive to decide how text-based general laws are translated into code, which implies both an interpretation process and a reduction process, since the rich openness of text is necessarily reduced to a specific reading of the text, which is then turned into machine-readable code.[218] Third, it also ensures that executive policies can be executed in a centralised and systemic way, whereby discretion that can be used to deviate from the codified policy is eliminated. In addition, once the infrastructure for algorithmic regulation has been implemented, the executive will have the ability to singlehandedly rewrite the code, which is malleable and can be adapted instantaneously. Underlying the deployment of algorithmic systems is an entire technical infrastructure comprising hardware, software and databases, which will likewise be controlled by the executive branch of power, and which will cement the automation of decision-making for years to come.

Consider, in this regard, the example of the algorithmic system used by the US Immigration and Customs Enforcement (ICE) to help assess whether an illegal immigrant should be detained. Under the Obama administration, such detainment typically only occurred if immigrants were caught crossing the border illegally or when they had a serious criminal record. Otherwise, they were in principle released on bond.[219] However, when Trump became president, an executive order was issued to put an end to this practice, and to instead insist on the detention of immigrants regardless of any criminal record. As a consequence, the ICE proceeded to modify the algorithmic tool and removed the possibility for the system to recommend 'release'.[220] From one day to the next, all public officials, by virtue of the change

[217] Restrepo Amariles (n 19).
[218] See *supra*, Section 4.1.1.
[219] Mica Rosenberg and Reade Levinson, 'Trump's Catch-and-Detain Policy Snares Many Who Call the U.S. Home' *Reuters* (20 June 2018) <www.reuters.com/investigates/special-report/usa-immigration-court/>.
[220] ibid.

in the algorithmic system, were only able to get a negative recommendation out of the system. Certainly, Trump's executive order in itself already required them to act accordingly, yet the layer of automation further diminished their agency to act differently in cases where a release on bond might nevertheless have been warranted in view of particular circumstances. Accordingly, it must be kept in mind that the decision to automate (part of) certain administrative acts in one legislature will inevitably also create affordances for the next legislature, as the infrastructure that enables it remains.

Furthermore, the lack of transparency that often surrounds algorithmic regulation reduces the ability of the other branches of power to exercise checks and ensure that power is balanced. Checks can also be complicated by the lack of technical expertise within the other branches, who lack skilled personnel to understand and scrutinise these systems. Since the beginning of the *trias politicas* doctrine and even more so in recent years,[221] scholars have argued that an asymmetry of power between the branches exists, in favour of the executive.[222] The efficiency and scalability of executive decision-making through the use of algorithmic regulation can further exacerbate this power asymmetry. Moreover, the fact that in virtually all states, the adoption of algorithmic systems is primarily an affair of the executive branch of power also means that its power increase is not counterbalanced by the potential use of such systems by the other branches (assuming that such counterbalancing is at all feasible).[223]

It can hence be concluded that the executive's use of algorithmic regulation reinforces existing power structures rather than rebalancing power, and that it seems to skew the balance further in favour of the executive. This holds true regardless of whether the executive branch purposely implements algorithmic systems to consolidate power, or whether it implements it with the intention to better serve the public interest.

4.1.6.b Privatising Legal Infrastructure

To ensure that public authorities uphold the principles of the rule of law, it is also important that private entities do not exercise undue power over public matters. This can be referred to as the separation of public power from private power. Many public authorities, however, still lack technical know-how to design and develop algorithmic systems themselves.[224] Accordingly, more often than not, the

[221] See *supra*, Section 3.3.6.

[222] See also Susan Rose-Ackerman, *Democracy and Executive Power: Policymaking Accountability in the US, the UK, Germany, and France* (Yale University Press 2021).

[223] See Reijer Passchier, *Artificiële intelligentie en de rechtsstaat* (Boom 2021).

[224] See Antonio Cordella and Leslie Willcocks, 'Outsourcing, Bureaucracy and Public Value: Reappraising the Notion of the "Contract State"' (2010) 27 Government Information Quarterly 82.

development of algorithmic systems used by public authorities is outsourced to private entities.[225] Given the stakes I described above (the translation exercise from text to code, the various interpretation choices, and the normative consequences), one might ask whether such outsourcing, in practice, risks providing private actors with an undue ability to shape public policy.[226] This pertains not only to the choices of interpretation, but also the choices of optimisation, model selection, data gathering, labelling and cleaning, and so on. To which extent does the outsourcing of these normatively relevant choices imply a privatisation of legal interpretation and application? And how can the translation process be verified, controlled and legitimised by the public officials who are actually in charge of the task, if their insufficient familiarity with algorithmic systems is what drove the outsourcing in the first place?

One can take this line of questioning a step further, and also inquire into the choices relating to the underlying infrastructure of the algorithmic system[227] which is, almost by definition, likewise controlled by private entities. As noted above,[228] infrastructural questions may sound boring, yet they matter a great deal. Together with the data and model of the system, the choice of infrastructure on which it is built likewise bears normative consequences, and can have an impact on individuals, groups and society at large.[229] While in-house knowledge to develop algorithmic systems is rare but existing, there are almost no public authorities that are also the full controller of the underlying infrastructure on which these systems operate. This implies a vulnerability, since once the system is in place and relied upon by public authorities, they will not only become dependent on the system's adequate functioning, but also on the adequate functioning of the infrastructure that enables it, and that can be altered by private entities who are not subjected to democratic oversight. In sum, one must heed the risks associated not only with the outsourcing of legal interpretation to private entities, but also with dependencies on 'legal infrastructure' more generally.

4.1.6.c Citizen Surveillance

Finally, public authorities' reliance on algorithmic systems also has an impact on the role that citizens and civil society can play to ensure that the separation of powers is upheld. Civil society contributes to the functioning of checks and balances by seeking information about how its representatives act, and by holding its representatives to account if they do not respect the rule of law, for instance during democratic

[225] See also *supra*, Section 3.3.6.
[226] See also Verkuil (n 117).
[227] See Diver (n 3) 20–21.
[228] See *supra*, Section 2.2.1.
[229] See also Julie E Cohen, 'Affording Fundamental Rights: A Provocation Inspired by Mireille Hildebrandt' (2017) 4 Critical Analysis of Law 76.

elections, or in court when seeking the judicial review of specific government actions.[230] However, when public authorities deploy algorithmic regulation, public scrutiny by civil society, media and the public at large can become more difficult, for the same reason that scrutiny by the other branches of power can become more difficult.[231] Many citizens also lack the technical skills to understand how algorithmic systems function. Public authorities hence need to ensure that, if information about the system and its functioning is provided, such explanation is understandable for non-experts while remaining sufficiently meaningful.

In addition, increased reliance on algorithmic systems is also accompanied by increased data-gathering on citizens, to enable the system to profile them and take administrative acts relating to them.[232] Beyond the risk that such information is reflected incorrectly or in a biased manner, and beyond the increased risk of data-leaks and other vulnerabilities, it is also possible that such information, along with its decision-making infrastructure, is at some point deliberately used against them. Consider the concerns that arose when Poland proclaimed it would henceforth keep a centralised registry of healthcare data of citizens, including data about whether a woman is pregnant, with the stated aim of enabling a faster and more personalised delivery of health services based on such information.[233] While the Polish government at the time sought to emphasise the beneficial goal behind such data collection,[234] civil society organisations were concerned that, in a country where abortion is near banned, such information could also be used to monitor women's compliance with abortion laws, and potentially lead to the establishment of automated red flags when women are no longer pregnant prior to their due date.

Regulations can be altered, and laws can change. Under a new government or a reversal of precedent case law,[235] actions that were once deemed a legal exercise of a fundamental right can become criminalised and vice versa. Yet through it all, data that was previously collected from citizens remains, as does the infrastructure that enables automated decision-making based on such data. The phenomenon of function creep that might accompany such infrastructure is well illustrated by an application of algorithmic regulation that is widely used in Belgium today, namely automated number-plate recognition (ANPR) cameras, which are essentially mass

[230] See *supra*, Section 3.3.6.

[231] See also Fink (n 165); Fink and Finck (n 109).

[232] See, e.g., Peeters and Widlak (n 44); Kennedy (n 149); Heather Broomfield and Lisa Reutter, 'In Search of the Citizen in the Datafication of Public Administration' (2022) 9 Big Data & Society 1.

[233] See '"Tool of Repression": Anger over Poland's New "Pregnancy Register"' *euronews* (6 June 2022) <www.euronews.com/2022/06/06/poland-s-government-criticised-over-pregnancy-register-amid-strict-abortion-laws>.

[234] Karolina Kocemba, 'Pregnancy Registry in Poland' (*Verfassungsblog*, 22 June 2022) <https://verfassungsblog.de/pregnancy-registry/>.

[235] Regarding the same subject matter, one can point to the US Supreme Court's overruling of *Roe v Wade* after fifty years, on 24 June 2022. See *Dobbs v Jackson Women's Health Organization*, 597 U.S. 2022.

surveillance tools.[236] These cameras have been deployed on the Belgian roads since many years to read number plates of passing cars and crossing them with a database containing the number plates of wanted vehicles. The cameras were initially installed after the terror attacks that took place in 2016, with the mere purpose of catching terrorists and other criminals. The infrastructure, for which substantial public investments were made, not only raises significant privacy concerns, but has thus far also not been effective, primarily due to a large percentage of false-positive alerts (in some cases up to 80 per cent)[237] and a lack of personnel to actually go after a car once it has been flagged.[238] This did not stop the government from incrementally extending the offences for which the cameras could be deployed, from the identification of stolen vehicles, and vehicles of which the owner did not pay a traffic fine, to most recently the identification of vehicles of which the owner did not pay off debts with the Ministry of Finance, including income tax, corporation tax, VAT or overdue alimony.[239] Another Belgian example concerns the installation of security cameras in the Jewish neighbourhood in Antwerp during the terrorist threat in 2015 and 2016 to protect the Jewish community. A few years later, during the Covid-19 pandemic in 2020, those same cameras were used to snoop on the community's compliance with the lockdown that was imposed, and especially with the ban on (religious) gatherings.[240]

Taking these examples one step further, one can thus imagine that the same infrastructure which facilitates scaled algorithmic decision-making in the so-called public interest can, under a worst case scenario, also be used by subsequent governments to oppress those very citizens, and specifically to target minorities, marginalised communities or political opponents. What happened in Afghanistan in the aftermath of the Taliban's return to power in August 2021 is telling in this regard. As reported by Human Rights Watch, before the Taliban's return

> foreign governments such as the United States, and international institutions, including United Nations agencies and the World Bank, funded and in some cases built or helped to build vast systems to hold the biometric and other personal data of

[236] Ian Warren and others, 'When the Profile Becomes the Population: Examining Privacy Governance and Road Traffic Surveillance in Canada and Australia' (2013) 25 Current Issues in Criminal Justice 565.

[237] See in this regard the investigation conducted by Comité P, Belgium's Official Police Monitoring Committee: Comité permanent de controle des services de police, 'Le fonctionnement de la police intégrée en matière de traitement des hits ANPR de plaques d'immatriculation volées' (2022) 15.

[238] Belga, 'Duur cameraschild langs snelwegen werkt amper: Tot 80 procent vals alarm' *De Morgen* (2 February 2022) <www.demorgen.be/gs-b84b968d>.

[239] See Belga, 'Belastingzondaars kunnen voortaan van de weg geplukt worden' *De Morgen* (19 August 2022) <www.demorgen.be/gs-b56328c5>. See particularly 'Wet houdende diverse fiscale bepalingen' of 5 July 2022, which introduces these extended grounds, accessible at www.ejustice.just.fgov.be/eli/wet/2022/07/05/2022032714/justel.

[240] See Matthias Verbergt, 'Camera's in joodse wijk controleren nu synagogegangers' *De Standaard* (13 March 2021) <www.standaard.be/cnt/dmf20210312_98151173>.

> various groups of Afghans for official purposes. In some cases, these systems were built for the former Afghan government. In others, they were designed for foreign governments and militaries.[241]

It is believed that several of these systems are now used by the Taliban with the aim of targeting journalists and political opponents.[242] While this example does not concern the use of algorithmic regulation in a liberal democracy, the algorithmic systems enabling it were placed there by the public authorities of liberal democracies who believed they were acting in the public interest.

Despite the stronger legal protection mechanisms and higher political stability in the EU, it would be short-sighted to assume that infrastructures built in European countries would be immune from the same fate if, over the longer term, authoritarian tendencies further increase, especially in Member States where the rule of law is already under threat. These examples hence show how important it is to consider a *long-term* perspective when rolling out algorithmic regulation infrastructures with large databases, as the normative pillars underpinning liberal democracies are inherently fragile. The deployment of algorithmic systems should hence go hand in hand with an assessment of the longer-term risks for individual and societal interests, and with mechanisms to rebalance the increased asymmetry of power that the unchecked use of such systems imply.[243]

4.2 ALGORITHMIC RULE BY LAW

In the previous section, I conducted a systematic analysis of how public authorities' reliance on algorithmic regulation can adversely impact each of the six rule of law principles, drawing on concrete illustrations. Let me reiterate that, while I do not claim that these adverse effects *always* manifest themselves, my analysis shows they *can*, and that this risk should therefore be pre-empted and addressed. Many of the

[241] 'New Evidence that Biometric Data Systems Imperil Afghans' (*Human Rights Watch*, 30 March 2022) <www.hrw.org/news/2022/03/30/new-evidence-biometric-data-systems-imperil-afghans>. The article lists six systems that were built by private companies for or with foreign governments or international institutions: (1) Afghan National Biometric System, used to issue Afghan national identity cards, known as e-Tazkira; (2) US Defense Department Automated Biometric Identification System (ABIS), used to identify people whom the US believed might pose a security risk as well as those working for the US government; (3) Afghan Automated Biometric Identification System (AABIS), used to identify criminals and Afghan army and police members; (4) Ministry of Interior and Defense Afghan Personnel and Pay Systems (APPS) for the army and police, into which the AABIS was integrated in early 2021; (5) payroll system of the National Directorate of Security, the former state intelligence agency; and (6) payroll system of the Afghan Supreme Court.

[242] ibid. See also the statement by Aziz Rafiee, the executive director of the Afghan Civil Society Forum, who commented that "*the international community might have thought it was helping us, but instead it played with our fate and ended up creating systems more dangerous than they were helpful*".

[243] I will further discuss these mechanisms *infra*, in Sections 4.3 and 6.2.2.

identified concerns are recurring across the six principles and are interlinked, since they stem from the combination of the risks inherent to algorithmic regulation on the one hand, and the role of the rule of law to tame public power on the other hand. In this section, I will therefore consolidate and summarise my findings, by proposing a theory of harm that conceptualises the adverse impact of algorithmic regulation on the rule of law. Conceptualising this harm can not only foster a better understanding of what is at stake, but it can also facilitate the evaluation of the legal framework's ability to counter it.

As announced in the Introduction, I propose to denote this theory of harm as *algorithmic rule by law*, to stress its deviation from the rule of law's ideal. Under the rule of law, public power is tamed by law, yet public authorities acknowledge the internal and external tensions that are inherent thereto, as well as the need to safeguard other EU values like respect for human rights and democracy. In contrast, under algorithmic rule by law, the law's power is channelled into a centralised algorithmic infrastructure that can be shaped and changed opaquely by a handful of people, and is prone to be wielded in a way that undermines the rule of law's very purpose – whether deliberately or not.

My analysis has brought to the surface at least five overarching problematic elements that characterise the threat of algorithmic rule by law. First, the illustrations indicated a prioritisation of algorithm-induced efficiency and procedural rationality over normative values like human rights and administrative justice ("*primacy of techno-rationality*") (Section 5.2.1). Second, rather than trained public officials, the outcome of administrative actions is determined by the handful of people who design and develop the algorithmic systems, who thereby gain significant influence over public decision-making ("*supremacy of coders*") (Section 5.2.2). Third, the analysis demonstrated how reliance on algorithmic regulation can reduce law's inherent openness and ambiguity to an overly formalised and narrow shape, leading to a legalistic approach instead, without the possibility to correct its hard edges where needed ("*automation of legalism*") (Section 5.2.3). Moreover, the opacity accompanying the systems' design and implementation processes tends to diminish the possibility to exert oversight over the executive's operations, and to ensure that constitutional checks and balances are maintained ("*deficit of accountability*") (Section 5.2.4). Finally, since algorithmic regulation rests on an underlying technical infrastructure, this introduces an important vulnerability in the legal system, which – as well as being instantly malleable – can also be deployed in a way that systemically undermines EU values ("*systemic vulnerability*") (Section 5.2.5).

While each of these elements is worrying in and of itself, they are interrelated and reinforce each other. Collectively, they can therefore be seen as symptoms of the broader problem that lies at the heart of this book: the risk that algorithmic regulation, under the guise of implementing law, actually serves inadvertently or deliberately to undermine the law's protective power and foster a rule *by* law approach instead, hence meriting the term *algorithmic rule by law*. I deliberately opt for a conceptualisation that focuses on the perversion of the *law*, rather than on the use of algorithms – therefore foregoing the use of terms like 'rule by algorithms' or 'algorithmic rule'. The core problem revealed by the analysis above stems from the way in which those responsible for the design, development and deployment of algorithmic systems may – under the veneer of legality – undercut its value and open the door to illiberal and authoritarian practices. In what follows, I conceptualise this threat by setting out its five problematic features, and outline how they erode the law's protective role.

4.2.1 *Primacy of Techno-rationality*

In Chapter 3, I described how the rule of law provides both procedural and substantive protection for citizens, by ensuring that public authorities duly consider their rights and interests and by empowering public officials to make appropriate trade-offs in between rules and discretion, thereby safeguarding individual justice. However, when algorithmic regulation is used, we can observe that the law's implementation is portrayed as a techno-scientific endeavour rather than a normative one.[244] Law is seen as an expression of rationality, and its application becomes a matter of mathematics rather than judgment and evaluation. Open-ended legal concepts such as 'exceptional' or 'reasonable', and even normative values like equality, are reflected into mathematical calculations and programmed into algorithmic systems.[245] Yet, as noted above, these concepts are not always uniformly understood, and their interpretation and codification embodies certain normative choices.[246] Notwithstanding this fact, pursuant to the logic of algorithms, the law's application is handled by a problem-solving approach, driven by efficiency rather than justice. By identifying optimal models and codifying optimal computations for the law's application, the 'solution' can be automated at scale, rendering individual judgment and assessment, and the time and resources that such assessments might require, redundant. In sum, the adoption of administrative acts, and of all the preparatory decisions to support this act, is reduced to a techno-scientific enterprise.

As a consequence, the law that is being algorithmically applied by public authorities is decoupled from the broader normative framework that it is part of, which in turn risks decoupling it from the overarching normative ends it should serve. Procedural rationality is hence favoured over substantive rationality, and normativity is being replaced by techno-rationality. This risk does not arise solely in algorithmic

[244] See Diver (n 3); Marijn Janssen and George Kuk, 'The Challenges and Limits of Big Data Algorithms in Technocratic Governance' (2016) 33 Government Information Quarterly 371; Niklas Andreas Andersen, 'The Technocratic Rationality of Governance – The Case of the Danish Employment Services' [2020] Critical Policy Studies 1.

[245] See Schartum (n 1) 315.

[246] See *supra*, Sections 3.3.1 and 4.1.1.

context, but in bureaucratic organisation more generally.[247] However, undeniably, algorithmic regulation can significantly exacerbate it.

Reliance on algorithmic regulation gives law, and the legal text that is being translated from law to code, an "*unwarranted aura of objectivity*".[248] While the notion of objectivity fits very well with the bureaucratic ideals of impersonality, rationality and efficiency, it is misplaced in the context of the law's application, and can be at odds with the ideal of individual justice. As the above illustrations made clear, the law's application is never truly 'objective', as open-ended legal concepts allow for a variety of legal interpretations.[249] Yet by essentialising a given interpretation and acting as if it is an objective one, public authorities not only reduce the role of the law but also sweep their underlying normative choices under the rug, all the while maintaining the aura of legality.

Accordingly, the positive and normative become conflated. Algorithmic regulation might present the application of a legal rule as something that is a positive interpretation of legislation: the law as it is. However, in the legal context, a purely positive interpretation only rarely exists. There is always some element of normativity in the way one interprets legal rules. And such interpretation, explicitly or implicitly, always requires a trade-off between different values and interests. Even Weber already emphasised that no rational scientific procedure exists to tell us which trade-offs to make between competing values.[250] Such trade-offs are always an inherently normative choice, and no layer of algorithmic modelling can change that, although it can obscure it.

Furthermore, a techno-scientific approach to law is inherently reductionist, since the richness of language, and the reality it represents, can never be wholly captured by mathematical models (whether knowledge- or data-driven). Yet public authorities' techno-optimism, coupled with the pressure of achieving efficiency gains and making budget cuts, might make them overlook this fact, even if it has important consequences for the individuals subjected to the system. Individuals who fall outside the model, for instance because they do not fit into any of the programmed categories of a knowledge-driven system, or because their situation was not picked up as a distinct pattern by a data-driven system, may be treated as an outlier, both statistically and legally. Crucially, in the context of public authorities, "*being*

[247] I have already discussed how scholars like Arendt and Bauman cautioned against it. See *supra*, Section 2.3.2.

[248] Hildebrandt, 'Algorithmic Regulation and the Rule of Law' (n 121) 3.

[249] Interpretations of legal rules are inherently contestable, and can hence be seen as a subjective exercise. As also noted by Julia Black, "*there is no inherent, fixed meaning to rules or to language; the meaning, and hence the application, of a rule is not an objective fact but is contingent on the interpretive community reading the rule*", in *Rules and Regulators* (n 6).

[250] See *supra*, Section 2.3.2. See also Michael W Spicer, 'Public Administration in a Disenchanted World: Reflections on Max Weber's Value Pluralism and His Views on Politics and Bureaucracy' (2015) 47 Administration & Society 24, 30.

excluded from the system also means being excluded from public services"[251] with highly problematic consequences, hence requiring the anticipation of this risk and the availability of alternative access routes to such services. Equally problematically, besides exclusionary classifications, individuals may also have been classified erroneously or based on discriminatory grounds. In addition, especially with data-driven systems, instead of being based on a *causal* relationship between the facts and the law, administrative acts can be taken based on how certain facts about an individual *correlate* with other facts that are not linked to the law at all. As noted by Langford, "*an individual's rights may be determined on the basis of predictions derived from the behavior of a general population group*",[252] thereby undermining the notion of individual justice.[253]

More generally, legal subjects are literally and figuratively dehumanised by being reduced to faceless datapoints subjected to mathematical rules.[254] This creates further distance between the public officials responsible for the adoption of an administrative act and the person subjected thereto, which in turn can diminish the sense of responsibility and empathy[255] that can help counter the excesses of procedural rationality. As discussed above, this distance (which is present in any bureaucratic form of organisation, but is significantly extended when relying on algorithmic regulation) undermines the 'internal morality' of public authorities. It may even deliberately be exploited to apply the law in an overly rigid manner, with the adverse consequences being felt especially by those already in a vulnerable situation.[256] Simultaneously, the fact that algorithmic regulation renders the contestability of administrative acts more difficult also makes it challenging to correct potential wrongs in the system.[257]

Finally, the logic of efficiency that underlies algorithmic regulation is likely to favour the optimisation of the operation of public authorities rather than the optimisation of the rights of individuals. As noted by Schartum, "*in mass administrative systems, choices of interpretations may easily be affected by expected effects on government budgets – for instance, by pushing interpretation of concepts to extremes*

[251] Peeters and Widlak (n 44) 176.

[252] Langford (n 7) 142.

[253] As defined by Reuben Binns, individual justice "*refers to the notion that each case needs to be assessed on its own merits, without comparison to, or generalization from, previous cases*". See Reuben Binns, 'Human Judgment in Algorithmic Loops: Individual Justice and Automated Decision-Making' (2022) 16 Regulation & Governance 197, 198.

[254] See also Li Huang, Zhi Lu and Priyali Rajagopal, 'Numbers, Not Lives: AI Dehumanization Undermines COVID-19 Preventive Intentions' (2022) 7 Journal of the Association for Consumer Research 63; Broomfield and Reutter (n 232).

[255] Sofia Ranchordas, 'Empathy in the Digital Administrative State' (2022) 71 Duke Law Journal 1341.

[256] Ranchordas and Scarcella (n 150).

[257] Karen Yeung, 'Why Worry about Decision-Making by Machine?' in Karen Yeung and Martin Lodge (eds), *Algorithmic Regulation* (Oxford University Press 2019).

to make possible reuse of data".[258] Recall in this regard also the pressure on public officials to meet KPIs, at the cost of ensuring individualised justice for persons subjected to administrative acts. The logic of efficiency and the logic of respect for individual rights and human dignity are therefore not necessarily aligned. Unfortunately, in the many illustrations discussed above, we must agree with Galligan that "*in the very nature of bureaucratic administration*", and a fortiori in the nature of algorithmic regulation, "*the logic of efficiency is more powerful than that of rights*".[259]

In sum, by relying on algorithmic regulation, the application of the law is reduced to a quantitative endeavour rather than a qualitative one. It is turned into a mathematical instrument and stripped away from its substantive notions, all in the name of efficiency, objectivity and consistency. Yet this can undermine the law's protective role, creating a semblance of legality without leading to justice. When the implementation of algorithmic regulation is framed as a mere positive interpretation and application of the law rather than a normatively relevant translation exercise, in the best case, public authorities risk remaining blind for these adverse consequences and, in the worst case, they deliberately use this blindness to push through problematic interpretations. Accordingly, when opting for reliance on algorithmic regulation, it is crucial that its normative role be acknowledged, and that appropriate mechanisms exist to curb the primacy of techno-rationality over justice.[260]

4.2.2 *Supremacy of Coders*

Under the EU conceptualisation of the rule of law, the principle of legality foresees that the law is adopted through a pluralistic democratic process based on political deliberation and civic participation. Subsequently, it should be applied by public authorities in a manner congruent thereto and in line with the authoritative interpretation of the law by independent courts. Especially in highly regulated societies, this typically implies that a wide range of competences are delegated to public authorities,[261] including discretionary powers to decide the optimal course of action to attain broadly formulated policy goals.[262] Yet the use of these delegated powers must occur in line with the rule of law's principles and, at least in theory, public officials are trained to do so. They are in principle hired based on their skills

[258] Schartum (n 1) 308.

[259] Denis J Galligan, 'Public Administration and the Tendency to Authoritarianism' in András Sajó (ed), *Out of and into Authoritarian Law* (Brill–Nijhoff 2002) 193.

[260] I will touch upon those mechanisms *infra*, in Sections 4.3 and 6.2.

[261] See *supra*, Section 2.3.3.

[262] Denis James Galligan, 'Senses of Discretion' in his *Discretionary Powers: A Legal Study of Official Discretion* (Oxford University Press 1990); Tony Evans, 'Professionals and Discretion in Street-Level Bureaucracy' in Peter Hupe, Michael Hill and Aurélien Buffat (eds), *Understanding Street-Level Bureaucracy* (Bristol University Press 2015).

and expert knowledge, and their ability to implement legislation and apply it to concrete cases based on their reasoned judgment and experience.

While there is no need to idealise the output produced by *all* public officials,[263] the fact that they are trained to carry out their tasks, given the significant impact of their actions on individual and societal interests, is important to stress.[264] This is particularly relevant given the power that public officials, as part of an organisation vested with public authority, can wield. Public officials are therefore typically also bound by administrative rules and specific deontological procedures relating to their professional and moral behaviour, to safeguard that their duties are carried out in the public interest.[265] Echoing the influential work of Jerry Mashaw, these rules and procedures are aimed at enabling 'bureaucratic justice', which includes not only bureaucratic rationality, but also the professional treatment of administrative cases and the exercise of moral judgment – thereby institutionalising normative values within administrations.[266] Recall in this regard also the discussion about the 'internal morality' within public authorities, which aims to ensure that procedural rationality does not overtake substantive rationality to the detriment of the rights and interests of individuals and society.[267] Public officials also act under the political responsibility of members of the executive, who exercise political oversight over their actions and enable democratic accountability, in addition to having their actions subjected to legal review by courts.

However, when public authorities rely on algorithmic regulation, they essentially re-delegate their decision-making power to what I have referred to above as 'coders': people who may have the technical skills to design and develop algorithmic systems, but who are not necessarily trained in public decision-making, nor in the responsibilities and delicate trade-offs this implies. These coders suddenly become the intermediary actors between public authorities and citizens.[268] While this shift of

[263] As discussed *supra*, in Section 1.2.3, my focus on the risks of algorithmic regulation does not imply a blind faith in human beings, or the misguided belief that decision-making by human beings is always free from prejudice or error.

[264] See also Evans (n 262).

[265] See *supra*, Section 2.3.

[266] See Jerry L Mashaw, *Bureaucratic Justice: Managing Social Security Disability Claims* (Yale University Press 1983). Mashaw also underlined the importance of internal governance and control mechanisms, and he considered judicial review – as an external mechanism of control – to be irrelevant or impertinent in most of the cases, given the remoteness of judges from bureaucratic realities. See in this regard Robert A Kagan, 'Varieties of Bureaucratic Justice: Building on Mashaw's Typology' in Nicholas R Parrillo (ed), *Administrative Law from the Inside Out* (1st edn, Cambridge University Press 2017) 248. Indeed, he found that "*the task of improving the quality of administrative justice is one that must be carried forward primarily by administrators*". See also Morgan and Yeung (n 6) 245.

[267] See Galligan, 'Public Administration and the Tendency to Authoritarianism' (n 259).

[268] See also David Freeman Engstrom and others, 'Government by Algorithm: Artificial Intelligence in Federal Administrative Agencies' (Administrative Conference of the United States 2020) <www.acus.gov/sites/default/files/documents/Government%20by%20Algorithm.pdf>.

power away from public officials has been denoted by some as *algocracy* or rule of algorithms,[269] I am wary of such conceptualisation, since it wrongly suggests that power is wielded by algorithmic systems.[270] In truth, power (implying here all the normative and political choices that relate to the implementation and application of the law and the adoption of administrative acts) lies in the hands of those who develop and design these algorithmic systems, or the coders. Speaking of the supremacy of coders would hence be more accurate, since the affordances of the technology are entirely shaped by the decisions underlying the algorithms' design, and hence by their coders.

As previously stressed, the transformation of text-based law to code implies a myriad of morally and politically relevant choices. Algorithmic systems "*only follow unambiguous rules, and there is no room for doubt or discretion*", even if "*it will almost always be possible to claim that other results are correct and legally valid, and thus there may be grounds to disagree that the interpretations embedded in the code should be held as correct*".[271] In the context of algorithmic regulation, discretion about the law's interpretation is centralised and moves upstream, away from public officials, to the handful of coders who translate, interpret and operationalise legal rules through the algorithms they design.[272]

Moreover, this translation process typically occurs in a frictionless manner, as the normative choices underlying it remain invisible, not only for the citizens subjected to the system, but also to the public officials that rely thereon for the purpose of taking administrative acts.[273] While this invisibility might give a semblance of impersonality and objectivity, it reduces the possibility for contestability.[274] Recall in this regard the claim by Peeters and Widlak that the 'digital cage' of public administration can hence not only extend to citizens, but also to public officials who see their discretionary actions constrained by the technology's architecture,[275] which is determined by coders. As noted by Yeung,[276] this absence of friction also

[269] See *supra*, Section 2.3.4.

[270] Similarly, regulation through algorithms has also been conceptualised through notions like *technological management*, the *rule of algorithms* or *algocracy*. See respectively Roger Brownsword, 'Technological Management and the Rule of Law' (2016) 8 Law, Innovation and Technology 100; Michael Meyer-Resende and Marlene Straub, 'The Rule of Law versus the Rule of the Algorithm' [2022] (Verfassungsblog, 28 March 2022) <https://verfassungsblog.de/rule-of-the-algorithm/>; John Danaher, 'The Threat of Algocracy: Reality, Resistance and Accommodation' (2016) 29 Philosophy & Technology 245; Lorenz, Meijer and Schuppan (n 124).

[271] Schartum (n 1) 306.

[272] See Bovens and Zouridis (n 115) 181. See also Burrell and Fourcade (n 42) 217.

[273] Recall in this regard, for instance, the example of the Polish unemployment algorithm, where the public officials using the system stated that they did not know the underlying logic of the system. See *supra*, Sections 4.1.2 and 4.1.3.

[274] Hildebrandt, 'Algorithmic Regulation and the Rule of Law' (n 121) 3.

[275] See Peeters and Widlak (n 44) 181.

[276] Yeung, 'Can We Employ Design-Based Regulation While Avoiding Brave New World?' (n 119) 16.

undermines public officials to exercise their agency and use their judgment, pursuant to their duty of acting in the public interest and in line with their deontological codes, for the seamlessness of the technology's design, in the name of user friendliness, might obliterate the possibility to do so.

At the same time, the outsourcing of discretion to coders occurs under a coat of legality, since, formally speaking, public officials are the ones who remain accountable for the decisions they make, even if they are no longer able to exercise much judgment in this regard. It is for this reason that the power wielded by coders can be seen as part of the larger threat posed by algorithmic rule by law. The fact that the translation of legislation to algorithms is considered as a mere techno-scientific enterprise rather than a normative task minimises the moral and political consequences attached to this process. In practice, however, the delegation of the law's implementation to coders also implies the delegation of public authority and moral responsibility.[277] Yet such delegation occurs without guarantees of adequate training, legal expertise, subjection to deontological codes, or even awareness of such responsibility and, as we shall see further below, without adequate accountability mechanisms for the power that comes with it.[278]

In sum, reliance on algorithmic regulation by public authorities entails a shift in power, whereby the interpretation of legal rules is delegated to coders rather than public officials hired based on their domain expertise and constrained to safeguard the public interest. It therefore also opens the door for these coders – or rather, for those who pay the salary of these coders – to opt for design choices that are problematic from a democracy and human rights-perspective, under the guise that it concerns a purely technical matter. Under a best case scenario, those problematic choices concern errors that can be rectified and hopefully do not cause irreversible damage (though we have seen that the scaled nature of the systems can make the adverse consequences extensive). Under a worst case scenario, those problematic choices deliberately use the veneer of the law, albeit in algorithmic shape, to implement illiberal and authoritarian practices at scale. Consequently, if public authorities wish to rely on algorithmic regulation, it is crucial to ensure that the upstream decisions of coders, regardless of whether they work for a private company to which the design of the system is outsourced or whether they work in-house, be subjected to review and oversight, both internally (to maintain public agency) and externally (to preserve public accountability).

4.2.3 *Automation of Legalism*

A third way in which algorithmic regulation can undermine the rule of law, concerns the way in which it disrupts the balance between rules and discretion.

[277] See also *supra*, Section 2.2.6. Moreover, see Yeung, 'Can We Employ Design-Based Regulation While Avoiding Brave New World?' (n 119); Yeung, 'Responsibility and AI' (n 209).

[278] See *infra*, Section 4.2.4.

This balance is indispensable for the law to carry out its protective function, as an overly rigid application of rules without discretion to ensure their contextualisation can lead to unjust outcomes.[279] The exercise of discretion, or the autonomous application of reasonable judgment,[280] should be aligned with the rule of law's principles and exercised based on an examination and assessment of the facts at hand.[281] Importantly, in undertaking this assessment, public officials rely not only on their specific expertise, but also on their *implicit* knowledge of society and human beings more generally.[282] Furthermore, this discretion can also serve as a correcting factor (and 'little goodness', as borrowed from Emmanuel Levinas[283]) in a situation where the provision of public services has been institutionalised and systematised, and might fail to deliver individual justice.[284] As also stressed by Binns, the need for individual justice or "*the notion that each case needs to be assessed on its own merits, without comparison to, or generalization from, previous cases*", requires a certain level of discretion to enable individualised assessments.[285] This is particularly relevant for the adoption of (individual) administrative acts, where public officials are required to apply general rules to individual cases and also when they rely on algorithmic systems to do so.[286]

However, the above analysis demonstrated that reliance on algorithmic regulation, which requires unambiguous and precise rules, can foster an overly strict interpretation of the law, which shifts the pendulum entirely away from 'discretion' all the way towards 'rules' instead of promoting their marriage. This does not result in the algorithmic system's conformity with *legality*, but in an automated form of *legalism*, with several problematic consequences. As defined above, legalism is characterised by a strict adherence to the law, based on the law's letter rather than its spirit.[287] While a rigid application of the law, regardless of its substantive ends or its concrete effects, can also be opted for without algorithmic systems, reliance on these systems *induces* a legalistic approach, in light of the reductive translation

[279] See *supra*, Section 2.3.3.

[280] See Galligan, 'Senses of Discretion' (n 262) 8.

[281] See in this regard also Lars Tummers and Victor Bekkers, 'Policy Implementation, Street-Level Bureaucracy, and the Importance of Discretion' (2014) 16 Public Management Review 527.

[282] See Diver (n 3) 8.

[283] See Emmanuel Levinas, *Is It Righteous to Be?: Interviews with Emmanuel Levinas* (Jill Robbins ed, Stanford University Press 2001) 116.

[284] See *supra*, Section 2.3.3.

[285] Binns (n 253) 198.

[286] Binns points out both epistemic and normative limitations of algorithmic decision-making systems when it comes to ensuring individual justice, without denying that the need for individual justice may at times conflict with other values, such as, for instance, consistency. See ibid 201 and following. Note that this potential for conflict is simply a reflection of the tensions that are inherent in a society organised on the basis of the rule of law, as discussed *supra*, in Section 3.4.

[287] See Shklar (n 22). See also Bankowski and Schafer (n 24). Note that HLA Hart also recalls in this regard the notion of 'formalism', see Hart (n 5) 129.

exercise it requires from open-ended legal concepts to codifiable rules. This condenses the law's pluralistic conceptualisation into a monistic straightjacket, which will be codified and essentialised. The only 'discretion' exercised in this context are the choices made by the coders when they take upstream decisions about the system's design and the law's translation. In doing so, they need to anticipate all situations to which the law may be applied, and the effects that their translation will have downstream, bearing in mind that all information that the system relies on must be rendered *explicit*. Yet, as noted above, reliance on algorithmic regulation often *disguises* the fact that interpretative choices are made, since all of these choices occur upstream and prior to the system's use.

Furthermore, it can also disguise the potential 'creative compliance' of the law by those developing the system, which McBarnet and Whelan conceptualise as a manipulation of the law "*to turn it – no matter what the intentions of legislators or enforcers – to the service of their own interests and to avoid unwanted control*".[288] Indeed, "*creative compliance thrives on a narrow legalistic approach to rules and legal control, on a formalistic conception of the law*",[289] which is precisely the risk identified with algorithmic regulation. While creative compliance can certainly also occur without reliance on algorithmic systems, their opaque and automated nature can both camouflage and facilitate this practice, on a very wide scale.

The above illustrations also demonstrated that discretion at the 'street-level' is significantly reduced, and one can hence no longer speak of discretion as the exercise of autonomous judgment based on a particular situation. Instead, judgment is replaced by mathematical rules and functions. Some might argue that discretion can be codified into the system, for instance by anticipating and programming different variations of a legal rule based on different criteria. Yet this can hardly be referred to as the act of 'judging', but should rather be seen as a "*replacement of discretion with a series of fixed cumulative criteria; that is, criteria that could be solved by collecting relevant machine-readable data*".[290] As explained by Schartum, modelling open-ended concepts – for instance, 'suitable employment', in the context of the evaluation of unemployment benefits – "*would require access to an unrealistically large number of types of data*".[291]

More generally, since reality and the human condition are not characterised only by a limited number of features, it would be impossible to anticipate all possible

[288] Doreen McBarnet and Christopher Whelan, 'The Elusive Spirit of the Law: Formalism and the Struggle for Legal Control' (1991) 54 The Modern Law Review 848.

[289] ibid 848. See in this regard also Karen Yeung's discussion of creative compliance, "*whereby technical compliance with rules may be achieved yet the underlying spirit and purpose of those rules might be simultaneously undermined*", in *Securing Compliance* (Hart Publishing 2004) 11. Yeung therefore draws a distinction between 'rule compliance', on the one hand, and 'substantive compliance', on the other hand, whereby the latter pays attention to the collective goals *behind* the rule rather than merely to the literal formulation of the rule itself.

[290] Schartum (n 1) 316.

[291] ibid.

situations in which the law may be applied in advance. As remarked by Hart, if "*everything would be known*" and if "*for everything, since it would be known, something could be done and specified in advance*", this would "*be a world fit for 'mechanical' jurisprudence*".[292] However, "*plainly this world is not our world; human legislations can have no such knowledge of all the possible combinations of circumstances which the future may bring*".[293]Accordingly, both from a practical and technical perspective, it may be difficult or unfeasible to automate the replacement of 'discretion', especially in a way that avoids the risk of "*creating an 'echo chamber' where old points of views become decisive even in new cases with new contexts*".[294] A legalistic approach thus overlooks or ignores the infinite variability of social contexts and interpretations, thereby hiding, but not undoing, the clash between the indeterminacy of rules and their algorithmic application.

Worryingly, algorithmic regulation not only reduces discretion at the street level, but it also creates a technological architecture that renders deviations from the law (or from its codified interpretation) technically unfeasible.[295] Accordingly, this eliminates the possibility for public officials to remedy potential adverse consequences of the law's rigid application, and restricts them to apply the rules in accordance with how they were programmed.[296] While algorithmic regulation can hence stand in the way of the 'softening' of the law's hard edges, it also prevents public officials to make corrections in case of an unjust situation. Put simply, the 'little goodness' that can correct the rough edges of an institutionalised legal system no longer has a place, and public officials can also no longer take up their role in 'speaking truth to power'.[297] It is moreover important to stress that reliance on algorithmic regulation instead does not prevent public officials to take arbitrary or unlawful decisions. It merely prevents them from taking decisions that deviate from whichever rules have been codified in the algorithmic system, without guaranteeing that those rules and outcomes in and of themselves are not arbitrary or unlawful.

Yet the problem goes further still. The prolonged attrition of public officials' autonomy – and the concomitant absence of the possibility to exercise discretion – might numb their ability to make a critical evaluation of the law's application in concrete cases, until their motivation and skill for reasoned judgment becomes superfluous.[298] Without the space to practise human agency, the question of

[292] Hart (n 5) 128.

[293] ibid.

[294] Schartum (n 1) 316.

[295] See in this regard Yeung, 'Can We Employ Design-Based Regulation While Avoiding Brave New World?' (n 119); Brownsword (n 270); Peeters and Widlak (n 44).

[296] Recall that adherence to the outcomes of an algorithmic system does not necessarily equal adherence to the law as such, even if that system is meant to have codified legal provisions.

[297] See in this regard also Thomas Elston and Gwyn Bevan, 'New Development: Scarcity, Policy Gambles, and "One-Shot Bias" – Training Civil Servants to Speak Truth to Power' (2020) 40 Public Money & Management 615.

[298] See *supra*, Section 2.3.2.

whether a certain legal interpretation or application leads to an unjust situation might not even pose itself.[299] As argued above, this, in turn, might lead to a problematic discharge of moral involvement and responsibility, for which agency is a precondition.[300] One might argue that this problem can be solved by ensuring that algorithmic regulation is relied upon only informatively rather than decisively. However, the above illustrations have shown that, even in those cases, in practice the space for agency is marginal, due to a high case load, the pressure to meet KPIs, the limited understanding of the system's operations, and more generally the impossibility of verifying the validity of recommendations pertaining to thousands or even millions of citizens. Accordingly, algorithmic regulation and the legalistic approach it induces might lead to the mindless execution of rules,[301] thereby reinforcing the hierarchical obedience to authority that already permeates bureaucratic organisation, and ultimately also to a *banalisation*[302] of its potentially adverse consequences.

It would be a mistake to ignore or make invisible the normative tensions that are inherent to the law. Yet it would be as problematic to make them invisible by disguising them as a techno-rational optimisation exercise, or to eliminate them altogether by opting for the codification of *one* interpretation over and above others, without an avenue for the reasoned judgment and potential contestability of such interpretation when inappropriate for the particular situation.[303] In the best case, the automation of legalism is an unintentional by-product of algorithmic regulation,

[299] See Yeung, 'Can We Employ Design-Based Regulation While Avoiding Brave New World?' (n 119). See also the emphasis on public agency in Endicott and Yeung (n 128).

[300] See also *supra*, Section 2.2.5.

[301] Diver (n 3) 13.

[302] This refers to Hannah Arendt's conceptualisation of the 'banality of evil', arguing that evil need not stem from a deliberately destructive intention, but that it can also arise from the execution of tasks without critical judgment or reflection about their morality, which can lead to a dangerous discharge of responsibility and thereby enable evil actions, particularly in a bureaucratic setting. See Hannah Arendt, *Eichmann in Jerusalem: A Report on the Banality of Evil* (Viking Press 1963). Recall in this regard also the experiment carried out by Milgram, discussed *supra*, in Section 2.2.6.

[303] While my analysis focuses on automation in the context of administrative actions, it should be noted that similar problems also arise in other contexts. Consider, for instance, the mass automation of content filtering on social media channels, where broad legal concepts such as 'hate speech' and 'illegal content' are codified into algorithmic systems in order to detect and take down problematic messages. It goes beyond the purpose of this book to analyse the use of such algorithmic systems in detail and compare their challenges with those used in the public sector, yet I nevertheless wish to point out that certain parallels can be drawn. These include, for instance, the need to cater for scaled and speedy decision-making on the one hand (the legal rules which provide protection against harmful content need to be upheld, despite the vast scale and speed at which data can be shared online), and the need to ensure individual justice on the other hand (the rights of individuals who share content and exercise their freedom of expression also need to be upheld, and any 'filtering' needs to occur in a transparent and contestable manner). These parallels might give rise to certain lessons or best practices that can be drawn from one area to the other – a subject that merits further research. For a discussion on some of the challenges of automated content filtering, see, e.g., Emma J Llansó, 'No Amount of "AI" in Content Moderation Will Solve Filtering's Prior-Restraint

and one that public authorities seek to remedy by safeguarding the discretion and autonomy of public officials. Yet in the worst case, the elimination of discretion, and the subsequent erosion of responsibility, can be used to prevent internal criticism, and to prevent the deviation from a problematic (or problematically codified) rule, despite its adverse impact. This approach might reinforce and automatise, at scale, illiberal and authoritarian interpretations of the law, while stifling the opportunity for critical reflection and remedial action. Therefore, if public authorities wish to rely on algorithmic regulation, they need to ensure that the realisation of the rule of law, which hinges on the sustainment of the tensions inherent thereto, rather than their dissolution, maintains the law's openness.

4.2.4 *Deficit of Accountability*

Ensuring public accountability is a central function of the rule of law. The legal system ensures that public authorities can be held to account whenever their actions infringe the principles of the rule of law, from the principle of equality to the prohibition on the arbitrary use of executive power, and secures the possibility of judicial review to challenge and remedy government actions whenever such infringement occurs.[304] It hence requires that public authorities comply with the law, and that they be held to account when they do not. However, as my analysis has shown, this function of the law can become more difficult to uphold in the context of algorithmic regulation.

First of all, the decisive aspect of public authorities' decisional action has shifted from 'street-level' to 'system-level',[305] as the choices that determine administrative acts have in fact been outsourced to coders. Yet this upstream move of discretion is not followed by an upstream move of accountability, given that these choices remain largely invisible. Indeed, as noted by Peeters and Widlak, the information architecture that enables algorithmic regulation "*is a less 'visible' form of rationalisation*".[306] This invisibility or opacity is not necessarily limited to the normative choices underlying the system's design and the law's translation, but often also encompass the system's mode of operation (especially in the case of complex data-driven systems) and at times even its existence.[307]

Such reduced transparency, along with the 'rational' framing, renders it much more difficult to contest certain normative decisions relating to algorithmic systems,

Problem' (2020) 7 Big Data & Society 1; Niva Elkin-Koren, 'Contesting Algorithms: Restoring the Public Interest in Content Filtering by Artificial Intelligence' (2020) 7 Big Data & Society 1.

304 See also *supra*, Sections 3.3.5 and 3.3.6.

305 Recall in this regard the discussion *supra*, in Section 2.3.4, and the conceptualisation proposed by Bovens and Zouridis regarding the wide-spread uptake of algorithmic systems by public authorities as 'system-level bureaucracy'. See Bovens and Zouridis (n 115).

306 Peeters and Widlak (n 44) 177–78.

307 See also *supra*, Sections 2.2.4, 4.1.1.c and 4.1.2.c.

and hence diminishes the opportunity to hold public authorities to account for their outcomes, especially when public officials *themselves* might not know how the systems function. Given the scale at which algorithmic regulation can operate, oversight over the systems' functioning to ensure no errors are made at the level of individual decisions is in any case challenging.[308] As noted by Schartum, "*if millions of individual decisions are made by the system, in the blink of an eye, it will generally not be feasible to manually check each output from the system, because it would take an army of case officers and extraordinary budgets to exercise meaningful controls*".[309] Moreover, by the time a problematic decision is taken, whether directly or based on an algorithmic recommendation, it may already be too late to counter potential adverse effects that may ensue therefrom. This renders the need for upstream control and oversight even more pressing,[310] not only to avoid potential errors, but also to ensure that the coders did not take too many liberties in the translation process from law to code, whether at their own initiative, the initiative of their private employer or the initiative of the executive that hired them (and may seek to entrench its power).

Yet this very need also raises a fundamental question: how can such upstream oversight be organised, and who can fulfil this role? Coders typically do not have domain expertise the way traditional public officials do, nor are they trained in or bound by the public sector's deontological codes if they are part of a private company to which the system's development is outsourced. In the case of the latter, they can still be said to act *on behalf of* public authorities, and public authorities could hence – through contractual means – hold them to account when they do not deliver what was agreed.[311] Yet for that to happen, the public authority first needs to know something is *off*, which is not easy if the relevant choices pertaining to the system's design are implicit and invisible. Accordingly, *internal* review and oversight is not always straightforward, even though the public authority that relies on

[308] See also Stefan Buijsman and Herman Veluwenkamp, 'Spotting When Algorithms Are Wrong' (2023) 33 Minds and Machines 541.

[309] Schartum (n 1) 307.

[310] I will come back to this need for institutionalised oversight *infra*, in Section 4.3 and in subsequent chapters.

[311] Consider in this regard the example of the Concentrix System used in the UK, designed to add capacity to the Revenue and Customs (HMRC) services to prevent or detect error and fraud in personal tax credits awards. Like many of the other examples, this system was adopted to save costs and reduce personnel, which could in theory be deployed elsewhere. However, the system was fraught with errors and decreased the intended 'customer service standard', and backlogs were significant. The HMRC actually had to reallocate public officials to start carrying out the tasks manually again. Furthermore, as an investigation by the National Audit Office noted, "*Concentrix stopped or amended tax credit awards in around 12% of cases investigated, of which 32% of these decisions were overturned following a mandatory reconsideration*". In November 2016, the HMRC decided to end the contract. See Report by the Comptroller and Auditor General, National Audit Office, 'Investigation into HMRC's Contract with Concentrix' (HM Revenue & Customs 2017) <www.nao.org.uk/wp-content/uploads/2017/01/Investigation-into-HMRCs-contract-with-Concentrix.pdf>.

algorithmic regulation is in theory publicly accountable for its functioning, regardless of whether it was developed in-house or procured. The difficulty of carrying out internal oversight, along with the fact that public officials have reduced agency over their decisions, is a worrisome combination of factors.

Moreover, while internal review is challenging, *external* review is even less straightforward. In theory, the legislative branch of power should be able to exercise democratic oversight of the executive's action to ensure it is aligned with democratically adopted legislation, and the judicial branch of power should be able to exercise judicial oversight over those actions in court.[312] Yet both types of oversight are difficult to achieve if the centre of gravity of the executive's action lays in the invisible normative design choices made by a set of coders through the system's architecture. Additionally, it should be borne in mind that, even if certain aspects of the system's design *are* visible, its operation is still not necessarily intelligible for non-technical experts (including most members of the legislative and judiciary branch of power). I also noted above how oversight and contestability are complicated for the natural and legal persons affected by the system and, more importantly, how the lack of the availability of *systemic* rather than mere individual review undermines the ability to challenge the societal harm that may be engendered through problematic algorithmic systems.[313]

Let me clarify that the risk of diminished accountability goes beyond the mere bypassing of the democratic process; it can also entail a deliberate misuse of 'democracy' (narrowly conceived as the will of the majority) to erode constitutional protections of minorities. Algorithmic regulation could potentially enable a tyrannic majority, under the guise of democracy and legality, to codify the interpretation of certain rights in a manner that erodes the law's protective role in constitutional liberal democracies. Recall in this regard that some EU Member States have indeed been relying on oppressive yet 'legally' adopted laws to erode the rights of minorities, and that the translation of these laws to code would hence enable them to apply such laws at scale, while simultaneously reducing visibility over their application, even if infringing EU law and human rights law.

To conclude, the fact that oversight by the legislator, the judiciary, the public and even at times the executive itself is made difficult risks diluting the constitutional checks and balances that tame the executive's power, and creates a problematic accountability deficit. Left unaddressed, over time, this deficit might further enlarge the asymmetry of power and information between the executive and the other branches, and thereby exacerbate the problem.[314] Unless algorithmic systems, and the normative processes underlying their design and deployment, are rendered

[312] See also Richard Bellamy (ed), *The Rule of Law and the Separation of Powers* (Ashgate/Dartmouth 2005).

[313] See *supra*, Section 4.1.5.

[314] See also Passchier (n 223); Malcolm Langford, 'Taming the Digital Leviathan: Automated Decision-Making and International Human Rights' (2020) 114 AJIL Unbound 141.

intelligible and controllable for non-coders, the contestability of the administrative acts they inform and adopt is undercut, as is the public accountability for their effects.[315] Once again, the protective role of the law, serving as a means to keep the executive's power in check and to protect human rights, risks being undermined. The difficulty to carry out internal and political oversight over these – normatively relevant – upstream design choices, despite their techno-rational coating, is problematic not only if the aim is to avoid erroneous translations and applications of the law, but also if the aim is to counter potentially abusive or arbitrary implementations, especially over the longer term. It must hence be ensured that algorithmic regulation cannot become a tool to bypass the democratic process and shortcut the principle of participation in law and policymaking, by securing accountability not only for the system's individual outcomes but also for the upstream decisions that shape these outcomes.

4.2.5 *Systemic Vulnerability*

There is one further characteristic of algorithmic rule by law that needs to be examined, which pertains to the underlying digital infrastructure that enables algorithmic regulation. Once such infrastructure has been put in place to implement and apply the law, by informing or adopting administrative acts, it should be kept in mind that it can also be altered, openly or behind the scenes. Unlike legal texts and policy implementation guidelines, which are often published in an official journal or a government website, software is inherently malleable, and can be changed by coders (or by hackers) with a few mouse clicks. When one considers the consequences in the long term, including the realisation that governments and policies change over time, one must also face the risk that this infrastructure may be used to implement policies that are normatively dubious, or plainly disregard EU or human rights law. Recall the example I mentioned above, about the algorithmic system deployed by the US Immigration and Customs Enforcement to help evaluate whether illegal immigrants should be detained or released on bail, and how from one day to the next, the system's functioning was altered following a change in policy by the Trump office.[316] The example of Belgium's reliance on ANPR cameras and the function creep accompanying their use is likewise a case in point.[317]

Let me complement those examples with a hypothetical illustration that builds on an existing use of algorithmic regulation, namely automated risk assessments to

[315] As argued by Hildebrandt "*Administrative decisions taken by code-driven regulation must thus always be contestable on the double basis of: 'the decision is based on legal conditions that do not apply because the system got the facts wrong', and 'the decision is based on a wrong interpretation of the relevant legal norms'*" in 'Algorithmic Regulation and the Rule of Law' (n 121) 3.
[316] Rosenberg and Levinson (n 219).
[317] See *supra*, Section 4.1.6. See also Belga (n 239).

detect and predict potential child abuse or neglect. As previously explained, such systems are used to identify families where (typically child welfare) authorities will prioritise their investigations, and may ultimately lead to the potential displacement of children away from their parents. Both in Europe and in the US, algorithmic regulation is already used for this purpose.[318] Now let me consider a development that in first instance seems unrelated: the rising state-sanctioned discrimination against LGBTQ+ persons in countries that are supposedly adhering to liberal democratic values, including Hungary and Romania.[319] All of these countries are, at least on paper, committed to human rights, democracy and the rule of law, yet by adopting legislation that curtails the rights and visibility of LGBTQ+ persons (for instance based on the view that it may cause 'damage' to children) they show that no algorithms need to be relied on to act in contradiction with those values.[320] Is it too far a stretch to hypothesise that information relating to such orientation (e.g. a registered same-sex partnership or marriage, or related proxies) could in these countries, at some point, be considered a risk-relevant parameter that should be added to the aforementioned algorithmic system, based on the reasoning that this information may contribute to a 'better' assessment of risks for children?

In such an example, one can imagine how much further-reaching discriminating policies could be if they are supported by an infrastructure of algorithmic regulation which allows the automated and systemic application of a policy, rather than being a mere piece of text that still needs to be implemented by (potentially critical) public officials. Add to this the other elements discussed above, namely that the choice to add this discriminatory risk-factor may be disguised as a merely techno-rational one, the supremacy of coders who can make these choices with little to no visibility and oversight, the deficit of accountability in terms of constitutional checks and balances, and the automation of obedience which side-lines critical reflection and technically prevents any correction by public officials who oppose such discriminating policies. Immediately, it becomes clear that what is at stake is not merely the risk of isolated instances of discrimination at the level of individuals, but the risk of a systemic breach of the rule of law, enabled by an algorithmic legal infrastructure that allows for instantaneous mass decision-making that can directly affect the population at large.

In EU legal doctrine, the concept of a 'systemic' deficiency of the rule of law has been developed to denote a situation in which a Member State infringes the law in a

[318] Reference can, for instance, be made to the Gladsaxe model used in Denmark to detect risk indicators for children in vulnerable families. This system has been put on hold after critical coverage in the press. See in this regard Kaun (n 93); AlgorithmWatch (n 62).

[319] See *supra*, Section 3.2.5 for a discussion thereof.

[320] See also Zoltán Kovács, 'Portrayal and Promotion – Hungary's LGBTQI+ Law Explained' *Euractiv* (24 June 2021) <www.euractiv.com/section/non-discrimination/news/portrayal-and-promotion-hungarys-latest-anti-lgbt-law-explained/>.

structural manner and at scale, rather than 'merely' episodically.[321] The systemic nature of the breach reflects the high threshold that needs to be reached before the procedure of Article 7 TEU (aimed at protecting EU values by suspending a Member States' rights deriving from the Treaties, including voting rights in the Council) can be triggered.[322] The consequences of this mechanism are severe: it has at times been referred to as the 'nuclear' option.[323] Occasional violations of the law therefore do not qualify for such standard, but only violations that are persistent or structural. As noted by Toggenburg and Grimheden, *"a solid debate on systemic deficiencies cannot stare at single legalistic elements in isolation but has to look at the 'combined effects of many developments'. Against a specific political background various legal developments can lead to a situation where 'the whole is greater than the sum of its parts'."*[324]

The threshold of a 'systemic' deficiency has also been used in the context of the two-step test developed by the CJEU to assess whether a European Arrest Warrant should be executed.[325] National judicial authorities can use this test to determine, based on the presence of systemic deficiencies relating to the independence of the judiciary in a given Member State, whether there are substantial grounds for believing that the person in respect of whom a European arrest warrant has been issued by that Member State, *"if surrendered, runs a real risk of breach of his or her*

[321] See, for instance, Armin von Bogdandy and Michael Ioannidis, 'Systemic Deficiency in the Rule of Law: What It Is, What Has Been Done, What Can Be Done' (2014) 51 Common Market Law Review 59.

[322] It should be noted that Article 7 TEU in fact speaks of a 'serious and persistent' breach, yet the CJEU and other EU institutions – along with legal scholars – typically have also used the term 'systemic'. See also Joined Cases C-354/20 PPU and C-412/20 PPU, 17 December 2020, EU:C:2020:1033, §69; Case C-216/18 PPU, LM, 25 July 2018, EU:C:2018:586, §§47–75; Joined Cases C-562/21 PPU and C-563/21 PPU, 22 February 2022, ECLI:EU:C:2022:100, §50. See also the references to 'systemic' threats and 'systemic' risks to the rule of law by the European Commission, 'Communication from the Commission to the European Parliament, the European Council and the Council: Further Strengthening the Rule of Law within the Union – State of Play and Possible Next Steps' (2019) COM/2019/163 final.

[323] See José Manuel Durão Barroso, 'State of the Union 2012 – Address Plenary Session of the European Parliament' (European Commission 2012), <https://ec.europa.eu/commission/presscorner/detail/en/SPEECH_12_596>. See also Sonja Priebus, 'Watering down the "Nuclear Option"? The Council and the Article 7 Dilemma' [2022] Journal of European Integration 1.

[324] Gabriel N Toggenburg and Jonas Grimheden, 'Managing the Rule of Law in a Heterogeneous Context: A Fundamental Rights Perspective on Ways Forward' in Werner Schroeder (ed), *Strengthening the Rule of Law in Europe: From a Common Concept to Mechanisms of Implementation* (Hart Publishing 2016) 225.

[325] See also Stefano Montaldo, 'On a Collision Course! Mutual Recognition, Mutual Trust and the Protection of Fundamental Rights in the Recent Case-Law of the Court of Justice' (2017) 2016 1 European Papers – A Journal on Law and Integration 965; Leandro Mancano, 'You'll Never Work Alone: A Systemic Assessment of the European Arrest Warrant and Judicial Independence' (2021) 58 Common Market Law Review 683.

fundamental right to a fair trial before an independent and impartial tribunal previously established by law".[326]

The need for an elevated threshold does not stem from the idea that sporadic infringements of the law are not problematic, but hinges on the fact that, in a well-functioning liberal democracy, with a legal system based on the rule of law, such infringements can in principle be overcome. That is, after all, the role of the law: providing both ex ante and ex post protection against violations of the law, and ensuring that governments who violate their legal obligations can be held to account. However, in a context where violations have become *systemic*, citizens can no longer count on the fact that the law will be able to fulfil this role, leading to a loss of trust in the legal system and in public institutions more generally.[327]

If we consider the adverse impact of algorithmic regulation on the rule of law based on the analysis carried out above, we can observe that this is precisely what is at stake here: the threat of a systemic deficiency in the rule of law, both literally and legally speaking. Literally, because the law's inability to properly play its protective role is exacerbated by the use of an algorithmic *system*, embedded in a networked infrastructure that enables its opaque automation and systematisation in a way that can undermine the rule of law's spirit. Legally, because the sheer scale at which this practice can take place, precisely due to the automation that enables mass decision-making, and the fact that it touches upon the very foundations of a Member State's legal system, can meet the threshold of a *systemic* breach of EU law.

Recall in this regard also the conceptualisation by Huq and Ginsburg of the broader phenomenon of 'constitutional retrogression':[328] a development that happens piecemeal by introducing gradual changes in the legal system that undermine liberal democratic values. They note that, whereas "*each of these changes may be innocuous or even defensible in isolation*", "*it is only by their cumulative, interactive effect that retrogression occurs.*"[329] Similarly, the gradual introduction of algorithmic regulation in an increasing range of domains in which public authorities make impactful decisions on individuals, without adequate safeguards, can result in such cumulative adverse impact on the rule of law, and on EU values in general.

[326] See, e.g., Case 480/21, *W O and J L v Minister for Justice and Equality*, Order of the Court of 12 July 2022, ECLI identifier: ECLI:EU:C:2022:592. Indeed, pursuant to Article 1(3) of the Framework Decision of the European Arrest Warrant, Member States' obligations to respect fundamental rights are not modified by anything contained in that Decision. See 2002/584/JHA: Council Framework Decision of 13 June 2002 on the European arrest warrant and the surrender procedures between Member States – Statements made by certain Member States on the adoption of the Framework Decision 2002 (OJ L).

[327] von Bogdandy and Ioannidis (n 321) 73.

[328] Aziz Huq and Tom Ginsburg, 'How to Lose a Constitutional Democracy' (2018) 65 UCLA Law Review 78, 83.

[329] ibid 97.

There is another, deeper, issue at stake here, which can be clarified by revisiting the concept of the 'little goodness' proposed by Emmanuel Levinas.[330] Recall that this 'little goodness' is juxtaposed to the systematised Goodness – with capital G – which relies on the legal and political system to enforce a set of ideas of which the current office-holder is convinced that it is the 'Good'. As history has shown, however, all systematisation of ideologies of the 'Good', no matter how benevolent, risk becoming a tool to do wrong precisely in the name of the good.[331] In the context of algorithmic regulation, such systematisation can take place literally, by codifying ideals into algorithmic systems that regulate the entire population. Yet this tends to essentialise *one* view of the good over others, and may have no place in a democratic and pluralistic society, especially if one considers the long-term consequences thereof.[332]

Accordingly, when we stop looking at the adverse effects that *one* problematic algorithmic system might have on the rights of one individual, or of one collective of individuals, and we start looking at the cumulative impact of algorithmic regulation across society, we are forced to confront the risk of a systemic threat to the rule of law, and to the normative foundations of liberal democracies more generally.[333] While these foundations are always fragile and do not require the use of algorithmic systems to be undermined, the intrinsic malleability of algorithmic regulation, which allows for scaled and instant decision-making at the level of the entire population, introduces a systemic vulnerability in the legal system. Consequently, the risk that this vulnerability is used in a way that inadvertently or deliberately undermines the rule of law in a 'serious and persistent' manner needs to be considered, ideally *before* the large-scale implementation of algorithmic systems in the public sector.[334]

4.3 CONCLUDING REMARKS

In this chapter, I have carried out a systematic analysis of how algorithmic regulation, when used by public authorities in the context of administrative acts, can

[330] See *supra*, Section 2.3.3.

[331] The book by Grossman, based on which Levinas' juxtaposition of the systematised Goodness versus the little goodness is based, particularly focuses on Nazism and Stalinism. See Vasily Grossman, *Life and Fate (1980)* (Robert Chandler tr, Vintage Classic 2017). See also Luc Anckaert, 'Goodness without Witnesses: Vasily Grossman and Emmanuel Levinas' in Michael Fagenblat and Arthur Cools (eds), *Levinas and Literature* (De Gruyter 2020).

[332] Consider also in this regard Isaiah Berlin's opposition against so-called 'monism', or "*the old perennial belief in the possibility of realising ultimate harmony*", whereby those in power are driven by a single ideal of perfection, both at individual and societal level, without any space for a pluralistic view of 'the good'. See Isaiah Berlin, *The Crooked Timber of Humanity: Chapters in the History of Ideas* (Henry Hardy ed, Fontana 1991) 8 and more generally Isaiah Berlin, *Liberty: Incorporating Four Essays on Liberty* (Oxford University Press 2002). See also Cécile Hatier, 'Isaiah Berlin and the Totalitarian Mind' (2004) 9 The European Legacy 767.

[333] This point has already strongly been made in Yeung, 'Responsibility and AI' (n 209).

[334] Smuha and others (n 57) 39.

adversely impact each of the six rule of law principles, by drawing on illustrations from existing applications. When conceptualising the rule of law and its principles in Chapter 3, I already noted that meeting their requirements entails inherent challenges, regardless of any use of algorithms. Yet the above analysis has demonstrated that reliance on algorithmic regulation can significantly exacerbate these challenges, and make compliance therewith even more difficult. As a consequence, the rule of law risks turning into *algorithmic rule by law*. The veneer of legality remains: algorithmic regulation, after all, aims to merely implement and apply the law in an optimised and more efficient way. However, the protective role of the law is hollowed out, and opens up weaknesses that can be exploited to undermine the rule of law's very purpose.

I outlined five problematic characteristics of algorithmic rule by law, thereby consolidating the common findings of the principle-by-principle impact analysis I conducted. Summarised, the law's application is being reduced to a techno-rational exercise (*primacy of techno-rationality*); its interpretation and translation to code is centralised and delegated to a handful of people with technical expertise who have the impossible task to anticipate all potential downstream situations, and whose upstream choices shaping the technology's affordance are largely invisible (*supremacy of coders*); discretion at the street-level is eliminated, leaving public officials without agency to counter the problem of law's over-generality and technically constrained to uncritically defer to the algorithmic outcomes (*automation of legalism*); public accountability mechanisms for the legality of the law's interpretation and application are eroded (*deficit of accountability*); and the infrastructure enabling algorithmic regulation introduces a significant vulnerability in the legal system, whereby a particular vision of the Good – despite potential adverse effects – can be systematised and risk leading to a systemic deficiency of the rule of law (*systemic vulnerability*).

Altogether, these characteristics can also exacerbate authoritarian elements in society, from the centralisation of power to the loss of transparency and accountability and the erosion of a sense of critical thinking and moral responsibility. Moreover, as the illustrations have shown, algorithmic regulation may also undermine human rights and foster illiberal practices, by limiting and infringing individual rights in the name of efficiency. The risk I see is not so much a sudden elimination of the law's protective function, but rather an erosion – and one that goes potentially unnoticed, given the veil of legality that surrounds algorithmic regulation, not least because of the European Commission's promotion of its uptake,[335] through the incremental reliance and dependence thereon for decisions that affect individual and societal interests. Accordingly, it can serve as a tool to attain the constitutional retrogression which Huq and Ginsburg conceptualised.[336]

[335] See *supra*, Section 2.3.5.

[336] Somewhat pessimistically, Huq and Ginsburg note that "*the constitutional safeguards against retrogression are weak*", and argue that "*the near-term prospects of constitutional liberal democracy hence depend less on our institutions than on the qualities of political leadership, popular resistance, and the quiddities of partisan coalitional politics.*" See Huq and Ginsburg (n 328).

I therefore argue that the irresponsible implementation of algorithmic regulation might foster the threat of algorithmic rule by law – whereby irresponsible means to disregard the risks I outlined, or with the deliberate aim of exploiting those risks. Let me stress that human beings are not devoid of error or ill intention, and that I hence do not argue that the regression of democracy and the erosion of the rule of law is *caused by* reliance on algorithmic regulation. Nor do I claim that the use of algorithmic regulation *necessarily* leads to a materialisation of the threat of algorithmic rule by law. My claim is merely that it can be exacerbated thereby, in light of the features inherent to algorithmic systems. Accordingly, if public authorities wish to rely on algorithmic regulation, the threat of algorithmic rule by law needs to be addressed. The fact that this technology provides the executive branch with more power and introduces stronger risks to the rule of law requires appropriate counterbalancing mechanisms.

The question is hence: does the current legal framework have sufficiently strong mechanisms in place to enable such counterbalancing?[337] Certainly, the law has its limits and it would be a mistake to consider legal rules as a panacea to all the identified problems. Yet it is worth asking which safeguards the EU legal order currently provides against the conceptualised threat. It goes beyond the purpose of this book to formulate detailed legal solutions. However, based on my analysis, a number of general conclusions can be made regarding the protection that the legal system should ideally provide.

First, given the vast scale of the harm that can arise from the problematic use of algorithmic regulation and the potential irreversibility of the damage, mere reliance on ex post remedies is insufficient. This does not mean that ex post remedies have no role to play in countering the identified threat. To the contrary, it is equally important to reflect on how they can be strengthened to ensure that not only individual but also systemic review of the executive's action through algorithmic regulation can be carried out. However, ex ante protection mechanisms are also needed, for instance in the form of certain requirements that should be fulfilled before algorithmic regulation can be used. In light of the importance of the decisions made during the design and implementation phase of algorithmic systems, oversight also needs to occur at the upstream level, rather than only at the level of the outcomes proposed or adopted by the system. The translation of legal rules and policies from law to code is not a techno-scientific matter, but an exercise that entails normative and political choices.[338] While the drive to rationality and efficiency might lead public authorities to ignore this fact, the principle of legality can only be secured by ensuring transparency, oversight and contestability over these important upstream choices (*prior and continuous oversight and accountability*).

[337] As my analysis in Chapter 5 will demonstrate, the answer to this question is negative. However, in Section 6.2, I will provide a number of recommendations to secure stronger safeguards against this threat.

[338] See *supra*, Section 4.1.1. See also Hildebrandt, 'Algorithmic Regulation and the Rule of Law' (n 121).

Second, one can argue that the mere choice of introducing algorithmic regulation, especially in certain sensitive domains, is already an administrative act that should be subjected to democratic oversight and judicial review in its own right. Given the potential consequences linked thereto, it is fair to claim that there should be no algorithmisation without representation (to paraphrase American revolutionists).[339] More generally, given the impact of algorithmic regulation on citizens, and given the fact that the principle of participation is increasingly recognised as essential also in public administration, citizens should be able to participate in – and give feedback on – important choices regarding the algorithmisation of the public sector (*public participation in algoritmisation*).[340]

Third, since the threat of algorithmic rule by law comes from reliance on algorithmic regulation by Member States, it is important that these safeguards, both ex ante and ex post, do not solely rely on public authorities of those very Member States. Ideally, safeguards can be invoked through both private and public enforcement mechanisms, ensuring that also citizens can play a role to hold the government's use of algorithmic regulation to account. Moreover, given the importance for the EU as a whole that Member States adhere to the rule of law, and given that not only national but also EU law can be inadvertently or deliberately infringed, one should also consider the role that EU institutions might play in mitigating and addressing the risk that Member States infringe the rule of *EU* law through reliance on algorithmic regulation (*private and public enforcement, at national and EU level*).

Fourth, the protective role of the law needs to be safeguarded by ensuring adequate individual and societal remedies against the scaled risks introduced by algorithmic regulation. Besides ensuring remedies for individuals who can be adversely impacted thereby, the fact that the rule of law's erosion leads to *societal* harm means that citizens and public interest groups should be able to counter this harm also without necessarily demonstrating individual harm. More generally, stronger checks and balances are also needed to ensure that the legislative and judicial branches of power, along with civil society and the public at large, can hold the executive accountable for its actions (*stronger checks and balances*).

Finally, attention should also be given to the role of public officials, and the importance of safeguarding their agency when applying legislation and taking administrative acts. The balance between rules and discretion, rigidity and fluidity,

339 The phrase 'no taxation without representation' was used by American colonists during British rule in the late eighteenth century.

340 Elsewhere, I drew a parallel with the need to ensure public participation and feedback in the context of environmental impact assessments, comparing the harm of public actions to the environment (for instance by allowing or establishing a polluting activity) to the harm that can ensue from AI's impact on societal interests. Just like environmental legislation provides public participation in decisions that affect the environment, so should such participation be foreseen in decisions that concern the implementation of algorithmic regulation when it can affect societal interests such as the rule of law. See in this regard Smuha, 'Beyond the Individual: Governing AI's Societal Harm' (n 209).

predictability and adaptability needs to be maintained. This means that, rather than operating seamlessly and restrictively, algorithmic regulation should allow for a certain level of friction that enables public officials to exercise critical judgment and maintain both actually and mentally a sense of responsibility for the outcome of public action. Furthermore, rather than viewing algorithmic regulation as a means to systematise 'the Good', opportunities for contestation and agonistic interpretations[341] need to be ensured, including the role of the 'little goodness' to soften the law's hard edges where need be (*contestation and internal critical reflection*).

[341] See in this regard Mireille Hildebrandt, 'Privacy as Protection of the Incomputable Self: From Agnostic to Agonistic Machine Learning' (2019) 20 Theoretical Inquiries in Law 83.

5

Legal Safeguards in the EU Legal Order

In Chapter 4, I analysed how algorithmic regulation (discussed in Chapter 2) affects the rule of law and its principles (discussed in Chapter 3), and identified a threat which I conceptualised as *algorithmic rule by law*, marking a deviation of the rule of law's ideal, facilitated by the use of algorithmic systems. In light of that analysis, let me now consider how the EU legal framework deals with this threat, and what safeguards it offers to counter it.

Two legal domains are of particular relevance in this regard: regulation pertaining to the protection of the rule of law (*the EU's rule of law agenda*), and regulation pertaining to (automated) personal data processing and the use of algorithmic systems (*the EU's digital agenda*). Each of these domains is vast and consists of a broad range of legislation, including not only primary and secondary EU law, but also soft law. In what follows, I therefore confine my investigation to those areas of legislation that are most relevant for the identified concerns, with a primary focus on binding legislation. In terms of safeguards, drawing on the conclusions of Chapter 4, I will be evaluating EU legislation based on whether it provides effective mechanisms enabling prior and continuous oversight and accountability over algorithmic regulation, also as regards the upstream choices; public participation mechanisms; private and public enforcement, at national and EU level; constitutional checks and balances; and the availability of contestability, as well as opportunities for internal critical reflection.

After some preliminary remarks about the EU's competence to take legal action in this field (Section 5.1), I respectively examine safeguards provided by regulation pertaining to the rule of law (Section 5.2), to personal data (Section 5.3) and to algorithmic systems (Section 5.4), before concluding (Section 5.5).

5.1 A NOTE ON EU COMPETENCES IN THE FIELD

Pursuant to the principle of conferral, the European Union can only act based on competences explicitly conferred to it.[1] Conversely, "*competences not conferred upon the Union in the Treaties remain with the Member States*".[2] Accordingly, whenever the EU seeks to undertake legal action, whether in the form of proposing the harmonisation of national legislation, or in the form of challenging a Member State's action in court, it needs to be able to rely on a legal basis to do so.[3] For each action at the EU level, whether preventative or mitigative in nature, one must hence first identify a legal basis that enables its execution.[4]

In addition, EU action is also constrained by the principles of subsidiarity and proportionality. Pursuant to the former, whenever the EU seeks to act in an area that does not fall under its exclusive competence, "*the Union shall act only if and in so far as the objectives of the proposed action cannot be sufficiently achieved by the Member States, either at central level or at regional and local level, but can rather, by reason of the scale or effects of the proposed action, be better achieved at Union level.*"[5] Pursuant to the latter, "*the content and form of Union action shall not exceed what is necessary to achieve the objectives of the Treaties*".[6] Collectively, the constraints posed by the principle of conferral, subsidiarity and proportionality can be considered as giving expression to the principle of legality at the level of the EU, underpinned by the fact that the EU legal order is based on the rule of law, and that the actions of EU institutions likewise need to adhere to its principles.[7]

This demarcation of competences is particularly relevant in an area that deals so intricately with a matter laying close to Member States' national identity (protected by Article 4(2) TEU[8]), namely the way in which national public authorities exercise their power and take administrative actions vis-à-vis their citizens. Accordingly, "*striking a balance between taking the effective action necessary to defend the Rule*

1 See Article 5(2) TEU, stating that "*under the principle of conferral, the Union shall act only within the limits of the competences conferred upon it by the Member States in the Treaties to attain the objectives set out therein. Competences not conferred upon the Union in the Treaties remain with the Member States*".

2 See Article 4(1) TEU.

3 Koen Lenaerts, Piet Van Nuffel and Tim Corthaut, *EU Constitutional Law* (Oxford University Press 2021) 84.

4 See also Annegret Engel, *The Choice of Legal Basis for Acts of the European Union: Competence Overlaps, Institutional Preferences, and Legal Basis Litigation* (Springer International Publishing 2018).

5 See Article 5(3) TEU.

6 See Article 5(4) TEU.

7 See Koen Lenaerts, Ignace Maselis and Kathleen Gutman, *EU Procedural Law* (Janek Tomasz Nowak ed, Oxford University Press 2015) 2. See also Theodore Konstadinides, *The Rule of Law in the European Union: The Internal Dimension* (Bloomsbury 2017).

8 Article 4(2) TEU states that the Union must respect Member States' national identities, "*inherent in their fundamental structures, political and constitutional, inclusive of regional and local self-government*".

of Law and respecting the limitations placed on the EU's competences is tricky".[9] At the same time, Article 4(3) TEU also enshrines the principle of sincere cooperation, demanding that the Union and the Member States shall, in full mutual respect, assist each other in carrying out tasks which flow from the Treaties. Furthermore, it also establishes the obligation for Member States to "*take any appropriate measure, general or particular, to ensure fulfilment of the obligations arising out of the Treaties or resulting from the acts of the institutions of the Union.*"[10] Member States can hence not invoke 'national identity' as an excuse to escape their obligations under EU law.[11]

This raises the question of how much 'diversity' EU Member States can maintain as regards the exercise of public power by national authorities, without overly endangering 'unity' in their respect for values that are considered to be common to all.[12] The answer to this question is highly complex, and not one that I will tempt to discuss in this book. Instead, I will formulate a different question, focusing on which EU obligations currently exist that relate to Member States' need to respect the rule of law, and that can provide protection against the risks posed by algorithmic regulation. After all, "*while the EU owes respect to its Member States' right to organize their government, the latter must observe the rule of law as it is understood in the EU legal order*".[13]

5.2 REGULATION PERTAINING TO THE RULE OF LAW

The EU legal framework counts several mechanisms that are aimed at ensuring Member States' compliance with the rule of (EU) law. In what follows, I respectively analyse the protection afforded by Article 2 TEU in combination with the procedure of Article 7 TEU (Section 5.2.1), the Conditionality Regulation (Section 5.2.2), and the role played by infringement procedures and challenges before national courts – including through the preliminary reference procedure (Section 5.2.3).

9 Kim Lane Scheppele, Dimitry Vladimirovich Kochenov and Barbara Grabowska-Moroz, 'EU Values Are Law, After All: Enforcing EU Values through Systemic Infringement Actions by the European Commission and the Member States of the European Union' (2020) 39 Yearbook of European Law 3, 8.

10 Article 4(3), §2.

11 Luigi Corrias, 'National Identity and European Integration: The Unbearable Lightness of Legal Tradition' (2016) 1 European Papers – A Journal on Law and Integration 383.

12 Note that 'United in Diversity' is also the EU's motto, which started being used from 2000 onwards. See also Jean-Marc Favret, 'L'union européenne: "L'unité dans la diversité". Signification et pertinence d'une devise' (2003) 39 Revue trimestrielle de droit européen 657.

13 Pekka Pohjankoski, 'Rule of Law with Leverage: Policing Structural Obligations in EU Law with the Infringement Procedure, Fines and Set-Off' (2021) 58 Common Market Law Review 1341.

5.2.1 Article 2 and 7 TEU

The rule of law is listed in Article 2 TEU as one of the foundational values of the EU, common to all Member States. It needs to be respected by states who aspire EU membership,[14] and it needs to be respected throughout a state's EU membership.[15] At the same time, the Treaty does not detail what, precisely, it means by 'to respect the value of the rule of law'. The drafters of the Treaty explained their selection for the values to be listed in Article 2 TEU based on the fact that these values "*have a clear non-controversial legal basis so that the Member States can discern the obligations resulting therefrom which are subject to sanction*".[16] Given that I had to develop an analytical framework in Chapter 3 to concretise, based on an extensive examination of legal sources, the rule of law requirements that Member States must meet when exercising public power, I would beg to differ.[17]

Be that as it may, Article 7 TEU provides a mechanism of protection in case the values listed in Article 2 TEU are threatened or infringed by a Member State. Although Article 7 TEU hence protects multiple values, it is typically referred to as the rule of law protection mechanism, since it not only protects the rule of law as one value amongst others, but it also consists of a legal provision that literally embodies the protective role of the law in a liberal democratic system. Article 7(1) TEU enables the Council, acting by a majority of four fifths of its members, to determine that there is a "*clear risk of a serious breach by a Member State of the values referred to in Article 2*". This determination must be based on a reasoned proposal by one third of the Member States, by the European Parliament or by the European Commission, and it can only be taken after the European Parliament consented. The mechanism of Article 7(1) TEU requires only the clear *risk* of a serious breach,[18] and hence serves as a warning mechanism.[19] In that case, the Council will hear the Member State in question and can address recommendations to it.[20] While I will not elaborate on this point here, it is worth highlighting that the analysis of Chapter 4 did indicate that the increasingly widespread use of algorithmic regulation, without the adoption of appropriate protection mechanisms to counter its risks, can entail a clear risk of a serious breach of the rule of law.

[14] See Article 49 TEU, stating that "*any European State which respects the values referred to in Article 2 and is committed to promoting them may apply to become a member of the Union.*"

[15] Gabriel N Toggenburg and Jonas Grimheden, 'Managing the Rule of Law in a Heterogeneous Context: A Fundamental Rights Perspective on Ways Forward' in Werner Schroeder (ed), *Strengthening the Rule of Law in Europe: From a Common Concept to Mechanisms of Implementation* (Hart Publishing 2016) 225.

[16] Praesidium, 'Draft of Articles 1 to 16 of the Constitutional Treaty' (The European Convention Secretariat 2003) CONV 528/03 11.

[17] See also the doubts raised in this regard by Toggenburg and Grimheden (n 15) 222.

[18] For a discussion of the meaning of this threshold, see *supra*, Section 4.2.5.

[19] See also Scheppele, Kochenov and Grabowska-Moroz (n 9) 8.

[20] Article 7(1) TEU.

Article 7(2) TEU goes a step further, as it enables the determination of the 'existence' of a 'serious and persistent' breach by a Member State of the values referred to in Article 2. In this case, however, the determination can only be made through a *unanimous* decision of the European Council, based on a proposal by one third of the Member States or by the Commission and after obtaining the consent of the European Parliament.[21] This is because the stakes of this determination are higher. Once a decision has been taken, Article 7(3) TEU enables the Council, acting by a qualified majority, to decide to suspend certain rights deriving from the application of the Treaties to the Member State in question, including voting rights in the Council. Before the determination of a 'clear risk' of a serious breach, or of the 'existence of a serious and persistent breach' of EU values, the Member State concerned always has the right to be heard and to submit its observations.

Thus far, the European Commission[22] and the European Parliament sought to trigger Article 7(1) against both Poland and Hungary,[23] and the Council has organised several hearings to hear the countries' positions. However, despite the calls by scholars, civil society organisations and even EU institutions to take further action,[24] and despite the fact that the concerns remain unaddressed (especially in Hungary),[25] the Council has come to the determination of neither a 'clear risk' nor the 'existence of a serious and persistent breach' of the rule of law. In addition, the Council's unwillingness to ensure that the Commission's recommendations to ameliorate the

[21] Article 7(2) TEU.

[22] In 2017, the European Commission triggered Article 7(1) for the first time in light of the clear risk of a serious breach of the rule of law by Poland. See European Commission, Reasoned proposal in accordance with Article 7(1) of the Treaty on European Union regarding the rule of law in Poland. Proposal for a Council decision on the determination of a clear risk of a serious breach by the Republic of Poland of the rule of law, COM(2017) 835 final, 20 December 2017.

[23] In 2018, the European Parliament adopted a resolution to determine the clear risk of a serious breach of the rule of law as regards Hungary. See 'European Parliament resolution of 12 September 2018 on a proposal calling on the Council to determine, pursuant to Article 7 (1) of the Treaty on European Union, the existence of a clear risk of a serious breach by Hungary of the values on which the Union is founded (2017/2131(INL)', 2018.

[24] R Daniel Kelemen and Kim Lane Scheppele, 'How to Stop Funding Autocracy in the EU' (*Verfassungsblog*, 10 September 2018) <https://verfassungsblog.de/how-to-stop-funding-autocracy-in-the-eu/>; Laurent Pech, 'The Rule of Law as a Well-Established and Well-Defined Principle of EU Law' (2022) 14 Hague Journal on the Rule of Law 107. See also Kerstin McCourt, 'European Commission Lacks Tenacity on the Rule of Law' (*Human Rights Watch*, 20 July 2022) <www.hrw.org/news/2022/07/20/european-commission-lacks-tenacity-rule-law>.

[25] In its resolution of 18 January 2024 on the situation in Hungary, the European Parliament stressed that its rule of law concerns have not been alleviated, and that it is '*strongly concerned about the further erosion of democracy, as well as the deterioration of the rule of law and the fundamental rights situation in Hungary*'. It also '*regrets the failure of the Council to make meaningful progress in the ongoing Article 7(1) TEU procedures*' and '*calls on the European Council and the Member States to take action and to determine whether Hungary has committed serious and persistent breaches of EU values under Article 7(2) TEU*'. See European Parliament resolution of 18 January 2024 on the situation in Hungary and frozen EU funds (2024/2512 (RSP)), 2024.

situation are implemented has led to much frustration.[26] Given the role of the Council (consisting of representatives from the twenty-seven EU Member States), the procedure in question is primarily political in nature. Considering the extensiveness of the procedure's potential consequences and the sheer symbolically weighty nature of its invocation, it is only considered a measure of last resort. Moreover, as long as there is at least one other Member State who vetoes the determination of the existence of a 'serious and persistent breach', the procedure of Article 7(2) stands no chance given the requirement for unanimity.[27]

The inability of Article 7 TEU to counter the ongoing rule of law threats in some EU Member States and, in particular, the reluctance to deploy its mechanism has been subjected to heavy criticism. It also pinpoints the dilemma that the EU and its Member States are faced with, in between maintaining the cooperation and goodwill of the Member States on other fronts, and ensuring adherence to the rule of (EU) law without further alienating infringing states. Either way, by the time Article 7 TEU finally comes into play, if ever, a lot of damage will already have been done.

One problem, which is also relevant to the risks identified in the context of algorithmic regulation, is that the erosion of the rule of law often occurs incrementally rather than suddenly.[28] However, as previously noted, incremental changes will rarely trigger a sufficiently strong counter-reaction so as to lead to the adoption of a measure which is deemed as far-reaching as Article 7 TEU. This gives rise to a tragic observation: the mechanism designed to avoid systemic breaches of the rule of law is, precisely because of the systemic and incremental nature of those breaches, unable to carry out its proper function.

Setting the ineffectiveness of Article 7 TEU aside, the EU's increased attention for the (dis)respect of the rule of law in Member States (perhaps precisely due to this ineffectiveness) did give rise to a number of soft-law initiatives that monitor the rule of law situation across the Union.[29] Indeed, in recent years, the Commission's rule of law toolbox has expanded, and now encompasses several evidence-gathering and documentation mechanisms based on rule of law-indicators. Examples are the

[26] See also Laurent Pech and Jakub Jaraczewski, 'Systemic Threat to the Rule of Law in Poland: Updated and New Article 7(1) TEU Recommendations' (2023), UCD Working Papers in Law, Criminology & Socio-Legal Studies Research Paper No. 13, 9.

[27] Scheppele, Kochenov and Grabowska-Moroz (n 9) 8. See also 'Four European Organisations of Judges Sue EU Council for Disregarding EU Court's Judgments on Decision to Unblock Funds to Poland' (AEAJ 28 August 2022) <www.rechtersvoorrechters.nl/uploads/2022/08/PRESS-RELEASE-EN-2022-08-28.pdf>.

[28] See also Kim Lane Scheppele, 'Autocratic Legalism' [2018] The University of Chicago Law Review 545; Aziz Huq and Tom Ginsburg, 'How to Lose a Constitutional Democracy' (2018) 65 UCLA Law Review 78.

[29] See European Commission, 'Communication from the Commission to the European Parliament, the European Council and the Council: Further Strengthening the Rule of Law within the Union – State of Play and Possible next Steps' (Brussels, 3 April 2019) COM/2019/163 final.

'European Semester',[30] the 'EU Justice Scoreboard',[31] and the annual 'Rule of Law Reports'[32] that essentially institutionalise a dialogue between the Commission and Member States. These mechanisms also provide useful information that could support the triggering of Article 7 TEU, the Conditionality Regulation or infringement actions, which I discuss in the following sections.[33] While non-binding, and not providing any guarantee that they will contribute to a successful triggering of the Article 7 TEU procedure, unlike the former, these initiatives are able to play a

[30] Introduced in 2011, the European Semester is the framework for integrated surveillance and coordination of economic and employment policies across the European Union. While it was initially mainly an economic exercise, it now also integrates other policy fields. It is not explicitly aimed at protecting 'the rule of law', yet its monitoring activities also cover areas that are relevant for the rule of law, including the European Justice Scoreboard. See also Amy Verdun and Jonathan Zeitlin, 'Introduction: The European Semester as a New Architecture of EU Socioeconomic Governance in Theory and Practice' (2018) 25 Journal of European Public Policy 137.

[31] The European Justice Scoreboard presents an annual overview of indicators on the efficiency, quality and independence of justice systems, and is meant to assist EU Member States in improving the effectiveness of their national justice systems through comparable data. Its findings feed into the annual rule of law reports. See also András Jakab and Lando Kirchmair, 'How to Develop the EU Justice Scoreboard into a Rule of Law Index: Using an Existing Tool in the EU Rule of Law Crisis in a More Efficient Way' (2021) 22 German Law Journal 936.

[32] The annual rule of law reporting mechanism was launched by the Commission in 2020, as part of its initiative to strengthen its rule of law toolbox. It is essentially a monitoring tool, meant to maintain a yearly dialogue with Member States as regards several areas that are of relevance to the rule of law, resulting in a report with data and conclusions on the state of the rule of law in each EU Member States (though no detailed recommendations or legal conclusions are made). Based on the Commission's rule of law methodology, these areas are: (1) justice systems; (2) the anti-corruption framework; (3) media pluralism; and (4) other institutional issues related to checks and balances. The Commission draws on data from Member States, case law, EU bodies, but also from the Council of Europe and other international organisations. See European Commission, 'European Rule of Law Mechanism: Methodology for the Preparation of the Annual Rule of Law Report' (2020) <https://commission.europa.eu/system/files/2020-09/2020_rule_of_law_report_methodology_en.pdf>.

[33] Recital 16 of the Conditionality Regulation, for instance, provides that, when the Commission seeks to identify potential breaches of the rule of law by Member States for the purpose of the triggering the regulation's mechanism,

> that assessment should be objective, impartial and fair, and should take into account relevant information from available sources and recognised institutions, including judgments of the Court of Justice of the European Union, reports of the Court of Auditors, the Commission's annual Rule of Law Report and EU Justice Scoreboard, reports of the European Anti-Fraud Office (OLAF) and the European Public Prosecutor's Office (EPPO) as relevant, and conclusions and recommendations of relevant international organisations and networks, including Council of Europe bodies such as the Council of Europe Group of States against Corruption (GRECO) and the Venice Commission, in particular its rule-of-law checklist, and the European networks of supreme courts and councils for the judiciary. The Commission could consult the European Union Agency for Fundamental Rights and the Venice Commission if necessary for the purpose of preparing a thorough qualitative assessment.

preventative role rather than a mere reactive one.[34] Furthermore, they enable the dissemination of information about the status of the rule of law in every EU Member State to the public at large, thereby contributing to transparency and potentially accountability at the national level too.

Regrettably, however, none of these initiatives currently have indicators about the potentially adverse impact of algorithmic regulation on the rule of law, or on the checks and balances that have been implemented to counter such impact. Quite to the contrary, if discussed at all, 'digitalisation' is presented as a desirable feature that Member States should ideally swiftly implement in light of the 'efficiencies' it can enable.[35] The risks attached to it, particularly in the area of public administration, are left unspoken and unmonitored, despite their *systemic* nature and potential contribution to the *systemic* breaches of the rule of law. In other words, the effects of algorithmic regulation on the rule of law remains a blind spot. As it currently stands, neither Article 7 TEU nor the soft-law mechanisms aimed at monitoring the rule of law situation seem to offer safeguards against the threat conceptualised under Chapter 4.

5.2.2 *The Conditionality Regulation*

Besides soft-law initiatives, the European Union also sought to expand its rule of law toolbox with binding mechanisms. The adoption of the Conditionality Regulation, or Regulation 2020/2092 of the European Parliament and of the Council of 16 December 2020 on a general regime of conditionality for the protection of the Union budget, can be seen as a highlight in this regard.[36] In addition to its legal relevance, I already noted in Chapter 3 that the Conditionality Regulation also has significant definitional relevance, as it provides "*the first comprehensive all-encompassing internal-oriented definition of the rule of law adopted by the EU co-legislators*".[37] While the European Commission had already proposed a conceptualisation of the rule of law and its six principles in 2019,[38] by means of the Conditionality Regulation, this conceptualisation was also formally adopted by the

[34] See also Toggenburg and Grimheden (n 15) 225.

[35] While the references to digitalisation are sporadic, the 2022 rule of law report, for instance, recommends several Member States to continue their digitalisation efforts (with particular focus on the justice system). See European Commission, 'The Rule of Law Situation in the European Union. 2022 Rule of Law Report.' (2022) COM(2022) 500 final <https://ec.europa.eu/info/sites/default/files/1_1_194062_communication_rol_en.pdf>.

[36] See, e.g., Antonia Baraggia and Matteo Bonelli, 'Linking Money to Values: The New Rule of Law Conditionality Regulation and Its Constitutional Challenges' (2022) 23 German Law Journal 131, 132.

[37] Pech (n 24).

[38] See also *supra*, Section 3.2.4.

European Parliament and the Council and enshrined in a piece of secondary legislation.[39]

The Regulation foresees a mechanism to suspend the transmission of EU funds to 'rogue'[40] Member States – or, more diplomatically, it conditions the transmission of EU funds to compliance with the rule of law. Its primary aim is hence to protect the EU budget and ensure the sound financial management thereof by Member States, while at the same time incentivising rule of law compliance through financial means. In essence, the regulation seeks to prevent that EU funds are being used for authoritarian or rule of law-infringing ends.[41] Some scholars[42] noted that the European Union already had a similar mechanism at its disposal through Regulation 1303/2013, laying down common provisions regarding the governance of a number of EU funds, including the European Regional Development Fund, the European Social Fund, the Cohesion Fund, the European Agricultural Fund for Rural Development and the European Maritime and Fisheries Fund.[43] Article 142 of that Regulation foresees a procedure for the suspension of payments by the Commission if, inter alia, "*there is a serious deficiency in the effective functioning of the management and control system of the operational programme, which has put at risk the Union contribution to the operational programme and for which corrective measures have not been taken*".[44] Based on the idea that "*surely, a country without the rule of law cannot generate effective management and control systems*", Kelemen and Scheppele argue that this provision already enabled the suspension of EU funds to rule of law-infringing Member States, yet they "*note with disappointment that the Commission has not yet had the will to use the power already in its hands*".[45]

Despite the seeming pre-existence of similar remedies, the adoption of the Conditionality Regulation, as a general regime of conditionality, was not without difficulty or controversy.[46] As soon as it was adopted, both Hungary and Poland

[39] ibid.

[40] See Laurent Pech and Kim Lane Scheppele, 'Illiberalism Within: Rule of Law Backsliding in the EU' (2017) 19 Cambridge Yearbook of European Legal Studies 3.

[41] See also Renáta Uitz, 'Funding Illiberal Democracy: The Case for Credible Budgetary Conditionality in the EU', BRIDGE Network – Working Paper 7 [2020] SSRN Electronic Journal <https://ssrn.com/abstract=3722936>.

[42] Kelemen and Scheppele (n 24).

[43] See Regulation (EU) no. 1303/2013 of the European Parliament and of the Council of 17 December 2013 laying down common provisions on the European Regional Development Fund, the European Social Fund, the Cohesion Fund, the European Agricultural Fund for Rural Development and the European Maritime and Fisheries Fund and laying down general provisions on the European Regional Development Fund, the European Social Fund, the Cohesion Fund and the European Maritime and Fisheries Fund and repealing Council Regulation (EC) no. 1083/2006 2013 (OJ L 347 20122013, p. 320). This Regulation has been amended multiple times since its adoption, the last time on 13 April 2022.

[44] See Article 142(1)(a) TFEU.

[45] Kelemen and Scheppele (n 24).

[46] Not only were negotiations between the Parliament and Council lengthy and challenging, but the Commission's initial proposal also received a negative opinion from the Council's Legal

challenged the validity of the regulation's legal basis before the Court.[47] They claimed that the EU did not have the legal competence to adopt a regulation that defines the rule of law or determines criteria to establish breaches thereof.[48] Moreover, they stated that the Regulation was not compatible with Article 7 TEU, which already, in their view, exhaustively, provides for a mechanism to protect the rule of law, thus precluding the EU to adopt another one.[49] As noted in Chapter 3, the EU does not have a 'general' legal competence to enforce the rule of law, and hence had to resort to a domain-specific legal basis. Given the link of the Regulation's suspension mechanism with the multi-annual financial framework (MFF), some have argued that the Regulation would need to be adopted under the MFF's legal basis, Article 312 TFEU, which requires adoption through unanimity in the Council.[50]

Instead, the Commission resorted to Article 322(1)(a) TFEU as the Regulation's legal basis, well aware that the unanimity requirement of Article 312 TFEU would prevent the Regulation to ever see the light of day, since Poland and Hungary would never agree to it. Article 322(1)(a) TFEU provides that the European Parliament and the Council, acting in accordance with the ordinary legislative procedure (i.e. without unanimity), can adopt regulations to set the financial rules determining "*the procedure to be adopted for establishing and implementing the budget and for presenting and auditing accounts*". Accordingly, the Conditionality Regulation can be seen as an example of the EU's use of legal competences in one particular field (e.g. the EU budget) to promote other aims in a more indirect way (e.g. the rule of

Service. See also Kim Lane Scheppele, Laurent Pech and R Daniel Kelemen, 'Never Missing an Opportunity to Miss an Opportunity: The Council Legal Service Opinion on the Commission's EU Budget-Related Rule of Law Mechanism' (*Verfassungsblog*, 12 November 2018) <https://verfassungsblog.de/never-missing-an-opportunity-to-miss-an-opportunity-the-council-legal-service-opinion-on-the-commissions-eu-budget-related-rule-of-law-mechanism/>.

[47] This legal challenge can be seen as part of the compromise in the European Council in December 2020, during which it was agreed that the implementation of the regulation would not be initiated before the CJEU could analyse its legality. See General Secretariat of the Council, 'European Council Meeting (10 and 11 December 2020) – Conclusions' (EUCO 2020). See also Baraggia and Bonelli (n 36) 132. Some scholars have argued that these Council conclusions were adopted *ultra vires* and constituted a violation of the principle of institutional balance by undermining the prerogatives of the Parliament, Council, Commission and Court of Justice. See, e.g., Alberto Alemanno and Marijn Chamon, 'To Save the Rule of Law You Must Apparently Break It' (*Verfassungsblog*, 11 December 2020) <https://verfassungsblog.de/to-save-the-rule-of-law-you-must-apparently-break-it/>.

[48] See Case C-157/21, *Republic of Poland v European Parliament and Council*, 16 February 2022, ECLI:EU:C:2022:98, §69.

[49] See ibid, §§87–88. Note that they also claimed that the Conditionality Regulation breaches the principle of legal certainty – i.e. a rule of law principle that the EU must respect, as part of its *horizontal* commitment to the rule of law – since it provides insufficient clarity as to how it would be applied to Member States. See ibid, §311.

[50] ibid, §83. See also Kelemen and Scheppele (n 24).

law), thereby overcoming the hurdles of potentially limited competences.[51] This approach, while not uncriticised, is not new. Various legislative initiatives which are based on Article 114 TFEU, aimed at advancing the harmonisation of the EU's internal market, also contribute (directly or indirectly) to the protection of fundamental rights, an area in which the EU's competences are also not generalised.[52]

In the past, the Court has already frequently been called upon to ensure that the EU does not overstep its competences by adopting an erroneous legal basis, and did not shy away from invalidating legislation where it deemed this to be the case.[53] However, in this case, the challenge raised by Poland and Hungary was unsuccessful, and the Court upheld the Regulation's validity. It found that the Regulation does not create a general rule of law protection mechanism, and only limits itself to those rule of law-infringements that are directly linked to the EU budget, hence remaining within the confines of Article 322 TFEU.[54] The Court also distinguished the Regulation's mechanism from the procedure in Article 7 TEU, which hence did not preclude its adoption.

With the Court's blessing, the Commission thus no longer faced an obstacle or excuse to launch the suspension mechanism.[55] In April 2022, it therefore announced the initiation of the procedure against Hungary[56] – the first step of a lengthy

[51] See also Baraggia and Bonelli (n 36) 134.

[52] For instance, before the enshrinement of Article 16 TFEU – granting the Union a specific legal basis to adopt regulation in the sphere of personal data processing, for instance the GDPR – the Union relied on Article 114 TFEU as the legal basis for its previous data protection directive (Directive 95/46/EC of the European Parliament and of the Council of 24 October 1995 on the protection of individuals with regard to the processing of personal data and on the free movement of such data (OJ 1995 L 281, p. 31)). See in this regard Case C-101/01, *Bodil Lindqvist*, 6 November 2003, ECLI:EU:C:2003:596. See also Gloria González Fuster, *The Emergence of Personal Data Protection as a Fundamental Right of the EU*, vol 16 (Springer International Publishing 2014). Similarly, environmental protection legislation has likewise been relying on Article 114 TFEU before a more specific legal basis was adopted in the Treaties. See also David Langlet and Said Mahmoudi, *EU Environmental Law and Policy* (Oxford University Press 2016); Geert van Calster and Leonie Reins, *EU Environmental Law* (Edward Elgar Publishing 2017).

[53] See for instance Case C-376/98, *Germany v European Parliament and Council*, 5 October 2000, ECLI:EU:C:2000:544, where the Court annulled Directive 98/43/EC of the European Parliament and of the Council of 6 July 1998 on the approximation of the laws, regulations and administrative provisions of the Member States relating to the advertising and sponsorship of tobacco products, pursuant to the fact that it was adopted based on an inappropriate legal basis. See also Stephen Weatherill, 'The Limits of Legislative Harmonization Ten Years after Tobacco Advertising: How the Court's Case Law Has Become a "Drafting Guide"' (2011) 12 German Law Journal 827.

[54] See Case C-157/21, *Republic of Poland v European Parliament and Council* (n 48), §130 and following.

[55] Note that this obstacle was primarily a *political* one, given the compromise solution reached by the European Council in its conclusions on 11 December 2020. See General Secretariat of the Council (n 47). See also Alemanno and Chamon (n 47).

[56] See Vlad Makszimov, 'Hungary: Commission Officially Launches Procedure Linking Bloc Funds to Rule of Law' *Euractiv* (27 April 2022) <www.euractiv.com/section/politics/news/

procedure.[57] Indeed, before the suspension mechanism could actually be implemented, the procedure set out by the Regulation had to be followed, including a written notification to the Member State concerned, setting out the factual elements and specific grounds on which the findings are based; the Member State's response and potential proposal of remedial measures; the Commission's notification of its intention to propose an implementing decision in case it considers the remedial measures to be insufficient; yet another opportunity for the Member State to share its observations, particularly regarding the proportionality of the Commission's envisaged measure; and, finally, an implementing decision by the Council acting by qualified majority, based on the Commission's proposal.[58] In March 2022, the Commission also adopted guidelines in which it set out how it will apply the regulation in more detail.[59]

Importantly, the suspension mechanism can only be invoked with regards to a limited set of rule of law-infringements that have a link with the EU budget, hence not providing a general suspension clause for all rule of law-infringements. After all, its purpose and its legal basis concern the protection of the EU budget rather than the rule of law in general. Article 3 of the Regulation sets out which Member State actions may be 'indicative' of breaches of principles of the rule of law for the purpose of the regulation, namely:

(a) endangering the independence of the judiciary;
(b) failing to prevent, correct or sanction arbitrary or unlawful decisions by public authorities, including by law-enforcement authorities, withholding financial and human resources affecting their proper functioning or failing to ensure the absence of conflicts of interest;
(c) limiting the availability and effectiveness of legal remedies, including through restrictive procedural rules and lack of implementation of judgments, or limiting the effective investigation, prosecution or sanctioning of breaches of law.

hungary-commission-officially-launches-procedure-linking-bloc-funds-to-rule-of-law/>. See also Nathalie Smuha, 'Een doosje vijgen na Pasen voor Viktor Orban' *De Standaard* (8 April 2022) <www.standaard.be/cnt/dmf20220407_97729796>.

57 The European Commission decided to postpone the initiation of the Conditionality Regulation's procedure against Hungary until the Court's judgment came out. However, on 20 October 2021, the European Parliament, fed up with the Commission's delay, submitted an action in court against the Commission for failure to act under Article 265 TFEU. On 18 May 2022 – after the Commission had announced the launch of the Regulation's suspension mechanism – the European Parliament informed the Court that it wished to discontinue its action, after which the President of the Court removed the case from the register. See Order of the President of the Court in Case C-657/21, *European Parliament v European Commission*, 8 June 2022.

58 See Article 6 of the Conditionality Regulation.

59 European Commission, 'Communication from the European Commission: Guidelines on the Application of the Regulation (EU, EURATOM) 2020/2092 on a General Regime of Conditionality for the Protection of the Union Budget' (2022) C(2022) 1382 final.

In addition to these 'general' indications, Article 4 sets out that action can be undertaken where it is established that "*breaches of the principles of the rule of law in a Member State affect or seriously risk affecting the sound financial management of the Union budget or the protection of the financial interests of the Union in a sufficiently direct way*".[60] To be deemed sufficiently direct, the breaches of the principles of the rule of law should fall under one of the following exhaustively listed categories:[61]

(a) the proper functioning of the authorities implementing the Union budget, including loans and other instruments guaranteed by the Union budget, in particular in the context of public procurement or grant procedures;
(b) the proper functioning of the authorities carrying out financial control, monitoring and audit, and the proper functioning of effective and transparent financial management and accountability systems;
(c) the proper functioning of investigation and public prosecution services in relation to the investigation and prosecution of fraud, including tax fraud, corruption or other breaches of Union law relating to the implementation of the Union budget or to the protection of the financial interests of the Union;
(d) the effective judicial review by independent courts of actions or omissions by the authorities referred to in points (a), (b) and (c);
(e) the prevention and sanctioning of fraud, including tax fraud, corruption or other breaches of Union law relating to the implementation of the Union budget or to the protection of the financial interests of the Union, and the imposition of effective and dissuasive penalties on recipients by national courts or by administrative authorities;
(f) the recovery of funds unduly paid;
(g) effective and timely cooperation with OLAF[62] and, subject to the participation of the Member State concerned, with EPPO[63] in their

[60] See Article 4(1) of the Conditionality Regulation.
[61] See Article 4(2) of the Conditionality Regulation.
[62] While OLAF – the European Anti-Fraud Office – is able to investigate potential cases of corruption relating to the use of EU funds, it does not have the competence to prosecute fraudsters. Instead, it passes on its investigation results to the Member State in which the fraudulent behaviour took place, so that its public authorities can take the necessary action. Evidently, such a set-up is not ideal if potentially problematic behaviour comes from Member States' public authorities themselves, or if their independence is doubted. See also Kelemen and Scheppele (n 24).
[63] The European Public Prosecutor's Office (EPPO) is the Union's independent public prosecution office, established by Council Regulation 2017/1939 in October 2017 pursuant to the mechanism of enhanced cooperation. It started its operations in June 2021 and is able to investigate, prosecute and bring to judgment crimes against the EU's financial interests. It is also able to exercise the function of prosecutor in the courts of Member States. However, given

investigations or prosecutions pursuant to the applicable Union acts in accordance with the principle of sincere cooperation;

(h) other situations or conduct of authorities that are relevant to the sound financial management of the Union budget or the protection of the financial interests of the Union.

Following the Regulation's application to Hungary, on 15 December 2022, the Council decided to freeze about €6.3 billion of budgetary commitments,[64] citing rule of law breaches pertaining to public procurement procedures and prosecutorial action, as well as conflicts of interest and concerns around the fight against corruption (though not the concerns around judicial independence). At the same time, inspired by the Conditionality Regulation's approach of financial incentivisation, the Commission also started relying on legal provisions in other funding mechanisms that tie a Member States' receipt of funding to certain conditions (such as the Resilience and Recovery Regulation[65] and the Common Provisions Regulation[66]), including the obligation to uphold the Charter of Fundamental Rights. On this basis, on 22 December 2022 the Commission decided to freeze about €21.7 billion of EU cohesion funds until Hungary adopted several measures regarding LGBTQI+ rights, academic freedom, asylum policies and judicial independence.[67]

These actions were initially applauded, yet the applause for the Commission was short-lived. A year later, on 13 December 2023, it decided to unblock €10.2 billion of the frozen EU cohesion funds, justifying its decision based on a 'thorough assessment' of Hungary's newly adopted measures to strengthen the judiciary's independence.[68] While critics have characterised those measures as mere window

that it is based on the mechanism of enhanced cooperation, it only has those powers in the Member States that explicitly opted in. Currently, twenty-two of the twenty-seven Member States are participating. The five non-participants are Hungary, Poland, Sweden, Denmark and Ireland (though the latter two have a general opt-out from the Union's activities in the area of freedom, security and justice (AFSJ)).

64 See Council Implementing Decision (EU) 2022/2506 of 15 December 2022 on measures for the protection of the Union budget against breaches of the principles of the rule of law in Hungary, ST/14247/2022/INIT, 2022.

65 Regulation 2021/241 of the European Parliament and of the Council of 12 February 2021 establishing the Recovery and Resilience Facility, OJ L 57, 18 February 2021.

66 Regulation (EU) 2021/1060 of the European Parliament and of the Council of 24 June 2021 laying down common provisions on the European Regional Development Fund, the European Social Fund Plus, the Cohesion Fund, the Just Transition Fund and the European Maritime, Fisheries and Aquaculture Fund and financial rules for those and for the Asylum, Migration and Integration Fund, the Internal Security Fund and the Instrument for Financial Support for Border Management and Visa Policy, PE/47/2021/INIT, OJ L 231, 30 June 2021.

67 For a detailed discussion of those actions and their legal basis, see pages 176–183 in Kim Lane Scheppele, 'The Treaties without a Guardian: The European Commission and the Rule of Law' (2023) 29 Columbia Journal of European Law 93.

68 The Commission, however, stressed that it "*will closely and continuously monitor, notably through audits, active engagement with stakeholders and in monitoring committees, the*

dressing, others have pointed to the politically strategic move of the Commission, as its decision to unfreeze the funds came a day before European leaders needed Hungary's cooperation to approve new aid to Ukraine.[69] In March 2024, the European Parliament therefore decided to challenge the Commission's decision before the Court of Justice, claiming that the Commission failed to fulfil its obligation to protect the EU budget and ensure that taxpayers' money is not misused.[70] If anything, this saga highlights that, despite the availability of *several* legal mechanisms to freeze EU funds, their application and effect are still highly dependent on the political willingness of EU actors and Member States to do so, and the bridging of political hurdles.

Let us, however, bracket this political aspect for a moment, and examine to what extent the Conditionality Regulation could at least theoretically serve as a mechanism to counter the threat of algorithmic rule by law. While it was certainly not conceived to offer protection in the specific context of algorithmic systems, it is worth asking whether it can nevertheless play a role in this context. Based on the contours set out above, a number of observations can be made.

First, given the Regulation's focus on the governance and sound management of EU funds, it appears to be most suitable in countering actions relating to fraudulent behaviour by officials or corrupt public procurement practices. Conversely, many of the examples discussed under Chapter 4, for instance in the area of social welfare or criminal risk assessments, would hence not easily fall under its scope. As regards the examination of tax fraud (an area in which algorithmic regulation is already widely used) the Regulation requires a link with the EU budget, and hence would not apply to all fraud examinations (for instance under points (c) and (e)). That said, the Court's judgment in *Ackerberg Fransson*[71] already clarified that, since the European Union's own resources include revenue from Member States' collection of VAT, the investigation and prosecution of tax fraud relating (even in part) to VAT affects the financial

application of the measures put in place by Hungary. If, at any point in time, the Commission considers that this horizontal enabling condition is no longer fulfilled, it may again decide to block funding." See European Commission, 'Commission considers that Hungary's judicial reform addressed deficiencies in judicial independence, but maintains measures on budget conditionality', Brussels, 13 December 2023, <https://ec.europa.eu/commission/presscorner/detail/en/ip_23_6465>.

69 Jakob Hanke Vela and Claudia Chiappa, 'Brussels vs. Brussels: EU Parliament to Sue Commission over Hungary Cash' (*Politico*, 12 March 2024) < www.politico.eu/article/parliament-sues-commission-over-unfreezing-of-hungary-funds/>.

70 Eddy Wax, '5 Questions about the EU Parliament Suing the Commission over Hungary Cash' (*Politico*, 18 March 2024), <www.politico.eu/article/5-questions-european-parliament-legal-action-commission-hungary-funds/>.

71 See Case C-617/10, *Åklagaren v Hans Åkerberg Fransson*, 26 February 2013, ECLI:EU:C:2013:105.

interests of the European Union.[72] It could hence reasonably be argued that, when public authorities deploy algorithmic systems to detect and prosecute tax fraud (including VAT), and they do so in a manner that does not comply with the six rule of law principles set out above, this would likewise fall under the Regulation's scope.[73]

Yet one can also raise a more straightforward example of where algorithmic regulation might play a role. When the analysis of elements and risks based on which a procurement contract is allocated (or not) occurs with the help of algorithmic systems,[74] one could argue that the potentially problematic design and use of these systems can adversely impact the rule of law in a way that is relevant for the purpose of the regulation. Procurement processes are increasingly supported by analyses carried out by algorithmic systems, and one can easily imagine that 'objectivity' might also be invoked to this end. And while such automation could make procurement processes more 'efficient',[75] at the same time, one might also imagine the risk that, whether through negligence or deliberate design choices, the outcomes of the automated process favour some tenderers over others. This scenario would, at least in theory,[76] fit rather neatly under Article 4(2)(a) of the Conditionality Regulation, and hence be susceptible to trigger (the first step of) the suspension mechanism. Accordingly, it appears that a number of applications of algorithmic regulation could relevantly fall under the scope of the Conditionality Regulation.

However, that fact in and of itself does not yet help us much further. Certainly, the Regulation could in theory disincentivise Member States to adopt algorithmic regulation in an irresponsible manner in the abovementioned areas. However, for this to be the case, Member States must first be aware of the risks posed thereby to the rule of law, which is not a given. Furthermore, these provisions will still not

[72] See for instance §22 of the Judgment, in which the Court states inter alia that

> Given that the European Union's own resources include, as provided in Article 2(1) of Council Decision 2007/436/EC, Euratom of 7 June 2007 on the system of the European Communities' own resources (OJ 2007 L 163, p. 17), revenue from application of a uniform rate to the harmonised VAT assessment bases determined according to European Union rules, there is thus a direct link between the collection of VAT revenue in compliance with the European Union law applicable and the availability to the European Union budget of the corresponding VAT resources, since any lacuna in the collection of the first potentially causes a reduction in the second.

[73] Recall that several examples discussed under Section 4.1 concerned uses of algorithmic regulation to detect fraud.

[74] See for instance Su Jin Choi and others, 'AI and Text-Mining Applications for Analyzing Contractor's Risk in Invitation to Bid (ITB) and Contracts for Engineering Procurement and Construction (EPC) Projects' (2021) 14 Energies 4632.

[75] See also Oihab Allal-Chérif, Virginia Simón-Moya and Antonio Carlos Cuenca Ballester, 'Intelligent Purchasing: How Artificial Intelligence Can Redefine the Purchasing Function' (2021) 124 Journal of Business Research 69.

[76] In practice, it would, however, be highly difficult to establish this connection, given a general lack of insight into such processes.

ensure that they set up appropriate transparency, control and oversight mechanisms over the algorithmic systems' design and deployment process. And while, in theory, the Regulation could provide a means to penalise Member States who do not take the risks emanating from algorithmic regulation seriously, by the time such penalisation arrives, a lot of damage may already have occurred – damage that could potentially have been prevented or at least mitigated in case of ex ante oversight. Furthermore, as already noted previously, any ex post remedy will in any case be dependent upon the realisation that the algorithmic system was inappropriately designed or used, a realisation that is difficult to achieve if the use of the system is not transparent and open to *systemic* review rather than mere individual review.[77]

Consequently, while the Conditionality Regulation can at least help prevent that *more* EU funds are made available to Member States that, with or without the assistance of algorithmic regulation, infringe the rule of law's principles, its relevance remains confined to areas that have an explicit link with the EU financial interests, and to Member States who disregard the rule of law to *such* extent that the Commission feels itself forced to launch the mechanism provided in the regulation. As a preventative tool for Member States who are negligent rather than deliberate in countering the adverse impact that their algorithmic systems can have on the rule of law, it will have little to no effect. It can thus be concluded that other safeguards, preferably of an ex ante character, are needed to address the threat of algorithmic rule by law.

5.2.3 *Infringement Actions and Proceedings before National Courts*

The two mechanisms I discussed above seek to counter, respectively, Member State breaches of EU values (including the rule of law) that are 'serious and persistent'; and Member State breaches of the rule of law that directly affect the financial interests of the EU. Yet when it comes to the protection of the rule of *EU* law (namely Member States' adherence to European Union law more generally), there are two other mechanisms that can be pointed out. The first concerns the infringement procedure enshrined in Articles 258–260 TFEU, which allows the European Commission or a Member State to seize the CJEU in case a fellow Member State failed to fulfil an obligation under the Treaties. The second concerns the ability to challenge a national act that breaches EU law before a national court, potentially through the preliminary reference procedure laid down in Article 267 TFEU. Both of these procedures enable the judicial review of the legality of Member States'

[77] To concretise: the tenderer who saw her bid refused in favour of a bid by someone who is openly pro-government – and who fears that something might be wrong with the algorithmic system used during the evaluation process – may, for instance, challenge this administrative act before a court. However, as noted *supra*, in Section 4.1.5, this court will not necessarily be able to carry out a systemic review of the way in which the government uses algorithmic systems to evaluate bids.

actions in light of their obligations under EU law.[78] Indeed, Member States are obliged to take "*any appropriate measure, general or particular, to ensure fulfilment of the obligations arising out of the Treaties or resulting from the acts of the institutions of the Union*,"[79] including obligations they might have under both primary and secondary EU legislation.

By virtue of the infringement procedure of Article 258 TFEU, the Commission may sue a Member State before the CJEU when it considers that it has failed to fulfil an obligation under the Treaties.[80] It must first deliver a reasoned opinion on the matter and give the State concerned the opportunity to submit its observations. In the absence of the State's compliance with the opinion within the period laid down by the Commission, it may take the matter to Court.[81] Article 259 TFEU also foresees that a Member State which considers that another State failed to fulfil an obligation under the Treaties can bring the matter to Court – after first passing by the Commission.[82] If the Court finds that the Member State has indeed failed to fulfil an obligation, the State shall be required to take the necessary measures to comply with the judgment of the Court.[83]

Importantly, if the Commission subsequently finds that the Member State did not comply with the Court's judgment, it may take the matter before the Court again, this time with the request that the Member State be imposed a lump sum or penalty payment.[84] Accordingly, the infringement procedure also provides the Commission with financial leverage to ensure that Member States comply.[85]

Note that the threshold for such a procedure does not consist of a 'serious', 'persistent' or 'systemic' breach of EU law, but simply of the failure to fulfil an obligation. This can also concern the mere obligation to transpose a directive into national law within the specified deadline.[86] It should be noted that the European Commission has discretion as to whether or not it decides to bring a case to court, and it has no obligation to do so.[87] That said, pursuant to Article 17(1) TEU, it is the Commission's task to ensure that EU law is duly applied.[88]

[78] See in this regard also Lenaerts, Van Nuffel and Corthaut (n 3), chapters 29 and 30. See also Matteo Bonelli, 'Effective Judicial Protection in EU Law: An Evolving Principle of a Constitutional Nature' (2019) 12 Review of European Administrative Law 35; Koen Lenaerts, 'New Horizons for the Rule of Law within the EU' (2020) 21 German Law Journal 29.

[79] Article 4(3), §2.

[80] See Lenaerts, Maselis and Gutman (n 7) 179.

[81] Article 285 TFEU.

[82] Article 259 §2 TFEU.

[83] Article 260(1) TFEU.

[84] Article 260(2) TFEU.

[85] See also Lenaerts, Maselis and Gutman (n 7) 208.

[86] ibid 169.

[87] ibid 179.

[88] Article 17(1) TEU provides that the Commission shall promote the general interest of the Union and take appropriate initiatives to that end. It shall ensure the application of the Treaties, and of measures adopted by the institutions pursuant to them.

Some have argued that the infringement procedure avenue constitutes an important tool for the Commission to counter rule of law infringements in the EU.[89] Others have claimed, however, that: "*despite ten years of EU attempts at reining in Rule of Law violations and even as backsliding Member States have lost cases at the Court of Justice, illiberal regimes inside the EU have become more consolidated: the EU has been losing through winning*".[90] Admittedly, the infringement procedure is not designed to address systemic deficiencies of the rule of law, but rather provides a mechanism to ensure the enforcement of Member States' *specific* EU law obligations. However, used tactically, it can serve to challenge Member States' actions that adversely impact the rule of law, and the Commission is increasingly doing so. The Court is thereby enabled to carry out a judicial review of the conformity of a Member State's actions with EU law, and to call out their illegality in case of non-conformity.[91]

Another, more indirect, route to enable judicial review of Member States' actions at EU level is provided by Article 267 TFEU, which establishes a procedure that can be initiated by natural and legal persons before their national courts, hence complementing public enforcement with private enforcement.[92] National courts play an essential role in the EU legal order, as they safeguard the application of EU law at the national level. Given the primacy of EU law and its direct effect in national legal orders,[93] national courts must interpret national acts in line with EU law, and must even leave them aside when they breach EU law.[94] When they are uncertain about the way in which they should interpret EU law to assess the validity of a national (administrative) act, a national court can initiate a preliminary reference procedure and seek guidance from the CJEU.[95] In theory, the Court can only express itself about the interpretation of EU (primary and secondary) law rather than taking a stance about the validity of the national act. However, it should provide the national court with all the information it needs to undertake that assessment by itself.[96] When based on such guidance, which is binding for all courts in the EU, the national

89 Pohjankoski (n 13). See also the discussion in Sonja Priebus and Lisa H Anders, 'Fundamental Change Beneath the Surface: The Supranationalisation of Rule of Law Protection in the European Union' (2024) 62 Journal of Common Market Studies 224, 235.

90 Scheppele, Kochenov and Grabowska-Moroz (n 9).

91 Through this mechanism, the Court is hence playing a pivotal role in the protection of the rule of law in Europe. See also John Morijn, 'Separate Charter Invocation as a New Enforcement Method: The Lex NGO Case' (2022) 59 Common Market Law Review 1137.

92 See Lenaerts, Van Nuffel and Corthaut (n 3) 768.

93 See also Bruno de Witte, 'Direct Effect, Primacy, and the Nature of the Legal Order' in Paul Craig and Gráinne de Búrca (eds), *The Evolution of EU Law* (Oxford University Press 2021).

94 See Lenaerts, Van Nuffel and Corthaut (n 3) 769. See for instance Case C-573/17, *Popławski*, 24 June 2019, ECLI:EU:C:2019:530, §§58–62.

95 See also Morten Broberg, 'Preliminary References as a Means for Enforcing EU Law' in András Jakab and Dimitry Kochenov (eds), *The Enforcement of EU Law and Values: Ensuring Member States' Compliance*, vol 1 (Oxford University Press 2017).

96 See Lenaerts, Maselis and Gutman (n 7) 233.

court concludes that a legal act at national level breaches EU law, it needs to set it aside.

The disadvantage of this procedure is that a natural or legal person already needs to be involved in a legal challenge before a national court in order to request a preliminary reference procedure. Moreover, the invalidation of the national act does not necessarily imply an invalidation of the public authority's working method more generally, as the judicial review is limited to the particular act in question rather than being systemic in nature, which showcases the limits of ex post judicial review rather than an ex ante preventative approach at the system level. But at least it offers natural and legal persons a legal avenue to protect the rights they derive from EU law, and to ensure that Member States fulfil their EU law obligations. In the context of Member States' citizen surveillance, for instance, this procedure has already proven to be effective in invalidating national (and even EU) legislation that undermines the fundamental right to privacy and data protection.[97]

The question then is: which EU law obligations are relevant for the context of algorithmic regulation deployed by public authorities, and can pertinently be the object of an infringement procedure or of a legal challenge before a national court? Indeed, to trigger the use of these procedures, a specific provision of EU law must be breached – hence requiring the existence of a relevant EU law provision in the first place.

There is currently no general EU regulation or directive setting out the obligations that public authorities must fulfil to comply with the rule of law when taking administrative acts, regardless of whether they do so through reliance on algorithmic systems. The functioning of public administrations largely remained a matter of national competence, given its entwinement with the exercise of national powers. In situations where algorithmic regulation by public authorities leads to infringements of purely domestic law rather than EU law, the procedures mentioned above cannot be invoked and national remedies – to the extent available – need to be relied on instead. That said, in a wide array of public sector domains, a link to EU law can nevertheless be established given the increasing harmonisation of national law in fields that influence public administration, thus rendering purely domestic situations ever more rare. The EU has, for instance, adopted legislation in the area of

[97] The Court, for instance, invalidated the Data Retention Directive (Directive 2006/24/EC) which it found to entail a wide-ranging and particularly serious interference with the fundamental rights to respect for private life and the protection of personal data, without that interference being limited to what is strictly necessary. See Joined Cases C-293/12 and C-594/12, Digital Rights Ireland and Seitlinger and Others, 8 April 2014, ECLI:EU:C:2014:238. It also invalidated Commission Implementing Decision 2016/1250 on the adequacy of the protection provided by the EU-US Data Protection Shield, in a case brought by a citizen in light of concerns that the Commission's Decision breached the fundamental right to data protection. See Case C-311/18, *Data Protection Commissioner v Facebook Ireland and Maximillian Schrems*, 16 July 2020, ECLI:EU:C:2020:559.

migration law,[98] social security,[99] public procurement,[100] environmental protection,[101] international transport and border control,[102] data (re)use[103] and criminal justice.[104]

Whenever Member States implement EU law, they must respect fundamental rights as enshrined in the Charter[105] (including, for instance, the right of defence, the presumption of innocence and the right to a good administration) as well as general principles of EU law.[106] Therefore, if public authorities rely on algorithmic regulation while implementing EU law in a way that breaches individuals' fundamental rights or general principles of EU law – for instance the general principle of equality, due to the discriminatory design or use of an algorithmic system – this constitutes the breach of a Member State's obligation that can become the object of an infringement action or preliminary reference procedure. Yet when does a public authority implement EU law?

The most obvious case concerns the situation in which Member States' public authorities act based on an EU regulation, directive or other legal act with binding force. To provide an example of an area of administrative law that has been (partially) harmonised, consider the domain of migration law, and more specifically the right to asylum. This right is enshrined in Article 18 CFREU, and has been

[98] See, e.g., Directive 2011/95/EU of the European Parliament and of the Council of 13 December 2011 on standards for the qualification of third-country nationals or stateless persons as beneficiaries of international protection, for a uniform status for refugees or for persons eligible for subsidiary protection, and for the content of the protection granted, 20 December 2011, L 337/9. See more generally Loïc Azoulai and Karin de Vries, *EU Migration Law: Legal Complexities and Political Rationales* (Oxford University Press 2014).

[99] See, e.g., Regulation (EC) no. 883/2004 of the European Parliament and of the Council of 29 April 2004 on the coordination of social security systems.

[100] See, e.g., Directive 2014/24/EU of the European Parliament and of the Council of 26 February 2014 on public procurement, OJ L 94, 28 March 2014.

[101] See, e.g., Directive 2011/92/EU of the European Parliament and of the Council of 13 December 2011 on the assessment of the effects of certain public and private projects on the environment, OJ L 26, 28 January 2012.

[102] See, e.g., Directive (EU) 2016/681 of the European Parliament and of the Council of 27 April 2016 on the use of passenger name record (PNR) data for the prevention, detection, investigation and prosecution of terrorist offences and serious crime, OJ L 119, 4 May 2016.

[103] See, e.g., Directive (EU) 2019/1024 of the European Parliament and of the Council of 20 June 2019 on open data and the re-use of public sector information (recast), OJ L 172, 26 June 2019.

[104] See, e.g., Directive 2012/13/EU of the European Parliament and of the Council of 22 May 2012 on the right to information in criminal proceedings; Directive 2013/48/EU of the European Parliament and of the Council of 22 October 2013 on the right of access to a lawyer in criminal proceedings and in European arrest warrant proceedings, and on the right to have a third party informed upon deprivation of liberty and to communicate with third persons and with consular authorities while deprived of liberty.

[105] See Article 51(1) CFREU.

[106] See Lenaerts, Van Nuffel and Corthaut (n 3) 684. See also Emily Hancox, 'The Relationship between the Charter and General Principles: Looking Back and Looking Forward' [2020] Cambridge Yearbook of European Legal Studies 22, 233–257.

further specified by secondary EU legislation that sets out which obligations Member States should respect vis-à-vis asylum applicants, and how they should evaluate an asylum application.[107] Accordingly, when a mistranslation from law to code (whether deliberate or inadvertent) occurs in the context of algorithmic regulation that helps assess asylum applications, this can give rise to an EU law infringement, both in terms of the public authority's failure to comply with the EU regulation or directive, and in terms of a potential breach of a fundamental right or general principle of EU law.

Besides harmonisation in vertical domains, there are also relevant pieces of legislation of horizontal nature. Consider, for instance, Council Directive 2000/43 that prevents discrimination based on racial or ethnic origin in a number of areas like social security and healthcare, thus setting out obligations that Member States must comply with.[108] When algorithmic regulation affects the rights of individuals based on their ethnicity, this can hence constitute a breach of EU law when the administrative act pertains to social security, the provision of healthcare, or another area of administration listed in the directive. Moreover, beyond situations of implementing EU legislation, the case law of the CJEU has indicated that also acts "*that constitute derogations from provisions of EU law, or acts adopted by the national authorities that only remotely are connected with EU law*",[109] can fall under the heading of 'EU law implementation'.[110]

Finally, some authors have argued that Article 2 TEU could in and of itself be understood as the basis for an EU law obligation based on which an infringement action can be launched in case of non-adherence to the rule of law.[111] For instance, Scheppele, Kochenov and Grabowska-Moroz have argued that Article 2 TEU could be relied upon to group isolated yet systemic infringements of EU law and, on that basis, to launch an infringement action, denoting this approach as a 'tool of militant

[107] See e.g. Directive 2013/32/EU of the European Parliament and of the Council of 26 June 2013 on common procedures for granting and withdrawing international protection (recast), 29 June 2013, L 180/60.

[108] See, for instance, EU Council Directive 2000/43/EC of 29 June 2000 implementing the principle of equal treatment between persons irrespective of racial or ethnic origin. See also Colm O'Cinneide and Kimberly Liu, *The Ongoing Evolution of the Case-Law of the Court of Justice of the European Union on Directives 2000/43/EC and 2000/78/EC: A Legal Analysis of the Situation in EU Member States* (Publications Office of the European Union 2019).

[109] Mihaela Vrabie, 'Judicial Review of Administrative Action at National Level under the EU Charter of Fundamental Rights and General Principles of EU Law' (2020) 18 Central European Public Administration Review (CEPAR) 25, 28.

[110] See, e.g., Case C-60/00, *Carpenter*, 11 July 2002, ECLI:EU:C:2002:434; Case C-36/02, *Omega*, 14 October 2004, ECLI:EU:C:2004:614; and Case C-208/09, *Wittgenstein*, 22 December 2010, ECLI:EU:C:2010:806. See also the abovementioned *Åklagaren v Hans Åkerberg Franson* case, C-617/10 (n 71).

[111] See, e.g., Scheppele, Kochenov and Grabowska-Moroz (n 9). See also Kim Lane Scheppele, 'Enforcing the Basic Principles of EU Law through Systemic Infringement Actions' in Carlos Closa and Dimitry Kochenov (eds), *Reinforcing Rule of Law Oversight in the European Union* (Cambridge University Press 2016).

democracy' through the launch of 'systemic infringement procedures'.[112] They believe that this approach could enable the Court, which has already shown itself an innovative protector of the principle of judicial independence by relying on Article 19(1) TEU, to play a more significant role in protecting other rule of law principles, which Article 7 TEU currently cannot due to the abovementioned political impasse. However, this understanding of Article 2 TEU is controversial, and as the authors themselves have noted, it is not widely supported.[113] Accordingly, the majority of scholars seem to consider that in order to be the object of an infringement procedure, the legal provision in question and the precise obligation it imposes on Member States needs to be more concrete, and cannot be brought under a collective Article 2 TEU umbrella.

That said, in December 2022, the Commission for the first time launched an infringement action against Hungary for rule of law-related breaches which not only cites violations of secondary EU legislation, but also the direct violation of Article 2 TEU itself.[114] Regardless of the outcome of this case, Bonelli and Claes point out that "*the autonomous enforceability of Article 2 TEU remains a controversial legal construction, one that, if accepted by the Court, could put its legitimacy and authority under strain*".[115] They also rightfully question whether "*the full judicialization of questions of 'values'*" is truly "*the most promising and effective response to the challenges that constitutional backsliding processes create*".[116]

Furthermore, notwithstanding the increasing harmonisation of national legislation, it should be stressed that a link with EU law cannot *always* be established, as there are still situations that are purely governed by domestic law. As I will discuss below,[117] this ups the game for any (new) EU legislative act that can provide safeguards for citizens whenever Member States deploy algorithmic regulation, as it can legally create a link with EU law (and hence with EU remedies) even in situations that are in principle considered domestic. Indeed, adopting EU legislation that governs the responsible use of algorithmic regulation by Member States in line with the rule of law would open up an avenue for the enforcement of these

[112] Scheppele, Kochenov and Grabowska-Moroz (n 9) 9–10.

[113] As the authors state: "*We recognise that most commentators have argued that only political mechanisms can be used to enforce the values of Article 2 TEU*". See ibid 8.

[114] The case concerns a new law that was introduced by the Hungarian government as a way of improving children's protection against paedophilia, while in effect containing several discriminating measures that specifically target the LGBTIQ+ community. See the Commission action brought on 19 December 2022 in Case C-769/22, *Commission v. Hungary*, still pending at the time of writing this book. See also Jannes Dresler, 'Der Brüsseler Testballon – Kommission betritt mit Klageschrift gegen Ungarns Anti-LGBTQ-Gesetz Neuland', (Verfassungsblog 21 February 2023) <https://verfassungsblog.de/der-brusseler-testballon/>.

[115] Matteo Bonelli and Monica Claes, 'Crossing the Rubicon? The Commission's Use of Article 2 TEU in the Infringement Action on LGBTIQ+ Rights in Hungary' (2022) 30 Maastricht Journal of European and Comparative Law 3, 4.

[116] ibid.

[117] See *infra*, Section 5.4.

provisions both through the infringement procedure of Articles 258–260 TFEU, and through legal challenges brought by individuals before national courts (with the associated preliminary reference procedure pursuant to Article 267 TFEU).

At the same time, the utility of these remedies, even in situations where a concrete obligation under EU law exists, must not be overstated. While the judicial review they enable can certainly play a role in the protection of the rule of (EU) law at Member State level, this is woefully insufficient to tackle the adverse effects of algorithmic regulation as identified in Chapter 4.

First, the ex post nature of these procedures means that the damage has already been done. As noted previously, if the damage is irreversible, any ex post remedy will be of little consolation to those adversely affected. If the damage is not (entirely) irreversible, in any event, a lot of time will inevitably pass between the damage caused and the judicial action. In the case of an infringement action, it typically takes the European Commission (which can decide to launch an action at its sole discretion) months if not years to collect sufficient evidence and arrive at a decision to initiate proceedings, if it decides to act at all.[118] In the case of a legal challenge brought by an individual before a national court, the speed of the potential remedy will depend on how swift the administration of justice in a particular country is organised. Moreover, the count starts not from the moment that problematic algorithmic regulation is used, but from the moment that someone is aware of such use and decides to bring a case.[119] By the time a condemning judgment arrives, significant harm can have occurred, and it may be too late to meaningfully remedy the situation. In addition, if the national court decides to stay proceedings to submit a request for a preliminary reference by the CJEU, the waiting time is extended by on average at least another year.[120] I invite the reader to reflect how much damage an infrastructure of algorithmic regulation, and the mass-decision-making it enables regarding millions of individuals, can cause in the time span of one year if left unaddressed.

Second, for an individual to bring a case before a court, she must not only be aware that algorithmic regulation is used (this is not straightforward given that many algorithmic applications are used in an untransparent manner[121]) but she must also have a sufficient incentive to start litigation.[122] If the damage at individual level is

[118] Recall that the Commission can initiate an infringement procedure at its own discretion. See Lenaerts, Van Nuffel and Corthaut (n 3) 784.

[119] See also *supra*, Section 4.1.5.

[120] Based on the Court of Justice's annual report of 2022, which includes statistical information about the court's activities, the average duration of proceedings that year was 16.4 months (and 17.3 months for requests for preliminary rulings). See Court of Justice of the European Union, 'Annual Report 2022 – The Year in Review' (CJEU 2023) 27, <https://curia.europa.eu/jcms/upload/docs/application/pdf/2023-04/qd-aq-23-001-en-n.pdf>.

[121] Emre Bayamlıoğlu, 'Contesting Automated Decisions: A View of Transparency Implications' (2018) 4 European Data Protection Law Review 433.

[122] As discussed *supra*, in Section 4.1.5.

relatively small, the person may be unwilling to incur time and costs to do so, even if the damage at societal level may be significant. Furthermore, in many jurisdictions one needs to be able to demonstrate individual harm to have standing in court, which may not always be easy to prove when the harm primarily manifests itself at societal level or over the longer term, rather than at individual level and in the short term.[123] And if individual harm can be proven (for instance when a right was erroneously denied) we have seen that courts may not always be well-equipped to deal with the *systemic* problems raised by the scaled use of algorithmic systems, as they are typically tasked with case-by-case reviews only.[124] This means that the upstream design choices will remain untouched. The person may be re-allocated her benefits that were wrongfully denied, but this does not necessarily mean that choices at the upstream level will become transparent and contestable, and that harm to other interests will be avoided.

Finally, to invoke the procedures discussed above, a link with EU law must first be argued. As explained, while such a link can often be found, there are also situations that may not be governed by current EU law, hence precluding reliance on an existing EU remedy. Moreover, even if such a link is present, in certain Member States, the executive power is already exercising undue influence on national courts, and compromised their independence and impartiality.[125] In those jurisdictions, which already showcase authoritarian tendencies, one can question the effectiveness of national judicial review as a means to prevent the exacerbation of those very tendencies.

For all these reasons, the mechanisms discussed above are inadequate to ensure that the implementation of algorithmic regulation by public authorities occurs in accordance with the rule of law, and that it does not exacerbate the threat of algorithmic rule by law. As stressed in Chapter 4, the extent and scale of the risks associated with algorithmic regulation require *preventative* action, inter alia through the organisation of ex ante and continuous oversight over the crucial decisions taken in the design and deployment process of algorithmic systems, rather than mere *remedial* action. Yet the currently available EU mechanisms that deal with the protection of the rule of (EU) law (Article 7 TEU, the Conditionality Regulation,

[123] Nathalie A Smuha, 'Beyond the Individual: Governing AI's Societal Harm' (2021) 10 Internet Policy Review 3, 9. See also Bart van der Sloot and Sascha van Schendel, 'Procedural Law for the Data-Driven Society' (2021) Information & Communications Technology Law 1.

[124] Abe Chauhan, 'Towards the Systemic Review of Automated Decision-Making Systems' [2021] Judicial Review 1.

[125] Werner Schroeder, 'The European Union and the Rule of Law – State of Affairs and Ways of Strengthening', in Werner Schroeder (ed), *Strengthening the Rule of Law in Europe: From a Common Concept to Mechanisms of Implementation* (Hart Publishing 2016); Jörg Polakiewicz and Julia Katharina Kirchmayr, 'Sounding the Alarm: The Council of Europe as the Guardian of the Rule of Law in Contemporary Europe' in Armin von Bogdandy and others (eds), *Defending Checks and Balances in EU Member States: Taking Stock of Europe's Actions* (Springer 2021).

or Articles 258–260 TFEU and 267 TFEU) are, in my view, not tailored to prevent the adverse impact of algorithmic regulation on the rule of law. This is not only so because they lack specific references to algorithmic systems as the potential cause of such adverse impact – and hence lack specific requirements as regards their use – but also because they only enable ex post solutions, which risk being too little too late. In sum, EU regulation pertaining to the protection of the rule of law does not seem to be sufficiently extended to tackle the risks of algorithmic regulation.

The question is now whether EU regulation that pertains to algorithmic systems can play a meaningful role in the protection of the rule of law. While there is, as of yet, no piece of EU legislation that deals specifically with public authorities' rule of law obligations in the context of algorithmic regulation, there are several regulations that apply to public and private organisations alike when they inform or take their decisions with the assistance of algorithmic systems.[126] For reasons of time and space, I will focus on the two most relevant ones for the purpose of my investigation: the General Data Protection Regulation (and neighbouring Law Enforcement Directive), which I discuss in Section 5.3, and the Artificial Intelligence Act, which I discuss in Section 5.4.

5.3 REGULATION PERTAINING TO PERSONAL DATA: THE GDPR

Few pieces of legislation are as relevant for the use of algorithmic regulation today as the General Data Protection Regulation (GDPR)[127] – and, in the context of

[126] Accordingly, when it comes to the regulation of algorithmic systems, instead of speaking of a legal vacuum, one can rather speak of legal gaps. Consider for instance the Machinery Directive which is relevant when algorithmic systems are embedded in hardware (Directive 2006/42/EC of the European Parliament and of the Council of 17 May 2006 on machinery, and amending Directive 95/16/EC (recast), OJ L 157, 9 June 2006), or the Digital Services Act (amending Directive 2000/31/EC) which touches upon algorithmic systems used in online platforms. More generally, the Product Liability Directive, for instance, also deals with liability questions related to certain algorithmic systems (Council Directive 85/374/EEC of 25 July 1985 on the approximation of the laws, regulations and administrative provisions of the Member States concerning liability for defective products OJ L 210, 7 August 1985). It can be noted that the European Commission also proposed a new directive to harmonise liability rules pertaining to AI systems. See the Proposal for a Directive of the European Parliament and the Council on adapting non-contractual civil liability rules to artificial intelligence (AI Liability Directive) 2022 [COM(2022) 496 final], which has not yet been adopted at the time of writing this book. See in this regard also European Commission, 'Commission Staff Working Document *Liability for emerging digital technologies*, accompanying the Communication from the Commission to the European Parliament, the European Council, the Council, the European Economic and Social Committee and the Committee of the Regions Artificial intelligence for Europe', SWD/2018/137 final, Brussels, 25 April 2018.

[127] Regulation (EU) 2016/679 of the European Parliament and of the Council of 27 April 2016 on the protection of natural persons with regard to the processing of personal data and on the free movement of such data, and repealing Directive 95/46/EC (General Data Protection Regulation) 2016 1.

criminal matters, the Law Enforcement Directive (LED).[128] The regime provided in these (highly similar) pieces of legislation shields individuals against infringements of their fundamental right to personal data protection,[129] by granting them protective rights and imposing obligations on organisations[130] that process their personal data.[131] Since a significant part of algorithmic systems used to inform or adopt administrative acts process personal data, these rights and obligations play an important role in this domain. The scope of application of the GDPR and LED is wider than algorithmic regulation though, as they apply to "*the processing of personal data wholly or partly by automated means*".[132] These legal instruments set out a dense legal framework and, in what follows, I will only point out some of its most relevant features.

Pursuant to their obligations under these legal instruments, when public authorities deploy algorithmic systems to inform or adopt administrative acts and in the course thereof process personal data, such data must be processed in line with a number of principles, including the principle of lawfulness, fairness and transparency; purpose limitation; data minimisation; accuracy; storage limitation; integrity

[128] Directive (EU) 2016/680 of the European Parliament and of the Council of 27 April 2016 on the protection of natural persons with regard to the processing of personal data by competent authorities for the purposes of the prevention, investigation, detection or prosecution of criminal offences or the execution of criminal penalties, and on the free movement of such data, and repealing Council Framework Decision 2008/977/JHA 2016.

[129] Article 8(1) CFREU and Article 16(1) TFEU provide that all individuals have the right to the protection of their personal data.

[130] The GDPR applies to private and public actors alike, though, given the focus of this book, I will only focus on the latter. The LED in principle only applies to 'competent authorities', meaning "*any public authority competent for the prevention, investigation, detection or prosecution of criminal offences or the execution of criminal penalties, including the safeguarding against and the prevention of threats to public security*" or "*any other body or entity entrusted by Member State law to exercise public authority and public powers for the purposes of the prevention, investigation, detection or prosecution of criminal offences or the execution of criminal penalties, including the safeguarding against and the prevention of threats to public security*". See in this regard Article 3(7) LED. Note that both pieces of legislation in principle do not apply to the processing of personal data in the course of an activity which falls outside the scope of Union law. See Article 2(2)(a) GDPR and Article 2(3)(a) LED.

[131] Personal data is defined broadly, as

> any information relating to an identified or identifiable natural person ('data subject'); an identifiable natural person is one who can be identified, directly or indirectly, in particular by reference to an identifier such as a name, an identification number, location data, an online identifier or to one or more factors specific to the physical, physiological, genetic, mental, economic, cultural or social identity of that natural person.

See Article 4(1) GDPR and Article 3(1) LED.

[132] As well as to "*the processing other than by automated means of personal data which form part of a filing system or are intended to form part of a filing system to any processing of personal data*". See Article 2(1) GDPR and Article 2(2) LED respectively.

and confidentiality; and accountability.[133] Moreover, the lawfulness of the data processing relies on the availability of a legal basis which, in the context of public authorities, will often come down to the fact that "*processing is necessary for the performance of a task carried out in the public interest or in the exercise of official authority vested in the controller*".[134]

5.3.1 *Need for a Legal Basis*

To legitimise such data processing, Member States should in principle adopt a law that sets out the purpose of the processing, and that contains more specific provisions about the types of data that are processed; the data subjects concerned; the entities to, and the purposes for which, the personal data may be disclosed; the purpose limitation; storage periods; and any processing operations and procedures.[135] This is also why the implementation of algorithmic systems by public authorities must have a lawful basis, which typically requires the adoption of a specific law that authorises the use of the system in line with the provisions of the GDPR (or the LED). The legal basis should indicate that the introduction of the algorithmic system, which can be invasive and impactful given the data processed and the scale at which it is deployed, is necessary and proportionate.

Importantly, the existence of a legal basis also renders it possible to subsequently challenge the system's use if the basis on which it was adopted does not provide sufficient protection against potential adverse impacts of the system, or is not in accordance with human rights law. This is precisely what happened in the Dutch SyRI case, which centred around an algorithmic system aimed at identifying natural and legal persons which, based on a set of risk-indicators, ought to be further examined for social security or tax fraud.[136] According to the government, the purpose of the system concerned "*the prevention of and combating the unlawful use of government funds and government schemes in the area of social security and income-dependent schemes, preventing and combating taxes and social security fraud and non-compliance with labour laws*".[137] The system allowed for the exchange of data amongst a variety of public authorities to facilitate the identification of fraud. Based on the system's risk-indications, a risk report was made concerning an individual's fraud potential. The SyRI-law defined a 'risk report' as

[133] See Article 5 GDPR. In the LED, these principles are formulated in a similar way, though with omission of the principle of transparency. See Article 4(1) LED.

[134] See Article 6(1)(e) GDPR.

[135] See Article 6(3) GDPR.

[136] See in this regard also Marvin van Bekkum and Frederik Zuiderveen Borgesius, 'Digital Welfare Fraud Detection and the Dutch SyRI Judgment' (2021) 243 European Journal of Social Security 323.

[137] *NJCM et al. en FNV v Staat der Nederlanden (SyRI Judgment)* [2020] Rechtbank Den Haag C-09-550982-HA ZA 18-388, ECLI:NL:RBDHA:2020:865, section 4.4.

> the provision of individualised information from [SyRI] containing a finding of an increased risk of unlawful use of government funds or government schemes in the area of social security and income-dependent schemes, taxes and social security fraud or non-compliance with labour laws by a natural person or legal person, and of which the risk analysis, consisting of coherently presented data from [SyRI], forms part.[138]

The system was already in use for years when, in 2014, a law was finally adopted to ensure a legal basis for its deployment, known as the SyRI-law. When the law was challenged in court, it was, however, found to be an insufficient legal basis to justify the system's use. The court concluded that it did not provide sufficient safeguards to protect individuals against the impact on their right to privacy, after which the government halted the system's use. For instance, the risk reports established by the system were put into a register.[139] This left a clear trace for other public authorities which risked stigmatising those individuals, even if the flagging turned out to be erroneous. Moreover, the persons concerned were not informed of the fact that a risk report was made about them (unless they specifically asked for this information by themselves).[140] And while the law also foresaw that public authorities had to justify the necessity and proportionality of the data exchange for the purpose of the risk analysis, no safeguards were included to ensure an adequate and comprehensive review of those justifications.

This case demonstrates that the GDPR is able to offer individuals protection by ensuring that the use of algorithmic systems needs to have an adequate legal basis. At the same time, it should be noted that the provisions of the GDPR, as such, do not necessarily provide insight (let alone participation) in any of the upstream decisions made by the coders, such as the assumptions that underlie the system, the interpretation and translation choices, or the model's optimisation function. Moreover, in many cases, the legal basis can be overly vague or provide overly extensive processing powers to avoid that the law must be amended whenever new processing activities take place, thus also undermining the protection it offers towards those subjected thereto.[141] Note that the processing of special categories of

[138] Article 65(2) SUWI Act or Wet structuur uitvoeringsorganisatie werk en inkomen. The implementation of that law was further specified through the Decree of 1 September 2014 to amend the SUWI Decree in connection with rules for tackling fraud by exchanging data and the effective use of data known within the government with the use of SyRI, Bulletin of Acts and Decrees 2014, 320.

[139] In line with the storage limitation principle, the law did foresee that the risk report could only be kept for as long as necessary to execute the relevant task, and for a maximum period of two years. See Article 65 of the law.

[140] *NJCM et al. en FNV v Staat der Nederlanden (SyRI Judgment)* (n 137), section 4.14.

[141] See, for instance, Degrave's observation that the law which is meant to provide a legal basis for the OASIS system – used by public authorities to identify fraud – is far too vague to comply with the GDPR, in Elise Degrave, 'The Use of Secret Algorithms to Combat Social Fraud in Belgium' (2020) 1 European Review of Digital Administration & Law 167.

personal data, such as data revealing racial or ethnic origin, political opinions, biometric data for the purpose of uniquely identifying a natural person, or data concerning a person's sexual orientation, is in principle prohibited, yet exceptions exist,[142] and public authorities can typically rely on them to exercise their functions if such processing is authorised by law.[143]

5.3.2 *Automated Decision-Making*

The GDPR and LED allocate certain rights to persons whose personal data is processed, such as the right to information about the data processing, the right of access to their data, the right to rectify their data and the right to erasure.[144] In addition to these general rights, natural persons also have specific rights in the context of automated decision-making. It should be pointed out that, for the purpose of the GDPR, automated decision-making is much broader than the adoption of an administrative act, but covers any type of decision taken through automated means, including profiling.[145] Accordingly, all intermediate decisions that are taken by automated means to inform an administrative act (for instance the automated classification of individuals in one category or another) also count as such.[146] Pursuant to Article 22 of the GDPR,[147] whenever a decision is being taken about an individual based solely on automated processing[148] which produces legal effects

[142] In this regard, it can also be noted that the AI Act (discussed *infra* in Section 5.4), establishes a specific legal basis to process such sensitive data '*to the extent that it is strictly necessary for the purpose of ensuring bias detection and correction in relation to the high-risk AI systems*', though several safeguards need to be fulfilled. See Article 10(5) AI Act.

[143] See Articles 9 and 10 GDPR. Note that, in this case, despite the existence of a legal basis, public authorities must provide appropriate safeguards for the fundamental rights and the interests of the data subject.

[144] See sections 2 and 3 of the GDPR.

[145] Article 4(4) of the GDPR defines profiling as "*any form of automated processing of personal data evaluating the personal aspects relating to a natural person, in particular to analyse or predict aspects concerning the data subject's performance at work, economic situation, health, personal preferences or interests, reliability or behaviour, location or movements*".

[146] See in this regard also the Court's interpretation of automated decision-making in case C-634/21, *OQ v SCHUFA Holding AG*, 7 December 2023, ECLI:EU:C:2023:957.

[147] Under the legal regime of the LED, individuals have no right to object to automated individual decision-making. Pursuant to Article 11(1) of the LED, this practice is prohibited unless authorised by Union or Member State law and providing "*appropriate safeguards for the rights and freedoms of the data subject, at least the right to obtain human intervention on the part of the controller.*" Nothing is, however, mentioned about a right to receive "meaningful information about the logic involved in the automated decision-making process", such as foreseen in Article 14 GDPR (see below).

[148] Recital 71, §2 of the GDPR also specifies that, in order to ensure fair and transparent processing in respect of the data subject,

> the controller should use appropriate mathematical or statistical procedures for the profiling, implement technical and organisational measures appropriate to ensure, in particular, that factors which result in inaccuracies in personal data are corrected and the

concerning her, or similarly significantly affects her, that individual has the right *not* to be subject to such decision.[149] While inclusion of the word 'solely' seemingly excludes situations where a decision is merely recommended by an algorithmic system and subsequently reviewed and adopted by a human being, such review should in principle be meaningful in order to warrant the exclusion. Merely "fabricating" human involvement will not do.[150]

Moreover, under those circumstances, the data controller[151] has the obligation to provide the individual concerned with information about the existence of automated decision-making and "*meaningful information about the logic involved*", as well as the significance and the envisaged consequences of such processing for her.[152] Recital 71 of the GDPR also states that "*such processing should be subject to suitable safeguards, which should include specific information to the data subject and the right to obtain human intervention, to express his or her point of view, to obtain an explanation of the decision reached after such assessment and to challenge the decision*". Yet given that recitals are non-binding, scholars disagree as to whether an actual individualised 'right to explanation' of an automated decision exists.[153]

These rights, along with other rights listed in the GDPR, can be restricted by Member State law as long as this restriction "*respects the essence of the fundamental rights and freedoms and is a necessary and proportionate measure in a democratic society to safeguard*" a range of interests, including national and public security, the prevention of criminal offences, and even – rather generally – "*other important objectives of general public interest of a Member State*".[154] In that case, the Member

risk of errors is minimised, secure personal data in a manner that takes account of the potential risks involved for the interests and rights of the data subject and that prevents, inter alia, discriminatory effects on natural persons on the basis of racial or ethnic origin, political opinion, religion or beliefs, trade union membership, genetic or health status or sexual orientation, or that result in measures having such an effect.

[149] Article 22(1) GDPR. Note, however, the argument by Aziz Huq *against* a right to a human decision (as it still seems "too early" to assume that human decisions will be globally superior to machine decisions). Instead, he suggests that a better option may be a right to a well-calibrated machine decision, in 'A Right to a Human Decision' (2020) 106 Virginia Law Review 611.

[150] Article 29 Data Protection Working Party, 'Guidelines on Automated Individual Decision-Making and Profiling for the Purposes of Regulation 2016/679' (last Revised and adopted on 6 February 2018, 2017) 17/EN WP251rev.01 21.

[151] Article 4(7) GDPR defines the controller as "*the natural or legal person, public authority, agency or other body which, alone or jointly with others, determines the purposes and means of the processing of personal data*".

[152] See Article 14(2)(g) GDPR.

[153] See, e.g., Sandra Wachter, Brent Mittelstadt and Luciano Floridi, 'Why a Right to Explanation of Automated Decision-Making Does Not Exist in the General Data Protection Regulation' (2017) 7 International Data Privacy Law 76; Bryce Goodman and Seth Flaxman, 'European Union Regulations on Algorithmic Decision-Making and a "Right to Explanation"' (2017) 38 AI Magazine 50; Margot E Kaminski, 'The Right to Explanation, Explained' (2019) 34 Berkeley Technology Law Journal 189.

[154] Article 23(1) GDPR.

State law should however contain provisions that describe the data processing activity and its purpose, as well as the safeguards to prevent abuse.[155]

Also noteworthy is the fact that, whenever a type of processing ("*in particular using new technologies*") is likely to result in a high risk to the rights and freedoms of natural persons, the controller shall, prior to the processing, carry out an assessment of the impact of the envisaged processing operations on the protection of personal data, referred to as a Data Protection Impact Assessment or DPIA).[156] Pursuant to Article 35(3)(a) of the GDPR, a DPIA is particularly required in the case of "*a systematic and extensive evaluation of personal aspects relating to natural persons which is based on automated processing, including profiling, and on which decisions are based that produce legal effects concerning the natural person or similarly significantly affect the natural person*".

Data controllers are, however, not obliged to make this assessment public, and input from the individuals concerned is only warranted "*where appropriate*" and "*without prejudice to the protection of public interests or the security of processing operations*".[157] Finally, to oversee compliance with these rights and obligations, the GDPR established national data protection authorities, acting "*with complete independence in performing its tasks and exercising its powers*", which is especially important when supervising the data processing activities of public authorities.[158]

5.3.3 *Evaluation: Necessary but Not Sufficient*

With this in mind, to which extent can the safeguards afforded by the GDPR help counter the adverse impact of algorithmic regulation on the rule of law? Unfortunately, the conclusion is not overly optimistic. Certainly, the GDPR establishes a critical and necessary set of EU obligations that Member States should respect (which can also become the object of a procedure under Articles 258–260 TFEU or Article 267 TFEU) and provides individuals with important rights they can directly invoke in a national court against public authorities. And since algorithmic regulation very often implies personal data processing, those rights and obligations are unquestionably relevant in this context. That said, these safeguards cannot be called comprehensive.

As observed by Maja Brkan, the provision that aims to protect individuals against the adverse effects of automated decision-making, by containing "*numerous*

[155] Article 23(2) GDPR. More generally, it should be noted that exceptions provided for in the GDPR must be interpreted strictly. See in this regard also §70 of the abovementioned PNR Judgment (Case C-817/19, *Ligue des droits humains ASBL v Conseil des ministres (PNR Case)*, 21 June 2022, ECLI:EU:C:2022:491).

[156] Article 35(1) GDPR.

[157] Article 35(9) GDPR.

[158] Articles 51 and 52 GDPR.

limitations and exceptions, looks rather like a Swiss cheese with giant holes in it".[159] While individuals should be informed of the fact that decisions are being made about them in an automated way, recall that the right not to be subjected to such decisions is only present in case of a 'solely' automated decision with 'legal effects' or similar, that exceptions exist in the 'public interest' and that no transparency is foreseen about the algorithm's functioning and the normative assumptions that underpin its design. In general, the GDPR contains no mechanisms that enable prior oversight over the upstream design of the algorithmic system (for instance to ensure its outcomes are accurate and non-biased); no obligatory mechanisms of public participation; no constitutional checks and balances as regards the translation from law to code; and no mechanisms that foster friction and internal critical reflection, for instance by mandating *meaningful* human oversight.

This is not to say that the GDPR and the LED, along with primary EU law protecting the rights to privacy and data protection, cannot play a role in ensuring that governments process the personal data of their citizens in a responsible manner, as previous legal challenges have demonstrated.[160] For instance, in June 2022, the CJEU was seized by a preliminary reference procedure regarding the Passenger Name Record (PNR) Directive and the Belgian law implementing it.[161] The case concerned the automated processing of passenger data by public authorities in the context of border control, enabled by the establishment of large databases to search and identify passengers involved in a terrorist offence or serious crime. While the Court found that the Directive poses an "*undeniably serious interference*" with the rights to privacy and data protection,[162] it nevertheless concluded it was compatible with the Charter, as it required the *predetermination* of the criteria based on which the database could be searched, and required these criteria to be non-discriminatory.[163] In the same breath, however, the Court noted that this "*requirement precludes the use of artificial intelligence technology in self-learning*

[159] Maja Brkan, 'Do Algorithms Rule the World? Algorithmic Decision-Making and Data Protection in the Framework of the GDPR and Beyond' (2019) 27 International Journal of Law and Information Technology 91, 97.

[160] For instance, in the abovementioned unlawful use of an algorithmic system in the Netherlands to detect fraud amongst child care benefit recipients, the Dutch data protection authority imposed a fine of €2.75 million on the Dutch Tax Administration, based on the fact that the authority had infringed the GDPR. See Autoriteit Persoonsgegevens, 'Tax Administration Fined for Discriminatory and Unlawful Data Processing' (8 December 2022) <https://autoriteitpersoonsgegevens.nl/en/news/tax-administration-fined-discriminatory-and-unlawful-data-processing>.

[161] See Case C-817/19 (n 155).

[162] Ibid., §111.

[163] More generally, the Court insisted on a narrow interpretation of the intrusive provisions of the Directive and the Belgian law implementing it, to ensure their proportionality. See also Thomas Wahl, 'CJEU: PNR Directive Valid if Limited to the "Strictly Necessary"' (*Eucrim*, 4 August 2022), <https://eucrim.eu/news/cjeu-pnr-directive-valid-if-limited-to-the-strictly-necessary/>.

systems ('machine learning'), capable of modifying without human intervention or review of the assessment process and, in particular, the assessment criteria on which the result of the application of that process is based as well as the weighting of those criteria."[164] It added that

> given the opacity which characterises the way in which artificial intelligence technology works, it might be impossible to understand the reason why a given program arrived at a positive match. In those circumstances, use of such technology may deprive the data subjects also of their right to an effective judicial remedy enshrined in Article 47 of the Charter, for which the PNR Directive, according to recital 28 thereof, seeks to ensure a high level of protection, in particular in order to challenge the non-discriminatory nature of the results obtained.[165]

Accordingly, the PNR judgment affirms the important role that EU privacy legislation can play in the context of algorithmic regulation, and the importance of transparency about the way in which individuals' data are being processed.[166]

At the same time, the lack of *ex ante* oversight mechanisms means that external accountability remains largely confined to an ex post stage, when the damage already occurred. Moreover, the focus lays primarily on harm to individual rather than to societal interests, such as the rule of law. It does not touch upon the intricacies of translating legal rules to code, nor does it provide more *systemic* remedies and oversight.[167] In sum, these legal instruments do not provide sufficient safeguards to counter the threat of algorithmic rule by law, or even properly to counter the risks raised by algorithmic systems more generally. While this conclusion may be rather glum, it was not only reached by other scholars, but also by the European Commission itself, who in February 2020, when it published its White Paper on AI,[168] observed that the current framework, including the GDPR, insufficiently protects people against the adverse impact of algorithmic systems.[169] Consequently, in April 2021, it put forward a proposal for an AI Act in order to fill these legal gaps. I will therefore examine this Act next.

[164] Case C-817/19 (n 155) §194.

[165] ibid., §195.

[166] For an overview of the relevance of data protection law in the context of algorithmic systems, and its interaction with the AI-specific rules of the AI Act, see also Nathalie A Smuha, 'The paramountcy of data protection law in the age of AI (Acts)' in EDPS (ed), *Two Decades of Personal Data Protection. What's Next?* (Publication Office of the EU 2024), 214–227.

[167] Smuha, 'Beyond the Individual' (n 123).

[168] See European Commission, 'White Paper on Artificial Intelligence – A European Approach to Excellence and Trust', COM(2020) 65 final, Brussels, 19 February 2020.

[169] In the Commission's own words, after having provided an overview of existing legislation and the risks not yet properly covered thereby "*the Commission concludes that – in addition to the possible adjustments to existing legislation – a new legislation specifically on AI may be needed in order to make the EU legal framework fit for the current and anticipated technological and commercial developments*"; see ibid 16.

5.4 REGULATION PERTAINING TO ALGORITHMIC SYSTEMS: THE AI ACT

The AI Act has been heralded as the first comprehensive regulation of AI systems in the world, aiming to tackle risks to people's health, safety and fundamental rights in a horizontal manner – including in the public sector, thus meriting a more extended discussion in this book. While the European Union has certainly not been the only jurisdiction partaking in the global race to AI regulation, other jurisdictions have thus far primarily focused their legislative efforts on sector- or application-specific regulations.[170]

After three years of extensive negotiations, and numerous amendments[171] suggested by the European Parliament and the Council (respectively in December 2022[172] and in June 2023[173]), the new regulation was formally adopted in 2024.[174] Much ink has already been spilled about the AI Act's merits and flaws, long before its adoption. Yet the question I am interested in here concerns the extent to which the AI Act's provisions are able to tackle the threat of algorithmic rule by law. Its novelty rendered it an ideal vehicle to introduce new legal safeguards to address the many concerns identified by scholars and civil society organisations over the past few years, and to bridge the gaps left open by the GDPR. However, does the new regulation fulfil this expectation?

170 China has, for instance, been an early adopter of AI regulation as well, with targeted rules for algorithmic recommendation systems, deepfakes, and generative AI services in particular. In this regard, see e.g. Angela Zhang, 'The Promise and Perils of China's Regulation of Artificial Intelligence', University of Hong Kong Faculty of Law Research Paper No. 2024/02, SSRN <https://ssrn.com/abstract=4708676>.

171 Generally speaking, the Council's amendment aimed to limit the AI Act's scope, while the Parliament instead sought to widen it, bringing to the fore a strong divergence in terms of their desired regulatory approach. That said, neither the Council nor the Parliament are monolithic entities, and in each of these institutions, different views exist. Moreover, finding alignment across Member States, as well as across political parties, has been far from evident.

172 The Council's general approach to the AI Act was formally adopted on 6 December 2022: Council of the European Union, 'Proposal for a Regulation of the European Parliament and of the Council Laying down Harmonised Rules on Artificial Intelligence (Artificial Intelligence Act) and Amending Certain Union Legislative Acts' (6 December 2022) <https://data.consilium.europa.eu/doc/document/ST-14954-2022-INIT/en/pdf>.

173 The Parliament's position on the AI Act was adopted in June 2023, after lengthy negotiations between the various political parties: European Parliament, 'Amendments Adopted by the European Parliament on 14 June 2023 on the Proposal for a Regulation of the European Parliament and of the Council on Laying down Harmonised Rules on Artificial Intelligence (Artificial Intelligence Act) and Amending Certain Union Legislative Acts (COM(2021)0206 – C9–0146/2021–2021/0106(COD))' P9_TA(2023)0236 <www.europarl.europa.eu/doceo/document/TA-9-2023-0236_EN.pdf>. In fact, already by the spring of 2022, a few thousands of amendments had been proposed by Members of Parliament. See Luca Bertuzzi, 'AI Regulation Filled with Thousands of Amendments in the European Parliament' *Euractiv* (2 June 2022) <www.euractiv.com/section/digital/news/ai-regulation-filled-with-thousands-of-amendments-in-the-european-parliament/>.

174 Regulation (EU) 2024/1689 of the European Parliament and of the Council of 13 June 2024 laying down harmonised rules on artificial intelligence and amending Regulations (EC) No 300/2008, (EU) No 167/2013, (EU) No 168/2013, (EU) 2018/858, (EU) 2018/1139 and (EU) 2019/2144 and Directives 2014/90/EU, (EU) 2016/797 and (EU) 2020/1828 (Artificial Intelligence Act).

To answer this question, I will respectively analyse the AI Act's scope and rationale (Section 5.4.1), its regulatory architecture (Section 5.4.2), the set of systems used by public authorities that fall under its provisions (Section 5.4.3), the requirements to which high-risk algorithmic regulation systems are subjected (Section 5.4.4), and the repercussions of its maximum approach to harmonisation (Section 5.4.5). Drawing on that analysis, I will assess the regulatory potential of the AI Act and conclude that it fails to provide a sufficient level of protection. Moreover, despite the critique provided thereon in Chapter 4, I argue that the AI Act effectively reinstates 'techno-supremacy' through its legal infrastructure, resulting in a relatively grim overall evaluation of this new regulation (Section 5.4.6).

5.4.1 *The AI Act's Goals and Scope*

5.4.1.a The AI Act's Origins

To understand the regulation's rationale, it is useful to briefly revisit its history. In essence, the AI Act builds on the work of the High-Level Expert Group on Artificial Intelligence, set up by the European Commission in June 2018 with the aim of drafting AI Ethics Guidelines[175] and Policy Recommendations.[176] At that time, one month after the GDPR came into force and modernised European privacy law, new legislation on the use of algorithmic systems seemed unnecessary, as it was the prevailing opinion at the Commission that existing rules already sufficed to protect individual and societal interests. Gradually, this stance changed, with the rise of both internal and external pressure to take action beyond the promotion of non-binding guidelines. Moreover, when submitting its deliverables in the spring of 2019, the High-Level Expert Group concluded that new legislation was needed to fill existing legal gaps, claiming that the risks posed by certain systems required stronger safeguards.[177] Concretely, the Expert Group proposed a risk-based approach[178] to

[175] High-Level Expert Group on AI, 'Ethics Guidelines for Trustworthy AI' (European Commission 2019) <https://digital-strategy.ec.europa.eu/en/library/ethics-guidelines-trustworthy-ai>.

[176] High-Level Expert Group on AI, 'Policy and Investment Recommendations for Trustworthy AI' (European Commission 2019) <https://digital-strategy.ec.europa.eu/en/library/policy-and-investment-recommendations-trustworthy-artificial-intelligence>.

[177] While the Group's Ethics Guidelines for Trustworthy AI already indicated a number of 'critical concerns' that required being addressed (see page 33 and following), in its Policy and Investment Recommendations it formulated more concrete guidance to the Commission as regards legal gaps (see page 37 and following).

[178] The group noted that "*'risk' for this purpose is broadly defined to encompass adverse impacts of all kinds, both individual and societal*", emphasising that this includes "*not only tangible risks to human health or the environment, but also intangible risks to fundamental rights, democracy and the rule of law, and other potential threats to the cultural and socio-technical foundations of democratic, rights-respecting, societies.*" See High-Level Expert Group on AI, 'Policy and Investment Recommendations for Trustworthy AI' (n 176) 38.

regulate AI,[179] combined with a principle-based approach that avoids over-prescriptiveness, and a precautionary approach "*when the stakes are high*", highlighting hazards to some of the EU's core values, such as human health, the environment and the democratic process.[180] It also noted that questions about which kinds of risks are deemed unacceptable "*must be deliberated and decided upon by the community at large through open, transparent and accountable deliberation*".[181] As regards the public sector in particular, the group stressed that safeguards were needed to protect "*individuals' fundamental rights, democracy and the rule of law*",[182] the alignment of which was more generally stressed across its deliverables.[183]

The Commission listened in part. It started mapping the legal gaps left open by existing pieces of legislation and, in February 2020, it outlined a blueprint for new AI-specific legislation through its White Paper on Artificial Intelligence.[184] After inviting feedback through a public consultation, the Commission put forward its proposal for an AI Act in April 2021, with clear references to the Expert Group's work. The Expert Group's Ethics Guidelines for 'Trustworthy AI' (a term coined by the experts to denote systems that are lawful, ethical and robust) listed seven key requirements that should be met throughout the life cycle of AI systems, based on fundamental rights.[185] In the Explanatory Memorandum of the AI Act, the Commission presented its proposal as providing "*a legal framework for trustworthy AI*"[186] and translated these key requirements into a series of legal requirements that should be met whenever AI systems are put into use or placed on the market.[187]

5.4.1.b Objectives and Legal Basis

The AI Act has the dual aim of harmonising Member States' national legislation to eliminate potential obstacles to trade on the internal market, and protecting the health, safety and fundamental rights of individuals against AI's adverse effects – in

179 ibid 37, 26.1.
180 ibid 38, 26.2.
181 ibid. Furthermore, the group proposed the adoption of a segment-specific methodology, whereby the protective measures of individuals against the adverse effects of AI would be tailored to, respectively, the private sector context and the public sector context. See ibid, 26.5.
182 ibid 19, 9.4.
183 See, e.g., High-Level Expert Group on AI, 'Ethics Guidelines for Trustworthy AI' (n 175) 35.
184 European Commission, 'White Paper on Artificial Intelligence – A European Approach to Excellence and Trust' (n 168).
185 High-Level Expert Group on AI, 'Ethics Guidelines for Trustworthy AI' (n 175) 14. See also Nathalie A Smuha, 'The EU Approach to Ethics Guidelines for Trustworthy Artificial Intelligence' (2019) 20 Computer Law Review International 97.
186 See Explanatory Memorandum of the proposed AI Act, section 1.1, §2.
187 See also Vera Lúcia Raposo, 'Ex Machina: Preliminary Critical Assessment of the European Draft Act on Artificial Intelligence' (2022) 30 International Journal of Law and Information Technology 88, 97.

that order. Indeed, as indicated by the AI Act's very first recital, and as the below discussion will highlight, the creation of an internal market for the free circulation of AI and the promotion of its uptake is the regulation's primary aim, with the protection of fundamental rights and other values being something to keep in mind while doing so.[188] Note that, despite the references thereto in the Expert Group's deliverables, the protection of the rule of law was not mentioned as an objective in the Commission's original proposal (an omission that scholars have criticised)[189] and is also barely mentioned in the AI Act's final version.[190]

Clearly, the regulation primarily pursues an internal market-oriented approach rather than a values-oriented one, in line with its underlying legal basis. Indeed, the Commission opted to rely on Article 114 TFEU (enabling the establishment and functioning of the internal market) as the Regulation's legal basis. This is not surprising, as the EU lacks a general legal basis to regulate (technology's adverse impact on) fundamental rights, democracy and the rule of law, and frequently relies on Article 114 TFEU to advance the protection of the interests for which it has no specific competence.[191] If the emphasis of the Regulation would have been on the protection of those values, Article 352 TFEU would arguably have been a more appropriate legal basis, as this Article allows the EU to adopt an act necessary to attain objectives laid down by the treaties whenever the treaties do not provide the

[188] Recital 1 of the AI Act – which has been lengthened by many amendments – reads as follows:

> The purpose of this Regulation is to improve the functioning of the internal market by laying down a uniform legal framework in particular for the development, the placing on the market, the putting into service and the use of artificial intelligence systems (AI systems) in the Union, in accordance with Union values, to promote the uptake of human centric and trustworthy artificial intelligence (AI) while ensuring a high level of protection of health, safety, fundamental rights as enshrined in the Charter of Fundamental Rights of the European Union (the 'Charter'), including democracy, the rule of law and environmental protection, to protect against the harmful effects of AI systems in the Union, and to support innovation. This Regulation ensures the free movement, cross-border, of AI-based goods and services, thus preventing Member States from imposing restrictions on the development, marketing and use of AI systems, unless explicitly authorised by this Regulation.

[189] See Nathalie A Smuha and others, 'How the EU Can Achieve Legally Trustworthy AI: A Response to the European Commission's Proposal for an Artificial Intelligence Act' (Social Science Research Network 2021) <https://papers.ssrn.com/abstract=3899991>.

[190] The only substantive article in which the rule of law is mentioned is Article 1(1) AI Act. While it sets out the AI Act's subject matter, the rule of law is clearly *not* the object of this regulation, thus making its inclusion mostly rhetorical.

[191] As previously noted, before Article 16 TFEU enshrined an EU legal basis to regulate the protection of personal data (based on which the GDPR was adopted), the harmonisation of national privacy legislation was based on Article 114 TFEU. Moreover, the Digital Services Act – which inter alia has the objective of protecting democracy and fundamental rights online – is likewise based on Article 114 TFEU. See Regulation (EU) 2022/2065 of the European Parliament and of the Council of 19 October 2022 on a Single Market for Digital Services and amending Directive 2000/31/EC (Digital Services Act), OJ L 277, 27 October 2022.

necessary powers of action for this purpose.[192] Reliance on this legal basis, however, requires unanimity in the Council and is hence typically avoided.[193]

By definition, a market-oriented legal basis entails certain limitations, as it renders regulatory intervention in the public sector (especially as regards law enforcement activities, public administration or the justice system) more difficult to justify. The legislator therefore also added Article 16 TFEU as a legal basis, yet only to the extent that, for the purpose of law enforcement, it contains specific rules on the protection of individuals' personal data which concern restrictions of "*the use of AI systems for remote biometric identification*", "*the use of AI systems for risk assessments of natural persons*" and "*the use of AI systems of biometric categorisation*".[194] One can still question whether the combination of Article 114 TFEU and, very limitedly, Article 16 TFEU constitutes a sufficient legal basis to extend the AI Act to the use of algorithmic systems by public administrations, yet I will not be delving further into this question here. For the remainder of my analysis, I will therefore proceed under the assumption that the AI Act's legal basis is valid.

5.4.1.c AI's Definition

Before turning to the regulatory framework and content of the AI Act, let me make a brief note on how it defines AI. As previously stressed, the definition of artificial intelligence constitutes an important battleground as it sets out the contours of the technological applications that fall under the law's scope, thereby also determining its regulatory relevance.[195] I shall not repeat here the definition's history which I discussed in Section 2.1.5, but merely zoom in on the final version of the

[192] See Article 352(1) TFEU, stating that

> If action by the Union should prove necessary, within the framework of the policies defined in the Treaties, to attain one of the objectives set out in the Treaties, and the Treaties have not provided the necessary powers, the Council, acting unanimously on a proposal from the Commission and after obtaining the consent of the European Parliament, shall adopt the appropriate measures. Where the measures in question are adopted by the Council in accordance with a special legislative procedure, it shall also act unanimously on a proposal from the Commission and after obtaining the consent of the European Parliament.

This is referred to as the so-called flexibility clause and requires that national parliaments are made aware of any legislative initiative proposed on that basis, considering the potential encroachment thereof on their legislative powers. See Article 352(2) TFEU and Article 5(3) TEU.

[193] The Parliament only needs to consent. Ibid. See also Theodore Konstadinides, 'Drawing the Line between Circumvention and Gap-Filling: An Exploration of the Conceptual Limits of the Treaty's Flexibility Clause' (2012) 31 Yearbook of European Law 227.

[194] Recital 3 of the AI Act.

[195] See also Bilel Benbouzid, Yannick Meneceur and Nathalie Alisa Smuha, 'Quatre nuances de régulation de l'intelligence artificielle: Une cartographie des conflits de définition' (2022) 232–233 Réseaux 29.

definition. To recap, AI is defined as a "*machine-based system that is designed to operate with varying levels of autonomy and that may exhibit adaptiveness after deployment, and that, for explicit or implicit objectives, infers, from the input it receives, how to generate outputs such as predictions, content, recommendations, or decisions that can influence physical or virtual environments*".[196]

Recital 12 of the AI Act clarifies that this covers knowledge- and data-driven methods alike. However, more narrowly than in the original proposal, it excludes from this definition "*simpler traditional software systems or programming approaches*" and "*systems that are based on the rules defined solely by natural persons to automatically execute operations*". It remains to be seen how this definition will be interpreted by the AI Act's implementers, but the recital raises doubts as to whether the algorithmic systems that are the subject of this book all fall under the AI Act's scope.[197] Throughout this section, I will assume it can reasonably be argued that they do, and use the term 'AI' interchangeably with algorithmic systems used for algorithmic regulation.

I do wish to stress, however, that this narrowing of AI's definition is rather unfortunate, as it creates the risk that harmful algorithmic systems can escape the AI Act's requirements through definitional gaps. This limitation is also unnecessary. Indeed, a broad definition of AI could have easily been maintained, since the systems that fall under the scope of the Act's requirements are not solely defined by this definition, but also by the regulation's specific provisions that categorise AI systems and impose different obligations per category. If the legislator's main focus had been the values it seeks to protect and the harmful conduct it wishes to avoid, it would not have mattered as much through which underlying algorithmic technique such harm occurred.

Let me also point out that the AI Act introduces a definition of general-purpose AI models, or models that are trained with a large amount of data using self-supervision at scale, that display significant generality and that are capable of "*competently performing a wide range of distinct tasks regardless of the way the model is placed on the market*" while also capable of being integrated into a variety of downstream systems or applications.[198]

[196] Article 3(1) AI Act.

[197] One can, for instance, wonder whether the Dutch system discussed under Section 4.1.4 to identify fraud based on blatantly discriminatory criteria (such as whether the individual is a taxi driver or hairdresser, or how high their level of education is) is still part of the AI Act's definition, as it concerns essentially a rule-based system with pre-defined rules and criteria that are automatically executed.

[198] See Article 3(63) AI Act. Unfortunately, this definition excludes "*AI models that are used for research, development or prototyping activities before they are placed on the market*". Since the AI Act was initially proposed before the launch of ChatGPT, when generative AI applications were not yet on the Commission's radar, there was no mentioning thereof in its original version. Yet the broad uptake of such applications during the AI Act's negotiations rendered their inclusion much more pressing, resulting in a new set of distinct requirements.

Finally, the regulation also introduces certain exceptions. AI systems and models that are developed and put into service for the sole purpose of scientific research and development fall outside its scope, as do systems that are used for national security, military and defence purposes. An exception also exists for AI systems that are released under free and open-source licences, unless they are placed on the market or put into service for a purpose that falls under one of the AI Act's explicit categories, which I will discuss next.[199]

5.4.2 *The AI Act's Regulatory Architecture*

There are many different ways of regulating (human behaviour related to) AI systems.[200] The drafters of the AI Act have let themselves be inspired by product (safety) legislation[201] instead of, for instance, legislation dealing with the protection of fundamental rights. The regulation hence treats AI as a product or service that must adhere to certain (primarily technical) requirements, meticulously set out in the regulation. The High-Level Expert Group's recommendation to adopt a principle-based approach to AI's regulation rather than an overly prescriptive one[202] has thus not been taken up. The legislator did take up the group's suggestion for a risk-based approach, by distinguishing different categories of AI systems based on the extent of risk[203] they raise to health, safety and fundamental rights,[204] and imposes different obligations for each risk category. The regulation's emphasis on *obligations*

[199] Article 2(12) AI Act.

[200] See also Nicolas Petit and Jerome De Cooman, 'Models of Law and Regulation for AI' in Anthony Elliott (ed), *The Routledge Social Science Handbook of AI* (Routledge 2021) 199.

[201] The AI Act is based on the New Legal Framework, which was adopted in 2008 and consists of three EU measures that are meant to improve the market surveillance of products and enhance the quality of conformity assessments: (1) EC Regulation No 765/2008 on accreditation and marketing surveillance; (2) Decision No 768/2008/EC on establishing a common framework for the marketing of products; and (3) EC Regulation No 764/2008 to strengthen the internal market for a wide range of other products not subject to EU harmonisation.

[202] See High-Level Expert Group on AI, 'Policy and Investment Recommendations for Trustworthy AI' (n 176) 38.

[203] Risk is defined in Article 3(2) AI Act as "*the combination of the probability of an occurrence of harm and the severity of that harm*". This definition has been criticised by scholars like Mireille Hildebrand, for when it comes to fundamental rights, the danger is the 'breach' of a right rather than 'harm'. It would hence be important to interpret this risk definition as also encompassing risks to rights breaches (and breaches of individual, collective and societal interests more generally).

[204] In its recitals, the regulation sparsely states that democracy, the rule of law and the environment are also values it seeks to protect. However, its substantive articles clarify that the risks it focuses on are primarily assessed in terms of their impact on health, safety and fundamental rights. This also explains, for instance, why certain systems – despite being included in the high-risk list – can still escape the high-risk obligations when they do "*not pose a significant risk of harm to the health, safety or fundamental rights of natural persons, including by not materially influencing the outcome of decision making*". See Article 6(3) AI Act.

for AI providers and deployers, with only a very limited number of new *rights* for those subjected to the systems, further reflects its market-oriented vision.

The AI Act distinguishes five[205] categories:

(1) AI practices that pose an unacceptable level of risk and that are hence prohibited (with exceptions) (*chapter II of the Act*);
(2) AI systems that must comply with a set of requirements due to posing a high risk to health, safety or fundamental rights, and that must undergo a conformity assessment prior to their use or placement on the market (*chapter III of the AI Act*). These consist of two subcategories: a) AI systems that are (incorporated into products that are) already subjected to existing product safety legislation (Annex I of the AI Act); and (b) 'stand-alone' AI systems (Annex III of the AI Act);
(3) AI systems subjected to additional transparency obligations due to their risk of deceit or intrusiveness (*chapter IV of the AI Act*);
(4) General-purpose AI models, including a sub-category of models that pose a systemic risk due to their scale and capabilities (*chapter V of the AI Act*); and
(5) AI systems that are considered to pose only a minimal or no risk.

The last one is a residual category, including all systems and practices that are not explicitly listed under one of the other categories. These systems are not subjected to any new requirements, but can become the object of voluntary codes of conduct and guidelines (*chapter X of the AI Act*). AI systems that fall under the first four categories are described and listed either directly in the AI Act's text or – in the case of high-risk systems – in annexes that can be updated over time.[206] The AI Act's drafters hence coupled a *risk-based* approach with a *list-based* approach, to which I will come back later.

Categories and their requirements can overlap. Some systems can, for instance, be subjected to both the requirements imposed on high-risk systems and to the

[205] Originally, four such categories were proposed, which the Commission eagerly represented by reference to a pyramid to stress that only a small number of systems are subjected to strict requirements, and that "*the vast majority of AI systems*" (those represented by the large base of the pyramid) are not subjected to any new requirements. See European Commission, 'Press Release – Europe Fit for the Digital Age: Commission Proposes New Rules and Actions for Excellence and Trust in Artificial Intelligence' (Brussels, 21 April 2021) <https://ec.europa.eu/commission/presscorner/detail/en/IP_21_1682>. A similar pyramidal approach had already been put forward by the German Data Ethics Commission, who differentiated five risk levels necessitating different regulatory requirements. See 'Opinion of the German Data Ethics Commission' (Data Ethics Commission of the Federal Government 2019). Over time, it became clear, however, that a pyramidal structure did not fit the bill to visualise the AI Act, as certain categories were overlapping, the new category of 'general-purpose AI models' was difficult to place, and the quantity of AI systems listed in certain categories did not always correspond to their place in the pyramid.

[206] See Article 7 AI Act.

additional transparency obligations. AI providers and deployers must self-assess the category under which their AI system falls. For high-risk systems listed in Annex III, they can even self-assess whether their system – though listed in the annex – is nevertheless exempt from the high-risk requirements if it, in their view, "*does not pose a significant risk of harm to the health, safety or fundamental rights of natural persons, including by not materially influencing the outcome of decision making*".[207] Coupled with the fact that the conformity assessment of virtually all high-risk systems can be carried out by the systems' providers themselves, this provides a high 'margin of appreciation' for the very actors the AI Act is supposed to regulate – a highly contentious point to which I will return.

Before discussing which applications of algorithmic regulation fall under the AI Act's respective categories, let me also briefly describe how the AI Act's requirements are enforced. The enforcement architecture of the AI Act is relatively complex, and involves several actors at different levels. The main action takes place at the national level. Member States must establish or designate an independent national competent authority (the role of which can also be undertaken by the data protection authority) to oversee the AI Act's requirements.[208] These take on the role of notifying authorities[209] and market surveillance authorities,[210] with the possibility for Member States to appoint different authorities for each task[211] as long as there is a "*single point of contact*".[212] The authorities' oversight primarily takes place ex post, when an investigation reveals that an AI provider or deployer did not comply with the regulation. To coordinate the activities of the national authorities, the AI Act also establishes a European AI Board, composed of Member States' representatives.[213]

While the Commission's initial proposal was limited to the above, both the Council and the Parliament underlined the need for a stronger enforcement role at the level of the EU, especially for systems that affect the EU population at large or

[207] Article 6(3) AI Act.

[208] See Article 70(1) AI Act.

[209] Notifying authorities play a role in the enforcement process of high-risk systems in particular. Pursuant to Article 28 of the AI Act, they are responsible for setting up and carrying out the necessary procedures for the assessment, designation and notification of conformity assessment bodies ('notified bodies') and for their monitoring. These bodies can act as an independent third-party that carries out conformity assessments of high-risk systems when system providers do not need or wish to do so themselves. Notified bodies must first submit an application for notification to the notifying authority, who will verify that they meet the conditions set out in Article 31 AI Act.

[210] Market surveillance authorities play the role of supervisory authority, and monitor organisations' compliance with the AI Act's requirements more generally. Often, the same authority will take on the role of both notifying authority and market surveillance authority.

[211] Article 70(1) AI Act.

[212] Article 70(2) AI Act

[213] Article 65 of the AI Act. Moreover, the European Data Protection Supervisor participates in the Board as an observer.

that cannot easily be monitored by individual states. This resulted in the establishment of an AI Office, housed at the European Commission.[214] The AI Office is responsible for the enforcement of the requirements imposed on general-purpose AI models. Moreover, it provides the secretariat for the Board, convenes the Board's meetings, and prepares its agenda.[215] To further complicate the landscape of relevant actors, Articles 67 and 68 also respectively set up an Advisory Forum and a Scientific Panel of Independent Experts. The former consists of a group of stakeholders that provide expertise and advice to the Board and the Commission.[216] The latter consists of experts that advise and support the AI Office in its enforcement tasks,[217] for instance by alerting it of possible systemic risks posed by general-purpose AI models or by developing methodologies to evaluate their capabilities.

Finally, let me point out three more characteristics of the AI Act's architecture. First, to expedite compliance monitoring of the Regulation's obligations, the AI Act establishes an EU-wide database, managed by the European Commission,[218] in which certain providers and deployers of AI systems need to register some basic information. Second, given the importance the EU attaches to AI-enabled innovation, the AI Act also provides measures 'in support of innovation', by setting up regulatory sandboxes in every Member State.[219] Third, compliance with the AI Act's requirements is facilitated by the establishment of harmonised standards (or common specifications).[220] Conformity therewith offers a presumption of conformity with the AI Act, which means that, in practice, the standards' interpretation of the AI Act's requirements can become the regulation's de facto authority. This approach is not without criticism, as European Standardisation Organisations are primarily populated by industry actors and technical experts, with little participation from civil society organisations and experts with an ethical or legal background.[221] More generally, one can also question whether requirements that are meant to ensure

[214] See Article 64 AI Act. Over time, the Office could be turned into a full-fledged Union agency if the Commission's evaluation of the Regulation's enforcement (which should be carried out seven years from the date of its entry into force) reveals enforcement shortcomings. See Article 112(13) AI Act.

[215] Article 65(8) AI Act.

[216] Article 67(1) AI Act.

[217] The scientific panel can also support the work of market surveillance authorities, pursuant to Article 68(3).

[218] Article 71 AI Act.

[219] Article 57 and following AI Act.

[220] Article 40 AI Act. In the absence of harmonised standards, the Commission can also adopt common specifications for the AI Act's requirements pursuant to Article 41 AI Act.

[221] See Nathalie A Smuha and Karen Yeung, 'The European Union's AI Act: Beyond Motherhood and Apple Pie?' in Nathalie A Smuha (ed), *The Cambridge Handbook of the Law, Ethics and Policy of AI* (Cambridge University Press). See also Joanna J Bryson, 'Belgian and Flemish Policy Makers' Guide to AI Regulation', KCDS-CiTiP Fellow Lectures Series: Towards an AI Regulator?, Leuven, 11 October 2022.

AI systems' alignment with fundamental rights can ever be captured by a set of technical standards.[222]

In what follows, let me now zoom in on the AI Act's merits and pitfalls specifically in the context of algorithmic regulation, and the risks it poses to the rule of law.

5.4.3 *Algorithmic Regulation in the AI Act*

To what extent is algorithmic regulation as defined in this book – namely reliance on algorithmic systems *to inform or take administrative acts* – covered by the AI Act? At the outset, it can be noted that the AI Act does not fundamentally distinguish between systems used by the private and the public sector when it comes to the *requirements* it imposes on AI systems. In most cases, these requirements are the same, regardless of whether a system is deployed by a private or a public actor. There are two notable exceptions: the obligation for public authority deployers to register the high-risk systems they use in the EU database, and the obligation to carry out a fundamental rights impact assessment pursuant to Article 27 of the AI Act.[223] That said, applications of algorithmic regulation can be found in all of the AI Act's categories, either explicitly (when a categorised system serves to inform or adopt administrative acts) or implicitly (when a categorised system *can* serve this purpose).

5.4.3.a Prohibited Practices

Article 5 of the AI Act enumerates eight practices that are prohibited in light of the unacceptable risk they pose.[224] Focusing only on the practices that are most relevant for the public sector, the AI Act prohibits generalised social scoring to evaluate or classify people based on their social behaviour (or based on their known, inferred or predicted characteristics), though only if it leads to their detrimental or unfavourable treatment in social contexts that are unrelated to those in which the data was collected, or to an unjustified or disproportionate treatment.[225] It also prohibits the use of AI systems to carry out risk assessments of natural persons that assess or predict the risk of a criminal offence based solely on the person's profiling or the assessment of her personality traits and characteristics. However, the prohibition does not apply

[222] For an extensive critique of this approach, see ibid.

[223] This obligation only applies to deployers of high-risk AI systems that are governed by public law, that provide public services, that evaluate people's creditworthiness or that analyse risks and prices relating to life and health insurance.

[224] The first two concern the subliminal manipulation of persons or groups or the exploitation of their vulnerabilities due to their age, disability or social or economic situation in a way that materially distorts their behaviour and can cause significant harm. Article 5(1)(a) and (b) AI Act. For a discussion on this topic, see also Rostam J Neuwirth, *The EU Artificial Intelligence Act: Regulating Subliminal AI Systems* (Routledge 2022).

[225] Article 5(1)(c) AI Act. While the Commission proposed such a prohibition only for public authorities, the Council and Parliament decided to expand this provision to private actors too.

to systems used "*to support the human assessment of the involvement of a person in a criminal activity, which is already based on objective and verifiable facts directly linked to a criminal activity*".[226]

Public and private actors are also not allowed to use AI systems that create or expand facial recognition databases through the untargeted scraping of facial images from the internet or CCTV footage,[227] or to use biometric categorisation systems that individually categorise natural persons based on their biometric data to infer their race, political opinions, trade union membership, religious or philosophical beliefs, sex life or sexual orientation. They can, however, still use the latter systems to infer other traits (as long as they comply with the GDPR and the LED), nor does this prohibition cover the "*labelling or filtering of lawfully acquired biometric datasets, such as images, based on biometric data or categorizing of biometric data in the area of law enforcement*", which is hence exempt therefrom.[228]

No prohibition is foreseen for public authorities' use of emotion recognition systems,[229] despite the fact that their use is scientifically so unsound that it is nearly impossible to come up with a single legitimate purpose for authorities to rely thereon.[230] Moreover, the prohibition on the use of facial recognition (or biometric identification systems) is so limited that it hardly merits this designation. It only applies to 'remote' and 'real-time' biometric identification, only in publicly accessible spaces, and only for the purposes of law enforcement (and thus not for the purposes of e.g. border control or other areas of public administration).[231] Furthermore, even this limited prohibition is subjected to exceptions, as remote biometric identification systems can still be used for the targeted search of victims or missing persons, the prevention of certain imminent threats, and the localisation or identification of (even) suspects of some criminal offences.[232]

Undoubtedly, this list of practices (very limited and full of exceptions) risks being incomplete, both in terms of problematic AI practices that already exist today, and

[226] Article 5(1)(d) AI Act.

[227] Article 5(e) AI Act.

[228] Article 5(g) AI Act.

[229] Pursuant to Article 5(f), these are only prohibited "*in the areas of workplace and education institutions, except where the use of the AI system is intended to be put in place or into the market for medical or safety reasons*".

[230] See, e.g., Thomas Bøgevald Bjørnsten and Mette-Marie Zacher Sørensen, 'Uncertainties of Facial Emotion Recognition Technologies and the Automation of Emotional Labour' (2017) 28 Digital Creativity 297; Lisa Feldman Barrett and others, 'Emotional Expressions Reconsidered: Challenges to Inferring Emotion from Human Facial Movements' (2019) 20 Psychological Science in the Public Interest 1.

[231] Article 5(h) AI Act.

[232] ibid. To make use of these exceptions, Article 5(2) does set out a number of safeguards that law enforcement authorities must implement, including the need to carry out a fundamental rights impact assessment and the need to request prior authorisation from a judicial authority or an independent administrative authority (though also there, exceptions are foreseen in case of a "*duly justified situation of urgency*").

practices that may pop up in the next few years. Article 5 will be subjected to a periodic assessment by the Commission of the need for amendments, which will be submitted to the Parliament and the Council. However, the only way to amend this list in practice would be to re-subject the regulation to the ordinary legislative procedure, which is unlikely to occur within the near future.

5.4.3.b Systems Requiring Additional Transparency

Three types of systems have additional transparency obligations, which in essence entail the mandatory disclosure that a person is subjected to such a system. First, systems that directly interact with natural persons – such as chatbots, which are increasingly used by public authorities to 'more efficiently' provide citizens with information – must be developed in such a way that people are informed they are interacting with an AI system.[233] Second, whenever public authorities deploy algorithmic systems for the purpose of emotion recognition or biometric categorisation, they are likewise required to inform individuals of the fact that they are being subjected thereto.[234] Last, the Article also imposes disclosure obligations on providers and deployers of systems that generate synthetic data or deepfakes, whether it concerns audio, image, video or text content.[235]

Note how, in line with the AI Act's focus on product requirements, this Article merely imposes obligations on AI providers and developers, rather than granting individuals a *right* to be informed. Furthermore, all of these provisions have exceptions where the system's use "*is authorised by law to detect, prevent, investigate or prosecute criminal offences*". Finally, it can be noted that this Article does not seem to be the object of a robust targeted periodic assessment or revision process.

5.4.3.c General-Purpose AI Models

The AI Act also imposes a set of obligations on providers of general-purpose AI models. Virtually all those providers are private actors, rendering these obligations less relevant for public authorities. That said, a growing number of authorities have started using systems that incorporate general-purpose AI models – referred to as 'general-purpose AI systems' in the AI Act – such as chatbots that help citizens to retrieve information, answer questions or fill in forms. This means these requirements are nevertheless relevant whenever authorities procure or develop such systems, especially for a high-risk purpose.

[233] Article 50(1) AI Act. An exception to this obligation is foreseen if "*this is obvious from the point of view of a natural person who is reasonably well-informed, observant and circumspect, taking into account the circumstances and the context of use*".
[234] Article 50(3) AI Act. The same, however, holds true for the private use of such applications, once again diminishing the distinction between private and public actors.
[235] Article 50(2) and 50(4) AI Act.

The AI Act's requirements for general-purpose AI models mainly concern tailored transparency measures to enable downstream AI providers that rely on those models to comply with their own obligations under the AI Act. Providers of such models must, for instance, draw up and keep up to date the model's technical documentation, including its training and testing process and the results of its evaluation.[236] They must also adopt a policy to ensure compliance with copyright law, and make available certain information and documentation to AI providers who intend to integrate the general-purpose AI model into their system (including information that enables those providers to have a good understanding of the capabilities and limitations of the model and to comply with their obligations under the AI Act).[237] In addition, they must make publicly available "*a sufficiently detailed summary about the content used for training of the general-purpose AI model, according to a template provided by the AI Office*".[238] Only the latter information is made accessible to the public at large, thus limiting the information that will be accessible for citizens who wish to learn more about the models underlying the systems used by public authorities.

As a reflection of the legislator's risk-based approach, providers of general-purpose AI models that pose a 'systemic risk' are subjected to additional obligations. These models must be notified to the Commission in order to be designated as such, akin to the gatekeeper designation process established by the Digital Markets Act.[239] General-purpose AI models that pose a systemic risk are defined as having "*high impact capabilities evaluated on the basis of appropriate technical tools and methodologies, including indicators and benchmarks*".[240] What, precisely, counts as a systemic risk is not defined. Furthermore, despite the constantly evolving nature of AI systems' computational capabilities, the drafters of the AI Act oddly enough decided to introduce a presumption of such capabilities "*when the cumulative amount of computation used for its training measured in floating point operations is greater than* 10^{25}". This rather arbitrary threshold can be amended by the Commission through delegated acts to ensure it keeps reflecting "*the state of the art*".[241]

Providers of general-purpose AI models must also perform model evaluations (including adversarial testing), and assess and mitigate possible systemic risks at Union level. They must report to national competent authorities any relevant information about serious incidents and corrective measures to address them, and

[236] See Article 53(1)(a) AI Act. The information that should be documented is set out in Annex XI of the Act.

[237] Article 53(1)(b) AI Act. The information that should be shared with those providers is set out in Annex XII of the Act.

[238] Article 53(1)(d) AI Act.

[239] Regulation 2022/1925 of the European Parliament and of the Council of 14 September 2022 on contestable and fair markets in the digital sector and amending Directives 2019/1937 and 2020/1828, OJ L 265, 12 October 2022.

[240] Article 51(1) AI Act.

[241] Article 51(1) and (3) AI Act.

ensure an adequate level of cybersecurity protection for the model and its physical infrastructure. Interestingly, despite the systemic risks they pose, and their use and integration by countless downstream providers and deployers (including public authorities), none of these obligations introduces the need for an independent verification of the model's compliance with EU law prior to its use.

5.4.3.d High-Risk Systems

Let me now turn to the category that is most relevant for the context of algorithmic regulation, namely high-risk AI systems. While the requirements that apply to such systems (listed in Articles 8 to 15 AI Act) are the same when it concerns a public or a private entity, Annex III does list numerous AI systems that are solely used in the public sector, reflecting the legislator's recognition that many such uses merit heightened attention and responsibility, given the asymmetrical power relationship between public authorities and individuals.

Annex III lists eight domains or purposes for which AI systems can be used. To be considered high-risk, a system must be explicitly listed as a use-case under one of the eight domain headings. While these lists can be updated by the Commission,[242] the headings themselves can only be altered by amending the regulation.[243] In other words, if an AI system does not fall under any of the eight listed domains, despite posing a high risk, it cannot be categorised as such without revisiting the entire legislative process.

Applications of algorithmic regulation covered by Annex III include, under the heading of 'biometrics' systems used for remote biometric identification, for biometric categorisation based on sensitive or protected attributes, and systems used for emotion recognition.[244] The heading of 'critical infrastructure' is relevant too, for it includes systems "*intended to be used as safety components in the management and operation of critical digital infrastructure, road traffic, or in the supply of water, gas, heating or electricity*".

Under the domain of 'education and vocational training', systems used for student admissions, to assign them to educational institutions, and to evaluate their learning outcomes are considered high risk. Returning to the illustrations of Chapter 4, this means that a system that would be similar to Ofqual's algorithm in the UK or the Admission Post Bac algorithm in France would be covered. The domain also includes systems to monitor and detect prohibited behaviour of students during tests, and to assess the level of education that an individual should receive or

[242] Article 7 AI Act sets out a procedure for this purpose, enabling the Commission to adopt delegated acts (pursuant to Article 97 AI Act) to add, modify or delete use cases of high-risk AI systems when certain conditions are fulfilled.

[243] See Article 112(11)(a) AI Act.

[244] Annex III, 1 AI Act. Systems that are merely used for biometric *verification* purposes are excluded from the high-risk list.

access.[245] To the extent public authorities rely on algorithmic regulation in recruitments, promotions, dismissals and the monitoring and evaluation of public officials, this is likewise considered as high risk, under the heading 'employment, workers management and access to self-employment'.[246]

Many of the other examples discussed in Chapter 4 fall under the heading 'access to and enjoyment of essential private services and essential public services and benefits'.[247] This includes systems used to evaluate the eligibility of natural persons for essential public assistance benefits and services, as well as systems to grant, reduce, revoke or reclaim them.[248] Furthermore, systems used to dispatch or to establish priority in the dispatching of emergency first response services by police, firefighters and medical aid (including emergency healthcare) are likewise included.[249]

As regards 'law enforcement', which has a separate heading, the annex covers an array of applications, including systems used to make an assessment of the risk of natural persons (re)offending or becoming victims of criminal offences, and systems used to profile natural persons in the course of criminal investigations. The list also includes systems that are used as polygraphs, and systems used to evaluate the reliability of evidence during investigations.[250]

AI applications for 'migration, asylum and border control management' are grouped under a separate heading, and include inter alia systems to assess risks related to security, irregular migration and the health of individuals; systems to examine applications for asylum, visa and residence permits, and to examine complaints associated thereto; systems used to assess the reliability of evidence; and systems used to detect, recognise or identify individuals. In addition, notwithstanding their scientific unsoundness, systems used as polygraphs or to detect the emotional state of natural persons are also included in this list rather than being prohibited, despite the highly vulnerable state of the individuals subjected thereto.[251]

The last heading of the annex is titled 'administration of justice and democratic processes'.[252] This includes two sets of systems: those used by a judicial authority to assist it with researching and interpreting facts and the law and applying the law to a concrete set of facts, and those used to influence the outcome of an election or referendum (or people's voting behaviour). Interestingly, in its position on the AI Act, the Parliament also suggested including AI systems used by an *administrative*

[245] Annex III, 3 AI Act.
[246] Annex II, 4 AI Act.
[247] Annex III, 5(a). Note how the word 'essential' was added before 'public services' during the AI Act's negotiations, raising the question whether a system used in the context of a service that a public authority does not consider as 'essential' might escape the list.
[248] Annex III, 5(a) AI Act.
[249] Annex III, 5(d) AI Act.
[250] Annex III, 6 AI Act.
[251] Annex III, 7 AI Act.
[252] Annex III, 8 AI Act.

body or on their behalf (and hence not only by a judicial authority) to research and interpret facts and the law, and apply the law to a concrete set of facts. This could have been an important addition, as it would have provided a broader basis to cover algorithmic regulation applications under the high-risk list. The Parliament's suggestion, however, was rejected, leaving out of scope decisions taken by administrative authorities under this heading.

Let me pause here for a moment and make some observations. The systems listed above are without a doubt liable to cause adverse effects on the rights and interests of individuals (and society) if not used responsibly. The fact that they are listed as 'high risk' and that they will be subjected to mandatory requirements which need to be fulfilled *before* their use is hence a positive development. However, as already hinted at, some of these applications can reasonably be found to pose an 'unacceptable' risk rather than a 'high' risk, and their use, especially in a public sector context, may merit being prohibited altogether.[253]

Second, this list appears to be legitimising the use of the systems it contains, as it provides that their use, though risky, is acceptable as long as the requirements attached thereto are fulfilled. Accordingly, public deliberation about whether certain of these applications should be used in the first place risks being bypassed. Some of these applications may require, in consonance with the GDPR, a separate legal basis in the form of a legislation that sets out the permissible uses of the technology, which would at least enable parliamentary debate and hence some level of democratic oversight prior to their implementation.[254] This, however, may not be the case for all these systems, and in any case depends on how (well) Member States fulfil their obligations under the GDPR, and how they interpret concepts like the 'public interest'.

Third, I have already noted that the requirements these high-risk systems must meet (discussed in more detail in the next section) are subjected to a conformity *self*-assessment. This means the AI Act foresees no *independent ex ante* oversight over why or how these systems are designed and used, despite the significance of the impact they can have when deployed at scale by public authorities.[255] On the one

[253] See Smuha and others (n 189) 30. After the Commission's proposal came out, various civil society organisations started campaigning not only to include in the Act a full ban on facial recognition, but also a ban on predictive policing more generally. See also 'AlgorithmWatch Signs Statement on Ban of Predictive Policing in the Artificial Intelligence Act' (*AlgorithmWatch*, 1 March 2022) <https://algorithmwatch.org/en/ban-predictive-policing-aia/>.

[254] Recall in this regard the abovementioned discussion of the SyRi system used in the Netherlands, where a national court found that the system's legal basis as described in the relevant national legislation was not sufficiently precise to justify its use. Accordingly, in some cases, the GDPR also provides some level of protection in this regard (yet this will depend on the legal basis based on which the data processing takes place). See *supra*, Section 5.3.1.

[255] Pursuant to Article 43(1) AI Act, this is only different for the high-risk systems listed under point 1 of Annex III, which in principle have to undergo a third party conformity assessment (set out in Annex VII). Exceptions are, however, foreseen in cases where the provider applies harmonised standards or common specifications. For the systems listed under points 2 to 8 of Annex III, an internal control mechanism (set out in Annex VI) suffices. See Article 43(2) AI Act.

hand, their inclusion in the high-risk annex signals the acknowledgement that the risk associated with these systems is *high*. On the other hand, however, independent oversight over their use and sound development is only possible ex post and, meanwhile, the system can simply be self-assessed (often by people who, as was already discussed above, have little clue about the intricacies of the application of general legal rules to specific cases).

Finally, this list-based approach to applications that constitute a high risk is deeply problematic, as it is bound to be under-inclusive, by overlooking other algorithmic systems that can *also* have an adverse impact on individual, collective and societal interests.[256] Why did the legislator not opt to include *all* algorithmic systems used to inform or adopt administrative acts? Can it not be reasonably argued that these systems are by definition 'high risk'? Or even more broadly, could one not consider including all systems that can have an adverse impact on fundamental rights, the democratic process and the rule of law? Undoubtedly, such broader formulation provides less legal certainty for providers and deployers subject to the AI Act. Would it not, however, offer more protection for individuals subjected to the adverse effects of algorithm regulation? In Chapter 4, I discussed the importance of letting the law play its role. This includes embracing its inherent tensions, and the push-and-pull marriage between discretion and rules, flexibility and stability, vagueness and precision, openness and closeness. The list-based approach of the AI Act, unfortunately, risks overly emphasising the latter.[257] This is worrisome since, as noted above, a legalistic approach tends not to lead to justice, but to legalism.

What is more, during the negotiations, the EU legislator included a provision that introduces a so-called filter for high-risk systems, which enables the circumvention of the high-risk requirements if system providers can argue that – despite falling under Annex III – their particular AI application does *not* pose a significant risk of harm to the health, safety or fundamental rights of natural persons. Accordingly, even if a system is classified as high risk by the AI Act, system providers can avoid the high-risk requirements if they *self*-assess that their system does not pose a significant risk.[258] To avoid abuse of this potential escape route, the AI Act does provide a

[256] See Smuha and others (n 189) 29. One could also point out the risk that this list is over-inclusive, but the additional exemptive layer that the Parliament and Council introduced when finalising the AI Act significantly decreases that risk.

[257] Admittedly, the Parliament did suggest including a set of general principles that are applicable to all AI systems, regardless of whether they appear on the high-risk list. These principles would have corresponded to the High-Level Expert Group's requirements for Trustworthy AI, whereby all actors falling under the AI Act would have had to 'make their best efforts' to develop and use AI systems in accordance therewith. This suggestion has, however, not been taken up in the final version of the AI Act, except for Recital 27 of the AI Act, which briefly mentions the Expert Group's seven requirements and notes that these "*should be translated, when possible, in the design and use of AI models*" and "*serve as a basis for the drafting of codes of conduct under this Regulation*".

[258] Article 6(3) AI Act. This article, along with Recital 53, further specifies the circumstances that would justify such an exclusion (e.g. the system is used to perform "*a narrow procedural task*",

procedure through which providers should justify their (rebuttable) exclusion from the high-risk requirements, and they still need to register their system in the EU database. Nevertheless, while the aim of this additional layer is to mitigate the over-inclusiveness of the high-risk list (yet not the under-inclusiveness), it will likely only add to the complexity of this Act's regulatory architecture, lead to more red tape, and diminish legal certainty for all those involved.[259]

For the sake of continuing my analysis, let me now, temporarily, bracket these concerns and examine the applications of algorithmic regulation that the AI Act *does* designate as high risk, arguably constituting the most relevant category in this context. To which extent do the requirements imposed on such systems provide protection against their adverse impact, particularly on the rule of law?

5.4.4 *High-Risk Algorithmic Regulation*

5.4.4.a Requirements for High-Risk Systems

Chapter III of the AI Act sets out the requirements that high-risk applications must comply with before being placed on the market or put into service. Article 9 provides that a 'risk management system' be established, implemented, documented and maintained, as part of a continuous iterative process running through the entire lifecycle of the system. This compels AI providers inter alia to identify and analyse the known and reasonably foreseeable risks associated with the system; to estimate and evaluate the risks that may emerge when the system is used in accordance with its intended purpose and 'under conditions of reasonably foreseeable misuse'; and to adopt 'appropriate and targeted risk management measures'.[260] The systems also need to be tested to identify the most appropriate risk management measures, based on their 'intended purpose'.[261]

Reflection on and documentation of those elements is to be welcomed. At the same time, technical developers that are not trained in concepts like fundamental rights and the rule of law will hardly be able to identify risks pertaining thereto. The proper identification of such risks, which enables subsequent measures of

"*to improve the result of a previously completed human activity*" or to "*perform a preparatory task to an assessment relevant for the purposes of the use cases listed in Annex III*").

[259] Unsurprisingly, the European Parliament's Legal Service also issued a 'damning' opinion on this addition, raising inter alia legal certainty as a core concern. This, however, did not stop the AI Act's negotiators from keeping it in. See in this regard Lucca Bertuzzi, 'AI Act: EU Parliament's Legal Office Gives Damning Opinion on High-Risk Classification "Filters"' (*Euractiv*, 19 October 2023) <www.euractiv.com/section/artificial-intelligence/news/ai-act-eu-parliaments-legal-office-gives-damning-opinion-on-high-risk-classification-filters/>

[260] See Article 9(2) AI Act. Such risk-assessments are frequently deployed as a regulatory solution also in other contexts, yet they are not devoid of criticism. For a critical examination thereof in the area of environmental protection, see, e.g., Kathleen Garnett, 'Novelty, Ignorance and the Unknown: Uncertain Science and the Frontiers of Science Doctrine' [2021] elni Review 11.

[261] Article 9(6) AI Act.

mitigation, necessarily requires input from others, including public officials who are trained in the law's application and who will be using the system, people with expertise about the ethical and legal impact of algorithmic systems and, most importantly, those who will be subjected to the system or can be adversely affected thereby. Unfortunately, the AI Act does not foresee the need to seek input and feedback from domain experts or from those who may be adversely impacted.

It can also be noted that Article 9(3) limits the risks that must be considered to "*those which may be reasonably mitigated or eliminated through the development or design of the high-risk AI system, or the provision of adequate technical information*". One can wonder what this means for risks that cannot be mitigated through the development and design of the system or by providing technical information. Are those risks simply to be ignored? Furthermore, Article 9(5) provides that any 'relevant residual risk' that cannot be eliminated or mitigated, as well as the 'overall residual risk' of the system, must be judged 'acceptable'. The judgment of whether or not a residual risk is acceptable hence resides solely with the system's coders, not with those who will be subjected thereto. Yet, as noted elsewhere, outsourcing the 'acceptability' of 'residual risks' to high-risk AI providers is hardly acceptable.[262]

As regards the requirement pertaining to data governance, Article 10 requires that the training, validation and testing data sets are subjected to appropriate data governance and management practices, which must include in particular: the relevant design choices; data collection processes; data preparation operations; the formulation of assumptions (with respect to the information that the data are supposed to measure and represent, which can be understood as the 'proxies' that are being used); an assessment of the availability, quantity and suitability of the data sets that are needed; the examination of possible biases as well as measures to detect and mitigate those biases; and the identification of relevant data gaps or shortcomings.[263] Furthermore, data sets must be relevant, sufficiently representative and 'to the best extent possible' free of errors and complete in view of the intended purpose. They should also have 'appropriate statistical properties', including as regards the persons or groups in relation to whom the system is intended to be used.[264] These elements (though not specific to the public sector) could in theory help provide insight into how legal provisions are being translated to code in the context of algorithmic regulation, as they force coders to be explicit about the design choices they make and the relevant assumptions underlying their 'translations'. There is, however, a catch.

First, this information need not be made public. Arguably, providers need to draw up technical documentation pursuant to Article 11 AI Act, which demonstrates that the system complies with the requirements. However, that documentation is only

[262] Smuha and others (n 189) 29. See also Smuha and Yeung (n 221).

[263] Article 10(2) AI act.

[264] Article 10(3) AI act.

meant to provide the relevant supervisory authorities with the necessary information to assess compliance ex post, in case an investigation ever arises. Citizens do not have access thereto, and it is not covered by the (rather minimalistic) information that providers and deployers are meant to include in the 'EU database of stand-alone high-risk systems'.[265] Arguably, if the provider is a public authority rather than a private company to which the system's development is outsourced (and perhaps also in that case), citizens could invoke a *national* right to access to information and submit an 'access to documents' request. However, as various illustrations in Chapter 4 have demonstrated, such a right does not always enable individuals to receive information about the system itself. More generally, the fact that such documentation is not rendered public-by-default whenever it concerns a system deployed to inform or take administrative acts is a missed opportunity. This may in part be due to the fact that the AI Act imposes a single set of requirements both to private and public actors, without acknowledging their crucial differences, particularly as regards the enhanced need of transparency in the public sector, which is meant to *controllably* act in the public interest.

Second, this article still leaves significant discretion to the system's coders. For instance, statistical properties should be 'appropriate', yet what that precisely means is left to the provider, and does not necessarily need to be spelled out or justified. Moreover, the formulation of relevant assumptions and proxies does not in itself prevent reliance on misguided proxies. As noted elsewhere, nothing in the AI Act seems to, for instance "*prevent public authorities from using arrest data as a proxy for crimes committed (while not all arrested persons are charged or convicted, and many crimes occur for which no arrests are made). Given that these assumptions are not publicly accessible, their misguided nature may not easily come to light.*"[266]

In order to enhance traceability and transparency, Article 12 requires record-keeping, while Article 13 imposes certain information obligations, requiring that high-risk systems be designed and developed in such a way to enable deployers to interpret a system's output and use it appropriately.[267] The system should also come with a set of instructions for use that provide, inter alia, information about the 'characteristics, capabilities and limitations of performance of the system'; 'foreseeable circumstances' that may lead to 'risks to the health and safety or fundamental

[265] See in this regard Annex VIII AI Act, which sets out the information that should be provided upon registration in the database, in accordance with Article 71. The AI Act's final version slightly expanded this list, which now includes not only a brief description of the system's intended purpose, but also of "*the components and functions*" it supports, as well as "*a basic and concise description of the information used by the system (data, inputs) and its operating logic*". Usefully, deployers that have a registration obligation must now also include a summary of the findings of their fundamental rights impact assessment pursuant to Article 27 (to which I will come back *infra*) and a summary of their data protection impact assessment pursuant to Article 35 GDPR or Article 27 LED.

[266] Smuha and others (n 189) 34.

[267] Article 13(1) of the AI Act.

rights'; 'when appropriate, its performance regarding specific persons or groups'; and human oversight measures (including technical measures) put in place to facilitate the interpretation out the system's output.[268] Note, however, that all this information is only meant to be provided to *deployers* of the system (*in casu*, the public officials who will be using it) rather than to those subjected to or affected by the system.[269] Once again, individuals adversely affected by algorithmic regulation have a much more limited role in the regulation.

Besides requirements around the accuracy, robustness and cybersecurity of the system in Article 15, and requirements of record-keeping and automatic logging in Article 12, the AI Act also contains a requirement on human oversight. Article 14 provides that high-risk systems should be designed and developed in a way that they can be effectively overseen by natural persons, and that such oversight should aim to "*prevent or minimise the risks to health, safety or fundamental rights that may emerge when a high-risk AI system is used in accordance with its intended purpose or under conditions of reasonably foreseeable misuse*".[270] The oversight measures must be commensurate to the risks, autonomy level and context of the system's use, and should either be put in place by the provider or by the deployer (or both) depending on what is most appropriate. [271] Pursuant to Article 14(4) of the AI Act, the system's deployers must be enabled to understand the system's relevant capacities and limitations; to monitor its operation so as to detect and address anomalies and dysfunctions; to remain aware of their possible tendency of automation bias; to 'correctly' interpret the system's output; to decide not to use the system or to otherwise disregard, override or reverse its output; and to intervene in its operation or interrupt it through "a 'stop' button or a similar procedure that allows the system to come to a halt in a safe state".

The intention behind this provision is certainly to be applauded, as it is aimed at mitigating the risk of 'mindless rule-following' identified under Chapter 4. As such, it could help public officials maintain their agency and hence their sense of responsibility for the administrative acts taken or informed by algorithmic systems. However, in many instances, a meaningful failsafe is impossible to secure in practice, given that the entire premise of data mining is aimed at generating insight that is beyond the capacity of human cognition. This inevitably also means that the human being who needs to exercise oversight over the system will often not be able to second-guess the validity of the system's outputs, except in limited cases where human intuition may detect obvious failures or outliers. Moreover, the problem of automation bias is unlikely to be overcome through this provision, despite the laudable intentions.[272]

[268] Article 13(3) AI Act.
[269] See in this regard also Smuha and others (n 189) 34.
[270] Article 14(2) AI Act.
[271] Article 14(3) AI Act.
[272] Smuha and others (n 189) 35.

It would therefore be important to ensure that this provision does not remain a dead letter, and that besides 'technical measures', deployers also implement 'non-technical' oversight measures, such as adequate education and training for public officials,[273] logging oversight activities and easily accessible review and redress mechanisms. While much will depend on the internal organisation of public authorities (and the importance they attach to speed and efficiency KPIs), it is to be hoped that this provision can nevertheless contribute to a more responsible use of algorithmic regulation by providing some friction and a much-needed opportunity for critical internal reflection.

5.4.4.b Additional Obligations for Deployers

In the original proposal, most of the responsibilities for high-risk AI systems fell on system *providers*.[274] In the final version of the AI Act, this has been somewhat rebalanced to also include obligations for system *deployers*.[275] The former are chiefly responsible for the conformity assessment of their system with the above high-risk requirements (and the concomitant affixation of the CE marking),[276] setting up a quality management[277] and ensuring documentation keeping and automated logs,[278] while the latter must take technical and organisational measures to use the

[273] During the negotiations, the drafters of the AI Act included a new article on 'AI literacy', which survived the final text. Article 4 of the AI Act now states that

> providers and deployers of AI systems shall take measures to ensure, to their best extent, a sufficient level of AI literacy of their staff and other persons dealing with the operation and use of AI systems on their behalf, taking into account their technical knowledge, experience, education and training and the context the AI systems are to be used in, and considering the persons or groups of persons on whom the AI systems are to be used.

The Act also goes on to define AI literacy in Article 3(56) as "*skills, knowledge and understanding that allow providers, deployers and affected persons, taking into account their respective rights and obligations in the context of this Regulation, to make an informed deployment of AI systems, as well as to gain awareness about the opportunities and risks of AI and possible harm it can cause*".

[274] Pursuant to Article 3(3) AI Act, a provider is defined as "*a natural or legal person, public authority, agency or other body that develops an AI system or a general-purpose AI model or that has an AI system or a general-purpose AI model developed and places it on the market or puts the AI system into service under its own name or trademark, whether for payment or free of charge*".

[275] One of the main criticisms of the Commission's original proposal (especially made by large tech companies) was the 'unbalanced' imposition of obligation on providers of AI systems, who may not always be able to know or control in which (potentially problematic ways) the systems are subsequently used by deployers of the system. Article 3(4) AI Act defines a deployer as "*a natural or legal person, public authority, agency or other body using an AI system under its authority, except where the AI system is used in the course of a personal non-professional activity*".

[276] Providers must draw up a declaration of conformity in accordance with Article 47 AI Act and affix a CE marking to their high-risk system to indicate conformity with the regulation. See Articles 16 and 43 AI Act.

[277] Article 17 AI Act.

[278] Articles 18 and 19 AI Act.

system in accordance with the provider's instructions for use, ensure human oversight, monitor the system, and keep the system's logs.[279]

Interestingly, certain deployers have a few additional obligations.[280] First, all deployers of high-risk AI systems referred to in Annex III "*that make decisions or assist in making decisions related to natural persons*" shall inform those persons that they are subject to the use of such system.[281] This is a highly important (new) obligation, especially when coupled with two rights introduced in the AI Act: the right for individuals to lodge a complaint with a market surveillance authority if they believe the AI Act is not complied with,[282] and the right for individuals to receive an explanation of a decision taken about them,[283] of which the combination could facilitate redress. Second, deployers of a post-remote biometric identification in the context of a criminal investigation must obtain ex ante judicial or administrative authorisation to do so.[284] Third, deployers of high-risk systems who are public authorities must register their use of a high-risk system in the EU database to make such use known.[285]

Finally, public authorities that deploy high-risk AI systems must also undertake a fundamental rights impact assessment (FRIA).[286] This obligation was fiercely advocated for by civil society organisations throughout the AI Act's negotiations, and the Parliament ultimately managed to push it through in Article 27.[287] Inspired by the

279 Article 26 AI Act.

280 When a high-risk system is deployed at the workplace, deployers who are employers shall inform workers' representatives and the affected workers that they will be subject to the use of the high-risk AI system. See specifically Article 26(7) AI Act.

281 Article 26(11) AI Act.

282 Article 85 AI Act.

283 Article 86 AI Act. It should, however, be pointed out that "*the right to obtain from the deployer clear and meaningful explanations of the role of the AI system in the decision-making procedure and the main elements of the decision taken*", only applies for a decision "*which produces legal effects or similarly significantly affects that person in a way that they consider to have an adverse impact on their health, safety or fundamental rights*". In theory, it is thus possible that a deployer has the obligation to inform individuals of the fact that they take a decision concerning them based on a high-risk system, without those individuals having the right to receive an explanation thereof if it cannot be said to produce legal effects or similarly affects them. Furthermore, Article 86(2) in any case precludes the right's application when exceptions are provided based on Union law or national law in compliance with Union law.

284 The additional safeguards concerning post-remote biometric identification used in the area of criminal investigations can be found in Article 26(8) AI Act.

285 The information they must provide is described in Annex VIII, section C. Apart from the deployer's contact details, it includes a summary of the findings of the fundamental rights impact assessment carried out under Article 27 of the AI Act and – where applicable – a summary of their data protection impact assessment.

286 See Article 27 AI Act.

287 See for instance European Center for Not-for-Profit Law (ECNL), 'Big Win for Fundamental Rights, as the European Parliament Adopts the AI Act' (ECNL 14 June 2023) <https://ecnl.org/news/big-win-fundamental-rights-european-parliament-adopts-ai-act>; Brussels Privacy Hub, 'More Than 150 University Professors from All Over Europe and Beyond Are Calling on the European Institutions to Include a Fundamental Rights Impact Assessment in the Future

concept of data protection impact assessments,[288] it is meant to force deployers to reflect on how their system can affect people's rights prior to its use, as well as to document and mitigate those effects. While this could constitute an important safeguard, the feedback gathered during the piloting phase of the Ethics Guidelines for Trustworthy AI revealed that most organisations, private or public, have no clue what such an assessment entails. Even for trained lawyers, assessing the impact of an AI system on all fundamental rights is not an easy task.

There are hence fears that this obligation will either be too difficult to comply with or, if interpretative guidance is provided, could turn into an empty box-ticking exercise leading to yet another façade of legality without any substantive protection. The latter unfortunately seems rather likely, since Article 27 provides a relatively rigid list of elements that the assessment should describe, and tasked the AI Office with developing "*a template for a questionnaire, including through an automated tool, to facilitate deployers in complying with their obligations under this Article in a simplified manner*". This reflects the legislator's desire to ensure the AI Act's measures can be implemented in an easy and straightforward manner, ideally with the help of some technical tools – even if there is nothing easy and straightforward about carrying out a proper assessment of the ways in which those systems can affect people's rights. This is an inevitably complex matter that requires the balancing of various interests and considerations, which cannot be bypassed through a simple checklist. Furthermore, the obligation's narrow focus on individual rights also neglects the societal interests that can be affected by such systems, especially by virtue of the systemic effects they can have on values like democracy and the rule of law.

5.4.5 *A Low Ceiling*

Considering these shortcomings, it is worth asking whether Member States can still remedy these gaps by adopting stronger safeguards through national legislation. In essence, this question comes down to whether the AI Act, and its aim to harmonise rules on algorithmic systems across the EU to establish an internal AI market, aspires a form of minimum or maximum harmonisation. Minimum harmonisation "*sets a common floor of regulation, which all Member States must respect, but it does not set a ceiling*", whereas maximum harmonisation "*serves as both floor and ceiling*".[289] The AI Act is directly applicable in national legal orders and

Regulation on Artificial Intelligence' (12 September 2023) <https://brusselsprivacyhub.com/2023/09/12/brussels-privacy-hub-and-other-academic-institutions-ask-to-approve-a-fundamental-rights-impact-assessment-in-the-eu-artificial-intelligence-act/>.

[288] Such an obligation was also already suggested by the High-Level Expert Group on AI in its Policy and Investment Recommendations (n 176) 40.

[289] Stephen Weatherill, 'Maximum versus Minimum Harmonization: Choosing between Unity and Diversity in the Search for the Soul of the Internal Market' in Niamh Nic Shuibhne and

Member States will need to ensure that individuals can benefit from the protection it affords.

However, can Member States go further than what the regulation requires and provide stronger safeguards against AI's adverse impact? If the AI Act seeks to ensure the maximum harmonisation of national rules, this would effectively prevent a Member State from addressing the AI Act's shortcomings, as that would be contrary to the regulation's objective and hence contrary to EU law.[290] As observed by Weatherill, this question thus expresses "*a battle for the soul of the internal market*",[291] as it essentially determines at which level regulatory power is held, and how much regulatory diversity the EU internal market can tolerate.

While the initial proposal of the AI Act still left the answer to this question somewhat ambiguous, the final version is more clear: "*This Regulation ensures the free movement, cross-border, of AI-based goods and services, thus preventing Member States from imposing restrictions on the development, marketing and use of AI systems, unless explicitly authorised by this Regulation*".[292] It hence appears that the AI Act is targeting the maximum harmonisation of national legislation, and that Member States cannot provide a higher level of protection by adopting stricter rules, as this may cause unwanted 'market fragmentation'. There are only few exceptions such as the protection of workers, for which the regulation states that it "*does not preclude the Union or Member States from maintaining or introducing laws, regulations or administrative provisions which are more favourable to workers in terms of protecting their rights in respect of the use of AI systems by employers*".[293] This explicit exception only seems to confirm the regulation's ceiling-imposing nature.

In theory, a maximum harmonisation approach is meant to ensure an *equal* level of protection in all Member States. Yet in practice, given the AI Act's deficiencies, this may in fact come down to an *equally low* level of protection of the rule of law. Certainly, the AI Act establishes EU law provisions that public authorities must comply with. It could thereby also serve as a basis to invoke EU remedies aimed at ensuring Member States' compliance with their EU law obligations.[294] However, the fact that it does not impose stronger obligations on Member States to ensure their use of algorithmic regulation does not lead to *algorithmic rule by law*,

Laurence W Gormley (eds), *From Single Market to Economic Union* (Oxford University Press 2012) 176.

[290] In the past, the CJEU has frequently been asked to offer guidance to national courts regarding Member State legislation that imposed stricter requirements on providers of goods and services than those imposed by EU law (a practice sometimes referred to as 'goldplating'), which in some cases also resulted in the national legislation's incompatibility with EU law precisely because it was aimed at maximum harmonisation. See, e.g., Joined Cases C-261/07 and C-299/07, VTB-VAB NV, 23 April 2009, ECLI:EU:C:2009:244.

[291] Weatherill, 'Maximum versus Minimum Harmonization' (n 289) 177.

[292] Recital 1 AI Act.

[293] Article 2(11) AI Act. This also includes encouraging and allowing the application of collective agreements that are more favourable to workers.

[294] See *supra*, Section 5.2.3.

inadvertently or intentionally, is a missed opportunity. And the fact that Member States may be legally unable to level this protection up through national legislation, unless they can argue it falls outside its scope, only makes this problem worse.

Admittedly, the AI Act does state that the harmonised rules it provides "*should be without prejudice to existing Union law, in particular on data protection, consumer protection, fundamental rights, employment, and protection of workers, and product safety, to which this Regulation is complementary.*"[295] It also mentions that a system's classification as 'high-risk' should not be interpreted as indicating the lawfulness of its use under other Acts of Union law or national law implementing Union law, "*such as on the protection of personal data, the use of polygraphs or the use of emotion recognition systems*".[296] However, the AI Act's clear intention to comprehensively regulate systems that pose a risk to fundamental rights makes it difficult to argue that an application listed in Annex III is nevertheless unlawful. While not excluded in principle, the person claiming such unlawfulness (for instance due to an incompatibility with a fundamental right) would have to surmount a significant burden of proof, which may only be met in the case where a national law exists that explicitly sets out the system's unlawfulness.[297] Moreover, in that case too, the risk still exists that an AI provider or deployer challenges the national law on internal market-based grounds, by claiming it constitutes an illegal market restriction for the very product the AI Act is meant to promote.[298]

Finally, the maximum ceiling imposed by the AI Act also has repercussions for Member States' participation in negotiations on AI regulation at the international level. For instance, during the Council of Europe's negotiations of a new Convention on AI and human rights, democracy and the rule of law,[299] which largely took place in parallel with the negotiations of the AI Act,[300] the Commission requested and

[295] See Recital 9 AI Act.

[296] See Recital 63 AI Act.

[297] I also made this point in Smuha (n 166).

[298] For a discussion of the relationship between internal market law and fundamental rights law, see also Stephanie Reynolds, 'Explaining the Constitutional Drivers behind a Perceived Judicial Preference for Free Movement over Fundamental Rights' (2016) 53 Common Market Law Review 643.

[299] This work was started by the Council of Europe's Ad Hoc Committee on AI (CAHAI) and continued by its Committee on AI (CAI). In Spring 2024, the CAI approved the 'draft Council of Europe Framework Convention on Artificial Intelligence and Human Rights, Democracy and the Rule of Law', along with a draft Explanatory Report. See also *supra*, Section 1.2.3.

[300] See Council Decision 2022/2349 of 21 November 2022 authorising the opening of negotiations on behalf of the European Union for a Council of Europe convention on artificial intelligence, human rights, democracy and the rule of law, ST/14173/2022/INIT, OJ L 311, 2 December 2022. When the Commission realised how fast the CAI's negotiations were advancing, and that the Convention could even be concluded before the finalisation of the AI Act, it quickly sought to postpone the Convention's negotiations. Officially, it requested its negotiation mandate to "*protect the integrity of Union law and to ensure that the rules of international law and Union law remain consistent*" (pursuant to Recital 7 of the Mandate). One could, however, also wonder to which extent the importance of being the *first* global

obtained a mandate to be the sole negotiator on behalf of EU Member States, rather than having Member States negotiating their own position.[301] From its request, it was evident that the Commission considers that matters related to the Council of Europe's Convention (meaning, matters related to AI's impact on human rights, democracy and the rule of law) to already be comprehensively dealt with under the AI Act. This assumption is, however, fanciful considering the inadequate attention to the rule of law in the AI Act, as well as its underwhelming protection of fundamental rights and democratic participation in decisions on AI's use. Nevertheless, the Commission wanted to ensure the Convention's alignment with the AI Act, thereby also precluding Member States to advocate for stronger protection. This is despite the fact that, as already hinted at, one could legitimately wonder whether the EU can claim the competence to exhaustively regulate aspects pertaining to algorithmic regulation in public administration on an internal market legal basis.

It hence appears that the EU legislator not only left open important legal gaps in the AI Act, but that it is also preventing Member States to fill these gaps, in the name of countering market fragmentation. This begs the question whether the Union's interest in being 'the first' AI legislator to reap the economic benefits of an internal market for AI are deemed more important than safeguarding its core values.

5.4.6 *Evaluation: The Return of Techno-supremacy*

Considering the above analysis, what should we now make of the AI Act in the context of the concerns identified in Chapter 4? Can it offer any help in countering the threat of algorithmic rule by law? Undoubtedly, the new regulation does introduce important legal safeguards to better protect individuals against the risks that *some* AI systems pose to their health, safety and fundamental rights. The establishment of a public enforcement mechanism; the introduction of prohibitions and requirements that must be met ex ante; as well as the inclusion of several rights for individuals that can fortify private enforcement channels are all to be welcomed. Furthermore, by imposing documentation and logging obligations that should facilitate ex post review, and by setting up an EU database to register the use of

legislator in this field played a role. See also Luca Bertuzzi, 'EU Commission postponed AI treaty negotiations with further delays in sight' *Euractiv* (5 October 2022), <www.euractiv.com/section/digital/news/eu-commission-postponed-ai-treaty-negotiations-with-further-delays-in-sight/>.

[301] This mandate was formally sought for matters falling within the exclusive competence of the Union, yet Article 2 of the Mandate also stated that "*to the extent that the subject matter of the negotiations falls partially within the competence of the Union and partially within the competence of its Member States, the Commission and the Member States shall cooperate closely during the negotiating process, with a view to ensuring unity in the external representation of the Union*".

high-risk systems by public authorities, the AI Act also enhances transparency around algorithmic regulation.[302]

However, overall, the protection the AI Act provides remains insufficient to meet the identified concerns. Its process is primarily based on self-assessments, and is not tailored to the specific risks arising in the context of algorithmic regulation. There are no proper mechanisms for public participation and input (for instance regarding the decision to deploy algorithmic regulation in the first place, or even just to help identify and assess the risks attached thereto); there are only limited transparency obligations towards those potentially affected by the systems; there is no obligation to make the extensive documentation of the system's functioning accessible to researchers, civil society organisations or the public at large; there are no provisions around the procurement of systems, or limitations as regards who should be able to undertake translations from law to code, with which training, and with which constitutional checks and balances; there are no ex ante independent oversight mechanisms, nor mandatory periodic audits that can help ensure continuous oversight; and there are no provisions that enable *systemic* review.

These substantive shortcomings are coupled with concerns around the AI Act's regulatory architecture. First, despite the role of the European AI Office, when it comes to public authorities' use of AI, oversight is primarily organised at the national level, which means the extent to which people can enjoy the AI Act's protection depends on the resources and skills of Member States. As the enforcement practice of the GDPR has shown, these vary significantly from one state to another.[303] And while national supervisory authorities ought to be independent, especially given their task to also review the actions of public authorities, experience with national data protection authorities has likewise indicated that such independence may not always be straightforward, even in countries that are not yet considered as undergoing 'an autocratic turn'.[304]

[302] In addition, geopolitically speaking, the regulation could act as a catalyst for others in the global regulatory arena for AI, as well as potentially offering the EU a first-mover advantage by setting the standard and aspiring to a 'Brussels effect' as described in Anu Bradford, *The Brussels Effect: How the European Union Rules the World* (Oxford University Press 2020); *Digital Empires: The Global Battle to Regulate Technology* (Oxford University Press 2023). See also Charlotte Siegmann and Markus Anderljung, 'The Brussels Effect and Artificial Intelligence' (Centre for the Governance of AI 2022). On the first mover advantage to regulate AI, see also Nathalie A Smuha, 'From a "Race to AI" to a "Race to AI Regulation": Regulatory Competition for Artificial Intelligence' (2021) 13 Law, Innovation and Technology 57.

[303] See, for instance, Johnny Ryan and Alan Toner, 'Europe's Enforcement Paralysis – ICCL's 2021 Report on the Enforcement Capacity of Data Protection Authorities' (Irish Council for Civil Liberties 2022) <www.iccl.ie/wp-content/uploads/2021/09/Europes-enforcement-paralysis-2021-ICCL-report-on-GDPR-enforcement.pdf>.

[304] In this regard, reference can, for instance, be made to the perceived concerns around the (lack of the) independence of the Belgian data protection authority. See Paul De Hert, 'Complete Independence of National Data Protection Supervisory Authorities: About Persons, Czars and Data Governance in Belgian Debates' (*European Law Blog*, 24 December 2021) <https://europeanlawblog.eu/2021/12/24/complete-independence-of-national-data-protection-supervisory-authorities-about-persons-czars-and-data-governance-in-belgian-debates/>. See also Belgian Data Protection Authority, 'A New Draft Law Threatens the Independence and Functioning of the BE

Second, the AI Act's reliance on conformity assessment and technical standardisation, as part of the New Legislative Framework (NLF) approach, is inadequate to deal with the rule of law risks posed by algorithmic regulation. As briefly noted above, this is an approach the Commission typically uses in the context of EU product regulation and safety standards. As such, it makes sense to subject high-risk systems that are already part of NLF legislation (listed in Annex I, including machinery, medical devices and toys), to the same compliance mechanisms as before, with the addition of the new requirements of the AI Act. However, applying the same model of safety legislation to the high-risk systems listed in Annex III is problematic, as the risks they pose – not only to fundamental rights, but also to societal interests such as the rule of law – are not comparable. AI systems are treated as tangible products which simply need to conform to technical requirements and have a 'CE' marking affixed to them, rather than socio-technological systems. This approach might work reasonably well for fridges and dishwashers, yet "*it is hardly appropriate for a digital technology which, on the Commission's own account, may pose significant risk to the protection of nontangible values*".[305] As noted elsewhere, while the "*text is infused with fundamental rights-language, it seems to take an overly technocratic approach to the protection of fundamental rights*",[306] by essentially translating those rights into a set of prescriptive rules, exhaustive lists, detailed technical safety standards, as well as handy templates and checklists. In addition, the reliance on harmonised standards that provide a 'presumption of conformity' in fact implies that the interpretation of the AI Act's requirements is outsourced to the (primarily technical experts of) standardisation organisations,[307] despite their lack of representativeness and democratic accountability.[308]

DPA' (March 2022) <www.dataprotectionauthority.be/citizen/a-new-draft-law-threatens-the-independence-and-functioning-of-the-be-dpa>; Belgian Data Protection Authority, 'Opinion on Preliminary Draft Law Amending the Act of 3 December 2017 Establishing the Data Protection Authority (AH-2022-0020)' (February 2022) <www.autoriteprotectiondonnees.be/publications/opinion-on-preliminary-draft-law-amending-the-act-of-3-december-2017-establishing-the-data-protection-authority.pdf>.

[305] Jeremias Adams-Prassl, 'Regulating Algorithms at Work: Lessons for a "European Approach to Artificial Intelligence"' (2022) 13 European Labour Law Journal 30, 49. See also Michael Veale and Frederik Zuiderveen Borgesius, 'Demystifying the Draft EU Artificial Intelligence Act' (2021) 22 Computer Law Review International 97, 102; Smuha and others (n 189) 39. See also Jérôme De Cooman, 'Humpty Dumpty and High-Risk AI Systems: The Ratione Materiae Dimension of the Proposal for an EU Artificial Intelligence Act' [2022] Market and Competition Law Review 49.

[306] Smuha and others (n 189) 9.

[307] While efforts are made to include civil society organisations in the discussions, they are not only a minority in these discussions, but they also have far less resources to take part therein, as well as less knowledge about the procedures of such standardisation organisations. See also Luca Bertuzzi, 'AI Standards Set for Joint Drafting among European Standardisation Bodies' *Euractiv* (30 May 2022) <www.euractiv.com/section/digital/news/ai-standards-set-for-joint-drafting-among-european-standardisation-bodies/>.

[308] See the critique thereon by Smuha and Yeung (n 221). See also Veale and Borgesius (n 305) 105.

Interestingly, and sadly, parallels can hence be drawn with one of the risks pointed out in Chapter 4, namely that reliance on algorithmic regulation may exacerbate a techno-scientific approach to the law.[309] As noted previously, the danger associated with *algorithmic rule by law* is that the legal protection of individuals and the translation from open-ended legal rules to code is seen as a mere techno-scientific enterprise, to the detriment of human rights, the rule of law, and other essential values. When the regulated risk concerns the safety of machines, food or pharmaceuticals, a techno-scientific approach is neither new nor surprising. In those areas, it is common for the legislator to set out broad norms stating the objective of protecting the health and safety of individuals, which are subsequently elaborated and complemented with detailed technical requirements by domain experts who translate the objective of 'safety' into quantifiable, measurable and demonstrable safety standards that need to be complied with.[310]

Yet when it comes to protecting fundamental rights or the rule of law, this type of approach falls woefully short, as it is unable to do justice to the intricate contextual assessment and balance it requires between various interests. Nevertheless, this is precisely the AI Act's approach, as it erroneously reduces "*the careful balancing exercise between fundamental rights to a technocratic process, thus rendering the need for such balancing invisible*".[311] In this way, legal concepts such as the right to non-discrimination and the principle of equality are considered as elements that can be embodied by technical standards expressed in quantifiable and measurable specifications, checked by an internal 'quality management process', and algorithmically programmed, thereby maintaining the primacy of techno-rationality.[312] Worse still, the fact that this assessment and quality management occurs entirely in-house, without external oversight or ex ante accountability mechanisms, leaves these translation decisions entirely in the hands of technical experts, thus maintaining the supremacy of coders set out above.[313]

Lastly, the ceiling imposed by the AI Act's maximum harmonisation means that Member States who want to offer a higher level of protection than the AI Act currently provides are practically unable to do so. Despite the regulation's laudable intentions, and despite its introduction of valuable new safeguards, the overall picture that results from this analysis is therefore still rather bleak when it comes to the AI Act's ability to counter the threat of algorithmic rule by law.

5.5 CONCLUDING REMARKS

In Chapter 4, I conducted a systematic analysis of the way in which algorithmic regulation can impact the core principles of the rule of law, and conceptualised the

[309] Just like in other regulatory domains, see e.g. Garnett (n 260).
[310] See also *supra*, Section 2.3.3.
[311] Smuha and others (n 189) 12.
[312] See *supra*, Section 4.2.1.
[313] See *supra*, Section 4.2.2.

threat emanating therefrom as *algorithmic rule by law*. I noted that this threat needs to be counter-balanced by appropriate legal safeguards, apt to address the challenges raised by public authorities' increased reliance on algorithmic regulation. In this chapter, I therefore critically assessed whether the current EU legal framework is up to this task, and respectively analysed legislation pertaining to the rule of law, and legislation pertaining to the risks posed by (personal) data processing activities and by algorithmic systems. Although various protection mechanisms exist, and while the AI Act should be able to make a relevant contribution in this regard, my evaluation leads me to conclude that these are insufficient to address the adverse impact of algorithmic regulation on the rule of law.

On the one hand, the legal domain pertaining to the rule of law does not consider algorithmic regulation to be a particular threat, and rule of law monitoring initiatives that can help trigger such legislation do not pay attention to it. Moreover, the legal mechanisms to protect the rule of law currently seem unable to tackle more than individual infringements or budget-related concerns, whereas the deployment of algorithmic regulation without adequate safeguards can result in, or exacerbate, systemic deficiencies. On the other hand, the legal domain pertaining to algorithmic systems does not consider the rule of law to be a particularly impacted value. It hence does not pay specific attention to the fact that algorithmic regulation can increase the executive's power, erode the protective role of the law and, given its systemic effects, undermine the normative pillars of liberal democracy. In other words, these two legal domains are currently not on speaking terms, despite the urgent need for them to enter into a serious dialogue.

This urgency is only exacerbated by the new AI Act, which aims to be future proof and on which hope has now been vested for years to come. Yet by seeking to put forward a comprehensive piece of legislation to deal with the risks of algorithmic systems in an exhaustive manner, the EU legislator's ambition, though praiseworthy in itself, undermines its own purpose. First, there is no such thing as an *exhaustive* way to tackle the risks posed by algorithmic systems, even if we would assume the EU would have such competences,[314] and the many gaps in the complex and legalistic list-based approach of the AI Act testify to that. Second, the Act appears to pre-empt stronger safeguards at Member State level, due to its objective to counter market fragmentation and ensure harmonised member state legislation. Third, it approaches the protection of fundamental rights and, to the extent these are on the radar, other values, as a technocratic endeavour, which can be solved by identifying the right technical standard that providers should implement, crowned by a CE marking. Fourth, the combination of a single set of requirements for applications

[314] Recall the fact that the EU, for instance, does not have a general competence to regulate matters pertaining to the rule of law – or pertaining to national public administrations – but instead needs to rely on specific competences that are indirectly linked thereto. See *supra*, Section 5.1.

used in the public sector and the private sector, with a few useful yet tailored exceptions, overlooks the particular rule of law-related risks that are associated with the former, and might explain the AI Act's disregard thereof. Instead, the regulation approaches the harm caused by algorithmic systems in an isolated fashion, assessing for each individual application which risks it can pose to each individual interest. Yet by looking at the trees, it risks overlooking the forest: the systemic, networked, long-term, widespread impact of algorithmic regulation on societal interests, including the preservation of the protective role of the law, and the integrity of the legal system as a whole.

Unfortunately, despite these flaws, the existence of the AI Act may nevertheless provide a false sense of security that the risks raised by algorithmic regulation are aptly dealt with, and that their use by public authorities can now be further promoted and sponsored in the name of efficiency and innovation. Some commentators even claimed that the AI Act is in fact overprotective, and "*may come at the price of digital innovation*",[315] seemingly forgetting that innovation is not an end in and of itself, but that the aim of regulating the risks of this technology is to delineate the contours in which socially beneficial innovation can thrive. Finally, it must be recalled that these developments occur against a background in which illiberal and authoritarian practices are on the rise, and in which the implementation of the law – whether in textual or algorithmic form – is already being used, inadvertently or deliberately, to further those problematic ends.

[315] Raposo (n 187) 88.

6

Conclusions

In this book, I set out to examine how public authorities' growing reliance on algorithmic regulation, defined as the use of algorithmic systems to inform or adopt administrative acts, might adversely impact the rule of law and erode its protective role in liberal democracy. I conceptualised this threat as *algorithmic rule by law*, and analysed to which extent the EU legal framework provides adequate safeguards to counter it, focusing both on legal provisions aimed at protecting the rule of law, and legal provisions aimed at tackling the risks associated with algorithmic systems. In this final chapter, I summarise my findings for each of the previous chapters and conclude that the threat of algorithmic rule by law is insufficiently taken into account (Section 6.1). Subsequently, I provide a number of recommendations that build on my analysis (Section 6.2). Finally, I formulate some concluding remarks, and defend the need to (re)embrace normative complexity – in algorithmic regulation, in regulation about algorithmic regulation and in society at large (Section 6.3).

6.1 SUMMARY

In Chapter 1, I introduced this book with the hypothesis that, despite the benefits that algorithmic regulation might generate, the technology's implementation by public authorities also implies significant risks, which may turn the state into an unchecked Algorithmic Leviathan. I specifically expressed the concern that reliance on algorithmic regulation might not only exacerbate the asymmetry of power between the government and its citizens, but also between the executive on the one hand, and the judicial and legislative on the other hand, by strengthening the executive's power, diminishing public accountability and undermining constitutional checks and balances. Importantly, I underlined that this concern arises within a broader context of rule of law-backsliding in several EU Member States, and a more general rise of authoritarian and illiberal tendencies across the world, including in liberal democracies. This concern led to an overarching research question:

which legal safeguards does the EU have in place to avoid that reliance on algorithmic regulation by public authorities, amidst a rule of law crisis, undermines the rule of law and results in *algorithmic rule by law*?

To answer this research question and verify my hypothesis, I first took a closer look at the concept of 'algorithmic regulation' in Chapter 2, by examining its technical and societal aspects, and how its use fits within the bureaucratic organisation of public authorities. In Section 2.1, I offered a technical description of algorithmic systems (which are the building blocks of algorithmic regulation) and set out their main characteristics, considering knowledge-driven and data-driven approaches alike and emphasising that algorithmic systems can rely on a mix of approaches. I also examined the definitional conundrums that surround the term artificial intelligence, noting that it can be defined differently depending on the time, context and definer, and that experts reasonably disagree on the type of systems that are deemed sufficiently 'intelligent' to fall under the AI-umbrella. I therefore decided to focus my investigation on all algorithmic systems deployed by public authorities to inform or adopt administrative acts, regardless of their underlying technical approach, and regardless of whether they are called 'AI'.

In Section 2.2, I then complemented the technical description of algorithmic systems with one that emphasises their socio-technical nature, and analysed several consequences of their societal embeddedness. For instance, I pointed out that, being the product of human developers and users, algorithmic systems can reflect human errors or bias, which can have vast consequences given the fact that they enable mass decision-making at population level. I also discussed the fact that algorithmic systems can function or be used in an opaque manner, and that they can undermine human agency and a sense of responsibility for the system's outcomes. Finally, I noted their dependency on data and proxies, which only ever provide a *partial* reflection of reality. I therefore stressed that, regardless of the systems' computational abilities, one should not overlook that the social phenomena they analyse can never be fully reduced to quantitative datapoints and numerical functions, especially when they concern something as complex as human nature.

Bearing these technical and societal aspects in mind, in Section 2.3 I described the role that algorithmic systems play within public authorities that are part of the executive branch of power, which first led me to examine how these authorities are organised, and how administrative acts are taken. To this end, I discussed the main characteristics of their bureaucratic environment (including traits like impersonality, efficiency, rationality and hierarchy) and examined some of the pitfalls associated therewith. I especially emphasised the risk that 'procedural' rationality gets prioritised over 'substantive' rationality, as an excessive focus on routinised procedures in the name of efficiency and objectivity might make public officials lose sight of the substantive aims those procedures are meant to achieve in the first place. I also discussed the warnings that the paradigm of public administration might not always align with the paradigm of individual rights, and that it can lead to authoritarian tendencies. The reason I elaborated on this topic is because it shows, regardless of any reliance on algorithmic systems, that the values of liberal democracy are fragile, especially when public authorities do not explicitly take them into consideration. At the same time, I pointed out the important role of discretion to counter-balance the rigidity of rules and procedures, as it allows public officials to contextualise laws of general applicability to particular cases in a way that preserves individualised justice, based on an appropriate trade-off of relevant interests. Moreover, the pitfalls of bureaucracy can also be countered by public authorities' 'internal morality' based on substantive values, as well as democratic oversight. Finally, I noted that public authorities' use of algorithmic systems is not a new development, though the systems' sophistication and their impact on the lives of individuals steadily increases over time. I also observed that the logic of algorithmic systems aligns rather well with the logic of bureaucracy, which, however, also foreshadowed that reliance thereon might reinforce the pitfalls of bureaucracy.

Having clarified the notion of algorithmic regulation, I then moved on to conceptualise, in Chapter 3, the rule of law. For this purpose, I started in Section 3.1 with a theoretical introduction to the concept, and I explained that it can be defined in various ways, from a list-based enumeration of the principles it entails, to a more succinct focus on the rule of law's overarching purpose and spirit, and particularly the role it plays in taming public power. I distinguished formal and substantive conceptions of the rule of law, linking these, respectively, to naturalistic and positivistic approaches to the law as such. Subsequently, I justified my reliance on a conception of the rule of law that combines both elements, given my focus on the role of the rule of law in liberal democracy, and its inherent entwinement with its values. Finally, I distinguished the rule *of* law from rule *by* law, describing the latter as a distortion of the former, whereby the law is merely used instrumentally as a tool of political power, regardless of the law's substantive aims and of the illiberal or authoritarian practices it might enable through the guise of legality.

As this book focuses on the EU legal order, in Section 3.2, I examined how the rule of law has been conceptualised in the EU, and explained that it heavily draws on the work of the Council of Europe, which lay the groundwork for a conception of the rule of law beyond the nation state. I observed that, in the EU legal order and the acquis of the Council of Europe alike, the rule of law encompasses both substantive and formal elements, which can be boiled down to six core principles, namely the principles of *legality*; *legal certainty*; *the prohibition of arbitrariness of the executive powers*; *equality before the law*; *effective judicial protection, with access to justice and review of government action by independent and impartial courts*; and *the separation of powers*.

These six principles constituted my starting point in Section 3.3, where I set out to concretise the requirements that the rule of law implies for public authorities of the executive branch of power more specifically. Drawing on legal sources that concretise these requirements, I developed a normative analytical framework that could subsequently enable me to assess how algorithmic regulation can impact the fulfilment of the rule of law's principles. For each of the six principles, I not only analysed the requirements they imply for public authorities, but I also examined the challenges associated therewith, observing that, just like the rule of law itself, these principles represent ideals that should be striven towards, yet can never be fully achieved due to the tensions they inherently bear. Essentially, striving to the rule of law's attainment can be likened to walking a tight rope, as a balance must continuously be found between stability and flexibility, precision and openness, rules and discretion. Undoing these tensions, for instance by opting for one of the two extremes instead of carrying out a balancing exercise, undoes the protective power of the law (leading either to rule *by* law or to arbitrary rule), since it is precisely by virtue of these tensions that the law can keep on fulfilling its role in an ever-changing environment marked by a plurality of often conflicting norms and interests.

In Chapter 4, I made a comprehensive assessment of how reliance on algorithmic regulation can undermine the rule of law's principles. For each of the six principles, I discussed in Section 4.1 some concrete examples that illustrate how public authorities' deployment of algorithmic systems can erode the law's protective power and enable illiberal and authoritarian practises, whether purposely or inadvertently. Even though the inherent pitfalls of bureaucracy discussed in Section 2.3 and the inherent tensions of the rule of law discussed in Section 3.3 already pose a challenge to public authorities' fulfilment of the rule of law's principles, my evaluation revealed that reliance on algorithmic regulation can significantly exacerbate those challenges. Importantly, I emphasised that my analysis does not allow me to conclude that *all* uses of algorithmic regulation are harmful for the rule of law and the values it protects per se, but it does support the conclusion that they *can* be harmful, and that this threat needs to be taken seriously, especially against the background of the EU's broader 'rule of law crisis'.

Since several risks were recurrent across the six principles, in Section 4.2 I consolidated the findings of my analysis and conceptualised the adverse impact of algorithmic regulation on the rule of law as *algorithmic rule by law*. I outlined five problematic characteristics of this threat, namely the fact that the law's application is being reduced to a techno-rational exercise (*primacy of techno-rationality*); that its translation from text to code is centralised and delegated to coders who shape the technology's affordance in a largely invisible way (*supremacy of coders*); that discretion at the level of public officials is near eliminated, which undermines their agency to counter the problem of law's over-generality and leaves them technically constrained to uncritically defer to the system's outcomes (*automation of legalism*); that accountability mechanisms for the validity and legality of the law's application are eroded (*deficit of accountability*); and, finally, that the technical infrastructure enabling algorithmic regulation introduces a significant vulnerability in the legal system which can lead to a systemic deficiency of the rule of law (*systemic vulnerability*).[1]

On that basis, and while acknowledging that legal solutions are a necessary but not a sufficient answer to these problems, I concluded that the legal framework needs to have adequate safeguards in place to counter the conceptualised threat. While a detailed account of how those safeguards should look like goes beyond the scope of this book, in Section 4.3 I nevertheless proposed that the legal framework should at least have meaningful and effective mechanisms that enable prior and continuous oversight and accountability over algorithmic regulation, also as regards the upstream choices; that it should enable mechanisms for public participation for questions around algorithmisation, with red lines to protect certain rights and values against a potential tyranny of the majority; that the enforcement mechanisms it offers should be both private and public, and both at national and EU level; that there should be strengthened constitutional checks and balances, including a role for public interest litigation; and that it should foster mechanisms for contestability, as well as the opportunity for internal critical reflection by the public officials who deploy the systems.

Keeping those broad safeguards in mind, in Chapter 5 I evaluated the adequacy of the current EU legal framework in countering the threat of algorithmic rule by law. After contextualising the EU's competences in this field in Section 5.1, in Section 5.2 I proceeded with an analysis of EU legislation that aims to protect the rule of (EU) law, by examining, respectively, the mechanism foreseen in Article 7 TEU, the Conditionality Regulation, and the judicial review enabled by Articles 258–260 TFEU and Article 267 TFEU. I concluded that, while these mechanisms (and especially the two latter) can contribute to the protection of the rule of law at Member State level, they are inadequate to effectively counter the risks associated with algorithmic regulation, which requires ex ante oversight. I also noted that EU rule of law monitoring mechanisms currently do not pay attention to the rule of law-risks associated with algorithmic regulation.

In Sections 5.3 and 5.4, I examined whether EU legislation that aims to protect individuals against the risks of algorithmic systems, whether in the context of automated personal data processing or reliance on 'AI' systems, offers better safeguards. I observed that the GDPR provides important protection mechanisms for individuals, yet concluded, along with the European Commission itself, that these are insufficient to protect them against the various risks of algorithmic systems. I subsequently assessed the AI Act and applauded its introduction of new requirements that must be implemented *before* a system's deployment. However, I concluded that the market-based and legalistic approach of this regulation left open significant legal gaps. It entirely ignores the particular risks posed by

[1] While my analysis focused on the use of algorithmic systems to inform and adopt administrative acts, these pathologies can also arise outside the context of the public sector, since they are to a large extent associated with the problems of automation more generally.

algorithmic regulation to the rule of law, and does not adequately deal with the threat of algorithmic rule by law. This is not only a missed opportunity given that the AI Act is meant to tackle the risks of algorithmic systems for years to come, but the Act also seemingly prevents Member States from introducing stronger protection mechanisms in view of the maximum harmonisation it aspires to achieve. More generally, I concluded that the legal domains pertaining to the rule of law and algorithmic systems, much like legal scholarship about these topics, are currently working in parallel rather than acknowledging the influence they have on each other, thereby overlooking their mutual risks.

In sum, the EU's *rule of law agenda* and its *digital agenda* – both a priority – are not merely misaligned, but they seem to be pursuing fundamentally antagonistic ends. This can have significant consequences both in the short and in the long term, as the Commission continues its promotion of Member States' uptake of algorithmic regulation under the false assumption that the risks associated therewith are comprehensively addressed by the new legal framework. Meanwhile, under the guise of the 'efficient implementation of the law', the EU is financing Member States' technical infrastructure for scaled algorithmic regulation in all public sector domains, and opens the door for the erosion of the very rule of law it seeks to protect. As I cautioned in the Introduction, at least two scenarios are thinkable. A Member State with intentions that are contrary to the values of liberal democracy might exploit this infrastructure to augment its power and scale its illiberal and authoritarian practices, while diminishing public scrutiny and accountability. Yet even a Member State with 'good' intentions might overlook the fact that the rule of law can be systemically undermined, along with the protective role it plays in liberal democracies, and that the infrastructure it puts in place can easily be abused by a next, less well-intentioned government.

In light of the above, it is crucial that a connection be made between the concerns around the ongoing erosion of the rule of law, and the concerns around the increased reliance on algorithmic regulation. In this book, I sought to establish a bridge between both by arguing that the former concerns can exacerbate the latter, which I conceptualised as the threat of algorithmic rule by law. It is my hope that this examination might foster further research in the intersection of these fields, as well as more attention from policymakers both at the European and national level for the issues at stake. The fact that reliance on algorithmic regulation keeps on increasing makes it essential that effective measures to counter the identified threat are adopted *with urgency*, ideally *before* the technology's adoption becomes even more widespread and its problematic implementation turns out to be irreversible.

6.2 RECOMMENDATIONS

Based on these findings, a number of general recommendations can now be made. First, policymakers and scholars need to take the threat of the algorithmic rule by law more seriously and acknowledge its risks since, without such awareness, no adequate counter-measures can be adopted (Section 6.2.1). Second, the current legal framework needs to be strengthened, which can be done in various ways (Section 6.2.2). Third, a number of neighbouring subjects are relevant for the identified threat and merit being the object of further research, which should hence be encouraged (Section 6.2.3). In what follows, I discuss each in turn.

6.2.1 *Acknowledging the Threat of Algorithmic Rule by Law*

A first recommendation that flows from this book concerns the need for EU institutions and Member States, as well as (legal) scholars focusing on these domains, to start interlinking the known rule of law problems with the known problems arising from algorithmic regulation. These two sets of problems, though being of mutual relevance, are currently insufficiently considered in combination. Yet by examining and addressing these problems in isolation, one fails to apprehend that they can reinforce each other and lead to an adverse impact that is greater than the mere sum of their risks.

The rule of law and the values of liberal democracy more generally are inherently fragile, and the European Commission's expanding rule of law initiatives over the past decade confirms its sensitivity for this fragility. However, the fact that the rule of law is not on the radar of the AI Act demonstrates that the EU may not be aware of the role that algorithmic regulation can play in its erosion, including in the erosion of the rule of *EU* law. After all, problematic translations from legal text to code might also have direct consequences for the law of the European Union, as such translations can occur in a way that erroneously or deliberately infringe or limit the rights that individuals derive from the EU legal order. Furthermore, the illustrations I provided in Section 4.1 are but a fraction of the many known uses of algorithmic regulation adopted by Member States where the rule of law's principles were breached – let alone the many unknown uses where this occurs. My analysis hence only revealed the tip of the iceberg, especially given the fact that many uses of algorithmic regulation by public authorities are simply not (yet) being communicated about.

Despite the higher level of transparency and accountability that one should expect when it comes to actions by public authorities, it is noteworthy that the AI Act to a large extent imposes a single set of obligations on AI providers from private and public organisations alike, seemingly downplaying the specific role of the rule of law in taming public power. It also overlooks the unique role that public authorities play in implementing and applying democratically adopted legislation, and that the application of laws to individuals *not* based on what they do, but based on what they *could* do – in light of predictions grounded in loose correlations with similar profiles – erodes the normative power of the law as such.[2] Since these

[2] This point is well made in Emre Bayamlıoğlu and Ronald Leenes, 'The "Rule of Law" Implications of Data-Driven Decision-Making: A Techno-Regulatory Perspective' (2018) 10 Law, Innovation and Technology 295. See also Mireille Hildebrandt, 'Algorithmic Regulation

concerns were not incorporated in the AI Act, it is unlikely that they will be dealt with at the EU level in the near future. Moreover, it is unlikely that Member States will individually be able to adopt stronger protection mechanisms in their national legal orders to anticipate and address these risks, given that the AI Act is meant to provide a ceiling rather than a floor of protection.

One particular difficulty that the EU might grapple with, and that also renders it more difficult for individuals to combat practices that adversely impact the rule of law, is that these practices typically occur under a veneer of legality. As discussed, the law itself is being used as a tool to erode the rule of law's protection of liberal democratic values. Furthermore, the adverse effects associated therewith tend to seep in incrementally and over the longer term, rather than instantaneously and easily discernibly. In contrast with, for instance, the harm caused by a massive oil leak, the harm caused by algorithmic rule by law is often not as tangible, visible, measurable or predictable,[3] which makes it more difficult to take decisive action. It is precisely the combination of the guise of legality and the incremental erosion of the rule of law that renders it so challenging to trigger a strong response. However, by acknowledging these risks and paying more attention to them in discussions on the rule of law and on algorithmic regulation alike, it is my hope that awareness on these issues will increase, and thereby also the possibility that stronger countermeasures will be adopted.

6.2.2 *Strengthening Legal Safeguards*

While this book does not seek to provide detailed recommendations as regards legal provisions that need to be amended or adopted to counter the threat of algorithmic rule by law, based on my analysis I can nevertheless mention some solutions that should be explored.

First of all, there are several ways in which EU legislation can be strengthened so as to provide better legal safeguards against the risks associated with algorithmic regulation. While the AI Act is now final, and it is too late to adapt its legalistic market-based approach, its provisions can still be interpreted in a way that maximises the protection it affords. This would be especially important as regards its transparency and accountability measures, where the need for more meaningful and effective mechanisms for public input and feedback should be considered, for instance as part of the mandatory fundamental rights impact assessments. This could help reveal risks that were overseen, and in some instances perhaps also lead to the

and the Rule of Law' (2018) 376 Philosophical Transactions of the Royal Society A: Mathematical, Physical and Engineering Sciences 20170355; Laurence Diver, 'Interpreting the Rule(s) of Code: Performance, Performativity, and Production' [2021] MIT Computational Law Report 2 <https://law.mit.edu/pub/interpretingtherulesofcode/release/1>.

[3] I also provided this example in Nathalie A Smuha, 'Beyond the Individual: Governing AI's Societal Harm' (2021) 10 Internet Policy Review 3, 10.

conclusion that it may be better not to use algorithmic regulation in a certain domain, or to do so differently. More generally, citizens should have more say in the process of algorithmisation, including the decisions to implement algorithmic regulation in the first place, while at the same time safeguarding the rights of minorities.

Second, beyond the AI Act, better use can be made of other legislation. Granted, as the analysis in Chapter 5 has shown, the current legal framework provides insufficient protection against the threat of algorithmic rule by law, especially considering the ex post nature of its mechanisms. This, however, does not mean that existing laws should be dismissed. When deployed strategically, ex post safeguards can still serve to mitigate potential harms. While they cannot always undo harm that already occurred, they can nevertheless contribute to the prevention of similar future harms. Both the GDPR and the LED, for instance, provide important safeguards to counter some of the risks associated with algorithmic systems, which can indirectly also counter their adverse impact on the rule of law's principles. At the same time, it is well known that EU privacy legislation is under-enforced, and that national data protection authorities often lack the necessary resources to properly carry out their tasks.[4] Their capacity should hence be expanded, especially given the high likelihood that their workload will considerably increase in the years to come in light of the omnipresence of algorithmic systems.

In addition to strengthening the enforcement of privacy legislation, mechanisms that serve to protect the rule of law can also be deployed more optimally. As already noted, the Commission has been criticised for not deploying the tools it already has in its rule of law toolbox. It can increase its recourse to infringement actions against Member States that adopt illiberal and authoritarian practices, whether they do so with or without algorithmic regulation. It should also be explored whether the Conditionality Regulation can be used to prevent Member States from implementing, especially with EU money, algorithmic regulation that adversely affects the rule of law's principles. Moreover, as part of its rule of law monitoring initiatives, the Commission can explicitly include attention to the risks raised by algorithmic regulation, which will in turn also force Member States to take these risks into consideration. Once the AI Act is applicable, despite its deficiencies, not only the Commission but also private individuals can challenge Member States' non-compliance with their obligations under the Act in court, and they should be encouraged to do so.

This brings me to a third recommendation, namely increasing people's literacy of the risks associated with algorithmic systems, and making them more aware of the fact that the outcomes of these systems are neither infallible nor incontestable. Improved education about the way in which algorithmic systems work is

4 See also European Digital Rights (EDRi), 'Civil Society Call and Recommendations for Concrete Solutions to GDPR Enforcement Shortcomings' (EDRi, 16 March 2022) <https://edri.org/wp-content/uploads/2022/03/EDRi-recommendations-for-better-GDPR-enforcement.pdf>.

indispensable to enable critical reflection on their use and output. Member States should hence not proceed with a wide-scale adoption of algorithmic regulation without priorly, or at the very least simultaneously, ensuring that public officials are trained to rely on them in a responsible manner and to ask critical questions about their functioning. It should, however, be noted that mere training and education is not enough to ensure public officials maintain their agency and sense of responsibility when deploying algorithmic systems. As already stressed, if the organisational environment in which the system is used excessively focuses on efficiency goals and KPIs, without facilitating the space, time and especially resources for reflection, procedural rationality will continue to be prioritised over substantive rationality. The protection of the rule of law, and of human rights and democracy more generally, hence needs to become part and parcel of the internal morality of public authorities, which can also imply that more resources need to be allocated for *human* decision-making to preserve the role of administrative discretion at the level of public officials.

Fourth, constitutional checks and balances need to be fortified. Legislators must become more familiar with the intricacies that accompany the implementation of algorithmic regulation and the translation choices this entails, and must take up their role of ensuring democratic oversight over its implementation and use. They, too, would hence benefit from better education about the opportunities and risks of algorithmic regulation, and particularly its impact on the rule of law. Similarly, judges that are tasked with carrying out judicial review of administrative acts that are informed or taken by algorithmic systems must have a better understanding of how these systems work, and be given the opportunity to review also the various upstream decisions that underlie the system's design, in order to tackle potential problems at the root. They should be able to conduct a systemic review rather than only focus their attention on the adverse impact on a single individual, given that the system's use can affect societal rather than mere individual interests. Simultaneously, it should be explored how individuals and civil society organisations can make use of strategic litigation in the public interest against the problematic deployment of algorithmic regulation, without the need to demonstrate individual harm to have standing.

Finally, it must also be acknowledged that legal safeguards to ensure accountability and oversight, even if strengthened, will always leave open the possibility that algorithmic regulation is inadvertently or deliberately used in a way that fosters illiberal and authoritarian practices. There are inherent limitations to what the law can do, and it would be a mistake to think that 'perfect' legislation exists or that it could solve the complex problems raised in this book. This means that reflection is also needed on whether, for some type of administrative acts, or in some public sector domains, the use of algorithmic regulation may need to be excluded altogether, given that it can exacerbate and scale the risks that are already inherent whenever public power is deployed.

6.2.3 *Promoting Further Research*

This book focused on the use of algorithmic regulation by national public authorities that are part of the executive branch of power. Given this scope limitation, there are several subjects that were not examined, even if they are relevant for the analysis of the impact of algorithmic systems on the rule of law. These subjects hence merit further examination in order to gain a deeper understanding of this impact, and their research should be promoted. In this section, I provide a brief description of some of those areas, which can also be read as a future research agenda.

A first area that requires further examination, concerns the deployment of algorithmic systems in the judiciary. While I noted that algorithmic systems are currently primarily used within the executive branch of power, there are also increasing uses of such systems to assist judges, for instance to make predictions about the risk of recidivism, or to peruse and compare past case law that can be of relevance for a judicial decision.[5] This raises important questions not only for the individuals that may be subjected to a biased or faulty algorithmic system, but also for the rule of law and particularly the principle of judicial independence and impartiality, a prerequisite for the judicial review of government action. It should also be noted that the introduction of such systems in the judiciary can be the result of a government decision to make the judicial system 'more efficient', with potential adverse effects on the principle of the separation of powers.[6] Considering that the independence of the judiciary is already being eroded in several EU Member States, it is important to conduct further research on the use of algorithmic systems in this domain, not only in terms of how individual interests can be affected, but also how it may affect the rule of law.

Second, closer attention should be paid to the potential adverse effects on the rule of law when the European Union itself relies on algorithmic systems.

[5] See, for instance, Julia Dressel and Hany Farid, 'The Accuracy, Fairness, and Limits of Predicting Recidivism' (2018) 4 Science Advances 1; Tania Sourdin, 'Judge v Robot? Artificial Intelligence and Judicial Decision-Making' (2018) 41 University of New South Wales Law Journal 1114; Carolyn McKay, 'Predicting Risk in Criminal Procedure: Actuarial Tools, Algorithms, AI and Judicial Decision-Making' (2020) 32 Current Issues in Criminal Justice 22; Jasper Ulenaers, 'The Impact of Artificial Intelligence on the Right to a Fair Trial: Towards a Robot Judge?' (2020) 11 Asian Journal of Law and Economics 1; Vilte Kristina Steponenaite and Peggy Valcke, 'Judicial Analytics on Trial: An Assessment of Legal Analytics in Judicial Systems in Light of the Right to a Fair Trial' (2020) 27 Maastricht Journal of European and Comparative Law 759.

[6] Consider in this regard the example Polish Ministry of Justice's introduction of the Random Allocation of Cases (RAC) System in the Polish judiciary as discussed in Bartosz Wilk, 'Mysterious Random Judge Allocation Algorithm' (*Sieć Obywatelska Watchdog*, 29 January 2019) <https://siecobywatelska.pl/mysterious-random-judge-allocation-algorithm/?lang=en>; Joanna Mazur, 'Automated Decision-Making Systems as a Challenge for Effective Legal Protection in European Union Law' (2021) 46 European Law Review 194; Fundacja Moje Państwo, 'Algorithm of the System of Random Allocation of Cases Finally Disclosed!' (22 September 2021) <https://mojepanstwo.pl/aktualnosci/773>.

As noted,[7] the Union, too, is subjected to the rule of law and must comply with its principles. In line with the general trend, EU institutions, bodies and agencies are increasingly adopting algorithmic systems to facilitate their tasks and enhance the efficiency of their decision-making processes.[8] Consider, for instance, the European Travel Information and Authorisation System (ETIAS).[9] This system is aimed at automating risk assessments regarding non-EU citizens who wish to enter the EU, and to make recommendations as to whether they should be allowed to enter.[10] According to Frontex' website, ETIAS will "*carry out pre-travel screening of travellers who enjoy from visa-free access to the Schengen Area, and thus allow Member States to deny authorisation to travellers considered to pose a security threat, a risk in terms of irregular migration or public health*".[11] Accordingly, the use of algorithmic regulation not only poses risks at the *national* level, but also at the *EU* level, and its impact on the EU rule of law should be further examined – ideally *before* its widespread adoption.

Third, while my investigation only focused on the robustness of the EU legal order, I noted that legislation at national level can also offer solace against the risk of algorithmic rule by law. In most Member States, provisions of constitutional and administrative law could, even if general in nature, potentially be applied to the use of algorithmic regulation, and be interpreted in a manner that provides stronger legal safeguards against the identified risks. A thorough examination of how individual Member States are currently dealing with those risks might not only reveal further gaps in protection, but could also lead to the identification of best practices that can be adopted by other jurisdictions.

A final area that merits closer attention is one that I mentioned only sporadically in this book, namely the reliance of public authorities on private companies to design and develop algorithmic systems. The focus of my analysis lay on how the dependency on such systems can increase the executive's power. However, when the executive outsources the upstream design and translation choices of algorithmic systems to a private company, or is otherwise dependent on a private company for its data or technical infrastructure, this can also significantly increase the power of that private company, as the latter can shape how public power is exercised by shaping the technology's affordances.[12] The Algorithmic Leviathan – mighty as it may be –

7 See *supra*, Section 3.2.3.

8 Note that the AI Act also applies to AI systems used by EU entities.

9 See also Regulation 2018/1240 of the European Parliament and of the Council of 12 September 2018 establishing a European Travel Information and Authorisation System (ETIAS) and amending Regulations no. 1077/2011, no. 515/2014, no. 2016/399, no. 2016/1624 and no. 2017/2226 2018.

10 Pedro Rubim Borges Fortes, Pablo Marcello Baquero and David Restrepo Amariles, 'Artificial Intelligence Risks and Algorithmic Regulation' [2022] European Journal of Risk Regulation 1, 2.

11 Frontex, 'ETIAS' (2024) <www.frontex.europa.eu/what-we-do/etias/about-etias/>. At the moment of this book's finalisation, the system is not yet operational, though its launch is expected for mid-2025.

12 See also Linnet Taylor, 'Public Actors without Public Values: Legitimacy, Domination and the Regulation of the Technology Sector' (2021) 34 Philosophy & Technology 897.

might hence in turn be dependent on an even mightier private company, which likewise raises important rule of law-concerns that require further scrutiny.

6.3 EMBRACING NORMATIVE COMPLEXITY

Let me conclude this book by taking a step back, and sharing a few broader reflections. Essentially, my analysis exposed that reliance on algorithmic regulation can disguise or obliterate the normative tensions that are inherent to the very concept of the rule of law and its principles, and thereby undermine the protective power of the law.[13] It might lead to an automated form of legalism – or the uncritical adherence to and execution of rules – by skewing the balance in favour of rules instead of discretion, resulting in their divorce rather than their marriage.

However, when examining the EU legal framework's aptness to counter the identified risks, I also recalled that a legalistic approach can arise in contexts outside algorithmic regulation, given the techno-rational features that underlie the AI Act. Its list-based methodology, along with its aspiration to reduce the protection of human rights (and the intricate trade-offs of interests this entails) to technical standards, may likewise result in a legalistic solution which fails to do justice to the complexity of the problem. Accordingly, on a meta level, even the rules that are supposed to counter the risks associated with algorithmic rule by law might show the same deficiency, whereby protecting human rights, democracy and the rule of law can turn into a technical checklist rather than being seen as a normative endeavour.[14]

Consequently, and rather ironically, one can observe the same deficiency both in the identified problem and in its proposed solutions. This deficiency comes down to the apparent need to eliminate normative tensions by settling down on a set of technical rules, whether algorithmically codified or part of a legalistic text, which allow us to forget about the complex normative questions that underlay those rules, and to just focus on their execution instead. In a way, this is not surprising. It is, after all, much easier to execute a set of pre-determined rules, than to be constantly faced with (the responsibility to make) difficult normative trade-offs, which requires confronting different interests, understanding various points of view and trying to balance them out on a continuous basis. However, that is precisely what the rule of law, along with its intrinsic tensions, is about, and what enables it to fulfil its protective role in a heterogenous society with inevitably conflicting norms.

[13] See *supra*, Sections 3.4 and 4.2 in particular.

[14] In the same vein, scholars have also remarked that, when public authorities are spurred to implement ethical guidelines when they develop and deploy algorithmic systems, there is a "*dangerous tendency where ethical deliberation is sometimes seen as an obnoxious bureaucratic box ticking exercise, instead of being considered as a vital part of the design and build-up of a data project*". See Lotje Siffels and others, 'Public Values and Technological Change: Mapping How Municipalities Grapple with Data Ethics' in Andreas Hepp, Juliane Jarke and Leif Kramp (eds), *New Perspectives in Critical Data Studies: The Ambivalences of Data Power* (Springer International Publishing 2022).

As discussed in Chapter 3, the rule of law requires a balance between stability and flexibility, vagueness and precision, generality and particularity, rules and discretion. This also means that the law will never be *perfectly* predictable, but that the navigation of these tensions can nevertheless allow it to provide *reasonable* predictability.

However, as the analysis of this book has shown, we are at risk precisely because we no longer seem to find a way to deal with these normative tensions, and instead prefer to search for an optimal solution that can be codified into an algorithmic system, and subsequently scaled with the click of a button. Algorithmic regulation promises simplicity, and a route to avoid the complex tensions of legal rules which are continuously open to multiple interpretations. Crucially, this same promise is also what is threatening the very foundations of liberal democracy today, as illiberal and authoritarian tendencies – along with populism – embody the very elimination of plurality in favour of simplicity. Autocratic leaders are hence exploiting this very feature of the law and, through a rule *by* law approach, seek to put forward *their* interpretation above others. And algorithmic regulation provides them with a tool to systematise and scale that interpretation, in the name of efficiency.

In sum, the threat encountered at the level of the rule of law, of which algorithmic regulation in public administration is an illustration, is the same one that threatens the very preservation of liberal democracy as a political system, namely the elimination of conflicting normative tensions in favour of essentialising a single view. Accordingly, the most important antidote to this threat is to (re)learn to embrace not only the normative tensions that are inherent to the law, but also the tensions that are inherent in a democratic society, which is marked by a plurality of views rather than by a single ideology. As long as we believe that there are multiple ways of living a 'good life' and that no one political view should oppress all others, the law's interpretation should not be essentialised and systematised. Any attempts to do so would undermine not only the rule of law, but also liberal democracy.

Yet if the law's normative tensions are to be maintained, along with the intricate balancing exercise this entails, it is even more important that this exercise is not simply outsourced to a handful of coders. Regardless of any future political developments, algorithmic regulation will inevitably play an ever bigger role in our society. It is therefore our collective responsibility to ensure that its adoption involves public participation, transparency, oversight and democratic accountability, and that it occurs in line with the trinity of human rights, democracy and the rule of law.

Bibliography

Aarvik P, 'Artificial Intelligence – A Promising Anti-Corruption Tool in Development Settings?' (Chr Michelsen Institute 2019)

Abdurahman JK, 'Birthing Predictions of Premature Death' (2022) 17 *Logic Magazine* <https://logicmag.io/home/birthing-predictions-of-premature-death/>

Ackerman B, 'The New Separation of Powers' (2000) 113 Harvard Law Review 633

Ada Lovelace Institute, AI Now Institute, and Open Government Partnership, 'Algorithmic Accountability for the Public Sector' (2021) <www.opengovpartnership.org/documents/algorithmic-accountability-public-sector/>

Adams-Prassl J, 'Regulating Algorithms at Work: Lessons for a "European Approach to Artificial Intelligence"' (2022) 13 European Labour Law Journal 30

Ala-Pietilä P and Smuha NA, 'A Framework for Global Cooperation on Artificial Intelligence and Its Governance' in Bertrand Braunschweig and Malik Ghallab (eds), *Reflections on Artificial Intelligence for Humanity* (Springer International Publishing 2021)

Alemanno A and Chamon M, 'To Save the Rule of Law You Must Apparently Break It' (*Verfassungsblog*, 11 December 2020) <https://verfassungsblog.de/to-save-the-rule-of-law-you-must-apparently-break-it/>

Alexander L, 'Scalar Properties, Binary Judgments' (2008) 25 Journal of Applied Philosophy 85

AlgorithmWatch, 'European Council and Commission in Agreement to Narrow the Scope of the AI Act' (*AlgorithmWatch*, 23 November 2021) <https://algorithmwatch.org/en/eu-narrow-scope-of-ai-act/>

'Automating Society Report 2020' (2020) <https://automatingsociety.algorithmwatch.org/wp-content/uploads/2020/12/Automating-Society-Report-2020.pdf>

'AlgorithmWatch Signs Statement on Ban of Predictive Policing in the Artificial Intelligence Act' (*AlgorithmWatch*, 1 March 2022) <https://algorithmwatch.org/en/ban-predictive-policing-aia/>

Allal-Chérif O, Simón-Moya V and Ballester ACC, 'Intelligent Purchasing: How Artificial Intelligence Can Redefine the Purchasing Function' (2021) 124 Journal of Business Research 69

Allas T, Dillon R and Gupta V, 'A Smarter Approach to Cost Reduction in the Public Sector' (McKinsey 8 June 2018) <www.mckinsey.com/industries/public-and-social-sector/our-insights/a-smarter-approach-to-cost-reduction-in-the-public-sector>

Allhutter D and others, 'Algorithmic Profiling of Job Seekers in Austria: How Austerity Politics Are Made Effective' (2020) 3 Frontiers in Big Data 1

Ananny M and Crawford K, 'Seeing without Knowing: Limitations of the Transparency Ideal and Its Application to Algorithmic Accountability' (2018) 20 New Media & Society 973

Anckaert L, 'Ethics of Responsibility and Ambiguity of Politics in Levinas's Philosophy' (2020) 97 Problemos 61

'Goodness without Witnesses: Vasily Grossman and Emmanuel Levinas' in Michael Fagenblat and Arthur Cools (eds), *Levinas and Literature* (De Gruyter 2020)

Andersen NA, 'The Technocratic Rationality of Governance – The Case of the Danish Employment Services' (2021) 15 Critical Policy Studies 425

Appel SM and Coglianese C, 'Algorithmic Governance and Administrative Law' in Woodrow Barfield (ed), *The Cambridge Handbook of the Law of Algorithms* (Cambridge University Press 2020)

Araujo T and others, 'In AI We Trust? Perceptions about Automated Decision-Making by Artificial Intelligence' (2020) 35 AI & Society 611

Arendt H, *The Human Condition* (University of Chicago Press (2019) 1958)

Eichmann in Jerusalem: A Report on the Banality of Evil (Viking Press 1963)

On Violence (Harcourt Brace and Company 1970)

Lectures on Kant's Political Philosophy (University of Chicago Press 1982)

Aristotle, *Nicomachean Ethics* (Terence Irwin tr, Hackett 1999)

Politics (Benjamin Jowett tr, Batoche Books 1999)

Aronson JD, 'The Utility of User-Generated Content in Human Rights Investigations' in Molly K Land and Jay D Aronson (eds), *New Technologies for Human Rights Law and Practice* (Cambridge University Press 2018)

Autoriteit Persoonsgegevens, 'Onderzoeksrapport Belastingdienst/Toeslagen: De verwerking van de nationaliteit van aanvragers van kinderopvangtoeslag' (2020) z2018–22445 <https://open.overheid.nl/documenten/ronl-71b93874-d34e-488a-9caf-9c455dec34a0/pdf>

'Tax Administration Fined for Discriminatory and Unlawful Data Processing' (8 December 2022) <https://autoriteitpersoonsgegevens.nl/en/news/tax-administration-fined-discriminatory-and-unlawful-data-processing>

Azoulai L and de Vries K, *EU Migration Law: Legal Complexities and Political Rationales* (Oxford University Press 2014)

Baehr P, 'The "Iron Cage" and the "Shell as Hard as Steel": Parsons, Weber, and the Stahlhartes Gehäuse Metaphor in the Protestant Ethic and the Spirit of Capitalism' (2001) 40 History and Theory 153

Bakó B, 'Hungary's Latest Experiences with Article 2 TEU: The Need for "Informed" EU Sanctions' in Armin von Bogdandy and others (eds), *Defending Checks and Balances in EU Member States*, vol 298 (Springer Berlin Heidelberg 2021)

Balaguer M, *Free Will* (MIT Press 2014)

Ball WWR, *A Short Account of the History of Mathematics* (4th edn, Dover Publications 1908)

Bankowski Z and Schafer B, 'Double-Click Justice: Legalism in the Computer Age' (2007) 1 Legisprudence 31

Banks G, 'Evidence-Based Policy Making: What Is It? How Do We Get It?' (2009) SSRN ANU Public Lecture Series, Productivity Commission <https://papers.ssrn.com/abstract=1616460>

Baraggia A and Bonelli M, 'Linking Money to Values: The New Rule of Law Conditionality Regulation and Its Constitutional Challenges' (2022) 23 German Law Journal 131

Bárd P and others, 'An EU Mechanism on Democracy, the Rule of Law and Fundamental Rights' (2016) CEPS Paper in Liberty and Security in Europe 247

Barfield W and Barfield J, 'An Introduction to Law and Algorithms' in Woodrow Barfield (ed), *The Cambridge Handbook of the Law of Algorithms* (Cambridge University Press 2020)

Barnard C, *The Substantive Law of the EU: The Four Freedoms* (6th edn, Oxford University Press 2019)
Barreno M and others, 'Can Machine Learning Be Secure?' in *Proceedings of the 2006 ACM Symposium on Information, Computer and Communications Security* (ACM 2006)
Barrett LF and others, 'Emotional Expressions Reconsidered: Challenges to Inferring Emotion from Human Facial Movements' (2019) 20 Psychological Science in the Public Interest 1
Barrett R and others, 'The Netherlands: Opinion on the Legal Protection of Citizens' (Venice Commission 2021) Opinion no. 1031/2021 CDL-AD(2021)031
Barroso JMD, 'State of the Union 2012 – Address Plenary Session of the European Parliament' (European Commission 12 September 2012) <https://ec.europa.eu/commission/presscorner/detail/en/SPEECH_12_596>
'Bart Somers vernietigt systeem trajectcontrole Bonheiden' *De Standaard* (14 January 2022) <www.standaard.be/cnt/dmf20220114_94712942>.
Barth TJ and Arnold E, 'Artificial Intelligence and Administrative Discretion: Implications for Public Administration' (1999) 29 The American Review of Public Administration 332
Bathaee Y, 'The Artificial Intelligence Black Box and the Failure of Intent and Causation' (2018) 31 Harvard Journal of Law & Technology 890
Bauman Z, *Modernity and the Holocaust* (Polity Press 1989)
Bavarian Broadcasting, 'Objective or Biased' (*BR*, 2021) <https://interaktiv.br.de/ki-bewerbung/en/>.
Baweja S and Singh S, 'Beginning of Artificial Intelligence, End of Human Rights' (*LSE Human Rights*, 16 July 2020) <https://blogs.lse.ac.uk/humanrights/2020/07/16/beginning-of-artificial-intelligence-end-of-human-rights/>.
Baxter G and Sommerville I, 'Socio-Technical Systems: From Design Methods to Systems Engineering' (2011) 23 Interacting with Computers 4
Bayamlıoğlu E, 'Contesting Automated Decisions: A View of Transparency Implications' (2018) 4 European Data Protection Law Review 433
Bayamlıoğlu E and Leenes R, 'The "Rule of Law" Implications of Data-Driven Decision-Making: A Techno-Regulatory Perspective' (2018) 10 Law, Innovation and Technology 295
Beadle R and Moore G, 'MacIntyre on Virtue and Organization' (2006) 27 Organization Studies 323
Beauchamp Z, 'Call It Authoritarianism' (*Vox*, 15 June 2021) <www.vox.com/policy-and-politics/2021/6/15/22522504/republicans-authoritarianism-trump-competitive>
Bedingfield W, 'Everything That Went Wrong with the Botched A-Levels Algorithm' (Wired UK, 2020) <www.wired.co.uk/article/alevel-exam-algorithm>
Begby E, 'The Epistemology of Prejudice' (2013) 2 Thought: A Journal of Philosophy 90
van Bekkum M and Borgesius FZ, 'Digital Welfare Fraud Detection and the Dutch SyRI Judgment' (2021) 23 European Journal of Social Security 323
Belga, 'Duur cameraschild langs snelwegen werkt amper: tot 80 procent vals alarm' *De Morgen* (2 February 2022) <www.demorgen.be/gs-b84b968d>
'Belastingzondaars kunnen voortaan van de weg geplukt worden' *De Morgen* (19 August 2022) <www.demorgen.be/gs-b56328c5>
Belgian Data Protection Authority, 'A New Draft Law Threatens the Independence and Functioning of the BE DPA' (March 2022) <www.dataprotectionauthority.be/citizen/a-new-draft-law-threatens-the-independence-and-functioning-of-the-be-dpa>
'Opinion on Preliminary Draft Law Amending the Act of 3 December 2017 Establishing the Data Protection Authority (AH-2022-0020)' (February 2022) <www.autoriteprotectiondonnees.be/publications/opinion-on-preliminary-draft-law-amending-the-act-of-3-december-2017-establishing-the-data-protection-authority.pdf>

Bellamy R (ed), *The Rule of Law and the Separation of Powers* (Ashgate/Dartmouth 2005)
Bellman R, *Dynamic Programming* (Princeton University Press 1957)
Benbouzid B, Meneceur Y and Smuha NA, 'Quatre nuances de régulation de l'intelligence artificielle: Une cartographie des conflits de définition' (2022) 232–33 Réseaux 29
Bengio Y, Courville A and Goodfellow I, *Deep Learning* (MIT Press 2016)
Ben-Shahar O, 'Data Pollution' (2019), 11 Journal of Legal Analysis 104–59
Ben-Shahar O and Porat A, *Personalized Law: Different Rules for Different People* (Oxford University Press 2021)
Benzécri J-P, *L'analyse des données. 2: L'analyse des correspondances* (Dunod 1973)
Berlin I, *The Crooked Timber of Humanity: Chapters in the History of Ideas* (Henry Hardy ed, Fontana 1991)
Liberty: Incorporating Four Essays on Liberty (Oxford University Press 2002)
Bernstein A and Rodriguez C, 'The Accountable Bureaucrat' (2023) 132 Yale Law Journal 6, 1600–90
Bersier Ladavac N, Bezemek C and Schauer F (eds), *The Normative Force of the Factual: Legal Philosophy Between Is and Ought*, vol 130 (Springer International Publishing 2019)
Bertuzzi L, 'AI Standards Set for Joint Drafting among European Standardisation Bodies' *Euractiv* (30 May 2022) <www.euractiv.com/section/digital/news/ai-standards-set-for-joint-drafting-among-european-standardisation-bodies/>
'AI Regulation Filled with Thousands of Amendments in the European Parliament' *Euractiv* (2 June 2022) <www.euractiv.com/section/digital/news/ai-regulation-filled-with-thousands-of-amendments-in-the-european-parliament/>
'Artificial Intelligence Definition, Governance on MEPs' Menu' *Euractiv* (8 November 2022) <www.euractiv.com/section/digital/news/artificial-intelligence-definition-governance-on-meps-menu/>
'AI Act: EU Parliament's Legal Office Gives Damning Opinion on High-Risk Classification "Filters"' *Euractiv* (19 October 2023) <www.euractiv.com/section/artificial-intelligence/news/ai-act-eu-parliaments-legal-office-gives-damning-opinion-on-high-risk-classification-filters/>
'Beware Spurious Correlations' (2015) *Harvard Business Review* <https://hbr.org/2015/06/beware-spurious-correlations>
Bignami F, 'From Expert Administration to Accountability Network: A New Paradigm for Comparative Administrative Law' (2011) 59 American Journal of Comparative Law 859
Bingham T, *The Rule of Law* (Penguin Books 2011)
Binns R, 'Human Judgment in Algorithmic Loops: Individual Justice and Automated Decision-Making' (2022) 16 Regulation & Governance 197
Bjørnsten TB and Zacher Sørensen M-M, 'Uncertainties of Facial Emotion Recognition Technologies and the Automation of Emotional Labour' (2017) 28 Digital Creativity 297
Black J, *Rules and Regulators* (Clarendon 1997)
'Learning from Regulatory Disasters' (2014) 24 LSE Law, Society and Economy Working Papers <http://eprints.lse.ac.uk/60569/1/WPS2014–24_Black.pdf>
Black M, 'The Gap Between "Is" and "Should"' (1964) 73 The Philosophical Review 165
Bloomfield BP and Vurdubakis T, 'IBM's Chess Players: On AI and Its Supplements' (2008) 24 The Information Society 69
Boden MA, 'The Social Impact of Artificial Intelligence' in Ray Kurzweil (ed), *The Age of Intelligent Machines* (Cambridge University Press 1990)
von Bogdandy A and Ioannidis M, 'Systemic Deficiency in the Rule of Law: What It Is, What Has Been Done, What Can Be Done' (2014) 51 Common Market Law Review 59

Bojarski Ł, 'Civil Society Organizations for and with the Courts and Judges – Struggle for the Rule of Law and Judicial Independence: The Case of Poland 1976–2020' (2021) 22 German Law Journal 1344

Bonelli M, 'Effective Judicial Protection in EU Law: An Evolving Principle of a Constitutional Nature' (2019) 12 Review of European Administrative Law 35

Bonelli M and Claes M, 'Crossing the Rubicon? The Commission's Use of Article 2 TEU in the Infringement Action on LGBTIQ+ Rights in Hungary' (2022) 30 Maastricht Journal of European and Comparative Law 3

Borry EL and Reuter TK, 'Humanizing Bureaucracy: Applying the Human Rights-Based Approach to Weber's Bureaucracy' (2022) 5 Perspectives on Public Management and Governance 164

Bottou L, 'From Machine Learning to Machine Reasoning' (2014) 94 Machine Learning 133

Bovens M and Zouridis S, 'From Street-Level to System-Level Bureaucracies: How Information and Communication Technology Is Transforming Administrative Discretion and Constitutional Control' (2002) 62 Public Administration Review 174

Bowker GC and Star SL, 'Building Information Infrastructures for Social Worlds – The Role of Classifications and Standards' in Toru Ishida (ed), *Community Computing and Support Systems: Social Interaction in Networked Communities* (Springer 1998)

Box GEP, 'Science and Statistics' (1976) 71 Journal of the American Statistical Association 791

Bozeman B, *Public Values and Public Interest: Counterbalancing Economic Individualism* (Georgetown University Press 2007)

Brachman RJ and Levesque HJ, *Knowledge Representation and Reasoning* (Elsevier 2004)

Bradford A, *The Brussels Effect: How the European Union Rules the World* (Oxford University Press 2020)

Digital Empires: The Global Battle to Regulate Technology (Oxford University Press 2023)

Brkan M, 'Artificial Intelligence and Democracy' (2019) 2 Delphi – Interdisciplinary Review of Emerging Technologies 66

'Do Algorithms Rule the World? Algorithmic Decision-Making and Data Protection in the Framework of the GDPR and Beyond' (2019) 27 International Journal of Law and Information Technology 91

Broberg M, 'Preliminary References as a Means for Enforcing EU Law' in András Jakab and Dimitry Kochenov (eds), *The Enforcement of EU Law and Values: Ensuring Member States' Compliance*, vol 1 (Oxford University Press 2017)

Broomfield H and Reutter L, 'In Search of the Citizen in the Datafication of Public Administration' (2022) 9 Big Data & Society 1

Brownsword R, 'Technological Management and the Rule of Law' (2016) 8 Law, Innovation and Technology 100

'Brussels Closes Case against Germany in EU Law Supremacy Dispute' (*POLITICO*, 2 December 2021) <www.politico.eu/article/brussels-closes-case-against-germany-in-eu-law-supremacy-dispute/>

Brussels Privacy Hub, 'More than 150 University Professors from All Over Europe and Beyond Are Calling on the European Institutions to Include a Fundamental Rights Impact Assessment in the Future Regulation on Artificial Intelligence' (12 September 2023) <https://brusselsprivacyhub.com/2023/09/12/brussels-privacy-hub-and-other-academic-institutions-ask-to-approve-a-fundamental-rights-impact-assessment-in-the-eu-artificial-intelligence-act/>

Bryson JJ, 'Belgian and Flemish Policy Makers' Guide to AI Regulation', KCDS-CiTiP Fellow Lectures Series: Towards an AI Regulator? (11 October 2022) <https://data-en-maatschappij.ai/en/publications/paper-belgian-and-flemish-policy-makers-guide-to-ai-regulation>

Buchanan C, 'Long Awaited Guidance on the Meaning of "Regulatory Act" for Locus Standi under the Lisbon Treaty' (2012) 3 European Journal of Risk Regulation 115

Buchholtz G, 'Artificial Intelligence and Legal Tech: Challenges to the Rule of Law' in Thomas Wischmeyer and Timo Rademacher (eds), *Regulating Artificial Intelligence* (Springer International Publishing 2020)

Bugarič B, 'The Rise of Nationalist-Authoritarian Populism and the Crisis of Liberal Democracy in Central and Eastern Europe' in Uladzislau Belavusau and Aleksandra Gliszczynska-Grabias (eds), *Constitutionalism under Stress* (Oxford University Press 2020)

Buijsman S and Veluwenkamp H, 'Spotting When Algorithms Are Wrong' (2023) 33 Minds and Machines 541

Bullock JB, 'Artificial Intelligence, Discretion, and Bureaucracy' (2019) 49 The American Review of Public Administration 751

Buolamwini J and Gebru T, 'Gender Shades: Intersectional Accuracy Disparities in Commercial Gender Classification', *Proceedings of Machine Learning Research* (2018) <http://proceedings.mlr.press/v81/buolamwini18a/buolamwini18a.pdf>

Burchardt D, 'Backlash against the Court of Justice of the EU? The Recent Jurisprudence of the German Constitutional Court on EU Fundamental Rights as a Standard of Review' (2020) 21 German Law Journal 1

Burgess M, 'UK Police Are Using AI to Inform Custodial Decisions – But It Could Be Discriminating against the Poor' (*Wired UK*, 1 March 2018) <www.wired.co.uk/article/police-ai-uk-durham-hart-checkpoint-algorithm-edit>

Burrell J, 'How the Machine "Thinks": Understanding Opacity in Machine Learning Algorithms' (2016) 3 Big Data & Society 1

Burrell J and Fourcade M, 'The Society of Algorithms' (2021) 47 Annual Review of Sociology 213

Buschor E, 'Performance Management in the Public Sector: Past, Current and Future Trends' (2013) 11 Tékhne 4

Calders T and Žliobaitė I, 'Why Unbiased Computational Processes Can Lead to Discriminative Decision Procedures' in Bart Custers and others (eds), *Discrimination and Privacy in the Information Society*, vol 3 (Springer Berlin Heidelberg 2013)

Calo R and Citron DK, 'The Automated Administrative State: A Crisis of Legitimacy' (2021) 70 Emory Law Journal 797

van Calster G and Reins L, *EU Environmental Law* (Edward Elgar Publishing 2017)

Canevaro M, 'The Rule of Law as the Measure of Political Legitimacy in the Greek City States' (2017) 9 Hague Journal on the Rule of Law 211

Carrera S and Mitsilegas V, 'Upholding the Rule of Law by Scrutinising Judicial Independence' (CEPS 2018)

Casey AJ and Niblett A, 'A Framework for the New Personalization of Law' (2019) 86 The University of Chicago Law Review 333

Chauhan A, 'Towards the Systemic Review of Automated Decision-Making Systems' (2021) 25 Judicial Review 285

Cheng H-F and others, 'How Child Welfare Workers Reduce Racial Disparities in Algorithmic Decisions', *CHI Conference on Human Factors in Computing Systems* (ACM 2022) <https://dl.acm.org/doi/10.1145/3491102.3501831>

Chin C and Robison M, 'How AI Bots and Voice Assistants Reinforce Gender Bias' (*Brookings*, 23 November 2020) <www.brookings.edu/research/how-ai-bots-and-voice-assistants-reinforce-gender-bias/>

Choi SJ and others, 'AI and Text-Mining Applications for Analyzing Contractor's Risk in Invitation to Bid (ITB) and Contracts for Engineering Procurement and Construction (EPC) Projects' (2021) 14 Energies 4632

Christakis T, 'French Council of State Discovers the "Philosopher's Stone" of Data Retention' (*about:intel*, 23 April 2021) <https://aboutintel.eu/france-council-of-state-ruling/>

Christensen J and others, 'Human Capital and Administrative Burden: The Role of Cognitive Resources in Citizen-State Interactions' (2020) 80 Public Administration Review 127

Clark M, 'Bad Software Sent Postal Workers to Jail, Because No One Wanted to Admit It Could Be Wrong' (*The Verge*, 23 April 2021) <www.theverge.com/2021/4/23/22399721/uk-post-office-software-bug-criminal-convictions-overturned>

Clarke R, 'Big Data, Big Risks' (2016) 26 Information Systems Journal 77

Cleppe P, 'An Overview of National Top Courts Challenging the Supremacy of EU Law, Brussels Report' (*Brussels Report*, 12 October 2021) <www.brusselsreport.eu/2021/10/12/an-overview-of-national-top-courts-challenging-the-supremacy-of-eu-law/>

Clifford C, 'Google CEO: A.I. Is More Important than Fire or Electricity' *CNBC* (1 February 2018) <www.cnbc.com/2018/02/01/google-ceo-sundar-pichai-ai-is-more-important-than-fire-electricity.html>

Cobbe J, Lee MSA and Singh J, 'Reviewable Automated Decision-Making: A Framework for Accountable Algorithmic Systems', *Proceedings of the 2021 ACM Conference on Fairness, Accountability, and Transparency* (Association for Computing Machinery 2021).

Cobbe J, Veale M and Singh J, 'Understanding Accountability in Algorithmic Supply Chains' (2023), *Proceedings of the 2023 ACM Conference on Fairness, Accountability, and Transparency*, 1186–97.

Cochran CE, 'Political Science and "The Public Interest"' (1974) 36 The Journal of Politics 327

Cochrane G, *Max Weber's Vision for Bureaucracy: A Casualty of World War I* (Springer International Publishing 2018)

Cohen JE, 'Affording Fundamental Rights: A Provocation Inspired by Mireille Hildebrandt' (2017) 4 Critical Analysis of Law 76

Between Truth and Power: The Legal Constructions of Informational Capitalism (Oxford University Press 2019)

'Turning Privacy Inside Out' (2019) 20 Theoretical Inquiries in Law 1

Čolaković A and Hadžialić M, 'Internet of Things (IoT): A Review of Enabling Technologies, Challenges, and Open Research Issues' (2018) 144 Computer Networks 17

Cole D, 'The Chinese Room Argument' in Edward N Zalta (ed), *The Stanford Encyclopedia of Philosophy* (Winter 2020, Metaphysics Research Lab, Stanford University 2020) <https://plato.stanford.edu/archives/win2020/entries/chinese-room/>

Comité permanent de controle des services de police, 'Le fonctionnement de la police intégrée en matière de traitement des hits ANPR de plaques d'immatriculation volées' (2022)

Conaghan J, 'Law, Harm and Redress: A Feminist Perspective' (2002) 22 Legal Studies 319

Cooman JD, 'Humpty Dumpty and High-Risk AI Systems: The Ratione Materiae Dimension of the Proposal for an EU Artificial Intelligence Act' (2022) 6 Market and Competition Law Review 49

Cordella A and Willcocks L, 'Outsourcing, Bureaucracy and Public Value: Reappraising the Notion of the "Contract State"' (2010) 27 Government Information Quarterly 82

Cormen TH and others, *Introduction to Algorithms* (3rd edn, MIT Press 2009)

Corrales J, 'The Authoritarian Resurgence: Autocratic Legalism in Venezuela' (2015) 26 Journal of Democracy 37

Corrias L, 'National Identity and European Integration: The Unbearable Lightness of Legal Tradition' (2016) 1 European Papers – A Journal on Law and Integration 383

Court of Justice of the European Union, 'Annual Report 2022 – The Year in Review' (CJEU, 2023) <https://curia.europa.eu/jcms/upload/docs/application/pdf/2023-04/qd-aq-23-001-en-n.pdf>

Craig P, 'Formal and Substantive Conceptions of the Rule of Law: An Analytical Framework' (1997) 3 Public Law 467

'Legality: Six Views of the Cathedral' in Peter Cane and others (eds), *The Oxford Handbook of Comparative Administrative Law* (Oxford University Press 2020)

Crawford K, *Atlas of AI* (Yale University Press 2021)

Crawford K and Joler V, 'Anatomy of an AI System: The Amazon Echo as an Anatomical Map of Human Labor, Data and Planetary Resources' (*Anatomy of an AI System*, 2018) <www.anatomyof.ai>

Creel K and Hellman D, 'The Algorithmic Leviathan: Arbitrariness, Fairness, and Opportunity in Algorithmic Decision-Making Systems' (2022) 52 Canadian Journal of Philosophy 26

Crooks P and Parsons TH (eds), *Empires and Bureaucracy in World History: From Late Antiquity to the Twentieth Century* (Cambridge University Press 2016)

Cummings M, 'Automation Bias in Intelligent Time Critical Decision Support Systems' (2014) *AIAA 1st Intelligent Systems Technical Conference*, 20–22 September 2004, Chicago, Illinois <https://doi.org/10.2514/6.2004-6313>

Custers B, 'Data Dilemmas in the Information Society: Introduction and Overview' in Bart Custers and others (eds), *Discrimination and Privacy in the Information Society*, vol 3 (Springer Berlin Heidelberg 2013) <http://link.springer.com/10.1007/978-3-642-30487-3_1>

Dahl RA, *On Democracy* (Yale University Press 1998)

Danaher J, 'The Threat of Algocracy: Reality, Resistance and Accommodation' (2016) 29 Philosophy & Technology 245

Darling Z, 'More than 30 Victims of Post Office IT Scandal Died Without Justice' (*The Justice Gap*, 15 February 2022) <www.thejusticegap.com/more-than-30-victims-of-post-office-it-scandal-died-without-justice/>

Dastin J, 'Amazon Scraps Secret AI Recruiting Tool That Showed Bias against Women' *Reuters* (San Francisco, 10 October 2018) <www.reuters.com/article/us-amazon-com-jobs-automation-insight-idUSKCN1MK08G>

Data Ethics Commission of the German Federal Government, 'Opinion of the German Data Ethics Commission' (2019) <www.bmi.bund.de/SharedDocs/downloads/EN/themen/it-digital-policy/datenethikkommission-abschlussgutachten-lang.pdf?__blob=publicationFile&v=5>

De Hert P, 'Complete Independence of National Data Protection Supervisory Authorities: About Persons, Czars and Data Governance in Belgian Debates' (European Law Blog, 24 December 2021) <https://europeanlawblog.eu/2021/12/24/complete-independence-of-national-data-protection-supervisory-authorities-about-persons-czars-and-data-governance-in-belgian-debates/>

De Hert P and others, 'Legal Safeguards for Privacy and Data Protection in Ambient Intelligence' (2009) 13 Personal and Ubiquitous Computing 435

De Raedt L, 'De artificiële-intelligentierevolutie en de impact ervan' in Pieter d'Hoine and Bart Pattyn (eds), *Wetenschap in een veranderende wereld: Lessen voor de eenentwintigste eeuw* (1st edn, Universitaire Pers Leuven 2020)

Degrave E, 'The Use of Secret Algorithms to Combat Social Fraud in Belgium' (2020) 1 European Review of Digital Administration & Law 167

Degrave E and Lachapelle A, 'Le droit d'accès du contribuable à ses données à caractère personnel et la lutte contre la fraude fiscale' (2014) 5 Revue Générale du Contentieux Fiscal 322

Delvaux M, 'Report with Recommendations to the Commission on Civil Law Rules on Robotics (2015/2103(INL))' (European Parliament 2017) A8–0005/2017

Dencik L and others, 'Data Scores as Governance: Investigating Uses of Citizen Scoring in Public Services' (Data Justice Lab, Cardiff University 2018) <https://datajustice.files.wordpress.com/2018/12/data-scores-as-governance-project-report2.pdf>

Dermine P, 'The New Economic Governance of the Eurozone: A Rule of Law Analysis' (PhD thesis, Maastricht University 2020)

The New Economic Governance of the Eurozone: A Rule of Law Analysis (Cambridge University Press 2022)

Dicey AV, *Introduction to the Study of the Law of the Constitution [1885]* (10th edn, Macmillan 1968)

Dickenson D, 'The Common Good' in Roger Brownsword, Eloise Scotford and Karen Yeung (eds), *The Oxford Handbook of Law, Regulation and Technology* (Oxford University Press 2017)

'DIGITALEUROPE's Initial Findings on the Proposed AI Act' (*DIGITALEUROPE*, 2021) <www.digitaleurope.org/resources/digitaleuropes-initial-findings-on-the-proposed-ai-act/>

Dignum V, 'The Myth of Complete AI-Fairness' in Allan Tucker and others (eds), *Artificial Intelligence in Medicine* (Springer International Publishing 2021)

Dijck J van, 'Datafication, Dataism and Dataveillance: Big Data between Scientific Paradigm and Ideology' (2014) 12 Surveillance & Society 197

Dindjer H, 'What Makes an Administrative Decision Unreasonable?' (2021) 84 The Modern Law Review 265

Diver L, 'Interpreting the Rule(s) of Code: Performance, Performativity, and Production' (2021) MIT Computational Law Report <https://law.mit.edu/pub/interpretingtherulesofcode/release/1>

Dixon R, 'Rule of Law Teleology: Against the Misuse and Abuse of Rule of Law Rhetoric' (2019) 11 Hague Journal on the Rule of Law 461

Dixon R and Landau D, *Abusive Constitutional Borrowing: Legal Globalization and the Subversion of Liberal Democracy* (Oxford University Press 2021)

'DN Debatt. "Är Sverige Redo Att Låta Maskiner Fatta Besluten?"' *Dagens Nyheter* (17 February 2019) <www.dn.se/debatt/ar-sverige-redo-att-lata-maskiner-fatta-besluten/>

Domingos P, *The Master Algorithm: How the Quest for the Ultimate Learning Machine Will Remake Our World* (1st edn, Penguin Books 2017)

van Domselaar I, 'The Perceptive Judge' (2018) 9 Jurisprudence 71

Dorani S, 'The Primacy of EU Law over French Law: EU Law Takes Precedence over National Law?' (CESRAN Int, 23 November 2021) <https://cesran.org/the-primacy-of-eu-law-over-french-law-eu-law-takes-precedence-over-national-law.html>

Downs A, 'The Public Interest: It's Meaning in a Democracy' (1962) 29 Social Research 1

Dragu T and Lupu Y, 'Digital Authoritarianism and the Future of Human Rights' (2021) 75 International Organization 991

Dresler J, 'Der Brüsseler Testballon – Kommission betritt mit Klageschrift gegen Ungarns Anti-LGBTQ-Gesetz Neuland' (*Verfassungsblog*, 21 February 2023) <https://verfassungsblog.de/der-brusseler-testballon/>

Dressel J and Farid H, 'The Accuracy, Fairness, and Limits of Predicting Recidivism' (2018) 4 Science Advances 1

Duan N, Tang D and Zhou M, 'Machine Reasoning: Technology, Dilemma and Future', *Proceedings of the 2020 Conference on Empirical Methods in Natural Language Processing: Tutorial Abstracts* (Association for Computational Linguistics 2020) <www.aclweb.org/anthology/2020.emnlp-tutorials.1>

Dunleavy P, 'New Public Management Is Dead – Long Live Digital-Era Governance' (2005) 16 Journal of Public Administration Research and Theory 467

Durkheim E, *L'éducation morale* (Alcan 1925)

Dworkin R, *Taking Rights Seriously* (Harvard University Press 1978)

Law's Empire (Hart Publishing 1998)

Dyzenhaus D, *The Constitution of Law: Legality in a Time of Emergency* (Cambridge University Press 2006)

'Preventive Justice and the Rule-of-Law Project' in Andrew Ashworth, Lucia Zedner and Patrick Tomlin (eds), *Prevention and the Limits of the Criminal Law* (Oxford University Press 2013)

Eidenmueller H, 'Why Personalized Law?' (Social Science Research Network 2021) SSRN Scholarly Paper ID 3969934 <https://papers.ssrn.com/abstract=3969934>

Eidenmüller H and Wagner G, *Law by Algorithm* (Mohr Siebeck 2021)

Eischen K, 'Opening the "Black Box" of Software: The Micro-Foundations of Informational Technologies, Practices and Environments' (2003) 6 Information, Communication & Society 57

Elkin-Koren N, 'Contesting Algorithms: Restoring the Public Interest in Content Filtering by Artificial Intelligence' (2020) 7 Big Data & Society 1

Elston T and Bevan G, 'New Development: Scarcity, Policy Gambles, and "One-Shot Bias" – Training Civil Servants to Speak Truth to Power' (2020) 40 Public Money & Management 615

Emanuilov I and Yordanova K, 'Do You Believe in FAIR-y-Tales? An Overview of Microsoft's New Toolkit for Assessing and Improving Fairness of Algorithms' (*CITIP blog*, 14 July 2020) <www.law.kuleuven.be/citip/blog/do-you-believe-in-fair-y-tales-an-overview-of-microsofts-new-toolkit-for-assessing-and-improving-fairness-of-algorithms/>

Emerson J, Satterthwaite ML and Pandey AV, 'The Challenging Power of Data Visualization for Human Rights Advocacy' in Molly K Land and Jay D Aronson (eds), *New Technologies for Human Rights Law and Practice* (Cambridge University Press 2018)

Endicott T and Yeung K, 'The Death of Law? Computationally Personalized Norms and The Rule of Law' (2022) 72 University of Toronto Law Journal 373

Engel A, *The Choice of Legal Basis for Acts of the European Union: Competence Overlaps, Institutional Preferences, and Legal Basis Litigation* (Springer International Publishing 2018)

van Engen N, Steijn B and Tummers L, 'Do Consistent Government Policies Lead to Greater Meaningfulness and Legitimacy on the Front Line?' (2019) 97 Public Administration 97

Engstrom DF and others, 'Government by Algorithm: Artificial Intelligence in Federal Administrative Agencies' (Administrative Conference of the United States 2020) <www.acus.gov/sites/default/files/documents/Government%20by%20Algorithm.pdf>

Eubanks V, *Automating Inequality – How High-Tech Tools Profile, Police and Punish the Poor* (Picador 2019)

European Center for Not-for-Profit Law (ECNL), 'Big Win for Fundamental Rights, as the European Parliament Adopts the AI Act' (14 June 2023) <https://ecnl.org/news/big-win-fundamental-rights-european-parliament-adopts-ai-act>.

European Commission. Joint Research Centre, *AI Watch, Artificial Intelligence for the Public Sector: Report of the '3rd Peer Learning Workshop on the Use and Impact of AI in Public Services', 24 June 2021* (Publications Office 2021) <https://data.europa.eu/doi/10.2760/162795>

'Commission Considers that Hungary's Judicial Reform Addressed Deficiencies in Judicial Independence, but Maintains Measures on Budget Conditionality', Brussels, 13 December 2023 <https://ec.europa.eu/commission/presscorner/detail/en/ip_23_6465>

European Digital Rights (EDRi), 'Civil Society Call and Recommendations for Concrete Solutions to GDPR Enforcement Shortcomings' (16 March 2022) <https://edri.org/wp-content/uploads/2022/03/EDRi-recommendations-for-better-GDPR-enforcement.pdf>

European Group on Ethics in Science and New Technologies (EGE), 'Statement on Artificial Intelligence, Robotics and "Autonomous" Systems'.

Evans T, 'Professionals and Discretion in Street-Level Bureaucracy' in Peter Hupe, Michael Hill and Aurélien Buffat (eds), *Understanding Street-Level Bureaucracy* (Bristol University Press 2015)

Evans T and Harris J, 'Street-Level Bureaucracy, Social Work and the (Exaggerated) Death of Discretion' (2004) 34 British Journal of Social Work 871

'Explained: What Bombshell Polish Court Ruling Means for EU' (*POLITICO*, 8 October 2021) <www.politico.eu/article/explained-poland-court-ruling-european-union-eu/>

Falk S, *Digital Government: Leveraging Innovation to Improve Public Sector Performance and Outcomes for Citizens* (Springer Berlin Heidelberg 2016)

Fallon RH, '"The Rule of Law" as a Concept in Constitutional Discourse' (1997) 97 Columbia Law Review 1

Favret J-M, 'L'union européenne : "l'unité dans la diversité". Signification et pertinence d'une devise' (2003) 39 Revue trimestrielle de droit européen 657

'Feedback to the European Commission's Regulation Proposal on the Artificial Intelligence Act' (DigitalPoland 2021) <https://digitalpoland.org/en/blog/2021/08/feedback-to-the-european-commission-s-regulation-proposal-on-the-artificial-intelligence-act>

Feinberg J, 'Harm to Others', in Joel Feinberg (ed), *The Moral Limits of the Criminal Law – Volume 1: Harm to Others* (Oxford University Press 1984)

Feldstein S, 'How Artificial Intelligence Is Reshaping Repression' (2019) 30 Journal of Democracy 40

The Rise of Digital Repression: How Technology Is Reshaping Power, Politics, and Resistance (Oxford University Press 2021) <https://academic.oup.com/book/39418>

Finck M, 'Automated Decision-Making and Administrative Law' in Peter Cane and others (eds), *The Oxford Handbook of Comparative Administrative Law* (Oxford University Press 2020)

de Fine Licht K and de Fine Licht J, 'Artificial Intelligence, Transparency, and Public Decision-Making' (2020) 35 AI & Society 917

Fink K, 'Opening the Government's Black Boxes: Freedom of Information and Algorithmic Accountability' (2018) 21 Information, Communication & Society 1453

Fink M and Finck M, 'Reasoned A(I)Administration: Explanation Requirements in EU Law and the Automation of Public Administration' (2022) 47 European Law Review 376

Fleck Z, Chronowski N and Bárd P, 'The Crisis of the Rule of Law, Democracy and Fundamental Rights in Hungary (Paper I)' (2022) 4 MTA Law Working Papers 1

Fortes PRB, Baquero PM and Amariles DR, 'Artificial Intelligence Risks and Algorithmic Regulation' (2022) 13 European Journal of Risk Regulation 357

Fosch-Villaronga E and others, 'A Little Bird Told Me Your Gender: Gender Inferences in Social Media' (2021) 58 Information Processing & Management 102541

'Four European Organisations of Judges Sue EU Council for Disregarding EU Court's Judgments on Decision to Unblock Funds to Poland' (AEAJ 28 August 2022) <www.rechtersvoorrechters.nl/uploads/2022/08/PRESS-RELEASE-EN-2022-08-28.pdf>

Fox J and Polborn M, 'On the Separation of Executive and Legislative Powers: Executive Independence, Liberty, and Social Welfare' (2021) 33 Journal of Theoretical Politics 430

Frontex, 'ETIAS' (2024) <www.frontex.europa.eu/what-we-do/etias/about-etias/>

Fuller LL, *The Morality of Law* (Yale University Press 1969)

Fundacja Moje Państwo, 'Algorithm of the System of Random Allocation of Cases Finally Disclosed!' (22 September 2021) <https://mojepanstwo.pl/aktualnosci/773>
Gailmard S and Patty JW, 'Formal Models of Bureaucracy' (2012) 15 Annual Review of Political Science 353
Gallie WB, 'Essentially Contested Concepts' (1955) 56 Proceedings of the Aristotelian Society 167
Galligan DJ, 'Discretionary Powers in the Legal Order', in DJ Galligan (ed), *Discretionary Powers: A Legal Study of Official Discretion* (Oxford University Press 1990)
'Fair Procedures in Discretionary Decisions', in DJ Galligan (ed), *Discretionary Powers: A Legal Study of Official Discretion* (Oxford University Press 1990)
'Senses of Discretion', in DJ Galligan (ed), *Discretionary Powers: A Legal Study of Official Discretion* (Oxford University Press 1990)
'Public Administration and the Tendency to Authoritarianism' in András Sajó (ed), *Out of and into Authoritarian Law* (Brill–Nijhoff 2002)
Gantman S, 'IT Outsourcing in the Public Sector: A Literature Analysis' (2011) 14 Journal of Global Information Technology Management 48
Garnett K, 'Novelty, Ignorance and the Unknown: Uncertain Science and the Frontiers of Science Doctrine' (2021) 21 elni Review 11
du Gay P, *In Praise of Bureaucracy: Weber, Organization, Ethics* (SAGE Publications 2000)
Gebru T, 'Race and Gender' in Markus D Dubber, Frank Pasquale and Sunit Das (eds), *The Oxford Handbook of Ethics of AI* (Oxford University Press 2020)
General Secretariat of the Council, 'European Council Meeting (10 and 11 December 2020) – Conclusions' (EUCO 2020)
Gerards J, 'Pluralism, Deference and the Margin of Appreciation Doctrine' (2011) 17 European Law Journal 80
Glasius M, 'What Authoritarianism Is … and Is Not: A Practice Perspective' (2018) 94 International Affairs 515
Glasius M and Michaelsen M, 'Illiberal and Authoritarian Practices in the Digital Sphere' (2018) 12 International Journal of Communication 3795
Glimm B and Kazakov Y, 'Classical Algorithms for Reasoning and Explanation in Description Logics' in Markus Krötzsch and Daria Stepanova (eds), *Reasoning Web. Explainable Artificial Intelligence*, vol 11810 (Springer International Publishing 2019)
Godfrey K, 'How the EU Can Better Avoid Bankrolling Authoritarianism' (*Carnegie Europe*, 4 March 2021) <https://carnegieeurope.eu/2021/03/04/how-eu-can-better-avoid-bankrolling-authoritarianism-pub-83992>
González Fuster G, *The Emergence of Personal Data Protection as a Fundamental Right of the EU*, vol 16 (Springer International Publishing 2014)
Goodman B and Flaxman S, 'European Union Regulations on Algorithmic Decision-Making and a "Right to Explanation"' (2017) 38 AI Magazine 50
Grabowska-Moroz B, 'The Systemic Implications of the Vertical Layering of the Legal Orders in the EU for the Practice of the Rule of Law' (Reconnect – Reconciling Europe with its Citizens through Democracy and Rule of Law 2020)
Griffiths TL, 'Understanding Human Intelligence through Human Limitations' (2020) 24 Trends in Cognitive Sciences 873
Gritsenko D and Wood M, 'Algorithmic Governance: A Modes of Governance Approach' (2022) 16 Regulation & Governance 45
Grogan J and others, 'The Crystallisation of a Core EU Meaning of the Rule of Law and Its (Limited) Normative Influence beyond the EU' (Reconnect – Reconciling Europe with its Citizens through Democracy and Rule of Law 2021)

Grossman V, *Life and Fate (1980)* (Robert Chandler tr, Vintage Classic 2017)
Günther WA and others, 'Debating Big Data: A Literature Review on Realizing Value from Big Data' (2017) 26 The Journal of Strategic Information Systems 191
Gurumurthy A and Bharthur D, 'Democracy and the Algorithmic Turn' (2018) 15 Sur – International Journal on human Rights 39
H2020, 'The Robots Are Coming to Clean up Our Nuclear Sites' (*CORDIS – European Commission*, 2019) <https://cordis.europa.eu/article/id/358596-the-robots-are-coming-to-clean-up-our-nuclear-sites>
Hallamaa J and Kalliokoski T, 'How AI Systems Challenge the Conditions of Moral Agency?' in Matthias Rauterberg (ed), *Culture and Computing* (Springer International Publishing 2020)
Hamilton A, Madison J Jay J and Goldman L, *The Federalist Papers, October 1787–May 1788* (Oxford University Press 2008)
Hancox E, 'The Relationship between the Charter and General Principles: Looking Back and Looking Forward' (2020) 22 Cambridge Yearbook of European Legal Studies 233
Hanke Vela J and Chiappa C, 'Brussels vs. Brussels: EU Parliament to Sue Commission over Hungary Cash' (*Politico*, 12 March 2024) <www.politico.eu/article/parliament-sues-commission-over-unfreezing-of-hungary-funds/>
Hänold S, 'Profiling and Automated Decision-Making: Legal Implications and Shortcomings' in Marcelo Corrales, Mark Fenwick and Nikolaus Forgó (eds), *Robotics, AI and the Future of Law* (Springer 2018)
Hanseth O and Monteiro E, 'Inscribing Behaviour in Information Infrastructure Standards' (1997) 7 Accounting, Management and Information Technologies 183
van Harn M and Zwaan KM, 'Kwantificeren is geen kwalificeren: De uitspraak van het Hof van Justitie inzake de vaststelling van willekeurig geweld (art. 15c-situaties)' (2021) 27 Nederlands tijdschrift voor Europees Recht 211
Hart HLA, *The Concept of Law* (3rd edn, Oxford University Press 2012)
Hasselbalch G, *Data Ethics of Power* (Edward Elgar Publishing 2021)
Hatier C, 'Isaiah Berlin and the Totalitarian Mind' (2004) 9 The European Legacy 767
Hayek FA, *The Road to Serfdom (1944)*, (Bruce Caldwell ed, Routledge 2008)
Heaven WD, 'Hundreds of AI Tools Have Been Built to Catch Covid. None of Them Helped' (*MIT Technology Review*, 30 July 2021) <www.technologyreview.com/2021/07/30/1030329/machine-learning-ai-failed-covid-hospital-diagnosis-pandemic/>
Henman P, 'Digital Technologies and Artificial Intelligence in Social Welfare Research: A Computer Science Perspective' in Michael Adler (ed), *Research Agenda for Social Welfare Law, Policy, Practice and Impact* (Edward Elgar Publishing 2022)
High-Level Expert Group on AI, 'A Definition of AI: Main Capabilities and Scientific Disciplines' (2018) <https://ec.europa.eu/futurium/en/system/files/ged/ai_hleg_definition_of_ai_18_december_1.pdf>.
'Ethics Guidelines for Trustworthy AI' (European Commission 2019) <https://digital-strategy.ec.europa.eu/en/library/ethics-guidelines-trustworthy-ai>
'Policy and Investment Recommendations for Trustworthy AI' (European Commission 2019) <https://digital-strategy.ec.europa.eu/en/library/policy-and-investment-recommendations-trustworthy-artificial-intelligence>
Hildebrandt M, *Smart Technologies and the End(s) of Law* (Edward Elgar Publishing 2015)
'Law as Information in the Era of Data-Driven Agency' (2016) 79 The Modern Law Review 1
'Algorithmic Regulation and the Rule of Law' (2018) 376 Philosophical Transactions of the Royal Society A: Mathematical, Physical and Engineering Sciences 20170355
'Privacy as Protection of the Incomputable Self: From Agnostic to Agonistic Machine Learning' (2019) 20 Theoretical Inquiries in Law 83

Law for Computer Scientists and Other Folk (Oxford University Press 2020)
'The Adaptive Nature of Text-Driven Law' (2021) 1 Journal of Cross-disciplinary Research in Computational Law 1 <https://journalcrcl.org/crcl/article/view/2>
'Understanding Law and the Rule of Law: A Plea to Augment CS Curricula' (2021) 64 Communications of the ACM 28
Hildebrandt M and Koops B-J, 'The Challenges of Ambient Law and Legal Protection in the Profiling Era' (2010) 73 Modern Law Review 428
Ho S and Burke G, 'An Algorithm That Screens for Child Neglect Raises Concerns' *Associated Press* (29 April 2022) <https://apnews.com/article/child-welfare-algorithm-investigation-9497ee937e0053ad4144a86c68241ef1>
Hobbes T, *Leviathan: Or the Matter, Forme and Power of a Commonwealth, Ecclesiasticall and Civil (1651)* (Project Gutenberg 2002) <www.gutenberg.org/files/3207/3207-h/3207-h.htm>
Höpfl HM, 'Post-bureaucracy and Weber's "Modern" Bureaucrat' (2006) 19 Journal of Organizational Change Management 8
Hsu F-H, *Behind Deep Blue: Building the Computer that Defeated the World Chess Champion* (Princeton University Press 2022)
Huang L, Lu Z and Rajagopal P, 'Numbers, Not Lives: AI Dehumanization Undermines COVID-19 Preventive Intentions' (2022) 7 Journal of the Association for Consumer Research 63
Huawei, 'Huawei Response on the European Commission's Proposal for a Regulation of the European Parliament and of the Council Laying Down the Harmonised Rules on Artificial Intelligence (Artificial Intelligence Act) and Amending Certain Union Legislative Acts' (*European Commission – Have your say*, August 2021) <https://ec.europa.eu/info/law/better-regulation/have-your-say/initiatives/12527-Artificial-intelligence-ethical-and-legal-requirements/F2665442_en>
Human Rights Watch, 'Automated Hardship: How the Tech-Driven Overhaul of the UK's Social Security System Worsens Poverty' (2020) <www.hrw.org/report/2020/09/29/automated-hardship/how-tech-driven-overhaul-uks-social-security-system-worsens>
Hume D, *A Treatise of Human Nature: Being an Attempt to Introduce the Experimental Method of Reasoning into Moral Subjects and Dialogues Concerning Natural Religion [1739]* (LA Selby-Bigge ed, Clarendon Press 1896)
Humphreys S, *Theatre of the Rule of Law: Transnational Legal Intervention in Theory and Practice* (Cambridge University Press 2010)
'Hungarian Civil Society Raises Alarm over NGO Law Change' (*Euractiv*, 22 April 2021) <www.euractiv.com/section/justice-home-affairs/news/hungarian-civil-society-raises-alarm-over-ngo-law-change/>
Huq A, 'A Right to a Human Decision' (2020) 106 Virginia Law Review 611
The Rule of Law: A Very Short Introduction (Oxford University Press 2024)
Huq A and Ginsburg T, 'How to Lose a Constitutional Democracy' (2018) 65 UCLA Law Review 78
Hurley D, 'Can an Algorithm Tell When Kids Are in Danger?' *The New York Times* (2 January 2018) <www.nytimes.com/2018/01/02/magazine/can-an-algorithm-tell-when-kids-are-in-danger.html>
Husson F, Josse J and Saporta G, 'Jan de Leeuw and the French School of Data Analysis' (2016) 73 Journal of Statistical Software 16
Hvidman U and Andersen SC, 'Impact of Performance Management in Public and Private Organizations' (2014) 24 Journal of Public Administration Research and Theory 35
Ignizio JP, *Introduction to Expert Systems: The Development and Implementation of Rule-Based Expert Systems* (McGraw-Hill 1991)

Jakab A and Kirchmair L, 'How to Develop the EU Justice Scoreboard into a Rule of Law Index: Using an Existing Tool in the EU Rule of Law Crisis in a More Efficient Way' (2021) 22 German Law Journal 936

Janssen HL, 'An Approach for a Fundamental Rights Impact Assessment to Automated Decision-Making' (2020) 10 International Data Privacy Law 76

Janssen M and Kuk G, 'The Challenges and Limits of Big Data Algorithms in Technocratic Governance' (2016) 33 Government Information Quarterly 371

Jasanoff S, 'Technologies of Humility: Citizen Participation in Governing Science' (2003) 41 *Minerva* 223

Joerges B, 'Do Politics Have Artefacts?' (1999) 29 Social Studies of Science 411

Johns F, 'Governance by Data' (2021) 17 Annual Review of Law and Social Science 53

Johnson GM, 'Algorithmic Bias: On the Implicit Biases of Social Technology' (2021) 198 Synthese 9941

Jørgensen RF, 'Data and Rights in the Digital Welfare State: The Case of Denmark' (2021) 26 Information, Communication & Society 123

'Junk Science Underpins Fraud Scores' (*Lighthouse Reports*, 25 June 2022) <www.lighthousereports.nl/investigation/junk-science-underpins-fraud-scores/>

Kaczynski PM, 'Poland, a LGBT-Free Zone?' *www.euractiv.com* (21 October 2021) <www.euractiv.com/section/politics/short_news/poland-a-lgbt-free-zone/>

Kaelbling LP, Littman ML and Moore AW, 'Reinforcement Learning: A Survey' (1996) 4 Journal of Artificial Intelligence Research 237

Kagan RA, 'Varieties of Bureaucratic Justice: Building on Mashaw's Typology' in Nicholas R Parrillo (ed), *Administrative Law from the Inside Out* (1st edn, Cambridge University Press 2017)

Kalberg S, 'Max Weber's Types of Rationality: Cornerstones for the Analysis of Rationalization Processes in History' (1980) 85 The American Journal of Sociology 1145

Kalluri P, 'Do Not Ask If Artificial Intelligence Is Good or Fair, Ask How It Shifts Power' (2020) 583 Nature 169

Kaminski ME, 'The Right to Explanation, Explained' (2019) 34 Berkeley Technology Law Journal 189

Kaun A, 'Suing the Algorithm: The Mundanization of Automated Decision-Making in Public Services through Litigation' (2021)25 Information, Communication & Society 2046

Kayser-Bril N, 'Austria's Employment Agency Rolls out Discriminatory Algorithm, Sees No Problem' (*AlgorithmWatch*, 6 October 2019) <https://algorithmwatch.org/en/austrias-employment-agency-ams-rolls-out-discriminatory-algorithm/>

Kelemen RD and Scheppele KL, 'How to Stop Funding Autocracy in the EU' (*Verfassungsblog*, 10 September 2018) <https://verfassungsblog.de/how-to-stop-funding-autocracy-in-the-eu/>

Kennedy R, 'The Rule of Law and Algorithmic Governance' in Woodrow Barfield (ed), *The Cambridge Handbook of the Law of Algorithms* (1st edn, Cambridge University Press 2020)

Knuutila A, 'Documents Relating to the Children's Safeguarding Profiling System – A Freedom of Information Request to Hackney Borough Council' (*WhatDoTheyKnow*, 15 January 2018) <www.whatdotheyknow.com/request/documents_relating_to_the_childr>

Köbis N, Starke C and Rahwan I, 'The Promise and Perils of Using Artificial Intelligence to Fight Corruption' (2022) 4 Nature Machine Intelligence 418 <www.nature.com/articles/s42256-022-00489-1>

Kocemba K, 'Pregnancy Registry in Poland' (*Verfassungsblog*, 22 June 2022) <https://verfassungsblog.de/pregnancy-registry/>

Kochenov DV and Morijn J, 'Strengthening the Charter's Role in the Fight for the Rule of Law in the EU: The Cases of Judicial Independence and Party Financing' (2021) 27 European Public Law 759

König PD, 'Dissecting the Algorithmic Leviathan: On the Socio-Political Anatomy of Algorithmic Governance' (2020) 33 Philosophy & Technology 467

Kononenko I and Kukar M, *Machine Learning and Data Mining* (Woodhead Publishing 2007)

Konstadinides T, 'Drawing the Line between Circumvention and Gap-Filling: An Exploration of the Conceptual Limits of the Treaty's Flexibility Clause' (2012) 31 Yearbook of European Law 227

The Rule of Law in the European Union: The Internal Dimension (Bloomsbury 2017)

Koops B-J, 'The (In)Flexibility of Techno-Regulation and the Case of Purpose-Binding' (2011) 5 Legisprudence 171

Körtvélyesi Z, 'The Illiberal Challenge in the EU: Exploring the Parallel with Illiberal Minorities and the Example of Hungary' (2020) 16 European Constitutional Law Review 567

Koutrakos P, 'Longing for Less Interesting Times? The German Federal Constitutional Court and the Supremacy of EU Law' (2020) 45 European Law Review 293

Kovács Z, 'Portrayal and Promotion – Hungary's LGBTQI+ Law Explained' *Euractiv* (24 June 2021) <www.euractiv.com/section/non-discrimination/news/portrayal-and-promotion-hungarys-latest-anti-lgbt-law-explained/>

Kranzberg M, 'Technology and History: "Kranzberg's Laws"' (1995) 15 Bulletin of Science, Technology & Society 5

Krygier M, 'The Rule of Law: Pasts, Presents, and Two Possible Futures' (2016) 12 Annual Review of Law and Social Science 199

'What's the Point of the Rule of Law?' (2019) 67 Buffalo Law Review 743

Kuziemski M and Misuraca G, 'AI Governance in the Public Sector: Three Tales from the Frontiers of Automated Decision-Making in Democratic Settings' (2020) 44 Telecommunications Policy 101976

'La détection par intelligence artificielle de piscines non déclarées va être généralisée en France' *Le Monde.fr* (29 August 2022) <www.lemonde.fr/pixels/article/2022/08/29/experimentee-dans-neuf-departements-la-detection-de-piscines-non-declarees-par-intelligence-artificielle-va-etre-generalisee_6139439_4408996.html>

La Porta R and others, 'Judicial Checks and Balances' (2004) 112 Journal of Political Economy 445

Langford M, 'Taming the Digital Leviathan: Automated Decision-Making and International Human Rights' (2020) 114 AJIL Unbound 141

Langlet D and Mahmoudi S, *EU Environmental Law and Policy* (Oxford University Press 2016)

Launchbury J, 'A DARPA Perspective on Artificial Intelligence' (DARPA, February 2017) <www.darpa.mil/about-us/darpa-perspective-on-ai>

Lee K-F, 'AI's Real Impact? Freeing Us from the Tyranny of Repetitive Tasks' (Wired, 2019) <www.wired.co.uk/article/artificial-intelligence-repetitive-tasks>

Lefort C, 'What Is Bureaucracy?' (1974) 22 Telos: Critical Theory of the Contemporary 31

Lenaerts K, 'The Autonomy of European Union Law' (2018) Il Diritto dell'Unione Europea 617

'New Horizons for the Rule of Law within the EU' (2020) 21 German Law Journal 29

Lenaerts K, Maselis I and Gutman K, *EU Procedural Law* (Janek Tomasz Nowak ed, Oxford University Press 2015)

Lenaerts K, Van Nuffel P and Corthaut T, *EU Constitutional Law* (Oxford University Press 2021)

Lequesne-Roth C, 'Livre blanc: La digitalisation du service public – Pour une éthique numérique inclusive' (Observatoire de l'éthique publique 2021)

Lessig L, *Code: And Other Laws of Cyberspace* (Basic Books 1999)

'The Law of the Horse: What Cyberlaw Might Teach' (1999) 113 Harvard Law Review 501

Levinas E, *Autrement qu'être ou au-delà de l'essence* (11th edn, Le Livre de Poche (2019) 1974)

Le temps et l'autre (11th edn, Presses Universitaires de France (2014) 1979)

Is It Righteous to Be?: Interviews with Emmanuel Levinas (Jill Robbins ed, Stanford University Press 2001)

Li J, 'The Leviathan's Rule by Law' (2015) 12 Journal of Empirical Legal Studies 815

Lighthouse Reports, 'People All Over the Netherlands Have Been Flagged for Welfare Fraud Based on a Crude Spreadsheet & Some Unscientific Prejudices. How Do We Know? We Took the Algorithm Apart & Rebuilt It. Score Yourself & See' (2022), <https://twitter.com/LHreports/status/1540598392300179456>

Linardatos P, Papastefanopoulos V and Kotsiantis S, 'Explainable AI: A Review of Machine Learning Interpretability Methods' (2021) 23 Entropy 18

Lipsky M, *Street-Level Bureaucracy: Dilemmas of the Individual in Public Services* (Russell Sage Foundation 1980)

Llansó EJ, 'No Amount of "AI" in Content Moderation Will Solve Filtering's Prior-Restraint Problem' (2020) 7 Big Data & Society 1

Lorenz L, Meijer A and Schuppan T, 'The Algocracy as a New Ideal Type for Government Organizations: Predictive Policing in Berlin as an Empirical Case' (2021) 26 Information Polity: The International Journal of Government & Democracy in the Information Age 71

Loughlin M, *Foundations of Public Law* (Oxford University Press 2010)

'The Apotheosis of the Rule of Law' (2018) 89 The Political Quarterly 659

Lust S, *Rechtsbescherming tegen de (administratieve) overheid. Een inleiding* (die Keure 2014)

MacIntyre A, *After Virtue: A Study in Moral Theory (1981)* (Bloomsbury Academic 2015)

Mader O, 'Enforcement of EU Values as a Political Endeavour: Constitutional Pluralism and Value Homogeneity in Times of Persistent Challenges to the Rule of Law' (2019) 11 Hague Journal on the Rule of Law 133

Magen A and Pech L, 'The Rule of Law and the European Union' in Christopher May and Adam Winchester (eds), *Handbook on the Rule of Law* (Edward Elgar Publishing 2018)

Makszimov V, 'Hungary: Commission Officially Launches Procedure Linking Bloc Funds to Rule of Law' *Euractiv* (27 April 2022) <www.euractiv.com/section/politics/news/hungary-commission-officially-launches-procedure-linking-bloc-funds-to-rule-of-law/>

Maley T, 'Max Weber and the Iron Cage of Technology' (2004) 24 Bulletin of Science, Technology & Society 69

Malleson K and Russell PH, *Appointing Judges in an Age of Judicial Power: Critical Perspectives from around the World* (University of Toronto Press 2018)

Mancano L, 'You'll Never Work Alone: A Systemic Assessment of the European Arrest Warrant and Judicial Independence' (2021) 58 Common Market Law Review 683

Mańko R, 'ECJ Case Law on Judicial Independence' (European Parliamentary Research Service 2021)

Mantelero A, *Beyond Data: Human Rights, Ethical and Social Impact Assessment in AI*, vol 36 (TMC Asser Press 2022)

Marcus G and Davis E, *Rebooting AI: Building Artificial Intelligence We Can Trust* (Penguin Random House 2020)
Mashaw JL, *Bureaucratic Justice: Managing Social Security Disability Claims* (Yale University Press 1983)
Mavrouli R, 'The Dark Relationship between the Rule of Law and Liberalism. The New ECJ Decision on the Conditionality Regulation' (2022) 7 European Papers 275
May L, *Ancient Legal Thought: Equity, Justice, and Humaneness from Hammurabi and the Pharaohs to Justinian and the Talmud* (Cambridge University Press 2019)
Mayer-Schönberger V and Cukier K, *Big Data: A Revolution that Will Transform How We Live, Work, and Think* (Houghton Mifflin Harcourt 2013)
Mazur J, 'Automated Decision-Making Systems as a Challenge for Effective Legal Protection in European Union Law' (2021) 46 European Law Review 194
McBarnet D and Whelan C, 'The Elusive Spirit of the Law: Formalism and the Struggle for Legal Control' (1991) 54 The Modern Law Review 848
McCarthy J and others, 'A Proposal for the Dartmouth Summer Research Project on Artificial Intelligence, 31 August 1955' (2006) 27 AI Magazine 12
McCorduck P, *Machines Who Think* (2nd edn, A K Peters, Ltd 2004)
McCourt K, 'European Commission Lacks Tenacity on the Rule of Law' (*Human Rights Watch*, 20 July 2022) <www.hrw.org/news/2022/07/20/european-commission-lacks-tenacity-rule-law>
McDonald H, 'Extinction Rebellion Calls Move to Class It as Organised Crime Group "Ridiculous"' *The Guardian* (6 September 2020) <www.theguardian.com/environment/2020/sep/06/extinction-rebellion-organised-crime-group-ridiculous-uk>
McIntyre N and Pegg D, 'Councils Use 377,000 People's Data in Efforts to Predict Child Abuse' *The Guardian* (16 September 2018) <www.theguardian.com/society/2018/sep/16/councils-use-377000-peoples-data-in-efforts-to-predict-child-abuse>
McKay C, 'Predicting Risk in Criminal Procedure: Actuarial Tools, Algorithms, AI and Judicial Decision-Making' (2020) 32 Current Issues in Criminal Justice 22
McKay L, *Toward a Rule of Law Culture: Exploring Effective Responses to Justice and Security Challenges* (Adewale Ajadi and Vivienne O'Connor eds, United States Institute of Peace 2015)
Meijer A, Lorenz L and Wessels M, 'Algorithmization of Bureaucratic Organizations: Using a Practice Lens to Study How Context Shapes Predictive Policing Systems' (2021) 81 Public Administration Review 837
Meijers M and van der Veer H, 'MEP Responses to Democratic Backsliding in Hungary and Poland. An Analysis of Agenda-Setting and Voting Behaviour' (2019) 57 Journal of Common Market Studies 838
'Memorandum of Understanding between the Council of Europe and the European Union' (Council of Europe and European Union 2007) <https://rm.coe.int/16804e437b>
Merry SE, 'Measuring the World: Indicators, Human Rights, and Global Governance' (2011) 52 Current Anthropology S83
Metzger GE, 'Legislatures, Executives, and Political Control of Government' in Peter Cane and others (eds), *The Oxford Handbook of Comparative Administrative Law* (Oxford University Press 2020)
Meyer-Resende M and Straub M, 'The Rule of Law versus the Rule of the Algorithm' (*Verfassungsblog*, 2022) <https://verfassungsblog.de/rule-of-the-algorithm/>
Meynen G, 'Why Mental Disorders Can Diminish Responsibility: Proposing a Theoretical Framework' in Bert Musschenga and Anton van Harskamp (eds), *What Makes Us Moral? On the Capacities and Conditions for Being Moral* (Springer Netherlands 2013)

Michalewicz M, Wierzchoń ST and Kłopotek MA, 'Knowledge Acquisition, Representation \& Manipulation in Decision Support Systems' (arXiv, 23 May 2017) <http://arxiv.org/abs/1705.08440>

Milgram S, *Obedience to Authority: An Experimental View* (Harper Perennial 2009)

Miller B, 'Is Technology Value-Neutral?' (2021) 46 Science, Technology, & Human Values 53

'Ministerial Declaration on EGovernment, Approved Unanimously in Malmö, Sweden, on 18 November 2009' (Malmö 2009) <www.mt.ro/web14/documente/date-deschise/reglementari/Ministerial-declaration-on-egovernment_Malmo_2009.pdf>

Mohamed S, Png M-T and Isaac W, 'Decolonial AI: Decolonial Theory as Sociotechnical Foresight in Artificial Intelligence' (2020) 33 Philosophy & Technology 659

Montaldo S, 'On a Collision Course! Mutual Recognition, Mutual Trust and the Protection of Fundamental Rights in the Recent Case-Law of the Court of Justice' (2017) 1 European Papers – A Journal on Law and Integration 965

Moosa IA, 'Blaming Suicide on NASA and Divorce on Margarine: The Hazard of Using Cointegration to Derive Inference on Spurious Correlation' (2017) 49 Applied Economics 1483

de Montesquieu, Baron, *The Spirit of the Laws (1748)* (Thomas Nugent tr, Hafner Publishing Company 1949)

Morgan B and Yeung K, *An Introduction to Law and Regulation: Text and Materials* (1st edn, Cambridge University Press 2007)

Morgan ML, *The Cambridge Introduction to Emmanuel Levinas* (Cambridge University Press 2011)

Morijn J, 'Separate Charter Invocation as a New Enforcement Method: The Lex NGO Case' (2022) 59 Common Market Law Review 1137

Moschella D, 'Machines Are Less Biased than People' (*Verdict*, 12 November 2019) <www.verdict.co.uk/ai-and-bias/>

Muellerleile C and Robertson SL, 'Digital Weberianism: Bureaucracy, Information, and the Techno-Rationality of Neoliberal Capitalism' (2018) 25 Indiana Journal of Global Legal Studies 187

Muir E, *EU Equality Law: The First Fundamental Rights Policy of the EU* (Oxford University Press 2018)

Muller C, 'The Impact of Artificial Intelligence on Human Rights, Democracy and the Rule of Law' (Council of Europe 2020) CAHAI(2020)06-fin <www.coe.int/en/web/artificial-intelligence/cahai>

Mumford L, 'Authoritarian and Democratic Technics' (1964) 5 Technology and Culture 1

Munger MC, 'Self-Interest and Public Interest: The Motivations of Political Actors' (2011) 23 Critical Review 339

Muñoz-González L and Lupu EC, 'The Security of Machine Learning Systems' in Leslie F Sikos (ed), *AI in Cybersecurity* (Springer International Publishing 2019) <https://doi.org/10.1007/978-3-319-98842-9_3>

Neff G and Nagy P, 'Talking to Bots: Symbiotic Agency and the Case of Tay' (2016) 10 International Journal of Communication 4915

Neuwirth RJ, *The EU Artificial Intelligence Act: Regulating Subliminal AI Systems* (Routledge 2022)

'New Evidence that Biometric Data Systems Imperil Afghans' (*Human Rights Watch*, 30 March 2022) <www.hrw.org/news/2022/03/30/new-evidence-biometric-data-systems-imperil-afghans>

Niklas J, 'Poland: Government to Scrap Controversial Unemployment Scoring System' (*AlgorithmWatch*, 16 April 2019) <https://algorithmwatch.org/en/poland-government-to-scrap-controversial-unemployment-scoring-system/>

Niklas J, Sztandar K and Szymielewicz K, 'Profiling the Unemployed in Poland: Social and Political Implications of Algorithmic Decision Making' (Panoptykon 2015) <https://panoptykon.org/biblio/profiling-unemployed-poland-social-and-political-implications-algorithmic-decision-making>

Nilsson NJ, *The Quest for Artificial Intelligence: A History of Ideas and Achievements* (Cambridge University Press 2009)

Nissenbaum H, 'Accountability in a Computerized Society' (1996) 2 Science and Engineering Ethics 25

van Noordt C and Misuraca G, 'Artificial Intelligence for the Public Sector: Results of Landscaping the Use of AI in Government across the European Union' (2022) 39 Government Information Quarterly 101714

Ntoutsi E and others, 'Bias in Data-Driven Artificial Intelligence Systems – An Introductory Survey' (2020) 10 WIREs Data Mining and Knowledge Discovery e1356

O'Cinneide C and Liu K, *The Ongoing Evolution of the Case-Law of the Court of Justice of the European Union on Directives 2000/43/EC and 2000/78/EC: A Legal Analysis of the Situation in EU Member States* (Publications Office of the European Union 2019)

OECD, 'A Data-Driven Public Sector: Enabling the Strategic Use of Data for Productive, Inclusive and Trustworthy Governance', vol 33 (2019) OECD Working Papers on Public Governance

The Path to Becoming a Data-Driven Public Sector (OECD 2019) <www.oecd-ilibrary.org/governance/the-path-to-becoming-a-data-driven-public-sector_059814a7-en>

'Recommendation of the Council on Artificial Intelligence' (2019) OECD/LEGAL/0449 <https://legalinstruments.oecd.org/en/instruments/OECD-LEGAL-0449>.

Ofqual, 'Awarding GCSE, AS, A Level, Advanced Extension Awards and Extended Project Qualifications in Summer 2020: Interim Report' 319 (13 August 2020) <https://assets.publishing.service.gov.uk/media/5f3571778fa8f5173f593d61/6656-1_Awarding_GCSE__AS__A_level__advanced_extension_awards_and_extended_project_qualifications_in_summer_2020_-_interim_report.pdf>

Olsen JP, 'Maybe It Is Time to Rediscover Bureaucracy' (2006) 16 Journal of Public Administration Research and Theory 1

O'Neil C, *Weapons of Math Destruction* (Penguin Books 2017)

Oswald M and others, 'Algorithmic Risk Assessment Policing Models: Lessons from the Durham HART Model and "Experimental" Proportionality' (2018) 27 Information & Communications Technology Law 223

Palonen K, 'Max Weber's Reconceptualization of Freedom Freedom and Foundations' (1999) 27 Political Theory 523

Parliamentary Assembly, 'Venice Commission's Rule of Law Checklist' (2017) Resolution 2187 (2017)

Parliamentary Assembly of the Council of Europe (PACE), 'Recommendation 2183 (2020) on Preventing Discrimination Caused by the Use of Artificial Intelligence' (PACE 2020) Recommendation

Parliamentary Inquiry Committee, 'Unprecedented Injustice' (House of Representatives of the States General 2020) 35 510, no. 1

Pasquale F, *The Black Box Society: The Secret Algorithms that Control Money and Information* (Harvard University Press 2015)

Passchier R, *Artificiële intelligentie en de rechtsstaat* (Boom 2021)

Payandeh M, 'Constitutional Review of EU Law after Honeywell: Contextualizing the Relationship between the German Constitutional Court and the EU Court of Justice' (2011) 48 Common Market Law Review 9

Pearl J, 'Graphical Models for Probabilistic and Causal Reasoning' in A Tucker and others (eds), *Computing Handbook* (Routledge 2014)

'The Seven Tools of Causal Inference, with Reflections on Machine Learning' (2019) 62 Communications of the ACM 54

Pech L, 'The Rule of Law as a Well-Established and Well-Defined Principle of EU Law' (2022) 14 Hague Journal on the Rule of Law 107

Pech L and Jaraczewski J, 'Systemic Threat to the Rule of Law in Poland: Updated and New Article 7(1) TEU Recommendations' (2023) UCD Working Papers in Law, Criminology & Socio-Legal Studies Research Paper No. 13

Pech L and Scheppele KL, 'Illiberalism Within: Rule of Law Backsliding in the EU' (2017) 19 Cambridge Yearbook of European Legal Studies 3

Peeters R and Widlak A, 'The Digital Cage: Administrative Exclusion through Information Architecture – The Case of the Dutch Civil Registry's Master Data Management System' (2018) 35 Government Information Quarterly 175

Pencheva I, Esteve M and Mikhaylov SJ, 'Big Data and AI – A Transformational Shift for Government: So, What Next for Research?' (2020) 35 Public Policy and Administration 24

Perez CC, 'The Deadly Truth about a World Built for Men – From Stab Vests to Car Crashes' *The Guardian* (23 February 2019) <www.theguardian.com/lifeandstyle/2019/feb/23/truth-world-built-for-men-car-crashes>

Invisible Women: Exposing Data Bias in a World Designed for Men (Vintage Publishing 2020)

Petit N and Cooman JD, 'Models of Law and Regulation for AI' in Anthony Elliott (ed), *The Routledge Social Science Handbook of AI* (Routledge 2021)

Pfander JE, 'Dicey's Nightmare: An Essay on The Rule of Law' (2019) 107 California Law Review 737

Pietsch W, *Big Data* (1st edn, Cambridge University Press 2021)

Pitt JC, '"Guns Do Not Kill, People Kill"; Values in and/or Around Technologies' in Peter Kroes and Peter-Paul Verbeek (eds), *The Moral Status of Technical Artefacts*, vol 17 (Springer Netherlands 2014)

Plato, *The Republic* (Benjamin Jowett tr, Dover Publications, Inc 2000)

Pohjankoski P, 'Rule of Law with Leverage: Policing Structural Obligations in EU Law with the Infringement Procedure, Fines and Set-Off' (2021) 58 Common Market Law Review 1341

Polakiewicz J and Kirchmayr JK, 'Sounding the Alarm: The Council of Europe as the Guardian of the Rule of Law in Contemporary Europe' in Armin von Bogdandy and others (eds), *Defending Checks and Balances in EU Member States: Taking Stock of Europe's Actions* (Springer 2021)

Połońska E and Beckett C (eds), *Public Service Broadcasting and Media Systems in Troubled European Democracies* (Springer International Publishing 2019)

Popa E, 'Human Goals Are Constitutive of Agency in Artificial Intelligence (AI)' (2021) 34 Philosophy & Technology 1731

Pope R, 'Universal Credit – Digital Welfare' (PT2 2020) <https://digitalwelfare.report/>

'Post Office Scandal: What the Horizon Saga Is All About' *BBC News* (22 July 2021) <www.bbc.com/news/business-56718036>

Praesidium, 'Draft of Articles 1 to 16 of the Constitutional Treaty' (The European Convention Secretariat 2003) CONV 528/03

'Presidency Conclusions – Copenhagen European Council' (European Council 1993) <www.europarl.europa.eu/enlargement/ec/pdf/cop_en.pdf>

Priebus S, 'Watering down the "Nuclear Option"? The Council and the Article 7 Dilemma' (2022) 44 Journal of European Integration 1

Priebus S and Anders LH, 'Fundamental Change Beneath the Surface: The Supranationalisation of Rule of Law Protection in the European Union' (2024) 62 Journal of Common Market Studies 224

Protect Democracy, 'The Authoritarian Playbook – How Reporters Can Contextualize and Cover Authoritarian Threats as Distinct from Politics-as-Usual' (2022) <protectdemocracy .org/project/playbook-media-primer>

Radin MJ, 'Reconsidering the Rule of Law' (1989) 69 Boston University Law Review 781

Ramraj VV, 'Democracy and Authoritarianism' in Peter Cane and others (eds), *The Oxford Handbook of Comparative Administrative Law* (Oxford University Press 2020)

Ranchordas S, 'Empathy in the Digital Administrative State' (2022) 71 Duke Law Journal 1341

Ranchordas S and Scarcella L, 'Automated Government for Vulnerable Citizens: Intermediating Rights' (2021) 30 William & Mary Bill of Rights Journal 373

Raposo VL, 'Ex Machina: Preliminary Critical Assessment of the European Draft Act on Artificial Intelligence' (2022) 30 International Journal of Law and Information Technology 88

Raymaekers B, *Ethiek, recht en samenleving* (LannooCampus 2013)

Raz J, 'The Rule of Law and Its Virtue' in J Raz (ed), *The Authority of Law: Essays on Law and Morality* (Oxford University Press 1979)

'The Law's Own Virtue' (2019) 39 Oxford Journal of Legal Studies 1

Redden J, Dencik L and Warne H, 'Datafied Child Welfare Services: Unpacking Politics, Economics and Power' (2020) 41 Policy Studies 507

Report by the Comptroller and Auditor General, National Audit Office, 'Investigation into HMRC's Contract with Concentrix' (HM Revenue & Customs 2017) <www.nao.org.uk/wp-content/uploads/2017/01/Investigation-into-HMRCs-contract-with-Concentrix.pdf>

Restrepo Amariles D, 'Algorithmic Decision Systems: Automation and Machine Learning in the Public Administration' in Woodrow Barfield (ed), *The Cambridge Handbook of the Law of Algorithms* (Cambridge University Press 2020)

'Algorithmic Decision Systems: Automation and Machine Learning in the Public Administration' (Social Science Research Network 2020) SSRN Scholarly Paper ID 3974564 289 <https://papers.ssrn.com/abstract=3974564>

Reuters, 'Hungary Restricts Sales of LGBT-Themed Children's Books' *Reuters* (6 August 2021) <www.reuters.com/world/europe/hungary-orders-shops-cover-up-lgbt-themed-childrens-books-2021-08-06/>

'Poland's Kaczynski Says Primacy of EU Law Undermines Sovereignty' *Reuters* (18 September 2021) <www.reuters.com/world/europe/polands-kaczynski-says-primacy-eu-law-undermines-sovereignty-2021-09-18/>

'Romania Must Reject Hungary-Style Anti-LGBT Bill, Rights Groups Say' *Reuters* (29 April 2022) <www.reuters.com/world/europe/romania-must-reject-hungary-style-anti-lgbt-bill-rights-groups-say-2022-04-29/>

Reynolds S, 'Explaining the Constitutional Drivers behind a Perceived Judicial Preference for Free Movement over Fundamental Rights' (2016) 53 Common Market Law Review 643

Rose-Ackerman S, *Democracy and Executive Power: Policymaking Accountability in the US, the UK, Germany, and France* (Yale University Press 2021)

Rosenberg M and Levinson R, 'Trump's Catch-and-Detain Policy Snares Many Who Call the U.S. Home' *Reuters* (20 June 2018) <www.reuters.com/investigates/special-report/usa-immigration-court/>

Rudin C and Radin J, 'Why Are We Using Black Box Models in AI When We Do Not Need To? A Lesson from an Explainable AI Competition' (2019) 1 Harvard Data Science Review <https://hdsr.mitpress.mit.edu/pub/f9kuryi8/release/6>

Russell SJ and Norvig P, *Artificial Intelligence: A Modern Approach* (3rd edn, Pearson 2016)

Ryan J and Toner A, 'Europe's Enforcement Paralysis – ICCL's 2021 Report on the Enforcement Capacity of Data Protection Authorities' (Irish Council for Civil Liberties 2022) <www.iccl.ie/wp-content/uploads/2021/09/Europes-enforcement-paralysis-2021-ICCL-report-on-GDPR-enforcement.pdf>

Sadurski W, 'Rule of Law v. the Rule of Men and Women: What's in the Distinction?: A Short Essay for Martin Krygier' (2019) 11 Hague Journal on the Rule of Law 377

Saposnik A and Aridan N, 'Introduction: Judicial Overhaul and Political Upheaval in Israel' (2023) 28 Israel Studies 1

Scalia A, 'The Rule of Law as a Law of Rules' (1989) 56 The University of Chicago Law Review 1175

Scarcello O, 'Authoritarian Constitutionalism: An Oxymoron? The Case of Costantino Mortati's Early Writings (1931–1940)' (2021) 3/21 Jean Monnet Working Paper <https://jeanmonnetprogram.org/wp-content/uploads/JMWP-03-Orlando-Scarcello.pdf>

Schartum DW, 'From Legal Sources to Programming Code: Automatic Individual Decisions in Public Administration and Computers under the Rule of Law' in Woodrow Barfield (ed), *The Cambridge Handbook of the Law of Algorithms* (1st edn, Cambridge University Press 2020)

Schedler A, 'Conceptualizing Accountability' in Andreas Schedler, Larry Diamond and Marc F Plattner (eds), *The Self-Restraining State: Power and Accountability in New Democracies* (Lynne Rienner Publishers 1999)

Scheppele KL, 'Enforcing the Basic Principles of EU Law through Systemic Infringement Actions' in Carlos Closa and Dimitry Kochenov (eds), *Reinforcing Rule of Law Oversight in the European Union* (Cambridge University Press 2016)

'Autocratic Legalism' (2018) 85 The University of Chicago Law Review 545

'The Treaties Without a Guardian: The European Commission and the Rule of Law' (2023) 29 Columbia Journal of European Law 93

Scheppele KL, Kochenov DV and Grabowska-Moroz B, 'EU Values Are Law, After All: Enforcing EU Values through Systemic Infringement Actions by the European Commission and the Member States of the European Union' (2020) 39 Yearbook of European Law 3

Scheppele KL, Pech L and Kelemen RD, 'Never Missing an Opportunity to Miss an Opportunity: The Council Legal Service Opinion on the Commission's EU Budget-Related Rule of Law Mechanism' (*Verfassungsblog*, 12 November 2018) <https://verfassungsblog.de/never-missing-an-opportunity-to-miss-an-opportunity-the-council-legal-service-opinion-on-the-commissions-eu-budget-related-rule-of-law-mechanism/>

Schlosser M, 'Agency' in Edward N Zalta (ed), *The Stanford Encyclopedia of Philosophy* (Winter 2019, Stanford University 2019) <https://plato.stanford.edu/archives/win2019/entries/agency/>

Schmitt C, *Legality and Legitimacy [1932]* (Duke University Press 2004)

Schmitter PC and Karl TL, 'What Democracy Is… and Is Not' (1991) 2 Journal of Democracy 75

Schroeder W, 'The European Union and the Rule of Law – State of Affairs and Ways of Strengthening', in Werner Schroeder (ed), *Strengthening the Rule of Law in Europe: From a Common Concept to Mechanisms of Implementation* (Hart Publishing 2016)

'The Rule of Law as a Value in the Sense of Article 2 TEU: What Does It Mean and Imply?' in Armin von Bogdandy and others (eds), *Defending Checks and Balances in EU Member States*, vol 298 (Springer Berlin Heidelberg 2021)

Schütze R, *European Constitutional Law* (Cambridge University Press 2012)

Sgaier SK, Huang V and Charles G, 'The Case for Causal AI' (2020) 18 Stanford Social Innovation Review 50

Shapiro SJ, 'The "Hart-Dworkin" Debate: A Short Guide for the Perplexed' (2007) Public Law and Legal Theory Working Paper Series <https://law.yale.edu/sites/default/files/documents/pdf/Faculty/Shapiro_Hart_Dworkin_Debate.pdf>

Shklar J, 'Political Theory and the Rule of Law' in Allan C Hutchinson and Patrick Monahan (eds), *The Rule of Law: Ideal or Ideology?* (Carswell 1987)

Legalism: Law, Morals, and Political Trials (Harvard University Press 1986)

Sie M, 'Self-Knowledge and the Minimal Conditions of Responsibility: A Traffic-Participation View on Human (Moral) Agency' (2014) 48 The Journal of Value Inquiry 271

Siegmann C and Anderljung M, 'The Brussels Effect and Artificial Intelligence: How EU Regulation Will Impact the Global AI Market' (Centre for the Governance of AI 2022) <www.governance.ai/research-paper/brussels-effect-ai>

Siffels L and others, 'Public Values and Technological Change: Mapping How Municipalities Grapple with Data Ethics' in Andreas Hepp, Juliane Jarke and Leif Kramp (eds), *New Perspectives in Critical Data Studies: The Ambivalences of Data Power* (Springer International Publishing 2022)

Simonofski A, Tombal T and Willem P, 'Policy Report on Big Data Policy of the Belgian Federal Administrations' (BELSPO 2020) <https://soc.kuleuven.be/io/digi4fed/doc/d1-2-policy-report-on-big-data-policy-of-the.pdf>

Sinnicks M, 'Leadership after Virtue: MacIntyre's Critique of Management Reconsidered' (2018) 147 Journal of Business Ethics 735

Sirendi R and Taveter K, 'Bringing Service Design Thinking into the Public Sector to Create Proactive and User-Friendly Public Services' in Fiona Fui-Hoon Nah and Chuan-Hoo Tan (eds), *HCI in Business, Government, and Organizations: Information Systems* (Springer International Publishing 2016)

Skitka LJ, Mosier KL and Burdick M, 'Does Automation Bias Decision-Making?' (1999) 51 International Journal of Human-Computer Studies 991

van der Sloot B and van Schendel S, 'Procedural Law for the Data-Driven Society' (2021) 30 Information & Communications Technology Law 304

Smuha NA, 'The EU Approach to Ethics Guidelines for Trustworthy Artificial Intelligence' (2019) 20 Computer Law Review International 97

'Beyond a Human Rights-Based Approach to AI Governance: Promise, Pitfalls, Plea' (2021) 34 Philosophy & Technology 91

'Laten we intelligenter zijn wanneer we het over Artificiële Intelligentie hebben' (*Knack Data News*, 11 March 2020) <https://datanews.knack.be/ict/nieuws/laten-we-intelligenter-zijn-wanneer-we-het-over-artificiele-intelligentie-hebben/article-opinion-1574905.html>

'Beyond the Individual: Governing AI's Societal Harm' (2021) 10 Internet Policy Review 1

'The Human Condition in an Algorithmized World: A Critique through the Lens of 20th-Century Jewish Thinkers and the Concepts of Rationality, Alterity and History' (Institute of Philosophy, KU Leuven 2021)

'From a "Race to AI" to a "Race to AI Regulation": Regulatory Competition for Artificial Intelligence' (2021) 13 Law, Innovation and Technology 57

'Een doosje vijgen na Pasen voor Viktor Orban' (*De Standaard*, 8 April 2022) <www.standaard.be/cnt/dmf20220407_97729796>

'The Paramountcy of Data Protection Law in the Age of AI (Acts)' in EDPS (ed), *Two Decades of Personal Data Protection. What Next?* (Publication Office of the EU 2024), 214

Smuha NA and others, 'How the EU Can Achieve Legally Trustworthy AI: A Response to the European Commission's Proposal for an Artificial Intelligence Act' (Social Science Research Network 2021) <https://papers.ssrn.com/abstract=3899991>

Smuha NA and Yeung K, 'The European Union's AI Act: Beyond Motherhood and Apple Pie?' in Nathalie A Smuha (ed), *The Cambridge Handbook of the Law, Ethics and Policy of AI* (Cambridge University Press)

Sneed MR, *Taming the Beast: A Reception History of Behemoth and Leviathan* (De Gruyter 2021)

Sorauf FJ, 'The Public Interest Reconsidered' (1957) 19 The Journal of Politics 616

Sourdin T, 'Judge v Robot? Artificial Intelligence and Judicial Decision-Making' (2018) 41 University of New South Wales Law Journal 1114

Spector H, 'Bureaucratization, Education and the Meanings of Responsibility' (2018) 48 Curriculum Inquiry 503

Spencer R, 'Got a Dirty, Dangerous, Dull Job? Let a Robot Do It and Keep Your Workers Safe' (2002) 20 Robotics World 14

Spicer MW, 'Public Administration in a Disenchanted World: Reflections on Max Weber's Value Pluralism and His Views on Politics and Bureaucracy' (2015) 47 Administration & Society 24

Stanley J, 'Pitfalls of Artificial Intelligence Decisionmaking Highlighted in Idaho ACLU Case' (*American Civil Liberties Union*, 2 June 2017) <www.aclu.org/blog/privacy-technology/pitfalls-artificial-intelligence-decisionmaking-highlighted-idaho-aclu-case>

Star SL, 'The Ethnography of Infrastructure' (1999) 43 American Behavioral Scientist 377

Stark L, 'Algorithmic Psychometrics and the Scalable Subject' (2018) 48 Social Studies of Science 204

Steponenaite VK and Valcke P, 'Judicial Analytics on Trial: An Assessment of Legal Analytics in Judicial Systems in Light of the Right to a Fair Trial' (2020) 27 Maastricht Journal of European and Comparative Law 759

Stevenson L, 'Artificial Intelligence: How a Council Seeks to Predict Support Needs for Children and Families' (*Community Care*, 1 March 2018) <www.communitycare.co.uk/2018/03/01/artificial-intelligence-council-seeks-predict-support-needs-children-families/>

Stivers C, 'Rule by Nobody: Bureaucratic Neutrality as Secular Theodicy' (2015) 37 Administrative Theory & Praxis 242

Sunstein CR and Vermeule A, *Law and Leviathan: Redeeming the Administrative State* (Harvard University Press 2020)

Suresh H, 'The Problem with "Biased Data"' (*Medium*, 26 April 2019) <https://medium.com/@harinisuresh/the-problem-with-biased-data-5700005e514c>

Sutton RS and Barto AG, *Reinforcement Learning: An Introduction* (2nd edn, MIT Press 2018)

'Systemic Backsliding of the Rule of Law in Hungary: State Control' (*Netherlands Helsinki Committee*, 19 April 2022) <www.nhc.nl/systemic-backsliding-of-the-rule-of-law-in-hungary-state-control/>

Szepesvári C, *Algorithms for Reinforcement Learning* (Morgan & Claypool Publishers 2010)

'Tallinn Declaration on EGovernment at the Ministerial Meeting during Estonian Presidency of the Council of the EU on 6 October 2017' (Talinn 2017) <https://digital-strategy.ec.europa.eu/en/news/ministerial-declaration-egovernment-tallinn-declaration>

Tamanaha BZ, *On the Rule of Law: History, Politics, Theory* (Cambridge University Press 2004)

'The History and Elements of the Rule of Law' (2012) Singapore Journal of Legal Studies 232

Taylor L, 'Public Actors without Public Values: Legitimacy, Domination and the Regulation of the Technology Sector' (2021) 34 Philosophy & Technology 897

Tennison J, 'How Does Ofqual's Grading Algorithm Work?' (n.p. 2020) <https://rpubs.com/JeniT/ofqual-algorithm>
Theodorou A and Dignum V, 'Towards Ethical and Socio-Legal Governance in AI' (2020) 2 Nature Machine Intelligence 10
Thogmartin D, 'Ensuring Reliable AI in Real World Situations' (Deloitte 2022) <www2.deloitte.com/content/dam/Deloitte/de/Documents/Innovation/DELO-8505%20Trustworthy%20AI%20Robust%20and%20Reliable_KS6.pdf>
Thomas R and Uminsky D, 'The Problem with Metrics Is a Fundamental Problem for AI' (2020) *Ethics of Data Science Conference 2020* <http://arxiv.org/abs/2002.08512>
Thompson DF, 'Designing Responsibility: The Problem of Many Hands in Complex Organizations' in Jeroen van den Hoven, Seumas Miller and Thomas Pogge (eds), *Designing in Ethics* (1st edn, Cambridge University Press 2017)
Thompson M, 'The French Educational Algorithm of Inefficiency' (Brown Political Review 8 November 2016) <https://brownpoliticalreview.org/2016/11/french-educational-algorithm/>
Tijsterman SP and Overeem P, 'Escaping the Iron Cage: Weber and Hegel on Bureaucracy and Freedom' (2008) 30 Administrative Theory & Praxis 71
Titcomb J and Field M, 'Sunak to Launch AI Chatbot for Britons to Pay Taxes and Access Pensions' *The Telegraph* (28 October 2023) <www.telegraph.co.uk/business/2023/10/28/rishi-sunak-launch-ai-chatbot-pay-taxes-access-pensions/>
de Tocqueville A, *Democracy in America (1835)* (Barnes & Noble 2003)
Toggenburg GN and Grimheden J, 'Managing the Rule of Law in a Heterogeneous Context: A Fundamental Rights Perspective on Ways Forward' in Werner Schroeder (ed), *Strengthening the Rule of Law in Europe: From a Common Concept to Mechanisms of Implementation* (Hart Publishing 2016)
Tomlinson J, Sheridan K and Harkens A, 'Judicial Review Evidence in the Era of the Digital State' (2020) 4 Public Law 740
'"Tool of Repression": Anger over Poland's New "Pregnancy Register"' *euronews* (6 June 2022) <www.euronews.com/2022/06/06/poland-s-government-criticised-over-pregnancy-register-amid-strict-abortion-laws>
Touriel A and Gadisseux T, 'Sondage RTBF : Un quart des Belges veulent la fin de notre démocratie parlementaire' *RTBF* (4 October 2021) <www.rtbf.be/article/sondage-rtbf-un-quart-des-belges-veulent-la-fin-de-notre-democratie-parlementaire-10852475>
Tridimas T, 'The General Principles of EU Law and the Europeanisation of National Laws' (2020) 13 Review of European Administrative Law 5
Tummers L and Bekkers V, 'Policy Implementation, Street-Level Bureaucracy, and the Importance of Discretion' (2014) 16 Public Management Review 527
Uitz R, 'Lessons from Sexual Orientation Discrimination in Central Europe' (2012) 60 American Journal of Comparative Law 235
'Funding Illiberal Democracy: The Case for Credible Budgetary Conditionality in the EU' (2020) BRIDGE Network – Working Paper 7, SSRN Electronic Journal <https://ssrn.com/abstract=3722936>
Ulenaers J, 'The Impact of Artificial Intelligence on the Right to a Fair Trial: Towards a Robot Judge?' (2020) 11 Asian Journal of Law and Economics 1
Ünver HA, 'Artificial Intelligence, Authoritarianism and the Future of Political Systems' (Centre for Economics and Foreign Policy Studies, JSTOR 2018) <www.jstor.org/stable/resrep26084>
Van Garsse S (ed), *Handboek Bestuursrecht* (Politeia 2016)

Veale M, 'Governing Machine Learning That Matters' (PhD thesis, University College London 2019) <https://discovery.ucl.ac.uk/id/eprint/10078626/1/book_final_corrected_mveale.pdf>

Veale M and Borgesius FZ, 'Demystifying the Draft EU Artificial Intelligence Act' (2021) 22 Computer Law Review International 97

Vedaldi A and others, *Explainable AI: Interpreting, Explaining and Visualizing Deep Learning* (Springer 2019)

Véliz C, *Privacy Is Power* (Bantam Press 2020)

Verberckmoes Y, 'Mogen verkeersboetes een verdienmodel zijn? Volgens experts is een grens overschreden' *De Morgen* (12 December 2021) <www.demorgen.be/gs-b72e332e>

Verbergt M, 'Camera's in joodse wijk controleren nu synagogegangers' *De Standaard* (13 March 2021) <www.standaard.be/cnt/dmf20210312_98151173>

'Privébedrijf achter trajectcontroles doet verkeersdrempels verdwijnen' (*De Standaard*, 11 December 2021) <www.standaard.be/cnt/dmf20211210_97898448>

'Verboden fraudescores bleven in gebruik bij gemeenten' *NRC* (25 June 2022) <www.nrc.nl/nieuws/2022/06/25/profileren-verboden-fraudescores-bleven-in-gebruik-bij-gemeenten-a4134660>

Verdun A and Zeitlin J, 'Introduction: The European Semester as a New Architecture of EU Socioeconomic Governance in Theory and Practice' (2018) 25 Journal of European Public Policy 137

Verkuil PR, *Outsourcing Sovereignty: Why Privatization of Government Functions Threatens Democracy and What We Can Do About It* (Cambridge University Press 2007)

Vetzo M, Gerards JH and Nehmelman R, *Algoritmes en grondrechten* (Boom juridisch 2018)

Viechnicki P and Eggers WD, 'How Much Time and Money Can AI Save Government?' (Deloitte Center for Government Insights 2017) <www2.deloitte.com/content/dam/insights/us/articles/3834_How-much-time-and-money-can-AI-save-government/DUP_How-much-time-and-money-can-AI-save-government.pdf>

Vigen T, *Spurious Correlations* (Hachette Books 2015)

Viljoen S, 'A Relational Theory of Data Governance' (2021) 131 The Yale Law Journal 573

Vincent J, 'Putin Says the Nation that Leads in AI "Will Be the Ruler of the World" – The Verge' *The Verge* (4 September 2017) <www.theverge.com/2017/9/4/16251226/russia-ai-putin-rule-the-world>

Vrabic M, 'Judicial Review of Administrative Action at National Level under the EU Charter of Fundamental Rights and General Principles of EU Law' (2020) 18 Central European Public Administration Review (CEPAR) 25

Wachter S and Mittelstadt B, 'A Right to Reasonable Inferences: Re-Thinking Data Protection Law in the Age of Big Data and AI' (2019) 2 Columbia Business Law Review <https://osf.io/mu2kf>

Wachter S, Mittelstadt B and Floridi L, 'Why a Right to Explanation of Automated Decision-Making Does Not Exist in the General Data Protection Regulation' (2017) 7 International Data Privacy Law 76

Wachter S, Mittelstadt B and Russell C, 'Bias Preservation in Machine Learning: The Legality of Fairness Metrics under EU Non-Discrimination Law' (2021) 123 West Virginia Law Review 105567 <www.ssrn.com/abstract–3792772>

'Why Fairness Cannot Be Automated: Bridging the Gap between EU Non-Discrimination Law and AI' (2021) 41 Computer Law & Security Review 105567

Wahl T, 'CJEU: PNR Directive Valid if Limited to the "Strictly Necessary"' (*Eucrim*, 4 August 2022), <https://eucrim.eu/news/cjeu-pnr-directive-valid-if-limited-to-the-strictly-necessary/>

Waldron J, 'Vagueness in Law and Language: Some Philosophical Issues' (1994) 82 California Law Review 509

'Is the Rule of Law an Essentially Contested Concept (in Florida)?' (2002) 21 Law and Philosophy 137

'The Rule of Law' in Edward N Zalta (ed), *The Stanford Encyclopedia of Philosophy* (Summer 2020, Metaphysics Research Lab, Stanford University 2020) <https://plato.stanford.edu/archives/sum2020/entries/rule-of-law/> 2

'The Rule of Law as an Essentially Contested Concept' in Jens Meierhenrich and Martin Loughlin (eds), *The Cambridge Companion to the Rule of Law* (Cambridge University Press 2021)

Warren I and others, 'When the Profile Becomes the Population: Examining Privacy Governance and Road Traffic Surveillance in Canada and Australia' (2013) 25 Current Issues in Criminal Justice 565

Wax E, '5 Questions about the EU Parliament Suing the Commission over Hungary Cash' (*Politico*, 18 March 2024), <www.politico.eu/article/5-questions-european-parliament-legal-action-commission-hungary-funds/>

Weatherill S, 'The Limits of Legislative Harmonization Ten Years after Tobacco Advertising: How the Court's Case Law Has Become a "Drafting Guide"' (2011) 12 German Law Journal 827

'Maximum versus Minimum Harmonization: Choosing between Unity and Diversity in the Search for the Soul of the Internal Market' in Niamh Nic Shuibhne and Laurence W Gormley (eds), *From Single Market to Economic Union* (Oxford University Press 2012)

Weber M, *Weber: Political Writings* (Peter Lassman and Ronald Speirs eds, Cambridge University Press 1994)

The Protestant Ethic and the Spirit of Capitalism (1905) (Stephen Kalberg tr, Blackwell 2002)

Economy and Society (1968) (Keith Tribe tr, Harvard University Press 2019)

Weiler JHH, 'Not on Bread Alone Doth Man Liveth (Deut. 8:3; Mat 4:4): Some Iconoclastic Views on Populism, Democracy, the Rule of Law and the Polish Circumstance' in Armin von Bogdandy and others (eds), *Defending Checks and Balances in EU Member States*, vol 298 (Springer Berlin Heidelberg 2021)

West R, 'Reconsidering Legalism' (2003) 88 Minnesota Law Review 119

Whitford AB, 'Decentralization and Political Control of the Bureaucracy' (2002) 14 Journal of Theoretical Politics 167

Wiącek M, 'Constitutional Crisis in Poland 2015–2016 in the Light of the Rule of Law Principle' in Armin von Bogdandy and others (eds), *Defending Checks and Balances in EU Member States*, vol 298 (Springer Berlin Heidelberg 2021)

Wilk B, 'Mysterious Random Judge Allocation Algorithm' (*Sieć Obywatelska Watchdog*, 29 January 2019) <https://siecobywatelska.pl/mysterious-random-judge-allocation-algorithm/?lang=en>

Wills T, 'Sweden: Rogue Algorithm Stops Welfare Payments for up to 70,000 Unemployed' (*AlgorithmWatch*, 25 February 2019) <https://algorithmwatch.org/en/rogue-algorithm-in-sweden-stops-welfare-payments/>

Winner L, 'Do Artifacts Have Politics?' (1980) 109 Daedalus 121

de Witte B, 'Direct Effect, Primacy, and the Nature of the Legal Order' in Paul Craig and Gráinne de Búrca (eds), *The Evolution of EU Law* (Oxford University Press 2021)

Wood DM, 'The Global Turn to Authoritarianism and After' (2017) 15 Surveillance & Society 357

Woolf H, Jowell J and Le Sueur AP, *De Smith, Woolf and Jowell's Principles of Judicial Review* (Sweet & Maxwell 1999)

World Justice Project, 'Rule of Law Index 2020' (World Justice Project 2020) <https://worldjusticeproject.org/sites/default/files/documents/WJP-ROLI-2020-Online_0.pdf>

Yeung K, *Securing Compliance* (Hart Publishing 2004)

'Can We Employ Design-Based Regulation While Avoiding Brave New World?' (2011) 3 Law, Innovation and Technology 1

'"Hypernudge": Big Data as a Mode of Regulation by Design' (2017) 20 Information, Communication & Society 118

'Algorithmic Regulation: A Critical Interrogation' (2018) 12 Regulation & Governance 505

'Five Fears about Mass Predictive Personalization in an Age of Surveillance Capitalism' (2018) 8 International Data Privacy Law 258

'Responsibility and AI: A Study of the Implications of Advanced Digital Technologies (Including AI Systems) for the Concept of Responsibility within a Human Rights Framework' (Council of Europe 2019) <https://rm.coe.int/a-study-of-the-implications-of-advanced-digital-technologies-including/168096bdab>

'Why Worry about Decision-Making by Machine?' in Karen Yeung and Martin Lodge (eds), *Algorithmic Regulation* (Oxford University Press 2019)

'Constitutional Principles in a Networked Digital Society' (2022) SSRN Electronic Journal 10 <www.ssrn.com/abstract=4049141>.

Yeung K and Bygrave LA, 'Demystifying the Modernized European Data Protection Regime: Cross-Disciplinary Insights from Legal and Regulatory Governance Scholarship' (2022) 16 Regulation & Governance 137

Young AL, *Democratic Dialogue and the Constitution* (Oxford University Press 2017)

Yuan Y and others, 'A Novel Multi-Step Reinforcement Learning Method for Solving Reward Hacking' (2019) 49 Applied Intelligence 2874

Zalnieriute M and others, 'From Rule of Law to Statute Drafting: Legal Issues for Algorithms in Government Decision-Making' in Woodrow Barfield (ed), *The Cambridge Handbook of the Law of Algorithms* (Cambridge University Press 2020)

Zhang A, 'The Promise and Perils of China's Regulation of Artificial Intelligence' (2024) University of Hong Kong Faculty of Law Research Paper No. 2024/02, SSRN <https://ssrn.com/abstract=4708676>

Zhu G, *Deference to the Administration in Judicial Review: Comparative Perspectives* (Springer International Publishing 2019)

Zuboff S, *The Age of Surveillance Capitalism: The Fight for a Human Future at the New Frontier of Power* (1st edn, PublicAffairs 2019)

Zuiderveen Borgesius FJ, 'Discrimination, Artificial Intelligence, and Algorithmic Decision-Making' (Council of Europe – Directorate General of Democracy 2018) <https://rm.coe.int/discrimination-artificial-intelligence-and-algorithmic-decision-making/1680925d73>

'Strengthening Legal Protection against Discrimination by Algorithms and Artificial Intelligence' (2020) 24 The International Journal of Human Rights 1572

Zuurmond A, *De Infocratie: Een Theoretische En Empirische Heroriëntatie Op Weber's Idealtype in Het Informatietijdperk* (Phaedrus 1994)

EU SOURCES

Article 29 Data Protection Working Party, 'Guidelines on Automated Individual Decision-Making and Profiling for the Purposes of Regulation 2016/679' (last revised and adopted on 6 February 2018 2017) 17/EN WP251rev.01

Committee on the Internal Market and Consumer Protection and Committee on Civil Liberties, Justice and Home Affairs, 'Draft Report on the Proposal for a Regulation of the European Parliament and of the Council on Harmonised Rules on Artificial Intelligence (Artificial Intelligence Act) and Amending Certain Union Legislative Acts' (European Parliament 2022) 2021/0106(COD)

Council of the European Union, 'Council Directive 85/374/EEC of 25 July 1985 on the approximation of the laws, regulations and administrative provisions of the Member States concerning liability for defective products'

'Council Directive 2000/43/EC of 29 June 2000 implementing the principle of equal treatment between persons irrespective of racial or ethnic origin'

'Council Framework Decision 2002/584/JHA of 13 June 2002 on the European arrest warrant and the surrender procedures between Member States – Statements made by certain Member States on the adoption of the Framework Decision 2002'

'Council Decision 2022/2349 of 21 November 2022 authorising the opening of negotiations on behalf of the European Union for a Council of Europe convention on artificial intelligence, human rights, democracy and the rule of law'

'Council General Approach: Proposal for a Regulation of the European Parliament and of the Council Laying down Harmonised Rules on Artificial Intelligence (Artificial Intelligence Act) and Amending Certain Union Legislative Acts' (6 December 2022) <https://data.consilium.europa.eu/doc/document/ST-14954-2022-INIT/en/pdf>

'Council Implementing Decision (EU) 2022/2506 of 15 December 2022 on measures for the protection of the Union budget against breaches of the principles of the rule of law in Hungary, ST/14247/2022/INIT, 2022'

Directive 95/46/EC of the European Parliament and of the Council of 24 October 1995 on the protection of individuals with regard to the processing of personal data and on the free movement of such data (OJ 1995 L 281, p. 31)

Directive 98/43/EC of the European Parliament and of the Council of 6 July 1998 on the approximation of the laws, regulations and administrative provisions of the Member States relating to the advertising and sponsorship of tobacco products, pursuant to the fact that it was adopted based on an inappropriate legal basis

Directive 2011/92/EU of the European Parliament and of the Council of 13 December 2011 on the assessment of the effects of certain public and private projects on the environment, OJ L 26, 28 January 2012

Directive 2016/680 of the European Parliament and of the Council of 27 April 2016 on the protection of natural persons with regard to the processing of personal data by competent authorities for the purposes of the prevention, investigation, detection or prosecution of criminal offences or the execution of criminal penalties, and on the free movement of such data, and repealing Council Framework Decision 2008/977/JHA 2016

Directive 2016/681 of the European Parliament and of the Council of 27 April 2016 on the use of passenger name record (PNR) data for the prevention, detection, investigation and prosecution of terrorist offences and serious crime, OJ L 119, 4 May 2016

Directive 2019/1024 of the European Parliament and of the Council of 20 June 2019 on open data and the re-use of public sector information (recast), OJ L 172, 26 June 2019

Directive 2003/4/EC of the European Parliament and of the Council of 28 January 2003 on public access to environmental information and repealing Council Directive 90/313/EEC, OJ L 41, 14 February 2003, pp. 26–32

Directive 2006/42/EC of the European Parliament and of the Council of 17 May 2006 on machinery, and amending Directive 95/16/EC (recast), OJ L 157, 9 June 2006

Directive 2011/95/EU of the European Parliament and of the Council of 13 December 2011 on standards for the qualification of third-country nationals or stateless persons as beneficiaries of international protection, for a uniform status for refugees or for persons eligible for subsidiary protection, and for the content of the protection granted, 20 December 2011, L 337/9

Directive 2012/13/EU of the European Parliament and of the Council of 22 May 2012 on the right to information in criminal proceedings; Directive 2013/48/EU of the European Parliament and of the Council of 22 October 2013 on the right of access to a lawyer in criminal proceedings and in European arrest warrant proceedings, and on the right to have a third party informed upon deprivation of liberty and to communicate with third persons and with consular authorities while deprived of liberty

Directive 2013/32/EU of the European Parliament and of the Council of 26 June 2013 on common procedures for granting and withdrawing international protection (recast), 29 June 2013, L 180/60

Directive 2014/24/EU of the European Parliament and of the Council of 26 February 2014 on public procurement, OJ L 94, 28 March 2014

European Commission, 'A Digital Agenda for Europe' (2010) Communication from the Commission to the European Parliament, the Council, the European Economic and Social Committee and the Committee of the Regions COM/2010/0245 final

'The European eGovernment Action Plan 2011–2015 – Harnessing ICT to promote smart, sustainable & innovative Government' 2010 (COM(2010) 743 final)

'A New EU Framework to Strengthen the Rule of Law' (2014) Communication from the Commission to the European Parliament and the Council COM/2014/0158 final

'EU eGovernment Action Plan 2016–2020 – Accelerating the digital transformation of government' 2016 (COM(2016) 179 final)

'Proposal for a Council decision on the determination of a clear risk of a serious breach by the Republic of Poland of the rule of law' 2017 (COM(2017) 835 final)

'Call for Applications for the Selection of Members of the High-Level Expert Group on Artificial Intelligence' (2018)

'Commission Staff Working Document *Liability for emerging digital technologies*, accompanying the Communication from the Commission to the European Parliament, the European Council, the Council, the European Economic and Social Committee and the Committee of the Regions Artificial intelligence for Europe', SWD/2018/137 final, Brussels, 25 April 2018

'Coordinated Plan on Artificial Intelligence' (2018) Brussels, 7 December 2018, COM(2018) 795 final

'Communication from the Commission to the European Parliament, the European Council and the Council: Further Strengthening the Rule of Law within the Union – State of Play and Possible next Steps' (Brussels, 3 April 2019) COM/2019/163 final

'2020 Rule of Law Report: The Rule of Law Situation in the European Union' (European Commission 2020) Communication from the Commission to the European Parliament, the Council and the European Economic and Social Committee of the Regions COM (2020) 580 final

'European Rule of Law Mechanism: Methodology for the Preparation of the Annual Rule of Law Report' (2020), <https://commission.europa.eu/system/files/2020-09/2020_rule_of_law_report_methodology_en.pdf>

'White Paper on Artificial Intelligence – A European Approach to Excellence and Trust' Brussels, 19 February 2020, COM(2020) 65 final

'2030 Digital Compass: The European Way for the Digital Decade' (2021) Communication from the Commission to the European Parliament, the Council, the European Economic and Social Committee and the Committee of Regions COM/2021/118 final

'Coordinated Plan on Artificial Intelligence: 2021 Review. Fostering a European Approach to Artificial Intelligence' (2021) Annex to the Communication from the Commission to the European Parliament, the European Council, the Council, the European Economic and Social Committee and the Committee of the Regions COM(2021) 205 final

'Press Release – Europe Fit for the Digital Age: Commission Proposes New Rules and Actions for Excellence and Trust in Artificial Intelligence' (Brussels, 21 April 2021) <https://ec.europa.eu/commission/presscorner/detail/en/IP_21_1682>

'Proposal for a Regulation of the European Parliament and the Council laying down harmonised rules on Artificial Intelligence (Artificial Intelligence Act) and amending certain Union legislative acts' 2021 [COM(2021) 206 final]

'The Rule of Law Situation in the European Union. 2021 Rule of Law Report' (European Commission 2021) COM(2021) 700 final

'Communication from the European Commission: Guidelines on the Application of the Regulation (EU, EURATOM) 2020/2092 on a General Regime of Conditionality for the Protection of the Union Budget' (2022) C(2022) 1382 final

'Proposal for a Directive of the European Parliament and the Council on adapting non-contractual civil liability rules to artificial intelligence (AI Liability Directive)' 2022 [COM(2022) 496 final]

'Recommendation for a Council Decision authorising the opening of negotiations on behalf of the European Union for a Council of Europe convention on artificial intelligence, human rights, democracy and the rule of law' 2022 [COM/2022/414 final]

'The Rule of Law Situation in the European Union. 2022 Rule of Law Report' (2022) COM (2022) 500 final

'Commission considers that Hungary's judicial reform addressed deficiencies in judicial independence, but maintains measures on budget conditionality', Brussels, 13 December 2023, <https://ec.europa.eu/commission/presscorner/detail/en/ip_23_6465>

European Parliament, 'European Parliament Resolution of 12 September 2018 on a Proposal Calling on the Council to Determine, Pursuant to Article 7(1) of the Treaty on European Union, the Existence of a Clear Risk of a Serious Breach by Hungary of the Values on Which the Union Is Founded 2018 (2017/2131(INL)'

'European Parliament Resolution of 17 September 2020 on the Proposal for a Council Decision on the Determination of a Clear Risk of a Serious Breach by the Republic of Poland of the Rule of Law (COM(2017)0835–2017/0360R(NLE))'

'Amendments Adopted by the European Parliament on 14 June 2023 on the Proposal for a Regulation of the European Parliament and of the Council on Laying down Harmonised Rules on Artificial Intelligence (Artificial Intelligence Act) and Amending Certain Union Legislative Acts (COM(2021)0206 – C9–0146/2021–2021/0106(COD))' P9_TA(2023)0236 <www.europarl.europa.eu/doceo/document/TA-9-2023-0236_EN.pdf>

'European Parliament Resolution of 18 January 2024 on the Situation in Hungary and Frozen EU Funds 2024 (2024/2512(RSP))'

European Union Agency for Fundamental Rights (ed), *Handbook on European Non-Discrimination Law* (Publications Office of the European Union 2018)

'Getting the Future Right – Artificial Intelligence and Fundamental Rights in the EU' (European Union Agency for Fundamental Rights 2020) <https://fra.europa.eu/en/publication/2020/artificial-intelligence-and-fundamental-rights>

Presidency of the Council (Czech Republic), 'Second Presidency Compromise Text on the Proposal for a Regulation of the European Parliament and of the Council Laying down Harmonised Rules on Artificial Intelligence (Artificial Intelligence Act) and Amending Certain Union Legislative Acts' (Council of the European Union 2022) 2021/0106(COD)

Regulation 2020/2092 of the European Parliament and of the Council of 16 December 2020 on a general regime of conditionality for the protection of the Union budget 2020

Regulation (EC) 883/2004 of the European Parliament and of the Council of 29 April 2004 on the coordination of social security systems

Regulation (EU) 2016/679 of the European Parliament and of the Council of 27 April 2016 on the protection of natural persons with regard to the processing of personal data and on the free movement of such data, and repealing Directive 95/46/EC (General Data Protection Regulation) 2016 1

Regulation (EU) 2018/1240 of the European Parliament and of the Council of 12 September 2018 establishing a European Travel Information and Authorisation System (ETIAS) and amending Regulations (EU) no. 1077/2011, (EU) no. 515/2014, (EU) 2016/399, (EU) 2016/1624 and (EU) 2017/2226 2018

Regulation (EU) 2021/241 of the European Parliament and of the Council of 12 February 2021 establishing the Recovery and Resilience Facility 2021

Regulation (EU) 2022/868 of the European Parliament and of the Council of 30 May 2022 on European data governance and amending Regulation (EU) 2018/1724 (Data Governance Act) 2022

Regulation (EU) 2022/1925 of the European Parliament and of the Council of 14 September 2022 on contestable and fair markets in the digital sector and amending Directives 2019/1937 and 2020/1828 (Digital Markets Act)

Regulation (EU) 2022/2065 of the European Parliament and of the Council of 19 October 2022 on a Single Market for Digital Services and amending Directive 2000/31/EC (Digital Services Act)

Regulation (EU) 1303/2013 of the European Parliament and of the Council of 17 December 2013 laying down common provisions on the European Regional Development Fund, the European Social Fund, the Cohesion Fund, the European Agricultural Fund for Rural Development and the European Maritime and Fisheries Fund and laying down general provisions on the European Regional Development Fund, the European Social Fund, the Cohesion Fund and the European Maritime and Fisheries Fund and repealing Council Regulation (EC) no. 1083/2006 2013

Regulation (EU) 2024/1689 of the European Parliament and of the Council of 13 June 2024 laying down harmonised rules on artificial intelligence and amending Regulations (EC) No 300/2008, (EU) No 167/2013, (EU) No 168/2013, (EU) 2018/858, (EU) 2018/1139 and (EU) 2019/2144 and Directives 2014/90/EU, (EU) 2016/797 and (EU) 2020/1828 (Artificial Intelligence Act)

Special Committee on Artificial Intelligence in a Digital Age (AIDA), 'Draft Report on Artificial Intelligence in a Digital Age' (European Parliament 2021) (2020/2266(INI))

COUNCIL OF EUROPE SOURCES

Committee of Ministers of the Council of Europe, 'Resolution (74) 29 on the Protection of the Privacy of Individuals vis-a-vis Electronic Data Banks in the Public Sector'

'Resolution 77(31) on the Protection of the Individual in Relation to the Acts of Administrative Authorities'

'Recommendation No. R (80) 2 of the Committee of Ministers Concerning the Exercise of Discretionary Powers by Administrative Authorities', Adopted by the Committee of Ministers on 11 March 1980 at the 316th meeting of the Ministers' Deputies, 1980

'Recommendation No. R (81) 19 of the Committee of Ministers to Member States on the Access to Information Held by Public Authorities'

'Recommendation No. R (87) 15 of the Committee of Ministers to Member States Regulating the Use of Personal Data in the Police Sector', Adopted by the Committee of Ministers on 17 September 1987 at the 410th meeting of the Ministers' Deputies (1987)

'Recommendation No. R (91) 10 of the Committee of Ministers to Member States on the Communication to Third Parties of Personal Data Held by Public Bodies', Adopted by the Committee of Ministers on 9 September 1991 at the 461st meeting of the Ministers' Deputies (1991)

'Recommendation Rec(2004)20 of the Committee of Ministers to Member States on Judicial Review of Administrative Acts'

'Recommendation CM/Rec(2007)7 of the Committee of Ministers to Member States on Good Administration' 2007

'Resolution CM/Res(2022)2 on the Cessation of the Membership of the Russian Federation to the Council of Europe'

'Terms of Reference of the Committee on Artificial Intelligence (CAI) Set up by the Committee of Ministers under Article 17 of the Statute of the Council of Europe and in Accordance with Resolution CM/Res(2021)3 on Intergovernmental Committees and Subordinate Bodies, Their Terms of Reference and Working Methods' (2021) CM (2021)131-addfinal <https://rm.coe.int/cai-terms-of-reference/1680a7b90b>

Council of Europe, 'The Council of Europe and the Rule of Law' (Council of Europe 2008) CM(2008)170

The Administration and You – A Handbook (Conseil de l'Europe 2018)

Council of Europe Ad Hoc Committee on Artificial Intelligence – CAHAI, 'Feasibility Study' (Council of Europe 2020) CAHAI(2020)23

'Possible Elements of a Legal Framework on Artificial Intelligence, Based on the Council of Europe's Standards on Human Rights, Democracy and the Rule of Law' (Council of Europe 2021) CM(2021)173-add <https://rm.coe.int/possible-elements-of-a-legal-framework-on-artificial-intelligence/1680a5ae6b>

Council of Europe, Framework Convention on Artificial Intelligence and Human Rights, Democracy and the Rule of Law [Vilnius, 5.IX.2024], <https://rm.coe.int/1680afae3c>

Venice Commission, 'Report on the Rule of Law – Adopted by the Venice Commission at Its 86th Plenary Session' (2011) CDL-AD(2011)003rev-e

'Study on Individual Access to Constitutional Justice – Adopted by the Venice Commission at Its 85th Plenary Session' (Council of Europe 2011) CDL-AD(2010)039rev

'Rule of Law Checklist' (Council of Europe 2016) Study no. 711/2013 CDL-AD(2016)007rev

Index

www.ingramcontent.com/pod-product-compliance
Lightning Source LLC
Chambersburg PA
CBHW050013281224
19607CB00004B/66

9 781009 427463